Companion to The Worshiping Church

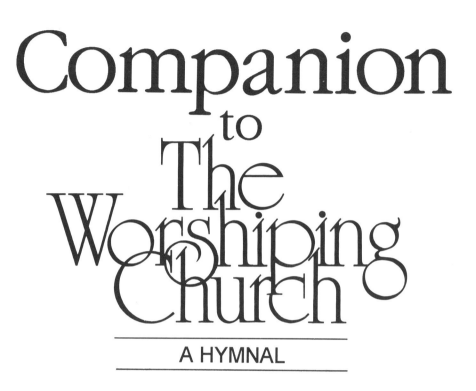

A HYMNAL

RICHARD J. STANISLAW
AND
DONALD P. HUSTAD

Hope Publishing Company
CAROL STREAM IL 60188

Foreword

*T*his *Companion* is based on the earlier work of editor Donald P. Hustad. Entries were used from his *Dictionary-Handbook to Hymns for the Living Church* (Hope Publishing Company, 1978) and are identified with the letter H. When the editorial changes were more than updates, the attribution is omitted. I take responsibility for the final versions.

Taylor University, where I served as Vice President for Academic Affairs and Dean of the University (along with the rank of Professor of Music) for all of the time period of this book's preparation, provided leave time in 1990, as well as computer support and very extensive library facilities. President Jay Kesler and Provost/Executive Vice President Daryl Yost gave personal encouragement and arranged institutional support—I am grateful! Taylor University Librarians Lois Weed, David Dickey, and Roger Phillips located numerous primary sources. They are better than detectives. H. Joanne Giger, Linda Mealy, Amy Joy Nordquist Muia, and many students helped type the data.

Mrs. Mary Louise Van Dyke of the Dictionary of American Hymnology, Oberlin College Library, and The Hymn Society, Oberlin, OH 44074 freely gave information which she has uncovered.

Informal help from the activities of The Hymn Society in the United States and Canada (National Headquarters, P. O. Box 30854, Texas Christian University, Fort Worth, TX 76129) and comparisons with their publications gave additional background. John Mann, Timothy Sharp, John P. Weigand, Vernon Wiley, and Carlton Young all graciously shared their hymn research.

William J. Reynolds, Mary Lou Reynolds and Donald P. Hustad, read several versions of the manuscript and offered valuable revisions.

King College, Bristol, TN, where I now serve as President, completed the scholarly undergirding of the project.

My wife, Rebecca Stanislaw, made phone calls, proofed my writing, and extensively edited the manuscript. In this same year she completed her PhD in English literature! This book is dedicated to her with love and appreciation.

Richard J. Stanislaw
King College
Bristol, Tennessee

The Worshiping Church: A Hymnal

Donald P. Hustad's association with Hope Publishing Company has produced leadership in congregational hymn singing for half a century. The new hymnal for which this book is a companion began with the determination of both publisher and editor to produce a compilation which met the needs of "thoughtful evangelicals." Repertoire would include historic hymnody and new congregational song; without embarrassment, it would contain the best of gospel music—the enduring songs of people of faith. The book would be contemporary in philosophy and appearance, using the language and addressing the issues of the 1990s, while carrying its singers into the next millennium. It would also sample the music of Christians in other parts of the world.

Editorial guidelines established specific criteria. Texts would be faithful to biblical Christianity. Language should be inclusive when referring to human beings; when referring to God, the scriptural examples would be retained, but new appropriate images would be added. Archaisms would be updated by "seamless mending," with living authors revising their own hymns. New paraphrases of scripture (especially psalms and historical canticles) would be included, some in poetic form and some to be spoken with musical responses. Texts would use capitalization, spelling, and punctuation in current forms; tunes would be singable, but not restricted to only those well known. The editorial committee (listed in the hymnal) would give advice, but final text and tune decisions would be made by the executive committee.

The hymnal is designed for congregational use, with extensive indexes and supporting material: brass parts, instrumental parts for brass, keyboards, and handbells, with festival arrangements of many titles; suggested medleys with introductions and interludes; service material; a concordance based on important words in each line of the hymns; a Worship Leaders' edition which gives full analyses of hymn texts and suggests when and how the hymns might be used; and this *Companion* for historical reference.

Hope Publishing Company began this project by sponsoring a symposium, "Hymns '84" (held at the Billy Graham Center of Wheaton College, July 25-26, 1984), which included full discussion of the current trends in hymn singing as perceived by the conferees and presenters Timothy Dudley-Smith, Lloyd John Ogilvie, Donald P. Hustad, and a group of other musical leaders (including representatives of other publishers): Kerchal Armstrong, Mary Kay Beall, Harold Best, Ken Bible, Fred Bock, Gordon Borror, Margaret Clarkson, Richard Dinwiddie, Wesley Forbis, Richard Gerig, Kurt Kaiser, Bruce Leafblad, Bryan Jeffery Leech, William Lock, Deborah

Loftis, Robert Posegate, Bernard Smith, Richard Stanislaw, Howard Stevenson, Jack Schrader, Robert Webber, John F. Wilson, Paul Wohlgemuth, and Don Wyrtzen, each of whom participated in discussion panels. Many of these church and education leaders served on the Editorial Committee for *The Worshiping Church: A Hymnal*; the first meeting was held immediately following the symposium, six years before the book was released.

At Hymns '84, "a symposium on hymns and hymn singing among evangelicals," a question was raised from the audience, "Is Hope Publishing Company working on a new hymnal?" Donald Hustad replied, "Hope is always working on a new hymnal." In this case, the project was not an "always" one, but an entirely new design and compilation.

Over the next years Hustad mailed dozens of surveys, first to establish the "core" of standard hymns, and then to decide on new literature (some of which will become the core of the future). Committee members examined hundreds of texts and tunes, and evaluated contemporary popular songs and worship choruses. The group met for several days in 1986 and again in 1988 to talk together about what well-loved hymns or songs should be retained (even if they did not measure up to our personal preferences), what language changes might be appropriate, and what was biblically accurate. We sang, we argued, we suggested, we discussed overhead projectors and taped orchestrations, and we fell in love again with congregational song. At one meeting we mourned the death in an automobile accident of our colleague and friend, Paul Wolgemuth, on December 28, 1987. This *Companion* was to have been his project.

The final contents reflect the diverseness of the literature (almost to the point of ambiguity) and the richness of our heritage. The hymns confront every major doctrinal theme and the selections encompass representative hymns from every category of singing— historical periods, differing liturgies, revivals, folk music, ethnic variety, geographic diversity. Styles include rounds, unison singing, jazz, four-part German chorales, Genevan psalms, African folk tunes, Jewish melodies, French carols, British traditional settings, orchestral borrowings, tunes written for these texts, tunes written for texts long forgotten, camp meeting songs, gospel songs, contemporary popular tunes, contemporary cerebral tunes, singalongs, strugglethroughs, and more.

The Worshiping Church; A Hymnal and its *Companion* are intended to help the congregation "sing with understanding." They trace traditions which began when the pre-creation "morning stars sang together" and which will continue into eternity when "the Spirit and the bride say 'come'"—an invitation to singing that will never end.

Richard J. Stanislaw   King College, Bristol, Tennessee, 1992

Table of Contents

Hymns by Title with Tunes
1

Authors, Composers, and Sources
196

Tune Index
380

Bibliography
395

Hymns by Title with Tunes

A Charge to Keep I Have   659
    Charles Wesley's hymn is based on Leviticus 8:35,"... keep the charge of the Lord, that ye die not." It first appeared in *Short Hymns on Select Passages of Holy Scripture* (1762). It has been pointed out that Wesley followed Matthew Henry's commentary on the scripture passage, almost phrase by phrase.   H

BOYLSON. First appearing in *The Choir* (1832), the tune was written by Lowell Mason as a setting for "Our days are as grass." Boylston is the name of a town in Massachusetts, Mason's native state, and also of a famous street in Boston.   H

A Hymn of Glory Let Us Sing   259
    Hymnum canamus gloriae was written by The Venerable Bede in the 8th century. This Latin hymn's earliest extant source is an 11th-century manuscript in the British Museum. The *Lutheran Book of Worship* (1978) English translation is the work of Elizabeth Rundle Charles (1858), revised by Benjamin Webb and later editors.

LASST UNS ERFREUEN; see **All Creatures of Our God and King** 356.

A Man There Lived in Galilee   88
    S. C. Lowry's text was first published in *Hymns and Spiritual Songs*, a collection for school worship (1926); it originally carried this refrain: "O Son of man, O more than man, / canst thou our comrade be? / Then help us all, who hear thy call, / to rise and follow thee." Its parallel construction makes it particularly effective as a strophic hymn.

TYROL (also **TYROLESE**). This Tyrolese tune (the Tyrol mountain people near Innsbruch, Austria, have a continuing musical heritage) may have been sung to a shepherd carol, "Ihr Hirten, stehet alle auf"; in the *Oxford Book of Carols* (1928) that carol is mentioned with the text "Out of the Orient." It is published with this text in *Anglican Praise* (supplement 1965).

A Mighty Fortress Is Our God   43
    Once called the "Marseillaise of the Reformation," this chorale is now sung by all Christians the world over. It was first published in Klug's *Geistliche Lieder* (1529). Martin Luther wrote it, probably at the time of the Diet of Speyer (1527), when the German princes made their formal protest against the attacks on their liberties and hence gained the name

"Protestants."

This translation, by Frederick H. Hedge in 1852, first appeared in W. H. Furness's *Gems of German Verse* (Philadelphia, 1853), and later the same year in *Hymns for the Church of Christ*, edited by Hedge and F. D. Huntington. H

EIN' FESTE BURG. The tune, whose name is derived from the first words of the German hymn, was probably developed along with the text. It first appeared in *Kirchen Gesänge* (Nuremberg, 1531) and later in the second edition of Klug's *Gesangbuch* (1535). It is probably the work of Martin Luther himself, and may have been adapted from an earlier source. The present version is based on the arrangement and harmonization of J. S. Bach. H

A Morning Prayer 360

Thomas Ken issued a *Manual of Prayers* for the students at Winchester College in 1674, with instructions to "be sure to sing the Morning and Evening Hymn in your chamber devoutly." This text appeared as the "Morning Hymn" in the 1695 edition. Note that the final stanza is our common "Doxology." H

TALLIS CANON; see **O Gracious Light, Lord Jesus Christ** 359.

A Purple Robe, a Crown of Thorn 217

First written October 1968 at Sevenoaks, Timothy Dudley-Smith's text was published in *Youth Praise 2* (1969); it was reworked in 1982 for *Hymns for Today's Church*. Stanza 3 has been omitted (with the author's permission): "Fast to the cross's spreading span, / high in the sunlit air, / all the unnumbered sins of man / I see my Savior bear."

A PURPLE ROBE. The tune was written for this text, then arranged for *Hymns for Today's Church* (1982), and adapted here, because of the omission of staza 3. The minor key and unique form provide a folk-like idiom.

Abide with Me, Fast Falls the Eventide 365

It was long thought—for a while debated—and recently confirmed that Henry Francis Lyte wrote this hymn in 1847 as he was about to leave his pastorate at Lower Brixham and take a trip to southern France in an unsuccessful effort to regain his health.

The opening words were inspired by Luke 24:29, "Abide with us: for it is toward evening, and the day is far spent." The poem appeared in a leaflet in 1847 and then in the *Remains of Henry Francis Lyte* (1850). H

EVENTIDE. There are conflicting stories about the writing of the tune, though it was composed for this text. William H. Monk's widow says it was written at a time of great sorrow one evening as she and her husband watched the setting sun. Another version says it was created in 10 minutes one night, at the end of a meeting of the committee that edited the first edition of *Hymns Ancient and Modern* (1861). Monk was music editor of that historic hymnal. H

Agnus Dei; see **Father, Grant Us Your Peace** 589 and **O Lamb of God** 833. The *Agnus Dei* Latin hymn became part of the Ordinary of the Mass (that is, the sections ordinarily used in every service) about the 7th century.

Ah, Holy Jesus, How Have You Offended? 231

The first source of this text, long attributed to St. Augustine, is now recognized as the writing of Jean de Fecamp, published 400 years after his death in a 15th-century devotional book entitled *Meditationes sanctorum patrum*. The hymn version (in German) by Johann Heermann first appeared in his *Devoti Musica Cordis* (c. 1630). The English translation by Robert D. Bridges (derived from both the Latin and German) appeared in his *Yattendon Hymnal* (1899). H

HERZLIEBSTER JESU. The music was composed by Johann Crüger and was found in his widely used *Gesangbuch* (1640). It may be based on the tune for the 23rd Psalm in the *Genevan Psalter* (1562) and/or on "Geliebter Freund" in Schein's *Cantional* (1627). Its title is derived from the beginning of the German version of the hymn. H

Alas! and Did My Savior Bleed? 208, 512

This poem of consecration by Isaac Watts first appeared in his *Hymns and Spiritual Songs* (July 1707) with the caption "Godly Sorrow Arising from the Sufferings of Christ." The hymn originally had six four-line stanzas, all of which have undergone alteration. The last phrase of stanza 1, "for such a worm as I," is frequently changed; the editors have chosen "for sinners such as I." Fanny Crosby testified that her "soul flooded with celestial light" at the time of her conversion, when this hymn was sung. H

HUDSON 512. The complete tune appeared in this form in *Songs of Peace, Love and Joy* (1885), compiled by Ralph E. Hudson, who was given credit for composing it. It seemed to be another example in the camp meeting tradition, in which a historic hymn was given a repeated refrain and a gospel-song-style tune. In the July 1980 issue of *The Hymn*, journal of The Hymn Society, Ernest K. Emurian quoted Phil Kerr (in *Music in Evangelism*, 4th ed.) as saying that Hudson "is supposed to have taken the melody of the chorus from an old southern plantation song." Emurian also supplied a photocopy of that song, a piece of sheet music discovered in the Library of Congress, entitled "Take Me Home," an anonymous poem with music by "Eugene Raymond" (a pseudonym for John H. Hewitt, "the bard of the Confederacy"), published in 1864 by Blackmar and Brother of Augusta, GA. The music was very much like the present refrain, and the opening words were:

Take me home to the place where I first saw the light,
    to the sweet sunny South take me home,
where the mockingbird sung [sic] me to rest every night.
    Ah! why was I tempted to roam!

It seems certain that Hudson wrote the refrain words, "At the cross, at the cross where I first saw the light," to fit his adaptation of the Hewitt tune, and then added simple music for Watts's stanzas.   H

MARTYRDOM 208. The tune "Martyrdom" first appeared in leaflet form in the late 18th century. It was set "in triple time" in R. A. Smith's *Sacred Music Sung in St. George's Church* (Edinburgh, 1825) where it was called an "old Scottish melody." After Hugh Wilson's death, a lawsuit declared him to be the rightful owner of the copyright, but the magazine *Choir* (July 1934) traced similarities in structure which indicate that Wilson may have adapted it from a traditional secular air, "Helen of Kirkconnel."   H

All Authority and Power   260
    Written in early 1971 while curate of Christ Church, Old Kent Road, first published in 1973 in *Psalm Praise* (for which it was commissioned), Christopher Idle calls this "an expanded meditation, not a paraphrase, on the four *all's* in Matthew 28:16-20." Minor word changes were made in 1987.

UNSER HERRSCHER. Sometimes called "Neander" after its composer, Joachim Neander, the tune originally appeared with the hymn "Unser Herrscher, Unser König" in the 1680 edition of the Glaubund Liebesübung.   H

All Creatures of Our God and King   356
    The original text is said to have been written by Francis of Assisi during the last months of his life (1225) when he was suffering intense pain and was almost blind. Known as "Canticle of the Sun," it may be the oldest religious poem extant in the Italian language. It expresses St. Francis's intense love of all creation. William Draper paraphrased the hymn for use at a Whitsuntide (Pentecost) festival at Leeds, England, sometime between 1899 and 1919; it was not published until 1926 when it appeared in a collection of Draper's hymns and in *School Worship*.   H

LASST UNS ERFREUEN. "Lasst uns erfreuen" is the beginning of the first line of an Easter hymn in *Ausserlesene Catholische Geistliche Kirchengesäng* (1623) for which this melody is used. It may have been derived from a folk tune or be based on the Strasbourg (1539) Psalm 36 tune. Widely used in German Roman Catholic settings, it came to English hymn repertoire with "Ye Watchers and Ye Holy Ones" in *The English Hymnal* (1906) with this Vaughan Williams arrangement.

All for Jesus! All for Jesus! 570
The hymn was written for Stainer's oratorio *The Crucifixion* (1887); originally it had an additional stanza. It was first performed on Ash Wednesday, February 24, 1887, in Marylebone Parish Church, London, but was not presented as a hymn in a congregational hymnal until *Hymns & Songs* (1969).

WYCLIFF. This tune by John Stainer, set to William Sparrow-Simpson's poem "All for Jesus," is the final hymn in the oratorio *The Crucifixion*. The tune, with the text, "Come Thou Fount of Every Blessing," was included in the *Church Hymnary* (1898).

All Glory Be to God on High 8
Based on the Latin canticle, *Gloria in Excelsis Deo*, which begins with the angels' song recorded in Luke 2:14, this hymn originated in a "Low German" rendering of the text in four stanzas of seven lines by Nikolaus Decius. According to Julian's *Dictionary of Hymnology*, it first appeared in the Rostock *Gesangbuch* (Leipzig, 1539). From the latter, Miss Catherine Winkworth made an early translation for the *Choral Book for England* (1863); this translation, by Gilbert E. Doan, was prepared for *Lutheran Book of Worship* (1978). H

MIT FREUDEN ZART. BOHEMIAN BRETHREN is another name for this tune, after the Bohemian Brethren's *Kirchengesänge*, compiled by Georg Vetter [or Stejc] (1566) in which it first appears in print. The melody may be older, from German or French folk sources; it has similarities to the tune for Psalm 138 in the Geneva Psalter (1551), probably a French folk tune.

All Glory, Laud and Honor 204
The original Latin text by St. Theodulph of Orleans is thought to have been written while he was in prison at Angers (*c.* 820 or 821). Tradition maintains that King Louis the Pious passed the prison and heard Theodulph sing the hymn and afterward set him free. The hymn has often been used in Palm Sunday processionals. The original Latin consisted of 78 lines from which this cento is taken. In its present form John Mason Neale's translation appeared in *Hymns Ancient and Modern* (1861). Its first printing was in the *Hymnal Noted* (1834) with the first line "Glory, and laud, and honor." H

ST. THEODULPH. The tune was composed by Melchior Teschner in 1613 for "Valet will ich dir geben," a hymn of consolation written by Valerius Herberger. It was published in *Ein andachtiges Gebet* (Leipzig, 1615). It was set to the above text and called ST. THEODULPH in *Hymns Ancient and Modern* (1861).　　　　　　H

All Hail the Power of Jesus' Name　　　　　　93, 95
This text by Edward Perronet consisted originally of eight stanzas, the first of which appeared in the November 1779 issue of the *Gospel Magazine*, Toplady's journal. The remaining seven stanzas appeared in the April 1780 issue. Often revised and altered, the version most frequently used is by John Rippon and appeared in his *Selection of Hymns from the Best Authors* (1787).　　　　　　H

DIADEM 93. James Ellor, a hatmaker by trade, directed the music at the Wesleyan Chapel, Droylsden, near Manchester and wrote this melody in 1838 at the age of 19. The tune is typical of the florid style of the period and is named for the phrase "royal diadem" in the first stanza.　　　H

CORONATION 95. This is the tune most often used with this text in America; it was composed by Oliver Holden in 1792 and first published in his *Union Harmony* (1793). The tune name refers to the words "Crown Him."　　　　　　H

All my life long I had panted; see **Satisfied** 511.

All People That on Earth Do Dwell　　　　　　317
Of all the English psalm versions now in use, this is the oldest. Based on Psalm 100, it was one of 25 paraphrases contributed by William Kethe to the Anglo-Genevan psalters of 1561. Very few changes have been made in the text throughout history; a fifth stanza Doxology, "To Father, Son and Holy Ghost," is omitted here.　　　　　　H

OLD HUNDREDTH. The melody is the best known and most widely used of all psalm tunes, and is attributed to Louis Bourgeois who either composed it or adapted an existing tune. In the French Genevan Psalter of 1551 it is set to Psalm 134, a metrical setting by Beze [or Beza]. In English books, it appeared with Psalm 100 beginning with William Kethe's version in *Four Score and Seven Psalms of David* (Geneva, 1561).　H

All Praise to Christ　　　　　　127
"All praise to thee, for thou, O King divine, / Didst yield the glory that of right was thine," was written by F. Bland Tucker (1938) for the Vaughan Williams tune SINE NOMINE (to which it was not allowed to be published). First publication with this tune, ENGELBERG, was in the

Episcopal Hymnal 1940; Tucker was a member of the editorial committee. The text has been substantially updated from the original.

ENGELBERG; see **When in Our Music God Is Glorified** 403.

All praise to thee, my God, this night; see **An Evening Prayer** 361.

All Shall Be Well! 236
   Written by Timothy Dudley-Smith, "All Shall Be Well" was published in *Anglican Praise* (1987), a supplement to the *Anglican Hymnal* (Church Society, London). H

SONG 46. Orlando Gibbons composed 16 tunes with figured bass (a shorthand for harmonies) for a planned book by George Withers, *The Hymns and Songs of the Church* (1623). The Company of Stationers opposed its publication because only psalmody was the approved form of worship, and it was not printed. Ralph Vaughan Williams discovered the tunes and used them in *The English Hymnal* (1906).

All the Way My Savior Leads Me 641
   These words came to Fanny Crosby after she had been the recipient of unexpected good fortune, and as she meditated on God's goodness. H

ALL THE WAY. Fanny Crosby sent her poem to Robert Lowry who composed the tune. It appeared first in *Brightest and Best* (1875), a Sunday School collection compiled by William H. Doane and Lowry, and was headed by the scripture "The Lord alone did lead him" (Deut. 32:12). H

All Things Are Yours 657
   Bryan Jeffery Leech wrote this hymn (spring 1989) for an Evangelical Covenant denominational fundraising drive, basing the text on John Greenleaf Whittier's "All Things are Thine."

GERMANY; see **Jesus, Thy Blood and Righteousness** 481.

All Things Bright and Beautiful 57
   Like most of the hymns of Mrs. Cecil Frances Alexander, this text was written to make biblical truth understandable to young minds. It appeared in her *Hymns for Little Children* (1848), and is based on the phrase in the Apostles' Creed describing God as "Maker of heaven and earth." H

VLEUGEL. The setting was published as an octavo anthem in *Better Choirs*, Grand Rapids, MI. Cornelius Vleugel is a 20th-century composer, probably of Dutch ancestry; no other information has been located.

All Things Come of Thee, O Lord 814
The text is 1 Chronicles 29:14, King James Version, part of David's last great prayer of thanksgiving shortly before his death and the enthronement of Solomon. H

[ALL THINGS]. This short unnamed tune is by Hope's staff composer John F. Wilson. It was composed as a choral response for the choir of First Methodist Church, La Grange, IL, and published in *Choir Praise* (Hope Publishing Company, 1967). H

All to Jesus I surrender; see **I Surrender All** 579.

All Who Love and Serve Your City 430
This first hymn of Erik Routley was written at Dunblane, Scotland (Oct. 1966), where he was part of a group of authors and composers in retreat to examine new church music directions. The hymn was first published in *Dunblane Praises II* (1967); it originally had one more stanza which has not been included in any hymnal publications.

CHARLESTOWN. The tune is from *Southern Harmony* (1835) where it was set to a text about blind Bartimaeus, but not attributed, so it is likely a folk tune gathered by "Singing Billy" Walker. It was reharmonized by Carlton Young for the *Methodist Hymnal* of 1964. Another tune, BIRABUS by Peter Cutts, was intended by Routley at the time of the text writing.

Alleluia 114
Folk-like in its simplicity, Jerry Sinclair's repetitious refrain became popular with early "Scripture songs" or "worship choruses" when it was first published in 1972.

ALLELUIA. Tune and text were created together.

Alleluia, Alleluia! Give Thanks to the Risen Lord 240
The song was written by Donald Fishel "spontaneously during a prayer time" (1971) at the guest house of The Word of God, a Catholic charismatic community in Washtenaw County, MI; stanza 3, "We have been crucified with Christ . . ." was added as a result of the author's adult baptism the previous year.

ALLELUIA NO. 1. The tune name was given by Fishel, who composed it at the Word of God community in Ann Arbor, near the University of Michigan campus; it was later arranged and a descant added by Betty Carr

Pulkingham (1974) and published in *Songs for Celebration* (1979) with voice leading adapted by George Mims and Charles Mallory.

Alleluia, Alleluia! Hearts to Heaven 254
Christopher Wordsworth wrote the text for *The Holy Year* (1862), with "Hallelujah" as the opening word; this revision is by the editors of *Hymns for Today's Church* (1982).

ODE TO JOY; see **Joyful, Joyful, We Adore Thee** 20.

Alleluia, Sing to Jesus 263
These words by William Chatterton Dix were written in 1866 (with additional stanzas) and first published in *Altar Songs, Verses on the Holy Eucharist, No. 7* (1867). The original title was "Redemption by the Precious Blood," based on Revelation 5:9. H

HYFRYDOL; see **Come, Thou Long-Expected Jesus** 135.

Am I a Soldier of the Cross 668
This text was written by Isaac Watts and appeared at the conclusion of a sermon on "Holy Fortitude," based on 1 Corinthians 16:13. It was published in Watts's *Sermons* (1721-24). H

ARLINGTON. This tune is adapted from the minuet in the overture to Thomas A. Arne's opera *Artaxerxes*, produced in London (1762). Its first appearance as a hymn tune is in Ralph Harrison's *Sacred Harmony, Vol. 1* (1784). H

Amazing Grace! How Sweet the Sound 502
John Newton's lines—a best loved hymn of many Christians—were written while he was curate at Olney, Buckinghamshire, England. His early life was one of immorality, debauchery, and failure. "Amazing Grace" could well be his own testimony of his conversion and his life as a Christian. The hymn first appeared in *Olney Hymns* (1779) in six four-line stanzas, and it bore the title "Faith's Review and Expectation"; Newton identified it as based on 1 Chronicles 17:16-17. The fifth stanza of the present version is anonymous and appears as the final verse in other hymns (e.g., "Jerusalem, my happy home" and "When I can read my title clear") in many early American collections. H
A 1990 Public Television special by journalist Bill Moyers studies this hymn in performance; it is available on video.

AMAZING GRACE. Warren Steel has found this early American melody in *Columbian Harmony; or Pilgrim's Musical Companion* (Cincinnati, 1829).

The first setting of Newton's hymn to this tune was done by William Walker of Spartanburg, SC, in his *Southern Harmony* (1835). The present form of the music is credited to E. O. Excell who included it in his *Make His Praise Glorious* (1900). H

Amens 820

The word "Amen" has been used for possibly 3000 years in both Hebrew and Christian worship, usually as a congregational response to prayer. It is said to mean, "So be it!" (1 Cor. 14:16). H

SINGLE is taken from music by Louis Bourgeois provided for the Psalm settings used in Geneva with Jean Calvin.

DRESDEN is sometimes attributed to Johann Gottlieb Naumann (1741-1801), and was presumably written for use in the royal chapel at Dresden. It appeared in the Zittau choir book, and the motif is heard in Mendelssohn's *Reformation Symphony* and Wagner's *Parsifal*. H

THREEFOLD (Danish) is of unknown origin, but widely used in Denmark's churches. H

THREEFOLD (traditional) is also of unknown origin. H

FOURFOLD is credited to John Stainer, though its first appearance cannot be documented. H

SEVENFOLD was written to be sung after the consecration prayer in the Eucharist. It was composed while John Stainer was organist at St. Paul's, London, and published in his *Choir-Book for the Office of Holy Communion* (1873).

America, the Beautiful 418

Katharine Lee Bates writes that her original poem was inspired by an expedition to the top of Pike's Peak in 1893. The opening lines came to her as she looked out over the "sea-like expanse of fertile country spreading away so far under the ample skies." A visit to the "alabaster city" at the Columbian Exposition in Chicago that same year was responsible for the last stanza. In 1904 Miss Bates rewrote the hymn simplifying the phraseology, and the revised version was first printed in the *Boston Evening Transcript* (Nov. 19, 1904). Further revision was made in 1918 to produce the present hymn. H

MATERNA. The tune was written by Samuel Augustus Ward in 1882 for the text "O mother, dear Jerusalem," hence the tune name meaning "motherly." In 1912 the president of the Massachusetts Agricultural College asked permission of Ward's widow to use the tune for Miss Bates's hymn. At least 60 tunes have been used with these words, but "Materna" is now the accepted setting. H

Amid the Thronging Worshipers 340

This paraphrase of Psalm 22:22-23 was published for the first time in *The Worshiping Church* (1990); except for the new fourth stanza, it is an adaptation of Laura A. Tate's versification in *The Psalter* (Eerdmans, 1927); it was prepared, though not used, for the Presbyterian Church (USA) *Hymnal.*

FOREST GREEN. This is an English folk tune as adapted by Ralph Vaughan Williams for the *English Hymnal* (1906). Its name is associated with Forest Green, Surrey, England, and the melody was originally called "The Ploughboy's Dream." H

An Advent Prayer 141

Paul Richardson wrote this prayer in 1986 as a benediction to a Lessons and Carols service, the annual yule log service at Southern Baptist Theological Seminary where he teaches. Its first publication is in *The Worshiping Church.*

An Evening Prayer 361

Bishop Thomas Ken published a *Manual of Prayers* (1674) for use by the boys at Winchester College in southern England, in which the note appeared: "Be sure to sing the Morning and Evening Hymn in your chamber devoutly." This and "A Morning Prayer," 360, were first published in the 1695 edition of the manual and revised by Ken in a 1709 edition. H

TALLIS CANON; see **O Gracious Light, Lord Jesus Christ** 359.

An Upper Room Did Our Lord Prepare 767

This 1973 hymn follows the narrative of John 13, borrowing one phrase from John 14:2 to include the reminder "till He come" (1 Cor. 11:26). Author Fred Pratt Green suggests singing the first two stanzas before the serving of the bread and cup with the last two following. The text was written for O WALY WALY in response to a request from John W. Wilson, who set the musical arrangement in *Hymns for Celebration* (1974); it was sung at the Service of Thanksgiving for John's wife, Mary.

O WALY WALY; see **When Love Is Found** 392.

And Can It Be That I Should Gain? 473

Charles Wesley's text was written shortly after his conversion (1738)

and was published that same year in *Psalms and Hymns* with the title "Free Grace." In his "Journal" for May 23, 1738, Wesley notes that he had difficulty in completing the hymn "because of Satan creating doubts about it . . . and causing him to feel he displeased God with its writing." He realized that it was the "device of the enemy to keep God from receiving the glory due him." It is said that the hymn was quoted to Wesley on his deathbed. H

SAGINA. Thomas Campbell's melody was one of 23 original tunes in his publication *The Bouquet* (1825). All the tunes were named after botanical terms; SAGINA was a plant that grew profusely on the thin rocky soil of the Roman Campagna. The music is typical of the "somewhat flamboyant" Methodist tunes of the period. It first became attached to this Wesley text in *New People's Hymnary* (1922). H

And the glory, the glory of the Lord; see **My Soul Glorifies the Lord** 351.

Angels Bright, Heavens High 323
Christopher Collins based this text on the Anglican canticle "Benedicite" (Song of the Hebrew Children), writing it in 1972 for *Psalm Praise* (1973), edited by Michael Baughen; he wrote it while Curate of Holy Trinity, Manchester.

SPARKLE. David G. Wilson composed the tune as part of the same project as the text (1971).

Angels from the Realms of Glory 174
James Montgomery wrote this poem for the Christmas Eve edition of his paper, *The Sheffield Iris* (1816), with the title "Good Tidings of Great Joy to All People." He revised it in 1825 and published it in his *Christian Psalmist*. In this form it has become universally popular. H

REGENT SQUARE. The tune was composed by Henry Smart for the English Presbyterian hymnal *Psalms and Hymns for Divine Worship* (London, 1867), which he edited. It was named for the Regent Square Presbyterian Church, known as the "cathedral of Presbyterianism in London." H

Angels We Have Heard on High 152
This anonymous French macaronic (vernacular and Latin) carol "Les anges dans nos campagnes" probably dates from the 18th century. The first publication in which it is known to have appeared was *Nouveau recueil de cantiques* (1855). It has become one of America's best known and loved Christmas carols, though the author of the English translation

is also unknown.   H

The translation first appeared in *Crown of Jesus*, "a complete Catholic manual of devotion, doctrine, and instruction" (*c.* 1862), an early book in English for Catholic worship.

GLORIA. The traditional French melody was usually associated with this historic carol, although it was used with another text in R. R. Chope's *Carols for use in the Church* (1875). The present version of text and tune appeared in *Carols Old and Carols New* (1916), edited by Charles L. Hutchins.   H

Apostles' Creed; see **The Apostles' Creed** 14.

Are You Weary, Heavy Laden?   453

In writing these lines, John Mason Neale is thought to have been inspired by four Greek words which he came across in his extensive reading in that language. The hymn first appeared in his *Hymns of the Eastern Church* (1862), where the first phrase was "Art Thou Weary, Art Thou Languid?" *Hymns for the Living Church* (1974) modernized the hymn's full text.   H

STEPHANOS. In early appearances, John Mason Neale credited the above hymn to St. Stephen the Sabaite, hence the tune name. The melody was written by Henry W. Baker and first appeared with the text in the Appendix to *Hymns Ancient and Modern* (1868).   H

Arise, My Soul, Arise   483

The hymn by Charles Wesley first appeared in *Hymns and Sacred Poems* (1742) under the title "Behold the Man." Ira D. Sankey claimed that it had been the direct instrumentality in the saving of thousands of souls.   H

LENOX. The tune, composed by Lewis Edson, was first printed in *The Chorister's Companion*, a collection of New England fuging tunes compiled by Simeon Jocelyn and Amos Doolittle (New Haven, 1782). Edson designed it with a typical homophonic opening of two lines and the second half presented in imitation (fugue-like: bass entering first, then tenor with the melody as it has survived in the hymn tune). It was reprinted in many of the popular singing school collections, including the shape-note books. It is named for a western Massachusetts town not far from Woodstock, where Edson lived at the end of his life.

As He Gathered at His Table   778

This Maundy Thursday hymn was written by Paul A. Richardson (1986) for a hymn competition conducted by the Music Department of the Southern Baptist Sunday School Board but was not the winning entry. This is its first publication (1990).

STUART. The tune is named for the author-composer's hometown and home church, Stuart (VA) Baptist Church.

As Jacob with Travel Was Weary One Day 637
This 18th-century carol was published in Bramley and Stainer's *Christmas Carols* (1871). According to Erik Routley in *The English Carol* (1958), it is "genuinely of the Evangelical Revival" tradition, with the "voice (though not the diction) of Charles Wesley." The text is based on the narrative of Genesis 28:10-12.

JACOB'S LADDER (also **JACOB'S VISION**). This tune may have been sung earlier with secular words, according to the *Oxford Book of Carols*, but since the 18th century it has been associated with the Jacob ballad. This harmonization by Knight is from *More Hymns for Today* (1980).

As Longs the Deer for Cooling Streams 331
This 1696 paraphrase of Psalm 42 is from Tate and Brady's *New Version of the Psalms of David* (London, 1696). The four stanzas in *The Worshiping Church* were stanzas 1, 2, 12, and the final doxology in Tate and Brady.

BELMONT. *The Historical Companion to Hymns Ancient and Modern* gives three possible antecedents for this melody. Most authorities agree that it is probably from William Gardiner's *Sacred Melodies* (1812), a collection of tunes to which English hymns have been set. H

As Sons of the Day and Daughters of Light 704
Idle identifies his source for the text as 1 Thessalonians 5:5-24—on Christian relationships. The hymn was written at Poplar, E. London, in 1975; sung for the institution service of the author as Rector of Limehouse, E. London, October 26, 1976; and was first published (with revisions) in *Hymns for Today's Church* (1982). The hymn responds to a survey of London clergy that indicated an under-representation of available hymns on the topic of the body of Christ.

LAUDATE DOMINUM. This is one of two tunes suggested by the text's author (the other is HOUGHTON). The tune, written for H. W. Baker's hymn "O Praise Ye the Lord" and used in Parry's anthem "Hear My Words" (1894), was composed for the Festival of the Salisbury Diocesan Choral Association. This harmonization was prepared by Parry for the 1916 edition of *Hymns Ancient & Modern*.

As Water to the Thirsty 608
Timothy Dudley-Smith found the idea for this text in Simon and Garfunkel's 1960s "Bridge Over Troubled Water"; he also credits some intuitive connection to Emma Bevan's "As the Bridegroom to His Chosen," itself based on a 14th-century text by John Tauler. The list of images grows from an extensive survey of Scriptures (*Lift Every Heart*, Hope Publishing Company, 1984). It was written at Bramerton (Feb. 1975) and first published, with OASIS, in *Partners in Praise* (Stainer & Bell, 1979).

OASIS. T. Brian Coleman composed this tune in 1979 for Dudley-Smith's hymn; it has appeared in several hymnals with this setting.

As We Gather Around the Table 770
Mark Blankenship wrote text and music for North Phoenix Baptist Church, Phoenix, AZ, the same week it was first sung (Christmas Eve 1973). Over 2,000 attended each of two services.

NORTH PHOENIX. The music was named for the church.

As with Gladness Men of Old 181
During his recovery from an illness, William Chatterton Dix wrote this hymn after reading the Gospel lesson for that particular day in the Epiphany season. It was published in *Hymns of Love and Joy*, a small personal collection (*c.* 1858), and then in the first edition of *Hymns Ancient and Modern* (1861). H

DIX. The source of the tune was a melody by Conrad Kocher in his collection of German hymns, *Stimmen aus dem Reiche Gottes* (1838). William H. Monk adapted the melody for this Dix hymn in *Hymns Ancient and Modern* (1861). The tune was named for the author, although Dix himself did not like the match. H

As Your Family, Lord, Meet Us Here 773
This anonymous text is in the spirit of folk "family" songs where a word or two is substituted with each stanza.

KUM BA YAH; see **Kum Ba Yah** 630.

Ask Ye What Great Thing I Know 224
The German hymn by Johann Schwedler, "Wollt ihr wissen was mein Preis?" (based on 1 Cor. 2:2 and Gal. 6:14), was first published in the *Hirschberger Gesangbuch* (1741) after the author's death. This most used English translation by Benjamin H. Kennedy first appeared in his collec-

tion of 1863, *Hymnologia Christiana*. Its first appearance in America was in the Dutch Reformed publication *Hymns of the Church* (1869).   H

HENDON. Henri A. C. Malan's tune was first published in his own collections in France, probably in 1827.   Lowell Mason is credited with bringing it to America, and he included it in his *Carmina Sacra* (1841). Hendon is a village in Middlesex, England; Malan may have visited there.
          H

At Calvary   510
     The words were written by William R. Newell while he was associated with Moody Bible Institute, Chicago. His thoughts took form one day on his way to a lecture, so he stepped into a room and wrote them down. Continuing on to his class he met Daniel B. Towner, director of the Music Department at the Institute, and handed him the words. Dr. Towner completed the tune immediately and it first appeared in *Famous Hymns* (1895).   H

CALVARY. The tune name is the traditional title of the hymn.

At the Cross; see **Alas! and Did My Savior Bleed?** 208.

At the Name of Jesus   266
     An invalid for the last 25 years of her life, Caroline Noel originally wrote this text for a book intended to be a comfort to others who were suffering, *The Name of Jesus and other Verses for the Sick and Lonely* (1870 ed.); it is based on Philippians 2:5-11.   H

CAMBERWELL. The above text version with Michael Brierly's tune was developed by the editors of *Jubilate Hymns* (1960) to fit a "20th-century folk mass." Geoffrey Beaumont has been sometimes credited with the tune, but he supplied only the two-measure stanza interlude and was involved in some early performances. An alternate tune, KING'S WESTON (set with "When the Church of Jesus" 722), was composed in 1925 for this text.

Awake, my soul, and with the sun; see **A Morning Prayer** 360.

Awake, O Sleeper, Rise from Death   449
     Bland Tucker's text was first drafted, November 1976, and revised June 21, 1977, for inclusion in *Hymns III* of the Church Hymnal Corporation (Augsburg, 1980).

MARSH CHAPEL. Commissioned by the editors for *The United Methodist Hymnal* (1989), Max Miller composed this tune for this text (1984).

Away in a Manger   147, 149
   This carol, attributed to Martin Luther by Murray (see below), is anonymous. An exhaustive study by Richard Hill entitled "Not so far away in a manger, forty-one settings of an American Carol," (*Music Library Assn. Notes*, Dec. 1945) asserts that the text was probably written by an anonymous author in Pennsylvania during the 19th century and sung by German Lutherans there. The hymn was first published in a collection authorized by the General Council of the Evangelical Lutheran Church in North America, *Little Children's Book* (1885). The third stanza is from Charles H. Gabriel's *Vineyard Songs* (1892).   H

AWAY IN A MANGER 147. In the second publication of this text, James Murray's *Dainty Songs for Little Lads and Lasses* (1887), this tune appears. Murray is almost certainly the composer and is the perpetrator of the inscription: "Luther's Cradle Hymn. Composed by Martin Luther for his children, and still sung by German mothers to their little ones."

CRADLE SONG 149. One of the most popular tunes used with this text in Great Britain, this tune was published in America in 1895 in a pamphlet of seven songs entitled *Around the World with Christmas: A Christmas Exercise*, with words arranged by E. E. Hewitt, and music by John R. Sweney and William J. Kirkpatrick. Kirkpatrick is credited with writing it, but it has enough "elegance" to be a folk melody.   H

Baptized in Water   758
   Michael Saward wrote the hymn in 1981 to "declare a whole range of baptismal theology, all of which stresses what God has done for us." It was intended to meet a need for baptism texts in *Hymns for Today's Church* (1982), where it was first published, and is part of a set of baptismal hymns. Saward suggests CRUSADER'S HYMN 115 as a tune setting.

BUNESSAN; see **Morning Has Broken** 362.

Battle Hymn of the Republic; see **Mine Eyes Have Seen the Glory** 416.

Be not dismayed whate'er betide; see **God Will Take Care of You** 619.

Be Still and Know   516
   This anonymous text and tune became popular around 1980. It is a
paraphrase of Psalm 46:10 and Exodus 15:26.

BE STILL AND KNOW. Hope Publishing Company Executive Editor,
Jack Schrader, prepared this arrangement (1988).   H

Be Still, My Soul   530
   The German hymn "Stille, mein Wille, dein Jesus hilft siegen," by
Katharina von Schlegel, originally had six stanzas based on Psalm 46:10
and 1 Thessalonians 4:17; it appeared in *Neue Sammlung Geistlicher Lieder*
(1752). The translation by Jane L. Borthwick has three of the original
stanzas. It was first published in Miss Borthwick's *Hymns from the Land of
Luther*, second series (1855).

FINLANDIA. The tune is from the tone poem "Finlandia" by Jean
Sibelius and was arranged in hymn form for the Presbyterian *Hymnal*
(1933). Another version appeared earlier in Scotland's *The Church
Hymnary, Revised* (1927).

Be Strong in the Lord   661
   Linda Lee Johnson wrote the text in response to a sermon on Joshua 1
by Rev. Neal Doty, Redwood Chapel Community Church, Castro Valley,
CA. She has used it as an encouragement for "friends who are going
through difficult times." It was sung at the memorial services for the
astronauts at Cape Canaveral, FL.

FETTKE. Tom Fettke composed the tune for this text in 1979, naming it
ELAVIL. First publication was as an octavo anthem.

Be Thou My Vision   532
   This 8th-century anonymous Irish poem was translated into English
prose by Mary E. Byrne and appeared in the journal *Erin*, Vol. II (1905).
The prose was put into verse by Eleanor H. Hull and published in her
Poem-Book of the Gael (1912).   H

SLANE. The tune was found in Patrick W. Joyce's *Old Irish Folk Music and
Songs* (1909), set to "With my love on the road." It was used with this
hymn text in the *Irish Church Hymnal* (1919). The present arrangement is
by Donald Hustad, editor of *The Worshiping Church*.
   Slane is a hill near Tara in County Meath, where St. Patrick is said to
have challenged the Druid priests by lighting the Paschal fire.   H

Because He Died and Is Risen 588

This Hebrew song, "Hevenu Shalom alechem" (welcome in peace), is widely known in Israel. Michael Baughen (1980) added the "peace of the New Testament" to what he has called a "catchy tune" and made it a favorite at All Souls Church, Langham Place, London, where it was published in *Church Family Worship* (1988), a hymnal supplement.

ISRAEL. Baughen arranged the folk tune for his adapted text.

Because He Lives 238

Author Gloria Gaither has written about this text in her book *Fully Alive* (Gaither Music, 1990). She and co-author Bill were "going through one of the most difficult times." He had been ill, they were expecting a baby, and world affairs seemed particularly dark. With the birth of their son came the realization that it is the "life" principle that makes the difference; this renewal resulted in this song with its memorable refrain. Originally, it had two additional stanzas which speak of the "newborn baby" and a final move to glory.

RESURRECTION. The tune was composed with the text.

Before the Cross of Jesus 215

According to the *Dictionary of American Hymnology*, Ferdinand Q. Blanchard's hymn first appeared in E. D. Eaton's *The New Hymnal of Praise* (NY: A. S. Barnes, 1937). It is a variation on the Clephane hymn across the page, 216.

ST. CHRISTOPHER; see **Beneath the Cross of Jesus** 216.

Beneath the Cross of Jesus 216

This text is part of a poem published anonymously in Edinburgh, Scotland (1872) in *Family Treasury*, a Scottish Presbyterian magazine. The editor added a comment that the hymn expressed "the experience, hopes and longings of a young lady lately released." The reference was to Miss Elizabeth C. Clephane, who had died three years earlier at the age of 39. H

ST. CHRISTOPHER. Frederick C. Maker composed the music for this hymn, and it first appeared in the supplement to the *Bristol Tune Book* (1881). The tune was presumably named for a 3rd-century martyr.

Bind Us Together 690

Bob Gillman says, "Whilst in a prayer meeting in a friend's house, I had the words of the chorus come to me which I sang out there and then." Written in 1974, it was first published in 1977 by Thankyou Music Ltd., East Sussex, England.

BIND US. Tune and text were composed together.

Bless His Holy Name   36
Andraé Crouch quotes Psalm 103:1 in this black-gospel setting (1973).

BLESS HIS HOLY NAME. Like many popular tunes, this was composed by Crouch with the text.

Bless the Lord, O my soul; see **Bless His Holy Name** 36 (above).

Blessed Assurance, Jesus Is Mine   514
This text by Fanny Crosby was written after she had listened to a new melody composed by her friend, Phoebe Palmer (Mrs. Joseph) Knapp. When asked what the melody said to her, Fanny Crosby replied, "Blessed assurance, Jesus is mine!" Words began to form and the result was this gospel hymn (which has been associated with Billy Graham Crusades). It first appeared in John R. Sweney's *Gems of Praise* (1873).   H

ASSURANCE. This is one of the instances in which a tune was the inspiration for a text, evidently a common practice in the 19th century. The two have remained together through the years.   H

Blessing and Honor and Glory and Power   257
From an eight-stanza hymn for Ascension Day, here are stanzas 8, 4, 5, and 7 (with a few alterations); this first verse was originally the final doxology. Titled "Into the Heaven of Heavens Hath He Gone," it was first published in Bonar's *Hymns of Faith and Hope* (third series, 1866).

O QUANTA QUALIA; see **Here from All Nations** 680.

Blest Be the God of Israel   332
Michael Perry rhymed this paraphrase of Zacharias's benediction (Luke 1:68-79) for *Psalm Praise* (1973) to fill the need for a "Benedictus."

Blest Be the Tie That Binds   708
The hymn's author, John D. Fawcett, having received a call to a church in London, resigned his pastorate in Wainsgate, Yorkshire, and was preparing to move, with personal belongings all packed and loaded. His congregation was grief-stricken at the thought of his leaving; he and his wife shared the feeling, so they changed their plans and decided to

remain. It has been said that this hymn was written as the result of this experience, and it first appeared in Fawcett's *Hymns adapted to the circumstances of Public Worship and Private Devotion* (1782).　　　　H

DENNIS. The tune first appeared in Mason and Webb's *The Psaltery* (1845) to the text, "How Gentle God's Commands." Lowell Mason adapted it from one found among the manuscripts of J. G. Nägeli, a Swiss music publisher; it was possibly Nägeli's setting of "O selig, selig, wer vor dir." It is thought to have been named for a town in Massachusetts.　　H

Bread of the World in Mercy Broken　　　　774
This communion hymn by Reginald Heber was first included in his collection, published posthumously, *Hymns Written and Adapted to the weekly Church Services of the Year* (1827). It was titled "Before the Sacrament."　　　　H

WAYFARING STRANGER. The first part of the melody appeared in the Georgia *Sacred Harp* (1844). The last section is quoted in Nathaniel Dett's *Folk Songs of the Negroes, sung at Hampton Institute* (1827). In both instances, the music is set to words other than the familiar folk text, "I'm just a poor wayfaring stranger."　　　　H

Break Forth, O Beauteous, Heavenly Light　　　　158
The first stanza is Johann Rist's hymn "Ermuntre dich, mein schwacher Geist" [Be cheerful, my faint spirit], published in *Erste Zehen Himmlische Lieder* [First Ten Heavenly Songs] (Lünebur, 1641) and translated (*c.* 1885) by John Troutbeck for Novello's edition of the Bach *Christmas Oratorio*. Rist wrote out of personal and community tragedy: he was pastor at Wedel (near Hamburg, Germany) during the Thirty Years' War. The other two stanzas were added by Fred Pratt Green (1986) at the request of the committee compiling *The United Methodist Hymnal* (1989). According to Carlton Young, Green's hymn was "based on a translation, but not his translation," rather a literal translation by a German pastor, Friedrich Hofmann, who was translating Green's poetry into German at the time of their working together.

ERMUNTRE DICH. The tune is named for the Rist hymn with which it has long been associated; Johann Schop probably composed it for this text (1641); he was the musical editor for Rist's book. Bach's harmonization is from the *Christmas Oratorio* (1734).

Break Thou the Bread of Life　　　　315
This hymn (first two stanzas) was written by Mary A. Lathbury in 1877 at the request of Bishop John H. Vincent, one of the founders of the Chautauqua Literary and Scientific Circle. It is based on Christ's feeding

the multitude and was intended to be used by groups devoted to Bible study. Tradition requires that it be sung at Sunday evening vespers at the Chautauqua assembly in New York.

Stanzas 3 and 4 were added by Alexander Groves and first appeared in the *Wesleyan Methodist Magazine* (London, Sept. 1913). H

BREAD OF LIFE. The tune (named for part of the first phrase) was composed in 1877 for the text by William F. Sherwin, choral director of the Chautauqua institution. It appeared in Chautauqua publications and then in *The Calvary Selection of Spiritual Songs* (1878). H

Breathe on Me, Breath of God 295

In Edwin Hatch's text, the Holy Spirit is addressed as "Breath of God" (from John 20:22). The hymn was first printed in a pamphlet, "Between Doubt and Prayer" (1878), and later in Dr. Allon's *Psalmist Hymnal* (1886). H

TRENTHAM. The tune was written by Robert Jackson, who was born at Trentham, Staffordshire, England. It was composed for Henry W. Baker's "O perfect life of love" and was first printed in *Fifty Sacred Leaflets* (1888 or 1894). (Equally trustworthy sources give both dates!) H

Brethren, We Have Met to Worship 802

Here is an early 19th-century camp meeting song. David W. Music has found this text in the *Spiritual Songster* (Frederick-Town, 1819), one of five texts attributed to George Atkins.

Stanza 3 was added by Bryan Jeffery Leech in the spirit of the "family" stanzas which are part of the camp meeting improvisation tradition. Leech notes that it was written quickly at Calvary Baptist Church, Santa Barbara, CA, on his way to lunch with John Coulombe (who had suggested he write another stanza).

HOLY MANNA. George Pullen Jackson has pointed out that, while the melody of lines 1, 2, and 4 are identical, the third phrase's tune has appeared independently with other words, such as "Come, ye sinners, poor and wretched." The tune name is derived from the words "holy manna" in stanzas 1, 2, and 4.

First known publication is in William Moore's *The Columbian Harmony* (1825), where it is claimed by Moore, although the tunebook compilers often attributed folk tunes with their own names. The melody is similar to a family of shape-note folk hymn tunes.

Brightest and Best of the Stars of the Morning 182

Published in the *Christian Observer* (1811, just before author Reginald Heber went to India as a missionary), "Brightest and Best" was given wider distribution in the posthumous collection which was Heber's special interest, *Hymns Written and Adapted to the Weekly Church Services of the Year* (London and New York, 1827), the first hymnal in the church year format.

MORNING STAR. The tune was part of an anthem by James Harding, composed for the Gifford Hall Mission in 1892. It was adapted to this text by Charles Hutchins for the *Episcopal Hymnal* (1894).

Built on the Rock   705

Copenhagen's old cathedral Church of Our Lady was in ruins in 1807 as a result of English bombardment of the Danish-Norwegian forces, a military retaliation against Napoleon's blockade. In that context, Nicolai F. S. Grundtvig wrote of the church built of "living stones," not the crumbled spires of Copenhagen. The text was published in his *Sang-Värk til den Danske Kirke* in 1837. It was translated by Carl Doving and appeared in the *Lutheran Hymnary* (1913) with five stanzas (the fourth is omitted here). The present version was adapted by Fred Hansen and appeared in the *Hymnal for Church and Home* (1927).

KIRKEN DEN ER ET. Ludvig Lindeman's tune, written for this text, first appeared in W. A. Wexel's *Christelige Psalmer* (1840). It has been noted that the tune has characteristics of Norse folk music, of which Lindeman was an avid scholar, collector, and publisher. "Kirken den er et gammelt hus" in Danish means "The church is an old house."   H

By Christ Redeemed, in Christ Restored   789

George Rawson wrote this hymn for *Psalms and Hymns for the use of the Baptist Denomination* (1858), a book he helped edit. The addition by Margaret Clarkson is in the spirit of Rawson's last stanza.

ALMSGIVING. This tune was composed by John B. Dykes for the hymn "O Lord of Heaven and Earth and Sea" by Christopher Wordsworth, and first published in Wordsworth's *The Holy Year* (1865), edited by William H. Monk.

Cast Thy Burden upon the Lord   815

The text is from Psalm 55:22 and 16:8. Originally set in German for the oratorio *Elias* [Elijah, No. 15] (1846), the simple refrain is sung to encourage Elijah as he faces the false prophets on Mount Carmel. The translation into English was by William Bartholomew, who worked closely with Mendelssohn for the seamless fit of text.

BIRMINGHAM. Felix Mendelssohn composed this chorale-like quartet for *Elias* [Elijah] (1846). Four soloists (angels) sing nearly unaccompanied—the organ and orchestra join by sounding a simple chord only on the last note of each phrase; the first violin gently plays an arpeggio as that chord is sustained (a fermata). BIRMINGHAM, England, was the location of *Elijah*'s first performance, August 26, 1846. The melody resembles MUNICH (310), a tune Mendelssohn would have known.

Channels Only 577

This hymn has been associated with the Inter-Varsity Christian Fellowship and the Keswick Convention movement in England and America. It was written by Mary E. Maxwell, of uncertain identity.   H

CHANNELS. Named from the first word of the refrain, this music was written by Ada Rose Gibbs and appeared with the text in her *Twenty-Four Gems of Sacred Song* (1900).   H

Children of the Heavenly Father 84

According to Swedish tradition, the original of this hymn was written by Carolina ("Lina") Sandell (later Berg) while seated on the branch of a large ash tree in the parsonage yard at Fräderyd, where she lived. The poem was first published in Sandell's anonymous *Andeliga daggdroppar* (Spiritual Dewdrops) in 1855. It appeared with this tune in *Lofsånger och Andeliga Wisor*, 1873. The translation by Ernst W. Olson was prepared for *Augustana Hymnal*, 1925.

A devotional study of the text by Donald Hustad appears in *Crusade Hymn Stories*.   H

TRYGGARE KAN INGEN VARA. It is a European custom to use the first text line as the tune name. *Song Book for Sunday Schools* (Stockholm, 1871) marked the first known appearance of this tune in print. Long thought to be a Swedish folk melody, it may be of English or of German origin, brought to Sweden in the Pietist movement of the late-19th century.   H

Christ Arose! 235

Robert Lowry wrote the text and tune in 1874 while he was pastor of a Baptist Church in Lewisburg, PA, and a professor of rhetoric at Bucknell University.   H

CHRIST AROSE. The complete hymn of Robert Lowry was first published in *Brightest and Best* (1875), edited by William H. Doane and Lowry.   H

Christ Be My Leader 107

An early hymn by the prolific Dudley-Smith, this was written at

Sevenoaks (1961) during the British interest in popular youth materials, at the request of Canon H. C. Taylor, editor of the *Anglican Hymn Book* (1965), where it was first published (to this tune). It is an explanation of John 14:6.

SLANE; see **Be Thou My Vision** 532.

Christ Beside Me 543

James Quinn adapted the text from St. Patrick's breastplate incantation. The breastplate expression was used to protect body and soul against evil; this quote is in an 11th-century manuscript, *The Irish Liber Hymnorum*. According to legend, St. Patrick and his company were made to look like deer (the breastplate is also called, "Faeth fiada," "the deer's cry") so they could approach Tara where the Druid fire-worshipers lived. It is unlikely that St. Patrick actually wrote the words, but they are ancient, shielding against pagan powers.

Father Quinn's version was published in his *New Hymns for All Seasons* (London, 1969), identified as a morning prayer.

BUNESSAN; see **Morning Has Broken** 362.

Christ for the World! We Sing 743

Samuel Wolcott, then pastor of the Plymouth Congregational Church, Cleveland, OH, gave this account: "The Young Men's Christian Association of Ohio met in one of our churches, with their motto, in evergreen letters over the pulpit, 'Christ for the World, and the World for Christ.' This suggested the hymn." Wolcott wrote it on the way home, February 7, 1869, according to William J. Reynolds (*Hymns of our Faith*, 1964). It was first published in Doane's *Songs of Devotion* (1870) to the tune ITALIAN HYMN.

ITALIAN HYMN; see **Come, Thou Almighty King** 5.

Christ has for sin atonement made; see **What a Wonderful Savior** 488.

Christ, High-Ascended 734

Timothy Dudley-Smith's text was written at Ruan Minor while the bishop was "on holiday" but doing preparation for Ascension Day (Aug. 1983). He was studying "passages in Acts and the Gospels, 1 Corinthians, Ephesians, Colossians, and 1 Peter, as well as certain Old Testament references," he recalls. It was first published in *Lift Every Heart* (Hope Publishing Company, 1984).

CHRISTE SANCTORUM; this is the tune recommended by the author; see **Christ Is the World's Light** 90.

Christ Is Alive! Let Christians Sing 243

Author Brian Wren writes: "Ten days after the assassination of Dr. Martin Luther King [April 1968], I and my congregation at Hockley, Essex [England], met to celebrate Easter. The hymn tried to do so with truth and integrity, in words that could be more widely applied." The last stanza was revised in 1978 "to remove the masculine metaphors."

First publication was in 1975 with a new tune by Peter Cutts, KEELE.

TRURO; see **Ride On, Ride On in Majesty** 205.

Christ Is Coming! Let Creation 271

The Handbook to the *Mennonite Hymnary* calls this "a Scottish hymn setting forth the glowing hope and expectation of the coming of Christ in glory." Based on Revelation 22:20, it was written by John R. Macduff and published in his *Altar Stones* (1853).   H

CWM RHONDDA; see **Guide Me, O Thou Great Jehovah** 634.

Christ Is Made the Sure Foundation 699

John Neale translated this early (6th to 8th century) anonymous Latin hymn of eight stanzas—5, 7, 8, 9, here. The hymn is used for the dedication of a church or other doxologies of celebration. The translation was published in Neale's *Medieval Hymns* (1851).

CHRIST CHURCH (SNYDOR). The tune was composed for this text on the occasion of the 200th anniversary of Christ Church, Alexandria, VA, George Washington's church. It was a commissioned work honoring Rev. William Snydor (alternate tune name), who is now on the staff of Washington National Cathedral.

Christ Is the World's Light 90

Originally titled "The Uniqueness of Christ," Fred Pratt Green's hymn was commissioned for this unique tune by the *Hymns and Songs* committee of the Methodist Church in Great Britain (1968). It has appeared in numerous hymnals (with minor word differences) and has been translated into French and German. It was honored as the only modern hymn sung at the founding of the United Reformed Church in Westminster Abbey (joining the Congregational and Presbyterian Churches, Oct. 5, 1972). Although Pratt Green agreed to some revisions toward inclusive language, he retains the expression, "our brother." Written for CHRISTE SANCTORUM, the text has also been sung to ISTE CONFESOR and to a Hungarian carol tune, CHRISTUS URUNKNAK.

CHRISTE SANCTORUM. This tune was selected by the hymnal committee for *Hymns and Songs* (1969) from *Paris Antiphoner* (1681). It also appeared in other hymnals in the intervening years including an influential singable version by La Feillée in *Nouvelle Méthode du Plain-Chant* (5th ed., 1752); in *Paris Antiphoner*, it is sung to "Ceteri numquam nisi vagiendo," a hymn for the Visitation of the Blessed Virgin, although its name is derived from its association with the medieval text, "Christe sanctorum decus angelorum" [Christ glory of the angels].

Christ the Lord Is Risen Today   234
   Entitled "Hymn for Easter Day," this text of Charles Wesley was first included in *Hymns and Sacred Poems* (1739). It was altered and published in Martin Madan's *Collection of Psalms and Hymns* (1760), a famous volume that influenced English hymnals for more than 100 years.   H

EASTER HYMN (also **WORGAN**). From *Lyra Davidica* (London, 1708), a collection of 22 tunes compiled by John Walsh, including this anonymous melody in two parts. Since its first appearance, it has been frequently revised and has appeared in many hymnals. In essentially the present form, it is found in Arnold's *Complete Psalmodist* (1741).   H

Christ The Victorious   685
   Carl Daw's hymn (1982) is a paraphrase of the Kontakion for the Departed from the Eastern Orthodox Memorial Service in the Order for Burial (*Book of Common Prayer*). The Kontakion began at least by the 6th century as chanted prose, often with dramatic first-person voices which paraphrased biblical characters; it evolved into formalized litanies for specific services.

RUSSIAN HYMN; see **God the Omnipotent** 685. Daw wrote the text specifically for this tune, he says, "for congregations unable to sing the traditional Kiev melody for the Kontakion."

Christ upon the Mountain Peak   180
   This was the second hymn (June 1962) written by Brian Wren—at Mansfield College, Oxford. First publication was in *New Church Praise* with a tune by Peter Cutts, SHILLINGFORD. Wren identifies it as portraying an "atmosphere of worship and adoration" rather than the "imagery or historical 'placing' of the transfiguration."

MOWSLEY. Cyril Taylor composed the tune as a replacement for Gauntlett's ST. ALBINUS, a "heavier" tune associated with the hymn "Jesus lives! no longer now / Can thy terrors, death, appall us." Taylor writes that he wanted to "incorporate the *Alleluia* in the tune—'take it in stride'—rather than tack it on at the end." Taylor, again: "MOWSLEY is a very small village in the south of Leicestershire. My father was rector of it, with another village one mile away, from 1915-1932, and I grew up there from age 7 to leaving home for ordination into the Church of England." The tune was first published in the *BBC Hymn Book* (1951).

Christory, We Do All Adore Thee 816

This is Theodore Baker's English translation of the *Adoramus Te*, an ancient expression of praise. Composed for choir, with its Latin text, it is the final section of Théodore Dubois's *Seven Last Words of Christ* (1867); it is simply titled "Prayer." The dramatic cantata for choir (with soprano, tenor, and baritone soloists) is still in print, available from G. Schirmer.

ADORE THEE. The tune and four-part setting are the final section of Théodore Dubois's *Seven Last Words of Christ* (1867), composed to the Latin text. The editors of Dubois's cantata suggest that organ "double the voices with very soft stops."

Christ, Whose Glory Fills the Skies 562

Charles Wesley published this text in his *Hymns and Sacred Poems* (1740) with the title "A Morning Hymn." For a time, it was attributed in error to Toplady because it appeared in his 1776 *Psalms and Hymns*.

DIX; see **As with Gladness Men of Old** 181.

Christ, Whose Purpose Is to Kindle 720

Elton Trueblood, influential Quaker writer, wrote the hymn about 1966. It appeared in his *Incendiary Fellowship* (1967) under the title "Baptism by Fire." Changes have been made in the text and in the order of stanzas, with the approval of the author. H

HYMN TO JOY; see **Joyful, Joyful, We Adore Thee** 20.

Christian, Do You Struggle? 660

This text is a free revision by Bert Polman of "Christian, dost thou see them," which may have been an ancient Greek hymn (with 253 stanzas) by Andrew of Crete (660-732). If so, it is one of the oldest hymns in *The Worshiping Church*. It may be based on the life of the monastery at Nar Sabe and the personal experience of Andrew (who was mute, then healed). It is more likely that the hymn was written by John Neale and included with his early Greek translations (1862), since no original has been found. The Neale text has had many small alterations in its years of use; this complete modernization was prepared (1985) for the Christian Reformed *Psalter Hymnal* (1987).

The antiphonal dramatic dialogue can be read effectively. The revision keeps the spirit of the Neale poem, emphasizing that the battle is "not against flesh and blood" but against the "powers of this dark world and against the spiritual forces of evil" described in Ephesians 6:10-18, according to Polman.

KING'S WESTON; see **When the Church of Jesus** 722, the tune Polman suggests for unison congregational singing.

Christian, Dost Thou See Them; see **Christian, Do You Struggle?** (above) 660.

Clap Your Hands 23

Words and music were written by Jimmy Owens as an audience-participation section of the youth musical "Come Together" (Lexicon, 1972). The text is a paraphrase of Psalm 47:1 and other references to hands which clap in praise.

CLAP YOUR HANDS. The tune was written with the text setting and had a pop-band-style accompaniment; this harmonization by Dale Grotenhuis made it more hymn-like.

Come, All Christians, Be Committed 578

Eva B. Lloyd's hymn was a winning text in the 1966 Southern Baptist hymn writing competition. It was written in 1963 in Maryville, MO, and first appeared in *Eight New Christian Service Hymns*, published by Broadman Press in 1966. Later it was included in *Worship Hymnal* (1971), the hymnbook of Mennonite Brethren in the United States. H

BEACH SPRING. James H. Wood wrote an anthem based on this early American melody, and it was published with the words "Come, Ye Sinners" in 1958 by Broadman Press; this hymn setting is part of his anthem arrangement. The original tune appeared in duple meter in *The Sacred Harp* (1844), attributed to B. F. White. H

Come by here; see **Kum Ba Yah** 630.

Come, Christians, Join to Sing 108

Originally titled "Come, Children, Join to Sing," this hymn appeared in *Sacred Melodies for Sabbath Schools and Families* (1843), edited by author Christian Henry Bateman. For many years the book was Scotland's "Sabbath School Hymnal." The first line has been changed to make the hymn available to all age groups. H

MADRID. The origin of the tune and its name are unknown, though some publications date it "17th century." In 1825 and 1826 it appeared in Philadelphia in arrangements by Benjamin Carr for piano solo, and for solo with chorus and accompaniment. The tune also appeared in *A Collection of Metrical Versions*, etc. by M. Burgoyne (London, 1827) with the title "Spanish Chant." This arrangement by David Evans appeared in *The Revised Church Hymnary* (1927). H

Come, Come, Ye Saints   595

In his diary for April 15, 1846, William Clayton recorded that he wrote a new song, "All is Well," while traveling with Brigham Young's "Latter Day Saints" from Nauvoo, IL, toward the Great Salt Lake in the west. Actually the refrain "All is well!" had appeared in a hymn about death and heaven, set to the same tune in *The Sacred Harp* (1844).

Only the first stanza of the present song is Clayton's, with slight revision. The rest is the work of Avis B. Christiansen, written at the request of Donald P. Hustad for inclusion in *Crusader Hymns* (Chicago: Hope Publishing Company, 1966). H

ALL IS WELL. While this tune is said to be a traditional English melody, it may very well be American in its origin. David W. Music has found the tune in *Revival Melodies*, or *Songs of Zion* (Boston, 1842), where the tune, in six-eight meter, is attributed to "C. Dingley" and set to the text "What's This That Steals Upon My Frame." This four-four meter version is in *The Sacred Harp* (1844). H

Come Down, O Love Divine!   304

This free translation of Bianco da Siena's lauda text, "*Discendi, amor santo*" by Richard F. Littledale (four of eight stanzas) is from *The People's Hymnal* (1867); it gained popularity with the Vaughan Williams tune, DOWN AMPNEY (1906).

DOWN AMPNEY. Ralph Vaughan Williams composed this tune for the above text; it is named for his birthplace.

Come, every soul by sin oppressed; see **Only Trust Him** 443.

Come, Holy Ghost, Our Souls Inspire   296

"Veni, creator Spiritus," the Latin original of this hymn, dates back to the 9th or 10th century and is often credited to Rabanus Maurus, Archbishop of Mainz. It has had wide liturgical use for a thousand years. The translation by John Cosin was taken from his *Collection of Private Devotions in the Practice of the Ancient Church* (1627). Bishop Cosin composed this hymn for the coronation of Charles I in 1625, at which he officiated. H

VENI CREATOR. Although this tune was first used for an Easter hymn by Ambrose, "Hic est diesverus Dei," it has been associated with this text since Maurus. This version is from *Vesperale Romanum* (Malines, Belgium, 1848).

Come, Holy Spirit, Heavenly Dove   298

This hymn by Isaac Watts based on Romans 5:5 appeared in his *Hymns and Spiritual Songs* (1707) under the heading "Breathing after the Holy Spirit: or, Fervency of Devotion Desired." Numerous alterations have been made to the text; Watts himself made some changes in a second edition.   H

ST. AGNES; see **Jesus, the Very Thought of Thee** 112.

Come into His Presence   122

This simple anonymous text and tune became popular in the 1970s. Earliest located publication is Ken Bible's *Cornerstone, A Treasury of Scripture Songs* (Lillenas, 1982) where it is listed as "unknown."

HIS PRESENCE. The tune is associated with these words.

Come, Let Us Praise the Lord   320

The text is a paraphrase of Psalm 95, the Psalm known as the *Venite* (its initial Latin word), by Timothy Dudley-Smith. It was first written at the request of Michael Baughen, editor of *Psalm Praise* (1973), but the author was not satisfied with this attempt, so it was not published in that book. Nine years later at Ruan Minor, Dudley-Smith says he "returned to this Psalm. Verses 1 & 2 were begun over breakfast and into the morning; verses 3 & 4 in the later afternoon after lunch at the beach. Revisions were finished after supper, and final polishing the following day" (1981).

DARWALL; see **Rejoice, the Lord Is King** 262, the tune the author suggests.

Come, Let Us Reason   456

Ken Medema wrote the Isaiah 1:18 setting (1971) for his recording *Fork in the Road* (1972), because the "album needed [a] last tune," he says.

COME LET US REASON. The tune was originally a secular love song, "Maybe if I Try," and was adapted by Medema for the Isaiah text.

Come, Let Us with Our Lord Arise   798

Charles Wesley's text, from *Hymns for Children* (1763), was titled, "For the Lord's Day." It is a summary of the Apostles' Creed. Originally it had four stanzas. About his children's hymns, Wesley wrote (1790): "they contain strong and manly [adult] sense, yet expressed in such plain and easy language as even children may understand. But when they do understand them they will be children no longer, only in years and in stature."

SUSSEX CAROL; see **On Christmas Night All Christians Sing** 168.

Come, Share the Lord 782
Bryan Jeffery Leech composed the tune (Christmas 1982, in England with his family) before having any words in mind. The following summer, a friend in Simi Valley, CA, suggested the theme "holy communion," and Leech wrote the text "within an hour."

DIVERNON. The tune is named for a street in Simi Valley where the lyricist-composer's friends, Ken and Audry Nelson, live and which Bryan Jeffery Leech identifies as "a second home." Words and music were first published as an anthem (Fred Bock Music, 1984).

Come, Thou Almighty King 5
For more than a hundred years the authorship of this hymn, originally titled "an hymn to the Trinity," was attributed to Charles Wesley, an idea that is strongly debated by Armin Haeussler in *The Story of Our Hymns*. It appeared first with George Whitefield's *Collection of Hymns* (*c.* 1757). It is now thought that the hymn was an imitation of the English national anthem, "God Save Our Gracious King," and for this reason the author chose to remain anonymous. For many years, these words were sung to the tune we know as "America." H

ITALIAN HYMN. The tune appeared for the first time with this text in *The Collection of Psalm and Hymn Tunes Sung at the Chapel of the Lock Hospital* (1769). Its name is derived from the nationality of the composer, Felice de Giardini. In the hymnals of Great Britain, the common tune name is "Moscow," presumably for the city in which the composer died. H

Come, Thou Fount of Every Blessing 45
Robert Robinson wrote the hymn in 1758 for the festival of Whitsunday (Pentecost). The lines reveal a deep gratitude to God for saving him from a life of dissipation, and were written while he was a pastor in Norwich, England. The text was first published in *A Collection of Hymns, Used by the Church of Christ in Angel-Alley, Bishopsgate* (1759). H

NETTLETON. "Hallelujah" was the first name of this tune in John Wyeth's folk hymn collection, *Repository of Sacred Music, Part Second* (1813). It has been attributed both to Wyeth and to Asahel Nettleton, a

19th-century New England evangelist. It has also been suggested that a friend of Nettleton composed the tune and named it in his honor.   H

Come, Thou Long-Expected Jesus   135

This text was first published by its author, Charles Wesley, in a small compilation of 18 poems, *Hymns for the Nativity of Our Lord* (1744).   H

HYFRYDOL. The tune was composed by the 20-year-old Rowland H. Prichard about 1830 and was first published in his *Cyfaill y Cantorion* (1844). The tune name means "Good cheer."   H

Come to Us, Creative Spirit   407

This text by David Mowbray, Vicar of Broxbourne, Hertfordshire, England, first appeared in his privately published, undated *Kingdom Come: Fifty Hymns for Parish Services* (1977) with the title "Creative Spirit." It was revised and printed in *Partners in Praise* (1979).

ANGEL VOICES. The tune was composed (1861) for the text "Angel Voices Ever Singing," the dedication hymn for the organ of Winwick Church, Warrington, England. The descant by John Barnard was written in 1985 and first published in 1987, *Hymns for Today's Church.*

Come, We That Love the Lord   22, 596

This hymn by Isaac Watts was first published in 10 stanzas in his *Hymns and Spiritual Songs, Book II* (1707), entitled "Heavenly Joy on Earth." During its history, several minor word changes have been made. The refrain (596) was added by Robert Lowry in the style of camp meeting choruses.   H

ST. THOMAS 22. This is only a fragment of a 16-line tune, "Holborn," in Aaron Williams's *Collection* (1763) and was probably written by him. This form (sometimes called "Williams") was first used in his *New Universal Psalmist* (1770).   H

MARCHING TO ZION 596. The tune and the words of the refrain "We're marching to Zion" were written by Robert Lowry in 1867. The complete song first appeared in *Silver Spray* (1868), a collection of Sunday School songs.   H

Come, Ye Disconsolate   613

Thomas Moore was the author of some 32 hymns, of which this is the only one still in common use. He was better known for such secular favorites as "Believe Me, If All Those Endearing Young Charms" and "The Last Rose of Summer." Two stanzas of this hymn appeared in Moore's

Sacred Songs (1816). Thomas Hastings added a third stanza and altered the other two somewhat (changing "shrine of God" to "mercy seat"); his revision was published in *Spiritual Songs for Social Worship* (1831) compiled by Hastings and Lowell Mason.　　　　　H

CONSOLATOR. Moore said the tune was a "German air" which inspired him to write the original text. It is unclear whether Samuel Webbe composed it or arranged an already existing melody, but it was first published in his *Collection of Motetts* (1792). It appeared with these words in *Spiritual Songs for Social Worship* (1831).

CONSOLATOR distinguishes it from the melody by Felix Mendelssohn, the tune earlier called CONSOLATION.　　　　　H

Come, Ye Sinners, Poor and Needy　　　　　451
This text by Joseph Hart, a Congregational minister, originally began "Come, ye sinners, poor and wretched." It was first published in his *Hymns Composed on Various Subjects* (1759) in seven six-line stanzas, with the heading "Come, and Welcome, to Jesus Christ." The refrain is part of an anonymous "Prodigal Son" hymn appearing in American collections in the 19th century, "Far, far away from my loving Father."　　　　　H

ARISE. The tune, named for the refrain text, is an American folk melody of unknown origin. Set to the folk hymn "Mercy, O Thou Son of David," a text about blind Bartimeus, it appears in William Walker's *Southern Harmony* (1835) with the tune name RESTORATION. Walker sets "Come, Ye Sinners" to two other tunes in the book.

Come, Ye Thankful People, Come　　　　　381
Henry Alford's hymn appears to have been written for the Harvest and Thanksgiving season, but it has a strong eschatological reference to the consummation of history as Jesus taught it in Matthew 13:36-43. Several alterations were made after the hymn first appeared in Alford's *Psalms and Hymns* (1844).　　　　　H

ST. GEORGE'S, WINDSOR. The tune was written by George J. Elvey for James Montgomery's text "Hark! the song of jubilee" and was first published in E. H. Thorne's *Selection of Psalm and Hymn-Tunes* (1858). In *Hymns Ancient and Modern* (1861) it appeared with Alford's words. The tune is named for the historic royal chapel at Windsor Castle, where Elvey served as organist and choirmaster for 47 years.　　　　　H

Comfort, Comfort Now My People　　　　　132
Johannes Olearius wrote this hymn on Isaiah 40:1-5 for John the Baptist's Day (June 24). It was first published in his *Geistliche Singe-Kunst* (Leipzig, 1671), a large and influential collection, about one-fourth writ-

ten by Olearius. The English translation by Catherine Winkworth appeared in her *Chorale Book for England* (London, 1863).

GENEVAN 42. The tune, from the Genevan Psalter (1551), was probably composed by Louis Bourgeois. Claude Goudimel, who was a contemporary of Bourgeois, set the psalm tunes in four-part hymn style (with the melody in tenor) along with other musical settings, including a contrasting and complex motet version of each tune.

Congregational Commitment to Parents   765
Daniel Sharp, a member of the editorial committee for *The Worshiping Church*, wrote this response for the dedication of his own son (1983). He and his wife had "waited 4 and 5 years for each of the boys" so it was a particularly special time at Grace Chapel, Lexington, MA. This is its first publication.

Cross of Jesus, Cross of Sorrow   214
William J. Sparrow-Simpson wrote the libretto for John Stainer's cantata, *The Crucifixion* (1887), of which this hymn is a part.   H

CROSS OF JESUS. John Stainer's tune appears with this hymn in *The Crucifixion*. In that choral work, it was evidently intended to be sung by the congregation.   H

Crown Him with Many Crowns   92
Matthew Bridges wrote the words of stanzas 1 and 4 in 1851 and published them with three others in the second edition of his *Hymns of the Heart* under the title "On His Head Were Many Crowns." The hymn was revised and additional stanzas written by Godfrey Thring for his *Hymns and Sacred Lyrics* (1874); stanzas 2 and 3 are Thring's.   H

DIADEMATA. The tune (whose name means "crowns") was written for this hymn by George Elvey and appeared in the Appendix to the first edition of *Hymns Ancient and Modern* (1868).   H

Day by Day   535
This text is from a longer reading attributed to St. Richard of Chichester (13th century) and preserved in various books of common prayer. The following words precede the hymn text: "Thanks be to Thee, O Lord Jesus Christ, for all the benefits which Thou hast given us; for all the pains and insults which Thou has borne for us. O most merciful Redeemer, friend, and brother, may we . . ."

GODSPELL. Stephen Schwartz used traditional church texts as the basis for many of the songs in the 1971 Broadway musical *Godspell*. This setting was used in a scene with the disciples as they prepared to follow Jesus.

Day by Day and with Each Passing Moment   367
    Carolina Sandell Berg, sometimes called "the Swedish Fanny Crosby," wrote this text in 1865. For a number of years she published a "Bible Calendar" of inspirational articles, and this song first appeared in her *Korsblomman* for 1866. Oscar Ahnfelt included it in his *Andeliga Sånger* (1872) with his musical setting. The English translation by Andrew L. Skoog is the most popular and accurate of all the versions available; it was used in *Mission Hymns* (1921) and *The Covenant Hymnal* (1931).   H

BLOTT EN DAG. Named for the first words of the Swedish version, the music was written for the text by Oscar Ahnfelt. It is said that Mrs. Berg lengthened each line for her original poem by one syllable, at Ahnfelt's suggestion, in order to give the song a "softer and more natural rhythm."   H

Day is dying in the west; see **O Lord Most High** 828.

Dear Lord and Father of Mankind   591
    "The Brewing of Soma," a 17-stanza poem by John Greenleaf Whittier, which first appeared in the *Atlantic Monthly* (April 1872), described the attempts pagan peoples make to worship their gods. "Soma" is an intoxicating drink which produced "a frenzy, a sacred madness, an ecstatic storm of drunken joy." Whittier, a Quaker, concludes his poem with six stanzas beginning "Dear Lord and Father of mankind," in which he extols the quietness of true Christian worship. The text was first used as a hymn by W. Garrett Horder, editor of an English Baptist hymnal, and of *Worship Song* (1884).   H

REST. The tune was composed for this text by Frederick C. Maker for publication in the *Congregational Church Hymnal* (London, 1887). It is named "Rest" because of the emphasis of the words.   H

Dona Nobis Pacem; see **Father, Grant Us Your Peace** 589 or **Holy Lord** 827.

Doxology; see **Praise God from Whom** 808, 809 and **All People That on Earth Do Dwell** 317.

Draw Me Nearer 534
Fanny J. Crosby wrote these words while visiting in the home of her musical collaborator, William H. Doane. They had been discussing the nearness of God. The words were written that same evening and entitled "Draw Me Nearer," based on Hebrews 10:22. H

I AM THINE. The tune was written by William H. Doane for the text. It first appeared with the words in *Brightest and Best* (1875), a Sunday School songbook compiled by Doane and Robert Lowry. H

Earth and All Stars 357
Herbert Brokering wrote the text for the 90th anniversary of St. Olaf College, Northfield, MN. His comments: "I tried to gather into a hymn of praise the many facets of life which emerge in the life of community. . . I visualize the rhyme and rhythm of the gospel [which] came to me in Nebraska and Iowa."

EARTH AND ALL STARS. The tune was composed (evidently for this text) by David Johnson (1968) and harmonized by Dale Grotenhuis (1984).

Easter Song 244
Anne Herring wrote words and music (1972) for the performing group "2nd Chapter of Acts" (recorded 1974). Based on Exodus 28:35 as well as Matthew 28:6, the hymn was composed in response to the "call of neighborhood church bells urging people to come worship the Lord, and [reminding of] the promise of new life." Herring notes that it has been widely used in Eastern Europe, even played in train stations behind what was then the iron curtain.

EASTER SONG. The tune was composed with the words (1972).

Emmanuel, Emmanuel 140
Bob McGee wrote tune and text (1976), but provides no information about circumstances. The sentiment references both Matthew 1:23 and Isaiah 7:14.

EMMANUEL. The popular tune was composed with the text.

Epiphany Prayer 184
Lawrence Hull Stookey's prayer for Epiphany (January 6) was commissioned for *The United Methodist Hymnal* (1989); he was a member of the revision committee. Epiphany season begins with the celebration of the arrival of the Wise Men at the house of the young child Jesus.

Eternal Father, Strong to Save 358
The Navy Hymn, written in 1860 by William Whiting, has been revised many times; by its first publishers (the compilers of *Hymns Ancient and Modern*, 1861), by the author himself in the Appendix to *Psalms and Hymns for Public Worship* (1869), and by others. It is a prayer for safety on the high seas.

In the *Missionary Service Book* (1937) Whiting's first and fourth stanzas were retained, with slight alterations, and a second and third stanza covering travelers by land and air were added, probably by Robert Nelson Spencer. H

MELITA. The tune was composed by John B. Dykes for the Whiting hymn and first published in the original musical edition of *Hymns Ancient and Modern* (1861). The name refers to the island (now called Malta) where St. Paul was shipwrecked, as mentioned in the King James Version of Acts 28:1. H

Eternal Light, Shine in My Heart 545
Christopher Idle based this hymn on a prayer of Alcuin (or Ealhwine) of the 8th century, enlarging the ideas with "touches of Bonhoeffer, the apostle Paul, and the Gospels," according to the author. It was written at Limehouse, East London, 1977, sung at the institution of Michael Saward as vicar of Ealing (1978), and first published in *Hymns for Today's Church* (1982).

JACOB. Jane Marshall composed this tune for this text (and for another, "How oft, O Lord," which fits it as well). The Idle text was distributed by *The United Methodist Hymnal* committee, seeking new tunes. This tune was used at the confirmation of a friend's daughter, prior to the first publication in *The Hymnal* (1982).

Every Eye Shall See 755
Authors Bill and Gloria Gaither call this "a proclamation of Romans 14:11 and Isaiah 45:23" and emphasize congregational participation: "This text of sacred scripture acts both as a comforting assurance and a disturbing warning, depending upon our choices, behavior, and commitment at any particular juncture on our journey. That is the reason we felt this song should take the form of a repeatable, sing-along chorus with a haunting, almost cyclical, melody."

EVERY EYE. William (Bill) Gaither composed the setting with the text.

Face to Face 684
Carrie E. Breck sent this poem to Grant C. Tullar in 1898 suggesting that he provide a musical setting for her words. Tullar had just written a

tune for his own text, "All for me the Savior suffered," while assisting in evangelistic services in the Methodist Episcopal Church in Rutherford, NJ. Mrs. Breck's poem fit his tune so perfectly that he discarded his own words and used hers.   H

FACE TO FACE. Grant C. Tullar wrote the tune for these words (as described above); first publication was in *Sermons in Song, No. 2* (NY: Tullar-Meredith, 1899).   H

Fairest Lord Jesus   115

Although it is known to have been written at least 15 years earlier (contained in a Münster manuscript), the original German text ("Schönster Herr Jesu") was first published in the *Münster Gesangbuch* (1677), with six stanzas and the Latin superscription, *Suspirium ad Jesum*. The anonymous English translation of this Roman Catholic hymn first appeared in Willis's *Church Chorals and Choir Studies* (New York, 1850). A fourth stanza was added by Joseph A. Seiss, and appeared as part of his full translation in *The Sunday School Book* of the American Lutheran General Council (Philadelphia, 1873).   H

CRUSADER'S HYMN (also **SCHÖNSTER HERR JESU, ST. ELIZA-BETH**, or **ASCALON**). The tune first appeared with the German text in a book of Silesian folk songs, Hoffman's *Schlesische Volkslieder* (Leipzig, 1842), evidently gathered by Hoffman as a folk tune sung by haymakers. It was first published in America in *Church Chorals and Choir Studies* (New York, 1850) edited by Richard Storrs Willis. The name refers to the erroneous tradition that German knights sang the hymn on their way to capture Jerusalem in the 12th century—a myth passed on by Willis and encouraged by its use in a setting composed by Franz Liszt, "The Legend of St. Elizabeth" (1862).

Faith of Our Fathers   692

Frederick W. Faber's hymn was written in two versions, one for England, the other for Ireland, and both versions appeared in his *Jesus and Mary* (1849). Both versions make it clear that for Faber the "faith of our fathers" is that of Roman Catholicism. However, the English version, with editing, is loved by evangelicals the world around, and Roman Catholics are now singing it.   H

ST. CATHERINE. Written by Henri F. Hemy, the tune was originally set to a Roman Catholic hymn in Part II of his volume *Crown of Jesus Music* (1864). The title of the hymn was "St. Catherine, Virgin and Martyr." James G. Walton made a new arrangement and used this adaptation in *Plain Song Music for the Holy Communion* (1874).   H

Father Eternal, Lord of the Ages 6

George B. Timm's hymn of worship, which speaks of the Trinity, Creator, Savior, and Sanctifier, was written in 1974 and first published in *English Praise, No. 45* (1975). It has also appeared in *Hymns for Today's Church* (1982) and the *New English Hymnal*. Each of the first three stanzas addresses a member of the Godhead, and the fourth speaks to the Three-in-One.

HARROW WEALD. The tune was composed by John Barnard (1979) for this text, first published in the *Hymns for Today's Church* (1982) and harmonized by Harry Grindle in 1989 for inclusion in *Sing and Pray*, a publication of the Sunday School Society of Ireland.

Father, Grant Us Your Peace 589

The Latin words are the end of the *Agnus Dei* section of the Mass, a traditional text from as early as the 7th century. The English is a singable set of words in the same spirit, by Ottilie Stafford, prepared (1983) for the *Seventh-Day Adventist Hymnal*, where it was first published.

DONA NOBIS PACEM. The tune is attributed to Palestrina or Mozart—but may not belong to either. The Latin text-tune has been sung as a three-voice canon since at least the 18th century. Melvin West arranged the accompaniment for the *Seventh-Day Adventist Hymnal* (1984) intending "maximum flexibility as well as interest for a pianist."

Father, I Adore You 4

Text and tune were written (1972) by Terrye Coelho "while driving a car and worshiping God" as she and her sister were traveling home from a Christian life conference; it was then performed and recorded by the "Jesus People" of Costa Mesa, CA, who formed Maranatha! Music.

MARANATHA. The tune name, which means "The Lord comes," is also the name of the publishing house. Singing it as a round brings the Trinity into a musical performance simultaneously.

Father, we love you; see **Glorify Your Name** 10.

Fill Us with Your Love; see **Jesu, Jesu, Fill Us with Your Love** 436.

Fear Not, Rejoice and Be Glad 592

The text is a paraphrase of Joel 2:22-28 by Priscilla Wright, written for a Bible study "as an expression of joy for what the Holy Spirit was doing among the body of believers at the Episcopal Church of the Redeemer in Houston, TX" (1971). Wright has used it with liturgical dance. It was recorded by Fisherfolk (1972) and published in *Sound of Living Waters* (1974).

CLAY. Wright composed the tune with the text; CLAY is a street on which she lived. It was harmonized by Dale Grotenhuis (1986).

Fire of God, Undying Flame 301
Albert F. Bayly wrote the text as a panorama of God's actions in the affairs of earth (April 1947). The hymn is altered for *The Worshiping Church*, using text changes supplied by Oxford University Press. H

SONG 13. Orlando Gibbons composed 16 tunes with figured bass (a shorthand for the harmonies) for a planned book by George Withers, *The Hymns and Songs of the Church* (1623). The Company of Stationers opposed its publication because only psalmody was the approved form of worship, and it was not printed. Ralph Vaughan Williams discovered the tunes and used them in *The English Hymnal* (1906). SONG 13 has also been known as GIBBONS, CANTERBURY, or SIMPLICITY in pre-1906 publications.

For Ages Women Hoped and Prayed 143
The hymn was written for advent during that season in 1986. Its author, Jane Parker Huber, intended to balance the wide selection for Christmas with this hymn of "waiting and wondering." She writes, "We still await the full advent of God's reign on earth, the overcoming of injustice, the feeding of the hungry, the coming of peace." Its rare focus on Mary in an "earthy and practical way" is intended to reflect "the heart-to-heart conversations of women in that Rome-dominated world."

VOX DILECTI. This tune was selected by the hymn's author and particularly fits the contrasts of the text; see **I Heard the Voice of Jesus Say 506.**

For All the Saints 751
Several of the hymns written by William Walsham How have gained wide popularity in England and America. This memorial hymn first appeared in *Hymns for Saints' Days, and Other Hymns* (1864), compiled by Earl Nelson, a nephew of England's heroic Admiral Nelson. The hymn originally had 11 stanzas and began, "For all thy saints." H

SINE NOMINE. Ralph Vaughan Williams composed the tune for this text's appearance in *English Hymnal*, 1906. Erik Routley reports that at first the tune was condemned as "jazz music," but more recently is judged to be one of the great tunes of the century and certainly contributed to the popularity of the hymn. The name SINE NOMINE means "without a name." H

For Beauty of Meadows 383
Walter Farquharson wrote the text in 1969 in the context of his rural-agricultural setting in Canada, emphasizing his "family heritage of treasuring creation and practicing stewardship." The original title, "For beauty of prairies," was changed to be less local, and some inclusive language was added; first publication was in *The Hymnal* of the United Anglican Church of Canada (1971).

ST. DENIO; see Immortal, Invisible, God Only Wise 62.

For Grace to Labor 396
Thomas More's economical 16th-century prayer is a short tribute to work. His influence was far greater than this one-line prayer. He worked as a lawyer, farmer, scholar, writer, and eventually, Chancellor of England.

For Grace to Serve Selflessly 667
Ignatius of Loyola, founder of the Jesuits, recorded this prayer of service (rather than a prayer of contemplation, by his own account) in his *Exercises* (*c.* 1640).

For the Beauty of the Earth 353
The inspiration for this hymn came one day when Folliott S. Pierpoint viewed the beauty around him from a hilltop near Bath, England. It was first published in Orby Shipley's *Lyra Eucharistica*, second edition (1864). Its original title, "The Sacrifice of Praise," is significant in that the hymn was originally written for the Eucharist. Changes in the text have made it suitable for general use. H

DIX; see As with Gladness Men of Old 181.

For the Bread Which You Have Broken 772
As a hymn scholar, Louis Benson recognized a need for post-communion service congregational material. This positive reminder of the meaning of the Lord's Supper is derived from 1 Corinthians 11:23-32, and is one of only two Benson hymns (see 192) to achieve wide use. It was written November 18-23, 1924, critiqued by Henry Sloan Coffin, published privately in the author's *Hymns Original and Translated* (1925), and then revised by Benson and by later editors.

FOR THE BREAD (also **KINGDOM**). The tune was composed for this text by V. Earle Copes (1960) and takes its name from the last line.

For the Fruit of All Creation 379
    Fred Pratt Green wrote the text (1970) at the suggestion of John W. Wilson for the tune EAST ACKLAM (composed in 1957 as an alternative to AR HYD Y NOS with the words "God That Madest Earth and Heaven") to respond to a need for a new "harvest hymn" (its original title). First published in the *Methodist Recorder* (Aug. 1970) as "For the fruits of his creation," with a footnote indicating how to gain permission for its use, the text quickly became popular around the world. It is also set to a tune by Emma Lou Diemer, SANTA BARBARA, in *The Lutheran Book of Worship* (1978) and as an anthem by Austin Lovelace (Choristers Guild).

AR HYD Y NOS; see Through the Love of God Our Savior 610.

For the Life That You Have Given 813
    Carl Daw was commissioned to write this text as an offertory response by Fourth Presbyterian Church, Chicago, IL (1987). It was first used there with a tune composed by Morgan Simmons, the organist-choirmaster.

PLEADING SAVIOR; see Jesus Calls Us o'er the Tumult 580.

For Your Gift of God the Spirit 285
    Margaret Clarkson first wrote this text at Severn River, Ontario (1959) in response to C. Stacey Woods's request for an InterVarsity hymn on the Holy Spirit; it was published in *Anywhere Songs* (InterVarsity Press, 1960). She revised it (1984) to remove archaisms.

BLAENWERN; see It Is Good to Sing Your Praises 325.

For Your Holy Book We Thank You 316
    Ruth Carter's sister, Bessie Carter, did not know that Ruth had written this hymn, so can provide no information.

IRBY; see Once in Royal David's City 161

Forth in Your Name, O Lord, I Go 397
    The text by Charles Wesley was first published in the Wesley brothers' *Hymns and Sacred Poems* (1749), one of the 43 "Hymns for Believers." It was titled "Before Work."

DANIEL. This Irish tune was arranged by Martin Shaw, who gathered many early folk tunes of the British Isles, and was first published in *Songs of Praise for Boys and Girls* (1930).

Gentle Mary Laid Her Child 156

Joseph S. Cook's text won first prize in a carol competition sponsored by the *Christian Guardian*. It first appeared in the Christmas 1919 issue of that magazine printed by the Methodist Book and Publishing House, Toronto, Canada. H

TEMPUS ADEST FLORIDUM. The tune is from the collection *Piae Cantiones* compiled by Theodoricus Petrus of Nyland, Finland (1582), where it is a spring carol with the opening Latin line "Tempus adest floridum." For many years it has been used with Neale's "Good King Wenceslas." The present harmonization was made by Sir Ernest Macmillan for the *Hymnary of the United Church of Canada* (1930), in which this text and tune appeared together for the first time. H

Give Me Jesus 551

Text and tune in nearly this form are printed in John W. Work's *American Negro Folk Songs and Spirituals* (Bonanza, 1940), a collection of oral tradition that Work gathered from his students at Fisk University. In addition to the stanzas in *The Worshiping Church*, Work includes a first stanza which indicates a "family" set of words: "I heard my mother say."

AFRICAN-AMERICAN NEGRO SPIRITUAL. The spiritual tune and various texts associated with the "Give me Jesus" refrain are evidently a call and answer folk song from the 19th century. Work's transcription of it has the voices in unison except for the three-word title-answer. *Slave Songs of the United States*, compiled by Allen, Ware, and Garrison (1867, reprinted by Peter Smith, 1951) includes "Tell My Jesus, 'Morning,'" a slave song which has some similarities in text and tune profile, but is unlikely to be very closely related. This arrangement by Alma Blackmon appeared in *Seventh-day Adventist Hymnal* (1985).

Give Thanks to the Lord 345
See **The Strife Is O'er, The Battle Done** 233.

Give Thanks with a Grateful Heart 496

Henry Smith wrote this text and music for a small church in Virginia (1978), and it was spread from church to church by singing. Integrity Music, Mobile, AL, recorded it on their album of the same title and first printed the song; it has become the publisher's "theme" and best known copyright.

GIVE THANKS. The music was composed with the text.

Give to Our God Immortal Praise   16
This is thought to be the best of Isaac Watts's three versions of Psalm 136, and it appeared in his *Psalms of David imitated in the Language of the New Testament* (1719).   H

DUKE STREET; see **Jesus Shall Reign** 745.

Give to the Winds Your Fears   618
Paul Gerhardt's German hymn based on Psalm 37:5 was printed in Johann Crüger's *Praxis Pietatis Melica* (1653) and has been translated into English more than 20 times. John Wesley's setting, which appeared in *Hymns and Sacred Poems*, 1739, has been slightly modernized by the editors of *The Worshiping Church.*   H

DIADEMATA; see **Crown Him with Many Crowns** 92.

Gloria, Gloria   825
The text is the Latin version of the first part of Luke 2:14, plus "alleluias"; see **Glory Be to God** 824.

GLORIA III. Brother Jacques Berthier's music to the traditional text was composed for the ecumenical monastic fellowship in Burgundy, France, known as the Taizé Community.

Gloria in excelsis; see **All Glory Be to God on High** 8 and **Glory Be to God on High** 824.

Glorify Your Name   10
The author-composer credits her family's move to north Louisiana (summer 1975) and the necessary adjustments as the inspiration for this song. It was "a needed change of pace and time for me to seek the Lord," she writes. Words and music, growing from her reading of John 17, were first published in a pamphlet for a pastor's conference (1976) and later revised (1981). This is a "family" song with single words interchanged in each stanza—designed for rote singing.

GLORIFY YOUR NAME. The repeated text and melody were composed together by Donna Adkins.

Glorious Things of Thee Are Spoken   694
This hymn first appeared (with five stanzas) in Book I of *Olney Hymns*, 1779, edited by William Cowper and John Newton, where its title was "Zion, or the City of God"; Newton attributed it to Isaiah 33:20-21.

Thought to be one of his greatest hymns, it was said to be the "only joyful hymn in the Olney collection."   H

AUSTRIAN HYMN. The tune is based on a Croatian melody, "Vjatvo rano se ja vstanem," according to William H. Hadow. Franz Joseph Haydn adapted it for the poet Hauschka's nationalistic hymn "Gott, erhalte Franz, den Kaiser" and it was first performed for the emperor's birthday on February 12, 1797. Haydn later used it as the theme for variations in the 2nd movement of his string quartet in C, Op. 76, No. 5. It is still considered an Austrian patriotic song.

Glory Be to God on High   824
    The *Gloria in excelsis Deo*, the "Greater Doxology" (cf. 807), is perhaps the most significant praise hymn in Christian history. It is the canticle to the Trinity, sung immediately after the *Kyrie* in all western eucharistic liturgies in every Sunday and feast-day service except during times of penitence, such as Advent and Lent. Its first section was written before 150 A.D. and the complete hymn has been used regularly since the 5th century.   H

WILLAN GLORIA. Healey Willan, expressing a strong interest in plainsong and historic musical idioms, composed settings (1928) for the English translation of this historic text while teaching theory at the University of Toronto and serving as precentor of the Church of St. Mary Magdalene.

Glory Be to God the Father   11
    This hymn of Horatius Bonar was written specifically for *Psalms and Hymns for Divine Worship*, 1867, a compilation of the English Presbyterian Church. However, it appeared first a year earlier in the writer's own volume, *Hymns of Faith and Hope*, 1866. In some churches the first stanza is sung at times in place of the traditional Doxology.   H

WORCESTER. Our research (and that of Concordia, the copyright holder) has not located any information on this tune.

Glory Be to the Father   805, 807
    The *Gloria Patri* (the opening words in Latin) is known as the Lesser Doxology in contrast to *Gloria in excelsis Deo*, the Greater Doxology. The ascription of praise to the Holy Trinity based on Matthew 28:19 may have been used in the days of the Apostles, certainly by the 2nd century. The second half of the text, however, did not come into being until after the Arian controversy in the 4th century. Since that time, in liturgical worship it has been sung after each psalm and canticle.   H

GREATOREX 805. The tune is from Henry W. Greatorex's *Collection of Psalm and Hymn Tunes* (1851). It was published when he was organist and director of music at Calvary Episcopal Church in New York City.   H

MEINEKE 807. Christoph Meineke published this tune to "Evening Prayer" in his *Music for the Church* (1844). The tune was composed for use in St. Paul's Church, Baltimore, MD.   H

Glory be to you, O Lord   810
The short text is a condensation of the *Gloria Patri* (above).

[GLORY BE]. Thomas Tallis's simple setting is from *Rejoice in the Lord*. H

Glory to the Father   806
The short text is a paraphrase of the *Gloria Patri* (above).

BETHEL PARK. John Erickson composed this setting (1984) out of his interest in 19th-century English cathedral music. It is named for his present home address.

Go, Tell It on the Mountain   151
Before 1840 no attempts were made to collect the songs of African Americans. George Pullen Jackson argues that black spirituals had their roots in camp meeting music and gospel songs, which in turn had their beginnings in the folk music of the British Isles that was perpetuated in Appalachia. Camp meetings were the only truly integrated events in antebellum America and their repertoire is collected in the shape-note tunebooks of the period. Other scholars present strong evidence that American "call and response" chants have been heard in African usage and were the prior influence on this style of both black and white spirituals.

The origin of this traditional spiritual is unknown. It is included in *American Negro Songs and Spirituals* (1940) by John W. Work III, where the footnote states that the stanzas were supplied years ago by his father, John W. Work, Jr., "in place of the original ones which could not be found."

GO TELL IT. The music continues to appear in different versions of both melody and harmony, clear marks of its folk tune origins. It has been pointed out that the melody of the stanzas resembles the white spiritual "We'll march about Jerusalem" and the refrain echoes George F. Root's "Tramp, tramp, tramp, the boys are marching."   H

Go to Dark Gethsemane 225

This text by James Montgomery portrays four of the final incidents in the life of Jesus; his agony in Gethsemane, his trial, his crucifixion, and his resurrection. From these, Montgomery draws lessons for Christian living. First published in 1822, the present text is the second and much-revised form which appeared in Montgomery's *Christian Psalmist* (1825) under the heading "Christ, our example in suffering." H

REDHEAD. The tune is named for its composer, Richard Redhead. It first appeared in his *Ancient Hymn Melodies and Other Church Tunes* (1853), bearing only the Roman numeral LXXVI. Consequently, it is sometimes called REDHEAD 76. H

God Be in My Head 837

The text is found in a book for home worship, a *Book of Hours* printed for Antoine Verard (France, *c*. 1497), "Jésus soit en ma tête." In English, it appeared in the *Book of Hours for the Blessed Virgin* (London, 1514, compiled by Richard Pynson), and a *Sarum Primer* (1558). It is a prayer which is "proper" before the daily offices, the services of worship which were part of monastic routines, and may have been used earlier as a *Lorica* (a prayer for protection engraved on a breastplate). Its first use as a hymn appears to be in the *Oxford Hymn Book* (1908).

FIELD. This anonymous tune is associated with the text.

God Be with You Till We Meet Again 839, 840

This text was written by Jeremiah E. Rankin while he was the pastor of the First Congregational Church in Washington, DC. There was no specific reason for its writing; he simply wanted to interpret the derivation of "good-bye" from "God be with you." It was first published with this tune in *Gospel Bells*, 1880, edited by J. W. Bischoff, Otis F. Presbrey, and Rankin. H

GOD BE WITH YOU 840. This tune was written at the request of the author (Rankin) by William G. Tomer, who was then director of music at the Grace Methodist Episcopal Church in Washington, DC. It has persisted as a favorite, despite criticism. As here, the traditional refrain has been omitted in several recent hymnals. H

RANDOLPH 839. The tune by Ralph Vaughan Williams was first published in the *English Hymnal* (1906). His association with the English Folk-Song Society (beginning 1904) no doubt influenced the style.

God Bless Our Native Land 421

The text is based on a German hymn by Siegfried Mahlmann, "Gott segne Sachsenland," published in *Zeitung für die elegante Welt* (1815). The first two lines of the English version were translated by Charles Brooks while he was a student at Harvard Divinity School; the balance of the English is the work of John S. Dwight, the Boston music critic.

AMERICA; see **My Country, 'Tis of Thee** 417.

God Has Spoken by His Prophets 311

George W. Briggs's words were written in 1952 and published by The Hymn Society of America in a pamphlet, "Ten New Bible Hymns" (1953). In conjunction with the National Christian Council and in celebration of the publication of the Revised Standard Version of the Bible, The Hymn Society had asked for new texts on the values and history of Holy Scripture. The 10 were selected from more than 300 entries.   H

ODE TO JOY; see **Joyful, Joyful, We Adore Thee** 20. This descant was composed for *The Worshiping Church* by its editor, Donald P. Hustad.

God Himself Is with Us 799

Gerhard Tersteegen is considered one of the great German hymnists and spiritual leaders in the Reformed tradition. Although he was never ordained, his simple, devout, mystical faith led him to minister to those in spiritual and physical need. His hymn "Gott ist gegenwartig" appeared in his *Geistliches Blumengartlein* (1729) and may be a paraphrase of a work by the French writer Labadie. The composite translation is the work of the editors of the Protestant Episcopal *Hymnal* (1940).   H

ARNSBERG (also **WUNDERBARER KÖNIG**). The tune was named for the German hymn to which it was first set, "Wunderbarer König, Herrscher von uns allen" (Wonderful King). It is credited to Joachim Neander, and appeared in his *Bundes-Lieder* (1680).   H

God in His Love for Us 385

Fred Pratt Green's text entitled "The Stewardship of the Earth" won a place in *Sixteen Hymns on the Stewardship of the Environment* (Hymn Society of America, 1973). It has since appeared in several hymnals. The original version included this additional stanza: "Casual despoilers, or high-priests of Mammon, / Selling the future for present rewards, / Careless of life and contemptuous of beauty; / Bid them remember: the Earth is the Lord's."

MORNING STAR; see **Brightest and Best of the Stars** 182.

God in Mercy Grant Us Blessing   344

This metrical version of Psalm 67 was intended by David Preston as "a harvest psalm leading to prayer for the worldwide spread of the knowledge of Israel's God." Written in 1980, it was first published in *The Book of Praises* (Carey Publications, 1986) along with other metrical psalms by Preston.

ZEUCH MICH, ZEUCH MICH. William Monk borrowed freely from other sources for his tunes and adapted them for his own use. This, from *Geistreiches Gesang-Buch* edited by E. P. Zühlen (Darmstadt, 1698), was sung to a text which provides the tune name.

God Is Here!   701

Fred Pratt Green titled this hymn "The Church of Christ" when he wrote it (1978) for Russell Schulz-Widmar, Co-director of Music at University United Methodist Church, Austin, TX. It was sung to the tune ABBOT'S LEIGH (70, 715) at the closing service of the church's eighth-month Festival of Worship, Music, and the Arts (1979).

BEECHER; see **Love Divine** 558.

God Is in This Place   791

Mary E. Caldwell wrote the text (May 1975) for an anthem (Fred Bock Music Co.) she composed for the dedication of the sanctuary at First Presbyterian Church, Santa Monica, CA. Marcia Hannah, organist, commissioned it; at her request, it refers to all aspects of the new sanctuary— symbols, windows, cornerstone, voices, and the world outside.

NUN DANKET (for the refrain); see **Now Thank We All Our God** 374.

God Is Love—His the Care   400

Percy Dearmer wrote this text for *Songs of Praise* (1925), a hymnal he compiled. It was designed for the tune then called THEODORIC [PERSONENT HODIE] and intended to "convey if possible some fundamental theology in a simple form."

PERSONENT HODIE [also **THEODORIC**]. The above text was written for this much earlier tune; see **On This Day Earth Shall Ring** 175.

God is Love, Let Heaven Adore Him   70

First printed in *Sermons and Hymns by Timothy Rees, Bishop of Llandaff* (1946), the hymn was soon included in the *BBC Hymn Book* and other collections.

ABBOT'S LEIGH. This tune was written by Cyril Taylor for the text "Glorious Things of Thee Are Spoken" (694). He notes that it has become "accepted pretty well throughout the English-speaking world as part of the furniture of public worship." In part, it is widely known because of its use on the BBC's "Songs of Praise" and "Sunday Half-Hour" during World War 2. First publication was in *Hymns Ancient and Modern* (1950, revised). Taylor explains:

> The BBC, at the beginning of World War Two, received letters asking why we had to use the tune of *Deutschland über alles* for 'Praise the Lord! ye heavens, adore him' and for 'Glorious things.' It was assumed that I wrote this to provide an alternative. I can only say that I cannot now remember having sat down with that deliberate intent, but of course the objective may have guided me subconsciously in that direction.

Taylor's obituary reports that "Cyril exploded with rage when people invariably sang the end of it incorrectly."

God Is My Great Desire   336
This metrical version of Psalm 63 was first published in *Book of Praises* (Leeds: Carey Publications, 1986) and *Lift Every Heart* (Hope Publishing Company, 1989). Timothy Dudley-Smith wrote it at Ruan Minor (Aug. 1982) for the tune LEONI at the request of David G. Preston, who had planned to use it in a collection. The hymn writer notes the recurring use of "s" and "t" as a poetic device anticipating the final word, "trust."

LEONI; see **The God of Abraham Praise** 66.

God Is So Good   75
This anonymous chorus appeared at least by the early 1970s and, because it is simple and memorable, quickly spread.

GOD IS SO GOOD. The tune is connected to the text.

God Is Working His Purpose Out   750
Written at Eton College by its assistant schoolmaster, Arthur Ainger (1894), this text was first printed as a leaflet; later, it was published in the Church Missionary Society *Hymn Book* (1899).

PURPOSE. The tune is from *Enlarged Songs of Praise* (Oxford University Press, 1931), edited by Martin Shaw, who composed it for this text.

God Moves in a Mysterious Way   73
The text appeared anonymously in John Newton's *Twenty-Six Letters on Religious Subjects* (1774) under the title "Light Shining out of Darkness"

(with six stanzas). In *Olney Hymns*, book 3 (1779), it was credited to William Cowper. It has been described as the finest hymn on God's providence ever written. The stanza omitted from *The Worshiping Church*: "Judge not the Lord by feeble sense, but trust him for his grace: behind a frowning providence he hides a smiling face." H

DUNDEE. Bearing the name FRENCH TUNE (still its name in Scotland), this melody was first used in *The One Hundred Fifty Psalms of David*, published by Andro Hart (Edinburgh, 1615), the first Scottish Psalter with melodies. It was one of 12 interchangeable "common tunes" (six still used today) that could be used with different psalms, rather than each being associated with a particular psalm. The Scottish name DUNDY TUNE was attached by Ravenscroft when it appeared in his *Psalmes* (1621), but the tune may have come from Geneva. Ravenscroft provided the four-part harmonization, with the melody given to the tenor and the other parts somewhat interchanged.

God of Creation, All-Powerful, All-Wise   48
Margaret Clarkson wrote this hymn in Toronto, Ontario, Canada, as her response to a Bible study on Acts 4:23-31 by Rev. Eric Alexander of Glasgow, Scotland. It was intended for the tune SLANE.

SLANE; see **Be Thou My Vision** 532

God of Grace and God of Glory   669
Written by Harry Emerson Fosdick for the opening service of New York City's Riverside Church, October 5, 1930, and the dedication service, February 8, 1931, the hymn appeared in H. Augustine Smith's *Praise and Service* (1932) set to the tune REGENT SQUARE. Dr. Fosdick was one of the principals in the fundamentalist-modernist struggle of the 1920s and 1930s, but these words can be the prayer of all true Christians. H

CWM RHONDDA; see **Guide Me, O Thou Great Jehovah** 634.

God of Love and Truth and Beauty   428
Timothy Rees's hymn was published in the *Mirfield Mission Hymn Book* (1922) and gained wide usage with the *BBC Hymn Book* (1951).

KANSFIELD. Although Eric Routley composed this tune for another text (1982), it fits the Rees hymn, which is (in stanza 1) reminiscent of Routley's often-repeated phrase "duty and delight" (itself a quote from a Watts hymn).

God of Our Fathers 419
Produced in 1876 and intended for the 100th anniversary of the Declaration of Independence, this text was later selected as the official hymn for the centennial celebration of the adoption of the Constitution. It was written by Daniel Crane Roberts while he was rector of St. Thomas' Episcopal Church, Brandon, VT, and originally sung to the tune RUSSIAN HYMN (427), with which it appeared in the Protestant Episcopal *Hymnal* (1892). H

NATIONAL HYMN. George William Warren, organist of New York City's St. Thomas' Church, composed this tune for this text. It was used at the Columbia celebration in St. Thomas' Church on October 8, 1892, and published in the revised musical edition of the Protestant Episcopal *Hymnal* (1894). H

God of Our Life 370
This poem by Hugh T. Kerr was written for the 50th anniversary celebration of the Shadyside Presbyterian Church, Pittsburgh, PA (1916). It was revised for inclusion in *The Church School Hymnal for Youth* (1928) and revised again in 1972. H

SANDON. Written by Charles Henry Purday for the hymn "Lead Kindly Light," this tune appeared in *Church and Home Metrical Psalter and Hymnal* (1860) which Purday edited. SANDON is an old English residence name. H

God of the Ages 363
Margaret Clarkson wrote this text (Nov. 1981) for a contest in *Christianity Today* magazine, in which it won first place (Aug. 1982). First publication as a hymn was in *Hymnal Supplement* (Agape, 1984). The author suggests BUNESSAN (362) as its tune.

BUNESSAN; see **Morning Has Broken** 362.

God sent his Son, they called him Jesus; see **Because He Lives** 238.

God the Father, Name We Treasure 766
Basil Bridge wrote this hymn for the baptism (May 5, 1975) of his first grandchild, Mark Christopher Hanson, son of Bridge's daughter Eleanor and her husband, Eric Hanson. The child's "name" suggested a trinitarian design for the text: Hanson was his father's name, Christopher means Christ-bearer, and the apostle Mark inspired the Gospel writers. It was first published in *More Hymns for Today* (1980).

LAUDA ANIMA; see **Praise, My Soul, the King of Heaven** 26; Bridge also suggests **NEANDER.**

God, the Omnipotent! 427

This text is a composite. Stanzas 1, 2, and 4 were written for the tune "Russian Hymn" by Henry F. Chorley in 1842, and were published in John Hullah's *Part Music*, 1842, with the title "In Time of War." In Great Britain the original first phrase is still sung: "God the All-terrible!"

During the Franco-Prussian War in 1870, John Ellerton wrote a similar hymn beginning "God the Almighty, in wisdom ordaining," which included the third stanza printed here. This hymn was published in Robert Brown-Borthwick's *Select Hymns for Church and Home*, 1871. The hymns appeared in a combined version in *Church Hymns*, 1871 (1874 ed.). Subsequent printings have received textual alterations.   H

RUSSIAN HYMN. The music was composed (1833) by Alexis F. Lvov at the request of Czar Nicholas for a truly Russian national hymn tune. Before this, the British melody "God Save the King" had been the setting for the Russian national song.   H

God, We Praise You! 39

This paraphrase of the ancient canticle *Te Deum laudamus* (dated from the 5th century) was written while Christopher Idle was "on holiday at Meols" (near Hoylake, Cheshire) in 1978, recovering from eye surgery which prevented his being in the sunlight. Having known the *Te Deum* "from boyhood," he chose to start as it did, by addressing God. In his metrical version, Idle deliberately included the major elements of the historic prayer: the Tersanctus (Holy, holy, holy), the "glorious catalogue of worshipers," the virgin birth, open heaven, and the concluding prayer. It was sung at the clergy conference at Ely (Feb. 1979), was published first in *Hymns for Today's Church* (1982), and in at least six hymnals since.

See also **Holy God, We Praise Your Name** 3, and a translation of the *Te Deum laudamus* 352.

RUSTINGTON. Named for the town in Sussex, England, where Hubert Parry last lived, the tune was first published in *The Westminster Abbey Hymn-Book* (1897) to Webb's text "Praise the Rock of Our Salvation."   H

God, Who Made the Earth and Heaven 366

Reginald Heber's hymn "God that madest earth and heaven" was published in his *Hymns* (1827) as one of two evening hymns; its first stanza is the beginning of this hymn, as well. Richard Whately added a stanza (the third, here) for his Dublin publication, *Sacred Poetry adapted to the Understanding of Children and Youth* (1838), basing his verse on the "Salve nos" antiphon. William Mercer, in *Church Psalter and Hymn Book* (1864), wrote the other two stanzas.

AR HYD Y NOS; see Through the Love of God Our Savior 610.

God, Who Stretched the Spangled Heavens 54

Catherine Cameron indicates she wrote the hymn "over a period of several months at a time when I was experiencing a new sense of direction, growth, and creativity in my life" (1965). She had in mind the Haydn tune AUSTRIAN HYMN (694). First publication was in *Contemporary Worship* (1969); it was altered before its next appearance in *Lutheran Book of Worship* (1978).

HOLY MANNA; see Brethren, We Have Met to Worship 802.

God, Whose Giving Knows No Ending 644

Robert L. Edwards's hymn was first published in *Ten New Stewardship Hymns* (Hymn Society, 1961). Quoted by Stulken, the author says:

"God, whose giving knows no ending" was written in the White Mountains of New Hampshire while we were summering at our cottage in the tiny town of Randolph in 1961. At that time the Hymn Society of America, of which my father was the President, was sponsoring a competition for stewardship hymns. In our family we were in the habit of listening to hymns on records from time-to-time during those days of leisure. One of them was set to the tune of HYFRYDOL [135], a tune unknown to me until that time. In some way the idea of writing a hymn text to that music gradually slipped into my mind, and in about a month I had my hymn.

BEACH SPRING; see Come, All Christians, Be Committed 578 [or **HYFRYDOL** 135].

God Will Take Care of You 619

Civilla D. Martin wrote the words one Sunday afternoon in 1904 while her husband was on a preaching assignment and she remained ill in bed in Lestershire, NY. Mr. Martin wrote the music when he returned that same day, and the hymn was sung in the evening. H

GOD CARES. W. Stillman Martin's tune appeared with his wife's words in *Songs of Redemption and Praise*, 1905, compiled by him with evangelist John A. Davis, founder and president of the Practical Bible Training School, Lestershire, New York. H

God, You Spin the Whirling Planets 51

Jane Parker Huber wrote this hymn for the 1979 National Meeting of United Presbyterian Women, using the conference theme, "In the Image of God." It was published in a booklet compiled for that meeting by Ann Lodge; the original title was "In God's Image," and the intended tune was AUSTRIAN HYMN (because of Haydn's "creation" connection); HYFRYDOL and IN BABILONE are also suggested by the author. Huber has slightly altered the grammar of the opening line since the premiere. The hymn has been translated into Spanish by Nanin Braulio of Puerto Rico.

HYFRYDOL; see Come, Thou Long-Expected Jesus 135.

God's Holy Ways Are Just and True 328

This metrical setting of Psalm 111 was written (1983-84) by Barbara Woollett in response to the "Jubilate Hymns" psalm project, was first sung at the Abere Bar Church (July 1984) where the author and her husband worship, and was first published in *Psalms for Today* (1984). She wrote the text for this tune.

LASST UNS ERFREUEN; see All Creatures of Our God and King 456.

God's Love Made Visible 179

Dave (jazz pianist) and Iola Brubeck's carol was composed as the 14th movement of a Mexican Christmas cantata, *La Fiesta de la Posada* (Shawnee Press, 1976), for Mary, the Wise Men, and children and adult chorus. The first performance was in Honolulu (1975), commissioned by the Honolulu Symphony Orchestra. This song introduces the piñata ceremony. Dave Brubeck writes that the music reflects "unshakable religious faith made evident in a strong sense of one's own worth and a deep respect for the shared values of one's own group—family, church, village. . . . It is this sense of *sharing* in an event that I have tried to capture. . ."

Iola Brubeck adds this recollection, "The composition 'La Fiesta de la Posada' was begun to commemorate the restoration of the California mission San Luis Rey, thus the Mexican influence on the music which depicts the reenactment of the Nativity story. The hymn . . . came almost as an afterthought. One hot summer day driving to Vermont, Dave and I were discussing the composition, when I said, 'You've told the story of the birth of Jesus, but you've not made a strong statement about the significance of his birth. It is God's love made visible.' Dave immediately said, 'Repeat that phrase.' 'God's love made visible.' 'Perfect in 5/4 time; it would go like this'—he hummed the tune. 'Now give me some verses.' We spent the rest of the drive working up verses in 5/4 rhythm and that evening Dave wrote down the melody."

"God's Love Made Visible" is recorded by the Dale Warland Singers

(CBS 36662) and *La Fiesta de la Posada* by Brubeck on *Live at Montreux* (Tomato 7018).

POSADA. The tune is named for the cantata (*posada* is Spanish for inn) and refers to the festival "depicting Joseph and Mary's search for lodging on the eve of her confinement, . . . reenacted from December 16 to Christmas Eve throughout Latin America and in [the U.S.] Southwest," according to Dave Brubeck.

Good Christian Friends, Rejoice 157
This text, a free rendering of the old German-Latin (macaronic, or bilingual) carol "In dulci jubilo," first appeared in John Mason Neale's *Carols for Christmastide* (1853). The earliest existing form of text and tune is in Leipzig University, Ms. No. 1305, *c.* 1400. The first published version is that in Klug's *Gesangbuch* (1535). H

IN DULCI JUBILO. The tune accompanied the text in the above-mentioned manuscript. It was published, much in its present form, in Klug's *Gesangbuch* (1535). H

Good Christian Men, Rejoice; see **Good Christian Friends, Rejoice** 157.

Good Christians All, Rejoice and Sing 255
Cyril Alington wrote this text for this tune. It was first published in *Songs of Praise* (London, 1931).

GELOBT SEI GOTT (also **VULPIUS**). The tune was first published in Melchior Vulpius's *Ein schön geistlich Gesangbuch* (Jena, 1609) with the text "Gelobt sei Gott in höchsten Thron" by Michael Weisse.

Good Shepherd, Take This Little Child 760
Claire Cloninger wrote the text on the occasion of a friend's child's dedication. She writes this account of her inspiration for the words: "After my niece Jenny was killed in an automobile accident, her mother had a dream of Jenny healed and peaceful, walking in a green meadow, holding the hand of a man in sandals and a white robe. . . . She knew with certainty that the Good Shepherd was now holding her little lamb."

AMY. Ken Barker composed the hymn setting for Cloninger's text at the request of Tom Fettke for *Hymnal for Worship and Celebration* (Word, 1986). The tune name was selected by Barker's wife, Brenda; it means "Beloved of God" and seemed to her to fit a child's dedication hymn.

Grace Greater than Our Sin 472
These words are by Julia H. Johnston. They appeared in *Hymns Tried and True*, compiled by D. B. Towner and published by Moody Bible Institute (Chicago, 1911). H

MOODY. The music was written for these words in 1910 by Daniel B. Towner, for many years head of the Music Department of Moody Bible Institute in Chicago. H

Great God, Your Love Has Called Us Here 779
When written (Apr. 1973), Brian Wren's hymn began, "Lord God, your love has called us here." Wren sees it as a "restatement in contemporary terms (but not a replacement) of Wesley's hymn, 'And can it be.'" This text was written in the same meter for a Routley tune, ABINGDON (which was attached to the Wesley text). First publication was in the United Kingdom Hymnal Supplement, *New Church Praise* (1975).
Stanza 2 was omitted by permission of the author; it is as follows: "We come with self-inflicted pains / of broken trust and chosen wrong, / half-free, half-bound by inner chains, / by social forces swept along, / by powers and systems close confined / yet seeking hope for humankind."

ST. PETERSBURG. The tune, by the Russian nationalistic composer, Dmitri Bortniansky, was written near the end of the composer's life and is named for the city where Bortniansky lived. It was first used with a text of Tersteegen in a Leipzig *Choralbuch . . . von Johannes Gossner*, edited by Johann Heinrich Tscherlitzky (1825). Tchaikovsky included it in his 10-volume edition of Bortniansky's music (1882) with a Russian hymn text. It has appeared (without the anacruses) as a British tune named WELLSPRING (1877) or WELLS, and in a German army hymnal.

Great Is the Lord 44
Husband and wife Michael W. Smith and Deborah D. Smith wrote the song based on Psalm 145:2-3 while he was keyboard player for Amy Grant (1982).

GREAT IS THE LORD. The tune was composed with the text.

Great Is the Lord Our God 335
This metrical setting of Psalm 48 was developed by the editors of CRC (Christian Reformed Church) publications for the *Psalter Hymnal* (1987). Several sources brought the text into contemporary language: Emily R. Brink, stanza 1; Bert Witvoet, stanza 2; editions of *A Selection of Metrical Versions of the Book of Psalms* (United Presbyterian, 1869), revised in 1887 and 1912, stanzas 3-5.

TERRA BEATA; see **This Is My Father's World** 384.

Great Is Thy Faithfulness 60

The text was written by Thomas O. Chisholm in 1923. According to him, there were no special circumstances which caused its writing—just his experience and Bible truth; it is a near-paraphrase of Lamentations 3:22-33. The hymn first appeared in *Songs of Salvation and Service,* 1923, compiled by William M. Runyan. It is the unofficial "school hymn" of Moody Bible Institute in Chicago, with which Dr. Runyan was associated for a number of years. H

FAITHFULNESS. The tune was written by William M. Runyan for these words. The name "Faithfulness" was chosen by him when it appeared in *Baptist Hymnal*, 1956. H

Greater Is He That Is in Me 525

Lanny Wolfe says that this simple chorus was written while he was traveling through Nevada on his way to Montana: "I was just riding in my car one day, and I had a moment of truth of the scripture that I had read all my life. It was just a realization of what that scripture really meant." First use was on the Benson Publications recording "Let's Sing a Song About Jesus," by the Lanny Wolfe Trio. Wolfe's habit was not to write out a song, but to teach it to the Trio by rote in the studio, correcting it as they experimented with the performance.

GREATER IS HE. The musical setting was composed with the text.

Greet Now the Swiftly Changing Year 372

This Slovak hymn was published in *Pisne duchovni stare i move* (Levoca, 1636) by Jurau Tranovsk—a book known as "Tranoscius." Jaroslav Vajda translated it for the *Worship Supplement* (1968) to the *Lutheran Hymnal*.

CHILDHOOD. The tune is from *A Students' Hymnal (Emynau'r Myfyrwyr); for use in Schools & Colleges* (1923), adapted by Walford Davies but attributed by him to "University of Wales," a collective group of up to five melodists which he calls "a small community of minds" but does not identify by name. In *A Students' Hymnal*, the tune is set to "It fell upon a summer day," a text about Jesus's blessing of the children—implying the "natural, interesting, life-like" performance the editor suggests. Davies calls for "rhythmic swing" in these tunes.

Guide Me, O Thou Great Jehovah 634

William Williams's text first appeared in his collection of Welsh hymns, *Alleluia* (1745), entitled "Strength to pass through the Wilderness." In *Crusade Hymn Stories*, Donald Hustad presents a complete analysis of the hymn and its imagery from the journey of the Israelites to the land of Canaan.

In his *Hymns on Various Subjects*, 1771, Peter Williams translated three of the stanzas into English. A year later the original author (or possibly his son John) made another English translation, retaining the first stanza of Peter Williams's version and adding a fourth. This hymn was first printed in 1772 in leaflet form and then included in Lady Huntingdon's *Collection*, 1772 or 1773. The first three stanzas of this second version are offered here. H

CWM RHONDDA. The tune (pronounced "coom rawnthuh") was composed by John Hughes in 1907 for the annual Baptist Cymanfau Ganu (Singing Festival) at Capel Rhondda, an industrial area in Pontypridd, Wales. It was first printed in Great Britain in the revised *Fellowship Hymn Book*, 1933. Interestingly enough, the tune was copyrighted in the United States in 1927 in an arrangement by E. Edwin Young that appeared in *The Voice of Thanksgiving No. 4* (Chicago: The Bible Institute Colportage Association, 1928). H

Hail the Day That Sees Him Rise 258
This "Hymn for Ascension Day" is by Charles Wesley and appeared with 10 stanzas in the Wesley brothers' *Hymns and Sacred Poems* (1739). The "Alleluias" were added in G. C. White's *Hymns and Introits* (1852). H

LLANFAIR. This simple Welsh melody is from an 1817 manuscript book of the Welsh singer Robert Williams, though he may not have written it. The arrangement by John Roberts is from Joseph Parry's *Peroriaeth Hyfryd* (1837). "Llanfair" is only the first part of the 58-letter name-description of Williams's home locality in Montgomery County, Wales. H

Hallelujah! What a Savior 226
The text and tune were both written by Philip P. Bliss and first appeared in *The International Lessons Monthly* (1875), and then in *Gospel Hymns No. 2* (1876). H

HALLELUJAH! WHAT A SAVIOR! The music was composed with his text by Bliss. The tune is also sometimes called GETHSEMANE. H

Happy the Home When God Is There 389
Entitled "The Happy Home," this hymn by Henry Ware, Jr. (sometimes called "the younger") first appeared in *Selections of Hymns and Poetry for the Use of Infant and Juvenile Schools and Families*, third edition (1846),

compiled by Mrs. Herbert Mayo. The authorship was obscure for some time and was finally clarified in the *Methodist Hymnal* (1935). H

ST. AGNES; see **Jesus, the Very Thought of Thee** 112.

Hark! the Herald Angels Sing 171
This text by Charles Wesley first appeared in *Hymns and Sacred Poems* (1739) beginning "Hark! how all the welkin rings." In succeeding years it underwent many alterations, appearing in its present form in George Whitefield's *Collection of Hymns for Social Worship* (1753). H

MENDELSSOHN. The music was taken with little adaptation from the second movement of Felix Mendelssohn's *Festgesang*, Op. 68, a *lied* for male chorus, composed in 1840 to commemorate the 400th anniversary of printing. The hymn setting was made by William H. Cummings and published in Chope's *Congregational Hymn and Tune Book* (1856). It has become the recognized tune for this hymn. H

Hark! the Voice of Love and Mercy 475
Jonathan Evans wrote the text in 1784. It was revised and language updated for *Hymns for Today's Church* (1982).

WESTMINSTER ABBEY [also **BELVILLE** or **LEXDEN**]. The tune is from Henry Purcell's extended SATB anthem "O God, Thou Art My God [Psalm 63]" (*c.* 1680-82). The anthem has repeated alleluias in the sixth movement. It was named WESTMINSTER ABBEY in *Hymns Ancient and Modern* (1950).

Have Mercy in Your Goodness, Lord (Psalm 51:1-10) 322
This metrical psalm portion was prepared by Christopher Webber for *A New Metrical Psalter* (1987), working from the 1979 *Book of Common Prayer*. His purpose "was to use contemporary English and the basic meters (SM, LM, & CM) so that the Psalms could be easily sung to familiar tunes." The texts have been used in other hymnals and in anthems published by Concordia.

JESU DULCIS MEMORIA. The tune is from a Trier manuscript (number 724) where it is the second plainsong setting for the Latin text, "*Jesu dulcis memoria.*"

Have Thine Own Way, Lord 584
Adelaide Pollard wrote this hymn in 1902 during a time when she was suffering "great distress of soul." Shortly before, she had tried unsuccessfully to raise funds for a missionary trip to Africa. A prayer meeting

had brought peace to her heart and complete abandonment of self in submission to God's will. The text first appeared in *Northfield Hymnal with Alexander's Supplement* compiled by George C. Stebbins (1907).   H

ADELAIDE. The tune was written for Adelaide Pollard's text in 1907 by George C. Stebbins, who included it in the hymnal mentioned above.   H

He is Born, the Divine Christ Child   177
This is an anonymous 19th-century French text.

IL EST NÉ. Named for its opening line in French, this 18th-century French tune (an air de chase [hunting song], *"La Tête Bizarde"*) predates its Christmas text. This arrangement by Donald P. Hustad is for *The Worshiping Church.*

He Is Coming Soon   281
The song was written "as a Christmas present to the Hurstbourne Baptist Church," Louisville, KY, where Phillip Landgrave was serving as minister of music (Dec. 1982); it was sung by a quartet of his family members. First publication was as an anthem in the Phillip Landgrave Choral Series (1984).

COMING SOON. The tune was composed with the text.

He Is Lord   97
This anonymous scripture song derived from Philippians 2:10-11 became popular around 1970.

HE IS LORD. This simple anonymous tune is associated with these anonymous words. Text and tune became popular in the early 1970s.

He Leadeth Me, O Blessed Thought   635
While still a young man, Joseph H. Gilmore served as a "pulpit supply" at the First Baptist Church in Philadelphia for a mid-week service, March 1862. He planned to give an exposition of the 23rd Psalm but could get no further than "He leadeth me." He saw in those words significance and beauty he had never before imagined. After the service, Gilmore penciled the hymn while being entertained in the home of one of the church's deacons, and eventually gave it to his wife. Months later she sent it to the *Watchman and Reflector*, a Boston paper, and they published it (Vol. XLIII, No. 49; Dec. 4, 1862) without Gilmore's knowledge; it was signed "Conto cook."   H

HE LEADETH ME. William Bradbury saw Gilmore's hymn in the *Watchman and Reflector* and set it to music. The text was also modified so as to provide a refrain. The tune first appeared with the text in Bradbury's *The Golden Censer* (1864).   H

He Lives   248
In *Forty Gospel Hymn Stories*, George Sanville (editor for the Rodeheaver Company) tells the story of the writing of this text and tune by Alfred H. Ackley. In 1933 a young Jew had asked him, "Why should I worship a dead Jew?" and Ackley had witnessed, "But Jesus lives!" The song first appeared in *Triumphant Service Songs* (Chicago: Rodeheaver, 1933).   H

ACKLEY. The tune was named for the composer, A. H. Ackley, by the editors of the *Baptist Hymnal* (1956).   H

He the Pearly Gates Will Open   683
There are conflicting reports about the origin of this hymn, especially its music. Elsie Ahlwén says that she knew the words of the refrain, "Han skall öppna pärleporten," in her native Sweden and sang them to "her own melody." She also says that, when she was conducting meetings in Chicago in 1930, an individual gave her a copy of Frederick Blom's complete hymn which "Blom had written in prison." He was jailed, presumably for drunkenness, during a period when he was estranged from God and the church. Ms. Ahlwén says that she selected five of the original nine verses, copyrighted them in Swedish, wrote her own melody and used it widely in her evangelistic meetings. She also secured a translation by "a Rev. Ohlson" of a Swedish Lutheran Church in Duluth, Minnesota.
An article appeared in Sweden's *Stridsropet* (War Cry), No. 52 (1960), written by Brigadier Oscar Blomgren of the Salvation Army. In a translation supplied by hymnologist J. Irving Erickson, Blomgren says:
In the winter of 1916, when we were stationed at Chicago's 7th Corps, Fred Blom made a surprise visit. (They had not seen him for about 14 years.) He was no longer a pastor but worked in the office of a travel agency. This was just before Christmas. Soon after New Year's he visited us again one afternoon. I had a severe cold and was confined to my bed. We noticed that Blom was not himself. He appeared sad and gloomy . . . My wife did her best to encourage our friend, cooked coffee and set a festive table.

During the Christmas season we had sung a carol that had become popular. It was a poem to which Alfred Dulin, a young musician from Norway who . . . had stayed with us, wrote a simple but beautiful melody. The poem had been taken from the Christmas edition of *From All Lands* (1906). My wife introduced the song to Blom and sang it several times for him. After a while, Blom picked up a guitar,

played a few chords and sang:
>Wonderful, festive, clear
>Star-filled Christmas night!
>Your wonders, every hour,
>Make the sorrowing heart glad.
>(Tr. from the Swedish)

Suddenly Fred Blom took out his pen, asked for a sheet of paper, and after an hour's silence had written five stanzas and a chorus to the song "The Pearly Gates." As a title he wrote "Because of the Blood." Elsie Ahlwén, a singing evangelist from Örebro, who visited America and held evangelistic meetings there in 1929-30, made use of the song and thereby popularized it. She called it "Pärleporten" and altered somewhat the words of the chorus. Fred Blom had written " . . . And surely will let me in," but Elsie Ahlwén used this version " . . . so that I may enter in."

Fred Blom wrote the song in my wife's songbook, signed it and added the date, 1917, and she has always kept that book in safekeeping.

It seems impossible to reconcile these two stories at this time. At any rate, it was a translation by Nathaniel Carlson which became accepted by English-speaking Christians and is used in *The Worshiping Church*.   H

PEARLY GATES. In our earlier hymnals, as in every publication of this song, Elsie Ahlwén is given credit for writing the music, but this will have to be reconsidered. We are inclined to think that she may have been honestly mistaken. Frederick Blom had returned to Sweden by 1921 and was again in the ministry. No doubt he used his song, whose melody had evidently been written by Alfred Dulin Olsen for another text. In those years, Elsie Ahlwén was a young woman in her teens, and she may have heard the melody along with the words—as she says, she knew the refrain in her native Sweden. Later, when the full text was given her, it is possible that a previously heard melody came to her spontaneously, and she may have honestly thought she had created it herself. See also the entry for Alfred Dulin Olsen in the biographies.   H

He took my feet from the miry clay; see **I Waited Patiently for the Lord** 341.

He Touched Me   410
With stanzas not included here, Bill Gaither wrote words and music (1963). He remembers this starting point of the idea:
>I was playing the piano for Doug Oldham during a week of revival ser-
>vices which he and his father, Dale, were conducting in Huntington,
>Indiana. We were discussing how dramatically God had worked in

our lives. Dale simply suggested to me, "Bill, you should write a song entitled, 'He Touched Me.'"

HE TOUCHED ME. The melody was composed with the text.

He Who Would Valiant Be; see **Who Honors Courage Here** 633.

He's Got the Whole World   518
The source of this traditional African-American spiritual is unknown.

WHOLE WORLD. One printing of this melody says it is taken from the "Marion Kerby Collection of Negro Exaltations."   H

Heal Me, Hands of Jesus   463
Michael Perry wrote this hymn in 1980 for the Jubilate team's *Hymns for Today's Church* (1982), to meet a need for hymns on healing. He says that the text "reflects a pastoral concern for the mentally ill and those who have burdens of anxiety which they cannot share." The first line originally read, "Heal me, hands of Christ," but the meter was adjusted for its first tune setting, by Norman Warren.

CAROL STREAM. John F. Wilson composed this setting for Perry's words (1988) and named the tune for the Illinois community where Hope Publishing Company is located.

Heal Us, Immanuel, Hear Our Prayer   411
Cowper titled this hymn, "Jehovah-Rophi. I Am the Lord that Healeth Thee—Exodus 15:26." Originally, along with older language, it had an additional stanza describing the woman healed (between stanzas 4 and 5). It was published in *Olney Hymns*, book 1 (1779), along with other hymns by Cowper and hymns by Newton.

BEATITUDO; see **O for a Closer Walk with God** 547.

Hear Our Prayer, O Heavenly Father   818
The words of the prayer response are very similar to those which frequently conclude a spoken petition in liturgical public worship.   H

Attributed to Frederic Chopin, the music setting is so short and simple that it could have come from many 19th-century sources.

Hear Our Prayer, O Lord   817
These words are derived from Psalm 143:1a. The final phrase echoes
the traditional "Dona nobis pacem" which closes the Agnus Dei of the
Mass—"Grant us thy peace."   H

George Whelpton's unnamed tune was written in 1897. It was published
in leaflet form and later in H. Augustine Smith's *Hymns for American Youth*
(1924).   H

Hear the bells ringing; see **Easter Song** 244.

Help Us Accept Each Other   437
A Bible study article by Mrs. Jackie Mattonen, written for the
Cumberland Presbyterian Church, gave Fred Kaan the idea for the hymn
(1974). Kaan knew her from their work together on the Executive
Committee of the World Alliance of Reformed Churches. The hymn was
included in *Cantate Domino*, new [CD III] edition (Bärenreiter, 1974;
Oxford University Press, 1975), "almost accidentally and at the last
moment," according to Kaan, placing it in a space that had been set aside
for another hymn, the owners of which had asked for fees the editors felt
were excessive.

BECK. Composer John Ness Beck was fond of the texts of Fred Kaan and
wrote this tune for the poem in 1977.

Here from All Nations   680
Christopher Idle's text is based on Revelation 7:9-17; it was written at
Poplar, E. London (1972), and first published in *Psalm Praise* (1973). Idle
notes that this is the most "in demand" of all his hymn texts.

O QUANTA QUALIA (also **REGNATOR ORBIS**). The tune was origi-
nally set to "Fumant Sabaeis," a hymn for the Feast of Purification, in
Paris Antiphoner (1681); it was later published to the text "Regnator orbis
summus" in a form more like the present singable Dykes setting, in La
Feillée's *Méthode du Plain-Chant* (a late edition, 1808) edited by François
David Aynes. Christopher Idle wrote "Here from All Nations" for this
tune at the suggestion of Richard Bewes, another member of the *Psalm
Praise* editors.

Here, Master, in This Quiet Place   408
Fred Pratt Green titled this hymn "Prayer for Healing" when he wrote
it at the request of the St. Barnabas Counseling Centre, an ecumenical
community of healing in Norwich, Norfolk, England; it was first sung at
the Centre to ST. BERNARD on that saint's day, June 4, 1974.

Here, O My Lord, I See You Face to Face   783
Horatius Bonar wrote this hymn at the request of his older brother, John J. Bonar, pastor of St. Andrew's Free Church, Greenock, Scotland. It was first printed in a leaflet distributed to the congregation following the observance of the Lord's Supper on the first Sunday in October 1855. It was later included in Bonar's *Hymns of Faith and Hope* (first series).   H

LANGRAN. James Langran wrote this music for "Abide with Me"; it first appeared in leaflet form (1861). Later, it was included in John Foster's *Psalms and Hymns Adapted to the Services of the Church of England* (1863). H

His Battle Ended There   253
Tom Colvin paraphrased this Chewa hymn about 1970 while he was serving in Malawi as Development Adviser to the Blantyre Synod (Presbyterian) of the joint development agency, the Christian Service Committee. It was published in Colvin's *Leap, My Soul* (1976). Originally an Angori (part of the Zulu) war song, it is Christianized to celebrate the resurrection. The text is in the spirit of victory and, suggests Colvin, "must be sung fast."

NCHEU. Named for the Angoni people of Ncheu, Malawi, this traditional war victory tune was adapted by Colvin around 1970 and published in *Fill Us With Your Love* (Agape, 1976).

His Name Is Wonderful   87
Author-composer Audrey Mieir describes a rehearsal for a Christmas pageant at her little Bethel Union Church, Duarte, CA, where the pastor was her brother-in-law. He responded to the scene of youth playing the familiar roles. Mieir writes (in Lindsay Terry's book):
> The pastor stood up and slowly lifted his hands toward heaven and said, "His name is Wonderful!" Those words electrified me. I immediately began writing in the back of my Bible. As I wrote I was thinking that God has something he wants said. I wrote a simple chorus and I sang it that night for the young people around the piano. They sang it immediately. It wasn't hard for them to learn. I never dreamed that it would go any further, but it has traveled around the world in many languages.

First publication was by Manna Music (1959).

MIEIR. The tune was composed to set this text; composer and author are one.

Holy God, We Praise Your Name   3
The hymn is a metrical paraphrase of the first line of the Latin "Te Deum" (*c.* 4th century; see also **God, We Praise You!** 39 and **You**

Are God, We Praise You 352). It appeared first in German in Maria Theresa's *Katholisches Gesangbuch* (Vienna, *c.* 1774). Four years later it was included in altered form in Ignaz Franz's *Gesangbuch*, where it is attributed to him. The English translation by Clarence A. Walworth is dated 1853 in *Evangelical Hymnal* (1880). However, its first authenticated appearance is in the *Catholic Psalmist* (Dublin, 1858). H

GROSSER GOTT, WIR LOBEN DICH [also **TE DEUM**]. The full history of this anonymous tune may be found in Wilhelm Baumker's *Katholische deutsche Kirchenlied* (vol. III, 285-87). It first appeared *c.* 1774 in *Katholisches Gesangbuch*. The present form of the melody was developed by J. G. Schicht in *Allgemeines Choralbuch* (Leipzig, 1819). The tune name is the first phrase of the German hymn. Donald Hustad's descant was composed for *The Worshiping Church*. H

Holy God, you have given us grace; see **Prayer for Trinity Sunday** 7.

Holy, holy, holy, holy is the Lord; see **Holy Is the Lord** 831.

Holy, Holy, Holy! Lord God Almighty 2
This paraphrase of Revelation 4:8-11 was written for Trinity Sunday by Reginald Heber, while he was vicar of Hodnet, Shropshire, England. The hymn first appeared in *Hymns of the Parish Church of Banbury* (3rd ed., 1826), the year of Heber's death. The next year it was published in his posthumous volume entitled *Hymns, Written and Adapted to the Weekly Service of the Year*. For devotional analysis see Colquhoun, *Hymns that Live*. H

NICAEA. The tune was written expressly for the hymn by John B. Dykes. It first appeared along with six other tunes by Dykes in *Hymns Ancient and Modern* (1861). The tune name refers to the Council of Nicaea which convened A.D. 325 and affirmed the doctrine of the Trinity in refutation of the Arian heresy. H

Holy, holy, holy, Lord God of Hosts; see **O Lord Most High** 828.

Holy Is the Lord 831
The setting of words from Isaiah 6:3 was part of Franz Schubert's "German Mass in F major," composed about 1826 but published posthumously (1845). The text, *"Heilig, Heilig,"* was in German, not Latin, an indication that it was to be sung in the vernacular. The English words, nearly identical to the German, are the traditional "trinitarian" explanation of "Holy, holy, holy."

HOLY IS THE LORD. Schubert set the German text in this four-part hymn form, intending it to be sung with great dynamic contrasts and *sehr langsam* (very slowly). It was published posthumously (1845); the date of composing is uncertain. It is true vocal music, composed by a trained singer. For woodwind and low brass instrumentation, see Schubert's *Werke*, Series 13, no. 7.

Holy Lord   827
The text is an adaptation of Isaiah 6:3, the cry of the angels around the throne of God.

DONA NOBIS PACEM; see **Father, Grant Us Your Peace** 589.

Holy, Lord God of Hosts   829
This is the Anglican form of the Sanctus—Isaiah 6:3, plus the *Gloria tibi* (glory be to thee, O Lord most high).

WILLAN SANCTUS. Healey Willan composed this setting (1928) as part of an Anglican Service of Holy Communion. He was professor of theory at the University of Toronto and precentor of the Church of St. Mary Magdalene—and expressed strong interest in plainsong and historic musical idioms.

Holy Spirit, Ever Dwelling   289
Timothy Rees's poem was published in the *Mirfield Mission Hymn Book* (1922), then revised by the author for *Sermons and Hymns by Timothy Rees, Bishop of Llandaff* (1946).

IN BABILONE. This traditional Dutch air is from *Oude en Nieuwe Hollantse Bîrenlities en Contradanseu* (*c.* 1710) and is similar to the tune "Vruechten" in *The Oxford Book of Carols*. It was arranged by Julius Röntgen and included in *The English Hymnal* (1906).   H

Holy Spirit, Light Divine   302
The editors of *Hymns for the Living Church* (1974) adapted the earlier title of Andrew Reed's hymn "Holy Ghost, with Light divine" to reflect the current usage of "Holy Spirit." The original hymn was included in Reed's *Supplement to Watts' Psalms and Hymns* (1817) with the title "Prayer to the Holy Spirit."   H

MERCY. This melody was early associated with Charles Wesley's "Depth of mercy, can there be," hence the tune name. It was arranged by Edwin P. Parker from Louis Gottschalk's piano piece, "The Last Hope" (1854).   H

Holy Spirit, Truth Divine 303
Samuel Longfellow wrote this text for his collection *Hymns of the Spirit* (1864), one of several books of his hymns. It was originally titled "Prayer for Inspiration" and represents the trinitarian bent of 19th-century Unitarians.

MERCY; see **Holy Spirit, Light Divine** 302 (above).

Hope of the World 434
This text by Georgia Harkness was awarded the first prize in a Hymn Society of America contest which attracted more than 500 entries. It was used as planned at the Second Assembly of the World Council of Churches, Evanston, IL (1954). First printed in the Hymn Society's bulletin, *Eleven Ecumenical Hymns* (1954), it soon appeared in *Baptist Hymnal* (1956) and *Worship and Service Hymnal* (1957) as well as later hymnals. H

VICAR. The tune was composed for this text (1963) by Vicar Earle Copes, for inclusion in the *Methodist Hymnal* (1964), and named for the composer's father. H

Hosanna, Loud Hosanna 203
All of Jeannette Threlfall's poems were written "at idle moments." This, her best known hymn, was first published in her volume, *Sunshine and Shadow* (1873). H

ELLACOMBE. The melody first appeared in the *Gesangbuch der Herzogl* (Wittenberg, 1784), number 1b. It came into English usage from a Mainz *Collection* (1833) edited by Xavier Ludwig Hartig, who dated the tune 1700 but gave no source. *Hymns Ancient and Modern* (1868 ed.) brought it into wide use in Great Britain. It bears the name of a village in Devonshire, England. H

How Blest Are the People (Psalm 32) 706
Barbara Woollett published this and other psalm paraphrases in her private collection, *Open Gates* (1985), for the "Jubilate Hymns" psalm project. She says of her approach, "As we base all our thinking on who God is and his unfailing love, the circumstances of life are brought into perspective to these great truths."

LOVE TO CHRIST; see **I Love You, My Jesus** 91.

How Blest Are the Poor in Spirit 603
Richard Avery and Donald Marsh wrote this text (paraphrasing the Sermon on the Mount, Mt. 5:3-12) and this tune in response to a felt

need for a "singable setting" of this "important teaching of Jesus" (1979). The authors suggest singing it lined out as well as straight through.

BEATITUDES. The tune was composed for the text and named for the Latin title of the "Blessed are" section of the Sermon on the Mount.

How Blest Are They Who, Fearing God 342
This paraphrase of Psalm 1 is from the *Psalter* (1912), published by the United Presbyterian Church in the United States, based on the psalter of 1875.

ST. ANNE; see **O God, Our Help in Ages Past** 78.

How Blest Are They Who Trust in Christ 673
Written by Fred Pratt Green with the caption "For a Memorial Service," the hymn was published in the *Methodist Recorder* (1972); in 1980 it was one of four (out of 457) entries accepted by The Hymn Society of America. The omitted third stanza was in the first publication: "They journey on! While we must stay, / our work not done, our time unspent; / what baffles us to them grows clear. / In Christ the Truth they are content."

How Clear Is Our Vocation, Lord 395
Fred Pratt Green titled this hymn "Our Christian Vocation." It was inspired (1981) by a request from Erik Routley for a new text for this tune. (Routley did not find Whittier's "Dear Lord and Father" a good match for REPTON.) Russell Schulz-Widmar suggested minor changes to the first draft before it was published in Green's *Hymns and Ballads* (Hope Publishing Company, 1982).

REPTON. The tune comes from C. Hubert Parry's oratorio, *Judith* (1888), where it sets a text describing the exodus, "Long since in Egypt's plenteous land." It first appeared as a hymn tune in *Repton School: Hymns for Use in Chapel* (1924).

How Firm a Foundation 612
These words first appeared in Dr. John Rippon's *A Selection of Hymns from the Best Authors* (1787) under the title "Exceeding Great and Precious Promises." The authorship was ascribed merely to "K." Later reprints gave "Kn" and "Keen." The author may be Richard Keen, a musician and precentor in the church pastored by Dr. Rippon, and composer of the tune to which the words were originally set. H

FOUNDATION. The source of the tune has been as much in question as the authorship of the text. However, it seems to have first appeared in

Joseph Funk's *Genuine Church Music* (1832), and later in *The Sacred Harp* (1844) where it was called BELLEVUE. It is generally agreed that it was one of the most widely sung folk hymn tunes in the South, and was used as a theme for the TV series "Wagon Train."   H

How Great Thou Art 21
More details of the following account appear in *Crusade Hymn Stories* (Hope Publishing Company, 1967): The original of this hymn was written in the summer (*c.* 1885) by Carl Boberg, a Swedish preacher, editor, and statesman. He was traveling home from Kronobäck and was inspired by the sound of church bells. The hymn was published in *Mönsterås Tidningen* (March 13, 1886) but Boberg set it aside until he heard it sung with the Swedish folk melody it now uses. He published it with this tune in *Sanningsvittnet* (1891). It appeared in a German version ("Wie gross bist Du") in Estonia (1907), and in a Russian translation from German by Ivan S. Prokhanoff (1912). Stuart K. Hine, a British missionary in western Ukraine, made this English translation of the Russian over a period of years (the fourth stanza was added in 1948) and it first appeared in a Russian gospel magazine, *Grace and Peace* (1949), a nearly new text when compared with Boberg's original. The song was popularized through its use in Billy Graham crusades.   H

O STORE GUD. The name consists of the first words of the original Swedish hymn text. This is a Swedish folk melody, to which Boberg's text was sung; it was first printed in *Sanningsvittnet* (1891) in 3/4 time. It was printed with its present rhythm in Svenska *Missionsförbundets Sångbok* (1894).   H

How I praise thee, precious Savior; see **Channels Only** 577.

How Long, O Lord? 339
Barbara Woollett writes, "This Psalm [13] paraphrase was written for my husband when he was suffering from a time of depression and confusion concerning his employment, and consequently over his own personal walk with the Lord." It was written in 1983 and included in a private collection of poems.

BINNEY'S. Eric Thiman composed this tune for a hymn by Thomas Binney, "Eternal Light." It was first published in *Congregational Praise* (1951).

How Lovely, Lord, How Lovely 333
Arlo Duba wrote this metrical paraphrase of Psalm 84 (1980) for MERLE'S TUNE while serving on the Presbyterian Psalter Task Force. He knew the tune and drafted the text while "flying home from a Task Force

meeting." The Task Force also had a part in some revisions which were first published in *Psalm Sampler* (Westminster Press, 1986).

MERLE'S TUNE. The tune was written for Michael Perry's text, "Blessed Be the God of Israel" and first published in the *Upper Room Worship Book* (1985). Merle is Hopson's older sister who was his first piano teacher.

How Majestic Is Your Name 61
Michael W. Smith (1981) wrote words and music while a staff writer at Meadowgreen Music Company. The song was nominated for a Dove Award (1983).

HOW MAJESTIC. The tune was composed with the text.

How Shall They Hear the Word of God? 740
This "proclamation" text was commissioned by BBC Radio for its 10th anniversary; Michael Perry based it on Romans 10:14. The first performance was in Winchester Cathedral (1981), with the text published in the program.

AUCH JETZT MACHT GOTT. The tune is from *Choralbuch* (1816), a collection of pieces for wind band by the theorist Heinrich Koch. It is named for a German text with which it has been sung. According to Carlton Young in *Companion To The United Methodist Hymnal* (1993), the tune was first matched with this text in *Worship* (3rd ed., 1986).

How Sure the Scriptures Are 312
Based on Hebrews 4, the hymn was written in response to a request from Scripture Union asking "for more texts about the Bible itself." It was written in Poplar, E. London (Sept. 23, 1976), for the Limehouse Pathfinders third birthday service and first published in the *All Souls, Langham Place Supplementary Hymn Book* (1980). It was more widely distributed in *Hymns for Today's Church* (1982) with a tune not recommended by the author, Christopher Idle.

DARWALL. This tune is suggested by the hymn's author, Christopher Idle; see **Rejoice, the Lord Is King** 262.

How Sweet the Name of Jesus Sounds 102
The words by John Newton were written while he was curate at Olney, Buckinghamshire, England. There, together with William Cowper, he produced the memorable volume, *Olney Hymns* (1779), containing 280 hymns by Newton and 68 by Cowper. This hymn was entitled "SOLOMON'S SONG. . . .The Name of Jesus" in the collection and was

based on a line from the Song of Solomon 1:3 (and so identified by Newton) "Thy name is as ointment poured forth." H

RACHEL. The editor of *Hymns for Today's Church* (1982), Drew Wilson, asked for a new tune for the familiar Newton text. David Peacock introduced the editorial team to Chris Bowater's 20th-century folk-like tune (reminiscent of "Drink to me only with thine eyes"). Noel Tredinnick was asked to arrange it for the hymn's publication. RACHEL is the oldest of Chris and Lesley Bowater's five children.

I Am His, and He Is Mine 602
George W. Robinson wrote these words which first appeared in *Hymns of Consecration and Faith* (1876). In commenting on the meaning of the hymn, Dr. Millar Patrick (in the Supplement to the *Handbook to the Church Hymnary*) quotes from Henry Martyn's *Cambridge Diary*: "Since I have known God in a saving manner, painting, poetry and music have had charms unknown to me before, for Religion has refined my mind and made it susceptible of impressions from the sublime and beautiful." H

EVERLASTING LOVE. James Mountain compiled the first edition of *Hymns of Consecration and Faith* (1876) and wrote the tune for these words for inclusion in that collection. H

I Am Not Skilled to Understand 480
This text was written by Dorothy Greenwell, commonly called "Dora," and was included in her *Songs of Salvation* (1873). It also appeared in Sankey's *Sacred Songs and Solos* under the caption "My Refuge, My Savior!" (2 Sam. 22:3). H

GREENWELL. This tune, named for the author of the text, was written by William J. Kirkpatrick and first appeared in *Songs of Joy and Gladness* (1885), compiled by W. McDonald, Joshua Gill, J. R. Sweney, and Kirkpatrick.
The name "Greenwell" is also used for another tune by Ernest B. Leslie which appears with Dora Greenwell's words in *Sunday School Hymnary* (1905). H

I am thine, O Lord; see **Draw Me Nearer** 534.

I Am Trusting Thee, Lord Jesus 524
This text by Frances Ridley Havergal was said to be the author's favorite of all her hymns. It was written at Ormont, Dessous, Switzerland, in 1874. A copy was found in her Bible after her death. H

BULLINGER. The tune was written by Ethelbert W. Bullinger in 1874 and first appeared in *Wesley's Hymns and New Supplement* (1877).　　H

I am weak, but Thou art strong; see **Just a Closer Walk with Thee** 561.

I Bind unto Myself Today　　　　　　　　　　　　　　　　1
These words are part of a nine-stanza *lorica* (prayer for the soul after death), traditionally ascribed to St. Patrick and widely used in churches and monasteries by at least 690. The earliest sources are two 11th-century manuscripts, available now as *The Irish Liber Hymnorum* (1897). The recitation may have been used as a protection "against all poison and envy" and "a guard against sudden death" according to the preface in the 11th-century manuscript. It was probably written in the early 5th century; it was translated by Cecil Frances Alexander for St. Patrick's Day 1889 and published in *The Writings of St. Patrick* (1889), edited by C. H. H. Wright.

I Cannot Tell　　　　　　　　　　　　　　　　　　　109
William Fullerton wrote this text for the LONDONDERRY AIR, following that tune's design. It was published in the *Baptist Church Hymnal* and the *Methodist Hymn Book* (both 1933), but was probably written earlier (perhaps 1920).

LONDONDERRY AIR. Also known as DANNY BOY (with words by Weatherly), this traditional tune is supposed to have originated in Northern Ireland, but its genealogy is unclear.

I come to the garden alone; see **In the Garden** 242.

I Come with Joy　　　　　　　　　　　　　　　　　　768
Brian Wren wrote this hymn (July 1968) for his congregation at Hockley "to sum up a series of sermons on the meaning of communion." Stanzas 2 and 3 were revised (1977) as a result of a "prompt from an American hymnal" to use more inclusive language.

DOVE OF PEACE. Austin Lovelace arranged this tune from William Walker's *Southern Harmony* (1854 ed.) where it sets the text "O Tell Me Where the Dove Has Flown." Walker attributes the "Treble by Wm. Houser" (the "Treble" is the soprano obligato line—the melody is in the tenor), so Walker is likely to have written down what was a folk melody, since he was in the habit of claiming tunes as his own compositions whenever appropriate. The text in Walker's book speaks of "religion" as the nest for the elusive Dove of Peace; so Lovelace's choice fits Wren's theme especially well.

I found free grace; see **I'm New Born Again** 494.

I Have Decided to Follow Jesus   576

This anonymous song appeared in the United States during the 1960s and was prominently featured in Billy Graham crusade meetings. It may have originated among national Christians in India.   H

ASSAM. It is reported that the melody has roots in Assam, a state in India where Christian missions have a long history.   H

I hear the Savior say; see **Jesus Paid It All** 489.

I Heard the Voice of Jesus Say   506

This text by Horatius Bonar was written while he was pastor at Kelso, Scotland. According to the author, it is based on John 1:16, "Of his fullness have all we received, and grace for grace." Others would suggest Matthew 11:28 and John 8:12. The hymn was originally published under the title "The Voice from Galilee" in Bonar's *Hymns Original and Selected* (1846).   H

VOX DILECTI. The tune (whose Latin name means "voice of the beloved") was written for this text by John B. Dykes and first appeared in *Hymns Ancient and Modern* (1868).   H

I Know a Fount   485

Oliver M. Cooke was a regular songwriter for the Salvation Army in England. This is evidently one of his contributions to their publications around the late 19th or early 20th century.

I KNOW A FOUNT. This very simple tune was composed with the text.

I Know Not Where the Road Will Lead   643

Evelyn Atwater Cummins wrote this text in response to hearing an early radio sermon by Dr. S. Parkes Cadman, "The King's Highway." She was home sick on that Sunday (1922) and says, "The title sort of stuck in my head, and I thought I would put down what the King's Highway meant to me."

NOEL [also **EARDISLEY**]. Sir Arthur Sullivan (1874) arranged and simplified an English folk tune which was associated with the text "Dives and Lazarus." The name NOEL was attached to the tune when it was connected with "It Came Upon the Midnight Clear." The French word NOEL may be derived from the Latin *natalis* (birthday) or *novellae* (news, i.e. the gospel).

I know not why God's wondrous grace; see **I Know Whom I Have Believed** 493.

I Know That My Redeemer Lives   239
This text appeared anonymously in George Whitefield's *Psalms and Hymns, extracted from Different Authors* (1775). Authorship was verified in the posthumous collection of Samuel Medley's lyrics, entitled *Hymns: The Public Worship and Private Devotions of True Christians, Assisted in Some Thoughts in Verse: Principally Drawn from Select Passages of the Word of God* (London, 1800).   H

DUKE STREET; see **Jesus Shall Reign** 745.

I Know Whom I Have Believed   493
The text by Daniel W. Whittle was based on 2 Timothy 1:12, and the refrain is a literal repetition of that verse (King James Version).   H

EL NATHAN. The tune was written by James W. McGranahan, song leader in evangelistic campaigns conducted by Major Whittle. Text and tune both appeared for the first time in *Gospel Hymns No. 4* (1883). "El Nathan" was a pseudonym used regularly by Daniel W. Whittle.   H

I Lay My Sins on Jesus   464
This text by Horatius Bonar is generally supposed to be his first hymn and it was written for children. He apologized that "it might be good gospel but it is not good poetry." Its first appearance was in his *Songs for the Wilderness* (1843).   H

CALCUTTA (also **WHITFIELD**). This anonymous tune appeared in the Sunday School Union's *The Sunday-Scholar's Tune Book* (London, 1869) and in Sir Arthur Sullivan's *Church Hymns* (1874), but its sources are earlier. It has been attributed to Heber, but Maurice Frost, English hymnologist, writing in *The Choir* (1991), is certain it was not Heber's composition. Frost traces it "to a benefit concert arranged by Thomas Moore at the Theatre Royal, Dublin, in 1811. It appears in a 'Melologue upon National Music' as a 'Greek Air resumed,' with a note, 'For this pretty Greek melody I am indebted to Mr. Gell who brought it with him from Athens.' A copy is in the British Museum, G. 806c(66)."

I Lift My Eyes to the Quiet Hills   81
Bishop Timothy Dudley-Smith wrote this as one of a pair of psalm settings for *Psalm Praise* (1968). The other is "Safe in the Shadow of the Lord" (513). "I Lift My Eyes" is based on the eight stanzas of the "pilgrim" psalm of ascents, Psalm 121.

UPLIFTED EYES. The tune was composed for these words in 1970 at the request of a congregation that wanted to sing Psalms in a style other than chanting. Elisabeth Crocker, a music student, and Michael Baughen collaborated on the setting. It was first published in *Psalm Praise* (1973) with the tune name, DAVOS; tune and text gained popularity in the United States through publication in InterVarsity's *Hymns II* (1976).

I Love Thy Kingdom, Lord   702
This text was inspired by Psalm 137:5-6 and is perhaps the oldest hymn written by an American which has remained in continuous use. The author, Dr. Timothy Dwight, revised *The Psalms of David* by Isaac Watts in 1800 and added 33 of his own paraphrases and hymns, including this one. It is apparent from stanza 1 that Dwight equates the "Kingdom" with the Church universal; stanza 4 interprets "Zion" similarly.   H

ST. THOMAS; see **Come, We That Love the Lord** 22.

I Love to Tell the Story   498
This hymn is part of a long poem of 50 stanzas in two parts by Arabella Catherine Hankey (also called Katherine Hankey), and was written during a long period of convalescence following a serious illness. Part I, dated January 29, 1866, is entitled "The Story Wanted" and is the source of the song "Tell me the old, old story." Part II, dated November 18, 1866, is called "The Story Told" and contained these lines, which were published in *The Old, Old Story* that same year.   H

HANKEY. The tune (named for the author of the text) was composed by William G. Fischer for these words. It first appeared in a pamphlet entitled *Joyful Songs, Nos. 1 to 3*, 1869. It was first published in a major volume titled *Music for Camp Meetings* in 1872.   H

I Love You, Lord   124
Author-composer Laurie Klein offers the following narrative of the writing of this worship chorus:
"I Love You, Lord" came as a gift during a very trying time. [Husband] Bill and I had moved to Oregon where he was attending school full-time. With no friends, money, church home, or driver's license, the days I spent with our one-year-old seemed endless. My time with the Lord was not only my "life-line"—it was one of my rare opportunities to talk to someone "older!" One extra-lonely morning I found myself praying, "Lord, I want to worship you. . . . I'm just so empty inside. Please give me something to sing that you would enjoy hearing." As I picked up my guitar, words and music came effortlessly.

I LOVE YOU, LORD. The tune was composed with the text.

I Love You, Lord, My Strength, My Rock 349
Fred Anderson's paraphrase of Psalm 18 was written (1984) for Pine Street Presbyterian Church, Harrisburg, PA, and first published in *Singing Psalms of Joy and Praise* (Westminster Press, 1986). It was prepared for the Presbyterian Church (USA) *Hymnal*, but was not used in that book.

FOREST GREEN; see **Amid The Thronging Worshipers** 340.

I Love You, My Jesus 91
The text has been found by David W. Music in Richard Allen's *Collection of Hymns and Spiritual Songs* (Philadelphia, 1801). Allen was the first bishop of the African Methodist Episcopal Church. Its infrequent appearances in American hymnals include those in *Free Methodist Hymnal* (1910) and *Baptist Hymnal* (1956).

LOVE TO CHRIST. The composer of this melody is also unknown. It appeared in *The Christian Harmony, or Songsters Companion*, compiled by Jeremiah Ingalls in 1805. Its infrequent appearances in American hymnals include those in *Free Methodist Hymnal* (1910), and *Baptist Hymnal* (1956). In previous Hope Publishing Company hymnals it was called I LOVE THEE.

I Must Tell Jesus 621
Both words and music of this hymn were written by Elisha Hoffman and appeared in *Pentecostal Hymns* (Chicago: Hope Publishing Company, 1894). Hoffman, one of the hymnal's editors, says that the song was inspired by the response of a parishioner whom he had counseled. "Yes," she exclaimed, echoing his own words, "I must tell Jesus!" H

ORWIGSBURG. The tune is named for Orwigsburg, PA, where author-composer Elisha Hoffman was born. H

I Need Thee Every Hour 538
This text by Annie S. Hawks was written in April 1872. She said she was so filled with a sense of nearness to the Master that, as she wondered how one could live without him, either in joy or pain, the words flashed into her mind. H

NEED. The tune and the refrain text were written by Mrs. Hawk's pastor, Dr. Robert Lowry. The complete hymn was first sung from a pamphlet at a November 1872 meeting of the National Baptist Sunday School Association in Cincinnati. Later, it was published in *Lowry's Royal Diadem* (1873). H

I serve a risen Savior; see **He Lives** 248.

I Sing the Mighty Power of God   52
This text, based on Psalm 19, appeared in the first hymnal written
exclusively for youth, *Divine Songs Attempted in Easy Language, for the Use
of Children* (1715). The book was in print for more than 100 years, and
was the "fountainhead of English children's hymnody." In this collection, author Isaac Watts titled the hymn "Praise for Creation and
Providence."   H

ELLACOMBE; see **Hosanna, Loud Hosanna** 203.

I stand amazed in the presence; see **My Savior's Love** 478.

I Surrender All   579
This text was written by Judson VanDeVenter while he was conducting a meeting at East Palestine, OH, in the home of George Sebring,
founder of the Sebring Campmeeting in Sebring, OH, and later the town
of Sebring, FL. The words were written in remembrance of the time
when, after a long struggle, the author dedicated himself completely to
Christian service.   H

SURRENDER. Winfield S. Weeden composed this melody for this text.
It first appeared in *Gospel Songs of Grace and Glory* (1896), compiled by
Weeden, VanDeVenter, and Leonard Weaver.   H

I Then Shall Live   507
Gloria Gaither wrote this text (1981) for FINLANDIA, noting "that
such expressive pieces of music make their way into the new generations
with power and relevance." She says she tries "to listen, with an ear
unprejudiced as possible, to the 'idea' that lies imbedded in the music
itself." The idea that came through she calls "tension" which parallels
"the tension in commitment to relationships that are worth the struggle."
The song was the conclusion of the Gaithers' musical, *God Has Always
Had a People* (Paragon, 1981).

FINLANDIA; see **Be Still, My Soul** 530.

I Waited Patiently for the Lord   341
The text is Psalm 40:1-11, with the refrain (response) taken from the
spiritual, "He Took My Feet from the Miry Clay, Yes, He Did." The spiritual is believed to have appeared first in a publication of the Rodeheaver
Hall-Mack Company and may have been "collected" by Frederick Hall,
who was associated with that organization.   H

YES, HE DID. The refrain is actually the first stanza of the spiritual (authentic or not) described above.

I Want Jesus to Walk with Me 642

Though the source of this American folk hymn is unknown, it is probably rooted in the antebellum rural camp meetings and may be either a black or white spiritual.

WALK WITH ME. This music has no refrain, so may have been adapted from an English folk tune brought to Appalachia by early settlers. H

I Want to Walk as a Child of the Light 539

Drawing on texts from the Old and New Testaments, Kathleen Thomerson wrote both words and music for the Fisherfolk Ministry at the Episcopal Church of the Redeemer, Houston, TX (summer 1966). The occasion was an unexpected visit to Houston to get away from heat in St. Louis (where a power shortage resulted in restricted air conditioning). It was first published in that church's hymnal and, soon after, as an anthem (Net Music, 1970).

HOUSTON. Thomerson composed the tune with the words: "As I wrote the words of the first stanza, I heard the melody to which they were to be sung. It is interesting that I did not hear any harmonies, only the melodic line. The harmonization was worked out later in my mind, and on a piano, without changing any of the melody."

I will arise and go to Jesus; see **Come, Ye Sinners, Poor and Needy** 451.

I Will Sing of My Redeemer 492

This text written by Philip P. Bliss was found in his trunk following the train wreck in which he and his wife lost their lives. The words first appeared in *Welcome Tidings, A New Collection for Sunday School* (1877). H

HYFRYDOL. The tune HYFRYDOL gives these historic words new life and meaning. In *Companion to Baptist Hymnal*, William J. Reynolds points out that it was used with Philip P. Bliss's "I will sing the wondrous story" in the Gipsy Smith Special Supplement to *Hallowed Hymns, New and Old*, compiled and edited by I. Allen Sankey (Biglow & Main, 1909). Also see **Come, Thou Long-Expected Jesus** 135.

In older hymnals, these words were sung to music written by James McGranahan, who followed P. P. Bliss as songleader for Evangelist D. W. Whittle. H

I Will Sing of the Mercies   30
The first stanza text is taken verbatim from Psalm 89:1, with repetitions; the second stanza is by Marie J. Post, first published in the Christian Reformed *Psalter Hymnal* (1987).

MERCIES. The music, mostly from oral traditions, became popular with United States youth groups in the late 1950s. Although identified as the work of James H. Fillmore, early 20th century, it is not in any of James H. Fillmore's collections. A similar melody is the beginning of a song by Fred A. Fillmore (whose middle initial is misprinted as E.) and may account for the confusion; Fred A. Fillmore's song with refrain was published in George B. Holsinger's *Gospel Songs and Hymns No. 1* (Elgin, IL, 1899) and was recently rediscovered by John P. Wiegand with the help of Joan Fyock. The complete song as it is now known has not been located in any of the older sources; it was published in *Let's Sing* (1960), Donald Hustad's arrangement.

I Will Sing the Wondrous Story   500
Francis H. Rowley wrote this text while he was conducting a revival at the First Baptist Church at North Adams, MA (1886), in the third year of his pastorate there. He was assisted by a young Swiss musician named Peter Bilhorn who suggested that Rowley write a hymn for which he would compose the music. The following night the words came without any particular effort. Ira D. Sankey says that he changed the first line from "Can't you sing the wondrous story" to its present form.   H

CECELIA. Arranger Jack Schrader heard this tune sung by a male quartet from a Lillenas book, *Men of God*, while he was a Moody Bible Institute student in 1960. It had appeared in one earlier Hope hymnal, *Sing Joyfully*, and was simply called "Folk Song" by the Lillenas publication. CECELIA is the name of the street in Brentwood, MO, where Schrader lived before he attended Moody.

I Wonder as I Wander   165
John Jacob Niles has claimed authorship of this Appalachian carol, although he earlier indicated that he "collected" it. Its first publication was with G. Schirmer (1934). It has been included in only one other hymnal, that of the United Church of Christ (1974). It does not seem to pre-date Niles, appearing in none of the 19th-century collections of shape-note tunebooks nor among the American folk songs gathered by Cecil Sharp.

I WONDER AS I WANDER. Tune and text share common heritage—John Jacob Niles. Donald Hustad adapted the carol for congregational singing (1984).

I'll Praise My Maker While I've Breath　　　　　79
Isaac Watts first wrote this Christianized Psalm 146 paraphrase for *Psalms of David* (1719), in six stanzas. It was then adapted by John Wesley in 1736, using only stanzas 1, 3, 4, and 6.

OLD 113th. First published in the *Strasburg Psalter* (1539), the tune was a Huguenot "Battle Song." It was widely known by several other names and has been sung to Psalms 119, 36, and 68, as well as to Psalm 113 and this setting of Psalm 146. Matthäus Greiter composed psalm settings around this time; this may be one of his.

I'm New Born Again　　　　　494
Evidently from the 19th-century United States, this black spiritual first appeared in *Folk Songs of the American Negro* (1907) complied by brothers John W. and Frederick J. Work for Fisk University.

NEW BORN AGAIN. Similar to other 19th-century African-American tunes, this version is associated with the "free grace" text.

If My People's Hearts Are Humbled　　　　　719
Clair Cloninger's text (1986) is a rhymed paraphrase of 2 Chronicles 7:14-15. Her father was State Chairman of the Louisiana Republican party for 12 years and, she writes, "We were taught political responsibility walks hand in hand with spiritual commitment." First publication was in the *Hymnal for Worship and Celebration* (Word, 1986) with a tune by Tom Fettke.

BEECHER; see **Love Divine, All Loves Excelling** 558

If You Will Trust in God to Guide You　　　　　636
Written by Georg Neumark (1641), this text was captioned, "A Song of Comfort: God will care for and help every one in his own time." The hymn was born out of a fortuitous change in Neumark's circumstances; following a time of hardship, he was appointed to a tutorship. Catherine Winkworth made two translations of the German original; this one appeared in her *Chorale Book for England* (1863).　　　H

WER NUR DEN LIEBEN GOTT (also called **NEUMARK**). The tune was written by Georg Neumark and appeared with this text in his *Fortgepflantzer Musikalisch Poetischer Lustwald* (1657). It has been set to no less than 400 different hymn texts.　　　H

Immortal, Invisible, God Only Wise　　　　　62
Walter Chalmers Smith's poem was first published in his *Hymns of*

Christ and the Christian Life in 1867. It is based on the doxology in 1 Timothy 1:17. A number of changes were made in the original text when it was included in Garrett Horder's *Congregational Hymns* (1884).   H

ST. DENIO. The tune (sometimes called "Joanna") first appeared with a hymn text in John Robert's *Caniadau y Cyssegr* (1839) and was called "Palestrina." It is based on a traditional Welsh ballad "Can Mlynedd i'nawr" ("A Hundred Years from Now"), which was identified in the *Welsh Folk Song Journal* (vol. 1, 1911).   H

Immortal Love, Forever Full   607
"Our Master" was the title of a 38-stanza poem by John Greenleaf Whittier, published in his *Tent on the Beach and Other Poems* (1867). The typical hymnal version (stanzas 5, 13, 14, 16 of the original) omits the first stanza, given here.   H

SERENITY. The musical setting was taken from a longer love song, "Waft, ye Winds," written by William Vincent Wallace (1856). Its earliest appearance as a hymn tune adaptation by Uzziah C. Burnap may have been in Robinson and MacArthur's *The Calvary Selection of Spiritual Songs* (1878). The same year it was printed in *The Hymnal of the Methodist Episcopal Church with Tunes.*   H

In Christ There Is No East or West   695
This text by Michael Perry grew from a line of the hymn 697 by John Oxenham (W. A. Dunkerly) bearing the same title. Perry intended to revise the older hymn but "soon realized that so radical must be the revision that an entirely new hymn might be constructed." Written about three years earlier, the hymn was first published in *Hymns for Today's Church* (1982).

McKEE. In 1939 Harry T. Burleigh adapted this tune from the spiritual "I know the angel's done changed my name." It was named to honor the rector of St. George's Church, New York City, where Burleigh was soloist for many years. The spiritual first appeared in print in the 1884 edition of *Jubilee Songs*, published by Fisk University; as a hymn tune it was included in the Protestant Episcopal *Hymnal 1940*.   H

In Christ There Is No East or West   697
This text was written by John Oxenham for "The Pageant of Darkness and Light" presented by the London Missionary Society for the missionary exhibition at the Agricultural Hall in London, 1908. It was first published in Oxenham's *Bees in Amber* (1913).   H

ST. PETER. Alexander Reinagle's melody was originally set to a version of Psalm 118 in his *Original Psalm Tunes, for Voice and Pianoforte* (c. 1836). It was named "St. Peter" in his *Collection of Psalm and Hymn Tunes* (1840) after St. Peter's-in-the-East, Oxford, where the composer was organist.   H

In Heaven Above   682
Laurentius Laurentii Laurinus wrote the original poem in 1622 at the time of his wife's death; it was appended to the funeral sermon. It was adapted by a fellow Swede, Johan Åström, into a lyric hymn almost 200 years later. Soon afterward, William Maccall (a Scot) gave us the English version.   H

I HIMMELEN (earlier called **HAUGE**). The Norse folk melody from Heddal was published by Ludvig Lindemann in *Aeldre og Nyere Norske Fjeldmelodier* (1853), then beautifully arranged by Edvard Grieg in one of his last writings, *Psalms* (1906). HAUGE [hedge] is a coastal town on the southern tip of Norway, about 125 miles from Grieg's home near Bergen; the current title, I HIMMELEN, means "in heaven" and connects the tune to this text.

In heavenly armor we'll enter the land; see **The Battle Belongs to the Lord** 672.

In Heavenly Love Abiding   521
This text by Anna Laetitia Waring was first published in *Hymns and Meditations* (1850) under the title "Safety in God" and the caption "I will fear no evil, for thou art with me" (Ps. 23:4).   H

NYLAND. The tune is a Finnish folk melody. It was arranged by David Evans and named for a province in Finland, appearing in *The Revised Church Hymnary* (1927).   H

In my life, Lord, be glorified; see **Lord, Be Glorified** 537.

In the Bulb There Is a Flower   678
Words and music were first written (Feb. 1985) as a choral anthem (Hope Publishing Company, 1986), then adapted as a hymn. Natalie Sleeth writes that she was "pondering the death of a friend (life and death, death and resurrection), pondering winter and spring (seeming opposites), and a T. S. Eliot poem which had the phrase, 'in our end is our beginning.' These seemingly contradictory 'pairs' led to the thesis of the song and the hopeful message that out of one will come the other whenever God chooses to bring that about." Dr. Ronald Sleeth, the author's late husband, heard it a month before his death and asked that it be sung at his funeral service, which it was.

PROMISE. The tune was composed with the text.

In the Cross of Christ I Glory 209

Based on Galatians 6:14, this text was written by John Bowring. Tradition has a disputed story (unlikely because the dates are in conflict) that Bowring was inspired by a view of the cross on the spire of the fire-gutted St. Paul's Church in the Portuguese colony of Macao (such a church facade does exist), on the coast of China (a colony returning to mainland China in 1999). The words appeared in Bowring's *Hymns* (1825) and the opening line was inscribed on his tombstone.

RATHBUN. Composed by Ithamar Conkey in 1849 while he was organist and choirmaster of the Central Baptist Church in Norwich, CT, the tune was named in honor of his soprano soloist, Mrs. Beriah S. Rathbun, the only choir member faithful on the particular Sunday; the interesting story appears in *Guide to the Pilgrim Hymnal*. The music first appeared in Greatorex's *Collection of Psalm and Hymn Tunes* (1851).

In the Garden 242

C. Austin Miles wrote this text and tune in March 1912. The editor of *Hymns for the Living Church* (1974) gives the account in *Crusader Hymn Stories* (1967). The hymn has often been categorized as "sentimental and erotic," but it is better appreciated when it is understood to be based on Mary Magdalene's experience, as she met Jesus in the garden outside the open tomb on Easter morning. H

GARDEN. The tune name comes from the traditional title for these words. This popular gospel song was first published in *The Gospel Message, No. 2* (Philadelphia: Hall-Mack, 1912). H

In the morning when I rise; see **Give Me Jesus** 551.

In the Name of the Lord 113

According to Phill McHugh, Gloria Gaither and Sandi Patti Helvering had worked on this chorus, then invited him to help with the final version. It was popularized by Sandi Patti in 1986 and won the Gospel Music Award, "Song of the Year" (1988).

NAME OF THE LORD. The tune was composed along with the words as a joint effort of the three musicians.

In the Presence of Your People 19

Brent Chambers wrote the words and music (1977) as a response to an evening of ethnic music and dance. The music came first, he notes, then the text (based on Ps. 22:3, 25) as a result of a suggestion from friend Dale Garratt who had also been at the concert. This is one of Chambers's first compositions published outside his native New Zealand. Text and tune appeared first in the Scripture in Song recording and songbook *Father, Make Us One* (Maranatha, 1978).

CELEBRATION. The tune was named by Garratt when she heard the Chambers melody.

Infant Holy, Infant Lowly   169
This is a very old Polish carol whose English translation was first published in a music magazine which Edith Reed edited, *Music and Youth* (Dec. 1921).

W ZLOBIE LEZY. The tune name is Polish for "in a manger lies" and has a long association with the text. Rosalind Rusbridge, whose husband provided the harmonization first published in the British *Baptist Hymnbook* (1960), writes: "I have been vainly trying to contact a Polish friend who sang the tune to me in Polish at Christmas out of an old Polish hymnbook"—so other information was not available. Rusbridge prefers that the last phrase be repeated.

Into My Heart   444
Harry D. Clarke, traveling music-evangelist, wrote words and music while a student at Moody Bible Institute (1924).

INTO MY HEART. The music was composed with the text by Clarke.

Iona Gloria   826
The text is a repetition of the first few words of the "Gloria" (Is. 6:3), plus "alleluias"; see **Glory Be to God**.

IONA. The source of this musical setting of the repeated Gloria may have been the monks of the abbey of St. Columba on Iona Island (off Scotland) *c.* 625-640 A.D. According to John F. Wilson, "Tradition says that as Columba's ships departed for preaching tours to the mainland, the song was echoed between the monks on shore and those on board."

It Came upon the Midnight Clear   170
This is one of the first carol-hymns written in America. The work of Edmund H. Sears, a Unitarian minister, it was first published in the *Christian Register*, December 29, 1849.   H

CAROL. Richard S. Willis's tune was originally used with "See Israel's gentle Shepherd stand." It is an adaptation of Study No. 23 in Willis's *Church Chorals and Choir Studies* (1850). H

It Is God Who Holds the Nations 415
Written in 1976, "A Hymn for the Nation" was commissioned by Norwich Cathedral during the celebrations of the Queen's Silver Jubilee (1977). The Archbishop of Canterbury's senior chaplain included it in the official Order of Service, so it came to be sung throughout Britain and parts of the Commonwealth, using the tune VISION, by Walford Davies. Harry Eskew, then editor of *The Hymn*, requested it for use in the United States and author Fred Pratt Green modified the third stanza to give it wider use. It is also available as an anthem by Austin Lovelace (Hope Publishing Company).

It Is Good to Sing Your Praises 325
The metrical Psalm 92 is from the United Presbyterian *Psalter* (1912).

BLAENWERN. The tune by William P. Rowlands (1905) is named for a farm in Pembrokeshire, Wales, where Rowlands recovered from a boyhood illness. It was composed during the Welsh revival (*c.* 1904-05) and published in Henry Haydn Jones's *Cân a Moliant* (1916).

It Is Well with My Soul 519
These words were written by Horatio G. Spafford following the loss of four daughters in an accident at sea. The family was scheduled to travel to Europe in November 1873. Being delayed by last minute business developments, Spafford sent his wife and the girls on ahead. In mid-ocean their ship, the French liner Ville du Havre, collided with an English sailing ship and foundered. Of the five, Mrs. Spafford only was rescued, and she cabled her husband "saved alone." Spafford started immediately for Europe and, while on the high seas near the scene of the tragedy, wrote this hymn. H

VILLE DU HAVRE. Philip P. Bliss wrote this tune for the text and it first appeared in *Gospel Hymns No. 2*, compiled by Ira D. Sankey and Bliss. It is named for the ship mentioned above. H

It only takes a spark; see **Pass It On** 739.

Jerusalem, My Happy Home 675
The original old-English version of this text is significant enough hymnologically to receive almost four pages (580-583) in Julian's *Dictionary*. Twenty-six stanzas appear in a British Museum manuscript that dates from about 1600. It has the title "A Song made by F. B. P. to

88

the tune of Diana." The initials are probably those of an unknown Roman Catholic priest, and the text closely resembles a passage in the meditations of St. Augustine, which was popular reading in the 16th century. The poem was first published in 1601 (in 19 verses) in *The Song of Mary the Mother of Christ, with a Description of Heavenly Jerusalem*. The present hymnal version is limited to four stanzas.   H

LAND OF REST. The tune is a traditional melody collected and arranged by Annabel Morris Buchanan in her *Folk Hymns of America*, 1938. Mrs. Buchanan states that she first heard it as a child from her grandmother, Sarah Ann (Love) Foster, who sang it to "O land of rest, for thee I sigh"; it appeared with those words in J. R. Graves's *Little Seraph* (1873). The tune may well be of Scottish or North of England origin, and was widely sung throughout the Appalachian region. Mrs. Buchanan is of the opinion that the spiritual "Swing Low, Sweet Chariot" may be derived from it.   H

Jerusalem the Golden   754

    Bernard of Cluny is best known for his poem "De Contemptu Mundi" ("On the Contemptibleness of the World") comprised of some 2,966 lines and written in the difficult pattern of dactylic hexameter. After completing the poem about 1145, Bernard said "Unless the Spirit of wisdom and understanding had flowed in upon me, I could not have put together so long a work in so difficult a meter."

    John Mason Neale's first translation of 95 lines from Bernard's poem appeared in his *Mediæval Hymns and Sequences* (1851), from which this cento is drawn. The fourth stanza was added in *Hymns Ancient and Modern* (1861) and was not found in the original Latin.   H

EWING. Alexander Ewing's tune was written in 1853 for a translation of Part IV of Bernard of Cluny's hymn "For thee, O dear, dear country." In *Hymns Ancient and Modern* (1861), the tune appeared with this text, and they have been coupled ever since.   H

Jesu, Jesu, Fill Us with Your Love   436

    Tom Colvin, missionary to Africa since 1959, gathered this traditional folk song at Chereponi, northern Ghana. The English text is his own, written in 1963 while he was a district pastor of the Presbyterian church there. First publication was in *Free to Serve* (Iona Community, 1968).

CHEREPONI. The tune was named for the area in Ghana, West Africa, where Colvin heard it sung by new Christians at a mission station. It was arranged by Charles Webb for the *United Methodist Hymnal* (1989). Gathered in 1963, it provided the paperback book title when it was published along with 33 other West African songs in *Fill Us With Your Love* (Agape, 1969).

Jesus Calls Us o'er the Tumult   580
Cecil Frances Alexander wrote this hymn for St. Andrew's Day 1852; it is based on Matthew 4:18-20. It first appeared in *Hymns for Public Worship* (1852). Interestingly enough, these words written by a woman were adopted as the official hymn of the Brotherhood of St. Andrew of the Protestant Episcopal Church in the United States and the Church of England in Canada. The second stanza (referring to Jesus's encounter with Andrew) is omitted in this volume and in most hymnals of non-liturgical churches. The current version combines each pair of stanzas into one (four become two).   H

PLEADING SAVIOR. The anonymous tune was first published in Joshua Leavitt's tunebook *The Christian Lyre* (1832), with the text "Now the Saviour standeth pleading," by John Leland. It entered the hymn tune repertoire through *The English Hymnal* (1906).

Jesus Came, the Heavens Adoring   194
The text may have been connected to a homily—Godfrey Thring often wrote a hymn as a reflection on one of his sermons. It appeared in the hymn collections which he edited.

LAUDA ANIMA; see **Praise, My Soul, the King of Heaven** 26.

Jesus Christ Is Risen Today   250
The Latin text is a composite of three sources, manuscripts in Prague, Engleberg, and Munich. The English translation was first published in John Walsh's *Lyra Davidica, or a Collection of Divine Songs and Hymns, partly new composed, partly translated from German and Latin Hymns: and set to easy and pleasant tunes* (1708); it was adjusted in John Arnold's *The Complete Psalmodist* (1749). The fourth stanza, by Charles Wesley, is from *Hymns and Sacred Poems* (1740).

LLANFAIR; see **Hail the Day That Sees Him Rise** 258.

Jesus, Come! for We Invite You   187
Christopher Idle wrote the text at Limehouse, East London, for Epiphany 1979 (few hymns were available on the "first miracle"); it was first published in *Hymns with the New Lectionary* (1980) and featured at the 1987 conference of The Hymn Society of America. Idle suggests several different tunes for this often used meter.

SICILIAN MARINERS; see **Lord, Dismiss Us with Your Blessing** 834.

Jesus Comes with All His Grace   468

Charles Wesley's text is from *Hymns and Sacred Poems* (1749) in the section of "Hymns for those that wait for Full Redemption." It originally had 11 stanzas; these five were numbers 1, 2, 3, 4, 8.

WÜRTEMBERG. The tune is similar to the melody of "Straf' mich nicht in deinem Zorn" in the appendix of *Hundert ahnmüthig und sonderbar geistlicher Arien* (Dresden, 1694). It has been attributed to Johann Rosenmüller, but that authorship is doubtful. Bach used the tune in Cantata 115 (*Mache dich, mein Geist, bereit*) and it appeared with variations in Jacobi's *Psalmodia Germanica* (1722) and later hymn collections.

Jesus Comes with Clouds Descending   283

In writing this hymn ("Lo, he comes") Charles Wesley was inspired by an earlier work of John Cennick (1752). The text on the second advent was first published in the Wesleys's *Hymns of Intercession for All Mankind* (1758), assigned to the second Sunday of Advent. The hymn has since been revised and is a combination of earlier texts.   H

BRYN CALFARIA. The name of the tune means Mount Calvary—from its association with a Welsh hymn on the crucifixion, "Gwaed dy Groes sy'n codi i fyny." It was written by William Owen for the second edition of his *Y Perl Cerddorol* (The Pearl of Music, 1954). Vaughan Williams used the tune in his *Three Preludes for Organ on Welsh Hymn Tunes* (1920).

Jesus' Hands Were Kind Hands   412

Margaret Cropper wrote the text (*c.* 1926) which was first published in her *Hymns and Songs for the Church Kindergarten* (*c.* 1930), a book prepared with A. R. B. Wylam for the St. James's Sunday School, Staveley, near Kendal, Westmorland, England.

AU CLAIR DE LA LUNE. This simple French folk tune, named for its moonbeam text, is at least 300 years old and may have been the work of Jean Baptiste Lully (1632-87).

Jesus, I Come   448

William T. Sleeper collaborated with George C. Stebbins in 1877 in writing "Ye Must Be Born Again." Consequently, when he finished the words for this invitation hymn, he sent them to Stebbins, who wrote the tune.   H

JESUS, I COME. The complete gospel song was first published in *Gospel Hymns No. 5* (1887) under the scripture text, "Deliver me, O my God" (Ps. 71:4).   H

Jesus Is All the World to Me   491
Will L. Thompson wrote both words and music of this hymn, which
appeared in his *New Century Hymnal* (1904).   H

ELIZABETH. Author-composer Will L. Thompson married Miss
Elizabeth Johnson in 1891 at East Liverpool, OH, and the tune is named
for her.   H

Jesus Is Coming Again   276
Author-composer John W. Peterson says that this "second advent"
song was written expressly for the first volume (1957) of the *Songster* choir
magazine he edited; the journal was published for several years by "Better
Choirs" and later by the Singspiration Company.   H

COMING AGAIN. Customarily John W. Peterson has written music for
his own words, and that is true of this song which sometimes appears
with the title "Coming Again."   H

Jesus is coming to earth again; see **What If It Were Today?** 275.

Jesus, Jesus, Jesus; see **There's Something About That Name** 104.

Jesus, Jesus, Jesus in the Morning   364
Here is an anonymous African-American folk song, evidently from the
19th century. It is in a "family" design with each new stanza changing a
few words.

JESUS IN THE MORNING. The tune is associated with this text.

Jesus, keep me near the cross; see **Near the Cross** 549.

Jesus Lives and So Shall I   246
Based on John 14:19, "Because I live, ye shall live also," Christian
Gellert's text "Jesus lebt, mit ihm auch ich" was published in his *Geistliche
Oden und Lieder* (Leipzig, 1757). The first appearance of this hymn in the
United States was in the *Plymouth Collection* (1855); the translation there
(as here) was by J. D. Lang and first appeared in *Aurora Australis* (Sydney,
1826); these are stanzas 1, 3, 4, and 6 of Lang's version.   H

ZUVERSICHT. The tune was named from the last line of the German
text "Dies ist meine Zuversicht," and appeared in the *Rungsche Gesangbuch*
without the name of the composer. In the 1668 edition of *Praxis Pietatis
Melica* the initials "J. C." (Johann Crüger) were included.   H

Jesus, Lover of My Soul 461

Charles Wesley wrote these lines in 1738 shortly after his conversion, and published them in *Hymns and Sacred Poems* (1740) with the heading "In Time of Prayer and Temptation." Because of the intensely personal nature of the hymn, John Wesley opposed its use in public worship.   H

ABERYSTWYTH. The city of Aberystwyth in North Wales gave this tune its name. The melody was composed by Joseph Parry, Professor of Music at University College in that city. It was set with another text in *Ail Tonau ac Emynau* (1879) and later put with Wesley's hymn in Parry's cantata *Ceridwen.*   H

Jesus Loves Me, This I Know 470

This poem, "The Love of Jesus," written by Anna Warner, was recited by a fictional character, Johnny Fax, in *Say and Seal* (1859), a Victorian moralistic novel Anna co-authored with her sister, Susan.

JESUS LOVES ME. William Bradbury composed the tune for these words and published them in his very popular book, *The Golden Shower* (1862).

Jesus my Lord will love me forever; see **Now I Belong to Jesus** 503.

Jesus, Name Above All Names 106

Naida Hearn says she "composed this chorus as she went about her household duties, doing the washing, and worshiping the Lord."

HEARN. The tune was composed with the text in 1974. Both were published in *Scripture in Song* (1978).

Jesus Paid It All 489

This text was written by Elvina M. Hall on the flyleaf of a hymnal one Sunday morning during a lengthy pastoral prayer. She gave the poem to her pastor and he in turn coupled it with a new tune written by the church organist, John T. Grape.   H

ALL TO CHRIST. John T. Grape's tune (named after the original title "All to Christ I owe") was written, he says, when his church was undergoing remodeling and the cabinet organ was left in his care. The resulting melody was approved by his wife, but criticized by his choir and other friends. It has achieved wide usage since Grape's pastor, a Rev. Schrick, coupled it with Mrs. Hall's words, and it was published in *Sabbath Chords* (1868).   H

Jesus, Priceless Treasure   119

The original German text by Johann Franck was first printed (with this tune) in Johann Crüger's *Praxis Pietatis Melica* (Frankfort, 1653). Both text and tune appear to be based on a secular love song, "Flora meine Freude," included in *Arien* (1641) by Alberti. Because of its sensual passion (and, perhaps, its associations), for a time it was not well received in Germany, but became popular in numerous European translations, including one in Latin commissioned by Peter the Great and translated from its Russian version. Catherine Winkworth brought it to English in *Chorale Book for England* (1863) but, according to her own testimony, struggled with the complex meter.

JESU, MEINE FREUDE. Crüger composed or arranged this tune (1653) for this text; it has become a classic chorale, perhaps because J. S. Bach used it in several cantatas, a motet (this setting, 1723), and an organ chorale prelude.

Jesus, Remember Me   822

The text is Luke 23:42, the cry of the penitent thief on the cross beside Jesus.

JESUS, REMEMBER ME. Brother Jacques Berthier's music to the brief text was composed for the ecumenical monastic fellowship in Burgundy, France, known as the Taizé Community.

Jesus Saves!   728

Priscilla J. Owens wrote these words for a missionary service in the Sunday School where she served faithfully for 50 years. They were originally sung to the music of "Vive le Roi" from Meyerbeer's opera, *Les Huguenots*, and first appeared in *The Revivalist* (1868).   H

JESUS SAVES. William Kirkpatrick wrote this tune for Miss Owens's words. It first appeared in *Songs of Redeeming Love* (1882), edited by John R. Sweney, C. C. McCabe, T. C. O'Kane, and Kirkpatrick.   H

Jesus Shall Reign   745

Isaac Watts first published this paraphrase of Psalm 72 in his *Psalms of David, Imitated in the Language of the New Testament* (1719). It was entitled "Christ's Kingdom among the Gentiles," and is said to have been translated into more languages and dialects than any of the other hymns Watts has written.   H

DUKE STREET. John Hatton, composer of this tune, lived on Duke Street in St. Helen's, England. His tune first appeared anonymously in *A Select Collection of Psalm and Hymn Tunes* compiled by Henry Boyd in

1793, under the heading "Addison's 19th Psalm." In 1805 it was included in William Dixon's *Euphonia* and was there attributed to Hatton.   H

Jesus, Stand Among Us   803
These lines were written by William Pennefather for the conferences which he began at Barnet and continued at Mildmay Park, London. The hymn was published posthumously in *Original Hymns and Thoughts in Verse* (1873).   H

BEMERTON [also **WEM IN LEIDENSTAGEN** or **FILITZ** or **CASWELL**]. Friedrich Filitz's tune first appeared in his *Choralbuch zu Kirchen und Hausgebrauch* (1847), set to the German hymn "Wem in Leidenstagen." BEMERTON was George Herbert's parish in Wiltshire, which seems to have no connection to this tune since it is known by other names in other appearances.

Jesus, the Very Thought of Thee   112
This hymn is called one of the most beautiful in the English language. The translation was derived by Edward Caswall from the Latin poem "Jesu, dulcis memoria," attributed to Bernard of Clairvaux, but now thought to be of British origin. It first appeared in Caswall's *Lyra Catholica* (1849). (See also **Jesus, Thou Joy of Loving Hearts** 121, another cento from the same Latin poem.)   H

ST. AGNES. The tune was composed by John B. Dykes for this text and was first published in Grey's *Hymnal for Use in the English Church* (1866). In order to differentiate between this tune and another used in England, it is sometimes called ST. AGNES, DURHAM. One of the early Christian martyrs, St. Agnes, was beheaded in 304 A.D. at the age of 13.   H

Jesus, Thou Joy of Loving Hearts   121
This text (like "Jesus, the Very Thought of Thee" 112) is taken from "Jesus, dulcis memoria," a long devotional poem attributed to Bernard of Clairvaux, but probably not written by him. The cento was translated by Ray Palmer for the *Sabbath Day Hymn Book* (1858).   H

QUEBEC. The tune was named "Whitburn" when it first appeared in J. Grey's *A Hymnal for Use in the English Church* (1866). It is said that in 1861 the *Penny Post* in London sought a tune for John Keble's "Sun of My Soul" and for a whole year received settings from many readers. The tune regarded as the best was unsigned. Sir Henry Baker finally claimed authorship after it was republished anonymously in Bishop Bickersteth's compilation in 1871. He had composed it in 1854, while still an undergraduate student at Exeter, Oxford.   H

Jesus, Thy Blood and Righteousness 481
Nicolaus Ludwig von Zinzendorf completed this hymn in 1739 on his return from visiting Moravian missionaries in the West Indies. The original German text, "Christi Blut und Gerechtigkeit," had 33 stanzas and appeared in appendix no. 8 to *Hernnhut Gesang Buch*. John Wesley's selective and free translation reduced the verses to 24; they were first published in *Hymns and Sacred Poems* (1740) under the title "The Believer's Triumph." These four stanzas are those most commonly used in the United States. H

GERMANY. The tune appeared in William Gardiner's *Sacred Melodies*, 1815. Gardiner attributed the tune to the German composer Ludwig van Beethoven, asserting: "It is somewhere in the works of Beethoven, but where I cannot now point out." More likely, it is the work of Gardiner himself. H

Jesus, Thy Boundless Love to Me 556
The original text was written by Paul Gerhardt and consisted of 16 nine-line stanzas. It was first published in the fifth edition of Johann Crüger's *Praxis Pietatis Melica* (1653). There have been many translations into English, John Wesley's paraphrase being the most popular. It first appeared in *Hymns and Sacred Poems* (1739) with nine stanzas, "Living by Christ"; in *The Worshiping Church* the first two and last are used. H

ST. CATHERINE; see **Faith of Our Fathers** 692.

Jesus! what a Friend for sinners; see **Our Great Savior** 89.

Join All the Glorious Names 85
Originally with 12 stanzas, this text by Isaac Watts was first published in Book I of his *Hymns and Spiritual Songs* (1707) under the caption "Offices of Christ." It is said to be one of the most impressive and exalted hymns that Watts ever wrote. H

DARWALL; see **Rejoice, the Lord is King** 262.

Joy to the World! the Lord Is Come 146
Isaac Watts's paraphrase of the second half of Psalm 98 first appeared in his *Psalms of David Imitated in the Language of the New Testament* (1719). It bore the caption, "The Messiah's Coming and Kingdom." H

ANTIOCH. The music first appeared in Lowell Mason's *Modern Psalmist* (Boston, 1839) with the notation "from Handel." It cannot be traced with any degree of certainty, though some have pointed out a resemblance to phrases in "Comfort Ye" and "Lift Up Your Heads" in *Messiah* (1742); it is probably Mason's own work. H

Joyful, Joyful, We Adore Thee 20
According to the author's son, this text was written in 1907 while Henry van Dyke was visiting Williams College in Massachusetts as a guest preacher. Evidently inspired by the beautiful Berkshire Mountains, he presented the manuscript to the college president (Garfield) one morning at the breakfast table, suggesting that it be sung to Beethoven's "Hymn to Joy." It was included in Van Dyke's Poems (3rd ed., 1911) and in *The Hymnal* (Presbyterian) that same year. H

ODE TO JOY. This is an adaptation of the principal theme of the final movement of Beethoven's Ninth Symphony, first performed in Vienna in 1824. The arrangement commonly used as a hymn tune was made by Edward Hodges, and appeared in Tuckerman's *Trinity Collection of Church Music* (1864). However, it had appeared in other versions and with other texts since at least 1846. H

Just a Closer Walk with Thee 561
This anonymous song has the flavor of a "modern spiritual" and began to appear in gospel songbooks in the late 1940s. It was a favorite in the "all night gospel singing" programs in the South. H

CLOSER WALK. The tune name is the traditional title for the song, taken from the refrain. H

Just As I Am, without One Plea 445
Charlotte Elliott wrote these words as a "simple, candid expression of trust and personal confession." She was ill at home, and the rest of the family was engaged at a bazaar to raise funds to build a college at Brighton, England. Her writings, along with this hymn, appeared in her *Invalid's Hymn Book* (1836). Miss Elliott received thousands of letters thanking her for this particular hymn, and in recent years it has been recognized as the invitation song in Billy Graham crusades. H

WOODWORTH. The music widely used for this hymn in America was written by William Bradbury. It was originally set to "The God of Love Will Sure Indulge" in *Third Book of Psalmody* (1849), better known as the "Mendelssohn Collection" by Thomas Hastings and Bradbury. The tune with this text appeared in the collections of *Gospel Hymns and Sacred Songs* (1875-1891) used by Moody and Sankey in their evangelistic campaigns. The coda was heard by Donald Hustad, editor of *The Worshiping Church*, while he was playing for a Billy Graham crusade in Denmark. H

Kind and Merciful God 455

Author Bryan Jeffery Leech gives this account:
This hymn was inspired by and adapted from the General
Confession of the Church of England. The tune originally
appeared in an early hymnal of the Evangelical Covenant Church. It
had a jerky rhythm and was written in a minor key which seemed at
odds with a text about being happy in God. So I decided to alter this
setting by smoothing out the rhythm, slowing it down, and wedding
it to a text of confession which suited its rather mournful feeling. It
was first published in *The Covenant Hymnal* (1973).

ELFAKER. Bryan Jeffery Leech adapted this Swedish folk tune to his text
(1973).

King of Kings and Lord of Lords 110

No information on this text and tune was discovered. The publishers,
Maranatha! Music, could supply only the date of writing (1980),authors'
names, Sophie Conty and Nomi Batya, and the fact that the hymn was
published in *Hymnal for Worship and Celebration* (1986), edited by Fettke.

KING OF KINGS. This Jewish-sounding melody may have been written
by Conty and Batya, although it is represented as an authentic Hebrew
folk song.

King of my life, I crown thee now; see **Lead Me to Calvary** 211

King of the Universe 67

Michael Saward's hymn was first sung at Dalton House Chapel,
Bristol, England, an Anglican training college for women's ministry, June
19, 1970, and first published in *Songs of Worship* (1979). He intended it to
be "a credal hymn of praise, drawing together a large range of titles and
attributes of God." The words were written for RUSSIAN HYMN to provide an alternative to the traditional text "God the Omnipotent!" (originally "God the All-Terrible"). The 1970 version was heavily revised for
Hymns for Today's Church (1982).

RUSSIAN HYMN; see **God the Omnipotent** 427.

Kum Ba Ya 630

Of African origins, the text and tune may have come from the coastal
lowlands of South Carolina; it is in the Gullah language, a patois spoken
by African-Americans living on the islands off South Carolina and in
northern Florida.

KUM BA YA. The tune resembles "Michael Row the Boat Ashore" which

Allen, Ware, and Garrison (*Slave Songs of the United States*, 1867) identify as a Port Royal Island song; they give a Hilton Head version, too, a heritage which fits with the language of the Gullahs from that geographic area. This tune appears consistently with the "Kum Ba Ya" text.

Lavish Love, Abundant Beauty   68
Peter Ellis was teaching a series of adult Bible studies on the Holy Spirit; this hymn was written (Sept. 9-18, 1985) to be sung following the lesson on "the work of the Holy Spirit in creation" and was used the evening of September 18. With revisions (the original first line was "Lavish love in living color"), it was published in *The Hymnal for Worship and Celebration* (Word, 1986).

Lead Me to Calvary   211
No information is available on the writing of this hymn by Jennie E. Hussey. It first appeared in *New Songs of Praise and Power*, No. 3 (Hall-Mack Company, 1921).   H

DUNCANNON. The tune was written for these words by William J. Kirkpatrick and was named for his birthplace, Duncannon, PA.   H

Lead On, O King Eternal   747
Ernest Warburton Shurtleff wrote these words on the occasion of his graduation from Andover Theological Seminary in 1887. The hymn met with instant success and was published the same year in his *Hymns of the Faith*.   H

LANCASHIRE. The tune was written for a missionary festival held at Blackburn, Lancashire, October 4, 1835, to celebrate the 300th anniversary of the Reformation in England. On that occasion it was used with the hymn "From Greenland's Icy Mountains." Composer Henry Smart was organist at Blackburn at the time and named the tune for the county. It first appeared in *Psalms and Hymns for Divine Worship* (1867).   H

Leaning on the Everlasting Arms   609
The text was written by Elisha A. Hoffman at the request of A. J. Showalter, composer of its accompanying tune. In an expression of sympathy to two former students, Showalter had quoted Deuteronomy 33:27, "The eternal God is thy refuge, and underneath are the everlasting arms." He was immediately impressed that the words could be the basis of a good song. He wrote the refrain and the music, and asked Hoffman to submit appropriate stanzas.   H

SHOWALTER. The tune was written by Anthony J. Showalter as described above. The complete hymn first appeared in *The Glad Evangel*

for Revival, Camp, and Evangelistic Meetings (1887), compiled by L. M. Evilsizer, S. J. Perry, and Showalter.　　　　　　　　　　　　　　　　　　H

Let All Mortal Flesh Keep Silence　　　　　　　　　　　167
This text is based on the "Cherubic Hymn" from the Liturgy of St. James of Jerusalem; used on October 23, the feast of St. James, as the bread and wine are presented, it was found in Eastern churches as early as the 5th century and is still associated with Orthodox worship. It may have been written by St. James the Less, first Bishop of Jerusalem; the present translation was made by Gerard Moultrie for the second edition of Shipley's *Lyra Eucharistica* (1864).　　　　　　　　　　H

PICARDY. The tune is a traditional religious French folk song, included in *Chansons populaires des provinces de France, IV* (1860) and is named for a province in the north of France; the original text, "Jesus Christ s'habille en pauvre," tells of Jesus disguised as a beggar looking for crumbs of kindness. The adaptation as a hymn tune arranged by Ralph Vaughan Williams appeared in the *English Hymnal* (1906).

Let All the World　　　　　　　　　　　　　　　　24
On his deathbed George Herbert handed a manuscript to his lawyer, Edmond Duncon, requesting that his brother read it and let it be published "if he thought it would be of advantage to any soul—if not, to burn it." *The Temple*, with this "Antiphon," was published the following year (1633), and is Herbert's principal literary work. "Antiphon" indicates the formal structure of the poem, with a refrain beginning and ending each stanza. Herbert's poetry was not intended for public worship, but the Wesleys used some 40 of the selections in their *Hymns and Sacred Poetry* (1739).　　　　　　　　　　　　　　　H

CONRAD; see **Through All the World Let Every Nation Sing** 738.

Let All Things Now Living　　　　　　　　　　　53
Katherine K. Davis (under the pseudonym John Cowley) wrote this text for the Welsh tune as a choral anthem with descant, published by E. C. Schirmer (1939).

ASH GROVE. This Welsh folk tune, also known as LLWYN ONN, outlines the tonic, dominant, and sub-dominant chords in sturdy sequence. Its English version is a ballad of a country lover; its Welsh text describes an accidental shooting by a bow hunter. It dates from as early as 17th-century harp books.

　　Davis's descant was composed for the choral anthem. She lists a Novello pamphlet, *Book of National Songs*, as her source of the tune.

Let Heaven Rejoice before the Living God   355
Hal M. Helms's text won the American Guild of Organists and Hymn Society of America award for "best combination of new text and new tune" (1986). He collaborated with Alan MacMillan at the Community of Jesus on Cape Cod, Orleans, MA.

ROCK HARBOR. Alan MacMillan composed the music, working with Hal Helms (1986).

Let the Song Go Round the Earth   726
Sarah Geraldine Stock wrote the text for the Church Missionary Society *Hymn Book* (1899), which she edited prior to her death in 1898. For the text she composed a tune MOEL LYS.

Let The Whole Creation Cry   40
This hymn originally had 10 stanzas and is an imitation of Psalm 148. It was written by Stopford A. Brooke, an Anglican clergyman, and was included in *Christian Hymns*, published in 1881 for his congregation.   H

LLANFAIR; see **Hail the Day That Sees Him Rise** 258

Let the Words of My Mouth   819
The text is Psalm 19:14.

BAUMBACH. Adolph Baumbach composed this unnamed tune about 1862.

"Let There Be Light!"   716
The theme of the 15th Baptist World Alliance Congress, Los Angeles, July 2-7, 1985, was "Out of Darkness into the Light of Christ." John Piper was requested to write a hymn undergirding this theme and he cast it to fit Bruce Leafblad's tune SOUTH PASADENA.

SOUTH PASADENA. Bruce Leafblad wrote the tune in 1969 for Isaac Watts's "Give to Our God Immortal Praise" for a class in hymnology taught by Charles C. Hirt at the University of Southern California. The class voted it the best tune.

Let Us Break Bread Together   776
As is true of folk songs, there is no known author or composer for this spiritual. In his book *Negro Slave Songs in the United States* (1953) Miles Mark Fisher suggested that after the Civil War it was sung by blacks as a communion hymn. It may be derived from a song they used to convene

secret meetings, when such gatherings were prohibited in the colony of Virginia. H

LET US BREAK BREAD. The history of the tune is lost in the traditions of black worship of the 18th and 19th centuries. John W. Work says it was first published by William Lawrence in 1928. Like many African-American spirituals, it has become known through choral arrangements. This harmonization was made by Carlton R. Young for *Methodist Hymnal* (1964). H

Let Us Build a House of Worship 793
Margaret Clarkson's text was written in Toronto (1977) at the request of St. Matthews Baptist Church, Louisville, KY, for promoting the planning and building of educational facilities. It was first published in Donald Hustad's *Jubilate! Church Music in the Evangelical Tradition* (Hope Publishing Company, 1981) where it was cited as an example of one of the "better hymns to come."

ST. MATTHEWS. Donald Hustad composed the tune for this text (it had first been sung to AUSTRIAN HYMN 694) and named it for the Louisville church.

Let Us Draw Near! 631
Margaret Clarkson wrote the text during her first year of teaching (Barwick, Ontario, 1936); it was published in *Clear Shining After Rain* (1962).

CROSSROADS. The tune was composed for this text but much later than the text (1987, 1989) by Kurt Kaiser. It was earlier called DRAW NEAR.

Let Us, with a Gladsome Mind 59
Written in 1623 when author John Milton was only 15 years old, this psalm paraphrase (with 24 stanzas) was published in his *Poems in English and Latin* (1645); it is one of Milton's 19 poetic versions of various psalms. These five stanzas are based on verses 1, 2, 7, and 15 of Psalm 136. H

MONKLAND. John B. Wilkes, organist at Monkland, gave this version of the music to his vicar, Henry W. Baker, editor of *Hymns Ancient and Modern* (1861). Its source is uncertain. In the archives of the Moravian church in London, a manuscript volume of hymn tunes ascribes the tune to John Antes. A longer variant can be found in choral form in Freylinghausen's *Geistreiches GesangBuch* (1704). H

Let Your Heart Be Broken 429
Bryan Jeffery Leech writes:
One of the great men in my own denomination, the late Clifford Bjorklund, suggested that I write a text for World Relief Sunday. It seemed like a very unpromising concept for a spiritual song. . . . And then it all turned around, and it occurred to me that what was important was our reaction to suffering and need. Then I remembered Bob Pierce's dictum, "Let your heart be broken," and the immense ministry of World Vision International [which Pierce founded]. And from this the song was born.

WYE VALLEY; see **Like a River Glorious** 594.

Lift High the Cross 229
This processional hymn is unique in that it begins and ends with the refrain. It was written by George W. Kitchin and Michael R. Newbolt and was included in the 1916 Supplement to *Hymns Ancient and Modern*.   H

CRUCIFER. Sydney H. Nicholson's tune was written for this text and appeared with it in the 1916 Supplement to *Hymns Ancient and Modern*. A "crucifer" is one who carries a cross in ecclesiastical processions.   H

Lift up your hearts unto the Lord; see **Sing Alleluia to the Lord** 771.

Like a River Glorious 594
Written by Frances Ridley Havergal at Leamington, England (1874), this text was published (without music) in her *Loyal Responses* (1878).   H

WYE VALLEY. This tune was written by James Mountain for these words; they first appeared together in his *Hymns of Consecration and Faith* (1876).   H

Like the Murmur of the Dove's Song 286
Carl Daw wrote the text specifically for Peter Cutt's tune BRIDE-GROOM, at the request of the committee for *The Hymnal* 1982 (Episcopal). It is available in anthem settings (Choristers Guild and Concordia) and has been translated into Spanish (*Albricias*, an Hispanic hymnal of the Episcopal Church). Daw began with the idea of the fou-word refrain and added the stanzas to address "how," "where," and "why."

BRIDEGROOM; see **Not for Tongues of Heaven's Angels** 597.

Living for Jesus a Life That Is True 569
Thomas O. Chisholm wrote these words (1917) at the request of C. Harold Lowden, who had composed the tune for another text and used it in a Children's Day service in 1915. Recognizing that the tune was worthy of stronger words, he sent it to Chisholm, suggesting the title "Living for Jesus." The hymn was published on single sheets in the spring of 1917, and later that same year it appeared in *Uplifting Songs*, compiled by Lowden and Rufus W. Miller. H

LIVING. The tune by C. Harold Lowden led to the writing of the words, "Living for Jesus" (see above). The composer chose the tune name for its appearance in *Baptist Hymnal* (1956). H

Lo! How a Rose E'er Blooming 163
This German carol may date from as early as the 15th century; its earliest source is a manuscript in St. Alban's, Trier, in a prayer book which belonged to Brother Conrad, the Carthusian of Mainz (1582-88). The text, published in *Alte Catholische Geistliche Kirchengesäng* (Cologne, 1599), had 23 stanzas. This translation is a composite of the work of Harriet Spaeth (1875) and Theodore Baker (1894).

ES IST EIN' ROS' ENTSPRUNGEN. This tune, as old as the text, was published in the same manuscript, *Alte Catholische Geistliche Kirchengesäng* (Cologne, 1599). Similar melodies appear in Psalm tunes and at least one secular song. The interesting harmonization, known nearly as well as the tune, is from Michael Praetorius's volume VI of *Musae Sionae* (1609).

Long Ago, Prophets Knew 142
Fred Pratt Green wrote (1970) this advent text for the 400-year-old tune at the request of John W. Wilson; it appeared in *Partners in Praise* (Oxford University Press).

PERSONENT HODIE; see **On This Day Earth Shall Ring** 175.

Long Time Ago in Bethlehem; see **Mary's Little Boy-Child** 178.

Lord, Be Glorified 537
Bob Kilpatrick wrote the song as a personal dedication for himself and his wife, Cindy, to sing before concerts (autumn 1977). It was first published and recorded in *Praise 3* (Maranatha Music, 1978).

GLORIFIED (also **LORD BE GLORIFIED**). The tune was written along with the words. It is a pentatonic melody (using only five notes). Perhaps because of its simplicity, it has been used in other cultures.

Lord, Dismiss Us with Your Blessing 834

The text is attributed to John Fawcett, a contemporary of George Whitefield, active in London revivals as a Methodist turned Baptist. According to Carlton Young in *Companion to the United Methodist Hymnal* (1993), this is "a version of a text that appeared without attribution under the title, 'Close of Service' in *A Supplement to the Shawbury Hymn Book*, 1773." In *Selection of Psalms for Social Worship* (1786), it is attributed to "F" which is J. Fawcett, according to the author's key, an admittedly uncertain claim. It was connected with the "O Sanctissima" tune in Little and Smith's *Easy Instructor* (1798), an influential American singing school book.

SICILIAN MARINERS. It seems that J. G. Herder found this tune sometime between 1788-99 in Italy. W. D. Tattersall included it in his *Improved Psalmody* (1794) and called it SICILIAN HYMN. Herder himself printed it with a Roman Catholic text in his *Stimmen der Völker in Liedern* (1807) under the heading [translated] "To the Virgin Mary. A Sicilian Boat Song." Wesley Milgate writes:

The earliest reported sighting [of this tune] seems to be in *The European Magazine and London Review* xxii, November 1792, pp. 385-6, where there is "We shall overcome" a Negro spiritual, to the tune "The Sicilian Mariner's Hymn to the Virgin."

Hooper and White add:

Today in Sicily the tune is unknown, but it does resemble some folk tunes of southern France. *The European Magazine* says that Sicilian sailors sing the hymn when the sun sets, and an 1866 source says that the Venetian gondoliers sang it, especially on St. Mary's Day.

Lord, Have Mercy upon Us 823

The text is a translation of the ancient Greek prayer which is used regularly in Lutheran, Anglican, Orthodox, and Roman Catholic worship.

MERBECKE. John Merbecke composed this setting for the communion service in the first Anglican *Book of Common Prayer* (1549). The service was drastically revised in 1552, and many scholars have expressed regret that this unique congregational chant never caught on in English worship.

Lord, Have Mercy upon Us 821

The text is a translation of the Greek invocation which is a part of the oldest Christian liturgies, based on the opening words of Psalm 51.

WILLAN KYRIE. Healey Willan composed this brief setting for the Church of St. Mary Magdalene (1928), while he was a theory professor at the University of Toronto. He had a keen interest in the use of plainsong and ancient musical forms.

Lord, I Want to Be a Christian   563

The origin of this text is uncertain. Eighteenth-century records show that a Presbyterian named William Davies was preaching in Virginia between 1748 and 1756. A slave came to him wanting to learn more about Jesus Christ and his duty to God and said, "Lord (sir), I want to be a Christian." In *Negro Slave Songs in the United States*, Miles Mark Fisher suggests that this spiritual could well have originated in Virginia about that time, so the story may be credible.   H

I WANT TO BE A CHRISTIAN. The tune first appeared in Frederick J. Work's *Folk Songs of the American Negro* (Nashville, 1907). George Pullen Jackson points out that the refrain is similar to the setting of "Come to me, sweet Marie" which he heard sung in rural Maine in the 1880s.   H

Lord, I Was Blind   499

The text is from a longer poem by William Matson, "The Inner Life" (1866); the language was revised for *Hymns for Today's Church* (1982) to avoid archaisms, such as "Thou" in "Lord, Thou has made." First publication was in *Supplemental Hymns*, compiled by Henry Allon (1868).

O WALY WALY; see **When Love Is Found** 392.

Lord Jesus Christ, Invited Guest   387

Michael Perry wrote this congregational prayer for the bride and groom for *Hymns for Today's Church* (1982) because the owners of the copyright to Gurney's "O Perfect Love" 388 refused to allow a text update.

Lord Jesus, Think on Me   462

This is the last of 10 odes written by Synesius of Cyrene (North Africa), presenting the Christian faith as seen by a man of neo-Platonist training. It was written in the early years of the 5th century.

The paraphrase by Allen W. Chatfield first appeared in *Hymns Ancient and Modern*, 1875, and later in his own *Songs and Hymns of Earliest Greek Christian Poets, Bishops, and Others translated into English Verse* (1876).   H

DAMON. This tune is often called SOUTHWELL and first appeared in William Damon's *Psalms of David* (1579), set to Psalm 45. The present arrangement varies considerably from the original.   H

Lord, Let Us Now Depart in Peace   842

Based on the Song of Simeon in Luke 2 (the "Nunc Dimittis"), these words may have been written by the music's composer, George Whelpton.   H

DISMISSAL. George Whelpton probably included this setting in a four-page leaflet of responses he published about 1900.　　　　　　　　H

Lord, Listen to Your Children Praying　　　　629
Author-composer Ken Medema was working as a music therapist in New Jersey (1970). As his youth fellowship met with him for prayer on behalf of a hospitalized young man, Medema began to hum, then sing, this chorus; the group joined in singing. Later he added stanzas (which are not included in *The Worshiping Church*).

CHILDREN PRAYING. The tune was improvised with the text.

Lord, Now Let Your Servant　　　　343
Written about 1972 and first used in London (1973), James Seddon's paraphrase of the song of Simeon was prepared for *Psalm Praise*, a collection of hymns based on the Psalms and Canticles of the *Book of Common Prayer*.

QUIETUDE; see **Speak, Lord in the Stillness** 585.

Lord of All Good, We Bring Our Gifts to You　　　　645
This hymn was written by Albert F. Bayly for a Christmas Fair at Eccleston Congregational Church where he was pastor (1950). First publication was in *Again, I Say, Rejoice* (1967).

MORESTEAD. Sidney Watson composed this hymn tune for Butler's "Lift Up Your Hearts," first published in *Hymns for Church and School* (1964). MORESTEAD is a village in Hampshire where Watson bicycled.

Lord of All Hopefulness　　　　369
Jan Struther (pseudonym of Joyce Torrens) wrote this text to be sung to SLANE for *Enlarged Songs of Praise* (1931).

SLANE; see **Be Thou My Vision** 532.

Lord of All Leisure Time　　　　398
The hymn was written for *The Worshiping Church* in response to editor Donald Hustad's challenge to Bryan Jeffery Leech (July 1988) to develop a hymn on this unexplored topic.

LEISURE TIME. John F. Wilson, editor at Hope Publishing Company, composed this tune for Leech's text for inclusion in *The Worshiping Church* (1990).

Lord of the Church, We Pray for Our Renewing   717
Written by Timothy Dudley-Smith at Ruan Minor, August 1976, this renewal hymn was first published in *Songs of Worship* (1980) to the author's suggested tune, LONDONDERRY AIR (109). The inspiration came while he was attending the National Evangelical Anglican Congress at Keele University nine years before the hymn was written (1967). The phrase, "Christ over all," in stanzas 1 and 4 was the motto of the Congress. "To turn to Christ" (stanzas 1-2) is found in the new Alternative Services of baptism and confirmation in the Church of England.

Lord, Our Lord, Your Glorious Name   319
The text is from the Presbyterian Church's *Psalter* (1912), and has been revised considerably.

CHAUTAUQUA. William F. Sherwin, director of music at the Chautauqua Assembly, composed this music for the text, "Day is Dying in the West" (see 828 for the refrain), in 1877. The tune is also called EVENING PRAISE.   H

Lord, Speak to Me, That I May Speak   574
This text was written by Frances Ridley Havergal at Winterdyne, England, April 28, 1872. It appeared first in a leaflet with the title "A Worker's Prayer" and the scripture reference, Romans 14:7. It was later published in Miss Havergal's *Under the Surface* (1874).   H

CANONBURY. The tune is an arrangement of one of Robert Schumann's piano pieces in his *Nachtstücke*, Opus 23, 1839. It is first found as a hymn tune in J. Ireland Tucker's *Hymnal with Tunes, Old and New* (1872). Canonbury is a street and a square in Islington, London.   H

Lord, Teach Us How to Pray Aright   628
James Montgomery's text was first published in Cotterill's *Selection* (1819), then revised by Montgomery himself in 1825—he often wrote quickly and revised later. An additional stanza was included between the present 3rd and 4th: "Give deep humility, the sense of godly sorrow give; a strong desiring confidence to hear thy voice and live." The editors of *The Worshiping Church* have made slight changes in language, as well as in the order of stanzas.

RICHMOND. The tune was first published in a collection of original hymns by Thomas Haweis, *Carmina Christo, or Hymns to the Saviour* (1792), with the text "O Thou, From Whom All Goodness Flows"; it included decorated repeats before the last line.

Lord, the light of your love is shining; see **Shine, Jesus, Shine** 721

Lord, We Bring to You Our Children 759
Author Frank von Christierson was baptized when he was two weeks old in the Lutheran Church of Lorisa, Finland. The text expresses his fondness for dedication of children. It was written about 1974, "too late for me to use," Christierson writes; he is now retired. He suggests HYFRY-DOL as another tune setting; if it is used, the four stanzas become two.

WYCLIFF. This tune by John Stainer was set to William Sparrow-Simpson's text "All for Jesus" as the final hymn in the oratorio *The Crucifixion* (1887). H

Lord, We Worship and Adore You 832
This experimental congregational worship piece was composed for the Lake Avenue Congregational Church, Pasadena, CA, where the author-composer was minister of music. It was designed for and first used as a performance project which was part of Bruce Leafblad's doctoral service (1976).

LAKE AVENUE. The tune is named for the church for which it was written.

Lord, Who Throughout These Forty Days 200
Claudia F. Hernaman wrote children's poems, and this unique temptation (Lenten) hymn was first published in her *Child's Book of Praise: A Manual of Devotion in Simple Verse* (1873).

LAND OF REST; see **Jerusalem, My Happy Home** 675.

Lord, Whose Love in Humble Service 426
Albert F. Bayly wrote this poem in response to an invitation by The Hymn Society of America to submit hymns on social welfare. It was named "Conference Hymn" for the second National Conference on the Churches and Social Welfare held in Cleveland, OH, October 23-27, 1961. The Hymn Society published it in *Seven New Social Welfare Hymns* (1961). It first appeared in a major volume in *The Methodist Hymnal* (1964). H

HYFRYDOL; see **Come, Thou Long-Expected Jesus** 135.

Lord, You Give the Great Commission 715
At the request of the senior class at Yale Divinity School, Jeffery Rowthorn wrote this ministry hymn. It was first sung on the eve of grad-

uation, May 1978. First publication was in *Laudamus* (Hymnal Supplement, Yale, 1980) and it has been widely reprinted.

ABBOTT'S LEIGH; see **God Is Love, Let Heaven Adore Him** 70.

Love Came Down at Christmas 153

Christina Rossetti's "Christmastide" was first published in her collection of 130 poems, *Time Flies: A Reading Diary* (1885), in a section called "Some Feasts and Fasts." It was based on the liturgical calendar and loosely related to her own copy of John Keble's *The Christian Year* (1827). The last lines originally read "Love to God and all men / Love the universal sign," which Rossetti herself updated to "love for plea and gift and sign" in a later edition.

Love Divine, All Loves Excelling 558

This hymn appeared under the heading "Jesus, show us thy salvation" in Charles Wesley's pamphlet *Hymns for those that seek, and those that have Redemption in the Blood of Jesus Christ* (1747). It had appeal from the beginning because so few hymns in those days expressed "the love of God." It also presents the Wesleyan doctrine of "Christian perfection" through an experience of "sanctification." H

BEECHER (also **ZUNDEL**). The tune was composed in 1870 by John Zundel, organist at the Pilgrim Congregational Church of Brooklyn, NY, when the famous Henry Ward Beecher was minister there. The church was widely known for great preaching, great organ playing, and great congregational singing. The tune was evidently named for the pastor and his brother Charles, both of whom worked with Zundel in publishing the *Plymouth Collection of Hymns* (1855); this text and tune were included in Zundel's *Christian Heart Songs, A Collection of Solos, Quartettes and Choruses of All Meters* (1870). H

Love divine, so great and wondrous; see **He the Pearly Gates Will Open** 683.

Loved with everlasting love; see **I Am His, and He Is Mine** 602.

Low in the grave he lay; see **Christ Arose!** 235.

Macedonia 737

These words were written by Anne Ortlund and won first prize in the contest to find a theme hymn for the World Congress on Evangelism, held in Berlin in 1966. It was first published in July 1966 in *Christianity Today*, sponsor of the Congress and the contest. The hymn's title is from

Acts 16:9, "Come over into Macedonia and help us." It has appeared in many hymnals and many languages around the world. H

ALL SAINTS NEW. Donald Hustad was chairman of the music committee and the hymn contest for the 1966 Congress on Evangelism; he chose this tune at that time for use with the text. The tune had been composed by Henry S. Cutler for Reginald Heber's "The Son of God Goes Forth to War" and was first published in *The Hymnal with Tunes Old and New* (1872). "New" was added to the tune name to avoid confusion with the earlier melody called "All Saints" in *Geistreiches Gesang-Buch, Darmstadt* (1698). H

Majesty, Worship His Majesty 98
Author Jack Hayford, pastor of the Church on the Way, Van Nuys, CA, was inspired by the royal family while traveling in Great Britain in 1977 during the silver anniversary of the coronation of Queen Elizabeth II, and related that image to Christ and His kingdom. A visit to Blenheim Palace, the birthplace of Winston Churchill, completed the setting for writing "Majesty," which Hayford recalls dictating to his wife as they drove away from Blenheim. It was later edited at the piano in their home, according to *Worship His Majesty* (Word).

MAJESTY. Hayford composed the music with the text.

Make a Joyful Noise 31
Jimmie Owens wrote words and music (1974) for the musical *If My People* (Lexicon, 1975). The text is a paraphrase of Psalm 98:4 and serves as part of the congregational praise and worship section of the musical, preparing for prayer for the nation.

JOYFUL NOISE. The tune was composed for these adapted words.

Make Me a Blessing 656
According to George S. Schuler, Ira B. Wilson wrote these words about 1909. Curiously, Wilson evidently could not remember having written them; further, he is best known as a composer, not a text writer. The song was first published in 1924 as a leaflet (with Schuler's music) and introduced at an International Sunday School Convention in Cleveland, OH. Later it appeared in *Songs of Evangelism* (1925), edited by Schuler, E. O. Excell, and W. E. Biederwolf (Chicago: Glad Tidings Publishing). H

SCHULER. In early printings, this setting is dedicated to the choir of Moody Memorial Church, Chicago. It was probably written during a period when its composer, George Schuler, directed that choir. H

Make Me a Captive, Lord 583
This text by George Matheson was based on the phrase "the prisoner of Jesus Christ" in Ephesians 3:1 and appeared in his *Sacred Songs* (1890) with the title "Christian Freedom." H

PARADOXY. Donald Hustad, co-author of this handbook, wrote the tune for these words; it was first published in *Tabernacle Hymns No. 5* (1953) as an alternative to the then-used tune LEOMINSTER. The harmony has been changed slightly for *The Worshiping Church* to avoid Hustad's earlier use of *fauxbourdon*. It is called PARADOXY because of the many paradoxes suggested in the text.

Make Me a Servant 653
Writer Kelly Willard tells this about the song: She had prayed specifically (1982) to be "made a servant" and received an answer to that prayer—she became pregnant. She remembers her response, "What is this, God, your idea of a joke?" She now believes that her prayer was answered through motherhood.

SERVANT. The tune was written with the text.

Make Room within My Heart, O God 559
Bryan Jeffery Leech writes that this was "my very first hymn, written as a poem and not with any idea in mind of its being sung. I seem to recall that I created it sometime during my seminary days in London (1951-55), but . . . kept it until 1970 when I showed it to the Editorial Committee of my denomination, the Evangelical Covenant Church of America. They voted its inclusion in *The Covenant Hymnal* (1973)."

KINGSFOLD; see **O Sing a Song of Bethlehem** 192.

"Man of Sorrows," what a name; see **Hallelujah! What a Savior** 226.

Marvelous grace of our loving Lord; see **Grace Greater than Our Sin** 472.

Marvelous message we bring; see **Jesus Is Coming Again** 276.

Mary's Little Boy-Child 178
Written by Jester Hairston as a solo-with-choir anthem (Bourne, 1956), the tune, capturing the calypso style of that era, gained popularity with choirs at historically black colleges and through recordings by Harry Belafonte. It is one of a large number of African-American spiritual-like compositions and spiritual arrangements by Hairston.

HAIRSTON. The tune was composed with the text (1956).

May the Grace of Christ Our Savior 841
Published (complete in two stanzas) in the "Short Hymns" section of *Olney Hymns* (1799), book 3, John Newton simply titled this setting, "2 Corinthians xiii. 14."

OMNI DEI. The tune was first published in David Corner's *Gross Catholisch Gesangbuch* [Large Catholic Hymnbook] (Nürnberg, 1631 and later editions) to the text *Omni die dic Mariae*, a hymn to the virgin.

May the Lord, Mighty God 843
The text is based on Psalm 29:11 and is sung to a variety of tunes.

WEN-TI. The tune is a Chinese melody located by Donald Hustad (in *Hymnal Supplement*, Hope Publishing Company, 1984) for use with this text. It probably was composed by Pao-Chen Li (1907-1979), a literary writer of Chinese art songs and choral works. The meaning of the name is obscure—it may be a location.

May the Mind of Christ My Savior 560
Written by Kate B. Wilkinson, of whom little is known, this devotional hymn was first included in *Golden Bells* (1925). H

ST. LEONARDS. A. Cyril Barham-Gould was living at St. Leonard's-on-Sea, England when he wrote this tune. It appeared with this text in *Golden Bells* (1925). H

Mine Eyes Have Seen the Glory 416
In December 1861, six months after the Civil War began, Julia Ward Howe and her husband traveled to Washington with Governor and Mrs. Andrews of Massachusetts. During the journey, she heard troops along the road singing "John Brown's body lies a-mouldering in the grave," and was reminded of this fine tune. James Freeman Clarke, her pastor and a member of the traveling group, suggested she write more fitting words. Mrs. Howe completed them that same night and showed them to Dr. Clarke a day or so later. *The Atlantic Monthly* issue of February 1862, printed the poem under the title "The Battle Hymn of the Republic." H

BATTLE HYMN. The source of the tune is unknown, though it has occasionally been attributed to William Steffe. It was associated with many different texts, including the camp meeting song "Say, brothers, will you meet us" and, according to Louis Elson in *National Music of America*, it was known in the South long before the Civil War. H

Moment by Moment   529
The song evidently developed from a chance remark of the preacher
Henry Varley to the American evangelist Daniel W. Whittle. Varley
expressed his feeling that the song "I Need Thee Every Hour" 538 was not
his favorite, because he needed Christ "every moment of the day." As a
result, Whittle penned "Dying with Jesus, by death reckoned mine";
"Moment by Moment" is the refrain.   H

WHITTLE. The music for D. W. Whittle's text was written by his daughter, May Whittle (early appearances of the song list her as "Mary"), who
married D. L. Moody's son, Will. Words and music were copyrighted in
1893 and first printed in leaflets. The song was published in Ira D.
Sankey's *Christian Endeavor Hymns* (Boston, 1894).   H

More Love to Thee, O Christ   555
Elizabeth Prentiss wrote these words in 1856 during a difficult time of
physical suffering and mental anguish. It has been called "a more explic-
itly Christian echo" of "Nearer, my God to Thee." Her husband said:
Like most of her hymns, it is simply a prayer put into the form of
verse. She wrote it so hastily that the last stanza was left incomplete,
one line having been added in pencil when it was printed. She did
not show it, not even to her husband, until many years after it was
written; and she wondered not a little that, when published, it met
with so much favor.
The original version of the third stanza was: Let sorrow do its work; send
grief and pain; / Sweet are thy messengers, sweet their refrain, / When
they can sing with me: More love, O Christ, to thee. At the request of
Donald Hustad, Margaret Clarkson wrote a new stanza in 1988. The
hymn was first printed in a leaflet in 1869.   H

MORE LOVE TO THEE. William H. Doane wrote this tune for the
hymn. Words and music appeared together in his *Songs of Devotion*
(1870).   H

Morning Has Broken   362
Songs of Praise Discussed (London, 1933) has this note about Eleanor
Farjeon's hymn which appeared first in *Songs of Praise* (1931):
There being no known hymn in this short dactylic meter, and some-
thing being also wanted on the theme of thanksgiving for each day as
it comes, Miss Farjeon was asked to make a poem to fit the lovely
Gaelic tune.
The information below shows that the first part of the comment was
incorrect. Nevertheless, the words (with this tune) became very popular
in the United States, partly as a result of a Cat Stevens recording (1972). H

BUNESSAN. According to James Moffat's *Handbook to the Church Hymnary* (1927), this tune "was noted down by Alexander Fraser from the singing of a wandering Highland singer. Its bold movements are in keeping with the freedom shown in Gaelic song." It was printed in *Songs and Hymns of the Gael* (1888) and appeared in the *Irish Church Hymnal* (1917) with the words "Child in the manger." David Evans's arrangement is from the *Church Hymnary* (Rev. ed., 1927), with the same Christmas text. The music first appeared with "Morning has broken" in *Enlarged Songs of Praise* (1931).　　　　　　　　　　　　　　　　　　　　　　H

Must Jesus Bear the Cross Alone?　　　　　　　　　　　658
Several authors contributed to this hymn as we know it. Stanza 1 is said to be an altered quatrain which originally appeared in Thomas Shepherd's *Penitential Cries* (1693). According to Julian's *Dictionary*, stanza 2 first appeared in a missionary collection published at Norwich, England (*c.* 1810), author unknown. Stanza 3 first appeared in *The Oberlin Social and Sabbath School Hymn Book*, compiled by George N. Allen (1844); Allen is given credit for some of these words.　　　　　H

MAITLAND. The tune was composed by George N. Allen and was included with the above text in his *Oberlin Social and Sabbath School Hymn Book* (1844). The tune is called CROSS AND CROWN in Henry Ward Beecher's *Plymouth Collection* (1855) and is identified as "a western melody." The hymn's popularity is credited to that appearance.　　H

My Country, 'Tis of Thee　　　　　　　　　　　　　　417
Several different accounts of this hymn's origin are available, more than one traceable to its author. The text was written by Samuel Francis Smith, a Baptist seminarian, and was first sung at the Independence Day exercises of the Boston Sabbath School Union, Park Street Church, July 4, 1831. Evidently Lowell Mason had brought a number of volumes of German songs to Smith requesting that he look them over and translate anything that was particularly appealing. Coming upon the tune, Smith was inspired to write this original patriotic text. The hymn was first published in *The Choir, or Union Collection of Church Music* (1832), compiled by Lowell Mason.　　　　　　　　　　　　　　　　　　　　　　H

AMERICA. The music is of unknown origin. Many authorities believe that it came from England, although it was also set to continental patriotic texts in Denmark, Sweden, and France. The first printed versions of the tune in its present form were in the *Thesaurus Musicus* (*c.* 1740-45) and *Harmonia Angelicana* (1743 or 1744). Edward Maginty in *The Musical Quarterly* (July 1934) traces the tune to plainsong ancestries, and Percy Scholes discusses it in the *Oxford Companion to Music* (1970), connecting it to tunes by Bull (early 17th century) and Purcell (17th century).

My Faith Has Found a Resting Place 495
According to Milburn Price in *Handbook to The Baptist Hymnal* (1992), "This text was written by Eliza E. Hewitt under the pseudonym Lidie H. Edmunds. It was first published in *Songs of Joy and Gladness, No. 2* (Boston and Chicago, *c.* 1890), under the title 'No Other Plea.' It apparently did not appear in another collection until 1944, when it was included in *Choice Hymns of the Faith*, a Plymouth Brethren hymnal."

LANDÅS. "Landås" is the name of a town in Norway. In the hymnal mentioned above, the music is listed as a Norse melody, arranged by William J. Kirkpatrick. Donald Hustad located the original melody set to "For Norge, kjempers födeland" (To Norway, mother of the brave) in Norsk Nasjonalmusikk (Norsk Musikforlag, Oslo, n.d.). The tune is credited to André Grétry (1741-1831), a Belgian opera composer, but has not been found in his works. H

My Faith Looks Up to Thee 552
Ray Palmer wrote these words as an expression of deep spiritual devotion shortly after graduating from Yale. Some time later, Lowell Mason met the author and asked him if he had anything to contribute to a book which he was about to publish. This text was given to him. The hymn with Mason's tune first appeared in *Songs for Social Worship* (1832), edited by Mason and Thomas Hastings. H

OLIVET. Lowell Mason wrote the tune specifically for these words. He once told the author: "Mr. Palmer, you may live many years and do many good things, but I think you will be best known to posterity as the author of 'My Faith Looks Up to Thee.'" "Olivet" is a variant of "Mount of Olives" and perhaps refers to the hymn's message. H

My God, How Wonderful Thou Art 65
Originally titled "The Eternal Father," these words were first published in Frederick W. Faber's *Jesus and Mary* (1849) and later in his *Hymns* (1861). The last two lines have been altered for *The Worshiping Church*. H

PYE. Written by Donald Hustad for these words in the cantata, *Celebration of Discipleship* (1976), the tune was recorded in Pye Studios, London. H

My hope is built; see **The Solid Rock** 517.

My Hope Is in the Lord 482
Norman J. Clayton wrote both the words and music of this hymn in 1945 in Malverne, New York. He first published it in *Word of Life Melodies, No. 2* (1945). H

WAKEFIELD. The tune was given the family name of composer Norman Clayton's mother, Mary Alice Wakefield.   H

My Jesus, I Love Thee   100, 101

These words were written by William Ralph Featherstone (possibly when he was converted) at the age of 16. He sent the hymn to his aunt, Mrs. E. Featherstone Wilson of Los Angeles, and she suggested it be published. In four stanzas, it was first published in *Primitive Methodist Magazine* (1862), then appeared anonymously in England in the *London Hymn Book* (1864). Shortly thereafter, it was included in American hymnals.   H

AFFECTION 100. E. F. Miller's tune has long been sung to General William Booth's "O Boundless Salvation! Deep Ocean of Love" in Salvation Army life, and is included in many evangelical British hymnals. Its style is similar to other 19th-century Methodist decorated tunes of the era (such as SAGINA or DIADEM).   H

GORDON 101. Adoniram J. Gordon composed the music for this text, which he found in the *London Hymn Book*. It first appeared in *The Service of Song for Baptist Churches*, 1876, compiled by S. L. Caldwell and Gordon.   H

My Lord of Light Who Made the Worlds   3

Christopher Idle wrote this text for the folk tune BARBARA ALLEN (his only recollection of a tune suggesting words to him) at Poplar in 1976, and it was first sung at the Limehouse Parish Church; he says it is "formed around the Three Persons of the Trinity." The hymn was first published in *The Christian Herald*, June 7, 1980, and later in other collections.

DOMINUS REGIT ME. The tune name, which means "The Lord rules me," is the Latin title for Psalm 23. The music was composed by John B. Dykes for the text "The King of Love My Shepherd Is"; that hymn was sung at the composer's funeral in 1876.   H

My Lord! What a Morning   279

This 19th-century spiritual in its original form may have read, "My Lord, what a mourning," according to poet James Weldon Johnson in *The Book of American Negro Spirituals* (1925). This idea is supported by the apocalyptic vision of Revelation 6:12-17, in which the words "and the stars of the sky fell to the earth" are found.

BURLEIGH. The tune name honors Harry T. Burleigh, the choral arranger who popularized many African-American spirituals.

My Lord, You Wore No Royal Crown   191

Author Christopher Idle says this about the writing of the hymn:
In 1978 I bought from a station bookstall a copy of Hans Küng's book
On Being a Christian, and began to read it on a family train journey on
holiday. I was moved by its fresh treatment of the person of Jesus,
and in particular Küng's description of four kinds of human leader—
the king, the revolutionary, the hermit, and the politician. The Lord
Jesus Christ, he said, fitted none of these categories; he stood and still
stands supreme, unique, alone. Back home in Limehouse . . . I wrote
this hymn text, where the first four stanzas correspond to Küng's four
categories of leadership, all transcended by our Lord, as the fifth and
sixth stanzas are meant to show.
First publication was in *Hymns for Today's Church* (1982); stanza 5 was
revised in 1988.

PUER NOBIS; see **O Love, How Deep, How Broad** 193. The author
suggests SPLENDOUR as another tune setting.

My Savior's Love   478

Both text and tune, written by Charles H. Gabriel, appeared in *Praises*
(1905), compiled and published by E. O. Excell.   H

MY SAVIOR'S LOVE. The tune title comes from the last phrase of the
text refrain.

My Song Is Love Unknown   202

Samuel Crossman was among the earliest writers of non-psalm
hymns; they were written to fit the psalm meters, however. This poem
was published in *The Young Man's Meditations, or some few Sacred Poems
upon Select Subjects and Scriptures* (London, 1664) with this comment: "A
Verse may find him whom a Sermon flies." Two centuries later it was first
used as a hymn in the *Anglican Hymn Book* (1868). Elizabethan language
was modernized by the editors of *Hymns for Today's Church* (1982).

**My Soul Glorifies the Lord [And the glory, the glory of the
Lord]**   351

The text is Isaiah 6:5.

MESSIAH. This simplified congregational refrain is from the first choral
section (No. 4) of Handel's *Messiah* (1742), a chorus which begins with
the alto section and is answered by the other voices.

My Tribute (To God be the glory)   46

Andraé Crouch wrote this popular tune for his black gospel singers,

The Disciples, recording and publishing it in 1971 (Light Records, Lexicon Music).

MY TRIBUTE. The tune was composed with the words and expresses the gospel pianistic style of the composer.

Nature with Open Volume Stands 222

With six stanzas (an enigmatic fourth is omitted here), this hymn was designated "For the Lord's Supper" and titled "Christ Crucify'd; The Wisdom and Power of God," in Isaac Watts's *Hymns and Spiritual Songs, 3rd Book* (1707). The fourth stanza reads: "Here I behold his inmost heart / where grace and vengeance strangely join, / piercing his Son with sharpest smart / to make the purchas'd pleasures mine."

GERMANY; see **Jesus, Thy Blood and Righteousness** 481.

Near the Cross 549

As were many of Fanny Crosby's poems, this text was written to fit an existing tune by William H. Doane. The completed hymn first appeared in *Bright Jewels* (1869) compiled by W. B. Bradbury, W. F. Sherwin, Chester G. Allen, and Doane. H

NEAR THE CROSS. William H. Doane wrote many tunes for Fanny Crosby's texts; in this instance, she wrote the text to fit his tune. H

Near to the Heart of God 542

It had been the custom of Rev. Cleland B. McAfee to write a hymn for each communion service in the Presbyterian church of which he was pastor. This hymn was written in 1901 after a great sorrow had come into his life in the death of two nieces from diphtheria. His church choir sang it on Saturday night outside his brother's quarantine house in Chicago, IL, and on Sunday morning at communion in the First Presbyterian Church of that city. H

McAFEE. This tune was written by Cleland B. McAfee for his text. The completed hymn first appeared in *The Choir Leader* (1903), a magazine of the Lorenz Publishing Company, Dayton, OH. H

New Songs of Celebration Render 32

Erik Routley paraphrased Psalm 98 for *Cantate Domino* (1974). The rhyme is treated in an anachronistic style similar to the French psalters of Marot and Bezé, so it particularly fits the style of the tune.

RENDEZ A DIEU. This Genevan tune for Psalm 118 (its French opening line), composed or gathered by Louis Bourgeois (editions from 1542 to 1557), is printed in psalters from Strasbourg (1545) and Lyon (1547); it also appeared in the psalter editions of Geneva (1551) and Edinburgh (1564). It was first associated with this Routley text in *Cantate Domino* (1974), although it was much earlier sung to an English metrical Psalm 118 by John Craig (1564).

Nicene Creed; see **The Nicene Creed** 15; also see **Of the Father's Love Begotten** 145.

No Other Plea; see **My Faith Has Found a Resting Place** 495.

Not All the Blood of Beasts; see **What Offering Shall We Give?** 490.

Not for Tongues of Heaven's Angels   597
    This expansion on 1 Corinthians 13 was written at Ruan Minor by Timothy Dudley-Smith (Aug. 1984) for Cutts's tune, at the request of Robert Batastini who was compiling a new hymnal, *Worship III*. It was first published, with this intended tune, in *New Songs of Praise* (1985).

BRIDEGROOM. Peter Cutts composed this tune (1967) for Erik Routley's text, "As the bridegroom to his chosen." Cutts reports that "Routley's grand piano wrote it" since Routley would not let him get up from the piano (in his house at Newcastle in northern England) until it was finished. Cyril Taylor suggested the current rhythmic design of the last phrase. It was first published in *100 Hymns for Today* (1969).

Not What These Hands Have Done   476
    The text written by Horatius Bonar appeared in his *Hymns of Faith and Hope* (1861) with the heading "Salvation through Christ alone."   H

ST. ANDREW. Joseph Barnby composed the tune in 1866 while he was organist of St. Andrew's Church, London. It was originally written for John S. B. Monsell's hymn, "Sweet Is Thy Mercy, Lord," and appeared unnamed with that text in Barnby's *Hymn Tunes* (1869). The tune name appeared with the music in the posthumous edition of *Hymn Tunes* (1897).   H

Nothing but the Blood of Jesus   471
    Robert Lowry wrote this text and tune, probably while he was pastor of the Park Avenue Baptist Church, Plainfield, NJ. It was first published in *Gospel Music* (1876) compiled by William H. Doane and Lowry, with the reference "Without the shedding of blood there is no remission of sin" (Heb. 9:22).   H

PLAINFIELD. Lowry's tune was named PLAINFIELD in *Baptist Hymnal* (1956) after the New Jersey town in which he served as pastor and where he died. H

Now I Belong to Jesus 503
This favorite gospel song was first published in *Word of Life Melodies, No. 1* (Gospel Songs, Inc., Norman Clayton Publishing Company, Malverne, NY, 1943). Words and music had been written by Norman J. Clayton that same year. H

ELLSWORTH. Ellsworth, a town in Connecticut, was a former residence of author-composer Norman Clayton. H

Now Let Us Learn of Christ 567
Christopher Idle's succinct text grows from themes in Ephesians; it was written at Poplar, E. London, 1976, just before Idle moved to Limehouse, and was first published in *Songs of Worship* (Scripture Union, 1980). The author says that some of his texts are "too long," but that this one is both "short and satisfying."

PARKSTONE. This is one of three tunes suggested by the text's author (the others: IBSTONE, GROWING). PARKSTONE was composed for this text by David Peacock (1980) and first published in *Hymns for Today's Church* (1982).

Now Thank We All Our God 374 [and 334]
Beginning "Nun danket alle Gott," the first two stanzas of this hymn were written by Martin Rinkart as a table grace for his family during the time of the Thirty Years' War in 17th-century Germany. The hymn was first published in Rinkart's *Jesu Hertz-Büchlein* (1636) and was sung at the conclusion of the Peace of Westphalia, ending that devastating war. The translation by Catherine Winkworth appeared in her *Lyra Germanica* (1858). H

NUN DANKET ALLE GOTT. The tune, with its title from the German text, has been associated with this hymn since they appeared together in Johann Crüger's *Praxis Pietatis Melica* (1647). While it bore no credits, it is believed that Crüger himself wrote the music. H

O beautiful for spacious skies; see **America the Beautiful** 418.

O Bless the Lord, My Soul! 71
Isaac Watts's paraphrase of Psalm 103 is from his *Psalms of David Imitated in the Language of the New Testament* (1719).

FESTAL SONG; see **Rise Up, O Saints of God** 670. Donald Hustad composed the descant for use with this Watts text.

O Breath of Life 299

The *Anglican Hymn Book* (1965) dates Bessie P. Head's hymn "ca. 1914," and it probably appeared first in leaflet form. It was included in Mrs. Head's *Heavenly Places and Other Messages* (1920) and in the *Keswick Hymn Book* (1937). This stanza is omitted in *The Worshiping Church*:

O Heart of Christ, once broken for us,
'tis there we find our strength and rest,
our broken contrite hearts now solace,
and let Thy waiting Church be blest. H

SPIRITUS VITAE. Mary J. Hammond wrote the music for these words, and it is named from the first words of the first stanza, "O Breath (Spirit) of Life." H

O Canada! 424

Judge Adolphe B. Routhier wrote the French text (before 1880) which is the national anthem of Canada, but it was not officially designated until July 1, 1980. The text which has become standard is the English translation by R. Stanley Weir, written in 1908.

O CANADA. The music to Canada's national anthem (*chant national*) was composed for St. John the Baptist Day, June 24, 1880, by a Montreal music theater composer, Calixa Lavallée. He was commissioned by the music committee of the Fête Nationales des Canadiens-français to set the French text by Routhier.

O Christ, the Great Foundation 709

Jubilate Group's editor, Michael Perry, has not located any details or the source of this hymn (*c.* 1936) which appears in *Hymns for Today's Church* (1982); the Christian Conference of Asia, the copyright holder, has "disappeared" along with information on its *Hymnal*. The text is evidently an extension of ideas in "The Church's One Foundation" (689) and is credited to a Chinese hymnist, Timothy Lew.

O Christians, Haste 731

Mary Ann Thomson began to write this hymn one night in 1868 as she sat up with one of her children who was ill. Her intention was to produce a missionary text to the tune which was then associated with Faber's hymn "Hark, hark, my soul, angelic songs are swelling," but it remained unfinished because she could not come up with a suitable refrain. Three years later she completed the work and it was first included in the

Protestant Episcopal *Hymnal* (1892). Donald Hustad made several alterations in the text (which originally began "O Zion, haste") in both *Hymns for the Living Church* (1974) and *The Worshiping Church*.   H

TIDINGS. The tune was composed by James Walch in 1875 as a setting for Faber's "Hark, hark, my soul." He felt that existing tunes (including Mary Thomson's favorite, mentioned above) were not adequate. It first appeared with the above text in *The Church Hymnal* (1894) and is named for a central word in the refrain.   H

O Come, All Ye Faithful   173
   Seven different manuscripts found in widely separated parts of Europe contain this hymn. All bear the signature of John Francis Wade, who made his living in the middle 18th century by copying and selling plainchant and other music. In Dom John Stephan's *Adeste Fideles; a study on its origin and development* (1947) sufficient evidence is presented for crediting the authorship to Wade. These stanzas are based on a translation by Frederick Oakeley made in 1841 and printed in Murray's *Hymnal* (1852). H

ADESTE FIDELES. The tune name is taken from the opening words of the original Latin hymn. The melody appeared in manuscript with this text in *Cantus Diversi*, a volume compiled by John Wade in 1751 for use in Roman Catholic homes and institutions. The present arrangement was published in *Essay on the Church Plain Chant*, 1782, by Samuel Webbe, organist at the Portuguese embassy in London; hence the tune is sometimes called "Portuguese Hymn."   H

O Come, Let Us Adore Him   126
The refrain of "O Come All Ye Faithful," is extended with "family" words of anonymous praise.

ADESTE FIDELES; see **O Come All Ye Faithful** 173 (above).

O Come, O Come, Emmanuel   133
   The liturgical practice from which this hymn developed reaches back to the 7th century, possibly earlier. The text is derived from the seven "Great O's" (antiphons) which were sung before and after the *Magnificat* in the office of Vespers, on successive days from December 17 to 23. The English translation (originally "Draw nigh, draw nigh, Emmanuel") first appeared in John Mason Neale's *Hymnal Noted* (1851).   H
   Henry S. Coffin added the fifth stanza in the same spirit when he revised the translation of the hymn (1916).

VENI EMMANUEL. The tune (whose Latin name means "Come, Emmanuel") is an adaptation or a composite of plainsong phrases taken from settings of the Kyrie. Thomas Helmore included this arrangement in the *Hymnal Noted, Part II* (London, 1854) and indicated that it was from a French missal in the National Library at Lisbon, Portugal.   H

O Come to Me, the Master Said   442
Written as a communion hymn at Ruan Minor, August, 1987, Timothy Dudley-Smith's text was published in the United States in *Songs of Deliverance* (Hope Publishing Company, 1988).

KINGSFOLD. This tune was recommended by Dudley-Smith; see **O Sing a Song of Bethlehem** 192.

O for a Closer Walk with God   547
The hymn was written by William Cowper. John Newton titled it, "Walking with God," based on Genesis 5:24. It was published, with the hymns of Newton, in *Olney Hymns* (1779). The original six stanzas were adapted and revised for *Hymns for Today's Church* (1982).

BEATITUDO. The tune was composed by John B. Dykes for the hymn, "How bright these glorious spirits shine," published in *Hymns Ancient and Modern* (1875). BEATITUDO, a word coined by Cicero, means "the condition of blessedness."   H
Another Cowper hymn is also sung to this tune: "Heal Us, Immanuel" 411.

O for a Thousand Tongues to Sing   130
Charles Wesley wrote this text on May 21, 1739, to commemorate the first anniversary of his "spiritual birth." The first stanza of the full 18-stanza hymn began "Glory to God, and praise and love." It first appeared in *Hymns and Sacred Poems* (1740).   H

AZMON. The tune first appeared anonymously in Lowell Mason's *The Modern Psalmist* (1839). It was one of many melodies picked up by Mason on a tour of Europe for the purpose of obtaining materials from distinguished composers for future publications. Among the composers visited was Carl G. Gläser. In The *Sabbath Hymn and Tune Book*, Mason called this tune DENFIELD and credited it to "C.G." Later he named it AZMON, a name mentioned in Numbers, chapter 34.   H

O God of Every Nation   422
This hymn by William W. Reid, Jr. won first place in The Hymn Society 1958 competition. It was published and sung at the Fifth World Order Study Conference, Cleveland, OH, November 18-21, 1958.

LLANGLOFFAN. First printed (anonymously) in *Hymnau a Thonau er Gwasanaeth yr Eglwys yng Nghymru*, edited by Daniel Evans (1865), this hymn tune was introduced to English-speaking churches in the *English Hymnal* (1906).

O God, Our Help in Ages Past   78

This paraphrase of Psalm 90 appeared in nine stanzas in Watts's *Psalms of David Imitated in the Language of the New Testament* (1719) under the title "Man Frail and God Eternal." The original hymn began with "Our" and John Wesley changed this to "O" in his *Psalms and Hymns* (1738). "Our" is still used frequently as the first word.   H

ST. ANNE. Set to Psalm 42, the tune first appeared anonymously in *A Supplement to the New Version of Psalms by Dr. Brady and Mr. Tate . . . the Sixth Edition, Corrected and Much Enlarged*, 1708. Croft is listed as composer in Philip Hart's *Collection* (London, 1720), and he was organist at St. Anne's Church, Soho, London, for which the tune is named.   H

O God, Who Gives to Humankind   399

Edward Burns wrote this text (*c.* 1969), first published in *Hymns for Today's Church* (1982), as "an exploration of the relationship between revealed truth and researched truth, between the fullness of what God has revealed in Christ and the open-ended search for truth which characterizes the scientific enterprise." Burns is a chemist and a theologian.

TALLIS CANON; see **O Gracious Light, Lord Jesus Christ** 359.

O God, Whose Will Is Life and Good   413

Harwicke D. Rawnsley wrote the hymn as "Father, Whose Will is Life and Good." It was first published in *A Missionary Hymn Book* (London: Society for the Promotion of Christian Knowledge, 1922).

CRIMOND; see **The Lord's My Shepherd, I'll Not Want** 330.

O Gracious Light, Lord Jesus Christ   359

An anonymous Greek hymn of the 3rd century, this text was translated by F. Bland Tucker (*c.* 1940). It was called "ancient" by St. Basil (*c.* 370); therefore, it was known before the 4th century. One of the oldest hymns in *The Worshiping Church*, it was intended to be sung for candle-lighting in the office of Vespers, and is still so used in Orthodox churches.   H

TALLIS CANON. Thomas Tallis provided settings for Archbishop Matthew Parker's *The whole Psalter translated into English Metre* (printed by

John Day, *c.* 1560) including this tune, written for Psalm 67. The tune should be sung as a canon (a "round") by starting the second part where indicated (four notes after the first). About this tune, when it was first published, Tallis wrote, it "goeth milde: in modest pace."

O Happy Day That Fixed My Choice 504
Originally entitled "Rejoicing in our Covenant engagements to God," this text was written by Philip Doddridge. It appeared posthumously without the refrain in Doddridge's *Hymns, founded on Various Texts in the Holy Scriptures* (1755). The hymn is said to have been chosen by Prince Albert, consort of Queen Victoria, to be sung on occasions when members of the royal family were confirmed. The refrain is anonymous.   H

HAPPY DAY. The refrain melody is from a popular song by Edward F. Rimbault entitled "Happy Land." The remainder is probably the work of other anonymous musicians. The full tune appeared in William McDonald's *The Wesleyan Sacred Harp* (1854) set to another hymn text, but the same refrain, "Happy day, happy day, when Jesus washed my sins away!"   H

O holy Dove of God descending; see **Spirit, Now Live in Me** 284.

O Holy Night 160
John S. Dwight, sometime Unitarian minister and active music critic, wrote this solo carol in the style of German *lied* texts which he greatly admired (mid 1800s). How this shy American minister-turned-musicologist connected his text with the music of a French music theatre composer is not clear; he may have heard the chanson and written these words for it.

CANTIQUE DE NOEL. The tune and French music-theatre-style accompaniment were composed by Adolphe-Charles Adam to a French text for Christmas midnight mass. Jack Schrader, staff composer for Hope Publishing Company, has adapted the solo setting for congregational use in *The Worshiping Church*.

O How Blest Are the Poor in Spirit 603
Richard Avery and Donald Marsh responded to a "felt need" for a "singable setting" of the "important teaching of Jesus, the Sermon on the Mount" (1979). Marsh suggests singing it by lining it out or singing it straight through as written.

BEATITUDES. The tune was composed with the words and named for its connection with the text from the Sermon on the Mount (Mt. 5:3-12).

O How He Loves You and Me!   479
    Kurt Kaiser habitually keeps a file of ideas for both lyrics and music;
he had "just scratched out the words, 'O how He loves you and me' and
put the paper away in the file." Later, he came back to it and found this
simple text and melody fit easily in his mind. When he sent it to be
copyrighted, he was told to add more original material, so he wrote stanzas which are not included here (1975).

PATRICIA. Patricia is Kurt Kaiser's wife; the melody was composed with
the text.

O, How I Love Jesus   509
    The stanzas of this hymn by Frederick Whitfield were first published
in leaflet form (1855) and appeared in the author's *Sacred Poems and Prose*
(1861). The refrain is probably anonymous.   H

O, HOW I LOVE JESUS. The tune is of unknown origin. It is found in
many collections published in America in the 19th century.   H

O Jesus, I Have Promised   648
    John E. Bode wrote this hymn in 1866 for the confirmation of his
daughter and two sons, with the first line, "O Jesus, we have promised."
It was printed in leaflet form by the Society for the Promotion of
Christian Knowledge (1868) and bore the title, "For the Newly
Confirmed." It was also included in the Appendix to *Psalms and Hymns*
(1869), published by the same society.   H

ANGEL'S STORY. Arthur H. Mann composed this tune as a setting for
"I love to hear the story which angel voices tell" by Mrs. E. H. Miller. It
first appeared in *The Methodist Sunday School Hymnbook* (1881).   H

O Lamb of God   833
    The text is an English translation of the Communion song "Agnus
Dei," commonly sung in Lutheran, Anglican, and Roman Catholic worship. It is based on John the Baptist's words: "Behold, the Lamb of God
who takes away the sin of the world!" (Jn. 1:29b)

WILLAN AGNUS DEI. Healey Willan composed this brief setting as
part of an Anglican Service of Holy Communion for the Church of St.
Mary Magdalene (1928), while he was a theory professor at the University
of Toronto. He had a keen interest in the use of plainsong and ancient
musical forms.

O Little Town of Bethlehem   154, 155
This text was inspired by Phillips Brooks's visit to the Holy Land in
1865. He was rector of Holy Trinity Church in Philadelphia and wrote
this much loved carol for the children in his Sunday School. It was sung
in their Christmas service in 1868, and included in *The Church Porch*
(1874), a Sunday School hymnal.   H

FOREST GREEN 154; see **Amid the Thronging Worshipers** 340.

ST. LOUIS 155. The tune was written at Brooks's request by the organist
of Holy Trinity Church, who also was the Sunday School superintendent.
Lewis Redner composed the tune and it was first sung on December 27,
1868. Tradition has it that Redner had delayed fulfilling his assignment
and that the tune came to him during the night before Christmas. Text
and tune appeared together for the first time in *The Church Porch* (1874),
edited by Dr. William R. Huntington. It has also been suggested that the
tune name is a "play" on Redner's first name and was chosen by Phillips
Brooks.   H

O Lord Most High   828
Mary A. Lathbury wrote the hymn "Day is Dying in the West" in
1877 at the request of Bishop John H. Vincent, founder of the
Chautauqua Assembly on Lake Chautauqua, NY. It was included in *The
Calvary Selection of Sacred Songs* (1878) and is still sung at each Sunday ves-
per service at the Chautauqua Assembly. This is the refrain of the hymn
and its tune.   H

CHAUTAUQUA; see **Lord, Our Lord, Your Glorious Name** 319 for
the full tune and description.

O Lord my God, when I in awesome wonder; see **How Great Thou Art**
21.

O Lord, our Lord, how majestic is your name; see **How Majestic Is
Your Name** 61.

O Love, How Deep, How Broad, How High   193
This anonymous, originally Latin hymn of 23 stanzas (15th century
or earlier) sometimes has been attributed to Thomas à Kempis (1380-
1471). Translated by Benjamin Webb (stanzas 2, 6, 9, 11, 12, 23), it was
published in *The Hymnal Noted, Part II* (1854).

PUER NOBIS; see **O Splendor of God's Glory Bright** 27.

O Love That Will Not Let Me Go 531

This text was written by George Matheson, June 6, 1881, while he was pastor of the Innellan Church, Argyllshire, Scotland. The nearly blind Matheson said that it was a time of severe mental anguish, and that he had the impression of having the words dictated by a small inner voice. The writing of the entire hymn took only about five minutes. It first appeared in the January, 1882, issue of *Life and Work*, a monthly magazine published by the Church of Scotland, and later was included in the *Scottish Hymnal* (1885).   H

ST. MARGARET. The tune was written for the text by Albert L. Peace and first appeared in the *Scottish Hymnal* (1885). Like the words, it was written very quickly. The composer said that "the ink of the first note was hardly dry when I had finished the tune." It has been surmised that the melody may be named for Margaret, Queen of Malcolm III of Scotland, who was canonized in 1251.   H

O Master, Let Me Walk with Thee 651

This text as originally written by Washington Gladden was a poem of three eight-line stanzas which appeared in a devotional column, "The Still Hour," in *The Sunday Afternoon* (1879), a magazine edited by Gladden. Charles H. Richards is responsible for turning the poem into a hymn by eliminating the second stanza and making the remaining two into four verses of four lines each. It appeared in Richards's *Songs of Christian Praise* (1880).   H

MARYTON. The tune was written by H. Percy Smith for the hymn, "Sun of My Soul," and first appeared in *Church Hymns with Tunes* (London, 1874).

O Perfect Love 388

Members of Dorothy Gurney's family were singing hymns at home in Ambleside, England, one Sunday evening in 1883. Her sister's favorite hymn tune was Dyke's "Strength and Stay" and she was bemoaning the fact that the words associated with it were not appropriate for her forthcoming marriage. Her complaint sent Mrs. Gurney (then Dorothy Blomfield) into the library with pencil and paper. Fifteen minutes later she came back with three stanzas of "O perfect Love." The text was first included in the Supplement to *Hymns Ancient and Modern* (1889).

Stanza 4 is the final doxology from John Ellerton's "O Strength and Stay," a paraphrase of the Latin "Rerum Deux tenax vigor." This was the hymn text sung by Mrs. Gurney's family on the occasion mentioned above.   H

O PERFECT LOVE (also **SANDRINGHAM**). The tune is arranged from an anthem composed by Joseph Barnby in 1889 (using this text) for the marriage of the Duke and Duchess of Fife. It first appeared as a hymn tune in *The Church Hymnary* (1898) and soon replaced "Strength and Stay" as a favorite for English weddings. Sometimes the tune is called SANDRINGHAM after a residence of the English royal family located in Norfolk.   H

O Sacred Head, Now Wounded   221
Ascribed to the 12th-century church leader, Bernard of Clairvaux, the Latin hymn "Salve caput cruentatum" was just one cento from a long poem addressed to seven parts of the body of the crucified Christ. Paul Gerhardt's free German translation "O Haupt voll Blut und Wunden" first appeared in *Praxis Pietatis Melica* (1656). James W. Alexander translated the Gerhardt version into English and this appeared in Leavitt's *The Christian Lyre* (1830) as well as Alexander's own *The Breaking Crucible, and other Translations* (1861).   H

PASSION CHORALE (also **HERZLICH TUT MICH VERLANGEN**). The tune was first set to a secular German song, "Mein G'müt ist mir ver-wirret," in Hans Leo Hassler's *Lustgarten Neuer Deutscher Gesäng* (1601). It was first used as a hymn tune in *Harmoniae Sacrae* (Görlitz, 1613) set to "Herzlich thut mich verlangen," a funeral hymn, then with Johann Hermann Schein's "Ach Herr, mich armen Sünder" (1625). It was set to the Gerhardt text in Crüger's *Praxis Pietatis Melica* (1656) and has been coupled with it and its translations ever since; this association has given it its name. The present harmonization by J. S. Bach is from his *St. Matthew Passion* (1729).   H

O say, can you see; see **The Star-Spangled Banner** 423.

O Sing a Song of Bethlehem   192
According to Carlton Young, in response to a perceived need for hymns about the life of Jesus, hymnologist Louis F. Benson wrote this hymn for *The School Hymnal* (1899), one of "a graded series of hymnals" under the topic, "Early life of Jesus."

KINGSFOLD. This English ballad melody, called "Dives and Lazarus" in *English County Songs* (1893), was first used as a hymn tune by Ralph Vaughan Williams in *The English Hymnal* (1908) to the text "I Heard the Voice of Jesus Say" (506). Vaughan Williams also used the tune as a theme and variations in his fantasia for strings and harp. Kingsfold is a village in Surrey, south of London. An Irish version of the tune is "The Star of County Down," used by Benjamin Britten; still another version appears in the *Crowley Carol Book* as "We are Poor Frozen-out Gardeners."

O Sons and Daughters, Let Us Sing   249

"L'aleluya du jour de Pasques" (The Easter Alleluia) was written in Latin by Jean Tisserand, a Franciscan monk who died in 1494 in Paris. It was first discovered in a small untitled book printed some time between 1518 and 1536. John Mason Neale translated the poem for his *Medieval Hymns and Sequences* (1851), the text beginning "Ye Sons and Daughters of the King." It has frequently been altered during the years of its use.   H

O FILII ET FILIAE. Named for its first line in Latin, this traditional French tune probably is contemporary with the text and associated with it in collections from the 17th and 18th centuries. The composer is unknown and it may have French folk roots, but its first printed appearance has been traced to *Airs sur les hymnes sacres, odes et noels* (Paris, 1623).   H

O Splendor of God's Glory Bright   27

The original Latin hymn "Splendor paternae gloriae" has been ascribed to St. Ambrose. In its complete form it is a morning hymn to the Holy Trinity and a prayer for help and guidance throughout the day. Its reference to Christ as "Light" was a favorite image in this period of Christian history, based on Hebrews 1:3. The earliest manuscript containing the hymn is from about 890 A.D., but it dates from much earlier. The English translation is a composite from many sources.   H

PUER NOBIS. Named from the Latin hymn "Puer nobis nascitur" in a 15th-century manuscript (the Trier Manuscript, later edited by Wilhelm Bäumker), the tune saw several variations. This version was adapted by Michael Praetorius for Volume VI of his *Musae Sioniae* (1609) and further edited by George Woodward in *Piae Cantiones* (1910 edition of the 1582 tunebook).

O the Deep, Deep Love of Jesus   477

In 1926, this was probably the best known hymn of S. Trevor Francis, who had died one year earlier at the age of 92; it was then that Pickering and Inglis, Ltd. of London and Glasgow released his collected works in a volume, *O the Deep, Deep Love of Jesus, and other poems*. The Irish *Church Hymnal* dates the hymn 1875. Its first publishing cannot be located, but it was included in *Song Companion to the Scriptures* (1911) compiled and published by G. Campbell Morgan, and in *Alexander's Hymns* (1913).   H

EBENEZER (also **TON-Y-BOTEL**). Written in 1896 as part of the extended anthem "Golau yn y glyn" (light and life in the valley), Thomas J. Williams's tune gained popularity during the Welsh revival of 1904-5. From there it became known in England, and the story was repeated that it had washed ashore in a bottle (hence, TON-Y-BOTEL). EBENEZER is a chapel in Rhos, Pontardawe, Wales, where the composer was a member at the time the tune was created.

O, When Shall I See Jesus? 278
John Leland may have written the text, known as "Faithful Soldier." It is not found in his collected writings, but some of his memorial poems are in this style, including a repeated expression. More likely, it was a call-and-answer folk song, sung by heart at camp meetings. The text first appeared in Eleazer Clay's *Hymns and Spiritual Songs* (Richmond, 1793), where it is credited to John Leland. *The Dictionary of American Hymnology* indicates that various versions of the hymn have appeared in almost 400 collections since 1793.

THE MORNING TRUMPET. The tune is credited to B. F. White both in Walker's *Southern Harmony* (1835), which White helped compile, and in White's *Sacred Harp* (1844).

O Word of God Incarnate 310
This text by William Walsham How, based on Psalm 119:105, first appeared in the 1867 supplement to *Psalms and Hymns*, compiled by How and Thomas Baker Morrell. H

MUNICH (also **MEININGEN**). The original chorale melody was found in *Neu-vermehrtes und zu Übung Christl. Gottseligkeit eingerichtetes Meiningisches Gesangbuch* (Meiningen, 1693), compiled by Niclaus Hassert and is one of several tunes sung to the text "O Gott, du frommer Gott." Felix Mendelssohn adapted it for the aria "Cast thy burden upon the Lord" (hymn 815) in his oratorio *Elijah* (1847); this hymn tune is based on Mendelssohn's version. H

O Worship the King, All Glorious Above 29
This hymn version of Psalm 104 is Sir Robert Grant's adaptation of an earlier setting by William Kethe which appeared in *Fourscore and seven Psalmes*, 1561. It was first printed in *Christian Psalmody*, 1833, edited by Edward Bickersteth. H

LYONS. The tune was introduced to English congregations through volume two of William Gardiner's *Sacred Melodies* (London, 1815), and in America through Oliver Shaw's *Sacred Melodies* (Providence, 1818). It has been credited to Johann Michael Haydn (or possibly Franz Joseph Haydn), though its exact source cannot be identified. H

O Zion, Haste; see O Christians, Haste 731.

Of All the Spirit's Gifts to Me   587

Fred Pratt Green wrote this hymn for a United Women's rally, Croydon, London, 1979; it was first sung at a session on the fruits of the Spirit to the tune for which it was written, RIPPONDEN by Norman Crocker; first printing was that same year in *Broadcast Praise*.

Of the Father's Love Begotten   145

Most of Aurelius Clemens Prudentius's 4th-century poems were written for personal devotional use. However, they have been freely drawn upon to provide the Western Church with some of its finest hymns. One of his major works *Cathemerinon*, in a section called *Hymnus omnis horae*, contains this hymn, "Corde natus ex Parentis." Parts of the hymn were sung at the service of Compline in the Christmas season in certain English churches. The translation by John Mason Neale appeared in *The Hymnal Noted* (1854) and was altered by Henry W. Baker in a trial edition of *Hymns Ancient and Modern* (1859). It resembles the Nicene Creed in content.   H

DIVINUM MYSTERIUM. The tune is a plainsong melody found in many European manuscripts from the 12th to 15th centuries, set to the text "Divinum Mysterium." It was a Sanctus "trope"—a musical interpolation in the medieval liturgy. This melody was associated with Neale's text in *The Hymnal Noted* (1854), and C. Winfred Douglas arranged the version which first appeared in *The Hymnal 1940*.   H

On a hill far away; see **The Old Rugged Cross** 484.

On Christmas Night All Christians Sing   168

According to the preface to *Oxford Book of Carols* (1928), this carol was published at Birmingham by J. Guest in *A New Carol Book*, undated, but "not much later than 1830."

SUSSEX CAROL. Ralph Vaughan Williams learned the tune from Harriet Verrall, of Monk's Gate, near Horsham, Sussex, England, and used it in his *Fantasia on Christmas Carols* (1912), then, in four-part harmony, in the *Oxford Book of Carols* (1928).

On Jordan's Bank the Baptist's Cry   136

Written in Latin by Charles Coffin, the hymn first appeared in his *Hymni Sacri* (1736) and *Paris Breviary* (1736). It was translated by John Chandler for *Hymns of the Primitive Church* (1837); Chandler's version is revised for *The Worshiping Church*.

PUER NOBIS; see **O Splendor of God's Glory Bright** 27.

On Jordan's Stormy Banks I Stand   674
Samuel Stennett, an English Baptist preacher, wrote this hymn which first appeared in John Rippon's *Selection of Hymns* (London, 1787) under the title "Heaven Anticipated."   H

PROMISED LAND. This is one of many traditional melodies used in America in the early part of the 19th century. Researchers have pointed out its resemblance to "I'll go and enlist for a sailor" in Sharp's *Morris Dances.* Its first appearance as a hymn dates back to William Walker's *Southern Harmony* (1835) where it is attributed to "Miss M. Durham." Rigdon M. McIntosh altered it (partly by changing the tonality from minor to major) and published it in *The Gospel Light* (1895), edited by H. R. Christie.   H

On This Day Earth Shall Ring   175
The text and tune came from the Swedish book *Piae Cantiones* (1582), brought to England by the British Minister to Stockholm, who gave it to John Mason Neale (about 1852). It appeared in the first section of the book, *[Cantiones] de Nativitate Domini* [Songs of the Nativity of the Lord]. This translation is by Jane M. Joseph, a student of Gustav Holst (early 20th century).

PERSONENT HODIE (also **THEODORIC**). The tune (melody only) is from the Swedish book, *Piae Cantiones* (1582), a collection of pre-Reformation melodies which came to England about 1852. It was printed with the Latin text translated here, so the association is a long one. The arrangement by Gustav Holst was first used in *Songs of Praise* (1925), then in the *Oxford Book of Carols* (1928).

Once in Royal David's City   161
Cecil Frances Alexander wrote these words to illustrate and interpret the phrase of the Apostles' Creed, "Who was conceived by the Holy Ghost, born of the Virgin Mary." It first appeared in her *Hymns for Little Children* (1848).   H

IRBY. Henry J. Gauntlett composed the tune for the text and it first appeared in his *Christmas Carols* (1849). He also prepared this four-part setting for *Hymns Ancient and Modern* (1861). "Irby" is the name of a village in Lincolnshire, England.   H

One Day   196
There is no information available concerning the writing of this hymn by J. Wilbur Chapman. The evangelist handed two poems (including this one) to Charles H. Marsh to be set to music. At the time (*c.* 1908)

they were working together in a Bible conference in Stony Brook, Long Island, NY.   H

CHAPMAN. Charles H. Marsh wrote the music for this text at the request of J. Wilbur Chapman, the author. In *Hymns of Our Faith*, William J. Reynolds quotes a letter from the composer in which he tells of a conflict regarding the ownership of the copyright. When the issue was settled, the copyright was controlled by The Rodeheaver Company, but Hope Publishing Company had special privileges pertaining to its use. The complete song was first published by Praise Publishing Company in *The Message in Song* (1911).   H

One is the race of mankind; see **One Race, One Gospel, One Task** 735 (below).

One Race, One Gospel, One Task   735
Margaret Clarkson wrote the hymn for the World Congress of Missions in Berlin, basing it on the theme of that Congress. The hymn was submitted as part of a contest which it did not win (1966)—Anne Ortlund's "Macedonia" (see 737) was chosen. The first and last stanza of this text became a secondary theme song for the occasion. Those original two stanzas were printed in *Christianity Today* (July 1966) and the complete hymn is in Clarkson's collection, *A Singing Heart* (Hope Publishing Company, 1987).

LOBE DEN HERREN; this is the author's suggested tune; see **Praise to the Lord, the Almighty** 77.

Only Trust Him   443
The original gospel song by John H. Stockton had five stanzas and first appeared in his *Salvation Melodies No. 1*, 1874. In its early printings, the refrain repeated the phrase "come to Jesus" three times. On board ship en route to Britain with D. L. Moody, Ira Sankey altered the hymn to tell "how" to come to Jesus—"only trust him." It was published in this form in 1875 in *Sacred Songs and Solos* (London) and in *Gospel Hymns and Sacred Songs* (New York).   H

MINERVA. Since John H. Stockton wrote both words and music, the tune is sometimes called STOCKTON. The name MINERVA has appeared occasionally, but its significance is unknown.   H

Onward, Christian Soldiers   748
This text was written by Sabine Baring-Gould in 1864 for a Children's Festival at Horbury Bridge, Yorkshire. The hymn was sung "in a procession with cross and banners" as the children marched from one village to

another, a traditional practice in 19th-century England. It was first published in *The Church Times*, October 15, 1864. The text should not be read as approval of human wars, but rather as a picture of God's struggle with, and final victory over, evil and death (Eph. 6). H

ST. GERTRUDE. Arthur S. Sullivan composed this tune for the text, and the full hymn appeared in the *Musical Times* (Dec. 1871) and in *The Hymnary* (1872). The tune name is said to be for Mrs. Gertrude Clay-Ker-Seymer, in whose home Sullivan was a visitor when he wrote the music. The composer frequently "canonized" his friends in this way. H

Open My Eyes, That I May See   557
   Both words and music were written by Clara H. Scott. The song first appeared in *Best Hymns No. 2* (1895), compiled by E. A. Hoffman and H. F. Sayles. H

SCOTT. The tune was named for the author-composer Clara H. Scott in *Baptist Hymnal* (1956). H

Open Our Eyes, Lord   536
   Robert Cull wrote text and tune in Hawaii (summer of 1975) in response to his need for a prayer song to "reach closed-hearted people" in a "religious school," which was a place where he sensed no fellowship. By his own account, he wanted to counter the desire for "entertainment" with a "cry of honest hearts." He had spent 30 minutes in prayer, when, he writes, "The song, like an answer to my prayer, 'fell into my head.'" It was first recorded on the Maranatha! Music *Praise II* album (1974) and has been translated and recorded in dozens of languages and settings.

OPEN OUR EYES. The tune was composed with the text; Cull says, "an answer to prayer."

Our Father   626
   The text is taken nearly verbatim from Matthew 6:9-13 with the repeated phrase "hallowed be thy name." It is a West Indian spiritual found in Edric Connor's *Collection* (1945).

CONNER. The tune is named for the one who discovered it. It appears to be thoroughly connected to this text in this particular folk setting.

Our Father, by Whose Name   393
   F. Bland Tucker first wrote this hymn (1939) for the Episcopal *The Hymnal 1940*, then revised it, changing its meter to fit the tune RHOSYMEDRE for the 1943 edition, a version which has been used in

several hymnals since. This was sung at Tucker's funeral, evidently at his request.

RHOSYMEDRE. The tune is named for RHOSYMEDRE, a parish near Ruabon, Clywd, where John David Edwards was vicar. It was probably composed by the compiler who included it in *Original Sacred Music, Composed and Arranged by the Rev. John Edwards, B.A., Jesus College, Oxford* (*c.* 1838); in that collection, it is named LOVELY and ends with an Alleluia. Ralph Vaughan Williams used it for one of his "Three Preludes on Welsh Hymn Tunes."

Our Father, which art in heaven; see **The Lord's Prayer** 632.

Our Great Savior 89
This interesting hymn by the Presbyterian evangelist J. Wilbur Chapman quotes many phrases from Charles Wesley's "Jesus, Lover of my soul." It might also be called a sequel to Isaac Watts's "Join all the glorious names," with its large number of names for Christ. It was written for and published with this tune in 1910 in *Alexander's Gospel Songs, No. 2* (Revell). H

HYFRYDOL. The tune by the Welsh composer Rowland H. Prichard was harmonized for this text by Robert Harkness, pianist in Dr. Wilbur Chapman's evangelistic campaigns. Also see **Come, Thou Long-Expected Jesus** 135. H

Our Savior's Infant Cries Were Heard 438
With the tune (below), this unique text was commissioned by Barium Springs (NC) Home for Children on the occasion of its bicentennial, 1991. Both text and tune were written in 1986. The commission asked Hal Hopson for a hymn; he, in turn, asked Thomas Troeger for a text about the care of children that would "be useful as a gift to the church from our celebration."

BARIUM SPRINGS HOME. Hal Hopson composed this tune for the Troeger text; both were commissioned by the Barium Springs Home for Children. *The Worshiping Church* offers its first publication.

Out in the highways and byways of life; see **Make Me a Blessing** 656.

Out of my bondage, sorrow and night; see **Jesus, I Come** 448.

Out of need and out of custom; see **The Gathering** 800.

Out of the Depths 465
This versification of Psalm 130 is from the *Psalter* of 1912.

SANDON; see **God of Our Life** 370.

Pass It On 739
One of the most successful sacred youth "musicals" of the recent past was *Tell It Like It Is*, co-authored by Kurt Kaiser and Ralph Carmichael and published by Lexicon Music (1969). In this popular work Kurt Kaiser wrote the song beginning "It only takes a spark." He gives this report: "There was a need for an invitation type number, and in keeping with our set guideline that the idiom had to be fresh, the words restated in current terminology an important doctrine, namely 'Go ye into all the world and preach the gospel.'"
The song has appeared in many folk songbooks and it is widely known, even by unchurched youth; its first inclusion in a major hymnal was Hope Publishing Company's *Hymns for the Living Church* (1974).   H

PASS IT ON. In this hymnal, the song's title is the tune name. In other publications, it is sometimes called BROOKS DRIVE after the street on which Kaiser lives in Waco, TX. He says that the song was written by the fireplace in the den of his home—"a peaceful setting and an important retreat for me." He has also expressed surprise at the popularity of what he calls a "simple tune."   H

Peace, Perfect Peace 598
While spending a summer holiday at Harrogate, England, in 1875, Edward H. Bickersteth heard the Vicar of Harrogate preach on the text "Thou wilt keep him in perfect peace whose mind is stayed on thee" (Isa. 26:3). That afternoon, while visiting an aged and dying relative, Dr. Bickersteth wrote this hymn and read it to him. The question-answer words have remained substantially as he originally wrote them. The hymn was first released in Bickersteth's *Songs in the House of Pilgrimage* (1875).   H

PAX TECUM. The tune (whose name means "Peace be with you") was written for these words by George Thomas Caldbeck. Dr. Charles Vincent revised and harmonized it for its first appearance in *The Hymnal Companion to the Book of Common Prayer* (2nd ed., 1877).   H

People Need the Lord 730
Greg Nelson and Phill McHugh report that they were "having lunch and both observed that the waitress seemed to be sad and lonely. When they reached the car they said, 'You know, people need the Lord,' and wrote the song that afternoon" (Nashville, fall 1982). It was popularized

by Steve Green (1984) and has been nominated Song of the Year for a Dove award as well as being used in choral octavos, solo sheet music, and at least one other hymnal. Two stanzas (only the refrain is in *The Worshiping Church*) are available through River Oaks Music Publishers.

PEOPLE NEED THE LORD. The music was composed with the text.

Powerful in Making Us Wise   305
Idle's text is based on 2 Timothy 3:15-17. First written at Poplar in response to a request from Scripture Union for more hymns about the Bible, this current text is a revision, written at Limehouse, E. London (1977), for the London Islington Conference and first published in *Songs of Worship* (1980).

O QUANTA QUALIA; see **Here from All Nations** 680. Idle also suggests EPIPHANY HYMN, YVONNE, LIVING WORD, or LIEBSTER IMMANUEL as possible tunes. Donald Hustad has written GUDS ORD for Idle's words, and it appears with them in *100 Hymns of Hope* (Hope Publishing Company, 1992).

Praise Awaits You, O God, in Zion [Psalm 65]   334
See **Now Thank We All Our God** 374.

Praise be to you, O Christ   810
This short phrase is the traditional response to a Gospel reading, since those books are a record of Jesus's words and acts.   H

[Praise be to you]. The John Playford musical phrase is from *Rejoice in the Lord*.   H

Praise God for the Harvest   373
Written in April 1968, Brian Wren's original version of this hymn was published in the UK Baptist Supplement *Praise for Today*; the subtitle is "All good gifts . . ." By October 1978, the author revised the text "because of its sexist language, its overoptimism about the uses of atomic power, and the blandness of its final stanza." The current strong expression "accepts the possibility that the Spirit of God can work out God's loving purpose in the conflicts of history," according to Wren.

ST. DENIO; see **For Beauty of Meadows** 383.

Praise God from Whom All Blessings 808, 809
Thomas Ken's familiar doxology is the closing stanza of his "Morning and Evening Hymns" (see **A Morning Prayer** 360); psalm settings traditionally were followed by a trinitarian doxology. Ken revised the text hymn to its present form in 1709.

OLD HUNDREDTH; see **All People That on Earth** 317.

Praise Him! Praise Him! 96
Fanny Crosby's text was first published by Biglow and Main in *Bright Jewels*, 1869, edited by W. B. Bradbury, W. H. Doane, W. F. Sherwin, and Chester G. Allen. It was originally titled "Praise, Give Thanks." H

JOYFUL SONG. The tune was written by Chester G. Allen for the first publication of these words and was first called ALLEN. H

Praise, My Soul, the King of Heaven 25, 26
This hymn of praise was published first in author Henry Francis Lyte's *Spirit of the Psalms* (1834), a collection of over 280 paraphrases of individual Psalms. Lyte wrote the hymns for his congregation in the small fishing village of Lower Brixham, Devonshire, where he was curate from 1823 until his death. Through the years, slight changes have been made in the text (a setting of Psalm 103). H

ANDREWS 25. This setting was first an SATB anthem (and is still available from G. Schirmer), strophic like the hymn, but with a rousing ending and interesting keyboard accompaniments and interludes; composer Mark Andrews called it LAUDA ANIMA and dedicated it to "Channing Lefebvre and the Trinity Alumni Association."

LAUDA ANIMA 26. The tune (whose name is Latin for "Praise, my soul") was composed for this text by John Goss. It was first published in Robert Brown-Borthwick's *Supplemental Hymn and Tune Book*, third edition with new Appendix (1869), with a set of varied organ accompaniments. H

Praise the Lord! 38
The first stanza is a traditional text from Psalm 113 (RSV), with the other three stanzas paraphrased from Psalm 113 by Marjorie Jillson (1971) to the music of Zimmermann.

LAUDATE PUERI. Heinz Werner Zimmermann, known for his sacred jazz compositions, composed this tune (one of a set, *Five Hymns*, Concordia, 1973) for choir or congregation. He "encourages talented pastors, music ministers, and congregation members to contribute their own prose stanzas."

Praise the Lord [Psalm 147]   338
See **Hail the Day That Sees Him Rise** 258.

Praise the Lord! O Heavens, Adore Him   17
The text is anonymous, first published in a four-page leaflet pasted
into the back of some 1796 or 1797 editions of *Psalms, Hymns, and
Anthems of the Foundling Hospital*, London.   Later editions carry the notation, "Music by Haydn," a reference to the AUSTRIAN HYMN. The hymn
is a paraphrase of Psalm 148, with "O" substituted here for the earlier
"ye."

AUSTRIAN HYMN; see **Glorious Things of Thee Are Spoken** 694.

Praise the Lord Who Reigns Above   49
Based on Psalm 150, the text first appeared in *A Collection of Psalms
and Hymns*, 1743 edition, published by John and Charles Wesley. It was
frequently credited to Augustus Toplady during the 19th century, and has
not appeared in standard hymnals as often as it deserves.   H

AMSTERDAM. The source of the tune is J. A. Freylinghausen's
Geistreiches Gesangbuch (Halle, 1704, 1714, and 1741) from which John
Wesley adapted six tunes. This one appeared in Wesley's *Foundery
Collection* (1742), the first Methodist hymnal, where it is erroneously
attributed to James Nares.   H

Praise the Name of Jesus   128
Roy Hicks, author-composer of this chorus, writes: "As pastor of a
small, struggling congregation in Eugene, OR, I was meditating on Psalm
18. The tune and the words 'came' to me during that prayer time. We
sang it the next Sunday" (1970). First publication was in the *Psalter*
(1972).

Praise the Savior, Ye Who Know Him   125
Typical of Thomas Kelly's hymns in its use of an unusual meter, this
text appeared in his *Psalms and Hymns extracted from Various Authors* (2nd
ed., 1806), entitled "Praise of Jesus." It was significant in the Moody-
Sankey campaigns of 1873-75 in Great Britain, and is still a favorite of
evangelicals in the United States and around the world.   H
A stanza omitted in *The Worshiping Church* is a delightful tongue-
twister:
> Then we shall be where we would be,
> Then we shall be what we should be;
> Things that are not now, nor could be,
> Soon shall be our own.

ACCLAIM. In Sankey's *Gospel Hymns No. 5* (New York, 1887) and *Sacred Songs and Solos* (London, 1873) this text is printed with another tune called a "German melody." However, in the enlarged edition (1903) of the London book, this melody appears with no identification. Through the years it, too, has become known as a "traditional German melody" and is named for the character of the text.   H

Praise to the Lord, the Almighty   77
This text, based on Psalms 103 and 150, is one of about 60 hymns written by Joachim Neander during his short life. Neander is widely regarded as the best poet of the Reformed Church in Germany and this is his best known hymn, published in his *Glaubund Liebesübung* (1680). The present translation by Catherine Winkworth appeared in her *Choral Book for England* (1863).   H

LOBE DEN HERREN. The tune ("Praise the Lord") is an adaptation of a melody which appeared in *Erneuerton Gesangbuch* (Stralsund, 1665) with the text, "Hast du den, Leibster"; it may be an earlier secular air, "Seh ich nicht blinkende." Neander chose it for his words in their first printing. The present version appeared with Catherine Winkworth's translation and was harmonized by Sterndale Bennett and Otto Goldschmidt. Bach used the tune as material for Cantatas 57 and 137.   H

Prayer for Trinity Sunday   7
This prayer (with more extended language) appears in the earliest editions of the *Book of Common Prayer*, including the authoritative 1559 Elizabethan version. It is designated The Collect for Trinity Sunday.

Prayer Is the Soul's Supreme Desire   620
At the request of Edward Bickersteth, James Montgomery wrote the text, "Prayer is the soul's sincere desire" (1818), for Bickersmith's *Treatise on Prayer* (1819). The poem originally had eight stanzas; two have been omitted in this hymnal with the current stanzas somewhat revised.   H

BEATITUDO; see **O for a Closer Walk with God** 547.

Precious Lord, Take My Hand   638
Thomas A. Dorsey, "the father of black gospel music," wrote words and music in response to the death of his first wife, Nettie (1932). Dorsey was in St. Louis, on the platform providing music for revival services, when he received a telegram with the news that his wife had died. He returned to Chicago immediately; his newborn son seemed to be healthy, but he also died that same night. Just days later, with a friend (Professor Frye at Madame Malone's College) he improvised the tune at the piano,

first using the expression "Blessed Lord" and then changing it to "Precious Lord."

Dorsey had successfully composed, recorded, and published many earlier gospel songs (for voice and piano), but this one achieved the widest acceptance.

PRECIOUS LORD, TAKE MY HAND. The tune, based on George N. Allen's MAITLAND ("Must Jesus Bear the Cross Alone" 1844), was written with the text (improvised before the words, no doubt) in a spiritual style. It was first published by Hill and Range (1938) after Dorsey had already sung it in ministry settings.

Redeemed, How I Love to Proclaim It!   505
Fanny J. Crosby's popular gospel song first appeared with William J. Kirkpatrick's tune in *Songs of Redeeming Love* (1882) edited by John R. Sweney, C. C. McCabe, T. C. O'Kane, and Kirkpatrick.   H

ADA. Shortly before *Hymns for the Living Church* (1974) went to press, this new tune was substituted for the traditional one composed by Kirkpatrick. It was written by A. L. Butler for the Singing Churchmen of Oklahoma, who presented it at the 1966 Southern Baptist Convention in Detroit. It was first published in *The Church Musician* (July 1967). The tune is named for Ada, OK, where Mr. Butler served as minister of music at First Baptist Church.   H

Rejoice in God's Saints   749
Fred Pratt Green's unique text "In Celebration of Saints" was written in response to a commission from the Dean of Norwich to celebrate the 600th anniversary of Mother Julian's cloistered life (1973). Green then revised the text (Oct. 1977) to express a broader view of the example of believers; it was sung on BBC Radio 4 in *The Daily Service* of Monday, September 21, 1981, to the tune OLD 104TH.

HANOVER; see **Ye Servants of God** 103.

Rejoice in the Lord Always   606
The text is Philippians 4:4 from the King James Version.

REJOICE. The anonymous tune is associated with this text and may go back to 1940-50 Youth for Christ rote-learning usage.   H

Rejoice, the Lord is King   262
This text first appeared in Charles Wesley's *Hymns for Our Lord's Resurrection* (1746). The refrain is based on Philippians 4:4, "Rejoice in

the Lord always: and again I say, Rejoice." The hymn has been recommended for processionals on Easter Day.   H

DARWALL. Sometimes called "Darwall's 148th," the tune was originally written by John Darwall for Psalm 148 in Aaron Williams's *New Universal Psalmist* (1770). It is the lone survivor of the 150 tunes written for that complete psalter.   H

Rejoice, Ye Pure in Heart   34
      This processional hymn by Edward H. Plumptre, written for a choir festival in May 1865 at Peterborough Cathedral, first appeared in 11 stanzas. The same year, Novello published it as a choral piece and it also appeared in the second edition of Plumptre's *Lazarus, and Other Poems.* It also was included in the Appendix to *Hymns Ancient and Modern,* 1868.
                                                                                 H

MARION. Named for the composer's mother, this tune was written by Arthur H. Messiter in 1883. It was first printed in the *Hymnal with Music as Used in Trinity Church* (New York, 1889), a collection edited by Messiter.
                                                                                 H

Renew Your Church, Her Ministries Restore   725
This hymn appeared as part of the Baptist Jubilee Advance, a five-year denominational program. It was written specifically for the second year's emphasis on "The Renewal of the Church: Imperative to Evangelism." It was composed while author Kenneth Cober was traveling across the country on trains and planes in denominational work, and was sung for the first time at the American Baptist Convention in May 1960.   H

ALL IS WELL; see **Come, Come, Ye Saints** 595.

Rescue the Perishing   736
      In 1869 Fanny Crosby visited a rescue mission in the slums of New York City and was greatly moved by the sad, desperate men around her. The song title, "Rescue the Perishing," had been suggested by William H. Doane a few days earlier, and while she sat in the mission the words began to form. Before she retired that night, the hymn was completed. H

RESCUE. Fanny Crosby sent these words to William H. Doane, who composed the music. The complete hymn first appeared in Doane's *Songs of Devotion* (New York: Biglow and Main, 1870).   H

Revive Us Again   723
      This hymn by William Paton Mackay, based on Habakkuk 3:2 and

144

Psalm 85:6, was written in 1863 and revised in 1867. The original text had five stanzas and refrain, and was included in *Gospel Hymns and Sacred Songs* (1875) compiled by P. P. Bliss and Ira Sankey, under the title "O Lord, revive thy work." H

REVIVE US AGAIN. This tune was composed by John J. Husband sometime around 1815 and was first used with another text, possibly secular. In *Gospel Hymns and Sacred Songs* (1875) it is set to Horatius Bonar's "Rejoice and be Glad!"; Mackay's text was listed as an alternate. Through the years Bonar's words have dropped out of common use and Mackay's hymn has been wedded to this tune. H

Ride On, Ride On in Majesty 205
This Palm Sunday hymn was written by Henry Milman, an Anglican clergyman and professor of poetry at Oxford. It was first published in Reginald Heber's posthumous volume *Hymns Written and Adapted to the Weekly Service of the Church Year* (1827) and designated for "The Sixth Sunday in Lent." H

TRURO. Appearing anonymously, the tune was included in *Psalmodia Evangelica: A Collection of Psalms and Hymns in Three Parts for Public Worship* (1789) published by Thomas Williams. "Truro" is the name of an ancient town and river in the southwestern part of Cornwall, England. H

Rise Up, O Men of God! 671
William Pierson Merrill wrote these words in 1911 after the editor of *The Continent* requested a hymn appropriate for the "brotherhood movement" of the Presbyterian Church. The author said he "got a start" from an article by Gerald Stanley Lee entitled "The Church of the Strong Men," and that the text was completed on a steamer on Lake Michigan. The hymn first appeared in the February 16, 1911, edition of *The Continent*. H

FESTAL SONG; see **Rise Up, O Saints of God!** 670 (below).

Rise Up, O Saints of God! 670
Norman O. Forness knew that the text committee preparing the *Lutheran Book of Worship* (1978) did not plan to include "Rise Up, O Men of God!"; he wrote a new text to the Walter tune and submitted it. As a next step, with that committee, he then revised and merged his and Merrill's text; but the editors were unable to gain permission for the revision from the copyright owners of the "men" hymn. The committee returned to the more complete new hymn which Forness had written in the mid 1970s—the version used here (with an additional second stanza on baptism which is not included in *The Worshiping Church*).

FESTAL SONG. The tune's name is related to its first association with the text "Awake and sing the song" in John Ireland Tucker's *The Hymnal with Tunes Old and New* (1872). William Walter's music was first used with "Rise up, O men of God" in *Pilgrim Hymnal* (1912); it is here coupled with Furness's new inclusive language text.

Rock of Ages, Cleft for Me 227

A single four-line stanza of this text (containing parts of the present first and third stanzas) first appeared in the *Gospel Magazine* published by Augustus Toplady in 1775. It came at the end of an article titled "Life—a Journey," a message of hope for all who had fallen into sin. The complete poem appeared in the same magazine in March 1776, with the heading "A living and dying Prayer for the Holiest Believer in the World." The same year it was No. 337 in Toplady's *Psalms and Hymns.* H

TOPLADY. The tune was composed for these words in 1830 by Thomas Hastings, and appeared with the title "Rock of Ages" in *Spiritual Songs for Social Worship*, 1831, edited by Hastings and Lowell Mason. The name was changed (to memorialize the text's author) and the rhythm was altered in Mason's *Sabbath Hymn and Tune Book* (1859). The editors of *The Worshiping Church* recommend REDHEAD 225 as an alternate tune for these words. H

Safe in the Shadow of the Lord 513

This metrical paraphrase of Psalm 91 forms a pair with "I Lift My Eyes to the Quiet Hills" 81. It was written at Sevenoaks for *Psalms Praise* (1970) and appeared there with another tune. Author Timothy Dudley-Smith indicates that the repeated "I trust in him," "is intended as an affirmation of confidence, the keynote of the text as it is of the psalm."

CREATOR GOD. Norman Warren had composed this tune for another earlier text (1964, first published in *Youth Praise*, 1966), but chose it for these Dudley-Smith words (1973), feeling that "it fitted perfectly—catching the mood of this metrical psalm." It is available on a 1978 Word recording, *Psalm Praise* (WST 9586).

Sanctus; see these settings in English: **Holy Lord** 827; **O Lord Most High** 828; **Holy Is the Lord** 831; **Holy, Lord God of Hosts** 829.

Satisfied 511

Keith Clark, founder of the Clark Hymnological Library at Houghton, NY, provides the information on this hymn and author. George Beverly Shea tells a story of his personal knowledge of the author in *Crusade Hymn Stories* (1967).

In the manuscript autobiography of Clara Tear Williams in the

Houghton College Library, she records: "About 1875 I was helping in meetings in Troy, Ohio where Prof. R. E. Hudson conducted the singing, when just before retiring one night he asked me to write a song for a book he was preparing to publish. Before sleeping I wrote 'Satisfied.' In the morning he composed the music."

In the original printing the refrain was "Hallelujah! I have found it— What my soul so long has craved!" The present version was found in the *Wesleyan Methodist Hymnal* (1910). The second line was originally "for a draught," and was changed to "for a drink" by Hope Publishing Company editors in *Crusader Hymns* (1966). H

SATISFIED. "Satisfied" was the original song title in the first printing in *Gems of Gospel Song* (1881) compiled by E. A. Hoffman, J. H. Tenney, and (composer) Ralph E. Hudson. H

Savior, Again to Your Dear Name 835

Author John Ellerton labeled his six-stanza hymn, "Evening (After Service, Sundays or Festivals)." It was written for the Festival of the Malpas, Middlewich, and Nantwich Choral Association (1866), then shortened for *Hymns Ancient and Modern* (1893); it is further updated for *The Worshiping Church*. The last stanza was sung at Ellerton's funeral.

ELLERS. Edward Hopkins composed this tune, designed for unison singing with organ accompaniment, for Ellerton's text in *The Supplemental Hymn and Tune Book* (3rd ed., 1869), then added hymn-style harmonization in the *Bradford Tune Book* (1872). It is somewhat unusual in its mixolydian beginning and cadence.

Savior, Like a Shepherd Lead Us 522

The authorship of this text is usually attributed to Dorothy A. Thrupp, although there is no positive proof that she wrote it. As the compiler of *Hymns for the Young* (London: Religious Tract Society, 4th ed., 1836) and author of many of its verses, she included this unsigned poem. It has sometimes been credited to Henry Francis Lyte. H

BRADBURY. The tune was composed by William B. Bradbury for these words. The full hymn first appeared in his Sunday School collection, *Oriola* (1859). H

Savior of the Nations, Come 138

This Latin advent hymn is attributed to Ambrose of Milan and is probably his, according to Augustine and other early scholars. It was translated into very literal German by Martin Luther (1523) and newly translated into English by Calvin Seerveld (1984).

NUN KOMM, DER HEIDEN HEILAND. The tune is named for its German opening line. Widely known, it is found with the Ambrose Latin text in the Einsiedeln *Hymnal* (12th or 13th century) and, with Luther's German text, in the *Enchiridia* (1524), a manuscript of music theory and musical examples, held in Erfurt, a Thüringian monastery and university in what was East Germany; Seth Calvisius prepared the harmonization in 1594, after the tune had already been published in several collections. Bach used it in two cantatas (36 and 62) and in organ settings.

Search Me, O God 458, 460
  J. Edwin Orr was known around the world as an evangelist and a student of "revival movements." He reports that he wrote this hymn in 1936 at a time of "inspiration during an intense movement of the Spirit" in Ngaruawahia, New Zealand. It first appeared in *All Your Need* (London: Marshall, Morgan and Scott, 1936). H

ELLERS 458; see **Savior, Again to Your Dear Name** 835.

MAORI 460. J. Edwin Orr says he first heard this melody and used it with these words in Ngaruawahia, New Zealand. He identifies it as a folk song of the Maori aborigines. It does resemble the songs of other Polynesian peoples, such as the Hawaiians. In the United States it has also appeared with the 1940s popular ballad "Now Is the Hour." H

Seek Ye First the Kingdom of God 447
  Karen Lafferty wrote this setting after attending a Bible study on the Matthew 6:33 text (1972). The second stanza, from the same section of scripture, was added anonymously—in the oral tradition by the "folk" singing it.

LAFFERTY. Karen Lafferty designed the simple melody for singing with guitar. She describes it as "as song in which people can put God's desire for their lives above their own."

Send Out Your Light and Your Truth 811
  The text is Psalm 43:3 from the King James Version.

LUX FIAT. The name means "instant light"; it is an excerpt from a choral composition by Charles Gounod or an adaptation from his works which found its way into the choral repertoire.

Shall We Gather at the River? 687
  Robert Lowry wrote text and music at his organ, at home in Brooklyn, NY (summer 1864), in response to many deaths in his congregation

because of an epidemic of illness. Seeing mourners, he meditated in this way: "At the parting of the river of death, shall we meet again at the river of life?"

HANSON PLACE. Lowry composed the setting with the text. The tune was named in *Baptist Hymnal* (1956) for the Hanson Place Baptist Church, Brooklyn, where Lowry was pastor when he wrote this hymn. Aaron Copland used text and tune as one of his "Early American Songs" for solo and orchestra, which he composed for William Warfield.

Shalom, My Friends, Shalom — 599
The Hebrew text (stanza 2) and melody come from anonymous sources. Donald Hustad's English words capture the spirit of the folk song.

SHALOM CHAVERIM. The tune is connected with the words in the oral tradition.

Shine, Jesus, Shine — 721
Graham Kendrick's words and music were written (1988) for the outdoor demonstrations which have characterized the Charismatic Renewal Movement of the United Kingdom. The song achieved wide popularity during the Billy Graham crusades of 1989.

SHINE, JESUS, SHINE. The tune was composed with the text.

Silent Night! Holy Night! — 164
The original text "Stille nacht, heilige nacht" was written by Joseph Mohr, assistant priest in St. Nicholas Church in Oberndorf, Upper Austria. It was first sung on Christmas Eve, 1818. Because of an organ breakdown, previous plans for the Christmas Eve service had to be abandoned. Mohr asked the organist Franz Gruber to set this text to music for choir, two voices, and guitar. This English translation by John Freeman Young, second bishop of the Episcopal Diocese of Florida, first appeared in Hollister's *The Sunday-School Service and Tune Book* (1863). H

STILLE NACHT. The tune is believed to have been written by Franz Gruber just a few hours before the Christmas Eve service of 1818. The organ repair man, Karl Mauracher of Zillerthal, heard it and passed it on to others; otherwise it might well have been forgotten. The earliest manuscript, dated 1833, is the composer's arrangement for chorus, orchestra, and organ. The descant was written by Donald Hustad years ago for a choral recording, and included in *The Worshiping Church*. H

Simply trusting every day; see **Trusting Jesus** 526.

Sing a New Song to the Lord   18

Timothy Dudley-Smith's paraphrase of Psalm 98 and its lively setting were written for *Psalm Praise* (London: Falcon Books, 1973). It is loosely based on an alternative Evening Prayer canticle in the *Book of Common Prayer*.

ONSLOW SQUARE. David G. Wilson composed this tune for this text at the organ of St. Paul's, Onslow Square in London, with its massive solo tuba pipes (fitting the trumpets mentioned in the third stanza); the name was added in 1979 for *Partners in Praise* (Stainer and Bell).

Sing Alleluia to the Lord   771

The title and last stanza were written by the composer of the tune, Linda Stassen (1974); first publication was in Maranatha! Music's *Praise* songbook (1978). Stassen wrote the song as an assignment for a music class at Calvary Chapel, Costa Mesa, CA. The first four stanzas of text may date as early as the 1st century (parts of the Lord's Supper congregational responses). The simple directness and historic connection have given it popularity in Chinese, Persian, Eskimo, and European language translations as well as in its original setting.

SING ALLELUIA. Linda Stassen composed this melody for her text and designed the male-female call and answer counterpoint (1974). Dale Grotenhuis arranged the setting and harmonized it for the *Psalter Hymnal* (Christian Reformed Publications, 1989); as a member of the revision committee for that hymnal, he is responsible for many of its harmonizations.

Sing, My Tongue, the Glorious Battle   228

The original Latin hymn by Fortunatus, *Pange lingua, gloriosi praelium* (*c.* 569), had 10 stanzas and would have been used in two groups of five stanzas each just after midnight and at dawn, Sunday through Thursday of Holy Week in Office worship. John Neale's translation in *Medieval Hymns* (1851) has been altered in its recent versions.

FORTUNATUS NEW. Written for this text, Carl Schalk's tune appeared first in *Spirit* (Mar. 1967).

Sing Praise to God Who Reigns Above   50

Johann Jakob Schütz's hymn "Sei Lob und Ehr dem Höchsten Gut" was first published in his *Christliches Gedenckbüchlein* (1675), a hymnal of encouragement to the Bohemian Brethren, the persecuted followers of John Huss. Frances E. Cox's translation was printed in *Lyra Eucharistica* (1864) and in her own *Hymns from the German* the same year.   H

MIT FREUDEN ZART; see **All Glory Be to God on High** 8.

Sing Praise to the Father 9
Margaret Clarkson's text, written in Toronto, was first published in *Chancel Choir, No. 3* (Hope Publishing Company, 1963) intended to be sung to another tune of her own composition, WILLOWDALE (in *Hymns for Praise and Worship*, 1984).

TO GOD BE THE GLORY; see **To God Be the Glory** 72.

Sing Praise to the Lord 346
This version of Psalm 149 from *Psalter* (1912) was altered for its inclusion in *Psalter Hymnal* (1989).

HANOVER; see **Ye Servants of God, Your Master** 103. The descant is from Alan Gray's *A Book of Descants* (1923).

Sing them over again to me; see **Wonderful Words of Life** 309.

Sing to the Lord a New Song 324
The text is directly from Psalm 98 (NIV); Hal Hopson adapted phrases to create the refrain.

[REFRAIN]. Hal Hopson prepared this refrain setting in 1984 together with music for stanzas; it was first published in *10 Psalms* (Hope Publishing Company, 1986).

Sing to the Lord of Harvest 375
The text was published in John S. B. Monsell's *Hymns of Love and Praise* (1866). Apparently Edward Klammer of Concordia Publishing House first combined this text with the Steurlein tune.

WIE LIEBLICH IST DER MAIEN. The tune, by Johann Steurlein, was first sung to a secular text of the good life, "Mit Leib bin ich umfangen"; it was published in Gregor Gunderreitter's *Davids Himlische Harpffen* (Nürnberg, 1581) using a hymn text. It is named for a spring song [Maien is the month of May] in a 17th-century source, *Handbuch der deutchen evangelischen Kirchenmusik*.

Sing the wondrous love of Jesus; see **When We All Get to Heaven** 697.

Sing We Now of Christmas   159
"Noël Nouvelet" is a traditional French carol from the 19th century or earlier.

NOËL NOUVELET. Martin Shaw harmonized this French folk carol tune for *The Oxford Book of Carols* (1928). Named for its initial French words, it is in the dorian church mode (the C# is really part of the key). Organ composer Marcel Dupré used the tune in his "Variations on a Nöel".

Sleepers, Wake; see **Wake, Awake, for Night Is Flying** 131.

Softly and Tenderly Jesus Is Calling   441
Will L. Thompson, "The Bard of Ohio," wrote this favorite invitation hymn. When Dwight L. Moody lay on his deathbed, Thompson paid him a visit. Moody feebly took his visitor's hand and said: "Will, I would rather have written 'Softly and tenderly Jesus is calling' than anything I have been able to do in my whole life." The hymn first appeared in J. Calvin Bushey's *Sparkling Gems Nos. 1 and 2 Combined* (Chicago, 1880). H

THOMPSON. To honor the author-composer of this gospel song, the editors of *Baptist Hymnal* (1956) named the tune THOMPSON.   H

So Send I You   732
Margaret Clarkson says that she wrote the original of this text when she was 22 years old. She had been teaching in northern Canada for three years, where she found almost no Christian fellowship. One night, reading the scriptures, she was reminded that this was her "missionary" obedience—to go where God sent her, regardless. She said that in later years she came to know that there is *joy* in obedience, and regretted the somber tone of the hymn which began "So send I You to labor unrewarded." She wrote another "optimistic" version and has stated her preference for this text, the one included in *The Worshiping Church.* The original text was written at Kirkland Lake, Ontario, in winter 1937-38 and first appeared in the Canadian magazine, *The Evangelical Monthly* (no longer in publication) in 1939. The new hymn was written while on vacation at the Severn River in 1962. Miss Clarkson says this of the current poem:

As I grew in knowledge of the Scriptures, I came to realize that this [original] text, written when I was only 22, was really very one-sided. . . . I used the same rhythm [for the new text] so that the stanzas could be used interchangeably. . . . I am happy to see that many of the newer hymnals are dropping that text in favor of the newer one, which undoubtedly is the more Biblical hymn.

TORONTO. John W. Peterson's share in this song is told in his own words.

A hand-copied version of the [1937] poem was handed me by a fellow

WMBI staff member with the suggestion that I read it on one of my radio programs. (I was responsible for twenty or so programs at the Moody Bible Institute station at the time.) I did use the poem and was so deeply moved by the power of the words that I took them with me on a Kansas vacation the following month. One day while improvising at the piano in my mother's home in Wichita, with the poem spread out before me, the melody came. Again I was deeply moved as I sang through the new song. I called in several members of my family and sang the number for them. Somehow I sensed that God would greatly use it. It was not till much later that I learned that the words had been written by Miss E. Margaret Clarkson.

The tune name is for Toronto, Canada, where Miss Clarkson has lived for many years. The completed song was first published in *Melody-Aire Low Voice Songs* (Moody Press, 1954). H

Soldiers of Christ, Arise 756
Based on Ephesians 6:10-20, these words of Charles Wesley appeared in *Hymns and Sacred Poems* (1749) with the title "The Whole Armour of God." The hymn originally contained 16 stanzas of eight lines each. H

DIADEMATA; see **Crown Him with Many Crowns** 92.

Songs of Thankfulness and Praise 190
Author Christopher Wordsworth, described his own text (1862), evidently intended for the last Sunday in Epiphany, as a "recapitulation of the successive manifestations of Christ, which have already been presented . . . throughout the season of Epiphany; and anticipation of that future great and glorious epiphany, at which Christ will be manifest to all, when he will appear again to judge the world."

ST. GEORGE'S, WINDSOR; see **Come, Ye Thankful People, Come** 381.

Soon and Very Soon 677
Andraé Crouch wrote this black-gospel song in 1976 for his concert and recording group, "Andraé Crouch and the Disciples."

SOON AND VERY SOON. As with many popular songs, the tune was composed with the text.

Speak, Lord, in the Stillness 585
These words were written by May Grimes while she was living in Pondoland, South Africa, and first published in her *Unseen Realities* (1920) where they carried these references: 1 Samuel 3:9, Psalm 62:1, and Job

4:16. The hymn is a favorite at the Keswick Convention in northern England and appeared in *The Keswick Hymn Book* (1936) as well as the InterVarsity hymnals in England and America.　　　　　　　　　　　H

QUIETUDE. Obviously named after the text's emphasis, this melody was written by Harold Green for Mrs. Grimes's words, and has always appeared with them.　　　　　　　　　　　　　　　　　　　H

Spirit, Now Live in Me　　　　　　　　　　　　　　　　284
Author-composer Bryan Jeffery Leech recalls that the hymn was written for the hymnal, *Hymns for the Family of God* (1976), of which he was associate editor.

LOIS. The tune was written with the text and is named for Lois Bock, wife of Fred Bock, the editor of *Hymns for the Family of God.*

Spirit of God, Descend upon My Heart　　　　　　　　290
This text, written by a London clergyman, George Croly, was not included in his *Psalms and Hymns for Public Worship* (1854) as many handbooks claim. Its first publication seems to be in the work of a contemporary, Charles Rogers's *Lyra Britannica* (1867).　　　　　　　　H

MORECAMBE. The tune was written in 1870 by Frederick Atkinson as a setting for "Abide with Me," and was first published in leaflet form. G. S. Barrett and E. J. Hopkins included it in their *Congregational Church Hymnal* (London, 1887). Morecambe is a well known town on Morecambe Bay in west England.　　　　　　　　　　　　　　　H

Spirit of Holiness　　　　　　　　　　　　　　　　287
Christopher Idle wrote this text (1975, rev. 1980) with its accompanying folk tune in mind—it fits the spirit of the "wind" as well as the meter of the tune. It was written at Poplar, E. London, May 18, 1975. A third stanza was originally included: "You came to convict us of wrong and futility, / closing all byways, directing us home: / now with us and in us, we welcome your company, / worship and praise you, for now you have come."

BLOW THE WIND SOUTHERLY. The traditional Tyneside sea chanty is from the North of England and was gathered in the 19th century by Cecil Sharp (published in *The Bishoprick Garland*). It is evidently a fragment of an earlier ballad.

Spirit of the Living God　　　　　　　　　　　　297
Daniel Everson composed the text of the first stanza and its matched

music in Orlando, FL (1926), responding to a sermon by Dr. Barron, a physician from Columbia, SC, who preached at a city-wide evangelistic crusade conducted by George Stephans. According to William J. Reynolds, in *Companion to the Baptist Hymnal* (1976), the crusade pianist Birdie Loes wrote out the setting and E. Powell Lee, Stephans's song leader, taught it to those attending. Printed as a single sheet, it was widely circulated and published anonymously in *Revival Songs* (1929). Michael Baughen added the second stanza as a corporate prayer in 1978, an expansion of the original theme; this stanza was first published in *Hymns for Today's Church* (1982).

SPIRIT OF THE LIVING GOD. The tune was composed with the original text (1926) and has been altered in various publications.

Spirit, Working in Creation 293
John Richards wrote the text to meet a topical need (1978). It has previously appeared in *Cry Hosanna* (1980) and the *Psalter Hymnal* (1989).

STUTTGART. The tune is probably by C. F. Witt; it first appeared (with the text, "Sollt' es gleich bisweilen scheinen," "Should it soon shine for a while," a reference to God's light in our lives) in *Psalmodia Sacra, oder, Andächtige und schöne Gesänge* (Gotha, Germany, 1715), edited by Witt and A. C. Ludwig. Henry C. Gauntlett adapted it for *Hymns Ancient and Modern* (1861) and named it, connecting it with the text, "Earth has many a noble city." John Richards suggests singing his text to John Stainer's ALL FOR JESUS 570.

Stand Up and Bless the Lord 41
Based on Nehemiah 9:5, the hymn was written by James Montgomery for the Red Hill Wesleyan Sunday School Anniversary observed in Sheffield, England, on March 15, 1824. The second line originally was "ye children of his choice." Montgomery gave the hymn wider use by changing it to "ye people" when it appeared in his *Christian Psalmist* (1825). It was changed to "you people" in *The Worshiping Church*. H

ST. MICHAEL. The original melody is the tune for Psalm 101 in the French Genevan Psalter, 1551. First known in England as the "Old 134th," it had many variants in later English and Scottish psalters. Largely forgotten in the 17th and 18th centuries, William Crotch revived and adapted the melody for use in his *Psalm Tunes* (1836) and named it ST. MICHAEL. H

Stand Up, Stand Up for Jesus 663
These words by George Duffield were inspired by the dying message of Dudley A. Tyng, a heroic and faithful Episcopalian minister in

Philadelphia during the great revival of 1858, usually known as "The Work of God in Philadelphia." The story is told completely in *Crusade Hymn Stories*, pages 19-20.

Tyng died as the result of an accident on the family farm. In his last moments he said to his father, "Stand up for Jesus; father, stand up for Jesus; and tell my brethren of the ministry wherever you meet them, to stand up for Jesus!" The following Sunday, after Tyng's death, George Duffield preached on Ephesians 6:14 in Temple Presbyterian Church, and the verses of the hymn were used as a concluding exhortation. The hymn first appeared as a leaflet for Sunday School children, but was badly garbled in the *Church Psalmist* (1858). In its present form it first appeared in *Lyra Sacra Americana* (1868). H

WEBB. This tune was probably first associated with this text in William B. Bradbury's *Golden Chain of Sabbath School Melodies* (1861). The music was composed by George J. Webb during a voyage from England to America, and was set to the secular words "Tis Dawn, the Lark is Singing." The song appeared in *The Odeon: A Collection of Secular Melodies* (1837), compiled by Webb and Lowell Mason. H

Standing on the Promises 306

R. Kelso Carter wrote these words and published them in *Songs of Perfect Love* (1886), compiled by John R. Sweney and Carter. H

PROMISES. The tune was written by R. Kelso Carter for his own text, and was first named in *Baptist Hymnal* (1956). In *Music in Evangelism*, Phil Kerr suggests that the martial flavor of the song may be due to Carter's association with the Pennsylvania Military Academy. H

Stir Your Church, O God, Our Father 718

Milburn Price wrote the text (1970) for the Church Music Department of the Southern Baptist Sunday School Board; it was updated for *The Worshiping Church*. Text and tune were first published in a supplement, "New Hymns for This Day" (Nashville, 1971).

MADILL. Aubrey Butler's tune was one of several composed for this text at the request of the Sunday School Board (1971). MADILL is a town in Oklahoma where Butler had been minister of music at First Baptist Church.

Surely Goodness and Mercy 639

This gospel song refrain, a paraphrase of part of Psalm 23, was written by John W. Peterson and Alfred B. Smith in Montrose, PA, in 1958. Mr. Peterson tells the story:

One day while improvising at the piano in my Montrose,

Pennsylvania studio, Alfred B. Smith, with whom I was associated at the time, walked in. For no particular reason that I can remember, we started to develop a new song. I would come up with a thought— then Al. In a short time "Surely Goodness and Mercy" was born. I had never worked with another writer in such a manner to compose a song. Later Al and I wrote two or three other numbers like that. That was the last of it.

Alfred B. Smith remembers more about the initial inspiration for the song. He adds a humorous touch:

It was written after receiving a letter from one of the descendants of P. P. Bliss telling of Bliss's first country school teacher, named Miss Murphy, whom he dearly loved. It told of her teaching the class (before they could read or write) to memorize the 23rd Psalm. When the part "surely goodness and mercy" was reached, little Philip thought it said "Surely good Miss Murphy shall follow me all the days of my life." This little incident focused our thoughts on the phrase which became the heart and title of the song.   H

SURELY GOODNESS AND MERCY. The tune name is the traditional title of the song (which originally had three stanzas). The completed composition was first published in *John Peterson's Folio of Favorites* (Grand Rapids: Singspiration, 1958).   H

Surely It Is God Who Saves Me'   327
Carl P. Daw, Jr. paraphrased *The First Song of Isaiah* (Isa. 12:2-6), Canticle No. 9 of the liturgy of Morning Prayer, for *The Hymnal 1982* (Episcopal); the text was then submitted to Urwin for a tune. It has been arranged as an anthem (Augsburg).

THOMAS MERTON. The tune is named for the late Roman Catholic mystic who was an influence on the composer, Ray W. Urwin. It was composed (1984) for the Daw paraphrase, in preparation for *The Hymnal 1982* (Episcopal), where it became one of the more popular tunes because of its folk-like design.

Sweet Hour of Prayer   623
The words of this hymn appeared in *The New York Observer*, September 13, 1945, a contribution by Rev. Thomas Salmon, who had recently come to the United States from England. He explained that the poem was written by W. W. Walford, a blind fellow-clergyman in Warwickshire.

There is some uncertainty about the identification of "W. W. Walford." William J. Reynolds, in his *Hymns of Our Faith*, gives a detailed account of research which suggests that this may be the work of William Walford of Homerton. It is the similarity between the hymn and Walford's book, *The Manner of Prayer* (c. 1842), that led to the conclusion. The first inclusion of the text in a hymnal was in the Baptist edition of

Church Melodies, compiled by Thomas Hastings and Robert Turnbull in 1859.   H

SWEET HOUR. The earliest publication to contain this tune, composed by William Bradbury for this hymn, is believed to be his compilation, *The Golden Chain* (New York, 1861).   H

Sweet, Sweet Spirit   291
The song was first published as sheet music by Manna Music, Inc., Burbank, California (1963). Doris Akers says that she wrote the words and music in Los Angeles, CA (1960). "After a very inspiring prayer service with the Sky Pilot Choir, where the Holy Spirit had made manifest His wonderful power, I said within myself, 'There's a sweet, sweet spirit in this place'—from whence words seemed to flow."   H

SWEET, SWEET SPIRIT. The editors of *Hymns for the Living Church* (Hope Publishing Company, 1974) chose to use the song's title as the tune name.   H

Take My Life and Let It Be Consecrated   568
This text by Frances Ridley Havergal was written on February 4, 1874, and first published that year in Snepp's *Songs of Grace and Glory* (Appendix), and in her own *Loyal Responses* (1878) under the heading "Self-consecration to Christ."

According to Miss Havergal's account, the words came to her during a night of personal praise and prayer, following a spiritual victory in her ministry.   H

HENDON; see **Ask Ye What Great Thing I Know** 224.

Take My Life, Lead Me, Lord   566
Text and music were written by R. Maines Rawls while flying from Nashville to Dallas. First publication was in *Songs for Fun and Fellowship No. 3* (Nashville, 1969).

LANGLEY. The tune was composed with the words and named for the author-composer's father, Langley A. Rawls.

Take Time to Be Holy   540
Ira D. Sankey says that William D. Longstaff wrote this hymn after hearing a sermon at New Brighton, England, on 1 Peter 1:10, "Be ye holy as I am holy." George C. Stebbins says it was written after a service at the Keswick Convention in the north of England, where the words, "Take

time to be holy," were quoted. It first appeared in an English publication about 1882, and later in *Hymns of Consecration*, used at Keswick.   H

HOLINESS. The tune was written for the text in 1890 by George C. Stebbins while he was in India for meetings and conferences. A friend had given him the poem, clipped from a periodical. Stebbins mailed the tune to Ira D. Sankey in New York, who included it in his *Winnowed Songs for Sunday School* (1890) and in the 1891 editions of *Gospel Hymns* and *Sacred Songs and Solos*.   H

"Take Up Your Cross," the Savior Said   655
   Charles William Everest's text was written in 1833 and published that year in his *Visions of Death and Other Poems*. It originally had six stanzas which have been reduced and considerably altered in various hymnals through the years. The editors of *Hymns for the Living Church* (Hope Publishing Company, 1974) changed the pronouns "thou" and "thy" to "you" and "your," etc. Otherwise the text is essentially that which appeared in *Hymns Ancient and Modern* (1861).   H

BOURBON. First published in Freeman Lewis's *The Beauties of Harmony* (Pittsburgh, 1814), then in William Moore's *Columbian Harmony* (Cincinnati, 1825) and William Hauser's [Houser] *Hesperian Harp* (1848), this gapped-scale tune is attributed to Freeman Lewis—who, like Moore, was a traveling singing school teacher using the four-shape shape-note system of teaching. Lewis and Moore print it with a Watts Maundy Thursday text, "'Twas on that Dark and Doleful Night." George Pullen Jackson places this tune in the family with KEDRON and notes that other texts were used with it in antebellum America. Louise McAllister's harmonization first appeared in *The Hymn* (Jan. 1953), and later in *The Pilgrim Hymnal* (1958).

Te Deum   3, 39, 352
   Te Deum laudamus, an extended Latin hymn written before A.D. 502, probably first for the Rule of St. Caesarius when he was Abbot of Lerins, provides a pattern for praise hymns in both Latin and the vernacular. It has been variously ascribed to Ambrose, Augustine, Niceta of Remesiana, and Hilary, but no evidence suggests they are the authors. The text is traditionally sung daily at the service of Matins throughout the year and for thanksgiving for some special blessing such as a coronation or consecration. See John Julian's *Dictionary of Hymnology* (1907; reprint, Dover, 1957) pages 1119-1134.

Teach Me Thy Way, O Lord   586
   Our inquiry to the last copyright holder, Mr. George Taylor of the Cross Printing Works, Stainland, Halifax, England, revealed that he had

no information about this song or its author-composer, B. Mansell Ramsey, because "all records were destroyed by fire in 1969." A brief article released in 1974 in *The Life of Faith* (the house organ of Marshall, Morgan & Scott Publications, Ltd., London) solicited information and brought a response that led to material that is included in the biography section. *The Anglican Hymn Book* (1965) dates the hymn 1919; it appeared in 1925 in a leaflet published by John T. Park, then in charge of the Cross Printing Works. This hymn came to be known in the United States through *Hymns* (1947) of the InterVarsity Christian Fellowship, and is no doubt based on Psalm 27:11. H

CAMACHA. The tune was also written by B. Mansell Ramsey and no doubt contributed much to the hymn's popularity. It is named for Ramsey's residence, Camacha, in Chichester, Sussex, where he lived and died. H

Tell All the World of Jesus 742
According to the wife of author James Seddon, this hymn was written at a time when he was traveling around the country on missionary deputation work; Seddon responded to the need for another missionary text. He had served in Morocco and was, in the 1960s, Home Secretary of the Church of England Missionary Society.

FAR OFF LANDS. The tune is from *Hemmets Koralbok* (1921)—a Bohemian Brethren melody associated with the Swedish text, "Hur Ljuvt det är att komma." The Bohemian Brethren were a migrating Czech group which also influenced Martin Luther's approach to music, so the traditions are extensive. The tune is named for its associations with missionary texts, as early as 1929 with Percy Dearmer's "Remember All the People."

Tell His Praise in Song and Story 347
Timothy Dudley-Smith's free paraphrase of Psalm 34 was written at Ruan Minor (Aug. 1976) for an early American tune, PLEADING SAVIOR 580 and 813. Bishop Dudley-Smith acknowledges his debt to Tate and Brady's *Psalms* (1696), to a phrase from Psalm 62:7, and to Bunyan's "Who would true valour see" in *Pilgrim's Progress* (1678).

HOLY MANNA; see **Brethren, We Have Met to Worship** 802.

Tell Me the Story of Jesus 199
This text, written by Fanny J. Crosby, first appeared in *The Quiver of Sacred Song* (1880) compiled by William J. Kirkpatrick and John R. Sweney, published in Philadelphia by John J. Hood. H

STORY OF JESUS. The music was composed by John R. Sweney and has appeared with this text since it was first published in 1880.　　H

Tell Out, My Soul　　　　　　　　　　350
　　Author Timothy Dudley-Smith based this text on the New English Bible translation of the Magnificat, Luke 1:46-55. He notes that it was "written at 84a, Vanbrugh Park, Blackheath, the first home of our married life, in May 1961." One of Dudley-Smith's first hymn texts, it was first published in the *Anglican Hymn Book* (1965); it has enjoyed extensive further publication and wide familiarity.

WOODLANDS. Walter Greatorex's tune was first published in the *Public School Hymn Book* (1919); it is one of the tunes suggested by the text's author and was published with these words in *100 Hymns for Today* (1969). The name is one of the school houses at Gresham's School in Norfolk where Greatorex was music director (from 1911) and, more than 60 years later, where Dudley-Smith was Archdeacon of Norwich (1973). The five-beat syllable at the end of the second phrase is unique to *The Worshiping Church*; many prefer the original version, with only one beat for that syllable (and a quick breath before the next phrase).

Ten Thousand Times Ten Thousand　　　　746
　　The magazine *Good Works*, VII (Mar. 1867) first carried this text in three stanzas by Henry Alford. That same year these stanzas were published in Alford's *Year of Praise*. The fourth stanza was added in *The Lord's Prayer Illustrated* (1870), compiled by F. R. Pickersgill and Alford.　　H

ALFORD. John B. Dykes composed this music for Alford's text in the revised edition of *Hymns Ancient and Modern* (1875).　　H

Thanks to God for My Redeemer　　　　380
　　This is one of the favorite thanksgiving songs of Swedish heritage. It was written by August Ludvig Storm, a Salvation Army officer, and first published in *Stridsropet* ("The War Cry"), December 5, 1891, and later in the Swedish Salvation Army songbook. The English translation by Carl E. Backstrom was made for *The Covenant Hymnal* (Chicago, 1931).
　　In his hymn commentary, *Sing with Understanding*, James P. Davies notes that author Storm gives thanks for many of the negative aspects of life—tears, storms and pain—and that he had himself experienced a partial paralysis from the age of 37.　　H

TACK, O GUD. The tune's name is the beginning of the original Swedish text. It was composed by John Alfred Hultman and published with its Swedish words in *Solskenssånger* (1910). The song quickly became popular in both Sweden and America.　　H

Thanks to God Whose Word Was Spoken 313
Reginald Thomas Brooks wrote this hymn for the Triple Jubilee of the British and Foreign Bible Society (1954). First publication was in *New Songs* (private publication of the Congregational Church, Surrey, England, 1962).

WYLDE GREEN. Peter Cutts composed the tune (*c.* 1955) for "God is love, by him upholden," a text he particularly liked that needed an adequate tune. It was used by the Hymn Society of Great Britain (1961-62) and published in the United States *Methodist Hymnal* (1964).

Thank You, God, for Water, Soil, and Air 382
Brian Wren wrote this text (Sept. 1973), for *New Church Praise*, to "make a Christian statement about ecological issues." It is available with a tune by Erik Routley, ALTHORP (Agape Publications, 1966).

The Apostles' Creed 14
During the Middle Ages (and as early as the 6th century), this brief formula of faith was attributed to the Twelve Apostles. Rufinus (*c.* 400) attributes the creed to earlier ages than his own (*"tradunt majores nostri"*), and the Council of Milan (*c.* 390 A.D.) calls it "the symbol of the apostles." It is probably not older than the Nicene Creed (325), which is the official establishing of the Trinity concept. See the *Catholic Encyclopedia* for more details of the Creed's history.

The Battle Belongs to the Lord 672
Jamie Owens-Collins wrote text and music as a result of a private worship time (1984) and a sense of the impact of 2 Chronicles 20:15.

THE BATTLE. The tune was composed with the text setting.

The Battle Is the Lord's! 741
This hymn was written by Margaret Clarkson (1960) as a result of meditating on the scriptures and on the idea of the sovereign will of God regarding missions. It was first published in *Hymns of the Christian Life* (1962) after she showed it to Dr. A. W. Tozer, author and pastor in the Christian and Missionary Alliance; he expressed his appreciation for it. Tozer was the speaker at a Bible Conference at Glen Rocks, near Parry Sound, Ontario, where it was written.

LEONI; see **The God of Abraham Praise** 66.

The Bond of Love   696
This short chorus was written for Otis Skillings's popular musical *Love* (1971), and was intended for the congregation to sing; stanzas were added after the initial composition and are available in *Exalt Him* (Lillenas).

BOND OF LOVE. Tune and text were composed together.

The Church's One Foundation   689
This text was written by Samuel Stone because of his admiration for the noble defense of the faith by Bishop Gray of Capetown, South Africa. A controversy arose from Bishop John William Colenso's book *The Pentateuch and Book of Joshua, Critically Examined.* The hymn appeared first in Stone's *Lyra Fidelium: Twelve Hymns on the Twelve Articles of the Apostles' Creed* (1866) where it contained seven stanzas. The present hymn with five stanzas appeared with the tune "Aurelia" in the 1868 Appendix to *Hymns Ancient and Modern.*   H

AURELIA. Samuel Sebastian Wesley's tune first appeared in *A Selection of Psalms and Hymns* (London, 1864), edited by S. S. Wesley and Charles Kemble. It was originally set to "Jerusalem the Golden." Wesley's wife suggested the tune name, taken from "aureus," Latin for "golden."   H

The Day of Resurrection   247
In the original Greek, this hymn is the first ode of the "Golden Canon" by John of Damascus. In Orthodox churches it is sung at midnight on Easter morn as the congregations, on a given signal, light their candles, filling the darkened churches with light, and shout, "Christos anesti" (Christ is risen!). The translation is a free setting by John Mason Neale which first appeared in his *Hymns of the Eastern Church* (1862).   H

LANCASHIRE; see **Lead On, O King Eternal** 747.

The Earth Belongs to the Lord   326
Hal Hopson adapted the text of Psalm 24:1-6 for use at First Presbyterian Church, Franklin, TN, where he was interim organist-choirmaster (1985). It was first published in *10 Psalms* (Hope Publishing Company, 1986).

SING, BELIEVERS. The tune was composed with the text adaptation.

The First Noel, the Angel Did Say   162
This carol is thought to be about 300 years old. "Nowell" is the old English spelling and refers to the joyous expression of greeting to celebrate the birth of Christ. The present text is taken from the nine original

verses published in William Sandys's *Christmas Carols Ancient and Modern* (1833). H

THE FIRST NOEL. The traditional tune for this text appeared with it in William Sandys's *Christmas Carols Ancient and Modern* (1833). The present harmonization by John Stainer is from Bramley and Stainer's *Christmas Carols New and Old* (1871). Routley, in *The English Carol* (1959), traces the unique lineage of this tune to an anonymous descant (possibly by Jeremiah Clark) in Playford's *Divine Companion* (1801).

The Gathering 800
Ken Medema wrote this text in 1977 for the tune AUSTRIAN HYMN (see Glorious Things of Thee Are Spoken 694), he says, "for a youth group from an uptight Baltimore Presbyterian Church, while in the swimming pool." They sang it that Sunday morning but their church "didn't like it." It was published in the musical *The Gathering* in 1977.

GATHERING. This tune was composed for the text as part of the musical *The Gathering* (1977).

The Gift of Love 593
Based on 1 Corinthians 13, this text-tune combination was composed as an anthem (Hope Publishing Company, 1972), then adapted as a hymn. The text was written (1971) with the tune in mind, because, according to Hal Hopson, "both had an intrinsic simplicity and yet a profound integrity that would make a convincing match."

THE GIFT OF LOVE. Author-composer Hal Hopson adapted and "Americanized" the English folk tune O WALY WALY (a love song in its earlier forms, but known to Hopson with "The Water is Wide") for this song of biblical love. It was first used by Hopson as an anthem (1972). See **When Love Is Found** 392.

The God of Abraham Praise 66
This text was written by Thomas Olivers while he was staying in the home of John Bakewell in Westminster, London (1770). It was inspired by hearing the "Yigdal" sung in the Great Synagogue, Duke's Place, London. The Yigdal is a Hebrew Creed by Maimonides (1135-1204), versified by Daniel ben Judah (mid-14th century). Olivers commented that he had given it a "Christian character" with his reference to the Holy Trinity. It was first published in a leaflet, "A Hymn to the God of Abraham" (*c.* 1770). H

LEONI (also **YIGDAL**). The tune is one of seven traditional melodies for the Yigdal. It is named for its transcriber, Meyer Lyon, the cantor of the

Great Synagogue who wrote it out for Olivers. Its origin is unknown but it is thought to be related to Spanish and Basque melodies. The Wesleys included both words and music in their *Pocket Hymn Book* (1785).   H

The Hands That First Held Mary's Child   144
Author Thomas Troeger says: The story of Joseph "came up in the lectionary. . . . Joseph has traditionally been relegated to the corners of the nativity scene, but the increasing attention to the nurturing role of men . . . inspired me to write about the part that he must have played in the birth of Jesus." Troeger notes that in this day of changing gender roles, men often care for children, so he sought to give Joseph that needed attention. The text (1985) is dedicated to Father Moynihan, priest at St. Joseph's Roman Catholic Church, Penfield, NY. Another musical setting (by Carol Doran) first introduced the words; FOREST GREEN 154 is a recommended tune in *The Worshiping Church.*

The Head That Once Was Crowned   268
This poem by Thomas Kelly was one of several hundred published in his *Hymns on Various Passages of Scripture* (London, 1820), a book that enjoyed eight editions.

ST. MAGNUS [also called NOTTINGHAM, BRENTFORD, NEWBOR-OUGH or BUCKINGHAM]. Jeremiah Clarke probably composed this tune; it was first published in Henry (son of John) Playford's *Divine Companion* (2nd ed., 1707) with a metrical text of Psalm 117. It is named for the Church of St. Magnus the Martyr, London, built by Christopher Wren in 1676.

The Heavens Declare the Glory of God   329
The brief refrain, arranged by Hope Publishing Company's staff composer, John F. Wilson, is the text of the opening words of Psalm 19.

[PSALM 19]. Benadetto Marcello composed this music (*c.* 1724) as part of one selection in a set of vocal-instrumental pieces (cantata-style) using Italian paraphrased texts of the first 50 Psalms. It has become a standard in organ repertoire as well as being sung with various English texts, including a translation from Italian during Marcello's own lifetime.

The King of Glory Comes   134
This text was written (1966) by a Chicago priest, Willard F. Jabusch, several years after Vatican II permitted the use of the vernacular in Roman Catholic services of worship. First publication was in *Hymnal for Young Christians* (1966).

PROMISED ONE. John Ferguson arranged (1973) the Israeli folk tune for the United Church of Christ *Hymnal* (1974).

The King Shall Come 277

This text, of unknown Greek Orthodox origin, was translated by John Brownlie and first appeared in his *Hymns from the East, being Centos and Suggestions from the Service Book of the Holy Eastern Church* (1907). H

MORNING SONG (also **CONSOLATION**). The tune appeared first in John Wyeth's *Repository of Sacred Music. Part Second* (Harrisburg, PA, 1812 or 1813; see facsimile of the 1820 second edition—Da Capo Press, 1964), a book influenced by Wyeth's musician friend, Rev. Elkanah Kelsay Dare. It is called CONSOLATION and carries the text of a morning song, "Once more, my soul, the rising day." Like many of Wyeth's selections, that text and melody were also included in *Kentucky Harmony* (1816); it appears in that historic book of American folk tunes with the name CON-SOLATION and is credited in the index to an unknown author, "Dean," which may be a mistaken "Dare."

The Kingdom of God Is Justice and Joy 712

This hymn by Bryn Rees (1973) was first published in *Praise for Today* (1974). A poetic, theological definition of "the Kingdom of God," it is important because there are few comparable hymns in the repertoire.

HANOVER; see **Ye Servants of God** 103.

The Lord Bless You and Keep You 845

The text is Numbers 6:24-26 from the King James Version.

BENEDICTION [also **CHORAL BLESSING**]. Peter Christian Lutkin composed this setting with its sevenfold amen as a choir anthem (1900), dedicated "to my friend William Smedley."

The Lord Is Here! 777

Written at Ruan Minor (Aug. 1985), Timothy Dudley-Smith's hymn was intended for the beginning of Holy Communion which uses these title words liturgically (1980 Service Book). It was published in *Songs of Deliverance* (Hope Publishing Company, 1988).

CRIMOND; see **The Lord's My Shepherd, I'll Not Want** 330.

The Lord Is in His Holy Temple 796

The text is Habakkuk 2:20 from the King James Version.

QUAM DILECTA. George F. Root, known more for his simple popular songs, composed this dignified setting (mid-19th century) and named it for the words in Latin of Psalm 81:4, "How lovely [are Thy tabernacles]."

The Lord My Shepherd Guards Me Well 615
Carl Daw was commissioned by St. Andrew's Episcopal Church, Amarillo, TX, to write this Psalm 23 paraphrase (1985) for an anthem arrangement by David A. White; it was premiered January 1986 for the Association of Anglican Musicians.

BROTHER JAMES' AIR. This is one of many tunes by James Leith Macbeth Bain, an itinerant preacher and mystic, who was known as "Brother James." It first appeared in Bain's tract *The Great Peace* (1915). Gordon Jacob's choral arrangement for the text "The Lord's My Shepherd, I'll Not Want" (Oxford University Press, 1934) made the tune very popular.

The Lord's My Shepherd, I'll Not Want 330
This metrical paraphrase of Psalm 23 is taken from the Scottish psalter of 1650 (*The Psalms of David in Meeter*) which was called the "Prince of Versions" because it contained the best of the psalters in existence at the time. It is still in use and remains the only version officially authorized by the Church of Scotland. The text is said to be a composite of seven extant versions of the psalms, including one by William Whittingham. H

CRIMOND. The music first appeared in the *Northern Psalter* (1872) and is now one of the most popular tunes for these words. The melody has been ascribed to David Grant, but research has determined that it was written by Jessie Seymour Irvine, daughter of a minister in Crimond, a parish in the northeastern part of Aberdeenshire, Scotland. She supposedly gave the tune to Grant for harmonization, and this is how the mix-up occurred. In the *Scottish Psalter* (1929) the tune was assigned to Miss Irvine, and this has been quite generally accepted.

A full discussion of this text and tune may be found in *The Baptist Hymn Book Companion* (London: Psalms and Hymns Trust, rev. ed., 1967).

The descant first appeared in an octavo arrangement, and most recently was included in *Hymns for Today's Church* (1982). H

The Lord's Prayer 632
The text is Matthew 6:9-13.

MALOTTE. Albert Hay Malotte composed this tune as a solo setting of the familiar text (G. Schirmer, 1935). It is his best known and most widely performed work, although he was a professional composer.

The Lord's Prayer; see also **Our Father** 626.

The Nicene Creed 15
This profession of faith used by the Roman Catholic Church, Eastern Churches, and mainline Protestant denominations dates to the Council of Nicaea (A.D. 325) and a revision by the Council of Constantinople (A.D. 381, the form which is generally used). In its Latin version it is part of the Ordinary of the Mass, one of the sections often set to music.

The Old Rugged Cross 484
The text for this hymn came to George Bennard during evangelistic services he was conducting in Michigan, as a result of his meditating on John 3:16 and praying for a full understanding of the cross. After many frustrated attempts to write and several experiences in which he saw the redeeming grace of God at work during those meetings, he was able to complete the poem. The song probably appeared first in leaflet form, and later in *Heart and Life Songs, for the Church, Sunday School, Home and Campmeeting* (1915), published by Hope Publishing Company for Chicago Evangelistic Institute and edited by Iva D. Vennard, Joseph H. Smith, and Bennard. H

OLD RUGGED CROSS. The tune was written simultaneously with the words by George Bennard. Homer Rodeheaver bought the copyright from the author, published it, and made contracts with various recording companies for its reproduction. For many years it was acknowledged to be America's favorite gospel hymn. H

The Savior Is Waiting 446
This invitation hymn was written by Ralph Carmichael for evangelistic services conducted by Dr. Lester Harnish at Temple Baptist Church in Los Angeles. It was first published in 1958 as a sheet music solo, by Sacred Songs, Inc. H

CARMICHAEL. Ralph Carmichael wrote both words and music of the hymn. The tune name was selected in his honor by the editors of *Hymns for the Living Church* (Hope Publishing Company, 1974). The harmonization by Don Hustad was copyrighted by Sacred Songs in 1966 and appeared in *Favorite Hymns of Praise* (Tabernacle Publishing Co., Chicago, 1967). H

The Solid Rock 517
This hymn of faith was written in 1834 as Edward Mote thought about the "Gracious Experience of a Christian." The refrain was conceived one morning as he was walking up Holborn Hill, London, and four

of the verses were completed the same day. He shared them that day in a visit with a Mrs. King, who was dying. The verses so met her spiritual need that he had a thousand copies printed and sent one to *Spiritual Magazine*, without any signature. The hymn appeared anonymously in an edition of hymns in 1836 compiled by a "Brother Rees" who was credited with authorship in a later edition introduced in 1837. Edward Mote included it and claimed authorship in his *Hymns of Praise* (1836) with the title "The Immutable Basis of a Sinner's Hope."   H

SOLID ROCK. The tune was composed by William Bradbury for this text (1863). It first appeared in his compilation, *The Devotional Hymn and Tune Book* (Phila., American Baptist Publication Society, 1864).   H

The Star-Spangled Banner   423
In 1814, Washington lawyer Francis Scott Key was asked by friends of a doctor being held by the British during the War of 1812 to help free him. The release was arranged, but Key was detained on a ship behind British lines on the night of September 13-14. From there, he observed the British bombardment of Baltimore and saw the flag flying over Fort McHenry at dawn—the inspiration for the poem.

STAR-SPANGLED BANNER. This tune of unknown origin appeared in *The Vocal Magazine* (London, 1778), set to the text "To Anacreon in Heaven," by Ralph Tomlinson. The tune was well known in America in the early 1790s; Key wrote "O Say, Can You See" to fit this melody. Text and tune were declared "The National Anthem" by an Act of Congress, March 3, 1931.

The Strife Is O'er, the Battle Done   233
The Latin antecedent of this hymn has been traced to the *Symphonia Sirenum Selectarum* (Cologne, 1695), where it appears anonymously (John Mason Neale in *Medieval Hymns*, 1851, considered it to be from the 12th century). In the original version, two "Alleluias" begin each stanza. Francis Pott translated it about 1859 and published it in his *Hymns Fitted to the Order of Common Prayer* (1861).   H

VICTORY. The music is an adaptation of the opening phrases of "Gloria Patri et Filio" from Palestrina's *Magnificat Tertii Toni* (1591). William H. Monk arranged it for the original musical edition of *Hymns Ancient and Modern* (1861). The title comes from the second phrase, stanza 1 of the English text.   H

The Trees of the Field   272
Steffi Geiser Rubin adapted Isaiah 55:12 for the recording and concert group, Liberated Wailing Wall (1975). She remembers "nothing special

about this particular song," but its memorable scripture and infectious tune have made it popular.

THE TREES OF THE FIELD. Rubin gave Stuart Dauermann the text (1975) and he wrote the tune for it (he also added a Hebrew text). Dauermann's composition fits the Hebrew-Christian folk music style of the performing group.

The vision of a dying world; see **Macedonia** 737.

The Works of the Lord Are Created 354

Christopher Idle based this hymn on the apocryphal text of Ecclesiasticus 42-43. It was written during his first month as Rector at Limehouse, E. London, 1976, and first printed in the All Souls Church, Langham Place, London, *Supplement* (1980), then published in *Hymns for Today's Church* (1982).

KREMSER. This is one of the tunes suggested by the author; see **We Gather Together** 376.

Then Moses and the Israelites Sang 318
See **Rejoice, Ye Pure in Heart** 34.

There Is a Balm in Gilead 611

George Pullen Jackson (in *White and Negro Spirituals*) reminds us that the phrase "sin-sick soul" is found in hymns of both Charles Wesley and John Newton. This traditional spiritual is traced to the Newton words:
How lost was my condition
    till Jesus made me whole;
there is but one Physician
    can cure a sin-sick soul.
In early American history the Newton text was associated with the Scottish folk tune "Banks of Sweet Dundee" with no refrain, though in African-American worship the words bore little resemblance to the original. The refrain evidently appeared in revival meetings and was published in the upstate New York *Revivalist* of 1868. The present form is based on the version in *Folk Songs of the American Negro* (Nashville, 1907), by Frederick J. Work and John W. Work, Jr. H

BALM IN GILEAD. The refrain, which gives the tune its name, is based on the words of Jeremiah 8:22: "Is there no balm in Gilead; is there no physician there?" H

There Is a Fountain Filled with Blood   467

Based on Zechariah 13:1 (its attribution in *Olney Hymns*) and written in 1770 or 1771 by William Cowper, this hymn first appeared in Conyer's *Collection of Psalms and Hymns* (1772) and was included in *Olney Hymns* (1779) with the title, "Praise for the Fountain Opened." Although the imagery of the text has been criticized and revised, this original remains in common use. The editors of *Worship and Service Hymnal* (Hope Publishing Company, 1957) adjusted the order of phrases in stanza 5 (from the seven original stanzas) to achieve a positive climax.   H

CLEANSING FOUNTAIN. Because its style is reminiscent of early American camp meeting songs, many scholars feel that the music is incorrectly attributed to Lowell Mason. Mason did write a similar tune called COWPER for this text (1830) which may have caused confusion. H

There is a name I love to hear; see **O, How I Love Jesus** 509.

There is a place of quiet rest; see **Near to the Heart of God** 542.

There is strength in the name of the Lord; see **In the Name of the Lord** 113.

There's a Quiet Understanding   788

Tedd Smith wrote words and music following an informal communion service which some 12 people shared in a hotel room after a Billy Graham crusade service in Oakland, CA (1972). The author-composer writes: "As we sat in a circle on the floor sharing communion, the feeling of being strangers disappeared and there seemed to come this quiet understanding of each other, a feeling of being with brothers and sisters and sensing the oneness Christ promised whenever two or three gather in His name. I went back to my room and wrote 'There's a Quiet Understanding' as a benediction to a meaningful evening."   H

QUIET UNDERSTANDING. Tedd Smith's words and music (copyrighted 1973) were first published as a choral octavo (Hope Publishing Company, 1974) then, as a hymn, in *Hymns for the Living Church* (1974). H

There's a Spirit in the Air   120

Brian Wren wrote this hymn for Pentecost 1969 in Hockley, Essex, England, and dedicated it "for Emma," who was under his guardianship until she turned 18 (she now lives in Scotland). He borrowed the alternating refrain repetitions from Isaac Watts. The hymn was first published in *Praise for Today* (London, 1974).

LAUDS. John W. Wilson composed this tune for another text and it was first published in *Hymns and Songs* (London, 1969). Wilson used it with

Wren's text in December 1972 at the annual celebration of the Royal School of Church Music.

There's a Sweet, Sweet Spirit; see **Sweet, Sweet Spirit** 291.

There's a Wideness in God's Mercy   486
This text is part of a 13-verse poem by Frederick W. Faber entitled "Come to Jesus" and beginning "Souls of men, why will ye scatter," published in his *Hymns* (1862). Faber included a shorter version in *Oratory Hymns* (1854).   H

WELLESLEY. The music was written by Lizzie S. Tourjée as her graduation hymn when she was a high school senior. Her father, Dr. Eben Tourjée, founder of the New England Conservatory of Music, named the tune for the newly established Wellesley College, which his daughter attended for one year. He included it in the *Hymnal of the Methodist Episcopal Church with Tunes* (1878), of which he was one of the editors.   H

There's Something about That Name   104
Co-author of the text, Gloria Gaither, remembers the meaning of the words rather than the actual circumstances of the writing:
"Something About That Name" came out of our personal experience with the effect and power of the name of Jesus in our everyday lives. We were inexperienced parents of small children, and often found ourselves calling on the name of Jesus when our babies woke in the middle of the night with a nagging fever. We witnessed the death of our much-loved grandparents one by one and were amazed and comforted to see how these saints died, repeating, even in the final delirium, the precious name of Jesus who had been their companion through all of the stages of life.

THAT NAME. The tune was composed with the text (1970) by William (Bill) Gaither who also co-authored the words.

These Are The Facts   466
As a member of the *Psalm Praise* team of writers, Michael Saward was given the task of preparing an "Easter canticle" to be an alternative to the traditional Anglican "Christ our Passover is sacrificed for us." It was written on Trinity Sunday, June 6, 1971, at his home in Beckenham, Kent, England, and appeared in *Psalm Praise* (Falcon Books, London, 1973). Rev. Saward specifically placed the fifth stanza as a repeat of the first, providing the hymn's conclusion.   H

YVONNE. YVONNE is the tune written for this Saward text—see 234 in *Hymns for the Living Church* (Hope Publishing Company, 1974). Although it is not associated with the Saward text, this editor suggests MORNING STAR, hymn 182, for use in *The Worshiping Church*; it works when beats 3 and 4 in measure 2 are connected with a slur.

They Asked, "Who's My Neighbor?" 435

At the encouragement of David Bridges, Jan Wesson wrote words and music of this children's hymn for a competition of The Hymn Society (spring 1981). It was published at the Society's national conference (June 1982) although it was first sung by Crievewood Methodist Church (Nashville, TN) children in an arrangement by Dan Boone (Jan. 1982).

WHO'S MY NEIGHBOR. Wesson titled her work, "My Neighbor," but concurs with this tune name.

Thine Is the Glory 251

The French hymn, "A toi la gloire" (*c.* 1884) by Edmond Budry, pastor in Vevey, Switzerland, was first published in the *Chants Evangeliques* (Lausanne, 1885). It was translated into English by Richard B. Hoyle (1923) and appeared in *Cantate Domino* (1925), the hymnal of the World's Student Christian Federation. In England the first line is sung "Thine be the glory." H

MACCABEUS. The hymn tune is adapted from a chorus in the original version of Handel's oratorio *Joshua* (1748). The music was transferred from *Joshua* to *Judas Maccabeus* (1751) and there it has remained, set to the words "See, the conquering hero comes." It appeared as a hymn tune about 1760 in Thomas Butts's *Harmonica Sacra* with Wesley's "Christ the Lord Is Risen Today." H

This Is a Time to Remember 792

The text by Bryan Jeffery Leech was written to be an anthem arrangement by Allan R. Petker (1982). Leech later selected it as a hymn for a minister's conference (1984); it was adapted by Roland Tabell for congregational use and first published in the Centennial Hymnal of the Evangelical Covenant Church (1985).

DUDLEY. The tune was composed by the author (with help from Howard Stevenson) along with the text for its anthem setting. It is named for Dudley Brient, of Frinton-on-Sea, Essex, England, Leech's brother-in-law's father.

This Is My Commandment 600

The text is John 15:11-12.

LOVE ONE ANOTHER. No information is available on this anonymous tune which gained popularity in the mid 1980s; it may be a true folk tune in the oral tradition, even though it appeared very recently. It was named by Donald P. Hustad.

This Is My Father's World   384
Written by Maltbie Davenport Babcock during his first pastorate in a Presbyterian church in Lockport, NY, this poem was inspired by his early morning walks when he was going out, as he would say, "to see my Father's world." It was published posthumously with other writings of Babcock in a small book called *Thoughts for Everyday Living* (1901). The hymn is only a short cento of the complete poem of 16 stanzas, which emphasizes the fatherhood of God. Mary Babcock Crawford's revision of her father's second stanza expands the hymn to include our larger responsibility for the world.   H

TERRA BEATA. The tune, whose name means "Blessed Earth," was written by Franklin L. Sheppard for the Babcock text. He believed it was inspired by a traditional English melody that he learned from his mother as a boy. It first appeared in his *Alleluia* (1915), a Sunday School collection. The tune is also called TERRA PATRIS—related to the hymn's first line.   H

This Is the Day   801
The first stanza text is a paraphrase of Psalm 118:24 by Les Garrett and was first published in *Scripture in Song* (Maranatha! Music, 1967). The other two stanzas appear to be anonymous.

THE LORD'S DAY. The music was written with the words although it has been called a folk melody and has been printed elsewhere with variations.

This Is the Threefold Truth   781
Based on an ancient triad of praise which has again found its way into liturgies, Fred Pratt Green's text (1980) was a response to those old "joyful cries."

ACCLAMATIONS. Jack Schrader was a new Hope Publishing Company editor when George Shorney handed him this and other Green texts with the instructions, "See if any of these strike a response with you, and give us a hymn tune." The design of the acclamations dictated the form of the music, and although the text has been set by others, this hymn tune has found wide use.

Those Who Love and Those Who Labor   394
Geoffrey Dearmer's hymn was first published in *Songs of Praise* (1925) as a paraphrase in the spirit of the "Agrapha"—sayings of Jesus which are attributed to him as if he had said them. Dearmer attributes the first two stanzas to *Logion 5* of the Oxyrhynchus papyri and the third to Logion 1; the Oxyrhynchus papyri were discovered by Grenfell and Hunt (1879 and 1903); Dearmer notes varied scholarly opinions "as to the possible authenticity and the date of the Oxyrhynchus *Logion*," some placing them about 140 A.D. The text is one of six in a set; three were published before 1925 and the others in *Songs of Praise Enlarged* (1925).

Thou Art Worthy   116
This song was improvised in an evangelistic meeting (1962) in Foursquare Church, Hillsboro, OR, in which the composer's son, Dick, was preaching. He had announced that his mother would receive favorite scriptures and write a setting for them before the end of the service—but she was not aware of his public offer. The evening ended and someone from the congregation asked for the song; it was after 10:00 p.m. Pauline Mills testified, "The Lord gave me the music" to the text of Revelation 5:9
Kathryn Kuhlman's choir popularized the song at the Shrine Auditorium, Los Angeles, CA.

WORTHY. The tune was composed as an improvisation for the scripture text.

Thou Didst Leave Thy Throne   198
This text based on Luke 2:7, "there was no room for them in the inn," was written for the choir and children of the parish school at St. Mark's, Brighton, England, by Emily E. S. Elliott, whose father was rector of the parish. It was first sung in 1864 from leaflets, and later printed in the *Church Missionary Juvenile Instructor* (1870) and in Miss Elliott's *Chimes for Daily Service* (1880).   H

MARGARET. The tune (also called **ELLIOTT**, for the author) was composed by Timothy R. Matthews for these words, and named by the composer for reasons unknown. It was first published in *Children's Hymns and Tunes* (1876).   H

Though I may speak with bravest fire; see **The Gift of Love** 593.

Through All the World   738
In 1967 Paul Liljestrand asked Bryan Jeffery Leech to write a new hymn for a missionary conference to be held at Calvary Baptist Church in New York City. It was first published with Liljestrand's music in the July

1970 issue of *The Hymn*, journal of The Hymn Society of America, and had its first hymnal inclusion in *Hymns for the Living Church* (Hope Publishing Company, 1974).　　　　　　　　　　　　　　　　　　　H

CONRAD. Paul Liljestrand wrote the tune for this text (1970) and named it after his father, Conrad Liljestrand.　　　　　　　　　H

Through It All　　　　　　　　　　　　　　　　　　　　616

A young woman soloist traveling with Andraé Crouch and the Disciples had captured the admiration of the leader of the group. But she unexpectedly left the performing tour and Andraé Crouch was seriously discouraged. A friend from the California Angels baseball team called and urged Crouch to continue the tour and work through the emotional wounds with prayer. Out of that disappointment came this song—first the refrain and its melody, then the stanzas (not included here). It was finished February 9, 1971, just minutes before an earthquake shook the San Fernando Valley where Crouch was composing.

THROUGH IT ALL. The music was composed at the piano along with the text.

Through the Love of God Our Savior　　　　　　　　　610

Mary Peters wrote this text for her collection *Hymns Intended to Help the Communion of Saints* (1847).

AR HYD Y NOS. This Welsh folk tune is a harp melody from as early as the 17th century; it means "on length of night." With English and Welsh text, it was published in Edward Jones's *Musical Relicks of the Welsh Bards* (Dublin, 1784), intended to be sung by a harpist with the audience joining on the refrain, "All Through the Night." Ralph Vaughan Williams first used it as a hymn in the *English Hymnal* (1906) with the Heber text "God, that madest earth and heaven" 366. The harmonization has been attributed to Luther O. Emerson (1906).

'Tis Midnight; and on Olive's Brow　　　　　　　　　220

These words, titled "Gethsemane," by William B. Tappan appeared in his *Poems* (1822) and also in *Lyra Sacra Americana* (1868) and later in many hymnals.　　　　　　　　　　　　　　　　　　　　H

OLIVE'S BROW. Written for this text and named for the first phrase, this music by William B. Bradbury first appeared in *The Shawm* (New York, 1853), compiled by Bradbury and George F. Root.　　　　H

'Tis So Sweet to Trust in Jesus   520
This text by Louisa M. R. Stead is believed to have been written out of the experience of sorrow because of the death of her husband.   H

TRUST IN JESUS. The tune was composed by William J. Kirkpatrick for these words. It appeared first in *Songs of Triumph* (1882), compiled by John R. Sweney and Kirkpatrick.   H

Trust and Obey   523
The hymn by John H. Sammis was the result of a suggestion by Daniel B. Towner. Professor Towner was singing in a series of meetings conducted by D. L. Moody in Brockton, MA. In a testimony service he heard a young man say, "I am not quite sure—but I am going to trust, and I am going to obey." Towner jotted down the words and sent them to his friend Sammis, who first wrote the refrain—a capsule version of the entire song—and later the verses.   H

TRUST AND OBEY. The tune was written by Daniel B. Towner for the text. The entire hymn first appeared in *Hymns Old and New* (Chicago: Fleming H. Revell Co., 1887).   H

Trust in the Lord   527
Roland Tabell remembers little about the writing of this adaptation of Proverbs 3:5-6 (*c.* 1970). First publication was in the *Covenant Press Songbook* (1981).

TABELL. The tune was composed for the scripture words.

Trusting Jesus   526
This text by Edgar Page Stites first appeared in a newspaper which was handed to D. L. Moody. In turn, the evangelist gave the clipping to Ira D. Sankey, his soloist and songleader, asking him to set it to music. Sankey agreed to do so on the condition that Moody would vouch for the doctrine taught in the verses. The evangelist said he would.   H

TRUSTING JESUS. The tune was composed by Ira D. Sankey for the text. Words and music first appeared in *Gospel Hymns No. 2* (1876).   H

To a Virgin Meek and Mild   139
Vigleik E. Boe and Oscar Overby wrote this text to a traditional Spanish melody. It appeared first as a choral octavo, published by Augsburg Publishing House (1935).

LO DESEMBRE CONGELAT. The tune is Catalonian, of unknown origin. Donald Hustad arranged the traditional tune with this text for inclusion in *The Christmas Story in Candlelight Carols* (Hope Publishing Company, 1962), and later for *The Worshiping Church.*

To God Be the Glory (for the things he has done); see **My Tribute** 46.

To God Be the Glory (great things he hath done)   72
This text was one of the new gospel songs written by Fanny Crosby and published in the collection *Brightest and Best* (1875), compiled by William Doane and Robert Lowry. Other songs in the collection were included in the more famous *Gospel Hymns* series, published by Ira D. Sankey, which consequently became widely known; "To God Be the Glory" was not included, and so was little known in America. Sankey introduced the song in Great Britain during his 1873-74 tour with D. L. Moody and included it in his *Sacred Songs and Solos,* published in England. It was printed in the *Greater London Crusade Song Book* for the Billy Graham Harringay Crusade in 1954 and introduced in the Nashville, TN, crusade the same year. Since then, this long forgotten American gospel song has become very popular in its homeland.   H

TO GOD BE THE GLORY. William H. Doane wrote the tune for this text, as he did for many of Fanny Crosby's poems; it was introduced by Moody and Sankey in Great Britain in 1873.   H

Turn Your Eyes upon Jesus   452
The story of this hymn, sometimes called "The Heavenly Vision," is in a booklet by its author-composer, Helen Howarth Lemmel. In 1928 she saw these words in a pamphlet entitled "Focussed" by a missionary, Lillias Trotter:
> So then, turn your eyes upon HIM. Look full into His face and you will find that the things of earth will acquire a strange, new dimness. . . .
> Suddenly, as if commanded to stop and listen, I stood still, and, singing in my soul and spirit was the chorus, with not one conscious moment of putting word to word to make rhyme, or note to note to make melody.

The stanzas are not included in *The Worshiping Church.* The entire hymn was first published in a pamphlet released by C. C. Birchard (London, 1918). The National Sunday School Union included it in *Glad Songs* (London, 1922), a collection of 67 numbers by Mrs. Lemmel. It became popular through its use that year at the Keswick Convention in the north of England. It first appeared in the United States in *Gospel Truth in Song, No. 2* (Chicago, 1924), published by Harry D. Clarke.   H

LEMMEL. The tune is named for the author-composer.

Two Fishermen 654

Suzanne Toolan, S.M., wrote this ballad text (1986) for her own earlier tune at the request of Bob Batastini, compiler of the GIA Publications hymnal *Worship*. This was her first attempt at text writing.

LEAVE ALL THINGS. Sister Suzanne Toolan wrote the tune to a poem of Rosaleen O'Sullivan, "The Call," for an ordination service (1970); it was later rematched to this text.

Up through Endless Ranks of Angels . 264

Hymnologist Jaroslav J. Vajda wrote the hymn (1973) to a Swedish tune; it was first published as a bulletin insert (Augsburg, 1974) with a tune by Carl Schalk, FORTUNATUS NEW 228.

ASCENDED TRIUMPH. Henry V. Gerike's tune was composed for this text—which he had heard sung to REGENT SQUARE—while he was attending summer school at Concordia Seminary, St. Louis, MO (1973). It is available in two choir settings, both published by Concordia (SAB concertato setting #982709; SATB with instruments #982324).

Wake, Awake, for Night is Flying 131

The text was written out of severe tragedy. Philipp Nicolai pastored in a village in Westphalia which suffered the loss of 1,300 people in one illness (1597-98). The hymn was published in *Frewden-Spiegel dess ewigen Lebens* (1599). The German text is an acrostic, with the initial of each stanza forming W. Z. G., the reverse of the initials of Nicolai's pupil, Graf zu Waldeck. Catherine Winkworth's translation is from *Lyra Germanica, II* (1858).

WACHET AUF. Little is known about Hans Sachs (*c.* 1494-*c.* 1576), poet and cobbler in Nuremburg, Germany. The popular tune was published in *Frewden-Spiegel* (1599); Nicolai adapted it to his own hymn text (of 1597), and the tune name is the beginning of that hymn. This harmonization is by Bach from his Cantata No. 140, "Wachet Auf" (1731). The melody also appears in the *Schübler Chorales* of Bach and in Mendelssohn's oratorio *St. Paul*.

We Are Called to Be God's People 710

Thomas A. Jackson wrote this text (1973) for AUSTRIAN HYMN for the church he then pastored, McLean Baptist Church, McLean, VA, a Washington suburb. It was first published in *Baptist Hymnal* (1975).

AUSTRIAN HYMN; see **Glorious Things of Thee Are Spoken** 694

We Are God's People   700
Bryan Jeffery Leech wrote this text July 4, 1975 ("a Britisher writing
on a dreary Independence Day") specifically for the Brahms symphonic
tune; it was published in *Hymns for the Family of God* (Paragon, 1976). He
selected the topic because "we have had so few popular hymns relating to
the church." Leech calls it his "favorite." It may be the only hymn to use
the word "transparently."

SYMPHONY. The tune and basic harmonization are from the theme of
the last movement of Brahms's *Symphony No. 1 in c minor, Op. 69*; a few
anacruses notes (the dominant) are omitted from the opening phrases.
Brahms called for an sFz on the half-note at midway ("O" in the text)
which also fits the hymn words. Brahms was 43 when he completed his
first symphony (1876), but had worked on it for nearly 20 years, having
used some of its preliminary ideas in piano works; first performance was
at Carlsruhe, November 4, 1876. Clara Schumann wrote that "it lacks
melody," an opinion history has disproved.
    Fred Bock worked with Bryan Jeffery Leech to adapt the text and tune
as a hymn. It was first published in Bock's *Hymns for the Family of God*
(Paragon, 1976).

We are one in the bond of love; see **The Bond of Love** 696.

We Are the Reason   474
    David Meece wrote words and music in 1980 in Nashville, TN; lyrics
were written in fifteen minutes the night before vocals were recorded. It
was first recorded on "Are You Ready?" in 1980.

MEECE. The text was written for this tune which had been composed
several months earlier.

We Believe in God Almighty   693
    David Mowbray's creed adaptation was written for this ancient tune.
He states that this is a "summary of the Nicene Creed, written . . . to provide a Confession of Faith set to music—suitable for all-age family worship." First used in parish worship at Hertfordshire (1977), it was published in *Hymns for Today's Church* (1982), then used in the BBC's "Songs
of Praise" for Pentecost, 1984.

DIVINUM MYSTERIUM; see Of the Father's Love Begotten 145.

We Bless the Name of Christ the Lord   761
    This baptism hymn was written by Samuel F. Coffman in 1926, and
was included in the Mennonite *Church Hymnal*, edited by J. D. Brunk and
S. F. Coffman (Scottdale, PA: Mennonite Publishing, 1927).   H

CANONBURY; see **Lord Speak to Me, That I May Speak** 574.

We Come as Guests Invited   784
Timothy Dudley-Smith wrote the communion service text at Ruan
Minor (Aug. 1975), taking expressions from Luke 22:19 and *The Book of
Common Prayer.* "The text," according to the author, "was originally writ-
ten in five verses of four lines each; and completed by the addition of
what is now the second half of verse 2."

PENLAN. This tune by the Welsh choral conductor, David Jenkins, was
composed for the wedding of a member of Parliament, T. E. Ellis (June 1,
1898) and named for the Penlan Congregational Church, Pwllheli, Wales.
First published in the Welsh magazine *Cymru* (May 1899) with a text written in memory of Ellis who had died just a year after the wedding, it
became widely used with the English words "In Heavenly Love Abiding"
521. The music shows both the Welsh folk background and English influence of Jenkins.

We Come, O Christ, to You   86
Margaret Clarkson wrote this text in the summer of 1946 after Stacey
Woods, Chairman of InterVarsity Christian Fellowship, had asked her to
provide a hymn for students. It was first sung in InterVarsity's first
American missionary conference, held in Toronto in December 1946. It
was first published in *Hymns*, 1947, an InterVarsity publication. Clarkson
thoroughly revised the hymn in 1984 to update the language.   H

DARWALL; see **Rejoice, the Lord Is King** 262.

We Gather Together   376
This "national hymn" was written by an unknown author at the end
of the 16th century in celebration of the Netherlands freedom from
Spanish rule. It was first published in Adrian Valerius's *Nederlandtsche
Gedenckclanck* (1626) with this tune. The English translation was made by
Theodore Baker and appeared in *Dutch Folk Songs* (1917), compiled by
Coenraad V. Bos.   H

KREMSER. Named for the arranger, Edward Kremser, this was one of six
tunes taken from Valerius's collection (above) and published in Kremser's
Sechs altniederländische Volkslieder (1877). Kremser had discovered and
revised the music after 250 years of neglect.   H

We Give Thee but Thine Own   649
An offertory hymn, the words by William How were written in 1858.

The hymn was not published until 1864 when it was included in *Psalms and Hymns*, second edition, edited by How and Thomas Baker Morrell.   H

SCHUMANN. Appearing first in the *Cantica Laudis*, published by Lowell Mason and George J. Webb in 1850, this tune was the setting for "Thou shalt, O Lord, descend." The German composer Robert Schumann has been credited with writing it, hence the name. However, the melody has not been found in any of Schumann's works.   H

We Give This Child to You   764
Carol Mayes wrote this hymn for the dedication of children in the context of a church which does not practice infant baptism. She says it was "for dear friends when they were blessed with a long-desired child." The hymn won first prize in the Seventh-day Adventist hymnal editors' search for new writers. It was written in 1974, first sung in 1976, and first published in the *Seventh-day Adventist Hymnal* (1984).

CARLISLE. The tune, formerly called INVOCATION, was first published in the *Collection of Psalm and Hymn Tunes Sung at the Chapel of the Lock Hospital* (1793), as a setting for the text "Come, Holy Spirit, Come" by Joseph Hart. It has passed through several hymnals with minor changes and other texts.

We Have a Gospel to Proclaim   714
Edward J. Burns wrote the hymn in 1968 in response to the Bishop of Blackburn's "Call to Mission." It was first used at the Call to Mission services in the Deanery of Chorley.

MENDON. The tune was found by Robert G. McCutchan in the *Methodist Harmonist* (1821) where it was called an "Old German Melody." Lowell Mason named the tune "Mendon" for a town in Worcester County, MA, when it appeared in the second edition of *The Choir* (1833).   H

We have heard the joyful sound; see **Jesus Saves!** 728.

We may not climb the heavenly steeps; see **Immortal Love, Forever Full** 607.

We praise Thee, O God; see **Revive Us Again** 723.

We Praise You, O God, Our Redeemer   377
Julia Cory wrote these words to the tune KREMSER at the request of the organist at Brick Presbyterian Church, New York City (Thanksgiving 1902); it was first published in 1910. It is clearly based on the older Thanksgiving hymn to this tune, "We Gather Together" 376.

KREMSER; see **We Gather Together** 376.

We Praise You with Our Minds 401

In the *Companion to the Baptist Hymnal* (1976), William J. Reynolds gives this description from the author, Hugh T. McElrath (summer 1962): My mind wandered; my interest lagged, and my thoughts kept turning to formulating some verses to fit the appealing Irish tune CLONMEL, which I had recently come to know and love. Being a teacher charged with the task of challenging minds, I was imbued with the idea of praising God with the mind as well as every other part of one's being. Taking Mark 12:30 as my inspiration and guide, I wrote all three stanzas of the hymn during the course of that afternoon. . . . I later revised it slightly and sent it in to the Southern Baptist Hymn Writing Competition of 1962, where it received honorable mention.

The hymn with the tune CLONMEL first appeared in *Christian Praise* (Nashville, 1964). It was revised again for inclusion in *The Worshiping Church.*

CLONMEL. Arranger William J. Reynolds says "CLONMEL is an Irish folk song known as 'The Flight of the Earls.' The melody first appeared as a hymn tune in the *Church and School Hymnal* (London, 1926). This arrangement appeared as a unison anthem for children in *The Church Musician* (March 1952). In *Congregational Praise* (London, 1951) Eric H. Thiman, the musical editor, named the tune for a small town in Ireland."

We Three Kings of Orient Are 185

Dr. John H. Hopkins, Jr. wrote both text and tune while he was rector of Christ Church, Williamsport, PA (*c.* 1857). The song, after quickly becoming popular in the United States, was published in England in Bramley and Stainer's *Christmas Carols New and Old* (1871) as the only American exemplar.

KINGS OF ORIENT. Hopkins composed both words and music in a ballad style, evidently intending the hymn to sound older than it is.

We Trust in You, Our Shield 573

Edith Cherry composed the text, probably in some association with the English Keswick movement.

STRENGTH AND STAY. The tune, composed by John B. Dykes for the hymn "O Strength and Stay," was first published in *Hymns Ancient and Modern* (1875). Some of Dykes's original but uncharacteristic chromaticism has been removed for *The Worshiping Church's* setting of the tune.

We Will Extol You   348
This versification of Psalm 145 follows the tradition of David's own Psalm text, "One generation shall praise Thy works to another" (vs. 4). The hymnwriter J. Nichol Grieve says, "Age shall to age pass on the endless song."

OLD 124th. The tune is from the *Genevan Psalter* (1551), a melody used in Calvin's day. It was composed (or, perhaps was a folk tune) for Psalm 124. Elaborate settings of this and other psalm tunes were composed by Claude Goudimel (16th century); this hymn-style harmonization is by C. Winfred Douglas.

We Will Glorify   118
Twila Paris wrote text and tune for her album *Keepin' My Eyes On You* (Milk & Honey, 1982), and the song reached "top 40" on MusicLine's Adult Contemporary Chart.

WE WILL GLORIFY. The music was composed with the song text.

We Worship and Adore You   33
No information has been found on this anonymous text and tune. It became popular around 1960.

We, Your People, Praise You   37
Kate Page, the author of this 1932 text, gives no information other than that she prefers the more formal expression "We, Thy People, Praise Thee."

ST. ANTHONY'S CHORALE. The music is derived from the second movement of F. J. Haydn's *Divertimento in B flat* for wind instruments (*c.* 1780), where it is titled "Chorale St. Antoni[i]"; the theme is the one used by Brahms in his orchestral "Variations on a Theme of Haydn." Edith Lowell Thomas first arranged it as a hymn for *Singing Worship* (Abingdon Press, 1935). This four-part setting is by Gary Alan Smith, a music editor for Abingdon Publishing House.

We're Marching to Zion; see **Come, We That Love the Lord** 596.

We've a Story to Tell to the Nations   733
Words and music by H. Ernest Nichol were written in 1896 and published that same year in *The Sunday School Hymnary*.   H

MESSAGE. H. Ernest Nichol made a practice of writing original tunes to his many Sunday School hymns, signing his correct name, but he used the pseudonym "Colin Sterne" (an anagram on his middle and last names) for the texts.   H

Welcome, Happy Morning   241

Venantius Fortunatus's 110-line Easter poem *Salva festa dies* (written about 582) was the first hymn to compare spring with the Resurrection, according to E. E. Messenger in *Latin Hymns of the Middle Ages* (1948). The translation by John Ellerton was included in Brown-Borthwick's *Supplementary Hymn and Tune Book* (1868) and Ellerton's own *Hymns* (1888); the editors of *Hymns for Today's Church* (1982) revised it.

NOEL NOUVELET; see **Sing We Now of Christmas** 159.

Were You There?   218

This text is anonymous and also appears as "Have you heard how they crucified, etc." George Pullen Jackson lists *Old Plantation Hymns* (1899), compiled by William E. Barton, as the earliest known printed source. Tradition ascribes its origin to black slaves who interpreted biblical stories in spontaneous song.   H

WERE YOU THERE? The tune also is anonymous and first appeared in *Old Plantation Hymns* (1899) with some differences from the present version. Its first printing in our familiar form was in Frederick J. Work's *Folk Songs of the American Negro* (1907). The folk melody was long known in the mainly white upper Cumberland region of Tennessee, and may have had earlier British antecedents.   H

What a fellowship, what a joy divine; see **Leaning on the Everlasting Arms** 609.

What a Friend We Have in Jesus   622

Joseph M. Scriven wrote these words (*c.* 1855) to comfort his mother in a time of sorrow, never intending them to have any wider use. A friend saw the manuscript when sitting with Scriven during the author's last illness. Scriven testified, "The Lord and I wrote it between us." The hymn evidently appeared first (and anonymously) in Horace L. Hasting's *Social Hymns, Original and Selected* (1865).   H

CONVERSE. Composed for these words by Charles Converse in 1868, this melody first appeared in *Silver Wings* (1870), compiled by "Karl Reden" (Converse's pseudonym). When Philip P. Bliss and Ira D. Sankey were completing the copy for their famous *Gospel Hymns and Sacred Songs* (1875), this hymn was substituted for another shortly before publication. Sankey later remarked that "the last hymn that went into the book became one of the first in favor."   H

What a Wonderful Savior 488
This hymn, both text and tune, were written by Elisha Hoffman and first appeared in *Gospel Hymns No. 6* (1891), published by Biglow and Main. H

BENTON HARBOR. The editors of *Baptist Hymnal* (1956) named the tune for the city of Benton Harbor, MI, where Hoffman was once pastor of the First Presbyterian Church. H

What can wash away my sin; see **Nothing but the Blood of Jesus** 471.

What Child Is This? 150
The text is taken from a longer Christmas poem, "The Manger Throne," written by William C. Dix (*c.* 1865). Lester Hostetler says (*Handbook to the Mennonite Hymnary*, 1949) that Dix "had been ill in bed on Epiphany Day, and after reading the Gospel for the day [Matt. 2:1-12], he wrote this hymn, finishing it by evening." H

GREENSLEEVES. The melody "Greensleeves" is a traditional English folk tune. In Chappell's *Popular Music of the Olden Time* (1855-59) it is associated with a great variety of texts, including the knight's "Lady of Greensleeves." It has been used with the carol "The old year now away is fled" since about 1642.

What Does the Lord Require? 571
Written in 1949, Albert F. Bayly's text, one of a series on Hebrew prophets, was first published in his anthology *Rejoice O People* (1950).

SHARPTHORNE. A tune called TYES CROSS, similar to SHARPTHORNE, was composed by Erik Routley for this text at Bayly's request; it was published in *Rejoice, O People*. In preparing *100 Hymns for Today*, the editor, John Dykes Bower, asked Routley to revise TYES CROSS because of its similarity to an earlier tune and SHARPTHORNE became that revision. It is named for a village near East Grinstead, Sussex, Routley's home area (and also near Tyes Cross)—not far from the home of author A. A. Milne and his Winnie the Pooh.

What Gift Can We Bring? 794
Hymnist-composer Jane Marshall wrote this hymn for the 25th anniversary of the Northaven United Methodist Church, Dallas, TX, her home church since 1957; publication was in the United Methodist *Supplement to the Book of Hymns* (1982) and in *The United Methodist Hymnal* (1989).

ANNIVERSARY SONG. The tune was composed with this text for the anniversary occasion.

What God Ordains Is Always Right   82
Based on Deuteronomy 32:4 (and chapter 33), this hymn was written in 1675 to help Samuel Rodigast's friend, the composer of the tune, Gastorius, when he was seriously ill. It was first published in the appendix to *Das Hannoverische Gesangbuch* (1676). Gracia Grindal translated it for the *Lutheran Book of Worship* (1978).

WAS GOTT TUT. Composed for this text (*Was Gott tut, das ist wohlgetan, es bleibt*) by Severus Gastorius, for whom Rodigast wrote the poem (1675), the tune was for a time thought to be by Pachelbel, a theory disproved by Johannes Zahn. First publication was in *Andächtige Elends-Stimme* (1697).

What If It Were Today?   275
Both words and music were written by Lelia N. (Mrs. C. H.) Morris. The song first appeared in *The King's Praises No. 3*, compiled by H. L. Gilmour, George W. Sanville, William J. Kirkpatrick, and Melvin J. Hill (Philadelphia: Praise Publishing, 1912).   H

SECOND COMING. The tune name was given first in *Baptist Hymnal* (1956).   H

What Offering Shall We Give   490
Isaac Watts's text was first published in his *Hymns and Spiritual Songs* (1709) with the title "Faith in Christ our Sacrifice."

What Wondrous Love Is This   212
The author of the text is unknown. It was first printed in Stith Mead's *A General Selection of the Newest and Most Admired Hymns and Spiritual Songs Now in Use* (Lynchburg, VA, 1811) and appeared with this tune in a number of 19th-century hymnals, including *Southern Harmony* (1840 ed.); the tune is attributed to James Christopher.

WONDROUS LOVE. From William Walker's *Southern Harmony* (1840 ed.), this tune has characteristics of traditional Anglo-American folk melodies of Elizabethan tradition; it has carried various sources including attribution to James Christopher of Spartanburg, SC—a possible source since both B. F. White and "Singing Billy" Walker could have known Christopher. George Pullen Jackson, in *The Story of the Sacred Harp, 1844-1944*, has pointed out its resemblance to a tune used for 250 years with a song about the pirate, Captain Kidd, but WONDROUS LOVE has its own distinctiveness.

When God the Spirit Came   688
Drawn from Acts 2 and Galations 5:22, this poem was written by
Timothy Dudley-Smith at Ruan Minor (Aug. 1977). He had in mind the
meter for VINEYARD HAVEN (a setting of "Rejoice, ye pure in heart").

When He Shall Come   273
Almeda J. Pearce wrote words and music at a time (1934) when her
husband, Rowan Pearce, was a traveling evangelist and visionary radio
Bible teacher who saw the potential of the new medium of radio. Study
of prophecy was particularly popular in the 1930s, 40s, and 50s, perhaps
because of the Depression and World War 2; yet this hymn has endured
to become a multi-generational statement of scriptural hope (Rev. 3:4,
7:9).

Pearce's daughter, Jeanne P. Hopkins, remembers that her mother had
a near-death experience and particularly "felt the presence of the Lord."
A hemophiliac, she had attempted to have a needed blood transfusion
from her husband, but because it was the wrong type, it did not seem to
help. Mrs. Pearce told of that "valley of the shadow" and of seeing the
hand of the Lord vividly. A second transfusion did function, but she
"didn't want to come back; she would never fear death, because the Lord
was there." That was the turning point in her ministry with Rowan and
resulted in both this hymn and an extensive live radio program that was
broadcast daily for nearly 30 years, then each Sunday for many more.

PEARCE. The music was composed with the text.

When I Can Read My Title Clear   681
This was a favorite hymn in 18th-century America, especially in the
South. Its British author, Isaac Watts, included it in his *Hymns and
Spiritual Songs* (1707). He titled it "The Hopes of Heaven our Support
under Trials on Earth."   H

PISGAH. Typical of the religious folk tunes sung in the South early in
the 19th century, around 1819 it was found in *Tennessee Harmony* credited to Alexander Johnson; this melody also appears in Leavitt's *Christian
Lyre* (1831) where it is credited to J. C. Lowry. It does not seem to be in
Kentucky Harmony (1816), although several tunes are similar to it and the
"Title Clear" text is used with a fuging tune called NINETY-FIFTH; the
text with NINETY-FIFTH is also in *Wyeth's Repository of Sacred Music. Part
Second* (1813). The *Sacred Harp* (1844) attributes this tune to both Lowry
and *Baptist Harmony* but uses the "Title Clear" text with three other tunes,
not PISGAH.

Pisgah is a mountain ridge near Mount Nebo, not far from the Dead
Sea, from which Moses viewed the land of Canaan; it is also an American
mountain in the Appalachians. In the United Kingdom the tune is
known as COVENANTERS and is sung to a metrical 23rd Psalm.

When I Survey the Wondrous Cross 213

This text by Isaac Watts, possibly based on Galatians 6:14, has been acclaimed by some as "the finest hymn in the English language." It first appeared in his *Hymns and Spiritual Songs* (1707) and was intended to be sung principally at Communion services. The original was altered somewhat and appeared in the enlarged edition of the same work in 1709.   H

HAMBURG. The music was written by Lowell Mason in 1824 and appeared in the third edition of the Boston *Handel and Haydn Society Collection of Church Music* (1825). Mason indicated that "Gregorian plainsong" was the source of the tune.   H

When In Our Music God Is Glorified 402, 403

Fred Pratt Green titled this poem "Let the People Sing!" when he wrote it (1972) at the request of John W. Wilson for Charles V. Stanford's tune ENGELBERG 403. All American hymnals include a minor change from the original text: "man's music" reads "our music."

CELEBRATION 402. Milburn Price composed this tune for Green's text. It was first published as an anthem (Van Ness Press, 1985).

ENGELBERG 403. Charles Villiers Stanford composed this tune for the text, "For All The Saints," *Hymns Ancient and Modern* (1904). For those words, Vaughan Williams's SINE NOMINE (751) has replaced Stanford's tune, but the Green text has effectively adopted it. John W. Wilson points out the need for the instrumental "Amen" chord to complete the climax of the melody—the high D.

When Love Is Found 392

Brian Wren wrote "When Love is Found" for two weddings which he could not attend—his brother Keith was marrying Sandra Michell in Bombay, India, and his friend Gill Todd was marrying Sri Lankan Percy Fernando in Scotland (1978)—and it is dedicated to the two couples. Wren had the tune O WALY WALY in mind when he wrote the text, "so that familiar music could carry the words." First publication was in *Mainly Hymns* (United Kingdom, 1983).

O WALY WALY. Several different tunes have carried the words "O Waly, Waly," a text of a lover who has been forsaken, which was printed as early as Allan Ramsay's *Tea Table Miscellany* (1724-32). The tune, of English origin, had come to the southern United States by the 19th century. The harmonization was prepared for Hope Publishing Company's *Faith Looking Forward* (1983) by staff composer John F. Wilson.

When Morning Gilds the Skies 99
The anonymous German hymn "Beim frühen Morgenlicht" was found in the Würzburg *Katholisches Gesangbuch für den öffentlich Gottesdienst im Biszthume Würzburg* (1828). It appears in other forms, leading to the conclusion that this was not the original source. Edward Caswall translated the hymn into English; it was published in six stanzas in Formby's *Catholic Hymns* (1854). Other stanzas were added in 1858, and various centos have been made for hymnal use. H

LAUDES DOMINI. The tune (Latin for "Praises of the Lord") was written by Joseph Barnby for this text and was published in the Appendix to *Hymns Ancient and Modern* (1868). H

When Peace like a river attendeth my way; see **It Is Well with My Soul** 519.

When the Church of Jesus 722
Fred Pratt Green was Superintendent Minister (pastoral) at Trinity Methodist Church, Sutton, London, when he wrote this text for a Stewardship Renewal Campaign, calling it "The Church in the World" (1968). It was his first widely sung hymn, published in *Hymns and Songs* (1969), just before his retirement from the active pastoral ministry into hymn writing. The Hymn Society of America introduced it in 1970 (with a misprint, "the war of traffic," rather than the "roar," which was corrected in *The Worshiping Church*).

KING'S WESTON. The tune was composed by Ralph Vaughan Williams for *Songs of Praise* (1925) for the text "At the Name of Jesus" 266. It is named for a country house and park on the River Avon, near Bristol, England. H
This hymn became associated with the tune in the Episcopal *Hymnal* (1940), a combination appreciated by Green.

When the King Shall Come Again 337
Christopher Idle based this hymn on Isaiah 35. The writer's motivation was a perceived need for "biblical words to the tune universally used for 'Good King Wenceslas.'" He noted that the tune was originally part of a spring carol. Although the text was written at Poplar, E. London, 1975, the author revised it in 1978, 1979, 1981, and 1989; its first widely circulated publication was in *Hymns for Today's Church* (1982). Idle himself sat on a hymnal editorial committee that rejected the text when it was presented anonymously, so this version represents the culmination of editing.

TEMPUS ADEST FLORIDUM. This is one of two tunes suggested by the author (the other is AVE VIRGO VIRGINUM); see **Gentle Mary Laid Her Child** 156.

When the Lord in Glory Comes 280
Timothy Dudley-Smith wrote the text at Sevenoaks (Jan. 1967) "on a late-night stroll" after hearing a television tune "with a pronounced beat, an emphatic rhythm." He sent the text to Baughen in Manchester and described to him the type of tune he had in mind, calling it in a "youth idiom." Text and tune were published in *Youth Praise, Book Two* (1969).

GLORIOUS COMING. Michael Baughen composed this tune for this text at Dudley-Smith's request for "a rag-time tune." The composer intended to build each stanza toward the climax. Composed in 1967, it was first published in *Youth Praise, Book Two* (1969).

When We All Get to Heaven 697
The author, Eliza E. Hewitt, was a regular attendant at the Methodist camp meeting at Ocean Grove, NJ. There she often met Emily D. Wilson, composer of this music. No doubt it was their mutual interest in the conference center that eventually produced this hymn. *Pentecostal Praises* (1898), compiled by William J. Kirkpatrick and Henry L. Gilmour, first brought it to public attention and wide use. H

HEAVEN. Emily D. Wilson wrote the music for the words of her friend, Hewitt. The tune name first appeared in the *Baptist Hymnal* (1956). H

When we walk with the Lord; see **Trust and Obey** 523.

Where Cross the Crowded Ways of Life 433
This "Prayer for the City" was written by Frank Mason North at the request of Caleb T. Winchester for a new missionary text to be included in the *Methodist Hymnal* (1905). The resulting hymn was based on a sermon Dr. North had preached on Matthew 22:9, "Go, therefore, into the highways." It was first printed in *The Christian City* (June 1903), the journal of the Methodist City Missionary Society, of which North was editor. H

GERMANY; see **Jesus, Thy Blood and Righteousness** 481.

Where the Spirit of the Lord Is 614
Words and music were created together by Steve Adams (1973, rev. 1983) and first published by Franklin House (1974).

ADAMS. The tune is named for the composer-lyricist.

While By the Sheep We Watched 166
This is a traditional German carol from the 19th century.

JUNGST. The German folk tune is named for its arranger, Hugo Jüngst (*c.* 1890).

While Shepherds Watched Their Flocks 172

A collection of 16 hymns titled *A Supplement to the New Version of the Psalms* (1700), compiled by Nahum Tate and Nicholas Brady, included this text. This hymn by Tate is the only one to have survived in common use. H

WINCHESTER OLD. The tune is printed in Thomas Este's *The Whole Book of Psalms* (1592). It may have been based on a similar melody by Christopher Tye in *Actes of the Apostles* (1553), a didactical biblical presentation of the first 14 chapters of Acts set to hymn-like tunes that later were adapted and reprinted for nearly another 200 years. The present arrangement is attributed to George Kirbye, a Suffolk, England, musician of the late-16th century. The counter-melody is from Alan Gray's *A Book of Descants* (1923).

Who Honors Courage Here? 633

Based on a scene in John Bunyan's *Pilgrim's Progress*, Michael Saward's paraphrase (1981) captures the spirit of the expression of courage by "Mr. Valiant-for-Truth" following his narration of the difficulties encountered in his pilgrimage: "I believed, and therefore came out, got into the Way, fought all that set themselves against me, and, by believing am come to this place."

Who Is He in Yonder Stall? 195

This text was written by Benjamin R. Hanby and was published in *The Dove, a Collection of Music for Day and Sunday Schools* (Chicago, 1866). For many years the song appeared with at least 10 stanzas, each only one line long. Donald Hustad introduced the present version in *Worship and Service Hymnal* (1957). H

LOWLINESS. The tune was composed by Hanby for his own words. The name is derived from the sentiment of the hymn's stanzas, which are in dramatic contrast to the refrain. H

Who Is on the Lord's Side? 666

Frances Ridley Havergal's hymn was written October 13, 1877, and entitled "Home Missions." It was based on 1 Chronicles 12:18 and first published in Miss Havergal's *Loyal Responses* (1878). H

ARMAGEDDON. The name is the location of the cataclysmic struggle which is associated prophetically with the end of history and mentioned in Revelation 16:16. The tune is a German melody credited to Luise Reichardt in Part II of *Layriz's Kern des deutschen Kirchengesangs* (1853). John Goss's adaptation appeared in the present form in *The Church Psalter and Hymn-book* (1872), set to "Onward, Christian Soldiers." H The editors of *The Worshiping Church* indicate that the choice of hymn number is coincidence.

Who's My Neighbor?; see **They Asked, "Who's My Neighbor?"** 435.

Wind Who Makes All Winds That Blow 294
The Spirit of God is described as a wind by Luke (Acts 2:2) in his narrative of the Day of Pentecost, and also by Jesus, when talking to Nicodemus (John 3:8). Author Thomas Troeger (1983) traces his inspiration "directly" to the text of Acts 2:1-13 and to

the influence of native American seminary students who have helped me to appreciate in fresh ways how the RUACH (the Hebrew word for Spirit and wind) is such a vital part of the materiality of our existence, breathing life into us, energizing our cells and very being. . . . My intention is to help renew our sense of the primal origins of the sense of Spirit which the ancient Hebrews and native Americans knew through wind and fire.

Troeger attributes the idea for this text to Father Sebastian Falcone, head of the St. Bernard's Institute, a Roman Catholic affiliate of Colgate Rochester (NY) Divinity School.

ABERYSTWYTH; see **Jesus, Lover of My Soul** 461.

Wise Men, They Came to Look 186
This text was written at Limehouse, E. London (Jan. 1981), and first published in *Hymns for Today's Church* (1982). Christopher Idle says that he was preparing for an Epiphany sermon and "realizing afresh (with the help of Prof. R. V. G. Tasker's commentary on Matthew's gospel) the richness of the familiar story of the coming of the Magi. The sermon outline became this hymn." Following a clergy conference at Ely where he introduced the text, Idle revised the hymn using suggestions from Archdeacon George Timms.

WER NUR DEN LIEBEN GOTT (the tune recommended by Idle); see **If You Will Trust in God to Guide You** 636.

Wonderful Grace of Jesus 497
While he was pastor of the Church of the Nazarene at Auburn, IL, 1916-1919, Haldor Lillenas wrote much music for the historic song evangelist Charles M. Alexander, including this choir selection. Homer Hammontree first introduced it in 1918 in the Bible Conference at

Northfield, MA, founded by D. L. Moody. It was published in *Tabernacle Choir* (1922), edited by R. J. Oliver and Lance Latham. It is listed as No. 95 in the index of *Conference Hymnal* (1919), compiled by Charles M. Alexander, but another song appears on those pages, evidently substituted at the last moment. H

WONDERFUL GRACE. Haldor Lillenas wrote the music for his text and often complained that most people sing it too fast. "A song should be performed in such a fashion that the words can be comfortably pronounced without undue haste," he said. Amazingly enough, he received only $5.00 for this composition, which has become popular the world around. Further, the copyright is owned by Hope Publishing Company, not the Lillenas company, which he founded. H

Wonderful Words of Life 309
This song was written by Philip Bliss at the request of publisher Fleming H. Revell, for the first issue of *Words of Life* (1874), a Sunday School paper. Two years later it was introduced in an evangelistic campaign which George Stebbins and Dr. George Pentecost were conducting in New Haven, CT. H

WORDS OF LIFE. The tune was composed by Bliss at the time he wrote the words; both were published in the magazine *Words of Life* (1874). H

Worthy Is the Lamb 230
Don Wyrtzen gives this account of his writing of the words and music:
In 1970, I was in Mexico City assisting evangelist Luis Palau conduct a series of crusades. As the messages were in Spanish, I spent the time during the sermons writing songs. One day, I became particularly impressed with the great truth of Revelation 5:12, and thought how effective this verse could be, if only the proper music was used to enhance it. I thought about the music used in the secular song "The Impossible Dream" and decided that a similar musical style would work well with these words. "Worthy [is the Lamb]" was first used in a musical [1973] titled "Breakthrough," in which I collaborated with John E. Walvoord. In more recent times, I have worked with Phil and Lynne Brower in producing an Easter musical based on this hymn.

WORTHY IS THE LAMB. The tune was composed with the text.

Write These Words in Our Hearts 812
The text is directly based on Jeremiah 31:33 with echoes of Proverbs 3:3 and 7:3.

[CHANT]. In the middle of an editorial meeting for *The Worshiping Church*, John F. Wilson jotted down this traditional chant tune and harmonized it.

Ye Servants of God, Your Master   103
The year 1744 was one of great tension, confusion, and unrest in England. The Wesleys and their Methodist followers were persecuted because they were accused of trying to overthrow the throne. This hymn was No. 1 in a collection published that year and entitled *Hymns for Times of Trouble and Persecution*. It was written by Charles Wesley and was based on Psalm 93:1-4 and Revelation 7:11-12.   H

HANOVER. The tune first appeared in *The Supplement to the New Version of Psalms* by Dr. Brady and Mr. Tate (6th ed., 1708). Although it was early ascribed to Handel, hymnologists now believe that it was written by William Croft. It was named "Hanover" at a time when Handel was assumed to be the composer and George III (of the house of Hanover) was on the British throne. Handel was court-conductor at Hanover (in Germany) in 1710-11.   H

Years I spent in vanity and pride; see **At Calvary** 510

You shall go out with joy; see **The Trees of the Field** 272.

Your Hands, O Lord, in Days of Old   409
Edward Plumptre wrote "Thine arm, O Lord, in days of old" for a leaflet (1864) printed by King's College Hospital, London, the college where he was a professor. He also included it in his *Lazarus, and Other Poems* (2nd ed., 1865) which gave it wider distribution.

ST. MICHAEL'S. This tune was first published in William Gawler's *Psalms and Hymns* (London, *c.* 1784-89), set to "Creator, Spirit," a text with a slightly different meter. The anonymous tune may have English or German folk song origins. Gawler was organist at an orphanage in Lambeth, so the *Psalms and Hymns* setting is designed for children's voices.

Authors, Composers, and Sources

Ackley, Alfred Henry (b. Jan. 21, 1887, Spring Hill, Bradford County, PA; d. July 3, 1960, Whittier, CA), a capable cellist, received his early musical training from his father, and later studied at the Royal Academy of Music, London, and with Hans Kronold in New York City; graduated from Westminster Theological Seminary, MD, and served Presbyterian churches in Pennsylvania and California, including a period as assistant to Dr. Hugh Thompson Kerr (editor of the Presbyterian Hymnal, 1933) at Shadyside Presbyterian Church of Pittsburgh, PA; in collaboration with his elder brother, Bentley, wrote words and/or music of perhaps 1000 hymns and gospel songs, and helped compile hymnals and song-books for the Rodeheaver Publishing Company; received the honorary DSacMus degree from John Brown University. H
He Lives, ACKLEY 248

Adam, Adolphe [Charles] (b. July 24, 1803, Paris, France; d. May 3, 1856, Paris), the son of a musician, was not encouraged by his father to develop his musical talents; followed a career in theater music, writing for the *Opera Comique* and the Paris grand opera while studying at the Paris Conservatoire (beginning in 1820); wrote many orchestral and vocal compositions and is best known for the ballet *Giselle*; won honorable mention, then second prize (1824-5) in the *Prix de Rome* contest; after suffering financial difficulties, then bankruptcy, became a journalist, but also taught composition at the Conservatoire.
O HOLY NIGHT 160

Adams, Stephen R. (b. Nov. 19, 1943, Woonsocket, RI); no other information has been located.
Where the Spirit of the Lord Is, ADAMS 604

Adkins, Donna Whobrey (b. June 18, 1940, Louisville, KY), the daughter of traveling gospel singers, Foster and Peare Whobrey, sang publicly at the age of two and was part of the family quartet at 12; attended Asbury College, Wilmore, KY (1959-60), and the University of Louisville (1961); is secretary to the Senior Pastor at Covenant Church, Pittsburgh, PA, and active in music there; is married to James Adkins, administrative pastor of Covenant Church, and they have two grown children.
Glorify Your Name, GLORIFY YOUR NAME 10

Ahlwén, Elsie R. (b. 1905, Örebro, Sweden) came to the United States as a young woman and studied at Moody Bible Institute, Chicago, IL; became an evangelist and worked among the Swedish-speaking people in Chicago and later, across the United States, preaching and singing; later married Daniel A. Sundeen, a business man, and they continued their ministry together while raising their family; retired to

live in Manchester, NH.   H
PEARLY GATES 683

Ahnfelt, Oscar (b. May 31, 1813, Gullarp, Skåne, Sweden; d. Oct. 22, 1882, Karlshamn, Sweden) grew up in a parsonage and shared good music and literature from his earliest years; received elementary education from his older brothers, then enrolled in the University at Lund; in 1840 began to study music in Stockholm and came under the influence of the religious revival led by Carl Rosenius; joined the movement and began traveling on a full-time basis, singing, playing, and preaching; was harassed in his activity because of the Conventicles Edict, but was vindicated in his ministry after a command performance before King Karl XV; met and married Clara Stromberg, who wrote many songs of her own; through the financial help of Jenny Lind, "the Swedish Nightingale," published his musical setting of words by Lina Sandell and others, beginning in 1850 and continuing through 12 editions by 1877, the volumes usually known as Ahnfelt's *Andeliga Sånger.*   H
BLOTT EN DAG 367

Ainger, Arthur Campbell (b. July 4, 1841, Greenwich, Kent, England; d. Oct. 26, 1919, Eton, Buckinghamshire), educated at Eton College and Trinity College, Cambridge, was assistant, then schoolmaster at Eton until 1901, where he wrote numerous hymns for the school's use.
God Is Working His Purpose Out 750

Akers, Doris Mae (b. May 21, 1922, Brookfield, MO), one of 10 children, attended high school and business college; has had no special training in music, but wrote her first gospel song at age 10, and has won many awards for singing, song writing, and choir directing; was affiliated with the Full Gospel church in Columbus, OH, where she still lives; has served as choir director, making outstanding recordings; has written over 300 gospel songs.   H
Sweet, Sweet Spirit,   SWEET, SWEET SPIRIT 291

Alcuin (also **Ealhwine, Falccus, Albinus**) (b. *c.* 735; d. *c.* 804), an 8th-century scholar at York, England, traveled to Rome; was spiritual guide for Charlemagne (from *c.* 780) and Abbot of St. Martin in Tours from 796 until his death; introduced the chanting of the creed into the Roman Catholic Mass.
Eternal Light, Shine in My Heart 545

Alexander, Cecil Frances Humphreys (b. 1818, Ballykean House, Redcross, Wicklow, Ireland; d. Oct. 12, 1895, at the Palace, Londonderry) specialized in writing hymns for children; the second daughter of a major in the Royal Marines, was born at Miltown House in County Tyrone, Ireland; in 1850, married the Rev. William Alexander, rector of the parish of Termonmongan who was appointed Bishop of Derry and Raphoe in 1867, and became (Anglican) Primate of all Ireland in 1893; before her marriage, published *Verses for Holy Seasons* (1846) and *Hymns for Little Children* (1848), her most famous collection which was printed in more than 100 editions;

also produced *Narrative Hymns for Village Schools* (1853), *Poems on Subjects in the Old Testament* (1854 and 1857), and *Hymns Descriptive and Devotional* (1858); contributed hymns to *Writings of St. Patrick* edited by C. H. H. Wright (1889), *Lyra Anglicana, Psalms and Hymns,* and *Hymns Ancient and Modern.* H
All Things Bright and Beautiful 57
I Bind unto Myself Today (para.) 1
Jesus Calls Us o'er the Tumult 580
Once in Royal David's City 161

Alexander, James Waddell (b. Mar. 13, 1804, Hopewell, VA; d. July 31, 1859, Sweetsprings, VA) was educated at Princeton University (then, College of New Jersey, 1820) and Seminary (1827); was pastor in Charlotte County, VA, then at First Presbyterian Church, Trenton, NJ, and Fifth Avenue Presbyterian Church, New York City, and others; taught at College of New Jersey and Princeton Theological Seminary; wrote for *The Princeton Quarterly Review* and produced over 30 books including translations (1861).
O Sacred Head, Now Wounded (tr.) 221

Alford, Henry (b. Oct. 7, 1810, Bloomsbury, London, England; d. Jan. 12, 1871, Canterbury) was born into a family which boasted five consecutive generations of clergymen, and was educated at Ilminster Grammar School and Trinity College, Cambridge; in 1833 was ordained in the Church of England, and served as curate to his father at Winkfield, Wiltshire, and then at Ampton; became vicar of Wymeswold, Leicestershire, in 1835, where he served for 18 years; was appointed dean of Canterbury

Cathedral, 1857; is best remembered for his four-volume commentary on the Greek New Testament; wrote many original hymns and translations which are found in *Psalms and Hymns* (1844), *Poetical Works* (1853), and *The Year of Praise* (1867). H
Come, Ye Thankful People, Come 381
Ten Thousand Times Ten Thousand 746

Alington, Cyril Argentine (b. Oct. 23, 1872, Candlesby, Lincolnshire, England; d. May 16, 1955, St. Leonards, Hertfordshire) was educated at Trinity College, Oxford (BA, 1893 and MA, 1895) and Marlborough School (DD, 1917); was ordained in the Church of England (deacon, 1899 and priest, 1901) and served at Eton College (1899-1908, and as headmaster, 1917-33), Shrewsbury School (1908-16), and was dean of Durham (1933-51); a scholar and author, was preacher for Oxford and chaplain to the King.
Good Christians All, Rejoice 255

Allen, Chester G. (b. 1838; d. 1878), despite the popularity of his tune JOYFUL SONG, remains basically unknown; contributed to several compilations of Sunday School songs, such as *Bright Jewels*, 1869, collaborating with William Bradbury, W. H. Doane, W. F. Sherwin, and others. H
JOYFUL SONG 96

Allen, David Jonathan (b. 1941); see **Fettke, Thomas E.**

Allen, George Nelson (b. Sept. 7, 1812, Mansfield, OH; d. Dec. 9, 1877, Cincinnati, OH) graduated

from Oberlin College in 1838 and stayed on as a member of the faculty, teaching music and geology until his retirement in 1865; initiated the choral and instrumental programs of music education which later developed into the famed Oberlin Conservatory of Music; contributed to several music collections and compiled *The Oberlin Social and Sabbath School Hymn Book* (1844). H
MAITLAND 658

Alleyne, Ellen; see **Rossetti, Christina**.

Ambrose of Milan (b. 340, Treves, or Trier, Germany; d. Apr. 4, 397, Milan, Italy) has been called the "Father of Church Song" because he wrote simple and expressive hymns which congregations could sing; the son of a Roman nobleman, was educated in preparation for a civil career; became governor of northern Italy and lived in Milan; at the death of the Arian bishop, was elected to the post by public acclamation at the age of 34, even though he had not yet been baptized; gave his fortune to the poor and to the church and became a staunch supporter of the Nicene (trinitarian) faith. H
O Splendor of God's Glory Bright 27
Savior of the Nations, Come (attr.) 138

Anderson, Fred R. (b. Dec. 27, 1941, San Bernardino, CA), son of a locomotive engineer and a secretary, graduated from Whittier High School, CA (1959), University of Arizona (in music, 1961), University of Redlands, CA (BMus in voice, 1963), Princeton

Theological Seminary (MDiv, 1973 and DMin, 1981); was pastor, Pompton Valley Presbyterian Church (1973-78) and Pine Street Presbyterian Church, Harrisburg, PA (since 1978); authored *Singing Psalms of Joy and Praise* (Westminster Press, 1986).
Amid the Thronging Worshipers (rev.) 340
I Love You, Lord, My Strength, My Rock (para.) 349

Andrew of Crete (b. *c.* 650, Damascus; d. *c.* 732, probably at Hierisuusu, near Mitylene, Greece) was mute from his birth until a miraculous healing while taking communion at age seven; a monk at age 20 or earlier, represented the Patriarch of Jerusalem, Theodore, at the Sixth Council of Constantinople (680-81) where he debated theological questions on the nature of Christ; stayed in Constantinople for a period of time and was appointed archbishop of the Isle of Crete by Philippus Bardesanes (between 711-714) and again went to Constantinople in 712, a session which condemned the sixth ecumenical council; later returned to the Orthodox position; led the defense of Crete against the invasion of Arabs; is credited with many hymns and may have written several long canons—poems of faith and biblical stories. Not all of the biographical information on St. Andrew is reliable, since myths have become attached to his name.
Christian, Do You Struggle (attr.) 660

Andrews, Mark (b. Mar. 21, 1875, Gainsborough, Lincolnshire, England; d. Dec. 10, 1939, Montclair, NJ) studied at

Westminster Abbey with John Thomas Ruck; emigrated to the United States (1902) where he was organist and choirmaster in Montclair, NJ, and an active composer of songs, and choral and instrumental music.
ANDREWS 25

Anselm, [*St.*] (b. 1033 or 1034, Aosta, Lombardy; d. 1109) was influenced by Lanfranc, famed theologian; was ordained in the Monastery of Bec (1060) and became Archbishop of Canterbury (1093); is credited with writing several hymns to the Virgin Mary; is called the founder of scholasticism.
Prayer of Aspiration to Christ 123

Antes, John (b. Mar. 24, 1740, Frederick, PA; d. Dec. 17, 1811, Bristol, England) was a Moravian minister and missionary, a watchmaker by profession, and a musician by avocation; was one of 11 children, the son of Heinrich Antes, who was active in buying land in Pennsylvania and Northern Carolina for Moravian settlements; received early training, academically and musically, in his own home, where his father had established a school for boys; in 1764 was "called for service" to the international headquarters of the Moravians in Herrnhut, Saxony; was ordained a Moravian minister in 1769 and spent the following 12 years in Egypt, the first American missionary to serve in that country; in 1781 left Egypt, spent two years in Germany and settled in Fulneck, England; composed a number of choral works for four voices and instruments, and some chorales, and is acclaimed as one of the finest early American composers of

sacred music.   H
MONKLAND (adapt.) 59

Arne, Thomas Augustine (b. Mar. 12, 1710, London, England; d. Mar. 5, 1778, London) was educated at Eton for a career in law, but chose music instead for his profession; won recognition as a composer when he wrote the music for Joseph Addison's *Rosamond*, 1733; wrote operas (e.g., *Comus*, 1738 and *Alfred*, 1740) and oratorios (*Abel*, 1744 and *Judith*, 1733); is remembered mostly for the song "Rule, Brittania!" (the finale from *Alfred*); was among the first to introduce women's voices into choral writing.
                                                       H
ARLINGTON 668

Åström, Johan (b. Nov. 20, 1767, Gäfle, Sweden; d. Feb. 29, 1844) lived during the "golden age of Swedish hymnody"; left fatherless at age 13, received early training from his mother, attended Uppsala University (MPh, 1794); ordained in 1793, was briefly pastor of the German church in Norrköping, then appointed rector (1805) at Tuna and Stavby and at Sigtuna and Altuna (1821); assisted Archbishop Johan Olof Wallin in preparing the *Swenska Psalm-Boken* [Swedish Psalmbook] (1816-18), and the 1819 edition contained 11 of his hymns and several translations.   H
In Heaven Above (adapt.) 682

Atkins, George (flourished 19th century); no information has been located.
Brethren, We Have Met to Worship 802

Atkinson, Frederick Cook (b. Aug. 21, 1841, Norwich, England; d. Nov. 30, 1896, East Dereham) was a boy chorister at Norwich Cathedral and later was assistant to Dr. Zechariah Buck, organist and choirmaster; received his MusB degree at Cambridge in 1867; served as organist-choirmaster at St. Luke's Church in Manningham, Bradford, at Norwich Cathedral (1881-85), and St. Mary's Parish Church in Lewisham (after 1886); composed a number of (Anglican) services, anthems, hymn tunes, and instrumental pieces.   H
MORECAMBE 290

Augustine   [Aurelius Augustinus] of Hippo (b. Nov. 13, 354, Thagaste, Algeria; d. Aug. 28, 430, Hippo) was the son of a pagan father and Christian mother; educated at Carthage (*c.* 372) in philosophy, Manicheism, and rhetoric, and then at Rome (382), was an orator in Milan; became a Christian (386) and was baptized by St. Ambrose (387); returned to Africa where he established a retreat community at Thagaste (until 391), then came to Hippo until his death; wrote extensively, including a treatise on music, *De musica*, influenced by Plato, and defending a complex theory of rhythm: *bene modulandi scientia* (the art of measuring well).
Jerusalem, My Happy Home (attr. or influenced) 675

Ausserlesene   Catholische Geistliche Kirchengesänge (1623), a widely used Catholic hymnal, was printed in Cologne [Kîln] by Peter von Brachel.
LASST UNS ERFREUEN 259, 328, 356

Avery, Richard (b. Aug. 26, 1934, Visalia, CA) is one-half of the "Avery and Marsh" team of contemporary worship specialists; was educated at the University of Redlands, CA (BA, 1956) and Union Theological Seminary (MDiv, 1960), and has had training in piano and choral music; in 1960 became pastor of First Presbyterian Church, Port Jervis, NY; has written over 50 hymns and contributed articles to *Presbyterian Life* (now *AD*), *Colloquy*, and other magazines; is co-founder with Donald Marsh   of   Proclamation Productions, Inc., and says of their creative activity: "We work together in producing our hymns, both writing words and music and exchanging ideas and self-criticism through the process."   H
O How Blest Are the Poor in Spirit, BEATITUDES 603

Babcock, Maltbie Davenport (b. Aug. 3, 1858, Syracuse, NY; d. May 18, 1901, Naples, Italy), a member of a socially prominent family, was educated at Syracuse University and Auburn Theological Seminary, where he excelled as a student, as an athlete, and also as a musician; was ordained a minister in the Presbyterian Church and served briefly in Lockport, NY, for 14 years in Baltimore, MD, and, in 1899, was called to the Brick Presbyterian Church of New York City; died in 1901 while on a trip to the Holy Land, so his pastorate at the Brick Church was cut short after 18 months; left a literary heritage which was collected and published shortly after his death, *Thoughts for Every-day Living* (1901).   H
This Is My Father's World 384

Bach, Johann Sebastian (b. Mar. 21, 1685, Eisenach, Germany; d. July 28, 1750, Leipzig) was undoubtedly the greatest musical genius to give his principal attention to music for the church; was born into an extremely gifted musical family, trained at Ohrdruf and Lüneburg, and served for a short time as organist at Arnstadt and Mählhausen; spent his professional and creative life in three cities: Weimar (1708-17), Anhalt-Cöthen (1718-23), and Leipzig (1723-50), where he was cantor of St. Thomas' Church; wrote almost 300 church cantatas and a great quantity of music for organ; provided settings for the Lutheran chorales which have been presented as models of four-part harmonization in music theory classes; was a devout Christian and felt himself divinely called to provide the best music for the worship of God. H

Recent discovery of Bach's Bible provides evidence in his own hand of his deep and personal faith in Christ.
ERMUNTRE DICH (harm.) 158
JESU, MEINE FREUDE (harm.) 119
PASSION CHORALE (arr.) 221
WACHET AUF (harm.) 131

Backstrom, Carl Ernest (b. May 2, 1901, Stockholm, Sweden; d. Sebring, FL, May 2, 1984) emigrated to the United States in 1907 with his parents, and the family became active in the Swedish Pilgrim Church (Covenant), Brooklyn, NY; after completing high school, worked at the Chase National Bank for four years; attended the University of Pennsylvania, Philadelphia, and North Park Theological Seminary, Chicago, graduating in 1926; took graduate work at the University of Chicago and was ordained in 1928; served Mission Covenant churches in Lincoln, NE, Lanyon, IA, and Youngstown, OH; in 1948 transferred his membership to the Presbyterian church; retired to Chautauqua, NY. H
Thanks to God for My Redeemer (trans.) 380

Bain, James Leith (b. c. 1840 [or 1860, according to some sources], Scotland; d. Sept. 19, 1925, Liverpool, England) was known as "Brother James," mystic and poet, sometime orthodox, agnostic, or divine healer; formed Brotherhood of Healers and published in that genre, 1906 and later; for some of his works, used the pseudonym "James MacBeth"; in later life worked in the slums of Liverpool.
BROTHER JAMES' AIR 615

Baker, Henry (b. June 16, 1835, Nuneham Courtney, Oxford, England; d. Feb. 1, 1910, Wimbledon, Surrey), the son of an Anglican clergyman, studied civil engineering at Winchester and Cooper's Hill and spent many years in India, building railroads; at the encouragement of John B. Dykes, completed a degree in music at Exeter College, Oxford (1867); released many of his tunes in W. Garrett Horder's *Worship Song*, 1905. H
QUEBEC 121

Baker, Henry Williams (b. May 27, 1821, Vauxhall, London, England; d. Feb. 12, 1877, Monkland, Hertfordshire) has a secure place in hymn history as the "editor-in-chief" of the historic *Hymns Ancient and Modern* (1861);

was educated at Trinity College, Cambridge, ordained in 1844 and appointed vicar at Monkland, near Leominster, and remained there until his death; served for almost 20 years as chairman of the committee which compiled *Hymns Ancient and Modern*; although criticized as "authoritarian and ruthless" in his editing decisions, no doubt profoundly influenced hymn singing of the Anglican communion, and thus all of Christendom, for almost a century.　　　　H
Of the Father's Love Begotten (trans.) 145
STEPHANOS 453

Baker, Theodore (b. June 3, 1851, New York, NY; d. Oct. 13, 1934, Dresden, Germany) first prepared for a career in business, but turned to music; studied at the University of Leipzig, where his doctoral dissertation (1881) was the first serious study of the music of the American Indian; returned to America in 1891 and served as literary editor and translator for G. Schirmer, Inc.; published *A Dictionary of Musical Terms* (1895) and the still-used *Baker's Biographical Dictionary of Musicians* (1900 and 1905); retired in 1926 and lived in Germany until his death.　　　　H
Christ, We Do All Adore Thee (English adaptation) 816
Lo! How a Rose E'er Blooming (trans.) 163
We Gather Together (trans.) 376

Barham-Gould, Arthur Cyril (b. 1891, England; d. Feb. 14, 1953, Tunbridge, Kent) was educated at Ridley Hall, Cambridge, and ordained in the Church of England in 1927; served as curate at All

Souls, Langham Place (1927-29) and Holy Trinity, Brompton (1932-36); was vicar of St. Paul's, Onslow Square (1936-53).　　　　H
ST. LEONARDS 560

Baring-Gould, Sabine (b. Jan. 28, 1834, Exeter, England; d. Jan. 2, 1924, Lew-Trenchard, Devon) was the oldest son of the squire of a large estate, and spent much of his early life in France and Germany; received degrees at Clare College, Cambridge, and was active in choir schools; was ordained in the Church of England in 1865 and served as curate of Horbury, writing many hymns for the children of the Horbury Bridge Mission; in 1881 inherited the family estate and was appointed rector of Lew-Trenchard, serving as country squire and parson for the rest of his life; published a great variety of books on travel, mythology, poetry, fiction, history, and theology; was a pioneer collector of English folk songs and collaborated in publishing *Songs and Ballads of the West* (1889-91), *A Garland of Country Song* (1894), and *English Folk-songs for Schools*.　　　　H
Onward Christian Soldiers 748

Barker, Kenneth Paul (b. Aug. 26, 1955, Dallas, TX), son of the editor of the NIV Study Bible, is active in church music (pianist, trumpeter, choir director, worship leader); was educated at Lake Highlands High School, Dallas, TX, West Texas State University (BMusEd, with honors), and University of North Texas (MMusEd); was trumpet instructor at Midwestern State University, Wichita Falls, TX (1978-79); was music editor, then director of

music publications, Word, Inc. (1979-89); has in print over a million copies of his anthems and numerous arrangements; served on editorial committee for *The Hymnal for Worship & Celebration* (Word, 1986).
AMY 760

Barnard, John (b. Apr. 20, 1948, Harrow, Wealdstone, Middlesex, England) was educated at Selwyn College, Cambridge (1966-69); was Deputy Headmaster of John Lyon School, Harrow, and Director of Music at St. Alban's Church, North Harrow; has published tunes and arrangements in *Hymns for Today's Church* and *Carols for Today* (Oxford University Press).
HARROW WEALD 6
ANGEL VOICES (desc.) 407

Barnby, Joseph (b. Aug. 12, 1838, York, England; d. Jan. 28, 1896, Westminster, London) as a boy was a precocious chorister at York Minster, becoming an organist at 12 and a choirmaster at 14; received the Fellowship degree at the Royal Academy of Music; was organist and choirmaster at St. Andrew's Church, Well Street, London, and then at St. Anne's, Soho, where the singing of the Bach passion music became an annual event; was appointed musical advisor to Novello and Company, 1861; served as precentor of Eton College (1875-92), resigning to become principal of the Guildhall School of Music; composed an oratorio, many anthems and liturgical services; edited five hymnbooks: *The Hymnary* (1872), *The Congregational Mission Hymnal* (1890), *The Congregational Sunday School*

Hymnal (1891), *The Home School Hymnal* (1893), and co-edited *The Cathedral Psalter* (1873); had his 246 hymn tunes published in one volume in 1897, after his death. H
LAUDES DOMINI 99
O PERFECT LOVE (also called SANDRINGHAM) 388
ST. ANDREW 476

Barnes, Edward Shippen (b. Sept. 14, 1887, Seabright, NJ; d. Feb. 14, 1958, Idyllwild, CA) was educated at Yale (BA) where he studied with Horatio Parker; studied in Paris with Vincent d'Indy and others; was organist-choirmaster at churches in New York City, Philadelphia, and Santa Monica, CA; wrote works for organ, choir, and congregation.
GLORIA (arr.) 152

Bateman, Christian Henry (b. Aug. 9, 1813, Wyke, Yorkshire, England; d. July 27, 1889, Carlisle) studied for the Moravian ministry and briefly pastored in that fellowship; served three Congregational churches in Scotland and England and then was ordained in the Church of England; from 1869 to 1894 was curate of St. Luke's, Jersey, vicar of All Saints', Childshill, and finally curate of St. John's, Penymyndd; edited *Sacred Melodies for Sabbath Schools and Families* (1843) (which had wide use in the Sunday Schools of Scotland) and *The Children's Hymnal and Christian Year* (1872). H
Come, Christians, Join to Sing 108

Bates, Katharine Lee (b. Aug. 12, 1859, Falmouth, MA; d. Mar. 28, 1929, Wellesley, MA) wrote one of our best known national hymns, "America the Beautiful"; was edu-

cated at Wellesley College, graduating in 1880; taught high school for six years, then joined the faculty at Wellesley and eventually became head of the English department; was the author or editor of approximately two dozen works and compilations, including a textbook, *History of American Literature* (1908), and volumes of poetry: *America the Beautiful* (1911), *Fairy Gold* (1916), and *The Pilgrim Ship* (1926).   H
America, the Beautiful 418

Batya, Nomi (b. Apr. 21, 1961); no other information has been located.
King of Kings and Lord of Lords 110

Bauchspiess; see **Gastorius, Severus**.

Baughen, Michael Alfred (b. June 7, 1930, Borehamwood, Hertfordshire, England), son of a steel company manager, was educated at Bromley County Grammar School and London University (BDiv); was Vicar and then Rector, All Souls Church, Langham Place, London (1970-82) and Bishop of Chester (1982 to the present); is writer or composer of over 35 hymns, songs, and hymn tunes; founded the Jubilate Group in the early 1960s to write and publish hymns for youth.
Because He Died and Is Risen, ISRAELI (arr.) 588
GLORIOUS COMING 280
Spirit of the Living God (vs. 2) 297
UPLIFTED EYES 81

Baumbach, Adolph (b. 1830, Germany; d. Apr. 3, 1880, Chicago, IL) received his musical education in his native Germany; emigrated to the United States in his mid-20s and taught piano and organ in Boston, and later in Chicago; published a collection of sacred music for quartet choirs.   H
[Unnamed tune] 819

Bayly, Albert Frederick (b. Sept. 6, 1901, Bexhill-on-Sea, Sussex, England; d. July 26, 1984, Chichester) for a brief period trained to be a ship builder at the Royal Dockyard School at Portsmouth, then received the BA degree from London University and studied for the ministry at Mansfield College, Oxford (1928); served Congregational churches in Northumberland, Lancashire, and Essex; writing hymns since 1945, published five books of verse, among them, *Again, I Say, Rejoice* (1967), *Rejoice Always* (1971), and *Rejoice in God* (1977); has also written several missionary pageants and librettos for W. L. Lloyd Webber's cantatas; was honored as a fellow of Westminster Choir College, Princeton, NJ (1968); died as the result of a heart attack while returning from the annual conference of The Hymn Society of Great Britain and Ireland.
      Bayly expressed his personal goals in an article in *The Hymn* (1969); he wished to write hymns "in small words and phrases, without bathos, without clichés, with a feeling for the proper dignity of worship and the rhythmic quality needed in a hymn . . . sensitive to the knowledge and modes of life and expression of his time."
Fire of God, O Sacred Flame 301
Lord of All Good 645
Lord, Whose Love in Humble Service 426
What Does the Lord Require? 571

Beck, John Ness (b. Nov. 11, 1930, Warren, OH; d. June 25, 1987, Columbus, OH) attended public schools in Warren, and at Ohio State University (BA and BSc in English, 1952); worked one year in student activities at State College of Washington; served two years in the army where he began arranging for music groups and returned to Ohio State University for degrees in composition (BMus and MA in music); was faculty member at Ohio State School of Music, but left to become manager and owner of retail sheet music store; later, was founder-partner of Beckenhorst Press (with John Tatgenhorst) and choir director at University Baptist Church, Columbus, OH; was a composer, conductor, theater director (including dance), artist, and teacher; died of cancer in Riverside Methodist Hospital.
BECK 437

Bede [also **Beda, Baeda**], **The Venerable** (b. 673, Tyne, now Jarrow County, Durham, England; d. May 26, 735, Jarrow) was writer of books on history, poetry, philosophy, possibly a tract on music, and at least 12 hymns; an orphan, was educated by Benedictines Biscop and Celfrith at the Wearmouth and Jarrow monasteries (near his place of birth); was ordained by St. John of Beverly (deacon, 691 or 692, and priest, *c.* 702); lived at the monasteries as a scholar, saying he "found it sweet either to learn, or to teach, or to write"; was called "Venerable" which indicates the first degree of Sainthood.
A Hymn Of Glory Let Us Sing 259

Beethoven, Ludwig van (b. Dec. 16, 1770, Bonn, Germany; d. Mar. 26, 1827, Vienna, Austria) brought "sonata form" classical music (symphonies, quartets, concerti, and sonatas) to full maturity; was born into a musical family and showed talent at a very early age; at 12, studied with Neefe, court organist, and became acquainted with the works of J. S. Bach; visited Vienna at age 17 and met Mozart, and later studied briefly with Haydn; from the age of 28 suffered deafness, which was total by age 45; during his mature years, wrote his most outstanding sacred works: *Christ on the Mount of Olives* (*c.* 1803), *Mass in C*, (1807), and *Missa Solemnis* (1818-23); is credited with several hymn tunes that are adapted from his larger works.   H
ODE TO JOY 20, 254, 311, 720

Benjamin; see **Stassen-Benjamin, Linda**.

Bennard, George (b. Feb. 4, 1873, Youngstown, OH; d. Oct. 10, 1958, Reed City, MI) wrote "The Old Rugged Cross," for many years acknowledged to be America's favorite gospel song; as a child, was converted while attending a Salvation Army meeting in Lucas, IA; at age 16, became the sole support of his mother and four sisters, when his father died; moved his family to Illinois, later married and he and his wife became workers in the Salvation Army; after several years, resigned to become a Methodist evangelist, preaching mostly in the north-central part of the United States and in Canada; in later years lived at Reed City, MI, where a twelve-foot wooden cross memorializes his contribution to hymnody.   H

The Old Rugged Cross, OLD RUGGED CROSS 484

Benson, Louis Fitzgerald (b. July 22, 1855, Philadelphia, PA; d. Oct. 10, 1930, Philadelphia) was educated as a lawyer (University of Pennsylvania) and then at Princeton Theological Seminary (where his library is housed); was ordained (1886) and pastored Church of the Redeemer, Germantown, Philadelphia, PA; lectured and wrote on hymnology at Princeton; edited *The Book of Common Worship of the Presbyterian Church in the United States* and several hymnals; authored his major work, *The English Hymn: Its Development and Use* (1915).
O Sing a Song of Bethlehem 192
For the Bread Which You Have Broken 772

Berg, Carolina V. Sandell (b. Oct. 3, 1832, Fröderyd, Sweden; d. July 27, 1903, Stockholm), who signed her hymns "L.S." (Lina Sandell), has been called "the Fanny Crosby of Sweden"; was very frail as a girl and spent a great deal of time with her father, who was a Lutheran minister; experienced a miraculous healing from paralysis at age 12; published several periodicals and 650 hymns during her lifetime; married C. O. Berg in 1867; credited much of the popularity of her hymns to the music written for them by Oscar Ahnfelt, a "spiritual troubadour" of his day; with the financial help of the famous Swedish soprano, Jenny Lind, published many of her songs in Ahnfelt's *Andeliga Sänger* (1850). H
Children of the Heavenly Father 84
Day by Day and with Each Passing

Moment 367

Bernadone, Giovanni; see **Francis of Assisi.**

Bernard of Clairvaux (b. *c.* 1090, Les Fontaines, near Dijon, France; d. Aug. 20, 1153, Clairvaux) was born of noble parents, and became one of the religious and political leaders of the 12th century; inherited his deeply religious nature from his mother, who died when he was 14; was educated at Chatillon, but rejected the life of worldly success; about 1112, entered the Cistercian monastery at Citeaux, bringing about 29 companions with him; in 1115 founded the monastery of Clairvaux, and remained as abbot until his death; was a very effective preacher, a brilliant theologian and wise counselor of both popes and kings; was canonized in 1174. H
Jesus, the Very Thought of Thee (attr.) 112
Jesus, Thou Joy of Loving Hearts (attr.) 121
O Sacred Head, Now Wounded (attr.) 221

Bernard of Cluny (12th century, Murles or Morlas, France) has often been confused with Bernard of Clairvaux; is believed to have been born of English parents, and to have lived as a monk at the abbey of Cluny during the time when Peter the Venerable was abbot (1122-56); in the cloistered setting, wrote *De Contemptu Mundi*, a satire of some 3000 lines condemning the follies and vices of his day and extolling the joys of the life immortal, and dedicated the work to Peter the Venerable. H
Jerusalem the Golden 754

Berthier, Jacques (b. June 27, 1923, Auxerre, Burgundy, France), son of musical parents, was first taught by his mother and his father, Paul Berthier, who was a composer and student of d'Indy; attended the César Franck School, Paris (1944); began writing for the Taizé Community through the influence of Gelineau; became organist, St. Ignace, Paris (1961); continues as resident composer at the Taizé Community while also writing for traditional Catholic liturgical services.
GLORIA III 825
JESUS, REMEMBER ME 822

Bianco da Siena (b. Anciolina, Tuscany; d. 1434, Venice) joined a religious order of unordained men (Jesuits in the Augustinian style) in 1367 and wrote a number of *laude spirituali* (vernacular devotional texts, set to "secular" tunes, which thrived in extra-liturgical gatherings but were not permitted to be used in official medieval worship).
Come Down, O Love Divine! 304

Bible, Ken (b. Mar. 7, 1950, Cincinnati, OH) graduated from Reading (OH) High School (valedictorian), College-Conservatory of Music at the University of Cincinnati, OH (BMus in composition, 1972, plus graduate work there in the same field); served as minister of music at Price Hill Church of the Nazarene, Cincinnati (1971-74), instructor in God's Bible School, Cincinnati (1973-75), and music editor at Lillenas Publishing Company (1975-77) where he became director (1977-90); since 1990, has continued part-time at Lillenas and writes music; wrote poetry under

the pseudonym of Peter Ellis.
Lavish Love, Abundant Beauty 68

Bickersteth, Edward Henry (b. Jan. 25, 1825, Islington, England; d. May 16, 1906, London), the son of a clergyman, was educated at Trinity College, Cambridge, and ordained in the Church of England in 1848; was curate and rector of several small parishes, and vicar of Christ Church, Hampstead (1855-85); was briefly Dean of Gloucester, and finally Bishop of Exeter, 1885-1900; authored 12 books, including *Psalms and Hymns* (1858), based on his father's *Christian Psalmody* (1833 and 1841); made a significant contribution to hymn singing in the *Hymnal Companion to the Book of Common Prayer* (1870, rev. 1877), which was adopted by most evangelical Anglican churches; wrote mostly subjective poems and John Julian says that his best works were his hymns for private devotion.   H
Peace, Perfect Peace 598

Blackmon, Alma Montgomery (b. July 25, 1921, Washington, DC), with the encouragement of her musical parents, at age five began publicly playing piano; from age 10 was organist and singer at First Seventh-day Adventist Church, Washington, DC; later was director of the Dupont Park Choir; served as assistant to conductors Robert Shaw and Howard Mitchell; taught in the Washington public schools, then Oakwood College, Huntsville, AL; directed several traveling choirs; lives in Memphis, TN, but has suffered twice from cancer.
GIVE ME JESUS (arr.) 551

Blanchard, Ferdinand Q. (b. July 23, 1876, NJ; d. Mar. 4, 1968, Cleveland, OH) graduated from Newlin (MA) High School, Amherst (BA), and Yale Divinity School; was awarded the DD from Amherst and Oberlin; was minister and then minister emeritus, Evangelical Congregational Church (1915-68) and National Moderator (1942-44); was chairman of the merger of Congregational and Evangelical Reformed Churches and National Chair of the Commission of Interchurch Affairs (1944-50).
Before the Cross of Jesus 215

Blankenship, Lyle Mark (b. May 11, 1943, Chicago, IL) was educated at Oklahoma Baptist University, Shawnee, OK (BM) and the University of Texas (MM); has been minister of music in Oklahoma City, OK, Fletcher, OK, Luling, TX, Belton, TX, Midland, TX, and in the North Phoenix Baptist Church, Phoenix, AZ (1972-74); has been music editor for the Baptist Sunday School Board since 1974.
As We Gather Around the Table, NORTH PHOENIX 770

Bliss, Philip Paul (b. July 9, 1838, Clearfield Co., PA; d. Dec. 29, 1876, near Ashtabula, OH) was born in a log house (the location marked by a plaque on route 255 near Hollywood, PA); as a boy worked on a farm and in lumber camps, and received his earliest musical training under J. G. Towner (father of D. B. Towner) and W. B. Bradbury; became an itinerant music teacher during the winter months and attended the Normal Academy of Music in Geneseo, NY, for several summers;

in 1864 sold his first song to Root and Cady, music publishers in Chicago, and was associated with them as a writer for four years; encouraged by D. L. Moody to become a singing evangelist, was associated with Major D. W. Whittle in revival meetings beginning in March 1874, traveling extensively throughout the midwest and south; on his way to an engagement in Moody's Tabernacle in Chicago, was killed trying to rescue his wife from the fire following a train wreck near Ashtabula, OH; wrote many successful gospel songs for George F. Root's collections; helped to compile *The Charm, a Collection of Sunday School Music* (1871), *Sunshine for Sunday Schools* (1873), *Gospel Songs, a Choice Collection of Hymns and Tunes, New and Old, for Gospel Meetings, Sunday Schools, Etc.* (1874), and (with Ira D. Sankey) *Gospel Hymns and Sacred Songs* (1875) and *Gospel Hymns No. 2* (1876).   H
Hallelujah! What a Savior, HALLELUJAH! WHAT A SAVIOR! 226
I Will Sing of My Redeemer 492
VILLE DU HAVRE 519
Wonderful Words of Life, WORDS OF LIFE 309

Blom, Frederick Arvid (b. May 21, 1867, near Enköping, Sweden; d. May 24, 1927, Uddevalla) as a young man received his certificate as a "chief mate" sailor; came to America in the 1890s and became an officer in the Salvation Army in Chicago; studied at North Park College and Seminary (1901-1904) and pastored a Mission Covenant Church; resigned his church in 1915, and later explained: "I drifted from God . . . and became embittered with myself, the world, and not the least with ministers who looked on me with suspicion because I was a member of the Socialist party"; was renewed in his faith at a Salvation Army meeting and appointed pastor of the Swedish Congregational Church, Titusville, PA; returned to Sweden in 1921 and served churches in the Swedish Covenant in Sater, Dalarna, and Rattvik; in 1926 became pastor of the Baptist Church in Uddevalla; evidently wrote a number of hymns but only this one is commonly known in America.

This information was supplied to Hustad by J. Irving Erickson, author of *Twice-Born Hymns* (Chicago: Covenant Press, 1976) and chairman of the commission which prepared *The Covenant Hymnal* (1973).   H
He the Pearly Gates Will Open 683

Boberg, Carl Gustaf (b. Aug. 16, 1859, Mönsterås, Sweden; d. Jan. 7, 1940, Kalmar), the son of a ship-yard carpenter, was a sailor for several years; was converted at the age of 19, attended a Bible school in Kristinehamn and was a lay preacher in his hometown for two years; was editor of the weekly *Sanningsvittnet* (Witness of the Truth) from 1890-1916; represented his district as a member of the Swedish parliament for 13 years between 1912 and 1931; published several books of poetry and many hymns, and was a member of the committees which compiled the first two hymnals of the Swedish Covenant.   H
How Great Thou Art (Swedish text attr.) 21

Bock, Fred (b. March 30, 1939,

Great Neck, NY), educated at Ithaca College (BSMusEd, 1960) and University of Southern California (MA, 1962), with an honorary doctorate, Taylor University (DHL, 1986); was founder and director for the music publishing division of Word, Inc., founder of Gentry Publications (educational music), founder of Fred Bock Music Company (church music), and owner of The Raymond A. Hoffman Company (elementary school operettas); for 14 years, was Minister of Music at Bel Air Presbyterian Church in Los Angeles, and is now at Hollywood Presbyterian Church; served as secretary of the Church Music Publishers Association and board member of Writers' Advisory Board of ASCAP; is editor of *Hymns for the Family of God* (Paragon, 1976) and *Worship His Majesty* (1987); lives in Tarzana, CA.
SYMPHONY (arr.) 700

Bode, John Ernest (b. Feb. 23, 1816, St. Pancras, London, England; d. Oct. 6, 1874, Castle Camps, Cambridge) was educated at Eton, Charterhouse and Christ Church, Oxford, where he was the first to receive the Hertford Scholarship (1835); served seven years as tutor in his college; was ordained in 1843 and became rector at Westwell, Oxfordshire, in 1847; in 1860 was appointed rector at Castle Camps, Cambridgeshire, and remained there until his death; delivered the Bampton Lectures at Oxford in 1855; was a gifted poet whose published works include *Ballads from Herodotus* (1853), *Short Occasional Poems* (1858), and *Hymns for the Gospel of the Day, for Each Sunday and the Festivals of Our*

Lord (1860).   H
O Jesus, I Have Promised 648

Boe, Vigleik Engebretson (b.
Mar. 30, 1872, Odda, Hardanger,
Norway; d. June 8, 1953,
Northfield, MN) was influenced by
devout parents (son of a lay preacher); immigrated to America in 1892;
studied at St. Olaf College (1895-
99) and United Church Seminary,
St. Paul, MN (1900-03); pastored in
Lutheran churches in Finley, ND
(1903-09, 1917-41), Staten Island,
NY (1909-15), and Osakis, MN
(1915-17); taught voice at St. Olaf
(1898-99); was a participating editor of the *Concordia Hymnal*
(Augsburg, 1932) which includes
two of his hymns.
To a Virgin Meek and Mild 139

Bohemian Brethren; see **All
Glory Be to God on High**.
MIT FREUDEN ZART 8, 50.

Bojaxhiu, Agnes Gonxha; see
Teresa [Mother].

Bonar, Horatius (b. Dec. 19,
1808, Edinburgh, Scotland; d. July
31, 1889, Edinburgh) is considered
to be the most eminent of the
Scottish hymnwriters, and was a
preacher of renown; received his
education at the University of
Edinburgh and at the age of 30 was
ordained at Kelso and put in charge
of the North Parish; in the ecclesiastical struggle of 1843, was actively involved in organizing the Free
Church of Scotland; pastored the
Free Church in Kelso, and
Chalmers Memorial Church,
Edinburgh (1866-83), and was
moderator of the General
Assembly, 1883; was keenly interested in the Second Coming of

Christ and edited the *Journal of
Prophecy* for many years; was also
one of the editors of *The Border
Watch*, the official publication of
the Free Church; wrote many
hymns, of which 100 have been
used in English-language hymnals;
wrote and/or published *Songs for
the Wilderness* (1843), *The Bible
Hymn Book* (1845), *Hymns, Original
and Selected* (1846), *Hymns of Faith
and Hope* (1857), *The Song of the
New Creation* (1872), and
Communion Hymns (1881).   H
Blessing and Honor and Glory 257
Glory Be to God the Father 11
Here, O My Lord, I See You 783
I Heard the Voice of Jesus Say 506
I Lay My Sins on Jesus 464
Not What These Hands Have Done
476

Book of Common Prayer, The
(1559) was restored by Elizabeth I
(following brief Latin use under the
Catholic Queen Mary) and by
Charles, after Cromwell; is the title
of all worship books in Anglican
churches worldwide, the Episcopal
Church (USA), and the Reformed
Episcopal Church (USA); is the
source of many of the enduring
liturgical prayers still in wide use in
other Christian traditions (with
denominational variations also in
numerous editions). The title
appeared with the first volume
(under Edward VI), edited by
Cranmer (1549).
A Baptism Prayer 189
A Litany of Thanksgiving 378
A Prayer for Confidence 80
A Prayer for Missionaries (Scottish
Book, 1912) 744
A Prayer for Unbelievers 727
A Responsive Song of Praise 321
Concerning the Scriptures 314
Prayer for Ascension Day 265

Prayer [Collect] for Trinity Sunday 7
Prayer of John Chrysostom 625

Borthwick, Jane Laurie (b. Apr. 9, 1813, Edinburgh, Scotland; d. Sept. 7, 1897, Edinburgh) was the eldest daughter of James Borthwick, manager of the North British Insurance Office, Edinburgh; traveled widely on the Continent and was encouraged by her father to use her linguistic gifts in translating; with her sister, Sarah (Mrs. Eric) Findlater, translated German hymns into English and published *Hymns from the Land of Luther* (4 eds., 1854-62); signed most of her hymns "H.L.L." (the initial letters of the words in the title of the collections); has been rated as second only to Catherine Winkworth in her German-English translations. H
Be Still, My Soul (trans.) 530

Bortniansky, Dimitri Stepanovich (b. Oct. 28, 1751, Glukhov, Ukraine; d. Oct. 10, 1825, St. Petersburg, Russia), Russian nationalistic composer, is known for his operas; was educated in Moscow and influenced by Italian opera (studied in Italy, 1768-79, financed by Catherine the Great); directed the Imperial Chapel Choir, for which he wrote liturgical music.
ST. PETERSBURG 779

Bourgeois, Louis (b. *c.* 1500-10, Paris, France; d. *c.* 1561 or shortly thereafter, Paris), a follower of John Calvin, left France and moved to Geneva in 1541, where he was cantor and choirmaster at St. Peter's Church; in 1542 was appointed by Calvin to be musical editor of the Geneva Psalter; in the successive editions (until 1557), provided suit-

able melodies for the psalms, some adapted from German and French secular sources, and some undoubtedly original tunes; wrote a book of music instruction, *La Droit Chemin de Musique* (1550); returned to Paris in 1557 and his last known activity was the publishing of a collection of harmonized psalm tunes in 1561. H
GENEVA 42 132
OLD HUNDREDTH (composed or adapted) 317, 808, 809
RENDEZ A DIEU (attr.) 32
SINGLE [AMEN] 820

Bowater, Christopher Alan (b. May 2, 1947, Birmingham, England) attended the Royal College of Music, London, where he earned several degrees; travels as director of Creative Ministries, offering workshops and song seminars in the United States, Canada, Malaysia, Australia, Singapore, and Europe; has recorded a number of albums, including "The Highest Honor" (Word).
RACHEL 102

Bowring, John (b. Oct. 17, 1792, Exeter, England; d. Nov. 23, 1872, Exeter) was born of Puritan stock and was affiliated with the branch of Unitarianism which believed that "Christ is all we know of God"; left school at the age of 14 to assist his father in the manufacture of woolen goods; traveled widely and gained proficiency in German, Dutch, Spanish, Portuguese, and Italian before he was 16; became one of the world's great linguists, able to converse in 100 languages, and to read some 200; had a keen interest in politics and became editor of the radical *Westminster Review* (1825); was a member of

Parliament and held several posts in foreign service, including the governorship of Hong Kong; was knighted by Queen Victoria in 1854; wrote many original poems and hymns and published *Matins and Vespers, with Hymns and Devotional Pieces* (1823) and a second collection, *Hymns as a Sequel to the Matins* (1825).   H
In the Cross of Christ I Glory 209

Bradbury, William Batchelder (b. Oct. 6, 1816, York, ME; d. Jan. 7, 1868, Montclair, NJ) was a pioneer in music for children, in the church and in the public school; as a young man, moved with his family to Boston, where he attended the Boston Academy of Music and sang in the Bowdoin Street Church choir under the direction of Lowell Mason; served as organist in the First Baptist Church, Brooklyn, and in 1841 became organist at the First Baptist Church, New York City; organized free singing classes, similar to those conducted by Mason in Boston, which resulted in the teaching of music in the New York City public schools; spent two years with his family in Europe (1847-49), studying in Leipzig with Ignaz Moscheles and Moritz Hauptmann; returning to the United States, devoted his time to teaching, conducting musical conventions, composing and editing; in 1854, with his brother founded the Bradbury Piano Company, later united with Knabe; from 1841 to 1867 published 59 music collections, including *The Young Choir* (1841), *The Psalmodist* (1844), *The Choralist* (1847), *The Mendelssohn Collection* (1849), *Psalmista* (1851), *The Shawm* (1853) and *The Jubilee* (1858).   H

BRADBURY 522
HE LEADETH ME 635
JESUS LOVES ME 470
OLIVE'S BROW 220
SOLID ROCK 517
SWEET HOUR 623
WOODWORTH 445

Brady, Nicholas (b. Oct. 25, 1659, Bandon, Cork County, Ireland; d. May 20, 1726, Richmond, Surrey, England) attended Westminster, Christ Church, Oxford University (1671), and returned to Ireland to Trinity College, Dublin (BA, 1685 and honorary BDiv and DDiv degrees); was ordained (1688) and served at Kinaglarchy, Cork, then Killmyne and Drinah; sent to London by the citizens of Bandon to represent their William of Orange grievances, preached and was appointed lecturer at St. Michael's, then the church of St. Catherine (1691), where he collaborated with Nahum Tate on the *New Version of the Psalms of David* (1696); until his death, he pastored at Richmond, Surrey.
As Longs the Deer for Cooling Streams (source) 331

Brahms, Johannes (b. May 7, 1833, Hamburg, Germany; d. Apr. 3, 1897, Vienna, Austria), son of a farmer and artisan, early performed on piano (by 1843) and continued as a performer and composer for all of his life—one of the few composers whose name is familiar to mass audiences; stylistically, is both Romantic and Classical, with influences from folk music in Hungary (refugees came through Hamburg) and from the active musical world of contemporary Europe (such as the Schumanns, Hoffmann, Joachim, Liszt) and the United

States; was court musician for the Prince of Lippe-Detmold (1854-59), director of the *Singakademie*, Vienna (1862-63), and director of the *Gesellschaft der Musickfreunde* (1872-75), with the balance of his time spent composing and performing—touring from homes in Hamburg (1859-62), Vienna (1862-97), Meingingen (from 1881), and from various summer homes; composed prolifically in nearly every medium.
SYMPHONY 700

Breck, Carrie E. (b. Jan 22, 1855, Walden, VT; d. Mar. 27, 1934, Portland, OR) spent her youth in Vermont, lived briefly in New Jersey and then moved to Portland, OR, where she remained for the rest of her life; was devoted to her family (a husband, Frank A. Breck, and five daughters); was a deeply committed Christian and life-long Presbyterian; according to Phil Kerr (*Music in Evangelism*), wrote more than 2000 poems, many while performing her household duties, though "she could not carry a tune and had no natural sense of pitch, but . . . had a keen sense of rhythm and loved music."   H
Face to Face 684

Bridge, Basil Ernest (b. Aug. 5, 1927, Norwich, Norfolk, England), son of a government officer and teacher, attended City of Norwich School and Cheshunt College, Cambridge University (MA); was ordained (1951) and served United Reformed Churches at Knowle, Warwickshire (1951-55), Bond Street and Abbots Road, Leicester (1955-74), Groby, Leicestershire (1974-76), and Stamford and Rourne, Lincolnshire (1976-89); is currently minister of the United Reformed Church, Harrold, Bedford, England.
God the Father, Name We Treasure 766

Bridges, Matthew (b. July 14, 1800, Malden, Essex, England; d. Oct. 6, 1894, Sidmouth, Devon) grew up in the Church of England, but came under the influence of the Oxford Movement, and, in 1848, like John Henry Newman and others, became a Roman Catholic; lived a number of years in Canada, but returned to England and died while at the Convent of the Assumption in Devon; besides his historical and political contributions, published *Hymns of the Heart* (1847) and *The Passion of Jesus* (1852); was introduced as a hymnist to American congregations by Henry Ward Beecher in the latter's *Plymouth Collection*, 1855.   H
Crown Him with Many Crowns (st. 1, 4) 92

Bridges, Robert Seymour (b. Oct. 23, 1844, Walmer, Kent, England; d. Apr. 21, 1930, Boar's Hill, Berkshire), poet laureate of England, was a scholar, musician and physician; was educated at Eton and Corpus Christi College, Oxford, and studied medicine at St. Bartholomew's Hospital in London; gave up medical practice in 1882 because of ill health and devoted his time to literature and hymnody; published many works, including *Shorter Poems* (1873), *Yattendon Hymnal* (1895-99), *A Practical Discourse on Some Principles of Hymn-Singing* (1899), *About Hymns* (1911), *Collected Essays* (1927-36), *Testament of Beauty*

(1929) and *Poetical Works* (1929-30); received an honorary LLD degree from the University of Michigan in 1924 and was awarded the Order of Merit in 1929.　H
Ah, Holy Jesus (trans. into English) 231

Brierley, Michael (b. July 29, 1932, Leicester, England) attended Bromsgrove School and Lichfield Theological College (BD with honors, London); is married, with two sons; has served parishes at Stourport on Severn (1960-62), Dines Green, Worcester (1962-71), Eastham and Rochjon (1971-79), and is currently Incumbent of St. Luke, Cradley Heath (1979-); is composer of several hymn tunes published by the Twentieth Century Light Music Group of the Church of England.
CAMBERWELL 266

Briggs, George Wallace (b. Dec. 14, 1875, Nottingham, England; d. Dec. 30, 1959, Hindhead, Surrey), according to Erik Routley (*Companion to Congregational Praise*), was the most prolific of the 20th-century's successful hymn writers; was educated at Emmanuel College, Cambridge, served as curate for a brief time in Wakefield, York, and then was a chaplain in the Royal Navy, 1902-09; was appointed vicar of St. Andrew's, Norwich, and in 1918, rector of Loughborough; from 1927-34, was canon of Leicester Cathedral, and from 1934 until his retirement in 1956, canon of Worcester; was one of the founders of The Hymn Society of Great Britain and Ireland; wrote many hymns and prayers for use in English schools and they appeared in *Songs of Praise*

(1925), *Prayers and Hymns for Use in Schools* (1927), *Little Bible* (1931), *Prayers and Hymns for Junior Schools* (1933), and *Songs of Faith* (1945). H
God Has Spoken by His Prophets 311

Brokering, Herbert F. (b. May 21, 1926, Beatrice, NE), according to the current entry in The Hymn Society files (courtesy of Mary Louise Van Dyke of the Dictionary of American Hymnology), graduated from Wartburg College (Waverly, OH), the University of Iowa (MA in Child Psychology), and Trinity (Lutheran) Seminary (Columbus, OH); after serving as a parish pastor in Pennsylvania, New York, and Texas, was national director for confirmation education of the American Lutheran Church; since 1970, has been a free lance educator and writer; has authored 33 books and collaborated with 40 composers, including Dave Brubeck, the composer of "Christ Carnival," an Easter cantata, for which he wrote the libretto; co-directed the film "Where Luther Walked"; is active in the Lutheran World Federation, the World Council of Churches, and the national office of the American Lutheran Church; is a traveling consultant, preacher, and writer.
Earth and All Stars 357

Brooke, Stopford Augustus (b. Nov. 14, 1832, Glendoen, Donegal, Ireland; d. Mar. 18, 1916, Ewhurst, Surrey, England) refused to copyright any of his hymns, saying "they are free, as I think all hymns ought to be, for the use of anyone who may care for them"; was educated at Kingstown, Kidderminster and at Trinity College, Dublin,

where he was awarded the Downs Prize and the Vice-Chancellor's Prize for English verse; took holy orders in London in 1857, and was appointed curate at St. Matthew's, Marylebone, and later at St. Mary Abbotts, Kensington, after which he became chaplain to the British embassy in Berlin; returned to London after two years, and resumed his ministry at the Chapel of St. James, York Street; in 1867 became chaplain to Queen Victoria, but in 1880 resigned from the Anglican Church to become an independent; published a volume of sermons and many books on English literature, besides *Riquet of the Tuft* (1880), *Poems* (1888), and *Christian Hymns* (*c.* 1878), edited for his own congregation.   H
Let the Whole Creation Cry 40

Brooks, Charles Timothy (June 20, 1813, Salem, MA; d. June 14, 1883) graduated from Harvard College and Divinity School (1832 and 1835); was ordained a Unitarian minister and served churches in Maine, Vermont, and Rhode Island.
God Bless Our Native Land (trans.) 421

Brooks, Phillips (b. Dec. 13, 1835, Boston, MA; d. Jan. 23, 1893, Boston) was one of America's greatest preachers in the last half of the 19th century, gifted in appearance and in personality; attended the Boston Latin School, and in 1855 received his AB degree from Harvard; studied for the ministry at the Episcopal Theological Seminary in Alexandria, VA, and was ordained in 1859; served the Church of the Advent in Philadelphia and three years later

became rector of Holy Trinity Church; in 1869 became rector of Trinity Church, Boston, where he served for 22 memorable years; had many of his sermons published, and they are still read widely; in 1885 received the DD degree from Oxford; had memorized 200 hymns as a child, and frequently quoted them in his sermons; in 1891 was consecrated Bishop of Massachusetts, but had served for only two years when death took him.   H
O Little Town of Bethlehem 154, 155

Brooks, Reginald Thomas (b. June 30, 1918, Wandsworth, London, England; d. Oct. 12, 1985) graduated from Mansfield College, Oxford University; was ordained a Congregational minister and served churches at Skipton and Bradford; later worked with the BBC's Religious Broadcasting division in radio and television.
Thanks to God Whose Word Was Spoken 313

Brownlie, John (b. Aug. 3, 1857, Glasgow, Scotland; d. Nov. 18, 1925, Crieff, Perth) received his schooling at the University of Glasgow and the Free Church College in the same city; served as assistant and later (1890) became minister in charge of the Free Church in Portpatrick, Wigtownshire; was active in the community's educational institutions and in 1901 became chairman of the governors of Stanrear High School; wrote many hymns and translations from Latin and Greek, which are found in *Hymns of Our Pilgrimage* (1889), *Zionward and Hymns of the Pilgrim Life* (1890),

Pilgrim Songs (1892), *Hymns from East and West* (1898), *Hymns of the Greek Church* (four series, 1900-06), and *Hymns from the East* (1907); also wrote the handbook *Hymns and Hymn-Writers of the Church Hymnary* (1899).   H
The King Shall Come (trans.) 277

Brubeck, Dave (b. Dec. 6, 1920, Concord, CA) is son of Howard "Pete" Brubeck, cattle rancher, and Elizabeth Ivey, pianist and music teacher (and brother of Howard, also a musician); "absorbed" Mexican folk music as a result of being born in a Spanish California town and raised on a cattle ranch that had been a Mexican land grant; studied at Ione (CA) High School, University of the Pacific, Stockton, CA, (BMus), and Mills College, Oakland, CA, with Darius Milhaud; was awarded honorary doctorates from University of the Pacific, Fairfield University, University of Bridgeport, Mills College, and Niagara University; served in Europe during World War 2 with Patton (1942-46); is married (Iola, below) with six children—son Chris (electric bass and trombone) is now a member of the Dave Brubeck Quartet; is known for his jazz piano work (the Dave Brubeck Quartet) and the large number of outstanding jazz musicians and groups he has assembled since 1946; is a widely traveled performer (who has given concerts for every president in the White House since Kennedy and performances from Australia to Europe to the Soviet Union); made many recordings and received many honors; authored several sacred publications, including *Light in the Wilderness, Beloved Son, Voice of the Holy Spirit, Gates of*

Justice (a civil rights commemorative), *Truth is Fallen* (with rock band), *la Fiesta de la Posada, Pange Lingua,* and *Mass to Hope.* Brubeck says, "The sacred pieces are particularly important to me. I'll keep on in that direction."
POSADA 179

Brubeck, Iola Whitlock (b. Aug. 14, 1923, Corning, CA) was educated at Shasta Union High School, Redding, CA, and University of the Pacific (BA); is editor or author of texts for husband Dave's cantatas and oratorios.
God's Love Made Visible 179

Buchanan, Annabel Morris (b. Oct. 22, 1888, Groesbeck, TX; d. Jan. 6, 1983, Paducah, KY) was a graduate of the London Conservatory of Music, Dallas, and studied privately with Emil Liebling, William C. Carl, Cornelius Rybner and others; taught music in Texas and Oklahoma and at Stonewall Jackson College in Abingdon, VA (now part of King College, Bristol, TN); did extensive research in the folk music of Appalachia and helped organize the annual White-Top Folk Festivals in Virginia; edited *Folk-Hymns of America*, published in 1938.   H
LAND OF REST (harm.) 200, 675

Budry, Edmond Louis (b. Aug. 30, 1854, Vevey, Switzerland; d. Nov. 12, 1932, Vevey) studied theology with the "Faculté libre" in Lausanne, Switzerland; for eight years was pastor at Cully and in 1881 went to the Free Church in Vevey, Switzerland, remaining for 35 years; wrote the words of over 60 chorales and many have

appeared in French hymnals; was active in translating German, Latin, and English hymns, and in writing poetry, to the end of his life.   H
Thine Is the Glory 251

Bullinger, Ethelbert William (b. Dec. 15, 1837, Canterbury, England; d. June 6, 1913, London) was a choirboy at Canterbury Cathedral and studied music with John Pyke Hullah and William H. Monk; was trained for the ministry at King's College, London, and became an accomplished Greek and Hebrew scholar, receiving an honorary DD degree from the Archbishop of Canterbury in 1881; composed several hymn tunes, but BULLINGER is one of the few that are still in use.   H
BULLINGER 524

Burleigh, Harry Thacker (b. Dec. 2, 1866, Erie, PA; d. Sept. 11, 1949, Stamford, CT) was one of the first black musicians to achieve professional success in "serious music" in America; as a boy, sold papers, ran errands, worked as a houseboy, and in the summers was a deck steward on a Great Lakes passenger boat; sang in the choir in St. Paul's Cathedral, Erie, PA; won a scholarship at the National Conservatory of Music, New York City, where he later taught for several years; was selected from some 60 applicants to be baritone soloist in the choir of St. George's Church (Episcopal) and remained for 52 years; received an honorary MA (Atlanta University) and DMus (Harvard University); was a charter member of the American Society of Composers, Authors, and Publishers; composed many songs and anthems,

and arranged negro spirituals.   H
McKEE (arr.) 695

Burns, Edward Joseph (b. May 16, 1938, Nelson, Lancashire, England) is the son of a father who was a bus conductor and a mother who was a housewife and hotel domestic; attended Baines Grammar School, Poulton-le-Fylde, Lancashire (1949-55), Liverpool University (BS in Chemistry, 1955-58), St. Catherine's College, Oxford (MA, Theology); has served parishes in St. Andre, Leyland, St. Peter, Burnley, St. James, Chorley; was Rural Dean of Preston, and is currently Vicar of Fulwood, Christ Church (since 1975); has written several hymns.
O God, Who Gives to Humankind 399
We Have a Gospel to Proclaim 714

Butler, Aubrey Lee (b. June 29, 1933, Noble, OK), called "Pete" by his friends, received his BMus degree at Oklahoma Baptist University and the MSM at Southern Baptist Theological Seminary, Louisville, KY; has served Southern Baptist churches as minister of music in Oklahoma City (1952-55), Middletown, KY (1955-57), Madill, OK (1957-60), Ada, OK (1960-83), and Prairie Village, KS (1983-86); in 1983, joined the faculty of Midwestern Baptist Theological Seminary, Kansas City, MO; served as president of Baptist Musicians of Oklahoma and as a member of the Board of Directors for the Baptist General Convention of Oklahoma; is a member of ASCAP; has written several hymn tunes, 14 anthems, and a cantata, *Something Wonderful*; served on the committee for *The Baptist Hymnal*

(1991). H
ADA 505
MADILL 718

Byrne, Mary Elizabeth (b. July 2, 1880, Dublin, Ireland; d. Jan. 19, 1931, Dublin) received her education at the Dominican Convent in Dublin and the University of Ireland; was an expert in the historic Gaelic language and employed by her country's Board of Intermediate Education as a researcher; contributed to the *Old and Mid-Irish Dictionary* and *Dictionary of the Irish Language*, and assisted in compiling the *Catalogue* of the Royal Irish Academy. H
Be Thou My Vision (trans.) 532

Caldbeck, George Thomas (b. 1852, Waterford, Ireland; d. Jan. 29, 1918, Epsom, Surrey, England) received training in England at the National Model School in Waterford and at Islington Theological College; wanted to be a missionary but ill health prevented his being accepted, so he returned to Ireland to become a schoolmaster and evangelist; in 1888 went back to London and became an independent itinerant preacher. H
PAX TECUM 598

Caldwell, Mary E. (b. Aug. 1, 1909, Tacoma, WA) is the daughter of E. S. Glockler and Alice Steinbach, and married to Philip G. Caldwell; was educated at the University of California at Berkeley (ABMus) and did graduate study in Munich, Germany, and at Julliard; received honors in college and from ASCAP, ACDA, and other arts societies; has over 200 choral compositions published; has served as organist/choirmaster in Dutch

Reformed, Baptist, Presbyterian, and Community churches, and is now organist emeritus at San Marino Community Church.
God Is in This Place 791

Calvisius, Sethus (b. Feb. 21, 1556, Gorsleben, near Sachsenburg, Thuringia, Germany; d. Nov. 24, 1615, Leipzig) was educated at Frankenhausen, Magdeburg, the University of Helmstedt (1579), and the University of Leipzig (1580); was Kantor at *Paulinerkirche*, Leipzig, then at Schulpforta, where he taught theory and composed; returned to Leipzig (1594) as Kantor of the *Thomaskirche*, and, briefly, at the university church; in addition to extensive music composition, including hymns and sacred choral works, he wrote on chronology and astronomy; published his main music theory book, *Melopoeia*, in 1592.
NUN KOMM, DER HEIDEN HEILAND (harm.) 138

Cameron, Catherine Arnott (b. Mar. 27, 1927, St. John, New Brunswick), daughter of a New York minister, Dr. John Sutherland Bonnell, is married to Dr. Stuart Oskamp; holds the BA from McMaster University and both the MA and PhD from the University of Southern California; a naturalized United States citizen, has been professor of social psychology at the University of La Verne, CA, since 1971.
God, Who Stretched the Spangled Heavens 54

Campbell, Thomas was evidently a native of Sheffield, England, who compiled a collection of 23 of his original tunes called *The*

Bouquet (1825). No additional information is available.
SAGINA 473

Carlson, Nathaniel (b. Apr. 17, 1879, Gothenburg, Sweden; d. Aug. 2, 1957, Minneapolis, MN) attended the Free Church Bible School, Chicago, and Northwest Bible College, Storm Lake, IA; a pastor in the Evangelical Free Church, was editor of *Chicagobladet* for several years; wrote many original hymns, both words and music, and translated many songs from Swedish into English; compiled three editions of *Songs of Trust and Triumph* (1929-32). H
He the Pearly Gates Will Open (trans.) 683

Carmichael, Ralph Richard (b. May 27, 1927, Quincy, IL), born in a minister's home, began to study violin at age four; graduated from high school and attended Southern California College, Costa Mesa, but, according to his own report, "failed college"; served as minister of music at Calvary Assembly, Inglewood, CA, beginning in 1946, and at Temple Baptist Church, Los Angeles, 1954; long active in professional music in Hollywood, wrote the musical scores for Billy Graham films: *Mr. Texas, For Pete's Sake, The Restless Ones* and *His Land*; is founder (1964) and President of Lexicon Music, Inc., and Light Records, producers of sacred music and recordings; has written some 200 songs in many styles and co-authored several popular trend-setting youth folk musicals, including *Tell It Like It Is, Natural High*, and *New Wine*; published *The New Church Hymnal* (1976). See his autobiography, *He's*

Everything to Me (Word, 1986). H
The Savior Is Waiting, CARMICHAEL 446

Carter, Russell Kelso (b. Nov. 18, 1849, Baltimore, MD; d. Aug. 23, 1926, Catonsville, MD) during his lifetime was successively a professor, a sheep rancher, a minister, an author and publisher, and a physician; as a student was an excellent athlete; graduated in the first class of the Pennsylvania Military Academy in 1867 and returned as professor (chemistry, natural science, civil engineering, and mathematics) for a number of years; in 1873-76 raised sheep in California; in 1887 was ordained into the Methodist ministry and became very active in the Holiness camp meetings; published widely in the areas of mathematics, science, and religion, as well as several novels; assisted A. B. Simpson in compiling *Hymns of the Christian Life* (1891) for use in churches of the Christian and Missionary Alliance; contributed some 68 original tunes and 52 poems to this hymnal; later in life, studied medicine and became a practicing physician in Baltimore. H
Standing on the Promises, PROMISES 306

Carter, Ruth (b. Aug. 22, 1900, Upper Clapton, London, England; d. Nov. 4, 1982, Clacton-on-Sea, Essex) is the daughter of James and Ethel Carter, lawyer and housewife; attended private school and Westhill Training College; was a schoolteacher and active in the United Reformed Church of Good Easter, Chelmsford, Essex.
For Your Holy Book We Thank You 316

Caswall, Edward (b. July 15, 1814, Yately, Hampshire, England; d. Jan. 2, 1878, Edgbaston, Birmingham), born in the vicarage at Yately, was educated at Marlborough and Brasenose College, Oxford; was ordained (Anglican Church) in 1839, and appointed curate of Stratford-sub-Castle, near Salisbury; during the Oxford movement, developed great interest in the Roman ritual and in 1847, resigned his pastorate and was received into the Roman Catholic Church; after his wife's death in 1849, became a priest and entered the Oratory of St. Philip Neri at Edgbaston, under Cardinal Newman; a prolific writer, is best known for *Lyra Catholica* (1849) which contained 197 translations of Latin hymns from the *Roman Breviary* and other sources.   H
Jesus, the Very Thought of Thee (trans.) 112
When Morning Gilds the Skies (trans.) 99

Cennick, John (b. Dec. 1, 1718, Reading, Berkshire, England; d. July 4, 1755, London), the son of Quaker parents, grew up in the Church of England; came under the influence of John Wesley and gave up his profession of surveyor to join the Methodist movement; was appointed teacher at Kingswood School, Bristol, and became a lay preacher; because of doctrinal differences, left the Wesleys and was associated with George Whitefield, but later joined the Moravian Brethren and was ordained by them (1749); as a Moravian preacher, traveled widely in Germany and Ireland; published *Sacred Hymns for the Children of God* (1741-42) and *Hymns to the Honor*

of Jesus Christ (1754) among other works.   H
Jesus Comes with Clouds Descending (influenced) 283

Chambers, Brent (b. Jan. 16, 1948, Napier, New Zealand) was educated at Colonso High School, Napier (1965), and at Bible College of New Zealand, Henderson, Auckland (1972-74); writes songs "full-time" but, in his words, "paints houses for a living"; with David and Dale Garrett, travels as a worship leader; has published more than 20 of his songs since 1976.
In the Presence of Your People, CELEBRATION 19

Chandler, John (June 16, 1806, Witley, Godalming, Surrey, England; d. July 1, 1876, Putney), son of Rev. John F. Chandler, was educated at Corpus Christi College, Oxford University (MA 1827); was ordained (1831) and followed his father as Vicar at Witley (1837); freely translated older hymns and wrote prose, including several books of meditations.
On Jordan's Bank the Baptist's Cry 136

Chapman, J. Wilbur (b. June 17, 1859, Richmond, IN; d. Dec. 25, 1918, Jamaica, Long Island, NY) was educated at Lake Forest (IL) University and Lane Theological Seminary; was ordained to the Presbyterian ministry and served as a pastor (Albany, NY, Philadelphia, and New York City) for almost 20 years; in 1905 became an evangelist, and for more than 10 years traveled extensively throughout the world, assisted by Charles M. Alexander, well known evangelistic singer and choir director; was the

first director of the Winona Lake (IN) Bible and Chautauqua Conference and was instrumental in starting similar conferences at Montreat, NC, and Stony Brook, Long Island, NY; in 1917 was elected moderator of the General Assembly of the Presbyterian Church, USA; published eight books and wrote a number of hymn texts. H
Our Great Savior 89
One Day 196

Charles, Elizabeth Rundle (b. Jan. 2, 1828, Tavistock, Devonshire, England; d. Mar. 28, 1896, Hampstead Heath, near London), the daughter of a Member of Parliament and wife of a lawyer, was educated at home with private tutors; wrote popular historic fiction as well as biographies of Luther, Wesley, and others; wrote hymns and translated others from Latin, German, and Swedish, many of which were published in *The Voice of Christian Life in Song* (1858, 1864).
A Hymn of Glory Let Us Sing (tr.) 259

Chatfield, Allen William (b. Oct. 2, 1808, Chatteris, Cambridge, England; d. Jan. 10, 1896, Much-Marcle, Hertfordshire) received training at Charterhouse School and Trinity College, Cambridge, where he achieved top class honors; ordained in 1832, was vicar at Stotfold, Bedford, and later at Much-Marcle, Hertfordshire, until his death; translated into Greek some hymns, the litany, the Te Deum, and other parts of the English Church offices; published *Songs and Hymns of the Earliest Greek Christian Poets, Bishops and Others,*

translated into English Verse (1876). H
Lord Jesus, Think on Me (trans.) 462

Cherry, Edith Adeline Gilling (b. Feb. 9, 1872, Plymouth, Devonshire, England; d. Aug. 29, 1897, Plymouth). The *Anglican Hymn Book* (1965) provides these dates; no additional biographical information on Cherry has been located, but she may be in the Keswick (England) theological tradition.
We Trust in You, Our Shield 573

Chisholm, Thomas Obediah (b. July 29, 1866, Franklin, KY; d. Feb. 29, 1960, Ocean Grove, NJ), educated in a small country school, became the teacher of that school at age 16; at 21, became associate editor of the weekly newspaper, *The Franklin Favorite*; in 1893 was converted under the ministry of Dr. Henry Clay Morrison (founder of Asbury College and Theological Seminary, Wilmore, KY); moved to Louisville at the persuasion of Morrison and became editor of the *Pentecostal Herald*; was ordained a Methodist minister in 1903 and served a brief pastorate at Scottsville, KY; in poor health, moved his family to a farm near Winona Lake, IN; became an insurance salesman, moving to Vineland, NY, in 1916; retired in 1953 to the Methodist Home for the Aged, Ocean Grove, NJ; wrote over 1200 poems, of which 800 were published, and many set to music. H
Great Is Thy Faithfulness 60
Living for Jesus a Life That Is True 569

Chopin, Frederic (b. Feb. 22, 1810, Zelazowa Wola, Poland; d. Oct. 17, 1849, Paris, France), son of a Polish mother and French father, composed for piano; attended Warsaw Conservatory; performed in Austria and Germany (with a reputation beyond) and settled in Paris; was a contemporary of Victor Hugo, Balzac, Heine, Delacroix, Liszt, Berlioz, and a close friend of George Sand (Aurore Dudevant), and other influential romantics; died at 39 of tuberculosis. [HEAR OUR PRAYER] (attr.) 818

Chorley, Henry Fothergill (b. Dec. 15, 1808, Blackley, Lancashire, England; d. Feb. 15, 1872, Westminster, Middlesex), born of Quaker stock, was largely self-taught; started in a commercial career, but soon discovered that his real interest and gifts lay in music and literature; began to write for the *Athenaeum* and later became its musical editor, as well as music critic for *The Times*; produced many literary works, including *Music and Manners in France and Germany* (1841), *Pomfret* (1845), *Roccabella* (1859), and *The Prodigy* (1866); left a manuscript autobiography, *Memoir and Letters*, which was published posthumously in 1873.   H
God the Omnipotent! 427

Christiansen, Avis Marguerite Burgeson (b. Oct. 11, 1895, Chicago, IL; d. Jan. 14, 1985, Chicago) collaborated with D. B. Towner in her first two songs, included in *Tabernacle Praises* (1916), the first release of Tabernacle Publishing Company; lived her entire life in Chicago, and for more than 60 years wrote sacred texts which have been set to music by many different composers; was married to Ernest C. Christiansen, a vice president of Moody Bible Institute; a long-time member of Moody Church, has written hundreds of gospel hymns and two volumes of poetry.   H
Come, Come, Ye Saints 595

Christierson, Frank von (b. Dec. 25, 1900, Lovisa, near Helsinki, Finland) attended San Jose (CA) High School, Stanford University (BA, Psychology, 1923), and San Francisco Theological Seminary (BD, 1929), was awarded Distinguished Alumnus (1983), and Fellow of The Hymn Society; has served as youth director, First Presbyterian Church, San Luis Obispo (1924-26) and pastor, Calvary Presbyterian Church, Berkeley (1929-34), Trinity Presbyterian Church, North Hollywood (1934-61), Celtic Cross Presbyterian Church, Citrus Heights, CA (1961-66), and interim pastorates since his 1966 retirement; published a hymnal collection, *Make A Joyful Noise* (1987), and is represented in Presbyterian, United Church of Christ, and Latter-Day Saints hymnals.
Lord, We Bring to You Our Children 759

Chrysostom, [St.] John (b. 354, Antioch, Greece; d. Sept. 14, 407, Comana, Pontus), son of a Christian family in high Greek society, studied under Andragathius and Libanius, who were not Christians; as a hermit-monk, lived in a cave on Mt. Sylpios; was ordained in Antioch (368) and became patriarch of Constantinople (398), but was

exiled (404) because of his uncompromising sermons; wrote *On the Priesthood* (before 386) and numerous sermons. The name, Chrysostom, means "golden mouth."
Prayer of John Chrysostom 625

Clarke, Harry D. (b. Jan. 28, 1888, Cardiff, Wales; d. Oct. 14, 1957, Lexington, KY) was left an orphan at an early age and had a very hard life as a youth; with the help of a brother, got to London, then Canada, and finally the United States, where he was converted; studied at Moody Bible Institute, Chicago, IL, in the early 1920s and was active in composing and music publishing; for a number of years was songleader for evangelist Harry Vom Bruch, and also for Billy Sunday in the last years of that evangelist's ministry; later founded the Billy Sunday Memorial Chapel, Sioux City, IA, and was pastor until 1945; in later life was active in evangelistic work and conferences, with headquarters in Garard's Fort, PA, and finally in South Milford, IN; wrote many songs and choruses, both words and music, which appeared in his *Gospel Truth in Song* (3 vols.) and *Songs of Glory*; eventually sold his copyrights to Hope Publishing Company.   H
Into My Heart, INTO MY HEART 444

Clarke, Jeremiah (b. *c.* 1659-73, London, England; d. Dec. 1, 1707, London) was a boy singer with John Blow of the Chapel Royal; was organist at Winchester College (1692-95) and St. Paul's Cathedral (from 1695); was a contemporary of William Croft and Henry Purcell

(with some confusion—the "Purcell *Trumpet Voluntary* and *Trumpet Tune*" are Clarke's work); was a prolific composer, whose patron was Queen Anne; composed vocal, keyboard, other instrumental, and psalm music.
ST. MAGNUS (attr.) 268

Clarkson, Edith Margaret (b. June 8, 1915, Melville, Saskatchewan, Canada) was educated at Riverdale Collegiate Institute, Toronto Teachers' College, and University of Toronto; taught elementary school for 38 years (mostly in Toronto), retiring in 1973; was a member of Presbyterian churches in Canada, and active in InterVarsity Christian Fellowship, publisher of several of her early hymns; a prolific and talented writer, has published scores of articles and 15 books, eight in translations. Textbooks include *Let's Listen to Music* (1944) and *The Creative Classroom* (1958); early childhood: *Susie's Babies* (1960), *Our Father* (1961), *Growing Up* (1962); devotional prose: *The Wondrous Cross* (1966), *God's Hedge* (1968), *Grace Grows Best in Winter* (1972, 1985), *Destined for Glory* (1983); and poetry: *Clear Shining After Rain* (1962), *Rivers Among the Rocks* (1968), *Conversations with a Barred Owl* (1975), *All Nature Sings* (1986), *A Singing Heart* (1987), which contains her collected hymn texts and three essays on hymnody; has composed music for some of her own texts.
By Christ Redeemed (st.6) 789
For Your Gift of God the Spirit 285
God of Creation, All-Powerful 48
God of the Ages 363
Let Us Build a House of Worship 793

Let Us Draw Near! 631
More Love to Thee, O Christ (st. 3) 555
One Race, One Gospel, One Task 735
Sing Praise to the Father 9
The Battle Is the Lord's! 741
So Send I You 732
We Come, O Christ, to You 86

Clayton, Norman John (b. Jan. 22, 1903, Brooklyn, NY) first worked on a dairy farm, then spent a number of years in a New York City office, later participated with his father in the construction business; during the depression, worked with a commercial bakery; in the early 1940s, was invited by Jack Wyrtzen to be organist for the Word of Life rallies in New York City and remained on Wyrtzen's staff for 15 years; published his own songbooks, 1945-59, and then merged with the Rodeheaver Company, joining them as a writer-editor; is a Baptist and has been a church organist for 50 years.   H
My Hope Is in the Lord, WAKEFIELD 482
Now I Belong to Jesus, ELLSWORTH 503

Clayton, William (b. July 17, 1814, Penwortham, Lancashire, England; d. Dec. 4, 1879, Salt Lake City, UT) was converted to Mormonism in 1837 and spent three years in missionary work in his native England; immigrated to the United States in 1840 and settled in Nauvoo, IL, serving as city treasurer and clerk of the Nauvoo Temple; was Joseph Smith's private secretary until the Mormon leader's death in 1844; was one of the group of pioneers who traveled to Utah with Brigham Young, reaching the site of Salt Lake City in 1847; was a member of the Nauvoo Brass Band, and later played second violin in the Salt Lake Theatre orchestra.   H
Come, Come, Ye Saints 595

Clephane, Elizabeth Cecilia (b. June 18, 1830, Edinburgh, Scotland; d. Feb. 19, 1869, Melrose, Roxburghshire) was author of "The Ninety and Nine," spontaneously set to music by Ira D. Sankey in one of D. L. Moody's services in Britain (1874); was a daughter of the sheriff of Fife, and grew up in the Free Church of Scotland; was affectionately called "Sunbeam" because of her humanitarian concerns; wrote at least eight hymns, printed posthumously (1872-74) in *The Family Treasury*, a Free Church magazine.   H
Beneath the Cross of Jesus 216

Cloninger, Claire (b. Aug. 12, 1942, Lafayette, LA), daughter of Charles (attorney) and Virginia (psychologist) de Gravelles, attended Lafayette High School, Louisiana State University (three years), and University of Southwestern Louisiana (BA and MA); has taught elementary school, been an advertising copywriter, and freelance songwriter and author; has composed and written 15 choir musicals and over 100 hymns, anthems, and praise choruses for Word, Inc. (since 1986) including "You Gave Me Love," her first recorded song (B. J. Thomas, 1979) and "The Gift Goes On"; lives with her husband in a self-constructed log cabin on a river bank in Baldwin County, AL.
Good Shepherd, Take This Little Child 760
If My People's Hearts Are Humbled 719

Cober, Kenneth L. (b. July 12, 1902, Dayton, OH), the son of missionary parents, grew up in Puerto Rico; received his education at Bucknell University and Colgate Rochester Divinity School; was pastor of First Baptist Church, Canandaigua, NY, and Lafayette Avenue Baptist Church, Buffalo, NY; has served the state conventions of American Baptists in New York, Rhode Island, and Connecticut, and was executive director of the Division of Christian Education, American Baptist Convention, 1953-70; has written many books on Christian education, including *The Church's Teaching Ministry* (1964); was a member of the joint committee for the *Hymnbook for Christian Worship* (1970); now retired at Penney Farms in Florida. H
Renew Your Church, Her Ministries Restore 725

Coelho, Terrye (b. Aug. 6, 1952, Camp Roberts, CA) attended Arizona State University and was trained as a medical assistant at Anaheim, CA; since becoming a Christian in 1971, has written lyrics for many Christian songs; married to James Strom (1978), and with their four children, live in Walnut, CA.
Father, I Adore You, MARANATHA 4

Coffin, Charles (b. 1676, Buzancy, Ardennes, northern France; d. June 20, 1749, Paris) studied Latin at Duplessis College (Paris); was a faculty member of the College of Beauvais (1701), then principal; was rector of the University of Paris (1718), and then returned to Beauvais.

On Jordan's Bank the Baptist's Cry 136

Coffin, Henry Sloan (b. Jan. 5, 1877, New York, NY; d. Nov. 25, 1954, Lakeville, CT) graduated from Yale University, New College (Edinburgh), the University of Marburg, and Union Theological Seminary; served as pastor at Bedford Park Prebyterian Church and Madison Avenue Presbyterian Church, both in New York City; taught theology and hymnology at Union Theological Seminary and, in 1926, became president; was elected Moderator of the Presbyterian Church USA (1943); authored several books on theology, and co-edited *Hymns of the Kingdom of God* (1910).
O Come, O Come, Emmanuel (stanza 5) 133

Coffman, Samuel Frederick (b. June 11, 1872, near Dale Enterprise, Rockingham Co., VA; d. June 28, 1954, Vineland, Ontario, Canada) spent his early years in Elkhart, IN, graduated from Elkhart High School, and attended Moody Bible Institute, Chicago, in 1894-95 and 1897-98; was ordained to the ministry in Chicago (1895) and moved to Vineland, Ontario (1896) to serve the Moyer Mennonite Church; in 1903 was ordained to the office of bishop and served Mennonite congregations in the Niagara district; in 1907 organized the Ontario Mennonite Bible School and served as principal until retiring in 1952; was appointed to the music committee of the Mennonite General Conference in 1911 and served the publishing division as hymn editor until 1947; assisted in publishing *Church and*

Sunday School Hymnal Supplement (1911), *Life Songs* (1916), *Songs of Cheer for Children* (1928), and *Life Songs No. 2* (1938); wrote a number of hymns, and four were included in the Mennonite *Church Hymnal* (1927), for which he edited the hymns and assisted in editing the music.   H
We Bless the Name of Christ the Lord 761

Coleman, T. Brian (b. Apr. 25, 1920, Walsend-on-Tyne, England); no other information has been located.
OASIS 608

Collins, Christopher (b. July 15, 1943, Worthing, Sussex, England) attended Whitgift School, S. Croydon, and University of Sheffield (BA with honors); has been curate in Anglican churches in Manchester (1965-71) and Wolverhampton (1971-74), and Vicar of St. John's, Fairfield, Liverpool (1974-81) and St. John's, Tunbridge Wells, Kent (since 1981).
Angels Bright, Heavens High 323

Columbian   Harmony (Cincinnati, 1825); see **Moore, William**.
HOLY MANNA 54, 347, 802

Columbian   Harmony;   or Pilgrim's Musical Companion, compiled by Benjamin Shaw and Charles H. Spilman (Cincinnati, 1829).
NEW BRITAIN 502

Colvin, Thomas [Tom] S. (b. April 16, 1925, Glasgow, Scotland) was educated at Allen Glen's High School, Glasgow and Glasgow University (Engineering, 1945);

served with the Royal Indian Engineers in Burma and Singapore; left the military to study at Trinity College Divinity School of Glasgow University (1961); was licensed as a minister (1951), Youth Secretary of Iona Community (1951-54), and ordained, Church of Scotland (1954); was a missionary to Blantyre, Malawi (1954-59, then Nyasaland), District Pastor of the Presbyterian Church at Tamale, Northern Ghana (1959-64), with the Church of Central Africa Presbytery in Blantyre, Malawi (1967-74), minister of the United Reformed Church at Sydenham, London (1976-84), with the World Council of Churches in Zimbabwe (1984-87), and is currently consultant to the Christian Council of Malawi (since 1987); is active in relief, refugee, rehabilitation, and long-term settlement programs; has gathered African hymns (published privately in Africa and, in the United States, by Agape), including some of his own translation, authorship, and musical arrangement; is married to Patricia Margaret McGregor.
Jesu, Jesu, Fill Us with Your Love, CHEREPONI (adapt.) 436
His Battle Ended There (para.), NCHEU (adapt.) 253
Humbly in Your Sight 575

Common Prayer, The Book of; see **Book of Common Prayer**.

Conkey, Ithamar (b. May 5, 1815, Shutesbury, MA; d. Apr. 30, 1867, Elizabeth, NJ) first served as organist and choir director at Central Baptist Church, Norwich, CT; in 1850 moved to New York City, where he had a brilliant career as bass soloist in Calvary

Episcopal Church and also took part in many oratorio presentations; was soloist and conductor of the quartet-choir at Madison Avenue Baptist Church in New York City for six years preceding his death.   H
RATHBUN 209

Conner, Edric (b. Trinidad, British West Indies; d. Oct. 16, 1968), operatic baritone and recitalist, has sung in Paris, Prague, Basel, Budapest, and the United Kingdom; a boxer and cricket player as well as a performer, he compiled *The Edric Conner Collection of West Indian Spirituals and Folk Tunes* (1945).
Our Father 626

Conty, Sophie (b. Dec. 12, 1960, Versailles, France); no other information has been located.
King of Kings and Lord of Lords 110

Converse, Charles Crozat (b. Oct. 7, 1832, Warren, MA; d. Oct. 18, 1918, Highwood, NJ) received his general education at Elmira Academy (NY) and in early life was associated with William B. Bradbury and Ira D. Sankey in compiling and editing Sunday School songbooks, using the pseudonym "Karl Reden"; later turned to "serious" music and studied in Europe at the Leipzig Conservatory, where he became well acquainted with Franz Liszt and Louis Spohr; returned to America in 1859 and studied law at Albany University; along with his successful law practice in Erie, PA, was active as a musician and writer, with interests that included philosophy and philology; wrote string quartets,

cantatas, chorales, hymn tunes, and other music, under many pen names.   H
CONVERSE 622

Cook, Joseph Simpson (b. Dec. 4, 1859, Durham Co., England; d. May 27, 1933, Toronto, Canada), after early education in England, attended Wesleyan College of McGill University in Montreal, Canada; was ordained to the Methodist ministry and later served the United Church of Canada.   H
Gentle Mary Laid Her Child 156

Cooke, Oliver Mark (b. July 13, 1873, Little London, Kennington, Berkshire, England; d. Mar. 5, 1945, West Ashford, Kent), according to Gordon Taylor, in *Companion to the Song Book of the Salvation Army* (1989), was son of Mark Cooke, a farm laborer, and moved with his family to London, studied music, and received the London College of Music certificate for organ playing; learned to play a cornet at the Borough Salvation Army Corps, and later served as bandmaster at Peckham, and then as song leader, first at Nunhead, and then at Lewisham; contributed his first song to *The War Cry* (Oct. 1888) and wrote regularly for *The Musical Salvationist* during the next 50 years.
I Know a Fount, I KNOW A FOUNT 485

Copes, Vicar Earle (b. Aug. 12, 1921, Norfolk, VA) received the BA degree from Davidson College, NC (1940), and a Masters in Sacred Music (1944) and Bachelor of Divinity (1945) from Union Theological Seminary, NY; ordained a Methodist minister, was

minister of music at Highland Park Methodist Church, Dallas, TX (1946-49), professor of organ and church music at Hendrix College, Conway, AR (1949-56), and professor, Cornell College, Mount Vernon, IA (1956-58); edited *Music Ministry* (1958-67) and chaired the department of church music at Birmingham Southern College (1967-73); since 1973, has served at Christ United Methodist Church, Dayton OH, and Wright State University, and is active in The Hymn Society.
FOR THE BREAD 772
OLD 113th (harm.) 79
VICAR 434

Corner, David Gregor (b. 1585, Hirschberg, Silesia; d. Jan. 9, 1648, Göttweig), educated at Prague (MA, 1609), Graz and Vienna (1614), served as a Roman Catholic parish priest and then entered the Göttweig Monastery (1631); became rector of the University of Vienna, which also awarded him the ThD (1624); compiled the *Gross Catolisch Gesangbuch* (Nürnberg, 1625 and later editions) and *Geistliche Nachtigal* (1631), collections of hymns to Mary which included tunes which may have been gathered folk melodies.
OMNI DEI 841

Cory, Julia Bulkley Cady (b. Nov. 19, 1882, New York, NY; d. May 1, 1963, Englewood, NJ) was the daughter of J. Cleveland Cady, an architect and superintendent of Sunday School at the Church of the Covenant, New York City, where, as a youth, she wrote hymns and carols; attended Bearly School and Reynolds School, New York City; was a member of Brick Presbyterian Church, New York City, and First Presbyterian Church, Englewood, NJ; married Robert Haskell Cory (1911) and had three sons.
We Praise You, O God, Our Redeemer 377

Cosin, John (b. Nov. 30, 1594, Norwich, England; d. Jan. 15, 1672, Westminster) was trained at Caius College, Cambridge, took Holy Orders and became chaplain to the Bishop of Durham (1624); served as archdeacon of East Riding, Yorkshire (1625-35), master of Peterhouse, Cambridge (1635-39), and vice-chancellor of Cambridge University (1639-40); was deposed by the "Long Parliament," and served as chaplain to the exiled royal family in France; following the Restoration, was made bishop of Durham and supervised extensive renovation of the cathedral and its library; a liturgical scholar, compiled *Collection of Private Devotions in the Practice of the Ancient Church called the Hours of Prayer* (1627); assisted in the revision of *The Book of Common Prayer* (1662), which contains his translation of "Veni, Creator Spiritus." H
Come, Holy Ghost, Our Souls Inspire (trans.) 296

Cowley, John; see **Davis, Katherine K.**

Cowper, William (b. Nov. 15, 1731, Berkhampstead, Hertfordshire, England; d. Apr. 25, 1800, East Dereham, Norfolk) was son of John C. Cowper, rector of the Great Hertfordshire parish and chaplain to George II, and a descendant of John Donne through his mother; was regarded by many as the leading English poet of his

day, especially for his translation of Homer in 1791; studied law at Westminster School and was admitted to the bar in 1754, but did not practice law because he feared appearing before the House to stand examination; suffered periods of ill health and depression throughout his life, and dreaded public appearances; lived mostly under the guardianship of Rev. and Mrs. Morley Unwin; spent his 19 most productive years at Olney, where he collaborated with John Newton in compiling the historic *Olney Hymns* (1779) with 67 of his texts in the collection. An unknown author inscribed on his tombstone in St. Edmund's Chapel, "Here, to devotion's bard devoutly just, Pay your fond tribute to Cowper's dust! . . . Sense, fancy, wit, suffice not all to raise So clear a title to affection's praise; His highest honors to the heart belong; His virtues formed the magic of his song."
God Moves in a Mysterious Way 73
Heal Us, Immanuel, Hear Our Prayer 411
O for a Closer Walk with God 547
There Is a Fountain Filled with Blood 467

Cox, Frances Elizabeth (b. May 10, 1812, Oxford, England; d. Sept. 23, 1897, Headington) is known chiefly for her hymns translated from the German; was assisted in her choice of hymns by Baron Bunsen, Prussian ambassador, 1841-54; published *Sacred Hymns from the German* (1841) and *Hymns from the German* (1864). H
Sing Praise to God Who Reigns Above (trans.) 50

Crawford, Mary Babcock (b. 1909), daughter of Maltbie D. Babcock, author of "This is My Father's World." No other information has been located.
This Is My Father's World (st. 2) 384

Crocker, Elisabeth (b. Apr. 15, 1950, Torquay, Devonshire, England) attended Torquay Girls' Grammar School, Manchester University, Royal Manchester College of Music, and Royal College of Music, London (MusB, ARMCM, GRSM); has been a freelance singer, soloist, and teacher, singing seven years with the BBC Singers; as a student, began collaborating with Michael Baughen at Holy Trinity Church, Rusholme, Manchester.
UPLIFTED EYES 81

Croft, William (baptized Dec. 30, 1678, Nether Eatington, Warwickshire, England; d. Aug. 14, 1727, Bath) in early life wrote secular music, but later became one of England's most significant composers of church music; was a boy chorister in St. James' Chapel Royal and studied organ under John Blow; was organist of St. Anne's, Soho, London, for 11 years; served (first with Jeremiah Clark and later alone) as organist of the Chapel Royal; in 1708 followed John Blow as organist of Westminster Abbey and composer to the Chapel Royal; contributed many tunes to *The Divine Companion* (1707) and the *Supplement to the New Version* (1708) which mark the transition from the older "Genevan" to the newer style of English psalmody. H
HANOVER 103, 346, 712, 749
ST. ANNE 78, 342

Croly, George (b. Aug. 17, 1780, Dublin, Ireland; d. Nov. 24, 1860, Holborn, England), a graduate of Trinity College, Dublin, took Anglican Holy Orders in 1804 and served in Ireland for six years; at age 30, moved to London and devoted himself with great success to literary work, writing novels, historical and theological works, dramas, poetry, and satires; was editor of *The Universal Review* and contributed frequently to such publications as *Blackwood's Magazine* and *Britannia*; in 1835 became rector at St. Stephen's and St. Bene't Sherehog, Walbrook, and during his ministry there, published *Psalms and Hymns for Public Worship* (1854).   H
Spirit of God, Descend upon My Heart 290

Cropper, Margaret Beatrice (b. Aug. 29, 1886, Kendal, England; d. Sept. 27, 1980, Kendal), according to David W. Music, was daughter of Charles James Cropper; wrote much poetry, drama, biography, and literary criticism, including *Flame Touches Flame* (1949), *Sparks among the Stubble* (1955), and *The Life of Evelyn Underhill* (1959), and dramatic works *Christ Crucified* (1932) and *Country Cottage* (1939).
Jesus' Hands Were Kind Hands 412

Crosby, Fanny Jane (b. Mar. 24, 1820, Putnam Co., NY; d. Feb. 12, 1915, Bridgeport, CT) was the most prolific and influential writer of gospel songs in American history, and was also a concert singer, organist and harpist; at the age of six weeks, was blinded for life because of improper treatment of an eye infection; began writing verse at the age of eight; studied at the New York City School for the Blind and later taught there, attracting the attention of prominent individuals, including United States presidents, because of her poetic gift; married Alexander Van Alstyne, a blind musician, who also taught at the New York school; wrote texts for the minstrel songs and cantatas of George F. Root and others, publishing several books of secular verse: *A Blind Girl, and Other Poems* (1844), *Monteresy, and Other Poems* (1849), and *A Wreath of Columbia's Flowers* (1858); at age 44 began to write hymns, producing perhaps 8500 texts, many set to music by the day's leading gospel song composers and published, mostly by the Biglow and Main Company; was also active as a devotional speaker and a counselor until she was past 90 years of age; wrote two autobiographies. See the biographical study *Fanny Crosby* by Bernard Ruffin (United Church Press, 1976).   H
All the Way My Savior Leads Me 641
Blessed Assurance, Jesus Is Mine 514
Draw Me Nearer (I am thine, O Lord) 534
Near the Cross (Jesus, keep me near the cross) 549
Praise Him! Praise Him! 96
Rescue the Perishing 736
Redeemed, How I Love to Proclaim It 505
Tell Me the Story of Jesus 199
To God Be the Glory 72

Crossman, Samuel (b. *c.* 1624, probably in Bradfield Monachorum, Suffolk, England; d. Feb. 4, 1683, Bristol) was educated at Pembroke College, Cambridge University; served the All Saints

Church, Sudbury (Anglican), along with a Puritan ("Dissenters") congregation; losing an attempt to revise *The Book of Common Prayer* so it would be acceptable to both Anglicans and Puritans, was ejected from his Anglican church through the Act of Uniformity (1662); later "conformed" to become chaplain to King Charles II (1665), then was appointed dean of Bristol Cathedral.
My Song Is Love Unknown 202

Crotch, William (b. July 5, 1775, Green's Lane, Norwich, England; d. Dec. 29, 1847, Taunton), a musical prodigy, gave a series of public recitals at the age of four; at age 11, studied at Cambridge with John Randall, and assisted him as organist at both Trinity College and King's College; began theological study at age 13 but decided to follow a musical career, accepting the position of organist at Christ Church, Oxford, while continuing musical studies; received the MusB and MusD degrees at Christ Church and served there (1787-1807) as professor of music; became the first principal of the Royal Academy of Music in 1822; wrote two oratorios, works for organ and piano, 10 anthems, and a number of books on the theory of music, but is remembered primarily for his 74 chants written for Anglican worship.   H
ST. MICHAEL (adapt.) 41

Crouch, Andraé (b. July 1, 1945, Los Angeles, CA) as a youth attended and played piano at Emmanuel Church of God in Christ where Bishop Samuel Crouch, his uncle, was pastor; started a choir at Christ Memorial Church (founded by his father), San Fernando Valley, while still in high school; counseled and directed a choir at Teen Challenge Center for drug rehabilitation, Los Angeles; studied at L.I.F.E. Bible College, then left to form a concert singing group, "Andraé Crouch and the Disciples"; became one of the first black composer-performers to receive national attention from the wider audience of American evangelicals, particularly through the encouragement of Tim Spencer of Manna Music and Ralph Carmichael of Lexicon Music and Light Records (Carmichael produced the initial recording); has received Grammy awards (1975, 1978, and 1979) and toured in Europe, Asia, and Australia, as well as in the United States.
Bless His Holy Name, BLESS HIS HOLY NAME 36
My Tribute, MY TRIBUTE 46
Soon and Very Soon, SOON AND VERY SOON 677
Through It All, THROUGH IT ALL 616

Crüger, Johann (b. Apr. 9, 1598, Grossbriesen, Prussia, near Guben, Germany; d. Feb. 23, 1662, Berlin), beginning in 1644, edited the first edition of *Praxis Pietatis Melica* ("the practice of piety through melody")—the most important contribution of the 17th century to hymnody; was educated at the Jesuit College of Olmutz, at the University of Regensburg (studied music under Paul Homberger) and completed his theological work at the University of Wittenberg; from 1622, served as cantor at St. Nicholas Cathedral in Berlin, where he organized and directed the choir; also taught at the *Gymnasium zum Grauen Kloster*, and

remained in Berlin until his death; in the *Praxis,* collected chorales and *magnificats* which are a prime source of Lutheran hymnody.   H
HERZLIEBSTER JESU 231
JESU, MEINE FREUDE 119
NUN DANKET ALLE GOTT 374
ZUVERSICHT 246

Cull, Robert [Bob] (b. May 24, 1949, Los Angeles, CA), son of salespersons, has served as an arranger-orchestrator (1971-83), as a pastor (1978-84), and now as a traveling musician; was educated at Medford (OR) High School and Southern California College (Costa Mesa); composed ballad "worship songs" and wedding songs.
Open Our Eyes, Lord, OPEN OUR EYES 536

Cummings, William Hayman (b. Aug. 22, 1831, Sidbury, Devonshire, England; d. June 6, 1915, London) at the age of seven sang in the choir at St. Paul's Cathedral and later at Temple Church; at 16, sang in the premiere performance of Mendelssohn's *Elijah* with the composer conducting; as an adult, was highly acclaimed as a tenor soloist in Great Britain and America, particularly for his performances of the Bach Passion music; served as organist at Waltham Abbey, professor of singing (1879-96) at the Royal Academy of Music, and subsequently followed Joseph Barnby as principal of the Guildhall School of Music; was renowned as a musicologist (an authority on Purcell), lecturer, and composer.   H
MENDELSSOHN (arr.) 171

Cummins, Evelyn Atwater (b. May 17, 1891, Poughkeepsie, NY;

d. Aug 30, 1971, Poughkeepsie) was educated at National Cathedral School (Washington, DC) and at Masters School (Dobbs Ferry, NY) and was married to Alexander Griswold Cummins, rector of Christ Church, Poughkeepsie; served as associate editor of *The Chronicle* and contributed articles to several magazines; became police commissioner of Poughkeepsie (1947), the first woman to hold such an office in New York.
I Know Not Where the Road Will Lead 643

Cutler, Henry Stephen (b. Oct. 13, 1824, Boston, MA; d. Dec. 5, 1902, Boston) received much of his musical training in England, where he became interested in cathedral choirs; returning to Boston, was organist at Grace Episcopal Church, and later at the Church of the Advent, where his choir of men and boys was the first to wear robes in this country; beginning in 1858, served as organist at Trinity Church, New York City for seven years, and then in several other churches in the East; retired in 1885 and returned to Boston; composed anthems, service music, and hymn tunes, and published the *Trinity Psalter* (1864) and *Trinity Anthems* (1865).   H
ALL SAINTS, NEW 737

Cutts, Peter Warwick (b. June 4, 1937, Birmingham, England) attended King Edward's School, Birmingham, Clare College, Cambridge University (BA with honors, 1961 and MA, 1965) and Mansfield College, Oxford (BA, 1963), and is the sole holder of a Diploma in Church Music,

University of St. Andrews; taught music at Huddersfield College of Technology and Oastler College of Education, Huddersfield, and was senior lecturer in Music, Bretton Hall College, Yorkshire (1968-89); is Director of Music, St. John's United Methodist Church, Watertown, MA, and teaches at Andover-Newton Theological School (since 1989); a popular teacher and man of humor as well as creativity, has composed some 80 hymn tunes with over 30 published.
BRIDEGROOM 286, 597
WYLDE GREEN 313

Damon [also **Daman**], **William** (b. c. 1540, Liége, Belgium; d. late 1591, Broad Street Ward, St. Peter-le-Poore parish, London, England) came to England with Thomas Sackville, Lord Buckhurst (1562), and was one of Queen Elizabeth's musicians (after 1579); composed and published *The Psalmes of David in English Meter* (printed by John Day, 1597), music in homophonic four-part settings, and several motets, an anthem, instrumental music, and the posthumous *Booke of Musicke* (1591), an influential psalter.
DAMON 462

Dare, Elkanah Kelsay (b. 1782; d. 1826), Methodist pastor, Freemason, and music editor for *Wyeth's Repository of Sacred Music. Part Second* (Harrisburg, PA, 1813; see facsimile of the 1820 2nd ed., Da Capo Press, 1964, where he is credited with 13 tunes); was dean of boys at Wilmington (DE) College; authored a theoretical work on music which is quoted extensively in the Wyeth introduc-

tion; may have been the most important musical composer-editor of the early United States rural singing school movement.
CONSOLATION (attr.) 277

Darwall, John (b. 1731, Haughton, Staffordshire, England; d. Dec. 18, 1789, Walsall, Staffordshire) received his education at Manchester Grammar School and Brasenose College, Oxford; in 1757 became curate and, later, vicar of St. Matthew's Church in Walsall, where he spent the rest of his life; composed two volumes of sonatas for the piano, and tunes for all of the 150 psalms (Tate and Brady's *New Version*, 1770) in three manuscript volumes; a few of the tune names were published in various psalters.   H
DARWALL 86, 262, 312, 320

Dauermann, Stuart (b. Sept. 15, 1944, Brooklyn, NY) became a Christian believer at age 18; attended Manhattan School of Music (Bachelors and MMusEd); taught junior high school in New York City; in the early 1970s, came to San Francisco to work with Jews for Jesus (for 15 years) and there composed much of the music for which he is known; in 1975 married Naomi Green, and, with three children lives in Altadena, CA; completed a Masters degree in Missiology at Fuller Theological Seminary (1992), and currently is "spiritual leader" of A Havat Zion Messianic Synagogue in Beverly Hills, CA.
THE TREES OF THE FIELD 272

Davies, Henry Walford (b. Sept. 6, 1869, Oswestry, England; d. Mar. 11, 1941, Warrington) was boy

singer at St. George's, Windsor, Great Park, then, after his voice changed, was organist there and at St. George's, Campden Hill, St. Anne's, Soho, Christ Church, Hampstead, and Temple Church, Cambridge (where he instituted a popular Bach cantata series); was educated at the Royal College of Music (a scholarship winner) and later was a professor there (1895-1903); continued his education at Cambridge University (DMus, 1898); became Professor of music at Aberystwyth (from 1919) and chairman of the National Council of Music for the University of Wales; was knighted (1922) and named Master of the King's Music (1934); edited or cooperated on hymnals: *In hoc signo* (1915), *Music and Worship* (1928), *Hymns of Western Europe*, and *A Students' Hymnal for Use in Schools and Colleges*, English and Welsh "Hymns of the Kingdom" along with "Psalms, Anthems and Carols" (1923) and a preface which gives insights on his neo-romantic approach to music.
CHILDHOOD (adapt.) 372

Davis, Katherine Kennicott (b. June 25, 1892, St. Joseph, MO; d. Apr. 20, 1980, Concord, MA) studied at Wellesley College, MA (BA and graduate study); taught piano, composition, and theory at Wellesley, then became a full-time composer and editor; is known best for her famous text "Little Drummer Boy," but also composed many choral selections, piano works, operas, and a cantata; used the pseudonyms of John Cowley and C. R. W. Robertson; was awarded an honorary doctorate from Stetson University, DeLand, FL.

Her personal library, given to the Choristers Guild, is located at the University of Lowell, MA.
Let All Things Now Living, ASH GROVE (desc.) 53

Davisson, Ananias (b. Feb. 2, 1780, Shenandoah County, VA; d. Oct. 21, 1857, Rockingham County, VA), widely traveled frontier singing school teacher and real estate entrepreneur, compiled several tunebooks, including the popular *Kentucky Harmony* (Harrisonburg, VA, five editions, 1816 to 1826; facsimile edition, Augsburg, 1976), which was used in Virginia and the "Western Country." The book (and, evidently, Davisson's teaching repertoire) included camp meeting folk hymns and New England anthems. It is unlikely that either of the two tunes attributed to him were composed by him. He attributes CONSOLATION (here called MORNING SONG) to "Dean," a possible misprint of Dare; tunes similar to PISGAH and the text of "When I can read my title clear" appear in *Kentucky Harmony*, but not this combination or tune.
MORNING SONG (attr.) 277
PISGAH (attr.) 681

Daw, Carl P., Jr. (b. Mar. 18, 1944, Louisville, KY), son of a Southern Baptist pastor, is an Episcopal priest (ordained 1981) and vicar-chaplain of St. Mark's Chapel, University of Connecticut, Storrs; holds PhD in English from the University of Virginia and also has taught at the college level; consultant for the *Episcopal Hymnal* (1982), is also published in other hymnals; published the hymn text anthology *A Year of Grace* (1990),

available from Hope Publishing Company.
Christ the Victorious 685
For the Life That You Have Given 813
Like the Murmur of the Dove's Song 286
Surely It Is God Who Saves Me (para.) 327
The Lord My Shepherd Guards Me Well (metrical Psalm) 615

Dearmer, Geoffrey (b. Mar. 21, 1893, London), son of Percy Dearmer (below), attended Westminster School and Christ Church, Oxford; published poetry, six hymn texts, and a drama, *St. Paul.*
Those Who Love and Those Who Labor 394

Dearmer, Percy (b. Feb. 27, 1867, London, England; d. May 29, 1936, London) was educated at Westminster School and Christ Church, Oxford; was secretary of the Christian Social Union, London (1891-1912) and chairman of the League of Arts; served as vicar of St. Mary the Virgin, Primrose Hill (1901-15); taught ecclesiastical art at King's College, London, and became a canon of Westminster (1931); published pastoral books, *The English Carol Book* (with Martin Shaw), and assisted in editing *English Hymnal, Songs of Praise* (with Martin Shaw and Ralph Vaughan Williams), and its handbook, *Songs of Praise Discussed* (1933).
God Is Love—His the Care 400

Decius, Nicolaus (b. *c.* 1490, Hof, Franconia, Bavaria, Germany; d. after 1546, circumstances unknown) received his training in a Latin school in Hof and the University of Leipzig; became a monk, and served as the provost of the Benedictine nunnery at Steterburg; later, was involved in the Reformation movement and entered the University of Wittenberg to study theology under Martin Luther in 1523; served as pastor in Stettin and Leibstadt and finally settled in Mühlhausen and this is thought to be the reason Luther never recognized his work; wrote a number of the earliest Lutheran hymns, two of which are found in almost all Lutheran hymnals, as well as in many others; died suddenly, possibly at the hands of his Roman Catholic enemies.   H
All Glory Be to God on High 8

Didaché (between the 1st and 3rd centuries), a book of early church ordinances and moral teachings; the prayers contained are very early (probably the 1st century), but the origins of the book are uncertain. The manuscript itself is dated 1056 and housed in the library of the Church of the Holy Sepulchre at Constantinople and is available in numerous translations and editions.
Prayer for the Church 691

Dingley, Charles (fl. 19th century) was a New York City music teacher, according to David W. Music.
ALL IS WELL (early version in six-eight meter) 595, 725

Dirksen, Richard Wayne (b. Feb. 8, 1921, Freeport, IL) was educated at Freeport High School (IL) and graduated with honors from Baltimore's Peabody Conservatory

of Music (1942); joined the staff of Washington Cathedral as assistant organist-choirmaster; was appointed the Cathedral's Director of Advance Program (1964), precentor of the cathedral, the first lay person to assume that high Anglican Church responsibility (1969), and organist-choirmaster (1978); composed extensively, including five operettas, an oratorio, and other works; was granted an honorary Doctor of Fine Arts from George Washington University (1980) and an honorary Doctorate in Music from Mount Union College, OH (1986); resides with his wife in Washington, DC, having retired April 1, 1991, following 49 years and 2 months of service to the Cathedral.
CHRIST CHURCH 699

Dix, William Chatterton (b. June 14, 1837, Bristol, England; d. Sept. 9, 1898, Axbridge, Somerset) was the son of a surgeon who wrote *Life of Chatterton* (the poet); trained at Bristol for a mercantile career and became manager of a marine insurance company in Glasgow; wrote a number of hymns, and versified many translations from the Greek, publishing *Hymns of Love and Joy* (1861), *Altar Songs, Verses on the Holy Eucharist* (1867), *A Vision of All Saints* (1871), and *Seekers of a City* (1878).   H
Alleluia, Sing to Jesus 263
As with Gladness, Men of Old 181
What Child Is This? (adapt.) 150

Doane, Gilbert E. (b. Sept. 14, 1930, Bethlehem, PA) was educated at Harvard College (BA in geology, 1952), Lutheran Theological Seminary, Philadelphia, PA (BDiv, 1955), the University of

Pennsylvania (MA in American Civilization, 1962), and Princeton Theological Seminary (1965-66); pastored in Philadelphia with campus ministries (1955-61) and now directs the Northeast Lutheran Campus Ministry (living in Ardmore, suburban Philadelphia); served on the Inter-Lutheran Commission on Worship (1967-78) and writes extensively—articles, sermons, reviews, and editorials.
All Glory Be to God on High (trans.) 8

Doane, William Howard (b. Feb. 3, 1832, Preston, CT; d. Dec. 23, 1915, South Orange, NJ) was Fanny Crosby's principal collaborator in composing the tunes for her gospel songs; received schooling at Woodstock Academy, where he conducted the school choir at age 14; as a youth, worked in a cloth manufacturing business with his father; later became the head of a large woodworking machinery plant in Cincinnati, and was a respected civic leader in that city; as an avocation, wrote songs, cantatas, and ballads, both secular and sacred; worked with Moody and Sankey in the cause of evangelism, and was superintendent of the Mt. Auburn Baptist Sunday School at Auburn, OH, for some 25 years; wrote more than 2200 gospel song tunes and edited over 40 songbooks, of which *Silver Spray* (1867) was probably the most famous and had the largest sale; left a fortune in trust which has been used in many philanthropic causes, including the construction of Doane Memorial Music Building at Moody Bible Institute, a facility which Donald Hustad had a part in designing.   H

I AM THINE 534
MORE LOVE TO THEE 555
NEAR THE CROSS 549
RESCUE 736
TO GOD BE THE GLORY 9, 72

Doddridge, Philip (b. June 26, 1702, London, England; d. Oct. 26, 1751, Lisbon, Portugal) was the youngest of 20 children, only two of whom survived infancy; was born into the family of a London merchant who suffered a great deal of religious persecution; orphaned at the age of 13, was offered the opportunity to study for the priesthood in the Church of England by the Duchess of Bedford, but chose instead to attend the nonconformist academy at Kibworth in Leicestershire; in 1729 became a minister at Northampton and for 22 years was head of an academy there; a man of great learning, wrote many theological books, of which *The Rise and Progress of Religion in the Soul* (1745) was the most notable, and was published in many editions and translated into many different languages; authored almost 400 hymns which showed unusual social and missionary concern for their time, all of them published in 1755, after his death; died in Portugal where he had gone for treatment for tuberculosis.   H
O Happy Day That Fixed My Choice 504

Dorsey, Thomas A. (b. July 1, 1899, Villa Rica, GA; d. Jan 23, 1993, Chicago, IL), son of an itinerant Baptist preacher, moved to Atlanta (1912) where he learned "blues" piano and vocal technique; went to Chicago (1919); became choir director at the Pilgrim Baptist Church (1932) where he served for many years; studied at the Chicago College of Composition and Arranging, while working as an agent for Paramount Records; recorded his compositions with King Oliver's Creole Jazz Band and Les Hite's Whispering Serenaders; formed his own Wildcats Jazz Band, which recorded with Ma Rainey (known as "Georgia Tom") and Tampa Red; organized the first gospel choir at Ebenezer Baptist Church, Chicago (1931), the Thomas A. Dorsey Gospel Songs Music Publishing Company (1931), and the National Convention of Gospel Choirs and Choruses (1932), the first devoted to black gospel music; toured with Mahalia Jackson and Roberta Martin; has written over 1000 songs and is called "the father of black gospel music."
Precious Lord, Take My Hand, PRECIOUS LORD 638

Douglas, Charles Winfred (b. Feb. 15, 1867, Oswego, NY; d. Jan. 18, 1944, Santa Rosa, CA) was one of America's foremost authorities on Gregorian chant; the son of a schoolteacher, first served as organist at the local Presbyterian church at the age of 16; received his higher education at Syracuse University and St. Andrew's Divinity School, Syracuse; was ordained an Episcopal priest in 1899 and did further study in England, France, and Germany, preparing him for the 40 years of work in which he dominated the liturgical, linguistic, and musical life of the Protestant Episcopal Church; founded the annual summer school of church music at Evergreen, CO, and served as director of music at the Community of St. Mary, Peekskill,

NY (from 1906) and chaplain of the Community of St. Mary, Kenosha, WI (from 1934); espoused the revival of plainsong in worship and was in great demand as a lecturer and writer on a variety of subjects; was musical editor of the Episcopal Church's *New Hymnal* (1916 and 1918) and its successor, *Hymnal 1940*; wrote *Church Music in History and Practice* (1937) which was revised in 1962 by Leonard Ellinwood.   H
DIVINUM MYSTERIUM (arr.)   145, 693
OLD 124th (harm.) 348

Douglas, Robert Franklin (b. 1941); see **Fettke, Thomas E.**

Doving, Carl (b. Mar. 21, 1867, Norddalen, Norway; d. Oct. 2, 1937, Chicago, IL) immigrated to the United States at the age of 23, and attended Luther College, Decorah, IA, and Luther Seminary, St. Paul, MN; pastored Norwegian Lutheran congregations in Montevideo and Red Wing, MN, and Brooklyn, NY; was a gifted linguist, and his language skills served him well in his final work as a city missionary in Chicago, visiting in the hospitals of various ethnic neighborhoods; was a member of a committee appointed by three Norwegian synods to compile the English-language *Lutheran Hymnary* (1913) which included 32 of his translations of German and Scandinavian hymns.   H
Built on a Rock (trans.) 705

Draper, William Henry (b. Dec. 19, 1855, Kenilworth, Warwickshire, England; d. Aug. 9, 1933, Clifton, Bristol), after schooling at Cheltenham College and

Keble College, Oxford (BA, 1877), was ordained in 1880, served various Anglican churches as curate, vicar, and rector; made significant literary contributions in the field of hymnology, specializing in translating hymns from Latin and Greek; published *Hymns for Holy Week* (1897)—translations from the Greek church, *The Victoria Book of Hymns* (1897), *Hymns for Tunes by Orlando Gibbons* (1925), and others; edited *Seven Spiritual Songs by Thomas Campion* (1919).   H
All Creatures of Our God and King (trans.) 356

Duba, Arlo D. (b. Nov. 12, 1929, Brule County, SD), son of farmers, earned degrees at University of Dubuque (BA, 1952) and at Princeton Theological Seminary (BD, 1955 and PhD, 1960); after serving as Assistant Professor and Chaplain at Westminster Choir College (1960-68), was Director of Admissions and Director of Chapel at Princeton Seminary (1969-82), and currently is Dean and Professor of Worship at Dubuque Seminary (1982-).
How Lovely, Lord, How Lovely 333

Dubois, Théodore (b. Aug. 24, 1837, Rosnay, Marne, France; d. June 11, 1924, Paris) was a composer, teacher, and organist; studied in France and Italy, and won *Prix de Rome* (1861); served as organist at Church of the Madeleine in Paris (Fauré followed him) and as *maître de chapelle* until 1877; taught harmony and composition (his theoretical works have endured) at the Conservatoire (1871-90) and became its director (1896-1905, again, followed by Fauré); wrote in

many genres, but only a few religious pieces are remembered, including "The Seven Last Words of Christ."
ADORE THEE 816

Dudley-Smith, Timothy (b. Dec. 26, 1926, Manchester, England), son of a Derbyshire schoolmaster who was a lover of poetry, was educated at Tonbridge School and Pembroke College, Cambridge; was ordained deacon (1950) and priest (1951), and served as curate in Erith, Head of the Cambridge University Mission in Bermondsey, editor of the monthly *Crusade*, and became editorial secretary of the Evangelical Alliance (1955-59); ministered at Kent, then with the Church Pastoral Aid Society (home missions), became archdeacon of Norwich, East Anglia (1973) and suffragan bishop of Thetford (1981); wrote hymns ("efforts at simplicity, vividness, and the communication of truth") which are widely published; served on editorial committees including that for *Psalm Praise* (London: Falcon Books, 1973); authored *Lift Every Heart: Collected Hymns 1961-1983 and some early poems* (Hope Publishing Company, 1984), a book of prayers, *Someone Who Beckons* (1978), *Songs of Deliverance* (Hope Publishing Company, 1988), and *A Voice of Singing* (Hope, 1993); retired in December 1991 and lives in Salisbury.
All Shall Be Well! 236
A Purple Robe, a Crown of Thorn 217
As Water to the Thirsty 608
Christ Be My Leader 107
Christ High-Ascended 734
Come, Let Us Praise the Lord 320
God Is My Great Desire 336

I Lift My Eyes to the Quiet Hills 81
Lord of the Church, We Pray for Our Renewing 717
Not for Tongues of Heaven's Angels 597
O Come to Me, the Master Said 442
Safe in the Shadow of the Lord 513
Sing a New Song to the Lord 18
Tell His Praise in Song and Story 347
Tell Out, My Soul 350
The Lord is Here! 777
We Come as Guests Invited 784
When God the Spirit Came 688
When the Lord in Glory Comes 280

Duffield, George, Jr. (b. Sept. 12, 1818, Carlisle, PA; d. July 6, 1888, Bloomfield, NJ) had a long Presbyterian heritage, studied at Yale University and Union Theological Seminary, and was ordained into the Presbyterian ministry (1840); was dedicated to building up small congregations, so served many pastorates in New York, New Jersey, Pennsylvania, Illinois, and Michigan; for seven years was a regent of the University of Michigan and for a time was editor of the *Christian Observer*, a Presbyterian family newspaper; in retirement lived in Bloomfield, NJ, with his son, the Rev. Samuel W. Duffield, author of *English Hymns, Their Authors and History* (1886). H
Stand Up, Stand Up for Jesus 663

Dulin, Alfred; see **Olsen, Alfred Dulin.**

Dunkerly, William Arthur; see **Oxenham, John.**

Dwight, John Sullivan (b. May 13, 1813, Boston, MA; d. Sept. 5,

1893, Boston) was educated at Harvard College and Divinity School; pastored the Northampton, MA, Unitarian Church for only one year and then withdrew from public ministry because of shyness; founded *Dwight's Journal of Music* (was editor for 30 years) and the Harvard Musical Association; admired the genteel German style and promoted its use in the United States.

O Holy Night 160
God Bless Our Native Land (trans.) 421

Dwight, Timothy (b. May 12, 1752, Northampton, MA; d. Jan. 11, 1817, Philadelphia, PA), a grandson of the historic preacher Jonathan Edwards, entered Yale University at the age of 13 and graduated with highest honors; so injured his eyesight with long hours of study by candlelight that, as an adult, he could read for only 15 minutes a day; served as chaplain in the Revolutionary Army and was a Congregational minister in Greenfield, CT; became President of Yale at the age of 43, was loved by the students and held in high esteem as an educator, teacher, preacher, and writer; revised Isaac Watts's *Psalms and Hymns*, adding 33 of his own texts to a completed work which was published in 1801 and known as "Dwight's Watts," the most popular hymnal in Presbyterian and Congregational churches in Connecticut in the early-19th century.   H
I Love Thy Kingdom, Lord 702

Dyer, Samuel (b. Nov. 4, 1785, Wellshire, England; d. July 20, 1835, Hoboken, NJ) was educated in England; came to America in 1811, and taught music and directed choirs in New York City and Philadelphia; after a brief return visit to England for further study and research, settled in Baltimore and seriously engaged in writing; was in much demand as a conductor of singing schools in the south and east and at one time was conductor of the New York Sacred Music Society; published church music materials under the titles: *New Selection of Sacred Music* (1817), *The Philadelphia Collection of Sacred Music*, (NY, 1828) and *Anthems* (1822 and 1834), all with several editions that are considered important contributions to hymnody.   H
MENDON (arr.) 714

Dykes, John Bacchus (b. Mar. 10, 1823, Kingston-upon-Hull, England; d. Jan. 22, 1876, Ticehurst, Sussex) at ten years of age played the organ in Hull, where his grandfather was minister; was trained at Wakefield and St. Catherine's College, Cambridge, and later in life received an honorary DMus degree from Durham University; after a brief pastorate, became a minor canon and precentor at Durham Cathedral; in 1862 became vicar of St. Oswald, Durham, and remained until his death; is credited with having written 300 hymn tunes, most of which first appeared in one of the editions of *Hymns Ancient and Modern* or Chope's *Congregational Hymn and Tune Book* (1857).   H
ALFORD 746
ALMSGIVING 789
BEATITUDO 411, 547, 620
DOMINUS REGIT ME 13
NICAEA 2
MELITA 358
O QUANTA QUALIA (harm.) 680

241

ST. AGNES 112, 298, 389
STRENGTH AND STAY 573
VOX DILECTI 143, 506

Edmunds, Lidie H. According to Milburn Price in *Handbook to the Baptist Hymnal* (1992), Lidie H. Edmunds is "a pseudonym used by Eliza Edmunds Hewitt."
My Faith Has Found a Resting Place 495

Edson, Lewis (b. Jan. 22, 1748, Bridgewater, MA; d. spring 1820, Woodstock, CT) was born into a Tory family of Salem, MA, which first moved to Bridgewater (in the East), then to western Massachusetts to avoid political tensions; trained as a blacksmith, but traveled as a singing school teacher in New York (where he lived beginning in 1776) and New England; compiled the *New York Selection of Sacred Music* (1809 and editions to 1816); moved back to Woodstock, CT, in 1817.
LENOX 483

Edwards, John David (b. Dec. 19, 1805 or 06, Penderlwyngoch, Gwnnw's, Cardiganshire, Wales; d. Nov. 24, 1885, Llanddoget, Denbighshire) was educated at Jesus College, Oxford University (1830) and became vicar of Rhosymedre, Denbighshire, North Wales (1843-85); published the first Welsh book of Anglican hymn tunes, *Original Sacred Music* (1836).
RHOSYMEDRE 202, 393

Edwards, Robert Lansing (b. Aug. 5, 1915, Auburn, NY) was educated at Deerfield Academy, Princeton University (BA, 1937), and Harvard University (MA, 1938) with additional work in history

toward the PhD; was an army captain in intelligence during World War 2 (1941-46), and returned to study at Union Theological Seminary, New York City (MDiv, 1949); has served First Congregational Church, Litchfield, CT (1949-56), and Immanuel Congregational Church, Hartford, CT (1956-80), where he is now minister emeritus; was active in church and community service, and attended the World Council of Churches meetings in Sweden and Kenya; is married to Sarah Alexander Edwards, also an ordained minister.
God, Whose Giving Knows No Ending 644

Ellerton, John (b. Dec. 16, 1826, Clerkenwell, London, England; d. June 15, 1893, Torquay, Devonshire) received his schooling at King William's College on the Isle of Man and Trinity College, Cambridge (BA, 1849 and MA, 1854); was ordained in 1850 and served as curate of Eastbourne and of Brighton, vicar of Crewe Greene, and rector of Hinstock (1872), of Barnes (1876), and of White Roding (1886), with a health-leave in Switzerland and Italy intervening (he suffered from paralysis); first wrote hymns for children in his parish at Brighton; became recognized as an authoritative hymnologist of his day; assisted in compiling the 1875 and 1889 editions of *Hymns Ancient and Modern, Church Hymns* (1871), and the *London Mission Hymn Book* (1884); wrote 68 hymns for special days and observances, and translated a large number which are still in use; published *Hymns for Schools and Bible Classes* (1859) and *Hymns,*

Original and Translated (1888).   H
God the Omnipotent! (st. 3-4) 427
Savior, Again to Your Dear Name
835
Welcome, Happy Morning! (trans.)
241

Elliott, Charlotte (b. Mar. 18,
1789, London, England; d. Sept.
22, 1871, Brighton), though an
invalid for the last 50 years of her
life, was one of Britain's outstanding women-hymnists in the 19th
century; through a long friendship
with the Geneva evangelist, H. A.
César Malan, was strongly influenced to devote her life to religious
and humanitarian writing; wrote
150 hymns which appeared in *The
Invalid's Hymn-Book* (1834), *Hours of
Sorrow* (1836), *Hymns for a Week*
(1839), *Psalms and Hymns for Public,
Private and Social Worship* (1838-
48), and *Thoughts in Verse on Sacred
Subjects* (1869).   H
Just As I Am, without One Plea 445

Elliott, Emily Elizabeth Steele
(b. July 22, 1836, Brighton,
England; d. Aug. 3, 1897, London)
was the niece of Charlotte Elliott
(above) and the daughter of an
Anglican clergyman; wrote a large
number of hymns for use in their
parish church in Brighton and also
in hospitals and infirmaries; was
editor for many years of *The Church
Missionary Juvenile Instructor*, in
which her hymns frequently
appeared; published *Chimes of
Consecration* (1873) and *Chimes for
Daily Service* (1880).   H
Thou Didst Leave Thy Throne 198

Ellis, Peter (b. Mar. 7, 1950,
Cincinnati, OH); see **Bible, Ken.**

Ellor, James (b. 1819, Droylsden,

Lancashire, England; d. Sept. 27,
1899, Newburgh, NY) learned the
hat-making trade as a youth in his
hometown; also had musical gifts
and directed the choir in the
Wesleyan Chapel at the age of 18;
came to the United States in 1843
and resumed hat-making; in later
life was blind.   H
DIADEM 93

Elvey, George Job (b. Mar. 27,
1816, Canterbury, England; d. Dec.
9, 1893, Windlesham, Surrey), born
into a musical family, was a boy
chorister at Canterbury Cathedral,
and studied with his brother
Stephen at the Royal Academy of
Music; was a capable organist at age
17, and at 19 was appointed "master of the boys" and organist at St.
George's Chapel, Windsor, serving
the royal family there for almost 50
years; was knighted by Queen
Victoria in 1871; composed two
oratorios, *The Resurrection and
Ascension* (1840) and *Mount Carmel*
(1886), as well as anthems and service music.   H
DIADEMATA 92, 618, 756
ST. GEORGE'S, WINDSOR 190,
381

Emerson, Luther O. (b. Aug. 3,
1820, Parsonsfield, ME; d. Sep. 29,
1915, Hyde Park, MA) was conductor of musical conventions and
composer of church music which
was popular but not enduring;
compiled and published seven
books of hymns and Sunday School
songs.
AR HYD Y NOS (harm. attr.) 366,
379, 610

Erickson, John Frederick (b.
Oct. 3, 1938, Ottawa, IL) was educated at Northwestern University,

Evanston, IL, and American Conservatory, Chicago, IL; published choral music, much of it influenced by his interest in English Cathedral style; now lives in Bethel Park, PA.
BETHEL PARK 806

Este (also **Est, Easte, East, Snodham**), **Thomas** (b. *c.* 1540; d. unknown) printed and published *Musica Transalpina* (1588), an influential book of English translations of Italian madrigals, as well as the works of Tallis, Byrd, and Morley, and *The Whole Book of Psalms*, which established styles of psalm printing and tune naming (giving the tunes names of places); in 1609, changed his name to Snodham.
WINCHESTER OLD 172

Evans, David (b. Feb. 6, 1874, Resolven, Glamorganshire, Wales; d. May 17, 1948, Rhosllan-nerchrugog, near Wrexham) received his education at Arnold College in Swansea, University College in Cardiff, and Oxford University (MusD); was organist at the Jewin Street Welsh Presbyterian Church in London; in 1903-39, served as professor of music at the University College, Cardiff; edited the Welsh musical periodical *Y Cerddor*, and was a leader in the Welsh singing festivals; composed *Alcestis* for chorus and string orchestra, and many cantatas and anthems; was musical editor of the *Church Hymnary* (rev. 1927), used in many English-speaking Presbyterian churches around the world.   H
MADRID (arr.) 108
NYLAND (arr.) 521
BUNESSAN (arr.) 362, 543, 758

Evans, Jonathan (b. *c.* 1749, Coventry, England; d. Aug. 31, 1809, Coventry). No other information has been located.
Hark! The Voice of Love and Mercy 475

Everest, Charles William (b. May 27, 1814, East Windsor, CT; d. Jan. 11, 1877, Waterbury, CT) graduated from Trinity College, Hartford, CT, and was ordained in 1842; served as rector of the Episcopal church in Hampden, CT, for 31 years; at the age of 19, published *Visions of Death and Other Poems* (1833); contributed texts to *Hymns Ancient and Modern* (1861).
"Take Up Your Cross," the Savior Said 655

Ewing, Alexander (b. Jan. 3, 1830, Old Machar, Aberdeen, Scotland; d. July 11, 1895, Taunton, Somerset, England) is remembered in hymnology for this one world-renowned hymn tune; an accomplished musician, studied the art in Heidelberg, but never pursued it professionally; studied law briefly at Marischal College, Aberdeen, and became a member of the Haydn Society and Harmonic Choir while there; served during the Crimean War (1855) and rose to the rank of Lieutenant-Colonel; a skilled linguist, served his government's foreign service in Australia and China.
                                    H
EWING 754

Excell, Edwin Othello (b. Dec. 13, 1851, Stark Co., OH; d. June 10, 1921, Chicago, IL), the son of a German Reformed pastor, worked as a plasterer and bricklayer as a young man; also had musical gifts,

and became popular as a singing school teacher; was converted while leading the music in a revival in the Methodist Episcopal Church; turned his interest to sacred music, studied under George F. and Frederick Root, and published gospel songbooks after moving to Chicago in 1883; was well known as a congregational song leader, working with Evangelist Sam Jones; composed music for over 2000 gospel songs and published some 90 songbooks; left a large number of copyrights, which were purchased by Hope Publishing Company in 1931 and combined with their affiliate, Biglow and Main, to become the Biglow-Main-Excell Company; became ill while assisting Gipsy Smith in a citywide revival in Louisville, KY, and died after returning to Chicago.   H
AMAZING GRACE (adapt.) 502

F. B. P. was an unknown Roman Catholic priest of the 16th century.
Jerusalem, My Happy Home 675

Faber, Frederick William (b. June 28, 1814, Calverly, Yorkshire, England; d. Sept. 26, 1863, London) was trained at Shrewsbury and Harrow and received higher education at Balliol and University Colleges, Oxford; in 1842 was ordained in the Church of England and served the parish of Elton, Hunts, as rector; in 1845, became a Roman Catholic and was eventually appointed superior of the Brompton Oratory in London; desired to produce hymns for Roman Catholics with the same appeal as Newton and Cowper's *Olney Hymns*; wrote 150 hymns, published in his *Hymns* (1849 and 1862), *Jesus and Mary—Catholic*

Hymns for Singing and Reading (1849 and 1852), *All for Jesus, or the Easy Ways of Divine Love* (1853), and *Oratory Hymns* (1854).   H
Faith of Our Fathers 692
My God, How Wonderful Thou Art 65
There's a Wideness in God's Mercy 486

Fallersleben, Heinrich August Hoffmann von; see **Hoffmann, Heinrich August**.

Farjeon, Eleanor (b. Feb. 13, 1881, Westminster, London, England; d. June 5, 1965, Hampstead, London) was born into a family that included a renowned English novelist and a famous actor; was educated privately, published her first book, *Nursery Rhymes of London Town* in 1916, and went on to write approximately 80 other works—novels, plays, poems, music, and books for children; received several awards, including the Carnegie Medal, Hans Christian Anderson International Medal, and Regina Medal; published many books, including *A Nursery in the Nineties* (1935), *Martin Pippin in the Daisyfield* (1937), *The Glass Slipper* (1944), *Silversand and Snow* (1951), and *The Last Four Years* (1958); became a Roman Catholic at the age of 70, and is the subject of biographies by Eileen H. Colwell (1961) and Denys M. Blakelock (1966).   H
Morning Has Broken 362

Farquharson, Walter H. (b. May, 30, 1936, Zealandia, near Rosetown, Saskatchewan, Canada), son of farmers, attended a country school in Zealandia, and high

245

school at Rosetown; graduated from the University of Saskatchewan (BA), St. Andrew's College, Saskatowa (BD), and New College of Edinburgh, Scotland; married Joan Casswell and had four children; as a "worker-priest," taught junior high school and was a K-12 principal (1961-89), while serving a rural church at Saltcoats-Bredenbury (United Church of Canada) and being president of the Saskatchewan Conference; has written over 100 hymns, including the children's collection, *Just Like Salt*.
For Beauty of Meadows 383

Fawcett, John (b. Jan. 6, 1740, Lidget Green, Yorkshire, England; d. July 25, 1817, Hebden Bridge, Yorkshire) was converted when he was 16 under the preaching of George Whitefield; joined the Methodist movement in the Church of England for a time; later united with the Baptists, was ordained in 1763, and served churches at Wainsgate and at Hebden Bridge as pastor; at Hebden Bridge, turned a part of his home into a school for neighborhood children; declined the presidency of the Baptist academy in Bristol, but founded the Northern Education Society (now Rawdon College); wrote essays and sermons, and *Devotional Commentary on the Holy Scriptures*, 1811; published *Hymns adapted to the Circumstances of Public Worship and Private Devotion*, 1782, whose 166 hymns were written to be sung at the conclusion of his sermons.   H
Blest Be the Tie That Binds 708
Lord, Dismiss Us with Your Blessing (attr.) 834

Featherstone, William Ralph (b. July 23, 1846, Montreal, Quebec; d. May 20, 1873, Montreal) is also listed as "William Rolf Featherston" and seems not to have left much historical record; evidently was a member, with his parents, of the Wesleyan Methodist Church (now St. James United Church) in Montreal, spending his life in that city.   H
My Jesus, I Love Thee 100, 101

Fécamp; see **Jean de Fécamp**.

Ferguson, John (b. Jan. 27, 1941, Cleveland, OH), son of an industrial engineer and homemaker, attended Charles F. Bush High School, Oberlin College (BMus, 1963), Kent State University (MA, 1965), and Eastman School of Music (DMA, 1976); taught at Kent State University (1965-78) and was organist at Kent, OH, United Church of Christ (1963-78); directed music at Central Lutheran Church in Minneapolis (1978-83), and, since 1983, has been at St. Olaf College, Northfield, MN; continues active as a performer with emphasis on hymn accompanying; has published anthems and organ compositions; was music editor for the United Church of Christ *The Hymnal* (1974), and has written two books on church music and one on organ building.
PROMISED ONE (arr.) 134

Fettke, Thomas E. (b. Feb. 24, 1941, Bronx, NY), son of a mechanic and a housewife, graduated from Oakland City College and California State University at Hayward (BA in Secondary Music Education); taught in public school and then at Redwood Christian

School; ministered in church music for 30 years, most recently at Redwood Chapel Community Church, Castro Valley, CA, and Danville (CA) Evangelical Free Church; has published over 800 compositions, arranged the accompaniment for several popular recordings, including Steve Green's *For God and God Alone*; was senior editor of *The Hymnal for Worship and Celebration* (Word, 1986); writes and arranges under the pseudonyms Robert F. Douglas and David J. Allen.

COME LET US REASON (arr.) 456
FETTKE (ELAVIL) 661
NAME OF THE LORD (arr.) 113
OPEN OUR EYES (arr.) 536
PEOPLE NEED THE LORD (arr.) 730
THE BATTLE (arr.) 672

Filitz, Friedrich (b. Mar. 16, 1804, Arnstadt, Thuringia, Germany; d. Dec. 8, 1876, Munich) earned a doctorate in philosophy; lived in Berlin, 1843-47, and the rest of his life in Munich; assisted in publishing a collection of 16th- and 17th-century chorales (1845); edited *Vierstimmiges Choralbuch* (1847) and *Versuch eines Allgemeine Evangelischen Gesang und Gebetbuch* (1846), a book of four-part settings for texts by his poet-friend von Bunsen. H
BEMERTON [also WEM IN LEIDEN-STAGEN, FILITZ, or CASWELL] 803

Fillmore, Fred Augustus (b. May 15, 1856, Paris, IL; d. Nov. 15, 1925, Cincinnati, OH) was a son of A. D. Fillmore, a preacher, music teacher, composer, and church music book compiler; showed musical talent at an early age;

attended public schools and an unidentified college; was brother of James Fillmore (below), and both of them were ministers and traveling music teachers (piano, organ, singing) who worked in Ohio, Indiana, Kentucky, Tennessee, Alabama, Missouri, and Pennsylvania; founded (with James) the Fillmore Bros. Publishing Company, Cincinnati, OH; composed gospel songs, anthems, and a popular *New Practical Organ Instructor*.
I Will Sing of the Mercies, FILLMORE (likely author-composer) 30

Fillmore, James Henry (b. June 1, 1849, Cincinnati, OH; d. Feb. 8, 1936, Cincinnati) was the son of A. D. Fillmore, an ordained minister (Christian Church) who was also a composer, publisher, and singing school teacher; at 16, when his father died, took over the music classes to support the family; with his brother, founded the Fillmore Bros. Publishing Company of Cincinnati; issued a periodical monthly, *The Musical Messenger*, and his hymns appeared in this publication as well as in many collections, of which *Songs of Glory* (1874) was first; wrote and published anthems, cantatas, and hymn tunes. H
I Will Sing of the Mercies, FILLMORE (attr. but unlikely) 30

Fischer, William Gustavus (b. Oct. 14, 1835, Baltimore, MD; d. Aug. 12, 1912, Philadelphia, PA) became interested in music as a youth, through attending a singing class in a German-speaking church in Philadelphia; while learning the bookbinding trade, devoted his evenings to musical study; became

a famous teacher and choral conductor, taught music at Girard College, Philadelphia (1858-68), then went into partnership with John E. Gould in a retail piano business; wrote over 200 gospel songs and was much in demand as a conductor and song leader for revivals, including the Moody-Sankey campaign of 1876.   H
HANKEY 498

Fishel, Donald E. (b. Nov. 1, 1950, Hart, MI) was raised a Methodist, but baptized a Roman Catholic in 1970; graduated from University of Michigan (BMus, 1972), and, as a student, was involved in the music of the charismatic community, The Word of God, at Ann Arbor, MI, and later became its orchestra conductor (1971-81); wrote for its Servant Publications (1973-81), composing extensively from 1980-82; since 1983 has been working as a computer systems programmer.
Alleluia, Alleluia! Give Thanks, ALLELUIA NO. 1 240

Forness, Norman O. (b. Jan. 5, 1936, Minot, ND) attended Pacific Lutheran University, Tacoma, WA (BA, 1958), Washington State University, Pullman (MA in history, 1960), and Penn State (PhD, 1964); came to Pennsylvania to attend graduate school and stayed to teach at Gettysburg College (since 1964) as associate professor; has also written a Christmas carol (Augsburg).
Rise Up, O Saints of God! 670

Fortunatus,   Venantius Honorius Clemantianus (b. *c.* 530, Treviso, near Venice, Italy; d. *c.* 609, Poitiers, France) was the

chief Latin poet of the age in which he lived, who eventually turned his gifts to the service of God; studied oratory and poetry at Ravenna; made a pilgrimage in 565 to the tomb of St. Martin of Tours, and met Queen Rhadegonda who persuaded him to settle at Poitiers; was admitted to the priesthood and in 599 became Bishop of Poitiers; wrote many hymns, including a volume, *Hymns for all the Festivals of the Christian Year*, which is lost.H
Sing, My Tongue, the Glorious Battle 228
Welcome, Happy Morning 241

Fosdick, Harry Emerson (b. May 24, 1878, Buffalo, NY; d. Oct. 5, 1969, Bronxville, NY) is remembered as "a fighting liberal" in the fundamentalist-modernist controversy of the 1920s, but has produced some helpful devotional studies and this fine hymn; was educated at Colgate University, Union Theological Seminary, and Columbia University, and was ordained to the Baptist ministry in 1903; served First Baptist Church, Montclair, NJ (1904-15); taught homiletics (1908-15) and occupied the chair of practical theology at Union (1915-46); was pastor of First Presbyterian Church, New York City (1919-26); in 1926 became pastor of Park Avenue Baptist Church, which later became Riverside Church; wrote 32 books, including the popular volume *The Meaning of Prayer* (1915), an autobiography, *The Living of These Days* (1956), and several hymns.   H
God of Grace and God of Glory 669

Foundery Collection (London, 1742), a collection of hymns and

tunes compiled by John Wesley; it was the first Methodist Hymnal.
Praise the Lord Who Reigns Above 49

Foundling Hospital, London; founded in 1738 by a Captain Coram for the education and care of orphans, it had an extensive music program; G. F. Handel gave benefit concerts there (including *Messiah*) and donated an organ. *Psalms, Hymns, and Anthems of the Foundling Hospital* (1774 and later editions) is known as *The Foundling Hospital Collection*.
Praise the Lord! O Heavens, Adore Him 17

Francis of Assisi [Giovanni Bernadone] (b. c. 1182, Assisi, Italy; d. Oct. 4, 1226, Assisi), the son of a prosperous cloth merchant, was a self-indulgent youth; because of a serious physical illness in his early 20s, turned his back on his wealth to devote his life to prayer, poverty, and caring for the needy; with his little band of followers, became a wandering preacher throughout all Italy; loved all living things and is known as "the patron saint of animals"; adapted Italian secular song to suit his spiritual purposes, creating the historic, folkish *laudi spirituali*, which endured in history to the 17th century; founded the Franciscan order of the Roman Catholic Church.   H
All Creatures of Our God and King 356
Lord, Make Me an Instrument 650

Francis, Samuel Trevor (b. Nov. 19, 1834, Cheshunt, Hertfordshire, England; d. Dec. 28, 1925, Worthing, Sussex) early in life moved with his family to Hull

where he received his basic education from his grandmother and aunt, with whom he lived for two years; was a member of the surpliced choir in the parish church of Hull, and began to write poetry at an early age; later affiliated with the "Plymouth Brethren" and a biography appears in H. Pickering's *Chief Men Among the Brethren* (1931); became a merchant in London, and wrote numerous hymns which appeared in various periodicals and religious newspapers, as well as the *Enlarged London Hymn Book* (1873); acted as assistant to Ira Sankey during the Moody-Sankey meetings (1873-75); became known as an effective devotional speaker, in Britain and around the world; authored *Gems from the Revised Version, with Poems* (1891), and *Whence-Whither, and Other Poems* (1898); had his collected verse published by Pickering and Inglis in 1926, *O the Deep, Deep Love of Jesus, and Other Poems*; died at Groombridge Nursing Home in Worthing, Sussex.   H
O the Deep, Deep Love of Jesus 477

Franck, Johann (b. June 1, 1618, Guben, Brandenburg, Germany; d. June 18, 1677, Guben) began to study law at the University of Königsburg, but, because of the Thirty Years' War, returned to Guben; worked as a lawyer and town leader; published his hymns in *Geistliches Sion* (Guben, 1674).
Jesus, Priceless Treasure 119

Franz, Ignace (b. Oct. 12, 1719, Protzau, Silesia; d. 1790) was a recognized German-Catholic hymnologist and compiler; studied in Glaz and Breslau; as an ordained priest,

was appointed chaplain at Gross-Glogau (1753) and archpriest at Schlawa; in 1766 became assessor of the apostolic vicar's office in Breslau, probably holding that position until his death; published ten books, of which the most significant is *Katholisches Gesangbuch* (c. 1774) containing 47 of his own hymns; also published a tunebook (1778).   H
Holy God, We Praise Your Name 3

Freylinghausen, Johann Anastasius (b. Dec. 2, 1670, Gandersheim, Brunswick, Germany; d. Feb. 12, 1739, Halle) attended the University of Jena (1689), but, attracted by Pietism, left and assisted August H. Francke, a Pietistic preacher, for 20 years at Glaucha; married Francke's daughter and moved with his father-in-law to Halle, where, at Francke's death (1727), became pastor of St. Ulrich's parish; compiled *Geistreiches Gesangbuch* (Halle, 1704), a book of German hymns and tunes of the Pietists.
MONKLAND 59

Fullerton, William Young (b. Mar. 8, 1857, Belfast, North Ireland; d. Aug. 17, 1932, Bedford Park, Middlesex, England) was reared an Irish Presbyterian but moved to London (1875) and joined W. H. Spurgeon's Baptist Tabernacle; studied at Pastor's College, which became Spurgeon's College, then traveled in evangelism and missions for 15 years and was Home Secretary of the Baptist Missionary Society; pastored at Melbourne Hall, Leicester.
I Cannot Tell 109

Funk, Joseph (b. Mar. 9, 1777,

Berks County, PA; d. Dec. 24, 1862, Singer's Glen, VA), from a Pennsylvania German Mennonite family, was active as a traveling music teacher, compiler, and publisher in the Shenandoah Valley, VA; wrote his most influential publication, a four-shape shape-note tunebook, *A Compilation of Genuine Church Music comprising a variety of meters, all harmonized for three voices together with a copius elucidation of the science of vocal music* (Winchester, VA, 1832).
FOUNDATION 612

Gabriel, Charles Hutchinson (b. Aug. 18, 1856, Wilton, IA; d. Sept. 14, 1932, Los Angeles, CA) was the most popular gospel song composer during the Billy Sunday-Homer Rodeheaver evangelistic crusades, 1910-20; grew up on an Iowa farm, where he taught himself to play the family's reed organ; at 16, taught in singing schools and soon became a recognized teacher and composer; was briefly music director of a Methodist church in San Francisco; in 1895 settled in Chicago and was active in composing and publishing, becoming associated with the Rodeheaver Hall-Mack Company in 1912; wrote words and music for many songs, often using the pseudonym "Charlotte G. Homer"; edited many compilations for different voicings and uses.   H
Away in a Manger (3rd stanza, comp.) 147
My Savior's Love, MY SAVIOR'S LOVE 478

Gaither, Gloria Sickal (b. Mar. 4, 1942, Battle Creek, MI), daughter of a minister, was educated at Alexandria (IN) High School,

Anderson (IN) University (BS *cum laude* in French, Sociology, and English, 1963), and Ball State University, Muncie, IN; holds four honorary doctorates; married neighboring English teacher Bill Gaither (below) in 1962, and has three children; as a result of the popularity of her songs and her traveling performances, was guided into recordings (40 albums), writing lyrics (over 500 songs and 10 musicals) and 10 books; received Dove Awards from the Gospel Music Association, including Song of the Year and Songwriter of the Year; lives in Alexandria, IN.

There's Something about That Name 104
In the Name of the Lord 113
Because He Lives 238
I Then Shall Live 507
Every Eye Shall See 755

Gaither, William [Bill] J. (b. Mar. 28, 1936, Alexandria, IN), reared in rural Indiana where he still lives, and attended Anderson (IN) University (BS in English Education, 1959) and Ball State University (MS in Guidance, 1961); taught high school for six years while traveling with his wife Gloria (above) and brother Danny as the Bill Gaither Trio (since 1962); composed over 500 songs with Gloria, recorded 40 albums, and performed on traveling tours, resulting in multiple Dove Awards from the Gospel Music Association (including Song of the Year and Songwriter of the Year) and induction into the Gospel Music Association Hall of Fame (1982); is active with Anderson University's Board of Trustees.

There's Something about That Name THAT NAME 104

Because He Lives RESURRECTION 238
He Touched Me HE TOUCHED ME 410
Every Eye Shall See EVERY EYE 755

Gardiner, William (b. Mar. 15, 1770, Leicester, England; d. Nov. 16, 1853, Leicester) inherited a hosiery manufacturing business, and successfully combined his business career with an unusual talent for music; was interested in musicians and took every opportunity to meet them and hear their performances; claimed to be the first to present Beethoven's music in England; introduced the concept of adapting classic works for use as hymn tunes; published *Sacred Melodies from Haydn, Mozart, and Beethoven, Adapted to the Best English Poets and Appropriated to the Use of the British Church* (2 vols., 1812 and 1815).   H

LYONS (compiler) 29
GERMANY 222, 433, 481, 657
BELMONT (compiler) 331

Garrett, Leslie (b. July 15, 1943, Matamata, New Zealand) received his education at Word of Faith Bible School and is pastor of the Christian Family Center in Maddington, Western Australia; published musical works, *Scripture in Song and Song of Praise*, and books, *Which Bible Can We Trust?* and *Best of All, God Is with Us.*

This Is the Day, THE LORD'S DAY 801

**Gastorius   [Bauchspiess],
Severus** (b. 1646, Öttern, near Weimar, Germany; d. 1678 [buried May 8], Jena) attended the Latin school, Weimar (where his father

251

taught) and the University of Jena, Germany (1667-70); became cantor at Jena and director of its choir school (*c.* 1675), and married the daughter of the former director, Andreas Zîll; was a friend of Samuel Rodigast, who wrote the text (1675) for Gastorius's only remembered tune.
WAS GOTT TUT 82

Gauntlett, Henry John (b. July 9, 1805, Wellington, Shropshire, England; d. Feb. 21, 1876, London) became organist in his father's church at Olney when he was nine, and later served as choirmaster; trained in law and was admitted to practice, but gave it up by 1844; served as organist and choirmaster for several leading congregations in the greater London area; was one of Britain's leading musicians in the mid-19th century and was interested in reform in organ design and the use of plainsong in liturgy; wrote much organ music, anthems, and perhaps 10,000 hymn tunes; compiled and published: *Hymnal for Matins and Evensong* (1844), *The Church Hymnal and Tune-book* (1844-51), *Cantus Melodici* (1845), *The Congregationalist Psalmist* (1851), and *Tunes, New and Old* (1868); was granted a doctorate in music in 1843 by the Archbishop of Canterbury because of the high quality of his work.   H
IRBY 161, 316
STUTTGART (adapt.) 293

Gawler, William (b. *c.* 1750, Lambeth, London; d. Mar. 15, 1809, Lambeth), a composer of choral and instrumental music, compiled and published *Hymns and Psalms* (1785-89) while organist at the Asylum of Refuge for French

Orphans at Lambeth, a home for fatherless girls.
ST. MICHAELS (comp.) 409

Geistliche   Kirchengesäng (Cologne, 1623); see **Ausserlesene Catholische   Geistliche Kirchengesänge**.
LASST UNS ERFREUEN 259, 328, 356

Gellert, Christian Fürchtegott (b. July 4, 1715, Hainichen, Saxony, Germany; d. Dec. 13, 1769, Leipzig), the son of a Lutheran clergyman-poet, entered the University of Leipzig to study theology; after graduation, served as assistant to his father, but physical and emotional weakness caused him to leave the ministry and become a private tutor; returned to the University to study and took a minor post on the faculty, lecturing in poetry and rhetoric and later, was professor of philosophy; was revered and loved by his students, among whom were Goethe and Lessing; wrote a book of popular *Tales and Fables* (1746-48) which had many printings and translations; published *Spiritual Odes and Songs* (1757), which contained 54 of his own hymns and was immediately successful.   H
Jesus Lives and So Shall I 246

Genevan Psalter (1551); Jean Calvin's approach to music was to sing only psalms and to sing them in unison. The collection of those psalms, with texts (metrical psalms) by two outstanding French poets, Marot and Beze, was the *Trente quatre Pseaumes de David,* known as the *Genevan Psalter.* It established a repertoire of tunes for psalm singing for all of Calvin's Europe

and came to America by way of the Presbyterian influence of Scotland and the Puritans. The American colonies' first book, *The Whole Book of Psalmes Faithfully Translated into English Metre*, known as the *Bay Psalm Book* (1640, printed by Stephen Day, who had one year earlier printed an almanac for 1639—which is not really a book) contained *Genevan Psalter* tunes with the names connected to the English words to which they were usually sung (often different Psalms from those sung with their earlier French texts).
GENEVAN 42nd 132
OLD HUNDREDTH 317, 808, 809
OLD 124th 348
ST. MICHAEL 41

Gerhardt, Paul (b. Mar. 12, 1607, near Wittenberg, Germany; d. June 7, 1676, Lüben) is one of the best loved hymn writers in the German tradition; was trained in the Elector's school at Grimma and the University of Wittenberg, where he was helped by Paul Röber and Jacob Martini to learn the purpose and use of hymnody; in 1642 became a tutor in the home of Andreas Barthold, an attorney in Berlin, and eventually married Barthold's daughter; knew Johann Crüger and published hymns in Crüger's *Geistliche Kirchenmelodien* (1649) and *Praxis Pietatis Melica* (1656); was ordained in 1651 and later served at Mittenwalde, Berlin, where Crüger was choirmaster, and at Lüben; in early life, suffered the terrors of the Thirty Years' War, and much of his life was marked with tragedy—four of his children died in infancy, his wife died after 13 years of marriage, and he was the center of theological and politi-

cal controversy under Frederick William I, Elector of Saxony; still reflects spiritual serenity in his "Cross and Comfort" hymns, of which translator Catherine Winkworth said: "The religious song of Saxony finds its purest and sweetest expression in his writing.
H
Give to the Winds Your Fears 618
Jesus, Thy Boundless Love to Me 556
O Sacred Head, Now Wounded (trans. Latin to German) 221

Gerig, Richard E. (b. May 25, 1922, Fort Wayne, IN) attended Wheaton College (AB with honors, 1949); taught music and broadcasting, Fort Wayne Bible College (1950-58); was minister of music, First Missionary Church, Fort Wayne (1954-58) and Wheaton Bible Church (1969-84); published choral music with Lillenas and Hope Publishing Company; retired from public relation duties (1958-88) at Wheaton College, and is now a Councilman for the city of Wheaton and has served other civic organizations; served as a member of the editorial committee of *The Worshiping Church*.
GLORIA (desc.) 152

Gerike, Henry V. (b. Aug. 17, 1948, Parkers Prairie, MN) studied with Paul Manz at Concordia College, St. Paul, MN (BA, 1970); taught at Concord Lutheran School, Pagedale, MO (1970-75), while also music director at Unity Lutheran Church, Ben Nor, MO; taught and directed music at St. Paul's Lutheran Church, Aurora, IL (1975-1979), and Grace English Lutheran Church and School, Chicago (1979-85); came to

Concordia Seminary in River Forest, IL, as a student (MDiv, 1991) and director of the choirs, a post he currently holds; has published choral and organ works with Concordia, GIA, and Mark Foster. ASCENDED TRIUMPH 264

Gesangbuch der Herzogl. Wirtemburgischen Katholischen Hofkapelle (Wittenberg, 1784) is a collection of hymns for use in the private chapel at Wirtemburg. ELLACOMBE 203

Giardini, Felice de (b. Apr. 12, 1716, Turin, Italy; d. June 8, 1796, Moscow, Russia) was a chorister at the Cathedral of Milan; played violin in opera orchestras in Rome and Naples and then gave concerts in Italy, in Germany (1748), and in London (1750); lived in England (1752-84), teaching, performing and conducting, and became impresario of the Italian Opera in London; a friend of nobility, including the Countess of Huntingdon, was commissioned to write hymn tunes for Martin Madan's *The Collection of Psalm and Hymn Tunes* (1769) and provided four tunes, but only this one has remained in use; suffered several reverses in his work in opera and went to Moscow in 1796, where he died less than three months after his arrival.   H ITALIAN HYMN 5, 743

Gibbons, Orlando (b. 1583, Oxford, England [baptized Dec. 25]; d. June 5, 1625, Canterbury) was son of the town musician; studied at King's College (where he was a choir singer at age 13); became organist of the Chapel Royal in 1605, a position held until the end of his life; received his education at Cambridge (MusB, 1606), and Oxford University (DMus, 1622); was organist at Westminster Abbey (from 1623); composed church music during the English protestant reformation, including over 25 verse anthems, full anthems, hymn tunes, and services, as well as instrumental suites, keyboard music, madrigals, and polyphonic *lieder*; wrote settings that are simple, syllabic, and usually in four parts; died suddenly of a stroke and was buried in Canterbury Cathedral. SONG 46 236 SONG 13 301

Gibbs, Ada Rose (b. 1865, England; d. 1905) spent her life in England and was evidently active in the Keswick Convention Movement; was married to William James Gibbs, sometime superintendent of the Central Hall (Methodist), Bromley, Kent, and was the mother of one of the former directors of Marshall, Morgan and Scott, Ltd., who owned this song's copyright; published *Twenty-Four Gems of Sacred Song*, whose preface is dated July 1, 1900.   H CHANNELS 577

Gillespie, James (20th century); no information has been located. WESTMINSTER ABBEY (desc.) 475

Gillman, Bob (b. June 16, 1946, Westham, London, England) attended a Roman Catholic primary school, and then a state secondary school; is managing director of his own printing company, founded in 1980; has written country and western music, with over

254

20 sacred selections published by Thankyou music of East Sussex. Bind Us Together, BIND US 690

Gilmore, Joseph Henry (b. Apr. 29, 1834, Boston, MA; d. July 23, 1918, Rochester, NY) served as private secretary to his father, Joseph A. Gilmore, governor of New Hampshire during the Civil War; was educated at Phillips Academy, Brown University, and Newton Theological Seminary; was ordained to the Baptist ministry in 1862, and served churches in Fisherville, NH, and Rochester, NY; for a short time, while serving his father, was also editor of the *Daily Monitor* in Concord, NH; was professor of logic and English literature at the University of Rochester (1868-1911); wrote and published in his academic discipline: *The Art of Expression* (1876) and *Outlines of English and American Literature* (1905); also published *He Leadeth Me, and Other Religious Poems* (1877). H
He Leadeth Me, O Blessed Thought 635

Gladden, Washington (b. Feb. 11, 1836, Pottsgrove, PA; d. July 2, 1918, Columbus, OH), educated at Oswego Academy and Williams College, was ordained into the Congregational ministry in 1860; served churches in New York and Massachusetts, and in 1882 began a pastorate at First Congregational Church, Columbus, OH, which lasted 32 years; was moderator of the National Council of Congregational Churches (1904-07) and an early proponent of the social implications of the gospel; was the author of some 32 works, including *The Christian Way* (1877), *Things New and Old* (1884),

Applied Christianity (1887), *Who Wrote the Bible?* (1891), *Art and Morality* (1897), *Christianity in Socialism* (1905), and *Recollections* (1909). H
O Master, Let Me Walk with Thee 651

Gläser, Carl Gotthelf (b. May 4, 1784, Weissenfels, Germany; d. Apr. 16, 1829, Barmen) received his first musical training from his father and later attended the *Thomasschule* in Leipzig where Johann A. Hiller was director; studied and taught piano and violin in Leipzig, then settled in Barmen where he added voice and choral music to his expertise, and was involved in composing and publishing. H
AZMON 130

Gordon, Adoniram Judson (b. Apr. 19, 1836, New Hampton, NH; d. Feb. 2, 1895, Boston, MA) was named for the pioneer Baptist missionary to India-Burma, and in turn is memorialized in the naming of Gordon College and Gordon-Conwell Seminary (near Boston); received his training at Brown University and Newton Theological Seminary, was ordained to the Baptist ministry (1863), and served the church at Jamaica Plain, MA, and, beginning in 1869, the Clarendon Street Baptist Church, Boston; was a close friend and supporter of D. L. Moody; edited *The Service of Song for Baptist Churches* (1871) and *The Vestry Hymn and Tune Book* (1872); and was editor of the monthly, *The Watchword*. H
GORDON 101

Goss, John (b. Dec. 27, 1800, Fareham, Hampshire, England; d.

May 10, 1880, Brixton) was a leader of English church music in the early-19th century, who was overshadowed only by Samuel Sebastian Wesley in effecting reforms in cathedral music and congregational song; began his career as a chorister in the Chapel Royal where he studied under Thomas Atwood; served as organist of Stockwell Chapel, St. Luke's in Chelsea, and then at St. Paul's Cathedral in London, succeeding Atwood; in 1827 became professor of harmony at the Royal Academy of Music and held this position for some 47 years; was appointed composer to the Chapel Royal (1856), knighted by Queen Victoria when he retired in 1872, and received an honorary MusD degree (Cambridge, 1876); wrote anthems, service music and hymn tunes, released in *Parochial Psalmody* (1826), *An Introduction to Harmony and Thorough Bass* (1833), *257 Chants, Ancient and Modern* (1841).
H
LAUDA ANIMA 26, 194, 766
ARMAGEDDON (arr.) 666

Gottschalk, Louis Moreau (b. May 8, 1829, New Orleans, LA; d. Dec. 18, 1869, Rio de Janeiro, Brazil) was America's first concert pianist and world-recognized composer; born to an English father and a French mother, was a child prodigy, sent to Paris to study at the age of 13; was predicted by Chopin, who attended his debut, to become a "king of pianists," and did win acclaim from music lovers throughout Europe, Latin America, and the United States; wrote many popular piano pieces, such as "The Dying Poet" and "The Last Hope" and included them in his recitals;

died of yellow fever in Rio de Janeiro, while performing at a festival of his music; composed several large works: a symphony, *La Nuit des Tropiques*, an overture, a cantata, and two operas.
H
MERCY 302

Goudimel, Claude [also **Godimel, Godimell, Godymel, Jodimel, Jodymel, Jodrymel, Jodimey**] (b. *c.* 1505, Besançon, France; d. Aug. 27, 1572, Lyons), Huguenot composer of settings of the Genevan psalm tunes (Calvin's psalm literature), often set several versions of the same tune, such as a polyphonic motet, a chorale-like harmonization, and a more complex but homophonic setting, in eight collections of music (1551-1572); studied at Paris University (1549), worked with the publisher, Nicolas du Chemin (1551-55), was in Geneva with Calvin, and lived in Metz (1557, left between 1565-67); returned to Besançon and to Lyon where he died in the St. Bartholomew's Day Massacre (and his body thrown into the Saône River); influenced Palestrina (although he was not his teacher), Jean Bavent, and nearly all psalter compilers since the 16th century; in addition to psalm settings, composed five masses, three settings of the *Magnificat*, and 10 motets. His complete works are collected and edited by Pidoux.
GENEVAN 42 (harm.) 132

Gounod, Charles F. (b. June 18, 1818, Paris, France; d. Oct. 18, 1893, Saint-Cloud) was born into a family in which his father was a painter and his mother, a pianist who gave him early instruction; followed classical studies and

entered the Paris Conservatoire (1836), and then studied in Rome (1839), Vienna (1842), Berlin, and Leipzig, where Mendelssohn introduced him to Bach's music; returned to Paris and studied for the priesthood (1846-48), although he was not known for a holy life; wrote operas (beginning in 1851), including *Faust* (1859); was most productive from 1855-65 when much vocal music was produced, but then the Franco-Prussian War drove his family to England (1870-74); returned to France where he influenced younger composers.
LUX FIAT 811

Grant, David (b. Sept. 19, 1833, Aberdeen, Scotland; d. July 30, 1893, Lewisham, London, England) was a tobacconist in Union Street, Aberdeen, Scotland, and an amateur musician who scored music for bands and arranged tunes for the *Northern Psalter*; was a member of the Footdee church and choir; is known today for his hymn tune RALEIGH and also for his harmonization of Jessie S. Irvine's CRIMOND.   H
CRIMOND (arr.) 330, 413, 777

Grant, Robert (b. 1779, Bengal, India; d. July 9, 1838, Dalpoorie, India) was the son of Charles Grant, a director of the East India Company; was educated at Magdalen College, Cambridge, and began to practice law in 1807; was elected to Parliament as representative from Inverness, Elgin, Norwich, and Finsbury, which had previously been represented by his father; was sympathetic to the Jews and (1833) introduced a bill granting them civil liberties; was made Judge Advocate General in 1832,

later (1834) was knighted and sent back to India as Governor of Bombay; was the author of 12 hymns which appeared in the *Christian Observer* and H. V. Elliott's *Psalms and Hymns*, and were published posthumously by his brother in a volume entitled *Sacred Poems* (1839).   H
O Worship the King (adapt.) 29

Grape, John Thomas (b. May 6, 1835, Baltimore, MD; d. Nov. 2, 1915, Baltimore) was a successful coal merchant in Baltimore, who, as he said, "dabbled in music for his own amusement"; directed the choir in the Monument Street Methodist Church, and later in the Hartford Avenue Methodist Church; wrote a number of hymn tunes, but only this one lives on. H
ALL TO CHRIST 489

Gray, Alan (b. 1855, York, England; d. 1935, York) studied at St. Peter's School, York, and Trinity College, Cambridge University—first for law and then for music (MusD); was musical director at Wellington College (1883) and then at Trinity College, Cambridge (1892); authored six major music publications, including *A Book of Descants* (1923), from which these descants are taken.
WINCHESTER OLD (desc.) 172
HANOVER (desc.) 346

Greatorex, Henry Wellington (b. Dec. 24, 1813, Burton-on-Trent, Derbyshire, England; d. Sept. 10, 1858, Charleston, SC) received early musical training from his father, Thomas Greatorex, a well-known teacher, composer, and organist at Carlisle Cathedral and Westminster Abbey during the

reign of King George IV; in 1839 came to America and was organist of Center Church, Hartford, CT, and later at St. Paul's Church and Calvary Church in New York City; died of yellow fever in Charlestown, SC, where he had gone to take another position; published a *Collection of Sacred Music* (1851) whose tunes were marked A. G., T. G. and H. W. G., signifying Anthony Greatorex (Henry's grandfather), Thomas Greatorex (his father), and himself.   H
GREATOREX 805

Greatorex, Walter (b. Mar. 30, 1877, Mansfield, Nottinghamshire, England; d. Dec. 29, 1949, Bournemouth) was educated at Cambridge where he was a chorister at King's College (1888-93); was assistant music master at Uppingham School, Rutland (1900-10), then music master at Gresham's School, Holt, Norfolk (1911-36).
WOODLANDS 350

Green, Fred Pratt (b. Sept. 2, 1903, Roby, near Liverpool, England) was son of a leather manufacturer and Wesleyan Methodist local preacher who provided a Christian home; was educated at Wallasey Grammar School, Huyton High School, and Rydal Methodist school at Colwyn Bay; following a year at Severn Valley Mission Circuit, studied at Didsbury Theological College, Manchester (1926-28), and was ordained (1928); went as Chaplain to Hunmanby Hall, a Methodist boarding school for girls where he met and married the French teacher, Marjorie Mildred Dowsett (1931); ministered in the Orley Circuit (1931-34),

Bradford, Manningham Circuit (1934-39), Ilford Circuit (1939-44), and North London's Finsbury Park Circuit; wrote a play *Farley Goes Out* (1928); was encouraged by Fallon Webb to write poetry, which is gathered in *This Unlikely Earth* (1952), *The Skating Parson* (1963), and *The Old Couple* (1976), and has been published in *The New Yorker*, *The Listener*, and many anthologies; became superintendent of the Dome Mission, Brighton (one of England's largest); was chairman of the Methodist York and Hull District (1957); returned to local ministry in the London Sutton Circuit (1964-69), then "retired" in Norwich; since 1969, has been an active poet and hymn writer, encouraged and influenced by Fallon Webb (a sometime hymn author), John W. Wilson (Director of Music at Charterhouse School), and Erik Routley (hymnographer); is a fellow of The Hymn Society and received the honorary doctorate from Emory University, Atlanta, GA (where his letters will be held at his death). See *The Hymns and Ballads of Fred Pratt Green* (Hope Publishing Company, 1982) for Green's comments on his hymn writing.
An Upper Room Did Our Lord Prepare 767
Break Forth, O Beauteous (alt. st. 2, 3) 158
Christ Is the World's Light 90
For the Fruit of All Creation 379
God in His Love for Us 385
God Is Here! 701
Here, Master, in This Quiet Place 408
How Blest Are They 673
How Clear Is Our Vocation, Lord 395
It Is God Who Holds the Nations 415

Long Ago, Prophets Knew 142
Of All the Spirit's Gifts to Me 587
Rejoice in God's Saints 749
This Is the Threefold Truth 781
When in Our Music God Is Glorified 402, 403
When the Church of Jesus 722

Green, Harold (b. Oct. 23, 1871, Helme, Yorkshire, England; d. Dec. 20, 1930, Umzimkalu, Cape Province, South Africa), the son of a minister, was born in the vicarage at Helme, near Huddersfield in Yorkshire; became a missionary to Pondoland in South Africa, serving with the South Africa General Mission; died there.   H
QUIETUDE 343, 585

Greenwell, Dorothy (b. Dec. 6, 1821, Greenwell Ford, Lanchester, Durham, England; d. Mar. 29, 1882, Clifton, Bristol) was born into a well-to-do family, but circumstances made it necessary for her father to sell the family estate; went to live with her two brothers, both clergymen, and then with her widowed mother in Durham, and finally alone in London, Torquay, and Clifton; had fragile health, but a keen mind and a loving heart and was especially interested in helping retarded children and outlawing vivisection; published many volumes of verse and devotional books, which have been compared to the writings of Thomas à Kempis, Fenelon, and Woolman, including *The Patience of Hope* (1860), *Carmina Crucis* (1869), and *Songs of Salvation* (1873).   H
I Am Not Skilled to Understand 480

Gregory I [Gregory the Great] (b. 540; d. 604), a high government official in Rome, gave his inherited wealth to charity; founded several Benedictine monasteries; became Pope (596); was interested in chant and encouraged its use, thus, many tunes were attributed to him (a 13th-century fresco at Subia shows the Holy Spirit as a dove dictating chant to him) and his plainsong style is known as Gregorian chant.
A Prayer for Living and Dying 686

Greiter, Matthäus (b. *c.* 1500, Aichach, Bavaria; d. Strasbourg, Dec. 20, 1550), educated at Freiburg University, became a chorister at Strasbourg Cathedral, then a monk, but later became a Lutheran (1542) serving as a pastor in several churches including St. Martin's and St. Stephen's; founded a choir school at the Strasbourg Cathedral; returned to Catholicism shortly before his death (possibly from the plague) and became Cantor of the Cathedral; co-edited and contributed to the *Strassburger Kirchenamt* (1525)—in which Calvin found and used four of his tunes (1539).
OLD 113th (attr.) 79

Grétry, André-Ernest-Modeste (b. Feb. 8, 1741, Liege, Belgium; d. Sept. 24, 1813, Paris) studied in Rome (1761-65), then lived in Geneva, composing sacred music; arrived in Paris (1767) where his interest and success in opera flourished, but the death of his daughters, failures of his works after 1785, and cultural upsets associated with the Revolution coincided to reverse his good fortune; wrote literary works in later years; because of lawsuits over his estate, was not finally buried until 1828, then was moved again in 1842 to a place

where, in front of the Liége opera house, his bronze statue stands.
LANDAS (ascr.) 495

Grieg, Edvard [Hagerup] (b. June 15, 1843, Bergen, Norway; d. Sept. 4, 1907, Bergen) studied piano with his mother from age six until he began attending the Leipzig Conservatory (1858); was influenced by the concerts of Clara Schumann; returned to Bergen (1862) as a successful piano performer; in Copenhagen (1863) developed an interest in Norwegian peasant culture and turned to romantic nationalism in his music; arranged a number of Norse folk tunes which have been set to hymn texts.
I HIMMELEN (arr.) 682

Grieve, James Nichol (b. 1868, Sunderland, County Durham; d. June 20, 1954, Liverpool, England); according to the *Historical Companion to Hymns Ancient and Modern*, was educated at Newcastle Royal Grammar School and Edinburgh University; was ordained in the Presbyterian Church of England, and served at Newbiggin-by-the-Sea and in Liverpool; published *The Scottish Metrical Psalter of 1650: A Revision* (1940).
We Will Extol You (para.) 348

Grimes, Emily May Crawford (b. May 10, 1864, Lambeth, Surrey, England; d. July 9, 1927, Folkestone, Kent) went as a missionary to Pondoland in South Africa in 1893; in 1904 married Dr. T. W. W. Crawford, a missionary of the Anglican church.   H
Speak, Lord, in the Stillness 585

Grindal, Gracia (b. May 4, 1943, Powers Lake, ND) graduated from Salem, OR, High School, Augsburg College (1965), and (after a year in Oslo, Norway) the University of Arkansas (MFA, 1969); was an editorial assistant at Augsburg Publishing House, and has taught poetry and writing at Luther College (1968-84); is Professor of Pastoral Theology and Ministry-Communication at Luther Northwestern Theological Seminary, St. Paul, MN (since 1984); was an editorial contributor to the *Lutheran Book of Worship* (1978) and a consultant for *The United Methodist Hymnal* (1989).
What God Ordains Is Always Right (trans.) 82

Grindle, Harry (b. Oct. 2, 1935, Bangar, Dann, N. Ireland) was educated at Dublin (MusB), Belfast (BA, MA), Dublin again (PhD), with other extensive musical training and performing; was the first Irish associate of the Royal School of Church Music; has served as organist and master of choristers, St. Anne's Cathedral, Belfast (1964-75), and senior lecturer in music, Stranmillis College of Education, Belfast (since 1975).
HARROW WEALD (harm.) 6

Grotenhuis, Dale (b. Dec. 1, 1931, Cedar Grove, WI), the son of an accountant, attended Cedar Grove High School, Calvin College (AB in Education), and Michigan State University (MA in Music); is widely published (choral, orchestral, band works) and has harmonized more than 50 settings in the Christian Reformed *Psalter Hymnal* (1989); was choral director at Lynden, WA, and Unity Christian

High Schools; is currently choral director at Dordt College, Sioux Center, IA.
CLAP YOUR HANDS (harm.) 23
CLAY (harm.) 592
EARTH AND ALL STARS (harm.) 357
SING ALLELUIA (harm.) 771

Groves, Alexander (b. 1842, Newport, Isle of Wight, England; d. Aug. 30, 1909, Henley-on-Thames, Oxfordshire) worked as a grocer and an accountant beginning at the age of 18; in 1887, worked for the Henley Savings Bank, where he served as a trustee for 10 years, later as auditor and bank actuary; a devout churchman, was organist at the Henley Wesleyan Chapel, and later was associated with the Church of England parish church there.   H
Break Thou the Bread of Life (stanzas 3 & 4) 315

Gruber, Franz Xaver (b. Nov. 25, 1787, Unterweizberg, near Hochburg, Austria; d. June 7, 1863, Hallein, near Salzburg) learned the linen weaving trade at his father's insistence, but his interest in music led him to study the violin and organ without his father's knowledge, and eventually to devote his life to the art; became a schoolmaster in a Roman Catholic school at Ansdorf and also organist at nearby Oberndorf, where Joseph Mohr, the author of "Silent Night," was priest; for approximately 30 years was organist and choral director at Hallein; wrote many compositions, but is best known for this simple hymn tune.   H
STILLE NACHT 164

Grundtvig, Nicolai Frederik Severin (b. Sept. 8, 1783, Udby, Seeland; d. Sept. 2, 1872, Vartov, Denmark) was one of Denmark's great hymnists, preachers, and educators; experienced a period of doubt during his "rationalistic" theological studies at the University of Copenhagen, but his faith was rekindled when he perceived the spiritual poverty of his people; became a teacher and then, an assistant to his father, an Evangelical Lutheran pastor; was ordained in 1811 and installed at Udby, but his controversial preaching caused him to be suspended for a period of 13 years; was fully reinstated in 1839 and appointed chaplain to the Vartov hospital, where he remained until his death; led in bringing reforms to Denmark's educational system, and has been called "the father of the public school in Scandinavia"; received the honorary title of Bishop from King Frederik VII in 1863; left five volumes of poems and hymns which were published after his death with the title (translated) *Hymns and Spiritual Songs.*   H
Built on the Rock 705

Gurney, Dorothy Frances Blomfield (b. Oct. 4, 1858, London, England; d. June 15, 1932, Notting Hill, London) had a long Anglican heritage—her father was rector of St. Andrew Undershaft, London, and her grandfather was Bishop Blomfield of Chester and London; married Gerald Gurney, a former actor who was ordained in the Church of England and was also the son of an Anglican clergyman and hymn writer; with her husband, became a Roman Catholic in 1919; wrote two vol-

umes of *Poems and A Little Book of Quiet*. H
O Perfect Love 388

Gwyllt, Ieuan; see **Roberts, John**.

Hairston, Jester (b. July 9, 1901, Belews Creek, NC), grandson of slaves, was raised in Homestead, near Pittsburgh, PA; attended University of Massachusetts, where he played football, but dropped out because of finances; after a period of working in steel mills, resumed study at Tufts University (BMus, *cum laude*, 1930); moved to New York City where he attended Julliard and was a music instructor; published at Harlem under the Federal Works Project (1930s); studied with the Russian composer Dmitri Tiomkin, and sang with the Hall Johnson Choir, becoming the assistant conductor (1933); went to Hollywood to record the soundtrack for *Green Pastures* and other films; holds five honorary doctorates and his music is widely published and performed by college choirs, including a CD history by the Belmont College Chorale; appeared on the radio show Amos 'n' Andy, in Tarzan movies, in *The Alamo, To Kill a Mockingbird, Lady Sings the Blues*, among other films; he was featured in a USO tour of Europe during World War 2, and with the Walter Schumann Choir at the College of the Pacific; in interviews, has called his "first love, spirituals"; also mentions that "we did rap in 1910," the generation he first heard singing; was seen on TV in *That's My Mama* and played the part of Rolly Forbes on the NBC sitcom *Amen*.
Mary's Little Boy-Child, HAIRSTON 178

Hall, Elvina Mabel (b. June 4, 1820, Alexandria, VA; d. July 18, 1889, Ocean Grove, NJ), with her husband Richard Hall, was a member of the Monument Street Methodist Church in Baltimore for more than 40 years; after Mr. Hall's death, married Rev. Thomas Myers of the Baltimore Conference of the Methodist Church, in 1885. H
Jesus Paid It All 489

Hammerken, Thomas; see **Thomas à Kempis**.

Hammond, Mary Jane (b. 1878, England; d. Jan. 23, 1964, St. Albans, Hertfordshire) died at Hilligdon Nursing Home on Hillside Road in St. Albans, Hertfordshire. No other information is available. H
SPIRITUS VITAE 299

Hanby, Benjamin Russell (b. July 22, 1833, Rushville, OH; d. Mar. 16, 1867, Chicago), the son of Bishop William Hanby of the United Brethren Church, was himself a minister in that church with a musical avocation that eventually became his lifework; was associated with George F. Root in music publishing in Chicago, co-editing *Chapel Gems*, 1866; wrote a number of Sunday School songs as well as secular lyrics (including the famous "Darling Nellie Gray" for which his sister wrote the music); died at the age of 34, just as his career was beginning. H
Who Is He in Yonder Stall? LOWLINESS 195

Handel, George Frederick (b. Feb. 23, 1685, Halle, Germany; d. Apr. 14, 1759, London, England) is sometimes described as "a German

musician who wrote Italian operas for English audiences"; showed unusual musical gifts at an early age; because of his father's desire that he become a lawyer, entered the University of Halle to study law, but quickly turned to music; studied organ, harpsichord, and music theory with Zachau, organist at the Halle Cathedral, and became his assistant; was violinist in the German opera for four years, then traveled through Italy, where he was inspired to write a number of his first operas; in 1713 settled in England (became a British subject in 1727) and enjoyed some 35 years of success in writing and producing "Italian" operas; later turned to the composition of oratorios which have won him lasting fame; also wrote instrumental and organ music in abundance, and three hymn tunes (for the Wesleys), but these settings listed below are adapted from other vocal works; was buried in the Poet's Corner of Westminster Abbey.   H
ANTIOCH 146
MACCABEUS 251
MESSIAH 351

Hankey, Arabella Catherine (b. 1834, Clapham, London, England; d. May 9, 1911, Westminster, London), usually known as "Kate," was born into the family of a banker who belonged to the evangelical "Clapham Sect" associated with William Wilberforce; throughout her life was interested and active in religious work—conducting Bible classes for shop girls, giving money from her writings to foreign missions, and visiting the sick in hospitals; published one important book, *The Old, Old Story and Other Verses* (1879).   H

I Love to Tell the Story 498

Harding, James Procktor (b. May 19, 1850, Clerkenwell, London, England; d. Feb. 21, 1911, London) was organist and choirmaster of St. Andre's Church, Thornhill Square, Islington, London, for 35 years as an amateur musician; was a clerk in England's internal revenue department, but also served as a pastor with the poor of Gifford Hall Mission; composed anthems and children's festival music.
MORNING STAR 182, 385

Harkness, Georgia Elma (b. Apr. 21, 1891, Harkness, NY; d. Aug. 30, 1974, Claremont, CA) is remembered as one of the leading women theologians of the last generation; was educated at Cornell University (BA) and Boston University (MA, MRE, PhD), Harvard University, Yale Divinity School, and Union Theological Seminary; an ordained Methodist minister, lectured in theology and philosophy of religion at Elmira College, Mount Holyoke College, Garrett Biblical Institute, Pacific School of Religion, and Japanese International Christian University; authored 18 books, three of which are collections of her prayers and poems.   H
Hope of the World 434

Harkness, Robert (b. Mar. 2, 1880, Bendigo, Australia; d. May 8, 1961, London, England) was the son of a minister but evidently not a confessing Christian when he was asked to join the Torrey-Alexander team as pianist, during their meetings in June, 1903, in his hometown in Australia; was led to Christ

by song leader Charles M. Alexander, a life-long specialist in "personal soul winning"; accompanied the singer and Dr. R. A. Torrey in round-the-world evangelistic tours, later working with Dr. J. Wilbur Chapman as well; after 1920, appeared in solo programs, entitled "The Music of the Cross"; wrote music for hundreds of gospel songs in his own harmonic style, which were introduced in their campaigns and later published; distributed for many years a correspondence course in "Evangelistic Piano Playing," which has been published in one volume by Lillenas Publishing Company. H
HYFRYDOL (arr.) 89

Hart, Joseph (b. 1712, London, England; d. May 24, 1768, London), well educated and the product of a Christian home, was a school teacher in London; lapsed into dissolute ways and agnostic thought, but was converted at the Moravian Chapel in London, 1757; became pastor of Jewin Street Chapel (Independent) in London, and was a popular preacher and ardent Calvinist; published *Hymns Composed on Various Subjects, with the Author's Experience*, 1759, for use in the Jewin Street Chapel. H
Come, Ye Sinners, Poor and Needy 451

Hassler, Hans Leo (b. Oct. 25, 1564, Nüremberg, Germany; d. June 8, 1612, Frankfurt-am-Main) learned the basics of music from his father and later studied organ and composition with Andrea Gabrieli at St. Mark's in Venice (1584); returning to his homeland in 1585, was organist to Count Octavian Fugger of Augsburg, and

then at the *Frauenkirche* in Nüremberg; later served Emperor Rudolph II and Prince Christian II of Saxony; composed both sacred and secular music, vocal and instrumental, and published: *Cantiones Sacrae* (1591), *Psalmen und christliche Gesang* (1607), and *Kirchengesänge, Psalmen und geistliche Lieder* (1608). H
PASSION CHORALE 221

Hastings, Thomas (b. Oct. 15, 1784, Washington, CT; d. May 15, 1872, New York, NY), the son of a physician, attended country school and taught himself the fundamentals of music; began directing choirs at age 18 and compiled sacred music collections; an albino, extremely near-sighted and not attractive of appearance, nevertheless, was an outstanding choral conductor; edited *The Western Recorder* (1823-32), a religious journal in which he published articles on the improving of church music; in 1832 moved to New York City to work with Lowell Mason and a number of churches in the development of the music of worship; assisted Mason in publishing *Spiritual Songs for Social Worship* (c. 1832); edited 50 collections, including *Church Melodies and Devotional Hymns and Poems*, and wrote 600 hymns and 1000 hymn tunes. H
TOPLADY 227
Come, Ye Disconsolate (st. 3) 613

Hatch, Edwin (b. Sept. 4, 1835, Derby, England; d. Nov. 10, 1889, Oxford), educated at King Edward's School, Birmingham and Pembroke College, Oxford, was confirmed in the Church of England and ordained in 1859; served as a parish

priest for a short time before moving to Toronto, Canada, where he became professor of classics at Trinity College; in 1867 returned to England as vice-principal of St. Mary's Hall, Oxford, and in 1884 became university reader in church history; was widely acclaimed for his Bampton Lectures (1880) and Hibbert Lectures (1888) on the history of the early church.　　H
Breathe on Me, Breath of God 295

Hatton, John (b. *c.* 1710, Warrington, Lancashire, England; d. Dec. 1793, St. Helens) has only a few lines in hymn history; was referred to as "John of Warrington" which gives the presumption of his birthplace; lived on Duke Street in St. Helens in the township of Windle, and was buried from the Presbyterian Chapel there on December 13, 1793.　　H
DUKE STREET 16, 239, 745

Havergal, Frances Ridley (b. Dec. 14, 1836, Astley, Worcestershire, England; d. June 3, 1879, Caswell Bay, near Swansea, Wales) was, for her 43 years, contemporary with America's Fanny Crosby, whom she admired, and their two lives had many things in common; was the youngest child of William Henry Havergal, vicar of Astley, Worcestershire; could read at the age of three and wrote poetry when she was seven; because of frail health, had limited formal education but developed great linguistic ability, being fluent in six or seven modern languages, as well as Hebrew and Greek; from the age of 14, was dedicated completely to the service of Christ; lived with her father until his death (1873) and then in Caswall Bay; was an inces-

sant writer, whose collected poems appeared in *Poetical Works* (1884) after her death.　　H
I Am Trusting Thee, Lord Jesus 524
Like a River Glorious 594
Lord, Speak to Me, That I May Speak 574
Take My Life and Let It Be Consecrated 568
Who Is on the Lord's Side? 666

Havergal, William Henry (b. Jan. 18, 1793, High Wycombe, Buckinghamshire, England; d. Apr. 19, 1870, Leamington, Warwickshire, England) was trained at Merchant Taylor's School and at St. Edmund's Hall, Oxford; took Anglican Holy Orders and became rector of Astley in Worcestershire; was seriously injured in an accident, so resigned his pastoral duties and turned to writing and publishing church music; returned to active ministry in 1842 as rector of St. Nicholas, Worcester, and from 1845 was honorary canon of Worcester Cathedral; wrote many hymns that were printed in leaflet form for special services in his church; in 1844, for the improving of psalm singing in the church, reprinted Ravenscroft's *Psalter* of 1611 and published *Old Church Psalmody* (1849) and *A Hundred Psalm and Hymn Tunes* (1859); wrote *History of the Old 100th Psalm Tune* (1854). H
WINCHESTER NEW (16, 132, 221)

Haweis, Thomas (b. Jan. 1, 1734, Redruth, Cornwall, England; d. Feb. 11, 1820, Bath) studied medicine but transferred to theology at Christ Church, Oxford, then at Magdalen College; became curate at St. Mary Magdalen's Church, Oxford, and assisted at Lock

Hospital, London, and other posts; published hymn collections, including *Carmina Christo*, or *Hymns to the Saviour*, and *Select Collection of Hymns* for the Countess of Huntingdon.
RICHMOND 628

Hawks, Annie Sherwood (b. May 28, 1835, Hoosick, NY; d. Jan. 3, 1918, Bennington, VT) resided in Brooklyn, NY, and was a member of the Hanson Place Baptist Church for many years; was encouraged to write hymns by her pastor, Robert Lowry; after the death of her husband, Charles H. Hawks, moved to Bennington, VT, where she lived with her daughter and son-in-law; wrote over 400 hymns, which were included in such compilations as *Bright Jewels*, *Pure Gold*, and *Royal Diadem*.   H
I Need Thee Every Hour 538

Haydn, Franz Joseph (b. Mar. 31, 1732, Rohrau, Lower Austria; d. May 31, 1809, Vienna) shared with Mozart the leadership of the western musical world in the late-18th century; received early training in the Roman Catholic choir school of St. Stephen's, Vienna; as music director to the court of the Esterhazys for most of his life, had financial security and musical resources to perform his vast output of timeless music; wrote over 100 symphonies, 22 operas, four oratorios, and much chamber music; in 1797 visited England and received many honors; an intensely pious man, ended all his music manuscripts with the words "Laus Deo" or "Soli Deo Gloria"; wrote no hymn tunes as such—those that exist are adapted from other works.
H

AUSTRIAN HYMN 17, 694, 710
ST. ANTHONY'S CHORALE 37

Haydn, Johann Michael (b. Sept. 14, 1737, Rohrau, Lower Austria; d. Aug. 10, 1806, Salzburg), the younger brother of Franz Joseph Haydn, was also a choirboy at St. Stephen's, Vienna; in 1757 became kappelmeister at Grosswardein; was musical director to Archbishop Sigismund at the cathedral of Salzburg from 1762 until his death; wrote more than 400 compositions for the church, including oratorios and music for organ with orchestra, few of which have been published.   H
LYONS (attr.) 29

Hayford, Jack W. (b. June 25, 1934, Oakland, CA), a graduate of L.I.F.E. Bible College, Los Angeles, CA (1956), and Azusa (CA) Pacific University (1970), has three honorary doctorates; is married to Anna Smith (whom he met at college); began his ministry in Fort Wayne, IN (1956-60), then served as youth director of the International Church of the Foursquare Gospel in Los Angeles (1960-65); served on the faculty of L.I.F.E. Bible College (1965-82), was Dean of Students (1965-70) and President (1977-82); has pastored the Church on the Way (First Foursquare Church), Van Nuys, CA (since 1977), with a weekly attendance over 10,000; is widely traveled as a speaker and influential in his church-sponsored pastors' seminars; broadcasts daily radio and weekly television programs.
Majesty, Worship His Majesty, MAJESTY 98

Head, Elizabeth [Bessie] Ann Porter (b. Jan. 1, 1850, probably in Norfolk, England; d. June 28, 1936, Wimbledon, Surrey), often listed as "Bessie Porter Head," was the wife of Albert Alfred Head, insurance broker of Henry Head Co., London, and Chairman of the Keswick Convention for several years; served with the YMCA in Swansea, South Wales, and as a missionary with the South Africa General Mission; a member of the Church of England, wrote many hymn texts, several of which appeared in the *Keswick Hymn Book* (*c.* 1937). H
O Breath of Life 299

Hearn, Naida O'Hara (b. Dec. 28, 1931, Palmerton North, New Zealand) is a housewife, mother, and professional music teacher (piano and theory) in New Zealand; graduated from Palmerton North Technical High School; is a church pianist, and has composed several gospel choruses.
Jesus, Name Above All Names, HEARN 106

Heber, Reginald (b. Apr. 21, 1783, Malpas, Cheshire, England; d. Apr. 3, 1826, Trichinopoly, India) is remembered for the impetus he gave to the cause of hymn (vs. psalm) singing in the Church of England, and for the new lyric quality he brought to hymn poetry; studied at the grammar school at Whitchurch, Bristow's Select School at Neasdon, Brasenose College, Oxford (honors), and was named a Fellow of All Souls' College, Oxford, in 1805; served as rector of his family's parish at Hodnet, Shropshire, 1807-23; was appointed Bishop of Calcutta

(1823) and had served there for only three years when he suddenly died at age 42; wrote many hymns during his Hodnet ministry, which were released from time to time in the *Christian Observer* and were published posthumously in *Hymns Written and Adapted to the Weekly Service of the Church Year* (1827). H
Brightest and Best of the Stars 182
Bread of the World in Mercy Broken 774
God, Who Made the Earth and Heaven 366
Holy, Holy, Holy! Lord God Almighty 2

Hebrew Melodies; with the continuing interest in the Jewish roots of Christianity and the visible witness in music of various Hebrew-Christian groups (such as Jews for Jesus), some of the folk repertoire has come into hymn literature. Of the tunes below, only LEONI (The God of Abraham Praise 66) has had a long hymn history.
ISRAELI 588
KING OF KINGS 110
LEONI 66, 336, 741
PROMISED ONE 134
 Shalom, My Friends, SHALOM CHAVERIM 599

Hedge, Frederick Henry (b. Dec. 12, 1805, Cambridge, MA; d. Aug. 21, 1890, Cambridge, MA) was sent to Germany to study at age 13, and graduated from Harvard Divinity School at 20; became a Unitarian minister and served churches in Maine, Rhode Island, and Massachusetts; also taught church history and German at Harvard, and shows his scholarly acumen in the monumental *Prose Writers of Germany*; published *Hymns for the Church of Christ* (1853); has been

the subject of two biographical studies: *Frederick Henry Hedge, A Cosmopolitan Scholar*, by Orie William Long (1940) and *Three Christian Transcendentalists*, by Ronald Vale Wells (1943).   H
A Mighty Fortress Is Our God (trans.) 43

Heermann, Johann (b. Oct. 11, 1585, Raudten, Silesia, Germany; d. Feb. 17, 1647, Lissa, Posen), the fifth and only surviving child of his parents, was educated at the St. Elisabeth Gymnasium at Breslau and the Gymnasium at Brieg, and for a short time at the University of Strassburg; became a pastor at Koeben in 1611 and remained during the terrors and hardship of the Thirty Years' War, though throat trouble forced him to give up preaching in 1634; wrote many hymns which show his spiritual serenity in spite of personal loss and danger; 16 of his hymns are translated into English.   H
Ah, Holy Jesus 231

Helmore, Thomas (b. May 7, 1811, Kidderminster, Worcester, England; d. July 6, 1890, Westminster, London), educated at Magdalen Hall, Oxford, was ordained an Anglican priest and served as curate, then vicar in Lichfield Cathedral; for 35 years was vice-principal and precentor of St. Mark's College in Chelsea; in 1846 was made master of the choristers in the Chapel Royal at St. James where he pioneered in the restoring of plainsong to liturgy; was musical editor of hymnals containing John Mason Neale's translations of Latin hymns, and translated Fetis's *Treatise on Choir and Chorus Singing* (1884); was one of

the editors of *The Hymnal Noted* (1851-54).   H
VENI EMMANUEL 133

Helms, Hal M. (b. July 10, 1923, Concord, NC), according to The Hymn Society, is a graduate of Furman University and Hartford Theological Seminary and an ordained minister in the United Church of Christ with a life-long interest in hymns; served as a pastor for 25 years in North Carolina, South Carolina, and Connecticut; in 1974, moved with his wife to the Community of Jesus on Cape Cod, Massachusetts, where his main responsibility at present is writing and editing.
Let Heaven Rejoice 355

Helvering, Sandi Patti [Patty] (b. July 12, 1956, Oklahoma City, OK), daughter of Ron and Carolyn Patty (also active in traveling music ministries), attended Crawford High School, San Diego, CA, and Anderson (IN) University (BA in music, 1979); as of 1991 had received 29 national awards from the popular music industry including 10 consecutive years for best female vocalist recording from the Gospel Music Association; divorced from her manager; is the mother of four children.
In the Name of the Lord,   NAME OF THE LORD 113

Hemy, Henri Frederick (b. Nov. 12, 1818, Newcastle-upon-Tyne, England; d. June 10, 1888, Hartlepool, Durham), born of German parents, was organist at St. Andrew's Roman Catholic Church in Newcastle, later taught music in Tynemouth and became professor of music at St. Cuthbert's College

in Ushaw, Durham; left the following publications: *Crown of Jesus Music* (1864, a popular volume among Roman Catholics), and *Royal Modern Tutor for the Pianoforte* (1858), a piano study book which went through many editions.   H
ST. CATHERINE 556, 692

Herbert, George (b. Apr. 3, 1593, Montgomery Castle, Wales; d. Mar. 1, 1633, Bemerton Rectory, Wiltshire) as a young man was a favorite in the court of James I; received his education at Westminster School and Trinity College, Cambridge, took Holy Orders and served for three notable years as rector of Bemerton, near Salisbury; left a major literary work, *The Temple*, a collection of mystical poems which was published posthumously (1633); was not known as a hymn composer during his lifetime (because of the psalm tradition), but 100 years later some 40 of his poems were included by the Wesleys in their *Hymns and Sacred Poetry* (1739).   H
Let All the World 24

Hernaman, Claudia Frances (b. Oct. 19, 1838, Addlestone, Surrey, England; d. Oct. 10, 1898, Brussels, Belgium), daughter of a Church of England clergyman and wife of a school inspector, wrote over 150 children's hymns; authored *The Child's Book of Praise: A Manual of Devotion in Simple Verse* (1873) and was co-editor of *The Altar Hymnal* (1884).
Lord, Who Throughout 200

Herring, Anne (b. Sept. 22, 1945, Grafton, ND) is a singer, recording artist, and writer for the folk-pop group Second Chapter of Acts; is

married to Buck Herring, recording producer.
Easter Song, EASTER SONG 244

Hesperian Harp (1848) is a shape-note tunebook compiled by George Hauser [or Houser], a physician who was also a traveling singing school teacher.
BOURBON (attr., but not the earliest publication) 655

Hewitt, Eliza Edmunds (b. June 28, 1851, Philadelphia, PA; d. Apr. 24, 1920, Philadelphia) was educated in the public schools and named valedictorian of her class at the Girls' Normal School, Philadelphia, where she spent her entire life; taught school a number of years; was intensely devoted to the Sunday School movement and gave much time to youth in the Northern Home for Friendless Children, and later in the Calvin Presbyterian Church, where she served as Sunday School superintendent; wrote many poems, some of which were first set to music by John R. Sweney and William J. Kirkpatrick, and later by B. D. Ackley, C. H. Gabriel, E. S. Lorenz, and Homer Rodeheaver; used the pseudonym Lidie H. Edmunds.   H
My Faith Has Found a Resting Place 495
When We All Get to Heaven 679

Hewitt, John Hill (b. 1801, New York, NY; d. 1890, Baltimore, MD), son of James Hewitt, a British emigrant, was a New York composer-promoter; studied at West Point, but left in the cadet rebellion of 1820; was a poet, actor, teacher, director, and author, whose musical career was mostly in Georgia, Virginia, and South Carolina, but

also in Baltimore; wrote Civil War songs which included "All Quiet Along the Potomac Tonight"; wrote an affective musical text, *Shadows on the Wall* (1877).
HUDSON 512

Hicks, Roy, Jr. (b. Dec. 21, 1943, Los Angeles, CA) attended North High School, Omaha, NE, and L.I.F.E. Bible College, Los Angeles, CA; was pastor of Parth Center Foursquare Church in Eugene, OR (1969-88) and Northwest District Supervisor of Foursquare Churches (1981-86); since 1988, has been Vice President and Missions Director for the same denominational group.
Praise the Name of Jesus 128

Hine, Stuart Wesley Keene [also **Keane**] (b. July 25, 1899, London, England; d. Mar. 14, 1989, Somerset) will long be remembered for his translation-paraphrase "How Great Thou Art"; was educated at Cooper's Company School, London; served in the British Army in France during World War 1; an ordained Methodist minister, was a missionary (1923-39) to Poland, Czechoslovakia, Romania, and Russia; during World War 2, worked with displaced persons in Britain; was retired in Somerset, England, and active in producing evangelical literature.   H
How Great Thou Art (trans.), O STORE GUD (arr.) 21

Hodges, Edward (b. July 20, 1796, Bristol, England; d. Sept. 1, 1867, Clifton, Bristol), a self-taught musician and organist in Bristol (1819-38), obtained his MusD at Cambridge (1825); emigrated to Canada (1838), then became direc-tor of music at Trinity Parish in New York City where he estab-lished his reputation as an organist and composer of service material and anthems; returned to England because of ill health (1863).
ODE TO JOY (adapt.)   20, 254, 311, 720

Hoffman, Elisha Albright (b. May 7, 1839, Orwigsburg, PA; d. Nov. 25, 1929, Chicago, IL), the son of devout Germans, was reared in a family that sang as part of their daily devotions; attended Central High School, Philadelphia, then Union Seminary (of the Evangelical Association) and became a minister of the Evangelical Church; was connected with the Evangelical Association publishing house in Cleveland, OH, for 11 years, and later was pas-tor of Evangelical churches and the Benton Harbor (MI) Presbyterian Church; served as editor of many music publications and was a gifted amateur writer of both words and music of gospel songs.
Leaning on the Everlasting Arms 609
What a Wonderful Savior, BENTON HARBOR 488
I Must Tell Jesus, ORWIGSBURG 621

Hoffmann, Heinrich August [von Fallersleben] (b. Apr. 2, 1798, Fallersleben, Hanover, Germany; d. Jan 29, 1874, Corvey, Westphalia, Germany) is described in *Grove's Dictionary* as a "German philologist, poet, hymn-writer and amateur composer"; received his education at Helmstedt, Brunswick, and at the University of Gottingen, and later studied Dutch literature in Holland; in 1835 was appointed

270

a professor at Breslau and later was librarian to Prince Lippe at Corvey; edited a significant history of German hymns, *Geschichte des deutschen Kirchenliedes* (Hanover, 1832 and 1854) and the famous *Schlesische Volkslieder mit Melodien* (Leipzig, 1842), a collection of Silesian folksongs, both sacred and secular, compiled with Ernst F. Richter (who edited the poetry). H CRUSADER'S HYMN (also ASCALON or SCHÖNSTER HERR JESU) 115

Holden, Oliver (b. Sept. 18, 1765, Shirley, MA; d. Sept. 4, 1844, Charlestown, MA), a carpenter by trade, moved to Charlestown, MA, in 1786 and helped to rebuild the city the British had burned; prospered financially, acquired large real estate holdings and opened a general store; was elected to the state legislature for six terms and served as pastor of the Puritan church; taught music and published several tunebooks, including *The American Harmony* (1792); *Union Harmony* (1793); *The Massachusetts Compiler* (1795); *Sacred Dirges, Hymns and Anthems* (1800), *The Modern Collection of Sacred Music* (1800), *Plain Psalmody* (1800), and *The Charlestown Collection of Sacred Songs* (1803); edited the sixth, seventh, and eighth editions of *The Worcester Collection* (1797, 1800, and 1803). H CORONATION 95

Holst, Gustav Theodore (b. Sept. 21, 1874, Cheltenham, England; d. May 25, 1934, London) received early musical training from his father; at the Royal College of Music in London, became friends with fellow student

Ralph Vaughan Williams, with whom he played sketches of compositions in process, a life-long practice; left RCOM (1898) to join the Carl Rosa Opera Company, touring with the Scottish Orchestra as trombonist; taught in several schools (1903-24), including the Royal College of Music, then turned to composition full time. PERSONENT HODIE (arr.) 142, 175, 400

Hopkins, Edward John (b. June 30, 1818, Westminster, London, England; d. Feb. 14, 1901, London), from a family of musicians, was a child singer with St. Paul's Cathedral and St. James Chapel Royal, singing for the coronation of William IV; studied organ with James Turles at Westminster Abbey and played there; was organist at Mitcham Church (at 16), St. Peter's, Islington, St. Luke's, Soho, and at Temple Church, which was a 55-year appointment and the place from which he composed, compiled several hymnals, and wrote a treatise on the organ. ELLERS is his only composition still in use. ELLERS 458, 835

Hopkins, John Henry, Jr. (b. Oct. 28, 1820, Pittsburgh, PA; d. Aug. 14, 1891, near Hudson, NY) was educated at the University of Vermont (AB, 1839 and MA, 1845) and General Theological Seminary (1850); in 1838 came to New York City to work as a reporter and to study law; taught music at General Seminary (1855-57) and edited the *Church Journal* (1853-68); designed stained glass and other church art; was ordained an Episcopal priest (1872), served Trinity Church, Plattsburg, PA (1872-76), and

Christ Church, Williamsport, PA (1876-87); published *Carols, Hymns and Songs* (1863, by 1882 in its 4th edition) and *Canticles Noted with Accompanying Harmonies* (1866). We Three Kings of Orient Are, KINGS OF ORIENT 185

Hopson, Hal Harold (b. June 12, 1933, Mound, TX), the son of a blacksmith and farmer, attended Gatesville (TX) High School, Baylor University (BA, received the Royalty Edwards scholarship in music) and Southern Baptist Seminary, Louisville, KY (MSM); became a minister of music in Nashville, TN (1969-83), and later taught church music at Westminster Choir College, Princeton, NJ (1983-84) and at Scarritt Graduate School, Nashville (1984-88); since 1986, has been organist-choirmaster, Church of the Advent, Episcopal, Nashville; is widely published with over 800 works in print, including many choral selections.
BARIUM SPRINGS HOME 438
MERLE'S TUNE 333
Sing to the Lord a New Song (ANTIPHON) 324
SING, BELIEVERS 326
The Gift of Love, GIFT OF LOVE 593

How, William Walsham (b. Dec. 13, 1823, Shrewsbury, Shropshire, England; d. Aug. 10, 1897, Leenane, County Mayo, Ireland) was known as the "Poor Man's Bishop" for the humanitarian work he did in the slums of East London; was educated at Wadham College, Oxford, and Durham University, ordained an Anglican priest (1847) and served at St. George's in Kidderminster, Holy

Cross in Shrewsbury, Whittington, and Oswestry; was appointed chaplain of the Anglican church in Rome (1865); became Suffragan Bishop of East London (1879), and the first bishop of Wakefield (1888); published *Daily Prayers for Churchmen* (1852) and *Psalms and Hymns* (1854); was co-editor (with Arthur Sullivan) of *Church Hymns* (Society for the Promotion of Christian Knowledge, 1871); wrote more than 50 hymns, a number of which are still in use.   H
For All the Saints 751
O Word of God Incarnate 310
We Give Thee but Thine Own 649

Howe, Julia Ward (b. May 27, 1819, New York, NY; d. Oct. 17, 1910, Newport, RI), followed the lead of her husband, Dr. Samuel Gridley Howe, in support of humanitarian causes; was a pioneer in women's suffrage, an ardent abolitionist, a pacifist, and social worker; frequently preached in the Unitarian fellowship, of which she was a member; wrote three volumes of poetry: *Passion Flowers* (1854), *Words of the Hour* (1856), and *Later Lyrics* (1866).   H
Mine Eyes Have Seen the Glory 416

Hoyle, Richard Birch (b. Mar. 8, 1875, Cloughfold, Lancashire, England; d. Dec. 14, 1939, London), a Baptist minister and scholar, served several pastorates in England, and in 1934 moved to the United States to take a teaching assignment at Western Theological Seminary; wrote the article on "The Holy Spirit" for the *Encyclopedia of Religion and Ethics*; was a close friend of Suzanne Bidgrain, who edited *Cantate Domino*, the hymn-

book adopted by the World Student Christian Federation.　H
Thine Is the Glory (trans.) 251

Huber, Jane Parker (b. Oct. 24, 1926, Jinan, China) was reared in a Victorian house on the campus of Hanover College in southern Indiana with a tradition of singing around the piano—both hymns and gospel songs; attended Wellesley College (1944-47), and Hanover College (BA, 1847-48); is married to William A. Huber and has six children and seven grandchildren as of 1989, and calls herself "homemaker and church volunteer"; an active Presbyterian, helped found St. Andrew's Church, Indianapolis, IN, and served on the committee for the Presbyterian hymnal *Psalms, Hymns, and Spiritual Songs* (1990); is unselfconsciously committed to inclusive language in her hymns. See her hymn collection and essays, *A Singing Faith* (Westminster Press, 1987).
God, You Spin the Whirling Planets 51
For Ages Women Hoped and Prayed 143

Hudson, Ralph E. (b. July 9, 1843, Napoleon, OH; d. June 14, 1901, Cleveland, OH) joined the Union Army and served as a nurse at the General Hospital, Annapolis, MD, during the Civil War; after discharge taught music at Mount Vernon College, Alliance, OH (1864-69); a licensed preacher in the Methodist Episcopal Church, was active in evangelistic work; was a singer, song writer, and compiler who established his own publishing company at Alliance, OH; compiled *Salvation Echoes* (1882), *Gems*

of Gospel Song (1884), *Songs of Peace, Love and Joy* (1885), and *Songs of the Ransomed* (1887), all of which were later combined into one volume titled *Quartette*; frequently set standard hymns to gospel song tunes, sometimes adding a refrain of his own.　H
At the Cross (ref.), HUDSON (attr.) 512
SATISFIED 511

Hughes, John (b. Nov. 22, 1873, Dowlais, Glamorganshire, Wales; d. May 14, 1932, Ton-teg, Llantwit Fardre, Pontypridd) lived in Llantwit Fardre most of his life; at age 12, went to work as a "door boy" at a local mine, Glyn Colliery; later became an official in the traffic department of the Great Western Railway; an active member of the Salem Baptist Church, and followed his father as deacon and precentor (music leader); wrote a large number of hymn tunes, Sunday school marches, and anthems.　H
CWM RHONDDA 271, 634, 669

Hull, Eleanor Henrietta (b. Jan. 15, 1860, Manchester, England; d. Jan. 13, 1935, London), founder and secretary of the Irish Text Society, served as president of the Irish Literary Society of London; authored several volumes on Irish literature and history.　H
Be Thou My Vision (versified) 532

Hultman, John Alfred (b. July 6, 1861, Hjärtlanda, Småland, Sweden; d. Aug. 7, 1942, Glendale, CA) showed an interest in music very early in his life; came to America with his family at the age of eight and settled on a farm in Essex, IA; taught school and direct-

ed the church choir in Fridhem, NE, and later became pastor of the church; 1879-81, studied at the Chicago Atheneum and served as choir director at the Douglas Park Covenant Church, then became an itinerant preacher and musician and traveled throughout the Midwest; in 1896-97 was on the music staff at North Park College and maintained an interest in this school throughout his life; while pastor of the Salem Square Church in Worcester, MA, continued giving concerts with his son Paul and founded the Hultman Conservatory of Music; moved to Sweden in 1909 and continued to concertize there and in the United States, becoming known as "The Sunshine Singer"; was also a writer and composer of hymns who published *Cymbalen* (1885) and collaborated with A. L. Skoog in producing *Jubelklangen* (1895); helped to compile *Sions Basun*, the first official hymnal of the Evangelical Mission Covenant Church.   H
TACK, O GUD 380

Hundert ahnmüthig-und son-derbahr geistlicher Arien; Geist-und Lehr-reiches Kirchen-und Hauss-Buch (Dresden, 1694), a collection of hymns and tunes for use in the church and home; the main part of the book has 100 selections and an appendix contains 35 more.
WUERTTEMBERG 468

Husband, John Jenkins (b. 1760, Plymouth, England; d. May 19, 1825, Philadelphia, PA) was a clerk at Surrey Chapel in his early years in Plymouth; came to America in 1809 and settled in Philadelphia, where he conducted

"singing schools" and served St. Paul's Protestant Episcopal Church as clerk; composed a number of hymn tunes and anthems, and supplied "an improved mode of teaching music" as a part of Andrew Adgate's *Philadelphia Harmony* (1790).   H
REVIVE US AGAIN 723

Hussey, Jennie Evelyn (b. Feb. 8, 1874, Henniker, NH; d. 1958, Concord) began writing poetry when she was very young; spent most of her life caring for an invalid sister on the farm where four generations of her Quaker ancestors had lived before her; toward the end of her life, she asked to be publicly baptized, a non-Quaker custom; late in life was stricken with crippling arthritis, and, according to Phil Kerr (*Music in Evangelism*), spent her last years in the Home for the Aged in Concord, NH.
Lead Me to Calvary 211

Hustad, Donald Paul (b. Oct. 2, 1918, Sioux Agency, Yellow Medicine Co., MN) at age one lost his father due to a hunting accident; lived with his mother and brother at the Boone Biblical College, Boone, IA, through high school; began to study piano at age four, and continued his education at John Fletcher College (BA, 1940) and Northwestern University (MMus, 1945 and DMus, 1963); earned diplomas as Associate of the American Guild of Organists (AAGO, 1969) and Fellow of the Royal College of Organists, London (FRCO, 1974); was a staff musician at WMBI, Chicago (1942-45) and musical director of "Club Time" (a program of hymns, with soloist

George Beverly Shea) on the ABC radio network (1945-53); taught at Olivet Nazarene College, Kankakee, IL (1946-50) and at Moody Bible Institute, Chicago (beginning in 1947), and was Director of the Sacred Music Department at Moody (1950-63); was organist for Billy Graham crusades (1961-67); served as professor of church music, Southern Baptist Theological Seminary (1966-86); as an editor for Hope Publishing Company, Chicago and Carol Stream, IL (1950-83), assisted in compiling *Tabernacle Hymns, No. 5* (1953), *Worship and Service Hymnal* (1957), *Youth Worship and Sing* (1959), and *Favorite Hymns of Praise* (1967); was co-editor with Cliff Barrows of *Crusader Hymns* (1966) and *Crusade Hymn Stories* (1967), and editor of *Fanny Crosby Speaks Again* (1977); was principal editor of *Hymns for the Living Church* (1974), *The Singing Church* (1985), *The Worshiping Church: A Hymnal* (1990), and *The Worshiping Church—Worship Leaders' Edition* (1991); authored *Dictionary-Handbook to Hymns for the Living Church* (1978, the basis for many entries in this Companion), and *Jubilate! Church Music in the Evangelical Tradition* (1981); served for a number of years as member of the Editorial Advisory Board and Columnist for *The Hymn*, and was honored as a Fellow of The Hymn Society of America (1989); retired in Louisville, KY, and continues as Senior Professor of Church Music, Southern Baptist Seminary, and emeritus editor, Hope Publishing Company.   H

BURLEIGH (arr.) 279
DIADEMATA (desc.) 756

FESTAL SONG (desc.) 71
GELOBT SEI GOTT (desc.) 255
GO TELL IT (arr.) 151
GROSSER GOTT, WIR LOBEN DICH (desc.) 3
HAMBURG (desc.) 213
I WONDER AS I WANDER (arr.) 165
IL EST Nê (harm.) 177
LO DESEMBRE CONGELAT (arr.) 139
MALOTTE (arr.) 632
MESSIAH (arr.) 351
ODE TO JOY (desc.) 311
PARADOXY 58
PROMISED LAND (arr.) 674
PYE 65
THE MORNING TRUMPET (arr.) 278
ST. ANNE (desc.) 78
ST. MATTHEWS 793
ST. THEODULPH (desc.) 204
Shalom, My Friends, Shalom (trans.) 599
SLANE (arr.) 48, 107, 369, 532
STILLE NACHT (desc.) 164
TRENTHAM (desc.) 295
WAYFARING STRANGER (arr.) 774
WIE LIEBLICH IST DER MAIEN (harm.) 375

Hymns for Today's Church, a publication of the Jubilate Group (1982), founded by Michael Baughen in Great Britain for the purpose of bringing historic hymnody to "a new generation" by tastefully revising archaic language while retaining the literary tone of the hymn—along with introducing new hymns. Text revisions and testing began in 1973; the publication is now in its second edition. The editorial staff of *Hymns for Today's Church*: Michael Baughen, Chairman, Michael Perry, Secretary; words committee: Michael Saward, Chairman,

Richard Bewes, Patrick Goodland, Kenneth Habershon, Christopher Idle, Alex Mitchell, Michael Perry, Clifford Roseweir, and James Seddon; many of these are individually represented in *The Worshiping Church* and have contributed to the group-revised texts. Hymns from *Hymns for Today's Church* have been reprinted in several United States hymnals through the work of George Shorney, President of Hope Publishing Company, Carol Stream, IL.

All for Jesus! All for Jesus! (rev.) 570

Alleluia, Alleluia! Hearts to Heaven (rev.) 254

Come Down, O Love Divine! (rev.) 304

Forth in Your Name, O Lord, I Go (rev.) 397

Hark! the Voice of Love and Mercy (rev.) 475

Lord, I Was Blind (rev.) 499

My Song Is Love Unknown (rev.) 202

O Christ the Great Foundation (rev.) 709

O for a Closer Walk with God (rev.) 547

Peace, Perfect Peace (rev.) 598

Prayer Is the Soul's Supreme Desire (rev.) 620

Songs of Thankfulness and Praise (rev.) 190

Ten Thousand Times Ten Thousand (rev.) 746

Welcome, Happy Morning (rev.) 241

What Offering Shall We Give? (rev.) 490

Idle, Christopher Martin (b. Sept. 11, 1938, Bromley, Kent, England) was educated at Elthan College (1956), St. Peter's College, Oxford (BA in English Literature,

1962), and Clifton Theological College, Bristol; was ordained in the Church of England, has served as curate in churches in Lancashire and London, as priest-in-charge of St. Matthias' Church, Poplar, London (1971-76), and as rector of Limehouse, London; since 1989 has served in a rural ministry at Oakley, Suffolk, and is rector of North Hartismere; is a prolific writer for magazines and newspapers on such subjects as "Christian communication, the Gospel, and peace," and was once jailed (1960) for participation in non-violent civil disobedience against nuclear weapons; has written and published over 100 hymn texts; is editor of *Anglican Praise* and *News of Hymnody*.

All Authority and Power 260

As Sons of the Day and Daughters of Light 704

Eternal Light, Shine in My Heart 545

God, We Praise You 39

Here from All Nations 680

How Sure the Scriptures Are 312

Jesus, Come! for We Invite You 187

My Lord of Light Who Made the Worlds 13

My Lord, You Wore No Royal Crown 191

Now Let Us Learn of Christ 567

Powerful in Making Us Wise 305

Spirit of Holiness 287

The Works of the Lord Are Created 354

When the King Shall Come Again 337

Wise Men, They Came to Look 186

Ignatius of Loyola (b. 1491, Loyola, Azpeitia, Spain; d. 1556), served as a page while a youth, and, by 1516 was in the court of

Navarre; was wounded in a war with France (1521), and, while recovering, read and learned from the lives of saints; traveled to Montserrat on a pilgrimage (1522) and to the Holy Land (1523), and returned to preach throughout Europe; founded the Society of Jesus (the Jesuits) to perform tasks for the Pope, including disciplined study and missionary efforts; wrote many meditations, including the influential small *Spiritual Exercises*, still in use at retreats.
For Grace to Serve Selflessly 667

Ingalls, Jeremiah (b. March 1, 1764, Andover, MA; d. April 6, 1828, Hancock, VT) was a cooper (barrel and cask maker), farmer, and amateur musician-teacher; operated an unprofitable tavern in Newbury, VT, then sold it and moved to Rochester, VT, and then to Hancock; was a deacon in the Congregational Church where he also directed the choir; compiled *The Christian Harmony; or, Songster's Companion*, Exeter, NH (1805).
LOVE TO CHRIST (editor, possibly composer) 91, 706

Irvine, Jessie Seymour (b. July 26, 1836, Dunottar, Kincardineshire, Scotland; d. Sept. 2, 1887, Crimond), the daughter of a minister, lived with her father in the manses at Dunottar, in Peterhead, and in Crimond, Aberdeenshire where she composed the tune CRIMOND for the metrical Psalm 23.   H
CRIMOND 330, 413, 777

Iverson, Daniel (b. Sept. 26, 1890, Brunswick, GA; d. 1977) was educated at Moody Bible Institute, University of Georgia, and

University of South Carolina; was a Presbyterian minister in Lumberton, NC, the organizing minister of Shenandoah Presbyterian Church, Miami, FL (1927-51), and served churches in Georgia and South Carolina; moved to Asheville, NC, in 1962 (he had retired in 1951) to continue preaching until his death.
Spirit of the Living God, SPIRIT OF THE LIVING GOD 297

Jabusch, Willard Francis (b. Mar. 12, 1930, Chicago, IL) received his education at Quigley Preparatory School, St. Mary of the Lake Seminary (BA, STB, MA), and Northwestern University, Evanston, IL (PhD in speech, 1986), with special training in music at the University of London and other studies in Germany and Israel; served as a parish priest, St. James Catholic Church, Chicago (1956-61); was a teacher, Quigley Preparatory School (1961-63), Niles College of Loyola University (1963-66), St. Mary of the Lake Seminary (professor, beginning 1968), and is now a University Chaplain at Calvert House, the Catholic center at the University of Chicago; has written over 80 hymn texts and 40 hymn tunes, articles, four books, and the collection *Sing of Christ Jesus*.   H
The King of Glory Comes 134

Jackson, Robert (b. May, 1840, Oldham, Lancashire, England; d. July 12, 1914, Royton, Oldham) was a teacher, composer, conductor, and organist; studied at the Royal Academy of Music; served as organist and choirmaster at St. Mark's, Grosvenor Square, London; in 1868 succeeded his father (who

had been there 48 years) as organist and choirmaster at St. Peter's Church, Oldham, remaining 46 years until his death.   H
TRENTHAM 295

Jackson, Thomas Albert (b. May 2, 1931, Baltimore, MD) studied at the University of Richmond (BA, 1953), Southeastern Baptist Theological Seminary (BD, 1957), and Johns Hopkins University (PhD, 1970); was ordained and has served Baptist churches in Fredericksburg, VA, Baltimore, MD, Reisterstown, MD, McLean, VA, and Wake Forest, NC (since 1988). We Are Called to Be God's People 710

Jacob, Gordon Percival Septimus (b. July 5, 1895, Norwood, near London, England; d. June 8, 1984, Saffron Walden, Essex) started his education at Dulwich College, but, in 1914, enlisted in the army and was a prisoner of war 1917-18; studied with Charles Stanford, Herbert Howells, and Adrian Boult at the Royal College of Music, where he later was appointed professor of composition (1926); earned the DMus at London University (1935) and received many other individual honors; was named editor of Penguin Scores in 1948, and is known for prolific compositions which range from light music and film scores to chamber music, brass band, and choral works; wrote a book on orchestration.
BROTHER JAMES' AIR (arr.) 615

Jean de Fécamp (b. *c.* 1000 near Ravenna; d. Feb. 22, 1079, Fécamp, Normandy) studied at Dijon under William, Abbott of St. Benignus;

accompanied his mentor to Fécamp, a seaport town near the present Le Havre, in Normandy, to reform the Abbey there and establish a Benedictine colony; succeeded William as head of the abbey (1028-1078); in later life took a trip to the Holy Land and was thrown into prison by the Turks; returned to France in 1076 and retired to Fécamp; wrote a number of ascetic works, many for the use of the widow of Emperor Henry III.   H
Ah, Holy Jesus 231

Jenkins, David (b. Dec. 30, 1848, Trecastle, Breconshire, Wales; d. Dec. 10, 1915, Aberystwyth) was orphaned early and became a tailor's apprentice; in the tonic sol-fa singing school movement showed musical talent; studied with Joseph Parry at Aberystwyth (1874), and at Cambridge (BMus, 1878); lectured (1893) in music at the University of Wales at Aberystwyth, and then became professor (1910); was active in the *eisteddfods* (choral festivals), conducting *Cymanfaoedd Ganu*; wrote songs, oratorio, and opera, as well as hymn tunes.
PENLAN 784

Jillson, Marjorie Ann (b. Oct. 29, 1931, Detroit, MI) studied at the College of Wooster, OH (BA in religion, 1953), and worked at Gallaudet College, Washington, DC; is a dental secretary in Detroit (since 1973) and active at Grosse Pointe Memorial United Presbyterian Church.
Praise the Lord! 38

John Chrysostom; see **Chrysostom**.
Prayer of John Chrysostom 625

John (also **Mansur**) **of Damascus** (b. *c.* 696, Damascus; d. Mar. 27 or Dec. 4, *c.* 749, 754, or 780), a theologian and hymnist who lived and worked at the St. Sabas monastery near Jerusalem, was educated principally by an Italian monk named Cosmos; was an iconolator, defending the use of icons and images in the church; organized the liturgical chants for the Eastern (Orthodox) Church, and is remembered for his hymns (canons) written for office worship on the festival days of the Christian Year; wrote the treatise *The Fountains of Knowledge.*　　H
The Day of Resurrection 247

Johnson, David N. (b. June 28, 1922, San Antonio, TX; d. Aug. 2, 1987, Phoenix, AZ) received his undergraduate degree from Trinity University, San Antonio, TX, and graduate degrees from Syracuse University (MMus and PhD); taught at Syracuse University, Alfred University, and St. Olaf College; was organist-choirmaster at Trinity Episcopal Cathedral, Phoenix, AZ, and professor of music at Arizona State University; in addition to hymn tunes, arrangements, and harmonizations (over 300 publications), wrote organ music and two manuals: *Instruction Book for Beginning Organists* and *Organ Teacher's Guide.* EARTH AND ALL STARS 357

Johnson, Linda Lee (b. Nov. 9, 1947, Seattle, WA) graduated from Roosevelt High School, Seattle, WA, and Chabot College, Hayward, CA; has been a lyricist (over 25 choral anthems) since 1978, and earlier was a church secretary and music copyist; describes herself as "involved in my husband's ministry and a mom who loves teenagers"; is married to Bruce D. Johnson, Superintendent, Redwood Christian Schools, and has a son and daughter.
Be Strong in the Lord 661

Johnston, Julia Harriette (b. Jan. 21, 1849, Salineville, OH; d. Mar. 6, 1919, Peoria, IL) at age six moved to Peoria, IL, where her father was pastor of the First Presbyterian Church until his death in 1864; remained in Peoria for the rest of her life, and was a leader in the First Presbyterian Sunday School for over 40 years; wrote lesson material for primary grades which was distributed by David C. Cook Publishing Company; published several books: *School of the Master* (1880), *Bright Threads* (1897), *Indian and Spanish Neighbors* (1905), and *Fifty Missionary Heroes* (1913); wrote approximately 500 hymn poems which were set to music by various composers.　　H
Grace Greater than Our Sin 472

Jones, David Hugh (b. 1900; d. Dec. 21, 1983); no further information has been located.
W ZLOBIE LEZY (harm.) 169

Joseph, Jane M. (b. *c.* 1894, London, England; d. 1929, London), studied at Norland Place School, St. Paul's Girls' School, Brook Green, Girton College, Cambridge, and later with Gustav Holst; directed choirs at Kensington and Caterham; composed all her life, beginning as a youth, including orchestral, choral, vocal solo, and piano music.
On This Day Earth Shall Ring (trans.) 175

279

Jubilate Group, founded in the early 1960s by Michael Baughen, with Richard Bews, Christopher Collins, Timothy Dudley-Smith, Christopher Idle, Gavin Reid, Edward Shirras, Michael Perry, Michael Saward, James Seddon, Norman Warren, and David Wilson, to write hymns and music for youth—the "new generation" no longer interested in traditional metrical hymnody and Anglican chant. The group found a publisher in The Church Pastoral Aid Society, who published *Youth Praise* (1966), *Youth Praise 2* (1969), and *Psalm Praise* (1973), all widely sold in England. With an enlarged group of authors and composers, they assembled *Hymns for Today's Church* (1982), which has provided many new texts and tunes in *The Worshiping Church* through the encouragement of George Shorney, President of Hope Publishing Company. Other Jubilate publications include *Church Family Worship* (1986, 1988), *Carols for Today* (1986), *Carol Praise* (1987), *Let's Praise* (1988), *Psalms for Today* and *Songs from the Psalms* (1989-90), and *Come Rejoice!* (1990). See the entries for individuals or hymnals for specific hymns.

Jüngst, Hugo (b. Feb. 26, 1853, Dresden, Germany; d. Mar. 3, 1923, Dresden) was a conductor, composer, and arranger; was educated at the Dresden Conservatory (1871-76) and founded the Dresden Male Choral Society, a group for which he arranged and composed; became well known as a leader of festivals. JUNGST (arr.) 166

Kaan, Frederic [Fred] H. (b. July 27, 1929, Haarlem, Holland) was the son of Herman Kaan, a Netherlands Railways worker, and Brandina Prinson; lived in Amersfoort, then in Zeist where he attended high school; during the Nazi occupation of Holland, as part of the Resistance, his family sheltered a Jewish woman and an escaped political prisoner; was only nominally Christian as a youth, but, through confirmation classes taught by J. M. van der Linde, joined the Reformed Church (1947); studied for the ministry at the State University of Utrecht (entered 1949), then at Western College at Bristol, London (1952-54); was ordained July 6, 1955, ministered at Windsor Road Congregational Church, Barry, South Wales (1955-1963), and followed that with an international ministry in over 60 countries; became active with Amnesty International and other housing and disarmament groups; pastored Pilgrim Church, Plymouth, England; was Minister-Secretary of the International Congregational Council, Geneva (1968-1970); served as editor of *Reformed Press Service* and *Reformed World*; was Moderator of West Midlands Province, United Reformed Church, England (1978-85); was awarded an honorary ThD, Reformed Theological Academy, Debrecen, Hungary; wrote his dissertation, "Emerging Language in Hymnody," for Geneva Theological College (PhD with distinction, 1984).
Help Us Accept Each Other 437

Kaiser, Kurt Frederic (b. Dec. 17, 1934, Chicago, IL) was born into a hymn-loving home: his father, Otto Kaiser, was chairman

of a hymnbook compilation committee of the Plymouth Brethren; received musical training at Northwestern University (BMus and MMus) and is a brilliant pianist (in concerts with George Beverly Shea, among others), arranger, composer, and conductor; for more than 30 years was associated with Word, Waco, TX, serving as Vice President and Director of Music, in charge of all recording; a deacon in the Seventh and James Baptist Church, has served as pianist for Sunday evening services; has written approximately 60 hymn texts and tunes in popular styles; collaborated in several musicals, including *Tell It Like It Is* (1969) and *God's People*; edited *Sing and Celebrate* (I and II); received the honorary Doctor of Sacred Music degree from Trinity College, Deerfield, IL (1973); still lives in Waco, TX, where he continues composing, conducting, and teaching.   H
CROSSROADS 631
Pass It On, PASS IT ON 739
O How He Loves You and Me, PATRICIA 479

Katholisches Gesangbuch [Catholic Hymnbook] (Vienna, *c.* 1774), a book published at the request of Maria Theresa (1717-80), empress of Austria and a devout Roman Catholic of the Hapsburg family.
GROSSER GOTT, WIR LOBEN DICH 3

Kelly, Thomas (b. July 13, 1769, Kellyville, Ireland; d. May 14, 1855, Dublin), who was a lifelong brilliant scholar, received his early education at Trinity College, Dublin; first studied for the bar, but

felt called to the ministry and took Anglican Holy Orders in 1792; because of his evangelical preaching, came into disfavor with the archbishop, left the established church and became an independent minister; wealthy, built a number of churches of his sect; published *A Collection of Psalms and Hymns* (1802), *Hymns on Various Passages of Scripture* (1804), and *Hymns by Thomas Kelly, Not Before Published* (1815); wrote at least 765 hymns, and in 1815 published a companion volume of tunes he had written in a variety of meters.H
Praise the Savior, Ye Who Know Him 125
The Head That Once Was Crowned 268

Kempis, Thomas à; see **Thomas à Kempis**.

Ken, Thomas (b. July, 1637, Berkhampstead, Hertfordshire, England; d. Mar. 19, 1711, Warminster, Wiltshire) was trained at Winchester College and New College, Oxford, ordained an Anglican priest (1662), and served several small churches in England; served at Winchester Cathedral and College (1669-79); published *Manual of Prayers for the Use of the Scholars of Winchester College* (1674); was briefly chaplain to Princess Mary and later, to the British fleet; in 1685 was made Bishop of Bath and Wells; was one of seven bishops imprisoned in the Tower of London for refusing to subscribe to James II's Declaration of Indulgence, was tried and acquitted; wrote much poetry, published in four volumes (1721, posthumously).   H
A Morning Prayer 360

An Evening Prayer 361
Praise God from Whom All
Blessings (Doxology) 808, 809

Kendrick, Graham (b. Aug. 2,
1950, Blisworth, Northamptonshire, England), son of a Baptist
minister, now lives in London and
is part of Ichthus Fellowship; has
served with Youth With a Mission,
leading outdoor singing; according
to Oxford University professor
David Cook, "is being sung all over
England, high church and low,
Anglican and Charismatic"; has
been active in public demonstrations called "Marches of Praise" or
"Make Way" marches through
streets, housing complexes, and
secular parades; authored songs
which have been featured on
"Praise Nine" and "Praise Ten"
recordings of Maranatha! Music,
and on Star Song's recording, "We
Believe," a "best-of" from his Make
Way label in Great Britain.
Shine, Jesus, Shine, SHINE, JESUS,
SHINE 721

Kennedy, Benjamin Hall (b.
Nov. 4, 1804, Summer Hill, near
Birmingham, England; d. Apr. 6,
1889, near Torquay, Devonshire)
was trained at King Edward's
School (Birmingham), Shrewsbury
School, and St. John's, Cambridge;
was a fellow at St. John's (1828-36)
and headmaster of Shrewsbury
School (1836-66); ordained in the
Church of England, served as
prebendary of Lichfield Cathedral,
rector of West Felton, Salop, and
canon at Ely; was very active in
writing, compiling, adapting, and
translating hymns (mostly from
German); published a *Psalter*, or the
Psalms of David, in English Verse,
1860, and *Hymnologia Christiana, or*

*Psalms and Hymns Selected and
Arranged in the Order of the Christian
Seasons*, 1863.   H
Ask Ye What Great Thing I Know
(trans.) 224

Kentucky Harmony (1816); see
Davisson, Ananias.

Kerr, Hugh Thompson (b. Feb.
11, 1871, Elora, Ontario, Canada;
d. June 27, 1950, Pittsburgh, PA)
received his schooling at the
University of Toronto and Western
Theological Seminary, Pittsburgh,
PA; was ordained into the
Presbyterian ministry and served
churches in Kansas and Illinois,
with a long tenure at Shadyside
Presbyterian Church (1913-46),
Pittsburgh, where he pioneered in
religious broadcasting; was elected
Moderator of the General Assembly
of the Presbyterian Church in the
U.S.A. (1930); served as chairman
of the committees for the
Presbyterian *Hymnal* (1933) and the
Presbyterian *Book of Common
Worship*.   H
God of Our Life 370

Kethe, William (b. *c.* 1530,
Scotland; d. 1594, Dorsetshire,
England) is believed to have been a
native of Scotland, but no record of
his early life is available; was in
exile in Frankfort and Geneva during the persecution under "Bloody
Mary" (1555-58); may have been
one of the scholars who worked on
the English-language Geneva
("Breeches") Bible (1560); served as
chaplain to the British troops
under the Earl of Warwick, at
Havre; returning to England, was
vicar of Childe Oxford, Dorsetshire
(1561-93); contributed 25 metrical
psalms to the Anglo-Genevan

Psalter (1561) which later appeared in the Scottish Psalter (1564-65). H
All People That on Earth Do Dwell 317
O Worship the King (excerpts) 29

Key, Francis Scott (b. Aug. 9, 1779, Pipe's Creek, Frederick Co., MD; d. Jan. 11, 1843, Baltimore, MD) graduated from St. John's College (1796) in law; moved to Washington, DC (1802) and, from there, was involved in the release of prisoners from the British during the War of 1812; wrote the "Star-Spangled Banner" from a British ship in the Baltimore harbor (Sept. 14, 1814); was United States Attorney for the District of Columbia (1833-41), settling a dispute between Alabama and the United States government over Indian lands; published a collection of his poetry in 1857.
The Star-Spangled Banner 423

Kilpatrick, Bob (b. Oct. 25, 1952, Louisville, KY), son of a retired Air Force chaplain, graduated from Wheatland High School (1970); became a traveling concert performer, recording artist, and publisher (Prism Tree Music and Bob Kilpatrick Music); was also music minister of Bethel Church, Redding, CA (1974-76).
Lord, Be Glorified, GLORIFIED 537

Kirchengesänge (Berlin, 1566), a Bohemian Brethren hymnal; see **All Glory Be to God on High** 82.
MIT FREUDEN ZART 8, 50.

Kirkpatrick, William James (b. Feb. 27, 1838, Duncannon, PA; d. Sept. 20, 1921, Germantown, PA)

received early musical training from his father and later studied with several recognized music teachers; was a fife major during the Civil War, and later a furniture dealer in Philadelphia (1862-78); edited his first music collection at age 21, *Devotional Melodies* (1859), and thereafter compiled some 100 books, collaborating mostly with John R. Sweney, but also with H. L. Gilmour and John H. Stockton, and publishing with the John J. Hood Company, Philadelphia; wrote many favorite gospel song melodies for his publications; was a life-long Methodist, associated first with Wharton Street M. E. Church and later as director of music for 11 years at Grace M. E. Church. H
CRADLE SONG 149
DUNCANNON 211
GREENWELL 480
JESUS SAVES 728
LANDAS (arr.) 495
TRUST IN JESUS 520

Kitchin, George William (b. Dec. 7, 1827, Naughton, Suffolk, England; d. Oct. 13, 1912, Durham, England), the son of a minister, was educated at Ipswich Grammar School, King's College School and College, and Christ Church, Oxford, where he later served as Censor and Tutor; from 1883-94 was Dean of Winchester, in 1894 became Dean of Durham and in 1909, Chancellor of Durham University; published many books on archaeology, biography, and history. H
Lift High the Cross 229

Klein, Laurie Brendemuehl (b. Nov. 29, 1950, Watertown, WI) attended Oconomowoc High School (1968), St. Olaf College (BA in Art, with honors, 1972), and

Whitworth College (1985-88 in Theater); tours as storyteller-musician with her husband, Bill.
I Love You, Lord 124

Knapp, Phoebe Palmer (b. Mar. 9, 1839, New York, NY; d. July 10, 1908, Poland Springs, ME), daughter of a Methodist evangelist, showed unusual musical talent as a young girl; at age 16 married John Fairfield Knapp, a successful business man and founder of the Metropolitan Life Insurance Company; was a close friend of Fanny Crosby and a generous leader in promoting evangelical and humanitarian causes; was mother of Joseph Palmer Knapp (d. 1951), president of Crowell-Collier Publishing Company; published over 500 gospel song tunes; is remembered as composer of the tune ASSURANCE and the music for "Open the Gates of the Temple," for both of which Fanny Crosby wrote the words.   H
ASSURANCE 514

Knight, Gerald Hocken (b. July 27, 1908, Wyngarvey, near St. Austell, Cornwall, England; d. Sept. 16, 1979, London) was an organ student at Truro School, Peterhouse, Cambridge (1926-29), College of St. Nicolas, Chislehurst, and the Royal College of Music (1929-31); was a World War 2 airman in the Royal Air Force; was organist at Truro Cathedral and Canterbury Cathedral (1937-52), and music editor for *Hymns Ancient and Modern Revised* (1950) and other publications.
JACOB'S LADDER (harm.) 637

Koch, Heinrich Christoph (b. Oct. 10, 1749, Rudolstadt, Germany; d. Mar. 19, 1816, Rudolstadt) studied violin and composition at Rudolstadt, Berlin, Weimar, Dresden, and Hamburg; was concertmaster at the court of Rudolstadt; compiled the influential theory texts *Versuch einer Anleitung zur Composition* (1782-93), *Musickalisches Lexikon* (1802), and a harmony *Handbuch* (1811), as well as a *Choralbuch* for wind instruments (1816) which has provided some hymn tunes.
AUCH JETZT MACHT GOTT 740

Kocher, Conrad (b. Dec. 16, 1786, Ditzingen, near Stuttgart, Germany; d. Mar. 12, 1872, Stuttgart) studied piano and composition in St. Petersburg, and later spent a year in Italy, becoming greatly interested in *a cappella* singing and the music of Palestrina; founded the School of Sacred Song in Stuttgart (1821) and became director of music in the collegiate church there, setting a standard for reforms in German church music; was author of *Die Tonkunst in der Kirche* (1823) and compiler of *Zionsharfe* (1855); also wrote two operas, an oratorio, and numerous smaller works.   H
DIX 181, 353, 562

Kremser, Edward (b. Apr. 10, 1838, Vienna, Austria; d. Nov. 26, 1914, Vienna) was chorusmaster of the Vienna Männergesangverein and a leader in choral singing in his day; composed many works for voices and instruments, and published the popular *Sechs Altniederländische Volkslieder* (1877); edited *Wiener Lieder und Tänze* (2 vols., 1912 and 1913).   H
KREMSER (arr.) 354, 376

Lafferty, Karen L. (b. Feb. 29, 1948, Alamogordo, NM), according to Carlton Young in H. Myron Braun's *Companion to the Book of Hymns Supplement*, was an oboist in the New Mexico All-State Symphony; graduated from Eastern New Mexico University (1970); continued singing in folk festivals and night clubs, but moved to Los Angeles (1971) and soon shifted to the music of the "Jesus movement"; sang at Calvary Chapel in Costa Mesa, CA, and recorded for Maranatha! Music; founded "Musicians for Mission" in Amsterdam, Netherlands (1981), a performing group touring Europe.
Seek Ye First the Kingdom of God, LAFFERTY 447

Landgrave, John Phillip (b. May 9, 1935, Marion, IN) was educated at Emory University, Atlanta, GA, Eastern Kentucky State College, Richmond (BA in music), The Southern Baptist Theological Seminary, Louisville, KY (BCM, MCM in voice, DMA), with post-doctoral studies at University of Southern California (1971-72), Indiana University (1978), England (1980), and in music missions in Europe, Africa, and the Far East (1986); has been minister of music in Kentucky, Alabama, California, England, and Georgia, and a traveling evangelist's soloist/songleader throughout the South, Southeast, and Southwest; has taught in workshops, clinics and international missions; since 1965, has been Professor of Church Music at The Southern Baptist Theological Seminary, Louisville; has extensively published compositions and arrangements, including works for the Third Army Band and Chorus

(1959-60), oratorios, folk musicals, cantatas, anthems, hymns, and other compositions.
He Is Coming Soon, COMING SOON 281

Lang, John Dunmore (b. Aug. 25, 1799, Greenock on Clyde, England; d. Aug. 8, 1878, Sydney, Australia), of Scottish ancestry, moved with his parents to Largs, Ayrshire, where he attended school; studied for the ministry at University of Edinburgh (MA, 1820, DD, 1825); traveled to Australia, then a prison colony, for ministry (1822), translating hymns during his journeys; served in the Scots' Church of Sidney, organizing a Synod in New South Wales (which later expelled him, then reinstated him); lectured and wrote extensively in Australia, England, and all of Europe; his writings include several books of translations, most done while he was at sea.
Jesus Lives and So Shall I (trans.) 246

Langran, James (b. Nov. 10, 1835, St. Pancras, London, England; d. June 8, 1909, Tottenham, London) was organist at St. Michael's, Wood Green (1856-59), Holy Trinity, Tottenham (1859-70), and All Hallows Church, Tottenham (1870-1909); taught music at St. Katherine's Training College, Tottenham (1878-1909); was music editor of *The New Mitre Hymnal* (1875) and composer of about 50 hymn tunes.
LANGRAN 783

Lathbury, Mary Artemisia (b. Aug. 10, 1841, Manchester, Ontario Co., NY; d. Oct. 20, 1913, East

Orange, NJ), the daughter of a Methodist minister, was a professional artist, as well as a writer and poet; served as general editor of youth publications for the Methodist Sunday School Union and much of her poetry first appeared in those journals; founded the youth movement known as the "Look-Up Legion"; was known as the "Poet Laureate of Lake Chautauqua" because of her close association with that New York conference—which still uses her hymn "Day Is Dying in the West" each Sunday evening.   H
Break Thou the Bread of Life 315
O Lord Most High 828

Laurinus,   Laurentius Laurentii (b. 1573, Söderköping, Sweden; d. Nov. 29, 1655, Häradshammar) studied at the University of Uppsala and received the master's degree at Wittenberg (1603); became headmaster of a school in Söderköping; was ordained, and later served as parish priest in Häradshammar and Jonsberg for 46 years, though he was blind for the last part of his life; wrote books in Swedish, German and Latin, and published *Musica rudimenta* (1622), Sweden's first textbook on singing; published *Haffenrefferi Compendium Locorum Theologicorum*, and included several of his songs in an appendix, including the popular "I himmelen."   H
In Heaven Above 682

Lavallée, Calixa (b. Dec. 28, 1842, Théodosie de Verchères [now Calixa-Lavallée], Quebec, Canada; d. Jan. 21, 1891, Boston, MA) was the son of Augustin Pâquet dit Lavallée, a band director and

instrument builder; studied in Montreal, and played piano, violin, and cornet as an itinerant theater musician (from 1857) in Canada, the United States, and as distant as Brazil; was a bandsman in the American Civil War (for the North), then taught in Quebec, California, Louisiana, and Massachusetts; was director of the New York Grand Opera House (c. 1870-72); after further study at the Paris Conservatoire (1873-75), returned to Montreal where he worked in church music and studio teaching, and unsuccessfully tried to begin a conservatory of music; composed comic operas, melodrama, choral and orchestral works, and light classics, including the widely performed piano piece *Le pappillon*, and a comic opera, *The Widow* (New Orleans, 1880); was commissioned to compose the tune for "O Canada!"
O CANADA 424

Leafblad, Bruce Harold (b. Oct. 28, 1939, Waukegan, IL) was educated at Central College, St. Paul, MN (BA in Music Education, 1962), Bethel Seminary, St. Paul (MDiv, 1966), University of Northern Colorado (MMus, 1967), and University of Southern California (DMA, 1976); served as minister of music at Lake Avenue Congregational Church, Pasadena, CA (1970-80); taught at Bethel College and Seminary, St. Paul (1980-83) and the Southwestern Baptist Theological Seminary, Fort Worth, TX (since 1983); participates in lectureships and workshops in worship throughout the United States; was a member of the editorial committee of *The Worshiping Church*.

Lord, We Worship and Adore You, LAKE AVENUE 832
SOUTH PASADENA 716

Leavitt, Joshua (b. 1794, Heath, MA; d. 1873, New York, NY) graduated from Yale and practiced law in Putney, VT; returned to Yale for ministry preparation and was ordained (1825) in the Congregational Church, Stratford, CT; served in anti-slavery and temperance societies; edited *The Christian Lyre*, a shape-note tunebook which he also published (1830).
PLEADING SAVIOR (ed.) 580, 813

Leech, Bryan Jeffery (b. May 14, 1931, Buckhurst Hill, Essex, England) in 1973 won first prize for the hymn "Let God Be God," used in the ecumenical evangelistic movement "Key 73"; was educated at London (England) Bible College, Barrington (MA) College (BA), and North Park Seminary (Chicago, IL), and has studied music theory at Westmont (CA) College; affiliated with the Evangelical Covenant denomination since coming to the United States in 1955 (ordained 1959), has served pastorates in Boston, MA, Montclair, NJ, and San Francisco and, recently, the Montecito Covenant Church in Santa Barbara, CA; a freelance writer and religious broadcaster since 1974, has written over 10 hymn texts and five hymn tunes (several included in contemporary hymnals), ballads, a musical play *Ebenezer*, and a musical adaptation of Dickens's "A Christian Carol"; co-authored the novel *It Must Have Been McNutt*, was an assistant editor of Fred Bock's best-selling *Hymns for the Family of God* (Paragon,

1976) and co-authored its *Hymnal Companion* (Paragon, 1979); was a member of the editorial committee for *The Worshiping Church*.   H
A Prayer for Unity in the Church 707
All Things Are Yours 657
Brethren, We Have Met to Worship (st. 3) 802
Come, Share the Lord, DIVERNON 782
Communion Service Call to Worship 769
Happy The Home When God Is There (adapt.) 389
Kind and Merciful God, ELFAKER (adapt.) 455
Let Your Heart Be Broken 429
Lord of All Leisure Time 398
Make Room within My Heart, O God 559
On Listening to God 627
Praise the Savior, Ye Who Know Him (adapt.) 125
Preparation for Giving 647
Spirit, Now Live in Me, LOIS 284
The People of God 804
This Is a Time to Remember, DUDLEY 792
Through All the World 738
We Are God's People 700

Leland, John (b. May 14, 1754, Grafton, MA; d. Jan. 14, 1841, Cheshire, MA), with little formal education, felt the call of God at the age of 20 and was licensed as a Baptist preacher (1775); worked in Orange, VA (1776-90), for the separation of the Episcopal Church from the state and the adoption of the state constitution (1776); returned to Cheshire, MA (1792), where he preached over 8,000 sermons and actively published evangelistic literature; took "the biggest cheese in America" (1,450 lbs.), a gift from the farmers of Cheshire,

by ox-cart, to President Jefferson, preaching along the way; baptized "one thousand three hundred and fifty-two," according to his own account in *The Writings of the late Elder John Leland, including Some Events In His Life, Written by Himself, with Additional Sketches, &c. by Miss L. F. Greene*, published posthumously by his niece (Lanesboro, MA; printed by G. W. Wood, New York, 1845, p. 513). It is unlikely that Leland is the author of "O When Shall I See Jesus," although he wrote many hymns.
O When Shall I See Jesus? (attr.) 278

Lemmel, Helen Howarth (b. Nov. 14, 1864, Wardle, Manchester, England; d. Nov. 1, 1961, Seattle, WA), daughter of a Wesleyan Methodist pastor in England, was brought to America in 1873, lived briefly in Mississippi and settled in Wisconsin; a brilliant singer, studied voice in the United States and Germany (four years), gave concerts and sang in churches, traveling widely; participated in Chautauqua groups in Illinois and Wisconsin in the early 1900s; taught studio voice in Milwaukee and Madison, WI, and later at Moody Bible Institute and the Bible Institute of Los Angeles; made her home in Seattle, WA, and was a member of Ballard Baptist Church; wrote about 500 hymns and much music for children.   H
Turn Your Eyes upon Jesus, LEM-MEL 452

Lew, Timothy T'ing Fang (b. Wenchaw, Chekiang, China, 1891; d. Aug. 5, 1947, Albuquerque, NM), according to William J. Reynolds in *Companion to Baptist Hymnal*, was

educated in China, at Yale University (BD), Columbia University (MA, PhD), and Union Theological Seminary, and lectured at American colleges and universities (1926-28); was elected chairman of the committee for the Chinese Union hymnal, *Hymns of Universal Praise* (1936); was the Chinese delegate to the World Council of Churches (1927-39); served in the legislative body of the Chinese government (1936-41); died while teaching at the University of New Mexico.
O Christ the Great Foundation 709

Lewis, Freeman (b. 1780; d. 1859) lived in Uniontown, PA; amateur musician and traveling teacher, and a surveyor by trade; compiled *The Beauties of Harmony* (1813, 1816, and 1818), a collection of camp meeting hymns used for instruction in singing schools.
BOURBON (attr.) 655

Liljestrand, Paul Frederick (b. May 15, 1931, Montclair, NJ) was, until recently, a professional concert artist under Columbia Artists Management—accompanist for other soloists, an organist, and a member of the duo-piano team Krellwitz and Liljestrand; received musical training at Juilliard School of Music (BS, 1952 and MS, 1953), and Union Theological Seminary's School of Sacred Music (SMM, 1958); was Chairman of the Sacred Music Department of Northeastern Collegiate Bible Institute and Minister of Music at Brookdale (NJ) Baptist Church; was Chairman of the Department of Music, Nyack (NY) College (1972-84); in 1966 became minister of music, Calvary Baptist Church, New York City,

where he currently is Director of Music and Fine Arts; has written and published in excess of 400 hymn tunes, cantatas, and anthems.
CONRAD 24, 738

Lillenas, Haldor (b. Nov. 19, 1885, Stord, near Bergen, Norway; d. Aug. 18, 1959, Aspen, CO) came to America as an infant, lived with his family in South Dakota for two years and then settled in Astoria, OR; was confirmed in the Lutheran Church at the age of 15; through the ministry of the Peniel Mission in Portland, was converted and called to preach; attended Deets Pacific Bible College in Los Angeles (later known as Pasadena College); married Bertha Mae Wilson, a song writer in her own right, and they were both elders in the Church of the Nazarene; completed three-year courses in harmony, counterpoint, and composition under Daniel Protheroe and Adolph Rosenbecker at the Siegel-Myers School of Music in Chicago; traveled as an evangelist, and then pastored churches in California, Illinois, Texas, and Indiana (1914-24); during his early years, supplied songs and choir music for many song evangelists such as Homer Hammontree, Arthur McKee, and Charles M. Alexander; in 1924 founded Lillenas Music Company in Indianapolis, IN, which was purchased by the Nazarene Publishing Company in 1930, with the founder staying on as music editor for 20 years; wrote some 4,000 texts and tunes; received the honorary doctorate (DMus) from Olivet Nazarene College, Kankakee, IL. H
Wonderful grace of Jesus, WONDERFUL GRACE 497

Lindeman, Ludvig Mathias (b. Nov. 28, 1812, Trondheim, Norway; d. May 23, 1887, Oslo) was acknowledged at his funeral as the man who "taught the Norwegian people to sing"; was born into a prominent Norwegian musical family, possibly of German descent; began to study theology, but gravitated to music and was organist for Our Savior's Church, Oslo, from 1839 until his death; is chiefly remembered as a collector of Norse folk melodies, an activity which was subsidized by the national government; prepared musical settings for the Norwegian Lutheran *Salmebog* (1869) which were released in 1877 as *Koralbog for den Norske Kirke.* H
I HIMMELEN (comp.) 682
KIRKEN DEN ER ET 705

Littledale, Richard Frederick (b. Sept. 14, 1833, Dublin, Ireland; d. Jan. 11, 1890, London, England) was educated at Trinity College, Dublin, ordained, and became curate in Norwich and London; translated hymns and compiled the *People's Hymnal* (1867); participated in the Oxford Movement with John Mason Neale.
Come Down, O Love Divine! 304

Liturgy of St. James (4th century), in Greek, the Syrian rite liturgy used on St. James's Day, October 23, is named in honor of St. James The Less, the first Bishop of Jerusalem, but was developed much later in Christian history.
Let All Mortal Flesh Keep Silence 167

Lloyd, Eva Brown (b. Mar. 9, 1912, Jameson, MO) received her higher education at Northwest

Missouri State University (B.S.), and University of Missouri at Kansas City (M.A.); taught in elementary and secondary schools in Missouri, and for 15 years taught English literature at Northwest Missouri University (Maryville); a Baptist, wife and mother, is involved in Christian education in the church, and has served as director of the Women's Missionary Union; has written five hymn texts and published both poetry and prose.   H
Come, All Christians, Be Committed 578

Lockhart, Charles (b. *c.* 1745, London, England; d. Feb. 9, 1815, Lambeth, London), a blind musician whose specialty was children's choirs, was organist at St. Katherine Cree, London (1766-1815), Lock Hospital Chapel (1772 and 1790-97), St. Mary's, Lambeth (1780) and Orange Street Congregational Chapel (1780-97); composed songs, anthems, and hymn tunes.
CARLISLE 764

Longfellow, Samuel (b. June 18, 1819, Portland, ME; d. Oct. 3, 1892, Portland) was educated at Harvard College (BA, 1839) and Harvard Divinity School; was ordained (1846) in the Unitarian Church and served churches at Fall River, MA, Brooklyn, NY, and Germantown, PA; wrote a biography of his famous brother, Henry Wadsworth Longfellow, and several books of hymns.
Holy Spirit, Truth Divine 303

Longstaff, William Dunn (b. Jan. 28, 1822, Sunderland, Durham, England; d. Apr. 2, 1894, Sunderland), the son of a wealthy shipowner, gave generously to phil-

anthropic causes; was associated with the Bethesda Free Chapel, serving as its treasurer; was a close friend of Moody and Sankey, and also William Booth, and may possibly have been a member of the Salvation Army for a time.   H
Take Time to Be Holy 540

Lovelace, Austin Cole (b. Mar. 26, 1919, Rutherfordton, NC) is one of America's leading church musicians today, a teacher, author, composer and organist-director; received his education at High Point College in North Carolina (AB, 1939) and Union Theological Seminary School of Sacred Music (MSM, 1941 and DSM, 1950) with an honorary doctorate awarded by High Point College (MusD, 1963); has served as minister of music in leading Methodist and Presbyterian churches in North Carolina, Nebraska, Illinois, and Colorado; was associate professor of church music at Garrett Theological Seminary, a lecturer in hymnology at Union Theological Seminary, adjunct faculty member at Iliff School of Theology and professor of organ at Temple Buell College, Denver, then minister of music, Lovers' Lane Methodist Church, Dallas, TX; lives now in Denver, retired from his most recent position with Wellshire Presbyterian Church (1976-86), but continues actively as a guest organist, lecturer, and conductor; has published *The Organist and Hymn Playing* (1962) and *The Anatomy of Hymnody* (1965); co-authored *Music and Worship in the Church* (1960, rev. 1976) with William G. Rice, and wrote the material on hymn tunes in *Companion to the Hymnal* (1970); has written extensively on

church music in periodicals; composed a great deal of sacred choral music and many hymn tunes, with over 600 compositions in print with 34 publishers; is past president and Fellow of The Hymn Society. H
DOVE OF PEACE (arr.) 768

Lowden, Carl Harold (b. Oct. 12, 1883, Burlington, NJ; d. Feb. 27, 1963, Collingswood, NJ), usually listed as "C. Harold Lowden," learned to play the violin as a boy and began writing songs at 12 years of age; was affiliated briefly with the Hall-Mack Company, and for 12 years served as musical editor for the Evangelical and Reformed Church Board; later established his own business in Camden, NJ; for eight years taught music at the Bible Institute of Pennsylvania (now Philadelphia College of Bible) and served as minister of music for the Linden Baptist Church in Camden, NJ, for 28 years; wrote a large number of hymn tunes and edited many collections. H
LIVING 569

Lowry, Joseph C. (early 19th century) was an American composer of shape-note tunes; little is known about him other than that he was a farmer.
PISGAH (attr.) 681

Lowry, Robert (b. Mar. 12, 1826, Philadelphia, PA; d. Nov. 25, 1899, Plainfield, NJ), a popular preacher and orator, is perhaps best remembered for his contribution in writing gospel hymns and tunes; was educated at Bucknell University and served Baptist pastorates in Pennsylvania, New York, and New Jersey; was also professor of litera-

ture at Bucknell University (1869-75) and received his D.D. degree there in 1875; succeeded William Bradbury as editor of Sunday School song collections, and collaborated with William H. Doane and others in many publications for Biglow and Main, New York City; compiled *Happy Voices* (1865), *Bright Jewels* (1869), *Royal Diadem* (1873), *Welcome Tidings* (1877), *Gospel Hymn and Tune Book* (1879), *Glad Refrain* (1886), and many others. H
ALL THE WAY 641
Christ Arose!, CHRIST AROSE 235
NEED 538
Nothing but the Blood of Jesus, PLAINFIELD 471
We're Marching to Zion (ref.), MARCHING TO ZION 596
Shall We Gather at the River? HANSON PLACE 687

Lowry, Somerset Thomas Corry (b. Mar. 21, 1855, Dublin, Ireland; d. Jan. 29, 1932, Torquay, Devonshire) attended Repton School and Trinity Hall, Cambridge; was ordained (1879) and served as curate at Doncaster, Yorkshire, and as Vicar at North Holmwood, Surrey, St. Augustine's Bournemouth, Wonston, St. Bartholomew's, Southsea, Hampshire, and retired at Bournemouth; wrote about 60 hymns which were published in periodicals and magazines, devotional books, and a collection, *Hymns and Spiritual Songs* (1926).
A Man There Lived in Galilee 88

Luther, Martin (b. Nov. 10, 1483, Eisleben, Saxony, Germany; d. Feb. 18, 1546, Eisleben) was the leader of the 16th-century Reformation in the "Lutheran" tradition and is credited with the

restoration of congregational participation in worship; was educated at Magdeburg, Eisenach, and Erfurt; entered the Augustinian convent at Erfurt and was ordained a priest (1507); taught at the University in Wittenberg, where (1517) he posted his 95 theses against papal abuses and corruption in the church; after a long open struggle, defending his preaching and writings, denied the supremacy of the Pope and broke with Rome; translated the Bible into German and developed liturgies for evangelical worship: *Formula missae*, 1523 and *Deutscher messe*, 1526; wrote 37 hymns and paraphrases, and composed tunes or adapted them for folk song sources; is the subject of an article by Walter Buszin, summing up his contributions to church music, *Musical Quarterly*, XXXII, 1946.   H
A Mighty Fortress Is Our God, EIN' FESTE BURG 43
Savior of the Nations, Come (trans.) 138

Lutheran Book of Worship (1978) is the most recent hymnal of the Inter-Lutheran Commission on Worship (Lutheran Church in America, The American Lutheran Church, The Evangelical Lutheran Church of Canada, The Lutheran Church-Missouri Synod), Augsburg Publishing House, Minneapolis; has influenced entries in *The Worshiping Church* and other hymnals of the past decade. *The Hymnal Companion to the Lutheran Book of Worship* by Marilyn Kay Stulken (Philadelphia: Fortress Press, 1981) is a particularly valuable reference for hymns of all traditions.
A Hymn of Glory Let Us Sing 259

Lutkin, Peter Christian (b. Mar. 27, 1858, Thompsonville, WI; d. Dec. 27, 1931, Evanston, IL), according to Mary Kay Van Dyke (Dictionary of American Hymnology, Oberlin), attended public school in Chicago and the choir school of St. James' Church, where he became organist at age 14; graduated from Syracuse University (DMus, 1900); was director of the theory department, American Conservatory (1885-95), and director of the newly established School of Music at Northwestern University, Evanston, IL (1896); was co-founder of the American Guild of Organists and president of the Music Teacher's National Association (1911 and 1920); served as commissioner with Methodist and Episcopal hymnals.
BENEDICTION 845

Lvov (also **Lwoff**), **Alexis Feodorovitch** (b. June 6, 1799, Reval (now Tallinn), Estonia; d. Dec. 16, 1870, Romanovo, near Kovno, Lithuania) studied music under his father, who was an authority on church music and folk song, conductor of the Russian Imperial Chapel choir, and a student of Bortniansky; served in the Russian army and reached the rank of major-general; followed his father as Director of the Imperial Chapel (1836-60), editing and publishing chants of the Russian church; was an excellent violinist and wrote music for strings; also wrote three operas, a violin method, and a great variety of church music; became deaf in 1867 and retired.   H
RUSSIAN HYMN 67, 427, 685

Lyon, Meyer (b. 1751; d. 1797, Kingston, Jamaica), also listed as "Meier Leoni," was cantor in various synagogues in London, including the great Synagogue (1768-72); entered the opera field (Drury Lane or Covent Garden) but was not successful, due to his lack of acting ability and his unwillingness to sing on Friday nights or Jewish festival days; in 1787 accepted the position of *chazan* (cantor) with the Ashkenazic (European) congregation at Kingston, Jamaica, and served there until his death. H
LEONI (arr.) 66, 336, 741

Lyra Davidica, or a Collection of Divine Songs and Hymns, partly new composed, partly translated from the High-German and Latin Hymns; and set to easy and pleasant tunes (London, 1708) is a collection of 22 hymns with tunes compiled by John Walsh.
EASTER HYMN 234
Jesus Christ Is Risen Today 250

Lyte, Henry Francis (b. June 1, 1793, Ednam, near Kelso, Roxburghshire, England; d. Nov. 20, 1847, Nice, France), orphaned as a child and never strong physically, struggled to acquire an education, and graduated from Trinity College, Dublin (1814); abandoned plans for a medical career in 1815, took Holy Orders in the Church of England, and served parishes in Wexford, Marazion, and Lymington; was appointed "perpetual curate" at Lower Brixham, Devonshire, and ministered to that fishing village for 23 years; wrote more than 80 hymns and paraphrases of psalms, which were published in *Poems, Chiefly Religious*

(1833) and *The Spirit of the Psalms* (1834). H
Abide with Me, Fast Falls the Eventide 365
Praise, My Soul, the King of Heaven 25, 26
Savior, Like a Shepherd Lead Us (attr.) 522

Maccall, William (b. Feb. 25, 1812, Largs, Ayrshire, Scotland; d. Nov. 19, 1888, Bexley Heath, near London, England) was educated at the University of Glasgow (MA, 1833) and the Presbyterian Academy at Geneva; served Unitarian churches in Lancashire and Devonshire; compiled and translated *Hymns of Sweden* (1868).
In Heaven Above (trans.) 682

MacDuff, John Ross (b. May 23, 1818, Bonhard, Perthshire, Scotland; d. Apr. 30, 1895, Chislehurst, Kent, England) received high school and university training in Edinburgh (later, the Universities of Edinburgh, Glasgow, and New York each awarded him honorary DD degrees); was ordained in the Church of Scotland (1842), served churches in Forfarshire, Perthshire, and Glasgow, and declined an offer by the crown to be appointed to the Cathedral Church of Glasgow; in 1871 resigned the pastorate to devote himself to writing; taking up residence at Chislehurst, Kent, produced many devotional books, such as *The Faithful Promise*, and *Morning and Night Watches*, which had enormous sales; was a member of the hymnal committee of the Church of Scotland, and wrote 31 hymns which appeared in *Altar Stones* (1853) and *The Gates of Praise* (1876). H
Christ Is coming! Let Creation 271

Mackay, William Paton (b. May 13, 1839, Montrose, Scotland; d. Aug. 22, 1885, Portree), educated at the University of Edinburgh, practiced medicine for a number of years; feeling called to the ministry, was ordained and became pastor of the Prospect Street Presbyterian Church, Hull (1868); wrote a number of hymns, 17 of which appeared in W. Reid's *Praise Book* (1872). H
Revive Us Again 723

Macmillan, Alan (b. Nov. 20, 1947, Nyack, NY), according to information from The Hymn Society, is the son of a Nyack College music professor and organist; began the study of the violin at the age of nine, went to high school at the Interlochen Arts Academy in Michigan; won the first prize in composition at Boston University where he received the BM, and then spent two years in the education of the mentally handicapped; completed the MM at Boston University, the PhD in music at Harvard, and taught Theory and Composition for two years at Boston University; in 1977, became Composer-in-Residence and Assistant Director of Music at the Community of Jesus (Orleans, MA) where he lives with his wife and two children; has received a number of commissions, and over 30 of his works are published by Paraclete Press.
ROCK HARBOR 355

Macmillan, Ernest Campbell (b. Aug. 18, 1893, Mimico, Ontario, Canada; d. May 6, 1973, Toronto) was the son of Dr. Alexander Macmillan, a Presbyterian minister and editor of the *Hymnary of the*

United Church of Canada (1930); was a child prodigy who played the organ in public at age 10, and studied later at the University of Toronto, University of Edinburgh, and Oxford University; attended the Wagner Festival in Bayreuth at the outbreak of World War 1 (1914) and was interned at Ruhleben prison camp for four years; during imprisonment, completed a major work based on Swinburne's ode, *England*, which earned him the MusD degree from Oxford University; after the war, returned to Canada and became conductor of the Toronto Symphony Orchestra (1931-56) and conductor of the Mendelssohn Choir (1942-57); was principal of the music Conservatory (1926-42) and Dean of the Music Faculty, Toronto University (1927-52); was knighted by George V in recognition of his service to Canada as composer, teacher, conductor, and organist; published several music textbooks, and volumes relating to Canada's indigenous Indian and French-Canadian music. H
TEMPUS ADEST FLORIDUM (arr.) 156, 337

Madan, Martin (b. 1726, Hertingfordbury, England; d. May 2, 1790, Epsom, Surrey), educated at Westminster School and Christ Church, Oxford, was admitted to the bar in 1748; was converted after hearing John Wesley preach, gave up law and was ordained to the Anglican ministry; served as chaplain at Lock Hospital, an institution "for the restoration of unhappy females"; was so disturbed by the problems of the patients that he wrote a treatise, *Thelyphthora* (1780), advocating

polygamy as the solution to the problem, thereby incurring so much criticism that he was forced to retire to Epsom; wrote few original hymns, but published *A Collection of Psalms and Hymns, Extracted from Various Authors* (1760) referred to as "The Lock Collection," which was the basis for many later hymnals. Also see Giardini. H
Jesus Comes with Clouds Descending 283

Mahlmann, Siegfried August (b. May 13, 1771, Leipzig, Germany; d. Dec. 16, 1826, Leipzig) studied law at the University of Leipzig, then opened a bookshop there and edited two newspapers; wrote songs—some for children.
God Bless Our Native Land 421

Maker, Frederick Charles (b. 1844, Bristol, England; d. Jan. 1, 1927, Bristol) spent his entire life in Bristol, beginning his musical career as a chorister in the cathedral; served as organist in several "free" churches in the city, with 28 years at the Redland Park Congregational Church; was visiting professor of music for 20 years at Clifton College and conductor of the Bristol Free Church Choirs Association; at the invitation of his organ teacher, Alfred Stone, contributed several hymn tunes to *The Bristol Tune Book* (1881); also wrote cantatas, anthems, and piano compositions. H
ST. CHRISTOPHER 216
REST 591

Malan, Henri Abraham César (b. July 7, 1787, Geneva, Switzerland; d. May 18, 1864, Vandoeuvres) was schooled at the College of Geneva, where his father was a professor; ordained in the Reformed Church, served as pastor of the Chapelle du Temoignage in Geneva; was bold and outspoken in preaching against the universalism and formalism of the Established Church, aroused opposition and resigned from his parish; founded a chapel on his own property and preached there for 43 years; made several evangelistic tours to Belgium, Scotland, France, and England, specializing in "personal soul winning"; wrote more than 1000 hymns and tunes, and published *Chants de Sion* (1841) which greatly influenced Protestant hymn singing in France. H
HENDON 224, 568

Malotte, Albert Hay (b. May 19, 1895, Philadelphia, PA; d. Nov. 16, 1964, Hollywood, CA), son of a choirmaster, studied piano and organ early; worked as a theater organist for silent motion picture houses in Europe while studying there; returned to Hollywood and founded a school to train theater organists (1927), but closed it after one year because of the addition of sound to motion pictures; joined the Walt Disney studio as a composer (1935) and later music director, composing the scores for 15 animated films during the 1930s; composed two ballets and much sacred music for choir and for solo, including "The Beatitudes," similar to the more famous "The Lord's Prayer" setting.
MALOTTE 632

Mann, Arthur Henry (b. May 16, 1850, Norwich, Norfolk, England; d. Nov. 19, 1929, Cambridge) was educated at

Norwich Cathedral and New College, Oxford; served briefly as organist at various churches and finally went to King's College Chapel (1876), Cambridge, where he held the position with distinction for 53 years; wrote many hymn tunes, anthems, and organ works; was an authority on the music of Handel and highly skilled in developing boys' choirs; was musical editor for Charles D. Bell's *The Church of England Hymnal* (1895). H
ANGEL'S STORY 648

Marcello, Benedetto (b. July 24 or Aug. 1, 1686, Venice, Italy; d. July 24 or 25, 1739, Brescia [birth date may have been confused with death date on his tombstone]) studied violin with his father, and voice and music theory with Gasparini; was encouraged by his mother to study law; spent some time in public service—on the Council of Forty, then as Governor of Pola (1730-37), and eventually as Chamberlain of Brescia (1738); wrote operatic political satire; composed prolifically for strings, voice, chorus, harpsichord, and organ, gaining wide popularity for his cantata-style settings of the first 50 Psalms (with varied vocal parts in Italian paraphrases by Giustiniani).
PSALM 19 329

Marsh, Charles Howard (b. Apr. 8, 1886, Magnolia, IA; d. Apr. 12, 1956, La Jolla, CA) wrote music for the gospel songs "One Day" and "Crowning Day" during his early twenties; the son of a Congregational minister, was born a few months after his parents had emigrated from England; after graduating from high school, was invit-

ed by J. Wilbur Chapman to be pianist at the Winona Lake Chautauqua and Bible Conference in Indiana; after some years of study, taught at the Bible Institute of Los Angeles (now Biola University) and then at the University of Redlands; went to France (1926-28) to study with Isidor Phillipp, Marcel Dupré, and Nadia Boulanger; returning to America, became President of the European School of Music and Art and organist-choirmaster of First Presbyterian Church in Fort Wayne, IN; in 1932 moved to Florida, taught organ at the Orlando College of Music, and became organist at the University of Florida in Gainesville; from 1936 until his death, served as organist-choirmaster at the St. James-by-the-Sea Episcopal Church in La Jolla, CA; a Fellow of the American Guild of Organists, was known also for his poetry and painting; wrote many songs, anthems, and instrumental works. H
CHAPMAN 196

Marsh, Donald Stuart (b. Sept. 5, 1923, Akron, OH) is a member of the "Avery and Marsh" duo, well known for workshops in contemporary worship; was raised by missionary parents in Asia (Singapore and Sumatra); attended Western Maryland University, the University of Houston (BS, MS), and the Theodora Irvine School of Drama; since 1946 has been active professionally as an actor, director, dancer, and choreographer in the New York City area although he no longer works actively in those endeavors; beginning in 1960 was appointed choirmaster and Director of Arts in Christian

Education at First Presbyterian Church, Port Jervis, NY; is an elder in the United Presbyterian Church (USA) and was a member of the Advisory Council for Discipleship and Worship for their General Assembly; is co-founder of Proclamation Productions, a drama group, and has written over 50 hymn texts and tunes.
O How Blest Are the Poor in Spirit, BEATITUDES 603

Marshall, Jane Manton (b. Dec. 5, 1924, Dallas, TX) is a graduate of Southern Methodist University (BMus, MMus; distinguished alumni award, 1965) where she also was on the faculty of the School of Music, in theory (1968-75) and then on the faculty of the Perkins School of Theology (1975-86), and where she received the first "Woman of Achievement" award; served on the music staff of United Methodist Churches in Northaven, TX, Corsicana, TX, and Dallas, TX, and of St. Andrews Presbyterian Church, Dallas, TX (1941-1960); is widely published in choral music and vocal collections; is frequently a guest conductor and worship presenter.
JACOB 545
What Gift Can We Bring? ANNIVERSARY SONG 794

Martin, Civilla Durfee (b. Aug. 21, 1866, Jordan, Nova Scotia; d. Mar. 9, 1948, Atlanta, GA) was a small town schoolteacher with some musical training; worked with her husband, Walter Stillman Martin (below), in his evangelistic campaigns throughout the United States, and collaborated with him in writing several gospel songs.   H
God Will Take Care of You 619

Martin, Walter Stillman (b. 1862, Rowley, Essex Co., MA; d. Dec. 16, 1935, Atlanta, GA), educated at Harvard University, was ordained to the Baptist ministry and later joined the Disciples of Christ; for a time taught Bible at the Atlantic Christian College (NC); in 1919 established his residence in Atlanta, GA, and conducted Bible conferences and evangelistic campaigns throughout the country; with his wife, Civilla Durfee Martin, wrote some gospel songs.   H
GOD CARES 619

Mason, Lowell (b. Jan. 8, 1792, Medfield, MA; d. Aug. 11, 1872, Orange, NJ) holds a special place in the history of church music and of music education in the United States; as a child learned to play several instruments, and at age 16, led the village choir and conducted singing schools; lived in Savannah, GA, for a while, working in a bank, studying harmony and composition, and serving the Independent Presbyterian Church as organist; in 1827 moved to Boston and became President of the Handel and Haydn Society and choir director of Bowdoin St. Church; in 1829 published *The Juvenile Psalmist*, or *The Child's Introduction to Sacred Music*; established the Boston Academy of Music (1833) and was eventually responsible for introducing music into the public school curriculum of Boston; pioneered in teaching music pedagogy for 25 years; compiled and published at least 80 music volumes which are listed in *Lowell Mason; the Father of Singing Among Children* (1946), by Arthur L. Rich; wrote more than 1100 hymn tunes and almost 500 arrangements of existing tunes, mostly from European sources. H

AZMON (arr.) 130
ANTIOCH 146
BOYLSTON 659
CLEANSING FOUNTAIN 467
DENNIS (arr.) 708
HAMBURG 213
OLIVET 552
SCHUMANN (attr.) 649

Matheson, George (b. Mar. 27, 1842, Glasgow, Scotland; d. Aug. 28, 1906, North Berwick, East Lothian) was almost blind by the time he was 18 years of age, but made a brilliant record at Glasgow Academy and Glasgow University; licensed as a Church of Scotland minister, was assistant at Sandyford Church, Glasgow, and then pastor of the Clydeside Church at Innellan, Argyllshire for 18 years; in 1886 was transferred to St. Bernard's Church in Edinburgh, where he remained a most popular and respected pastor until he was forced to retire in 1899 because of ill health; wrote many theological and devotional volumes, and one book of verse, *Sacred Songs* (1890).H
O Love That Will Not Let Me Go 531
Make Me a Captive, Lord 583

Matson, William Tidd (b. Oct. 17, 1833, West Hackney, London, England; d. Dec. 23, 1899, Portsea, Hampshire) studied at St. John's College, Cambridge; was secretary of the European Freedom Committee (1853); through a conversion experience, joined first the Methodists and then the Congregationalists; studied theology at Cotten End Institute and was ordained in 1860; pastored at Havant, Gosport, Stratford

(East London), Rothwell (Northamptonshire), Portsmouth, and Salisbury Green.
Lord, I Was Blind 499

Matthews, Timothy Richard (b. Nov. 4, 1826, Colmworth, near Bedford, England; d. Jan. 5, 1910, Tetney, Lincolnshire) was educated at Bedford Grammar School and Caius College, Cambridge, and studied organ with George Elvey; ordained an Anglican minister (1853), was curate at St. Mary's, Nottingham, then rector of North Coates, Lincolnshire, until he retired in 1907; composed more than 100 hymn tunes, and published *Tunes for Holy Worship* (1859), *The Village Church Tune Book* (1859), *Congregational Melodies* (1862), *Hymn Tunes* (1867), *The Village Organist* (1877), and *North Coates Supplemental Tune Book* (1878). H
MARGARET 198

Maurus, Rabanus; see **Rabanus Maurus**.

Maxwell, Mary E. (b. Oct. 4, 1837, England; d. Feb. 4, 1915, Richmond, Surrey) is not identifiable for a certainty, but her hymn is associated with the Keswick Convention in north England. Records show that a prolific author named Mary Elizabeth Braddon was born on October 4, 1837, was educated at home by private tutors, and married John Maxwell in 1874. She died February 4, 1915 at Richmond, Surrey.

The Rev. Alan Luff, Secretary of The Hymn Society of Great Britain and Ireland, has written:

One must regret a tendency for hymn scholars to ignore the

type of hymnody to be found in "Keswick." It is partly a result of a feeling that we do not have much sympathy with it and that we should therefore be led to make adverse criticisms of it. But we ought to be able to see it as a branch of hymnody that ought not be ignored, while at the same time hoping that those in sympathy with it will make their own efforts to produce the kind of background material that you are seeking. Fortunately, this effort is being made and we have received the above information from Mr. Andrew J. Hayden of Tonbridge, Kent, England.　　　H
Channels Only 577

Mayes, Carol (b. Feb. 19, 1924, Loma Linda, CA) is a high school graduate with an AA in secretarial science and a year of study in music and journalism; is a talented music performer (soprano and pianist), who has been vocationally active in secretarial, editorial, and word processing management.
We Give This Child to You 764

McAfee, Cleland Boyd (b. Sept. 25, 1866, Ashley, MO; d. Feb. 4, 1944, Jaffrey, NH) received his schooling at Park College, Parkville, MO, and Union Theological Seminary; returned to Park College to teach and also served as pastor and choir director of the college church; served pastorates in Chicago and Brooklyn (1901-12); was professor of systematic theology (1912-30) at McCormick Theological Seminary, Chicago, and later became secretary of the Presbyterian Board of Foreign Missions (1930-36); following his

retirement in New Hampshire, remained active lecturing, preaching, teaching, and writing.　　H
Near to the Heart of God, McAFEE 542

McAllister, Louise (b. 1913, Louisville, KY; d. 1960, Richmond, VA), a pianist, teacher, composer, and writer, was daughter of a professor of English Bible (at the Louisville Presbyterian Theological Seminary, and later, the Union Theological Seminary, Richmond); was educated at the Collegiate School, Richmond, and Mary Baldwin College, and studied privately with Mrs. Crosby Adams and John Powell; harmonized folk hymn melodies which have appeared in several hymnals.
BOURBON (harm.) 655

McDonald, William (b. Mar. 1, 1820, Belmont, ME; d. Sep. 11, 1901, Monrovia, CA) at the age of 19 was a local preacher in the Methodist Episcopal Church; was active in ministry in the Maine, Wisconsin, and New England Conferences and was editor of the *Advocate of Christian Holiness*; edited and published *Western Minstrels* (1840), *Wesleyan Sacred Harp* (1855), *Beulah Songs* (1870), and *Tribute of Praise* (1874).　　H
O Happy Day That Fixed My Choice, HAPPY DAY (ed. ref.) 504

McElrath, Hugh Thomas (b. Nov. 13, 1921, Murray, KY) was educated at Murray State University (BA), Southern Baptist Theological Seminary (BSM, MSM), and Eastman School of Music, Rochester, NY (PhD); also pursued sabbatical studies in Bologna, Italy, Oxford, England, and Zürich,

Switzerland; teaches at Southern Baptist Theological Seminary, Louisville, KY (since 1948), in voice, musicology, and hymnology; has been a church musician since the 1940s in churches in North Carolina and Kentucky; co-authored *Sing with Understanding* (1980), and co-ordinated the writing for *Handbook to the Baptist Hymnal* (1992); was a member of the hymnal committees for *Baptist Hymnal* (1975) and *The Baptist Hymnal* (1991); is active in The Hymn Society in the United States and Canada, and in 1991 was made a Fellow of the Society.
We Praise You with Our Minds, O Lord 401

Mcgee, Bob (b. June 18, 1949, Vancouver, British Columbia, Canada); no other information was located.
Emmanuel, Emmanuel 140

McGranahan, James (b. July 4, 1840 near Adamsville, PA; d. July 7, 1907, Kinsman, OH) had only a limited formal education, but quickly developed musical skills and at age 19 was teaching music; after brief study at Bradbury's Music School, Geneseo, NY, was associated with J. G. Towner in music conventions and singing schools in Pennsylvania and New York; later studied with George F. Root and taught in his institutes; after the sudden death of P. P. Bliss (1877), became song leader in the evangelistic campaigns conducted by Major D. W. Whittle in England and America; had a beautiful tenor voice and a commanding personality, and pioneered in using men's choirs in his meetings; collaborated with Ira Sankey, George C.

Stebbins, and other musicians in many publications, including *The Gospel Male Choir*, 2 vols. (1878, 1883), *The Choice, Harvest of Song, Gospel Choir*, and *Gospel Hymns* (Nos. 3, 4, 5 and 6).   H
EL NATHAN 493

McHugh, Phillip [Phill] James (b. Apr. 25, 1951, Aberdeen, SD), son of a farmer and housewife, graduated from Roncalli High School (1969); has received Dove Award nominations; writes for River Oaks Music Company; is staff writer for Meadowgreen Music.
In the Name of the Lord, NAME OF THE LORD 113
People Need the Lord, PEOPLE NEED THE LORD 730

McIntosh, Rigdon McCoy (b. Apr. 3, 1836, Maury Co., TN; d. July 2, 1899, Atlanta, GA) attended Jackson College, Columbia, TN; studied music with L. C. and Asa Everett, and was associated with them in publishing books and teaching singing schools; in the 1860s began a 30-year relationship as music editor for the publishing house of the Methodist Episcopal Church, South; was briefly head of the Music Department of Vanderbilt University, and in 1877 accepted a similar appointment at Emory College, Oxford, GA; in 1895 left education and established the R. M. McIntosh Publishing Company; was an accomplished teacher, composer, choral director, and editor, whose publications include *Hermon: the Methodist Hymn and Tune Book, Prayer and Praise, Christian Hymns, Gospel Grace, McIntosh's Anthems, Glad Tidings, Living Songs,* and *Songs of Service.* H
PROMISED LAND (arr.) 674

Mead, Stith was compiler of *A General Selection of the Newest and Most Admired Hymns and Spiritual Songs Now in Use* (Lynchburg, VA, 1811).
What Wondrous Love is This 212

Mechtild of Magdeburg (b. *c.* 1209, Saxony; d. *c.* 1282-94, Helfta), a mystical poet of noble parents, became a Beguine at Magdeburg (1230) in the Dominican order, a lay-sisterhood who took no vows, hence could leave and marry; after 40 years, left Magdeburg for a Convent at Helfta (1270); wrote extensively in German and may have influenced Dante with her vivid descriptive language.
Praising God of Many Names 64

Medema, Ken (b. July 12, 1943, Grand Rapids, MI) graduated from Grand Rapids Christian School and Michigan State University (BA, MMus); blind himself, was music therapist at Fort Wayne State Hospital (1965-67); was Graduate Research Assistant, Michigan State University (1967-69) and Director of Activity Therapy, Essex County Hospital Center, Cedar Grove, NJ (1969-72); currently gives concerts, a "Traveling Minstrel," in his words; has numerous publications, including several musicals, solo and instrumental works.
Come, Let Us Reason, COME LET US REASON 456
Lord, Listen to Your Children Praying, CHILDREN PRAYING 629
The Gathering, GATHERING 800

Medley, Samuel (b. June 23, 1738, Cheshunt, Hertfordshire, England; d. July 17, 1799, Liverpool, Lancashire), was the son of a schoolteacher who was a friend of Isaac Newton; served as a midshipman in the Royal Navy and was wounded off Port Lagos (1759); was converted after reading a sermon by Isaac Watts and joined the Eagle Street Baptist Church; pastored Baptist churches at Watford and Liverpool, the latter ministry being especially successful; edited *Hymns* (1785), *Hymns on Select Portions of Scripture* (1785 and 1787), *Hymns* (1794), and *Hymns: The Public Worship and Private Devotions of True Christians, Assisted in Some Thoughts in Verse, Principally Drawn from Select Passages of the Word of God* (1800); is the subject of a biography, *A Memoir* (1833), written by his daughter Sarah, and containing 44 additional hymns.   H
I Know That My Redeemer Lives 239

Meece, David (b. May 26, 1952, Houston, TX) is the son of Roger and Joyce Meece; graduated from Peabody Conservatory of Music (BMus in piano performance, 1975); has 10 albums, including Best Album of the Year in 1990 for "Learning to Trust"; is married with two children.
We Are the Reason, MEECE 474

Meineke, Christoph (b. May 1, 1782, Oldenburg, Germany; d. Nov. 6, 1850, Baltimore, MD), sometimes listed as Charles Meineke, was the son of Karl Meineke, organist to the duke of Oldenburg; in 1810 left Germany for England, then came to the United States in 1820; served as organist of St. Paul's Episcopal Church in Baltimore, MD, until his death; published *Music for the*

Church . . . Composed for St. Paul's Church, Baltimore, by C. Meineke, Organist (1844). H
MEINEKE 807

Mendelssohn-Bartholdy, Felix (b. Feb. 3, 1809, Hamburg, Germany; d. Nov. 4, 1847, Leipzig), grandson of the Jewish philosopher Moses Mendelssohn, was born into a wealthy Jewish-Christian home (the hyphenated name was the result of his father's conversion), his father a banker, his mother a talented artist and musician who gave her children their first musical training; in 1811 moved with his family to Berlin, where all were baptized in the Lutheran church; a prodigy, made his first public appearance as a pianist at age nine, and had written five symphonies by the time he was 12; one of Germany's greats in the early-19th century, is credited with reviving interest in the music of J. S. Bach (he conducted the *St. Matthew Passion* at age 20, the first since Bach's death); traveled widely and was feted as a brilliant performer, conductor, and composer (as well as a painter and writer); although he died at 38, wrote prolifically in almost every *genre* (except opera)— symphonies, chamber music, concertos, organ and piano music, vocal music, and much sacred music, including the oratorios *St. Paul* and *Elijah*; is credited with hymn tunes that are adapted from other works. H
MENDELSSOHN 171
NUN DANKET ALLE GOTT (harm.) 374
BIRMINGHAM 815

Merbecke [or **Marbeck**], **John** (b. *c.* 1505-10, Windsor?, England;

d. *c.* 1585, Windsor?) was listed as a clerk of St. George's Chapel, Windsor, in 1531 (date of birth may be earlier than 1505), where he was also organist until his death; was arrested for heresy (1543) because he took a Calvinist position and compiled a concordance of the English Bible among other theological projects; was released on a reprieve by Henry VIII, and returned to his Protestant scholarship, producing, along with other things, a concordance to replace the one confiscated (unpublished, but the basis of a 900-page shorter version); in the concordance preface, writes that his church music training was a waste; with the rule of Edward VI (to whom the concordance is dedicated), Calvinism was less dangerous; completed his degree at Oxford (BMus, 1549) and composed the first comprehensive musical setting for uniform worship, *The Booke of Common Praier Noted* (London, 1550; in facsimile, 1939), his last extant music; later criticized the use of choral and instrumental music in church (after 1574).
MERBECKE 823

Mercer, William (b. 1811, Barnard Castle, Durham, England; d. Aug. 21, 1873 Sheffield) worked with James Montgomery and John Goss to compile *The Church Psalter and Hymn Book* (1855), a widely used hymnal in the Anglican Church of the middle 1800s.
God, Who Made the Earth and Heaven 366

Merrill, William Pierson (b. Jan. 10, 1867, Orange, NJ; d. June 19, 1954, New York, NY), convert-

ed at age 11, was successively a member of a Congregational and a Dutch Reformed Church; was educated at Rutgers College and Union Theological Seminary, and ordained to the Presbyterian ministry (1890); served churches in Philadelphia and Chicago, and then (1911) became pastor of the Brick Presbyterian Church in New York City where he remained until his retirement (1938); wrote many hymns as well as a number of theological books, including *Footings for Faith* (1915), *Christian Internationalism* (1919), *The Common Creed of Christians* (1920), *The Freedom of the Preacher* (1922), *Liberal Christianity* (1925), *Prophets of the Dawn* (1927), *The Way* (1933), and *We See Jesus* (1934).   H
Rise Up, O Men of God 671

Messiter, Arthur Henry (b. Apr. 1, 1834, Frome Selwood, Somersetshire, England; d. July 2, 1916, New York, NY) received his early education from private tutors, and his first musical training from McKorkell and Kerfell in Northampton at age 17; in 1863 came to the United States and sang in the choir at Trinity Episcopal Church, New York City; served as organist in churches in Poultney, VT (where he also taught), and Philadelphia; in 1866 accepted responsibility for the music at Trinity Church, New York City, where he served for over 31 years; as a model of Episcopalian musicianship, received the honorary DMus degree, St. Stephen's College, Annandale, NY; edited *Psalter* (1889), *Choir Office Book* (1891), and *Hymnal with Music as Used in Trinity Church* (1893); composed a number of anthems and wrote *A*

History of the Choir and the Music of Trinity Church (1906).   H
MARION 34

Mieir, Audrey Mae Wagner (b. May 12, 1916, Leechburg, PA) began writing songs at 16 years of age; was educated at L.I.F.E. Bible College; married Charles B. Mieir (1936); was ordained in the Church of the Foursquare Gospel (1937); travels as preacher, pianist, choral director, recording artist, and clinician; has been vice-president of Mieir Music Foundation, Hollywood, CA, since 1960; is active on Christian television with Trinity Broadcasting, Tustin, CA.
His Name is Wonderful, MIEIR 87

Miles, C. Austin (b. Jan. 7, 1868, Lakehurst, NJ; d. Mar. 10, 1946, Pitman, NJ) was educated at the Philadelphia College of Pharmacy and the University of Pennsylvania, and was an active pharmacist for many years; released his first gospel song, "List, 'Tis Jesus' Voice," through the Hall-Mack Publishing Company, Philadelphia, who encouraged him to write others; in June 1898, went to work full-time with Hall-Mack and remained for 37 years as editor and manager, continuing in an editorial capacity when the company merged with Rodeheaver in 1935; composed several cantatas and anthems, but said, "It is as a writer of gospel songs I am proud to be known, for in that way I may be of the most use to my Master whom I serve willingly although not as efficiently as is my desire."   H
In the Garden, GARDEN 242

Miller, Emily F. Huntington (b. 1833, Brooklyn, CT; d. 1913) was

the daughter of Rev. Thomas Huntington; graduated from Oberlin College (BA) and married Professor John E. Miller (1860); was co-editor of *The Little Corporal* and *Army Bells* magazines (late 1860s).
AFFECTION 100

Miller, Max (b. Oct. 21, 1927, Fullerton, CA), son of an osteopathic physician and a nurse, was educated at Fullerton (CA) Union High School, University of Redlands (BMus and MMus), and Boston University (PhD); was active in the American Guild of Organists; served as organist, First Methodist Church, Pasadena, CA (1949-51), and organist-choirmaster, Grace Cathedral, Topeka, KS (1954-55); taught at Washburn University, Topeka (1954-55), and, since 1955, has been at Boston University (currently is chair of the organ department).
MARSH CHAPEL 449

Mills, Pauline Michael (b. Oct. 13, 1898, Portland, IN), daughter of Otto and Ella Michael, graduated from L.I.F.E. Bible College and was ordained; wrote over 300 songs including love songs and scripture settings; has six children; her daughter, Leah N. Payne (Tulare, CA), reports that she traveled widely, speaking to women's groups and churches, but is now in a convalescent home.
Thou Art Worthy, WORTHY 116

Milman, Henry Hart (b. Feb. 10, 1791, London, England; d. Sept. 24, 1868, Sunninghill, Berkshire) was the son of King George II's physician; received schooling at Eton and Brasenose College, Oxford; was ordained in 1817 and

served churches in Reading and Westminster; was professor of poetry at Oxford University for a number of years, and in 1849 was appointed Dean of St. Paul's Cathedral; contributed 13 texts in Reginald Heber's *Hymns* (1827); published his own collection, *Selection of Psalms and Hymns* (1837).   H
Ride On, Ride On in Majesty 205

Milton, John (b. Dec. 9, 1608, London, England; d. Nov. 8, 1674, London) is best known as the brilliant blind English poet who wrote the literary masterpieces *Paradise Lost* (1667) and *Paradise Regained* (1671); was educated at St. Paul's School and Christ College, Cambridge; in 1649 was appointed "Latin Secretary" under Oliver Cromwell, responsible for translating letters of the British government to foreign powers; became totally blind when he was 44, but continued his work until Cromwell abdicated; escaped the scaffold, which was the fate of most Cromwell followers, because of his fame and acceptance as a writer; wrote 19 paraphrases of various Psalms, intended for private devotional use; is credited with helping to develop the hymn styles of Isaac Watts and Charles Wesley.   H
Let Us, with a Gladsome Mind 59

Mims, George Ellis (b. 1938, Houston, TX) is an active church musician, arranger, and editor with the Episcopal Church; studied at Baylor University (BMus, viola and church music, 1961) and Union Theological Seminary (MSM, conducting and organ, 1967); is a recording artist, organist, and director of the St. George Singers; since

1989, has been Music Director, St. Philip's Episcopal Church, Charleston, SC.   H
Alleluia, Alleluia! Give Thanks (adapt. arr.) 240

Mohr, Joseph (b. Dec. 11, 1792, Salzburg, Austria; d. Dec. 4, 1848, Wagrein) will forever be remembered as author of the Christmas hymn "Stille Nacht! heilige nacht!"; was a boy chorister in the cathedral choir at Salzburg, where the Mozarts had served a generation before; in 1815 was ordained in the Roman Catholic church and went to St. Nicholas Church, Oberndorf, for two years as assistant priest, and it was here he wrote his famous carol; after several other assignments, became vicar at Hintersee (1828) and then at Wagrein (1837), where he stayed until his death.   H
Silent Night! Holy Night! 164

Monk, Edwin George (b. Dec. 13, 1819, Frome Selwood, Somersetshire, England; d. Jan. 3, 1900, Radley, Abingdon, Berkshire) was organist at Midsomer Norton Parish Church and at Christ Church, Frome; became the first precentor and master of music at St. Columba's College (1844-47); after a year conducting the Oxford University Motet and Madrigal Society, became precentor of St. Peter's College, Radley (1848-59); was organist of York Minster (1859-83), and Oxford University examiner in music (1871-83); wrote songs and anthems, and published hymns and chants; retired to Radley in 1883.
ANGEL VOICES 407

Monk, William Henry (b. Mar. 16, 1823, Brompton, London, England; d. Mar. 1, 1889, Stoke Newington, London) was music editor for the first three editions of the historic English hymnal *Hymns Ancient and Modern* (1861, 1875, and 1889); first studied music with private instructors; served as organist for several London churches and was finally appointed to St. Matthias, Stoke Newington, a position he held until his death; during the same years, taught music at King's College, London, at the School for the Indigent Blind, the National Training School for Music, and Bedford College; was given the honorary DMus degree, Durham University (1882); was editor of the *Parish Choir* (1840-1851) and contributed some 50 hymn tunes to *Hymns Ancient and Modern* (1861, 1875, and 1889).   H
DIX (harm.) 181, 353, 562
EVENTIDE 365
ST. THEODULPH 204
VICTORY (arr.) 233
ZEUCH MICH, ZEUCH MICH 344

Monsell, John Samuel Bewley (b. Mar. 2, 1811, St. Colomb's, Derry, Ireland; d. Apr. 9, 1875, Guildford, Surrey, England) received his education at Trinity College, Dublin; was ordained (1834) and served several parishes in Ireland; in 1853 went to England as vicar of Egham, Surrey, and later (1870), rector of St. Nicholas, Guildford; was accidentally killed by falling masonry during roof repairs at St. Nicholas; published 11 volumes of poetry, including some 300 hymns; was a strong advocate of "more fervent and joyous" congregational singing.   H
Sing to the Lord of the Harvest 375

Montgomery, James (b. Nov. 4, 1771, Irvine, Ayrshire, Scotland; d. Apr. 30, 1854, Sheffield, Yorkshire, England), the son of the only Moravian minister in Scotland, was educated at Fulneck Seminary near Leeds; made little progress in school and was dismissed because of his preoccupation with writing poetry; was apprenticed to a baker, but ran away and eventually settled in Sheffield (1792) and became associated with the *Sheffield Register*; later became editor and owner of the newspaper (the previous editor having been jailed for his political positions) and changed its name to *Sheffield Iris*; was outspoken and influential in many humanitarian causes, especially opposition to slavery; also sponsored the singing of hymns in Anglican worship, and the causes of foreign missions and The British Bible Society; wrote more than 400 hymns which appeared in his *Songs of Zion* (1822), *The Christian Psalmist* (1825), and *Original Hymns for Public, Private and Social Devotion* (1853). H
Angels from the Realms of Glory 174
Go to Dark Gethsemane 225
Lord, Teach Us How to Pray Aright 628
Prayer Is the Soul's Supreme Desire 620
Stand Up and Bless the Lord 41

Moody, May Whittle (b. Mar. 20, 1870, Chicago, IL; d. Aug. 20, 1963, Northfield, MA), the daughter of Evangelist D. W. Whittle (an associate of D. L. Moody), was actually named "Mary" but chose to be known as "May"; at age 15 attended the Girl's School founded by Moody in Northfield, MA, and later, Oberlin College (1888-89), followed by a year at the Royal Academy of Music, London (1890-91); had a singing voice of "rare sweetness and richness of quality" and assisted her father and D. L. Moody in their evangelistic campaigns; married William R. Moody (son of the evangelist) on August 29, 1894, and they were the parents of six children, two of whom died as infants; lived at Northfield, MA, where Will Moody was head of the Northfield Schools and the Mount Hermon Conference center founded by his father; was co-editor (with Charles M. Alexander) of *Northfield Hymnal, No. 3.* H
WHITTLE 529

Moore, Thomas (b. May 28, 1779, Dublin, Ireland; d. Feb. 25, 1852, Chittoe, near Bath, England) was educated at Trinity College, Dublin, and in London, where he studied law (1799); was appointed to the Admiralty Court of Bermuda (1803); when a debuty embezzled funds, went into a self-imposed exile; returned to England (1822) and wrote poetry, a biography of Byron, and hymns to be sung to existing folk or popular tunes.
Come, Ye Disconsolate (st. 1, 2) 613

Moore, William has not left much record in biographical history; according to *Hymns of Our Faith*, he compiled *The Columbian Harmony*, containing 180 pages of music, 17 pages of introductory instructional material, and the credit: "William Moore, West Tennessee, Wilson County, March, 1825"; signed 18 tunes in the volume, including HOLY MANNA, two of which are named for his

home town and the nearby county seat, LEBANON and WILSON.   H
BOURBON (comp.) 655
HOLY MANNA 54, 347, 802

More, Thomas (b. Feb. 7, 1477, London, England; d. July 6, 1535, London) was educated at St. Anthony's, Threadneedle Street, and with John Morton, Archbishop of Canterbury and Chancellor of England, the post More later held; studied classics at Oxford, then returned to London to study law and joined the legal society of Lincoln's Inn (1496); chose the priesthood over his father's wishes; married Jane Colt (*c.* 1504-5) who died in 1511 leaving four children; wrote a history that influenced Shakespeare and *Utopia* which influenced all of western political science; began a political career by helping calm a London riot (Mayday, 1517), then worked with Erasmus and eventually King Henry VIII, who made him Chancellor of England and later beheaded him for refusing to accept the King as the Head of the Church; was canonized by the Roman Catholic Church (May 19, 1935) and assigned the feast day of July 9.
For Grace to Labor 396

Morris, Lelia Naylor (b. Apr. 15, 1862, Pennsville, Morgan Co., OH; d. July 23, 1929, Auburn, OH) moved with her family to Malta, OH, as a child; after her father's death, with her mother and sister, opened a millinery shop just across the Muskingum River, in McConnelsville; married Charles H. Morris and the two were very active in the Methodist Episcopal Church and in holiness camp meetings; first encouraged by H. L.

Gilmour, wrote more than 1000 hymns and many tunes as well, continuing even after she was old and blind.   H
What If It Were Today? SECOND COMING 275

Mote, Edward (b. Jan. 21, 1797, London, England; d. Nov. 13, 1874, Southwark, London), as a youth, was moved by the preaching of John Hyatt of Tottenham Court Road Chapel; became a successful cabinetmaker in a suburb of London, and was dedicated to the work of the church; wrote over 100 hymns, published in his *Hymns of Praise, A New Selection of Gospel Hymns, Combining All the Excellencies of Our Spiritual Poets, with many Originals* (1836) (this may be the first use of the term "gospel hymn," though most of the contents were hymns of praise); in 1852 became pastor of the Baptist church in Horsham, Sussex, served for 21 years, and is buried in the churchyard.   H
The Solid Rock 517

Mother Teresa of Calcutta, see **Teresa**.

Moultrie, Gerard (b. Sept. 16, 1829, Rugby, England; d. Apr. 25, 1885, Southleigh), in his hymn activity was influenced by the Oxford (high church) movement of the Anglican Church; was trained at Rugby School and Exeter College, Oxford (MA, 1856); was ordained into the Anglican priesthood, held various chaplaincies, became vicar of Southleigh (1869) and warden of St. James' College, Southleigh (1873); edited and published *Hymns and Lyrics for the Seasons and Saints' Days of the*

Church (1867), *Cantica Sanctorum, or Hymns for the Black Letter Saints' Days in the English and Scottish Calendars* (1880), and other volumes.　H
Let All Mortal Flesh Keep Silence (adapt.) 167

Mountain, James (b. July 16, 1844, Leeds, York, England; d. June 27, 1933, Tunbridge Wells, Kent) trained for the ministry of the "Countess of Huntingdon's Connexion" (Anglican churches influenced and supported by the Countess) at Rotherham College, Nottingham Institute, and Cheshunt College, with further study in Heidelberg and Tübingen, Germany; was ordained and served a pastorate at Great Marlow, but poor health interrupted his ministry; was greatly influenced by the visit of Moody and Sankey in the early 1870s and gave himself to evangelism in Britain and worldwide (1874-89); pastored the Countess of Huntingdon's church, Tunbridge Wells (1889-97); became a Baptist, founding St. John's Free Church at Tunbridge Wells; wrote many religious books and articles, and a number of hymn texts, but is better known for his tunes; shows the influence of Ira Sankey in his *Hymns of Consecration and Faith* (1876).　H
WYE VALLEY 429, 594
EVERLASTING LOVE 602

Mowbray, David (b. May 1, 1938, Wallington, Surrey, England) attended Dulwich College, Fitzwilliam of Cambridge (MA), and London (external) (BD); has served as Curate of St. Giles, Northampton (1963-66), Lecturer at St. Mary, Watford (1966-70),

Vicar at Broxbourne with Wormley, Hertfordshire (1970-84), and All Saints, Hertfordshire (since 1984); published his hymn texts with Jubilate and Stainer & Bell.
Come to Us, Creative Spirit 407
We Believe in God Almighty 693

Murray, James Ramsey (b. Mar. 17, 1841, Andover, MA; d. Mar. 10, 1905, Cincinnati, OH), the son of Scottish immigrants, studied with Lowell Mason and his contemporaries at the Musical Institute in North Reading, MA; was a Union soldier in the Civil War; served as a music editor for Root and Cady, Chicago, and John Church Company, Cincinnati; published several Sunday School songbooks with many of his own tunes.
AWAY IN A MANGER 147

Nägeli, Johann (**Hans**) **Georg** (b. May 26, 1773, Wetzikon, near Zurich, Switzerland; d. Dec. 26, 1836, Wetzikon) has not left a clear record in history either as to birth date (1768 in some sources) or first name (Johann or Hans); was a pioneer music educator who strongly influenced Lowell Mason, and founded a school of music in Zurich known as the Swiss Association for the Cultivation of Music; was also a music publisher who released excellent editions of the works of J. S. Bach, Handel, Frescobaldi, and other composers; published his theories of music education in *Gesangbildungslehre nach Pestalozzischen Grundsätzen* (1810).　H
DENNIS 708

Neale, John Mason (b. Jan. 24, 1818, London, England; d. Aug. 6, 1866, East Grinstead, Sussex)

brought much of the rich treasury of ancient Greek and Latin hymns into English-language worship in the mid-19th century; was educated at Trinity College, Cambridge, and ordained in 1841; in 1846 became warden of Sackville College, East Grinstead (a home for indigent old men), and remained there until his death (because of ecclesiastical opposition to his "high church" views, was made caretaker rather than chaplain— with meager compensation); was founding father of one of the first nursing homes in England, the Sisterhood of St. Margaret; a liturgical scholar and linguist, translated many early Greek and Latin hymns, which may be more beautiful and meaningful in English than in the original; also wrote a large number of original hymns which appear, along with the translations, in *Medieval Hymns and Sequences* (1851), *The Hymnal Noted* (1852 and 1854), *Hymns of the Eastern Church* (1862), and *Sequences, Hymns, and other Ecclesiastical Verses* (1866); unrecognized by his native country, was given an honorary DD degree by the University of Hartford, CT.   H
All Glory, Laud and Honor (trans.) 204
Are You Weary, Heavy Laden? 453
Christ Is Made the Sure Foundation (trans.) 699
Christian, Do You Struggle? 660
Good Christian Friends, Rejoice (para.) 157
Jerusalem, the Golden (trans.) 754
O Come, O Come, Emmanuel (trans.) 133
O Sons and Daughters, Let Us Sing (trans.) 249
Of the Father's Love Begotten (trans.) 145

Sing, My Tongue, the Glorious Battle (trans.) 228
The Day of Resurrection (trans.) 247

Neander, Joachim (b. 1650, Bremen, Germany; d. May 31, 1680, Bremen), called "the Paul Gerhardt of the German Calvinists," was trained at the Padagogium in Bremen, where his father taught, and later at the Gymnasium Illustre; a part of the rebellious student life of his day, became convicted by the preaching of Theodore Under-Eyck in St. Martin's Church, Bremen, and was converted; tutored at Frankfurt and Heidelberg, and in 1674 was appointed rector of the Latin School at Düsseldorf, sponsored by the Reformed Church; was briefly suspended from the school because of his Pietist associations and activity; in 1679 went back to Bremen to serve as an unordained assistant to Under-Eyck at St. Martin's Church; died at age 30 of tuberculosis; wrote some 60 hymns, many of which express his love of nature, and provided tunes for several; published *Geistreiches Bundes-und-Dank-Lieder,* and A *und Ω Joachimi Neandri Glaubes und Liebesübung* (1680).   H
Praise to the Lord, the Almighty 77
ARNSBERG 799
UNSER HERRSCHER 260

Nelson, Gregory Allan (b. Sept. 10, 1948, Bismarck, ND) is the son of Corliss and Irene Nelson, contractor and homemaker; was educated at Bismarck (ND) High School, University of North Dakota, Grand Forks, and Mary College, Bismarck (BA in Social Science, 1972) where he was an

honor student and received the outstanding student music award; taught high school at Bismark (1969, 1971-76); owned (1976-79), then continued to manage Spirit Records and Hartson Records (1979-80); has served as minister of music in Nazarene, Lutheran, and United Methodist churches; is a free-lance songwriter (since 1980) in Nashville; published with Word, Sparrow, and Benson.
People Need the Lord, PEOPLE NEED THE LORD 730

Neumark, Georg (b. Mar. 16, 1621, Langensalza, Thuringia, Germany; d. July 18, 1681, Weimar) received his early education at Schleusingen and Gotha; on his way to study law at the University of Königsberg, was robbed, so was forced to take a tutorship in Kiel for two years; finally reached Königsberg and stayed five years, studying law and poetry; had several years of scant employment, but in 1652 was appointed court poet, librarian, and registrar to the Duke of Weimar, and later secretary of the ducal archives; was blind during the last year of his life; produced 34 hymns, many written in times of difficulty and misfortune; left one principal volume of sacred and secular songs, *Fortgeflantzter Musikalisch-Poetischer Lustwald* (1657). H
If You Will Trust in God to Guide You 636
WER NUR DEN LIEBEN GOTT 186, 636

Neuvermehrtes und zu Übung Christl. Gottseligkeit eingerichtetes Meiningishches Gesangbuch (Meiningen, 1693)

was compiled by Niclaus Hassert. MUNICH [also MEININGEN] 310

Newbolt, Michael Robert (b. 1874, Dymock, Gloucestershire, England; d. Feb. 7, 1956, Bierton, Buckinghamshire) received his education at St. John's College, Oxford, and was ordained an Anglican priest in 1900; served as assistant curate at Wantage, and then as vicar of St. Mary's in Iffley; was principal of the Missionary College in Dorchester for several years; later served churches in Brighton and Chester, and was licensed to officiate in the Diocese of Oxford. H
Lift High the Cross (alt.) 229

Newell, William Reed (b. May 22, 1868, Savannah, OH; d. Apr. 1, 1956, DeLand, FL) was educated at Wooster College and at Princeton and Oberlin Theological Seminaries; served several pastorates and then became assistant superintendent of Moody Bible Institute in Chicago; at the suggestion of Dwight L. Moody, for many years held regular Bible classes in several different cities, commuting between them by train; was a popular conference speaker who published expositions of many books of the Bible. H
At Calvary 510

Newton, John (b. July 24, 1725, London, England; d. Dec. 21, 1807, London) went to sea with his father at age 11 and later served in the Royal Navy; captained a slave ship and, by his own admission, led a life of dissipation and wretchedness; was converted through reading *The Imitation of Christ* by Thomas à Kempis, and

the experience of a stormy night at sea; was ordained an Anglican minister when almost 40 years of age, and went to Olney as curate; with William Cowper, produced the historic *Olney Hymns* (1779) to which he contributed some 280 poems and Cowper, 68; later, was rector at St. Mary's, Woolnoth, London; wrote this epitaph which appears on his gravestone in the churchyard at Olney: "John Newton, Clerk, Once an infidel and libertine, A servant of slaves in Africa, was by the rich mercy of our Lord and Saviour, Jesus Christ, preserved, restored, pardoned, and appointed to preach the faith he had long labored to destroy."   H
Amazing Grace! How Sweet the Sound 502
Glorious Things of Thee Are Spoken 694
How Sweet the Name of Jesus Sounds 102
May the Grace of Christ Our Savior 841

Nichol, Henry Ernest (b. Dec. 10, 1862, Hull, England; d. Aug. 30, 1926, Skirlaugh, York) studied civil engineering, but gave it up in favor of music; received the BMus from Oxford (1888); wrote primarily for Sunday School anniversary services (both words and music); often used the pseudonym "Colin Sterne," derived from the letters of his last and middle names.   H
We've a Story to Tell to the Nations, MESSAGE 733

Nicholson, Sydney Hugo (b. Feb. 9, 1875, London, England; d. May 30, 1947, Ashford, Kent) received schooling at Rugby School, New College, Oxford, and the Royal College of Music; was organist at Barnet Parish Church, at Lower Chapel, and at Eton College, then assistant organist at Carlisle Cathedral, and organist at Manchester Cathedral and Westminster Abbey; in 1927 founded the School of English Church Music and served as Director until his death; was knighted in 1938; served as musical editor of the later editions of *Hymns Ancient and Modern*; published *Boys Choirs* (1922), *A Manual of English Church Music* (1923, with George L. H. Gardner), *Quires and Places Where They Sing* (1932), and *Peter—The Adventures of a Chorister* (1944).   H
CARLISLE (descant) 764
CRUCIFER 229

Nicolai, Philipp (b. Aug. 10, 1556, Mengeringhausen, Waldeck, Germany; d. Oct. 26, 1608, Hamburg) was the son of a Lutheran pastor whom he later assisted at Mengeringhausen; studied at Erfurt (1575), Wittenberg (Bachelors, 1576-79, DDiv, 1579); pastored at Herdecke but left because of unsympathetic Roman Catholic leadership and a Spanish invasion (1586); served in Niederwildungen and there wrote part of the Formula of Concord (a treatise on the Lord's Supper); pastored at Altwidungen and then at Unna, Westphalia (1596-98 and 1600), where a great plague took hundreds of lives; fled Spanish invasion of Westphalia and pastored St. Catherine's, Hamburg (1601-08), where he died of "the fever."
Wake, Awake, for Night Is Flying, WACHET AUF (adapt.) 131

Niles, John Jacob (Apr. 28, 1892; d. Mar. 1, 1980, Black Hill Farm,

Lexington, KY), son of John Thomas and Lula Sarah Niles, gathered Appalachian folk music since age 15; studied at the Cincinnati Conservatory (1919) and the University of Lyon and the Paris Schola Contorum, and holds many honorary doctorates; was first an opera singer (debut 1920), then an active ballad performer (first recording with RCA, 1940) and instrument maker; began a book of ballads in 1935, which was finally published in 1961 (Houghton Mifflin) with cautions about the distinctions between "public-domain folk material" and his "composed love songs and carols," probably a reference to "I Wonder as I Wander"; taught briefly at Curtis, Eastman, Juilliard, and other music schools; deposited his works at the University of Kentucky and in the Library of Congress, including the published volumes: *7 Kentucky Mountain Songs* (1929), *7 Negro Exaltations* (1929), *Songs of the Hill Folk* (1934), *10 Christmas Carols* (1935), *More Songs of the Hill Folk* (1936), *Ballads and Tragic Legends* (1937), *The Anglo-American Ballad Study Book* (1945), *The Anglo-American Carol Study Book* (1948), and *The Shape-Note Study Book* (1950).
I Wonder as I Wander, I WONDER AS I WANDER (collected or composed) 165

Noel, Caroline Maria (b. Apr. 10, 1817, London, England; d. Dec. 7, 1877, St. Marylebone, London) was the daughter of a Church of England clergyman who was also a hymnodist; wrote hymns as a youth and again late in life when she was ill; authored *The Name of*

Jesus and other Verses for the Sick and Lonely (1861).   H
At the Name of Jesus 266

North, Frank Mason (b. Dec. 3, 1850, New York, NY; d. Dec. 17, 1935, Madison, NJ) received the BA and MA degrees from Wesleyan University, CT, and was ordained in the Methodist Episcopal Church (1872); served churches in Florida, New York, and Connecticut (1872-92); was editor of the *Christian City* and corresponding secretary of the New York Extension and Missionary Society of his denomination, and in 1919 became secretary of the Board of Foreign Missions; acted as president of the Federal Council of Churches of Christ in America (1916-20); wrote a number of hymns for special occasions.   H
Where Cross the Crowded Ways of Life 433

Oakeley, Frederick (b. Sept. 5, 1802, Shrewsbury, England; d. Jan. 29, 1880, Islington, London) is principally remembered for his translation of "Adeste Fideles"; was educated at Christ Church, Oxford, and made a Fellow of Balliol (1827); was ordained in 1826 and served at Lichfield Cathedral, Whitehall, and Margaret Chapel, London; was a leader of the Oxford Movement in the Church of England and eventually became a Roman Catholic; was appointed a canon of Westminster Procathedral (1852) and worked among the poor in that area; translated hymns from the Latin and published several volumes of prose and poetry.   H
O Come, All Ye Faithful (trans.) 126, 173

Olearius, Johannes G. (b. Sept. 17, 1611, Halle, Germany; d. Apr. 24, 1684, Weissenfels), son of a hymnwriter, was educated at the University of Wittenberg (MA, 1632 and DD, 1643); after a term as superintendent at Querfurst (1637-43), became court preacher to Duke August of Sachsen-Weissenfels (1643-80), and, after Duke August's death, continued in a similar position at Weissenfels until his own death; wrote hymns and a Bible commentary, and compiled a German hymnal containing over 1200 hymns (302 of his own), *Geistliche Singe-Kunst* [Spiritual Artsongs] (Leipzig, 1671).
Comfort, Comfort Now My People 132

Olivers, Thomas (b. 1725, Tregynon, Montgomeryshire, Wales; d. Mar., 1799, London, England) was orphaned at the age of four and grew up without much care; was apprenticed to a shoemaker, but led a restless, undisciplined life until he was converted through a sermon of George Whitefield in Bristol; in 1753 became an itinerant Methodist preacher, traveling more than 100,000 miles on horseback during 25 years of ministry; served with John Wesley and was appointed supervisor of the Methodist Press (1775); was discharged by Wesley in 1789 for "errors and unauthorized insertions" in the *Arminian Magazine*; retired in London.   H
The God of Abraham Praise 66

Olsen, Alfred Dulin (b. 1894; d. 1960). Little information is available about this individual. The *Metodistkirkens Salme Bok* [Methodist Church Song Book]

(Norsk Forlagsselskap A/S, Oslo, 1987) gives his name as listed above and dates the writing of PEARLY GATES as 1920. The Swedish hymnal *Segertoner* (Förlaget Filadelfia, Stockholm, 1988) calls him simply "Alfred Dulin" and gives the birth/death dates listed above, with the composing date, 1917; the authors-composers index identifies him as a Salvation Army officer in Norway and the United States.   H
He the Pearly Gates Will Open. PEARLY GATES 683

Olson, Ernst William (b. Mar. 16, 1870, Skåne, Sweden; d. Oct. 6, 1958, Chicago, IL) immigrated to America at age five, and his family settled in Nebraska, then moved to Texas; graduated from Augustana College; was editor of various Swedish weekly publications for about 12 years; became associated with Engberg-Holmberg Publishing Company, Chicago (1906) and later with the Augustana Book Concern (Lutheran), where he remained more than 35 years; wrote several books, including *A History of the Swedes in Illinois*; translated 28 hymns and wrote four original texts for *Augustana Hymnal* (1925); was a member of the hymnal committee for *Service Book and Hymnal* (1958).   H
Children of the Heavenly Father (trans.) 84

Orr, James Edwin (b. Jan. 12, 1912, Belfast, Ireland; d. Apr. 29, 1987, Asheville, NC) left Ireland in 1933 and became active in worldwide evangelism; was ordained an American Baptist minister (1940) and educated at Northwestern University (MA, 1941), Northern

Baptist Seminary (1943), Oxford University (DPhil, 1948), and UCLA (EdD, 1971); served as chaplain in the Air Force in the Southwest Pacific (1943-46); received honorary degrees from a seminary in India and the University of South Africa; became a professor in the School of World Missions at Fuller Theological Seminary, Pasadena, CA (1967); wrote six hymn texts and a score of books on revivals in church history. H
Search Me, O God 458, 460

Ortlund, Anne (b. Dec. 3, 1923, Wichita, KS) grew up on army posts where her father (Brig. Gen. Joseph B. Sweet) and mother held Bible classes for officers and their wives and led many to Christ during 40 years of service; earned her B.M. degree at the University of Redlands (CA) and holds the A.A.G.O. certificate of the American Guild of Organists; is married to Raymond C. Ortlund, for many years pastor of Lake Avenue Congregational Church in Pasadena, CA; served as organist for the "Old Fashioned Revival Hour" broadcast, and its successor "The Joyful Sound"; is the author of the booklet *Up with Worship*, and has written 80 anthems, sacred and secular solos, instrumental works, and 25 hymn texts and tunes; travels with her husband in conference ministry. H
Macedonia 737

Overby, Oscar R. (b. Sept. 25, 1892, Cooperstown, ND; d. June 17, 1964, Minneapolis, MN) attended Concordia College, Moorhead, MN (1910-1915), studied music at the New England Conservatory, Boston (1915-16), Northwestern Conservatory of Music, Minneapolis (1917), and St. Olaf College, Northfield, MN (graduated 1921); taught at Concordia College Academy (1912-15), Park Region College, Fergus Falls (1919-20), and at St. Olaf College (1921-50), where he collaborated with F. Melius Christiansen on arrangements (1940-49); was also guest choral conductor at Frances Shimer College, Mt. Carroll, IL (1948-49); served as executive director of church music with the Evangelical Lutheran Church (1949-64); wrote many hymn booklets and articles.
To a Virgin Meek and Mild 139

Owen, William (b. Dec. 12, 1813, Bangor, Caernarvonshire, Wales; d. July 20, 1893, Caernarvon), son of a slate quarry miner, also worked in the mines at Bethesda, Wales; began composing at age 18 and published *E Perl Cerddorol* (The Pearl of Music, 1854, with later editions in 1886 and 1892); was choir director and precentor at Caeathrow Chapel.
BRYN CALFARIA 283

Owens, Jimmy (b. Dec. 9, 1930, Clarksdale, MS), son of a salesman, graduated from Central High School, Jackson, MS, and attended Millsaps College, Jackson, MS; performed with Jackson Symphony (1940s) and in several jazz bands; arranged for Stan Kenton's Collegiate Neaphonic Orchestra (1960s and 1970s); for twelve years was church music director at Oakland's Neighborhood [CMA] Church (now Cathedral at the Crossroads), Castro Valley, CA; ministers with Stuart McBirnie, Glendale, CA, and Christian Center

Church (now Melodyland Christian Center) with Ralph Wilkerson, Anaheim, CA; is a composer, arranger, conductor, producer of 11 musicals (published by Lexicon, Word, Sparrow, Maranatha! Music, and Benson), including *If My People, The Witness,* and *Come Together,* and arranger-producer of over 70 recording albums; with his wife, Carol, founded and directed a traveling training program, School of Music Ministries International, Lindale, TX.
Make a Joyful Noise, JOYFUL NOISE 31
Clap Your Hands, CLAP YOUR HANDS 23

Owens, Priscilla Jane (b. July 21, 1829, Baltimore, MD; d. Dec. 5, 1907, Baltimore) was for 49 years a public school teacher, spending her entire life in Baltimore; as a faithful member of the Union Square Methodist Church, wrote most of her hymns for the Sunday School; frequently released her poetry and prose in the *Methodist Protestant* and the *Christian Standard.* H
Jesus Saves! 728

Owens-Collins, Jamie (b. Sept. 27, 1955, Castro Valley, CA), daughter of songwriters Jimmie (above) and Carol Owens, was music minister and recording artist for several companies for over 20 years; currently travels independently, teaching worship and music in Europe, New Zealand, Canada, and elsewhere; lives in Newbury Park, CA, with her husband, and operates Fairhill Music Company, representing other performers.
The Battle Belongs to the Lord, THE BATTLE 672

Oxenham, John (b. Nov. 12, 1852, Cheetham, Manchester, England; d. Jan. 23, 1941, Worthing, Sussex) was born William Arthur Dunkerly, and trained at Old Trafford School and Victoria University in Manchester; traveled extensively in Europe, Canada, and America in connection with his business; lived in the United States for two years and, returning to England, published the London edition of the *Detroit Free Press*; began writing under a pseudonym as an avocation and, because his work was so well received, eventually devoted his full time to literary work; is credited with some 40 novels and several books of poetry and prose; was long active at the Ealing Congregational Church, London, teaching a Bible class and serving as a deacon. H
In Christ There Is No East or West 697
In Christ There Is No East or West (inspired) 695

Page, Kate Stearns (b. Aug. 21, 1873, Brookline, MA; d. Jan. 19, 1963, New York, NY) taught preschool music at the Diller-Quaile School, New York, NY, and collaborated with Angela Diller on several published compositions; also taught at Dennison House Settlement School, Boston, MA, and Parke School, Brookline, near Boston.
We, Your People, Praise You 37

Palestrina, Giovanni Pierluigi da (b. *c.* 1525, Palestrina, Italy; d. Feb. 2, 1594, Rome), who derives his name from his birthplace, was a leading composer of church music in the 16th century; began as a

choirboy in the Cathedral of St. Agapit, and eventually became Chapel Master of the Julian Choir in St. Peter's, Rome; is credited with 100 masses, 200 motets, offertories, hymns and other liturgical materials which are bound in 33 volumes (Breitkopf and Härtel, 1862-1903); because of his composing genius, is credited with rescuing Catholic church music from the restrictive reforms dictated by the Council of Trent in 1562.   H
DONA NOBIS PACEM (attr.) 589
VICTORY 233

Palmer, Ray (b. Nov. 12, 1808, Little Compton, RI; d. Mar. 29, 1887, Newark, NJ) received schooling at Phillips Academy and Yale University; as a Congregational minister, served churches at Bath, ME, and Albany, NY; was appointed corresponding secretary of the American Congregational Union in 1865 and served until his retirement; edited *Hymns and Sacred Pieces* (1865), *Hymns of My Holy Hours and Other Pieces* (1868), and *Poetical Works* (1876); contributed a number of original hymns and translations from Latin to *Sabbath Hymn-Book* (1858); permitted no revision of his texts, and made it a habit to take no compensation for their use.   H
Jesus, Thou Joy of Loving Hearts (trans.) 121
My Faith Looks Up to Thee 552

Paris Antiphoner, 1681, is a French collection of Latin texts and primarily plainsong (chant) tunes.
CHRISTE SANCTORUM 90, 734
O QUANTA QUALIA 257, 305, 680

Paris, Twila (b. Dec. 28, 1958, Springdale, AR) is the oldest of four children of Inez and Oren Paris, who is pastor of the Missions Network Center of Youth With a Mission, Elm Springs, AR (her grandfather and great-grandfather were traveling evangelists); has been a songwriter and performer for 11 popular recording albums since 1981 (Milk & Honey, Benson, Star Song); was married to Jack Wright in 1985 and lives in Fayetteville, AR, near both of their families.
We Will Glorify, WE WILL GLORIFY 118

Parker, Edwin Pond (b. Jan 13, 1836, Castine, ME; d. May 28, 1925, Hartford, CT), educated at Bowdoin College and Bangor Theological Seminary, served the Center Church (Congregational), Hartford, CT, for 50 years; wrote at least 200 hymns after the age of 56 and edited a number of hymn collections.   H
MERCY (arr.) 302

Parry, Charles Hubert Hastings (b. Feb. 27, 1848, Bournemouth, England; d. Oct. 7, 1918, Rustington, Sussex) was educated at Eton (where as a schoolboy he also passed the Oxford Bachelor of Music degree), Exeter College, Oxford (BA 1870); worked at Lloyd's Register because his artist father objected to a music career; became professor of composition and music history at the Royal College of Music in 1883, succeeding Sir John Stainer, then became director in 1884, succeeding Sir George Grove with whom he worked on the Grove's *Dictionary of Music and Musicians*; was awarded

the honorary doctor of music degrees from Cambridge (1883), Oxford (1884), and Dublin (1891), and the doctor of civil law degree from Durham (1894); became a knight (1898) and a baronet (1902); was a teacher, scholar, writer, as well as composer of five symphonies, choral and organ works, and hymn tunes; had wide interests, which included science, theater, and yachting.　　　H
LAUDATE DOMINUM 704
REPTON 395
RUSTINGTON 39

Parry, Joseph (b. May 21, 1841, Cyfarthfa, Wales; d. Feb. 17, 1903, Cartref, Penarth, Glamorganshire) was a Welsh musician who came to America as a boy of 13 and received his first musical training in classes conducted by fellow workers in the Danville, PA, iron works; later attended a summer music school in Geneseo, NY; returned to Wales and won several Eisteddfod contests (Swansea, 1863; Llandudno, 1864; Chester, 1866); studied at the Royal Academy of Music in London and received BMus and DMus degrees from Cambridge University; after a brief return to the United States (1871-73), was appointed professor of music at the University College in Aberystwyth, and finally at the University College, Cardiff; wrote oratorios, cantatas, anthems, and some 400 hymn tunes.　　　H
ABERYSTWYTH 461

Patrick, St. (b. *c.* 372 to 389, Bannavem Taberniae, Britain; d. March 17, 466 [or 461], Ireland) was from a three-generation Christian family, the son of a Roman; was captured by slave traders and taken to Ireland where he learned the language and had time for mystic devotional life; following his escape, may have studied at Lerins; was ordained and consecrated Bishop of Ireland, and returned to Ireland as a missionary. See his *Confessions.*
I Arise Today 371
I Bind unto Myself Today 1
Christ Beside Me (attr.) 543

Patti, Sandi; see **Helvering, Sandi Patti**.

Peace, Albert Lister (b. Jan. 26, 1844, Huddersfield, England; d. Mar. 14, 1912, Blundellsands, Liverpool), a child prodigy, was organist at the parish church of Holmfirth, York, at age nine; received BMus and DMus degrees from Oxford and was organist of Glasgow Cathedral (1879-97); went to St. George's Hall, Liverpool, as successor to William T. Best and remained until his death; was a Fellow of the Royal College of Organists (1866) and is said to have played more dedicatory recitals on new organs than any other organist of his time; edited a number of volumes for the Church of Scotland: *The Scottish Hymnal* (1885), *Psalms and Paraphrases with Tunes* (1886), *The Psalter with Chants* (1888), and *The Scottish Anthem Book* (1891).　　H
ST. MARGARET 531

Peacock, David (b. Aug. 9, 1949, Bradford, England), son of a clergyman, earned the BMus and a certificate in Education; was coordinator of Christian Aid Project (1972-74), music director, BBC Television (1973-74), teacher (1974-85); has been Minister of Music, Upten Vale Baptist Church, Torquay,

Dovershire (since 1985); is music editor (*Hymns for Today's Church* and others), composer, arranger, and orchestrator.
PARKSTONE 567

Pearce, Almeda Jones (b. Jan. 4, 1893, Carlisle, PA; d. July 25, 1986, Lancaster, PA) early displayed musical talent and played piano in her church, sang soprano with her three sisters, and accompanied voice students at nearby Dickinson College (including concert baritone soloist John Charles Thomas); briefly studied in New York at the Walter Damrosch School of Music; returned to Carlisle and married the baritone in the Methodist church quartet, evangelist Rowan Pearce, also a sometime student at Dickinson; in addition to ministry at the Collingswood (NJ) Methodist Church, taught (with her husband), on a small radio station in Camden, NJ, a Bible study in the Keswick tradition called "Christian Voices," which included the music ministry of Almeda and the three children (singer-trombonist Bill Pearce is one of the sons). Daughter Jeanne P. Hopkins recalls the family's getting up early for the daily live broadcasts from 1932 to the 1960s, at which time they became Sunday only. Almeda prepared the music and influenced such other ministries as that of Ruth and Percy Crawford. Hopkins's memory is one of "Mother's devotion to the Lord."
When He Shall Come, PEARCE 273

Pennefather, William (b. Feb. 5, 1816, Dublin, Ireland; d. Apr. 30, 1873, Muswell Hill, London, England) was born of titled parents and educated at Westbury College near Bristol and at Trinity College, Dublin (BA, 1840); was ordained in 1841 and served Anglican churches at Ballymacugh, Kilmore, and Mellifont in Ireland; moved to England (1848) and ministered in Walton, Aylesbury, and Barnet and East London, where he established the Mildmay Religious and Benevolent Institution, a center of religious work; produced several volumes, including *Hymns, Original and Selected* (1872) and *Original Hymns and Thoughts in Verse* (1873, posthumously). Also see his *Life and Letters* (1847). H
Jesus, Stand Among Us 803

Perronet, Edward (b. 1726, Sundridge, Kent, England; d. Jan 2, 1792, Canterbury) is remembered for the text "All hail the power of Jesus' name," which is included in most English-language hymnals and in many translations; received his early education under a tutor of his father's vicarage and prepared to be a clergyman in the Church of England; was a strong evangelical whose poem *The Mitre*, 1757, attacked certain practices of the Church; associated with reformers like John and Charles Wesley and Selina, Countess of Huntingdon, but eventually withdrew from the Anglican Church; spent his last years as pastor of a dissenting congregation in a small chapel at Canterbury; wrote several volumes of poems and versified scripture. H
All Hail the Power of Jesus' Name 93, 95

Perry, Michael Arnold (b. Mar. 8, 1942, Beckenham, Kent, England) attended Dulwich,

London, Cambridge, and Southampton Colleges (BD, MPh); served as Vicar of Bifferne, Southampton (1972-81), Rector of Eversley, Hampshire (1981-89), and, since 1989, as Vicar of Tonbridge, Kent; is editor of *Carols for Today, Carol Praise, Church Family Worship, Come Rejoice,* and other publications; wrote texts which have appeared in several hymnals, including those of the Jubilate Group, musicians and "wordsmiths" with whom he writes new hymns and "writes back" existing hymns, noting that "if we don't update, they are going to die."

Blest Be the God of Israel (para.) 332

Heal Me, Hands of Jesus 463

How Shall They Hear? 740

In Christ There Is No East or West 695

Lord Jesus Christ, Invited Guest 387

Peters, Mary Bowly (b. Apr. 17, 1813, Cirencester, Oxfordshire, England; d. July 29, 1856, Clifton, Bristol) was the daughter of Richard Bowly and wife of Rev. John McWilliam Peters; wrote most of her hymns before she was 30; authored a seven-volume work, *The World's History from the Creation to the Accession of Queen Victoria.* Through the Love of God the Savior 610

Peterson, John Willard (b. Nov. 1, 1921, Lindsborg, KS) was born into a musical family, members of a Mission Covenant Church and active in Christian radio; during World War 2 was a pilot in the Army Air Force in Asia; received training at Moody Bible Institute

and American Conservatory of Music, Chicago (BMus, 1951); received an honorary DD degree (1971) from Western Conservative Baptist Seminary and the SacMusD (1967) from John Brown University; was a staff musician, WMBI, Chicago (1950-54); in 1954 joined Alfred B. Smith as an editor and composer for Singspiration, Montrose, PA, and in 1963 became president of the company when it was acquired by Zondervan Publishing House, Grand Rapids, MI; now lives in Scottsdale, AZ, where he manages the John W. Peterson Music Company; has edited several hymnals, including *Great Hymns of Our Faith* (1968), and written more than 1000 texts and tunes; has published more than 25 cantatas and musicals, which have sold some eight million copies.   H

Jesus Is Coming Again, COMING AGAIN 276

Surely Goodness and Mercy, SURELY GOODNESS AND MERCY 639

TORONTO 732

Piae Cantiones (Nyland, Finland, 1582) is a collection of 74 Latin hymns and carols with melodies for use by Protestants (topics are seasonal for the church year). A few texts have alternate tunes and 12 tunes are harmonized in two, three, or four parts. The book was edited by Theodoricus [Didrik] Petri (of Danish descent and Swedish influence) of Abo, Finland, while he was a student at the university of Rostock. *Piae Cantiones* was brought to England by the British Minister to Stockholm and given to John M. Neale about 1852; it became the source for continental folk song-based hymn tunes. It is available in a newer, but anachro-

nistic, edition by G. R. Woodward, with historic preface, notes, and some "corrections" (London: Plainsong and Medieval Music Society [Broude], 1910); Woodward notes the similarity between Petri's work and that of Lucas Lossius (1553-79), a Lutheran compiler from Lüneberg, Germany, who evidently influenced Petri.
On This Day Earth Shall Ring 175
PERSONENT HODIE 142, 175, 400
TEMPUS ADEST FLORIDUM 156, 337

Pierpoint, Folliott Sanford (b. Oct. 7, 1835, Bath, Somerset, England; d. Mar. 10, 1917, Newport, Gwent) took his early schooling at Bath, with higher education at Queen's College, Cambridge; for a time was master of the classics at Somersetshire College; contributed hymns to the *Lyra Eucharistica* and *The Hymnal Noted*; published several volumes of poems, including *The Chalice of Nature, Songs of Love,* and *Lyra Jesu* (1878). H
For the Beauty of the Earth 353

Piper, John Stephen (b. Jan. 11, 1946, Chattanooga, TN) is senior pastor, Bethlehem Baptist Church, Minneapolis, MN; was educated at Wheaton College, IL (BA, 1968), Fuller Seminary (BD, 1971), and University of Munich (DTh, 1974); taught at Bethel College, St. Paul, MN; in addition to writing hymns, has published *Love Your Enemies* (Cambridge Univ. Press, 1979), *The Justification of God* (Baker, 1981), *Desiring God* (Multnomah, 1987), *What's the Difference?* (Crossway, 1990), and *The Pleasures of God* (Multnomah, 1991).
"Let There Be Light!" 716

Playford, John (b. *c.* 1623, Norwich, England; d. Nov., 1686, London) was a music publisher and keeper of a bookshop near Temple Church, London, which was a gathering place for musicians including Pepys and Purcell; composed and arranged glees, catches, and instrumental music; is known for collections including *Psalms and Hymns in Solemn Musick* (1671) and *The Whole Book of Psalms* (1677).
[PRAISE BE TO YOU, O CHRIST] 810

Plumptre, Edward Hayes (b. Aug. 6, 1821, Bloomsbury, London, England; d. Feb. 1, 1891, Wells, Somerset) was trained at King's College, London, and University College, Oxford; became a Fellow of Brasenose College; ordained (1846), was chaplain at King's College, where he later taught pastoral theology and exegesis; also served as Dean of Queen's College, Oxford, prebendary of St. Paul's, rector of Pluckley and vicar of Bickley in Kent, and Dean of Wells; was a member of the Old Testament Revision Committee for the English Revised Version of the Bible; wrote several volumes of verse and translated many hymns. H
Rejoice, Ye Pure in Heart 34
Your Hands, O Lord, in Days of Old 409

Pollard, Adelaide Addison (b. Nov. 27, 1862, Bloomfield, IA; d. Dec. 20, 1934, New York, NY) was born "Sarah" but chose the name Adelaide; received her education in schools in Denmark, IA, and Valparaiso, IN, and the Boston School of Oratory; taught in girls' schools in Chicago and became well known as an itinerant Bible teacher; taught at the Missionary Training School in New York City (Christian and Missionary Alliance) for eight years; was interested in missions and spent a few months in Africa before the outbreak of World War 1; passed her last years in the East, still ministering, though she was in poor health most of her life; wrote a number of hymns, but only "Have Thine Own Way, Lord" has remained popular.

H

Have Thine Own Way, Lord 584

Polman, Bert (b. Aug. 28, 1945, Rozenburg, The Netherlands), the son of a preacher, spent two years as a child in Indonesia, then immigrated to Canada in 1955; was educated at Dordt College, Sioux Center, IA (BA, 1968), University of Minnesota (MA, 1969, PhD in musicology, 1981, writing on the music of the Christian Reformed Church); taught music at Ontario Bible College, Toronto (1975-85), and has been music professor and administrator at Redeemer College, Ancaster, Ontario, since 1985; is a specialist in hymnology and liturgics, and hymnologist for the Christian Reformed *Psalter Hymnal* (1987) and principal contributor to its companion, which is soon to be released; was a member of the editorial committee of *The Worshiping Church*; is currently preparing a children's hymnal for the Christian Reformed Church; is active in The Hymn Society, and presently serves as Hymn Research Chairman.
Christian, Do You Struggle? (rev.) 660

Post, Marie J. (b. Feb. 8, 1919, Jenison, MI; d. May 24, 1990,

Grand Rapids, MI) attended Calvin College; taught junior high school in Grand Rapids; was known as a poet with Grand Rapids Press and wrote for devotional and church magazines; has several publications, including a collection, *I Had Never Visited An Artist Before* (1977); served on the revision committee of the *Psalter Hymnal* of the Christian Reformed Church; died on Ascension Day.
I Will Sing of the Mercies (2nd stanza) 30

Pott, Francis (b. Dec. 29, 1832, Southwark, London, England; d. Oct. 26, 1909, Speldhurst, Kent, England) made important contributions to hymnody through his translations from the Latin; graduated from Brasenose College, Oxford (BA, MA), was ordained in 1856 and served as curate in parishes in Somerset and Sussex; was rector of Northill, Bedfordshire (1866-91); was forced to retire because of deafness, and afterward was active in research and writing; was a member of the original committee for *Hymns Ancient and Modern* (1861); edited *Hymns Fitted to the Order of Common Prayer* (1861) and *The Free Rhythm Psalter* (1898).   H
The Strife is O'er, the Battle Done (trans.) 233

Praetorius, Michael (b. Feb. 15, 1571, Kreutzberg, Thuringia, Germany; d. Feb. 15, 1621, Wolfenbüttel), whose name is a Latin form of the original family name Schulz, was the son of a Lutheran pastor; attended the University of Frankfurt-an-der-Oder, then returned to be organist (1604); served in the court of Heinrich Julius of Halberstadt and

as prior of the Ringelheim Monastery; published three large and significant sources for Protestant church music, *Syntagma Musicum* (1614-19).
PUER NOBIS (harm.) 27, 136, 193
ES IST EIN' ROS' ENTSPRUNGEN (harm.) 163

Prentiss, Elizabeth Payson (b. Oct. 26, 1818, Portland, ME; d. Aug. 13, 1878, Dorset, VT) was a schoolteacher for some years; in 1845 married R. George Lewis Prentiss, a Presbyterian-Congregational minister, who became professor of homiletics and polity at Union Theological Seminary, New York; as a teenager, contributed to the *Youth's Companion*; published a number of works, including *Stepping Heavenward* (1869), *Religious Poems* (1873), and *Golden Hours, or Hymns and Songs of the Christian Life* (1874). H
More Love to Thee, O Christ 555

Preston, David G. (b. Nov. 1, 1939, London, England), the son of a sports journalist, was educated at Oxford University (MA) and Ahmadu Bells University, Nigeria (PhD); was lecturer in French language and literature at Ahmadu Bells University (1968-79); wrote Psalm paraphrases, including those in *The Book of Praises* (Leeds: Carey Publications, 1986).
God in Mercy Grant Us Blessing (Psalm 67) 344

Price, Shelby Milburn (b. Apr. 9, 1938, Electric Mills, MS) attended the University of Mississippi (BMus), Baylor University (MMus), the University of Southern California (DMA), and Princeton

Theological Seminary; taught at the University of Southern California (1966-67) and at Furman University (1967-81; music department chair, 1972-81); has served churches in Mississippi, Texas, California, South Carolina, and Kentucky, and was Dean of the School of Church Music at Southern Baptist Theological Seminary, Louisville, KY (1981-93); currently Dean, School of Music, Samford University, Birmingham, AL; has numerous published choral compositions and hymn texts and tunes; co-authored with William J. Reynolds, *A Survey of Christian Hymnody* (Hope Publishing Company, 3rd ed., 1987) and a writer for *Companion to the Baptist Hymnal*.
CELEBRATION '85 402
Stir Your Church, O God, Our Father 718

Prichard, Rowland Hugh (b. Jan. 14, 1811, Y Graienyn, near Bala, Wales; d. Jan. 25, 1887, Holywell, Flintshire) is best known as the composer of the tune HYFRYDOL, which he wrote when about 20 years of age; spent most of his life in Bala, North Wales, where he was well known as a choir director and amateur musician; in 1880 moved to Holywell to become an assistant loom tender at the Welsh Flannel Manufacturing Company; in 1844, published *Cyfaill y Cantorion* (The Singer's Friend) which contained most of his tunes. H
HYFRYDOL 51, 89, 135, 263, 492

Prudentius, Marcus Aurelius Clemens (b. 348, Spain; d. *c.* 413) is known only from what he said about himself in a short, poetic

introduction to his writings; was a Spaniard from a good family, who studied and practiced law and became a judge, and was eventually made chief of Emperor Honorius's imperial bodyguard; at age 57 was conscious-stricken because of his self-centered life, entered a monastery, and spent the rest of his days in meditation, prayer, and writing; left the historic volumes *Liber Cathemerinon* (hymns for the hours of the day) and *Liber Peristephanon* (14 hymns honoring martyrs).				H
Of the Father's Love Begotten 145

Psalter (1912) was prepared by a cross-section of Presbyterians and Christian Reformed Church leaders as a revision of the Psalter of 1895, which had been revised and enlarged from an earlier book by the Reformed Presbyterians. The book was compiled in stages—a draft was readied in 1905 and returned to the working committee. These combined groups presented their work to the Presbyterian Church in the United States and the Psalter was adopted in 1912; the Christian Reformed Church adopted a very similar collection (with some additional material) in 1914.
Amid the Thronging Worshipers (Psalm 22:22-31) 340
How Blest Are They Who, Fearing God (Psalm 1) 342
It Is Good to Sing Your Praises (Psalm 92) 325
Lord, Our Lord, Your Glorious Name (Psalm 8) 319
Out of the Depths (Psalm 130) 465
Sing Praise to the Lord (Psalm 149) 346

Psalter Hymnal (1987) is the most recent hymnal of the Christian Reformed Church; contains metrical versions of every Psalm, plus hymns and other congregational materials.
Great Is the Lord Our God 335

Pulkingham, Betty Carr (b. Aug. 25, 1928, Burlington, NC) is the daughter of Leo Carr, a lawyer and judge, and Betty Knott (Carr), teacher and homemaker; attended Burlington High School (1945), University of North Carolina, Greensboro (BS in Music—Piano, Theory, *magna cum laude*, 1949), and Eastman School of Music, Rochester, NY (1949); has taught at the School of Fine Arts, University of Texas, Austin, and Austin High School; has been choir director at various churches; is a founding member of Community of Celebration, Berkshire, England (1974); is co-editor of songbooks, *Sounds of Living Waters, Fresh Sounds,* and *Cry Hosanna,* and producer for Fisherfolk recordings; currently resides in Aliquippa, PA, with her husband, Rev. Graham Pulkingham, at the Community of Celebration; has six children; has worked with such publishers as Hope Publishing Company, Royal School of Church Music (United Kingdom), and Mel Bay Publications.
ALLELUIA NO. 1 (arr.) 240

Purcell, Henry (b. 1659, London, England; d. Nov. 21, 1695, London), son of a musician, is one of the finest composers to set English text; was chorister of the Chapel Royal (1869-73) and later was appointed its composer (1677) and organist (1682-95); studied organ building with Hingston, and composition with Humfrey and

Blow; was organist at Westminster Abbey (1679-95); wrote extensively (see Zimmerman's analytical catalogue, MacMillan, 1963) including ceremonial music for coronations (1685 and 1689); is buried in Westminster Abbey.
WESTMINSTER ABBEY 475

Purday, Charles Henry (b. Jan. 11, 1799, Folkestone, Kent, England; d. Apr. 23, 1885, London), during a long career, was a singer (performed at Queen Victoria's coronation), music teacher, publisher, lecturer, and conductor; was actively involved in reforming the music copyright laws; for many years served as precentor at the Scottish Church in London's Covent Garden; wrote a number of popular songs and contributed to *Grove's Dictionary of Music and Musicians*; published *The Sacred Musical Offering* (1833), *A Few Directions for Chanting* (1855), *A Church and Home Tune Book* (1857), and *Copyright, a Sketch of Its Rise and Progress* (1877).   H
SANDON 370, 465

Quinn, James (b. Apr. 21, 1919, Glasgow, Scotland) received the MA with honors at St. Aloysius' College, Glasgow (1935-39), was a member of the Society of Jesus (1939-41), studied at Heythrop College, Oxfordshire (1941-44), and became classics master at Preston Catholic College (1944-48); completed theology studies at Heythrop (1948-52), and was ordained a Jesuit priest (1950); taught at several colleges; was active in exchanges with Protestant groups and ecumenical commissions; wrote articles in *New Catholic Encyclopaedia*, and authored *The*

Theology of the Eucharist (1973) and a hymn collection, *New Hymns for All Seasons* (1969).
Christ Beside Me (adapt.) 543

Rabanus Maurus (b. 776, Mainz, Germany; d. Feb. 4, 856, Winkel-on-the-Rhine, near Fulda, Hesse) was born of noble parents and educated at Fulda and Tours under Alcuin; in 803 became director of the Benedictine Abbey school at Fulda; was ordained a priest in 814 and made a pilgrimage to Palestine; became Archbishop of Mainz, 847, and later was proclaimed a saint; left extensive biblical commentaries, other scholarly works, and many Latin poems.   H
Come, Holy Ghost, Our Souls Inspire (attr.) 296

Ramsey, Benjamin Mansell (b. 1849, Richmond, Surrey, England; d. Aug. 31, 1923, West Wittering, Chichester, Sussex) "was for many years a well known teacher in the Bournemouth area; a prolific composer of part-songs and pianoforte pieces and a writer of hymns and carols and on musical theory; retired from active professional life in 1916; during the last year of his life was in poor health, but organized and conducted a choral society in the village of Chichester" (from an obituary notice in the *Musical Times*, Oct. 1, 1923).   H
Teach Me Thy Way, O Lord, CAMACHA 586

Rankin, Jeremiah Eames (b. Jan. 2, 1828, Thornton, NH; d. Nov. 28, 1904, Cleveland, OH) received his education at Middlebury College (VT) and Andover Theological Seminary; was ordained a Congregational minister

(1855), and served churches in New York, Vermont, Massachusetts, Washington, DC, and New Jersey; returned to Washington, DC, as President of Howard University (1889); left many publications (mostly gospel songbooks) including *Gospel Temperance Hymnal* (1878), *Gospel Bells* (1883) and *German-English Lyrics, Sacred and Secular* (1897).   H
God Be with You 839, 840

Ravenscroft, Thomas (b. *c.* 1582 or 1590; d. *c.* 1633) was a boy chorister at St. Paul's Cathedral; received the BMus from Cambridge University (1605); served as music master at Christ's Hospital (1618-22); published many works, including the round "Three Blind Mice," but is best known for his *Whole Book of Psalmes* (1621) in which he introduced 105 tunes (many from the continent, 51 harmonized by him, and two probably composed by him) which became for many years the standard musical version of the psalter in England; may have initiated the practice of naming tunes after cities and other locations.
DUNDEE (harm.) 73

Rawls, Rooks Maines (b. July 12, 1916, Lake Butler, FL) studied at Mercer University (AB) and George Peabody College (now Vanderbilt) and Scarritt College; served in Georgia Baptist Convention Church Training (1938-43) and Alabama Baptist Convention Church Training and student ministries (1943-44); retired in 1981 from The Baptist Sunday School Board, Nashville, TN, and makes his home in Brentwood, TN.
Take My Life, Lead Me, Lord 566

Rawnsley, Hardwicke Drummond (b. Sept. 28, 1851, Shiplake, Henley-on-Thames, England; d. May 28, 1920, Grasmere) was the son of an Anglican clergyman; attended Balliol College, Oxford (BA, 1875, MA, 1883); was ordained (1875) and served St. Barnabas', Bristol (1875-78), Low Wray, Lancashire (1878-83), Crosthwaite (1883-1917), and was honorary canon of Carlisle (1893); published hymns, poetry, and historic books.
O God, Whose Will Is Life and Good 413

Rawson, George (b. June 5, 1807, Leeds, England; d. Mar. 24, 1889, Clifton, Bristol) was educated at Manchester Grammar School; a congregationalist, he assisted with compiling the *Leeds Hymn Book* (1853) and *Psalms and Hymns for the use of the Baptist Denomination* (1858); wrote many hymns, including some under the pseudonym "A Leeds Layman."
By Christ Redeemed 789

Reden, Karl; see **Converse, Charles C.**

Redhead, Richard (b. Mar. 1, 1820, Harrow, Middlesex, England; d. Apr. 27, 1901, Hellingly, Hailsham, Sussex), during the Tractarian movement in the Church of England, pioneered in the revival of Gregorian chant; was a chorister at Magdalen College, Oxford, and studied organ with Walter Vicary; for 25 years was organist at Margaret Chapel, London (now All Saints', Margaret Street); in 1864 became organist at St. Mary Magdalen Church, Paddington, where he served for 30

years; with his pastor, Canon Frederick Oakeley, was co-editor of the first Gregorian psalter used in the Anglican church, *Laudes Diurnae* (1843); published *Ancient Hymn Melodies and Other Church Tunes* (1853).   H
REDHEAD 225

Redner, Lewis Henry (b. Dec. 15, 1831, Philadelphia, PA; d. Aug. 29, 1908, Atlantic City, NJ) was a very successful real estate broker in his native Philadelphia; was successively organist of four different churches including Holy Trinity, where he shared a notable ministry with rector Phillips Brooks and also was Sunday School superintendent; remained a bachelor all his life, making his home with his sister. H
ST. LOUIS 155

Reed, Andrew (b. Nov. 27, 1787, London, England; d. Feb. 25, 1862, London) is remembered as the founder of The London Orphan Asylum, The Asylum for Fatherless Children, The Asylum for Idiots, The Infant Orphan Asylum, and The Hospital for Incurables; received schooling at Hackney College and was ordained a Congregational minister in 1811; was the first pastor of the New Road Chapel (St. George's-in-the-East) and, when the building became too small, was responsible for building Wycliffe Chapel, remaining there until 1861; composed 21 hymns, and in 1817 published a supplement to Isaac Watts's *Psalms and Hymns*, and later, *The Hymn Book* (1842).   H
Holy Spirit, Light Divine 302

Reed, Edith Margaret Gellibrand (b. Mar. 31, 1885,

Islington, Middlesex, London, England; d. June 4, 1933, Barnet, Hertfordshire) studied at St. Leonard's School in St. Andrews and the Guildhall School of Music, London; with Percy Scholes, edited *The Music Student and Music and Youth*; edited *Panpipes* (for children) and wrote *Story Lives of the Great Composers*.
Infant Holy, Infant Lowly (trans.) 169

Rees, Bryn Austin (b. Sept. 21, 1911, Chelsea, London, England; d. Aug. 4, 1983, Epping, Essex) was educated at Neath Grammar School, Wales, and Hackney and New College, London; was ordained a Congregational minister (1935), pastored in Sawbridgeworth (Hertfordshire), Ipswich (Suffolk), Felixstowe (Suffolk), Muswell Hill (London), Woodford Green and Epping (Essex); was a Royal Air Force Chaplain; wrote anthems and an Easter cantata, *The Saviour*, as well as hymns.
The Kingdom of God Is Justice and Joy 712

Rees, Timothy (b. Aug. 15, 1874, Llanon, Dyfed, Wales; d. Apr. 29, 1939, Llandaff) studied at St. David's College, Lampeter, Wales, and St. Michael's College, Aberdare; was ordained (1897) and became curate of Mountain Ash (1897), then chaplain at St. Michael's (1901), and served in the armed services during World War 1; joined the Community of the Resurrection (1907) and then became Warden (1922) and Bishop of Llandaff (1931); published hymns and sermons.
God of Love and Truth and Beauty 428

God Is Love, Let Heaven Adore Him 70
Holy Spirit, Ever Dwelling 289

Reichardt, C. Luise (b. Apr. 11, 1779, Berlin, Germany; d. Nov. 17, 1826, Hamburg), daughter of the composer-teacher Johann Friedrich Reichardt, studied with her father and made her debut as a singer in Berlin in 1794; settled in Hamburg (1814) and taught in a vocal academy; suffered misfortune in the death of her fiancé shortly before the wedding and later, the loss of her voice; wrote many songs, some of which remained popular for many years.   H
ARMAGEDDON 666

Reid, William Watkins, Jr. (b. Nov. 12, 1923, New York, NY), the son of a hymnodist, was educated at Oberlin (OH) College (BA) and Yale Divinity School (BDiv); served in the United States Army Medical Corps (1943-45) and was a prisoner of war in Germany; pastored Methodist churches in North Dakota, and then in Wyoming, PA, and Wilkes-Barre, PA (District Superintendent, 1978); has published several hymns and articles.
O God of Every Nation 422

Reimann, Heinrich (b. March 14, 1850, Rengersdorf, Silesia [now Klodzko, Poland]; d. May 24, 1906, Berlin, Germany), son and student of musician Ignaz Reimann, studied at Breslau (1870-75) and directed the choral society; taught at Strehlen, Wohlau, Ratifor, and Berlin; left for Leipzig but returned to Berlin (1887); was a composer and biographer; wrote extensively as a music critic, sometimes using the pseudonym Erich Reinhardt,

and performed as organist and choral director; taught theory at Kaiser-Wilhelm-Gedächtniskirche.
MIT FREUDEN ZART (harm.) 8, 50

Reinagle, Alexander Robert (b. Aug. 21, 1799, Brighton, Sussex, England; d. Apr. 6, 1877, Kidlington, Oxfordshire) was born into a family of musicians—his grandfather had been "trumpeter to the King," his father was a distinguished cellist, and his uncle, Alexander Reinagle, was a renowned pianist, composer, and conductor in America; served as organist of St. Peter's-in-the-East, Oxford, 1822-53; wrote a large amount of music and published collections of hymn tunes in 1836 and 1840.   H
ST. PETER 697

Repository of Sacred Music; see **Wyeth, John**.

Revival Melodies, or Songs of Zion (Boston, 1842) is a tunebook recently discovered by David W. Music.
ALL IS WELL (early version in six-eight meter) 595, 725

Reynolds, William Jensen (b. Apr. 2, 1920, Atlantic, IA) is the son of George Washington Reynolds, an evangelistic singer and church musician, and Ethel (Horn) Reynolds; was educated at Southwest Missouri State College (AB), Southwestern Baptist Theological Seminary (MSM), and George Peabody College (EdD); did further study at Westminster Choir College, and Regent's Park College, Oxford; served as minister of music, First Baptist Church, Oklahoma City, OK (1947-55); was

employed by the Church Music Department, Baptist Sunday School Board, Nashville, TN (1955-80) and serves as professor of church music, Southwestern Baptist Theological Seminary (1980-); was a member of the hymnal committee for the *Baptist Hymnal* (1956), and general editor of the Baptist Hymnal (1975), and *The New Broadman Hymnal* (1977); is author of *Hymns of Our Faith* (1964), *Companion to Baptist Hymnal* (1976), and *Songs of Glory* (1990), and co-author (with Milburn Price) of *A Survey of Christian Hymnody* (Hope Publishing Company, 3rd ed., 1987), and a contributor to *Handbook to The Baptist Hymnal* (1992); member of ASCAP and NARAS; among his more than 600 compositions are cantatas, anthems, choral arrangements, hymn tunes, and children's songs; since 1979, has written a weekly newspaper column, "History of Hymns"; in 1992 was honored as a Fellow of The Hymn Society, an organization he served as president (1978-80). H
CLONMEL (arr.) 401

Richard of Chichester, (St.) [born **Richard Wyche, de Wych,** or **De Wicio**] (b. *c.* 1198, Droitwich, Worcestershire, England; d. April 3, 1253, Dover, Kent) studied at Oxford (MA), Paris, and possibly Bologna; became Chancellor of Oxford and then Chancellor to the Archbishop of Canterbury, Edmund of Abingdon (1236-40); was ordained at Orléans Dominican School and made Bishop of Chichester (1244); was canonized January 28, 1262; is the subject of a biography written by the Dominican friar Ralph Bocking

(*c.* 1270).
Day by Day (attr.) 535

Richards, John (b. Jan. 2, 1939, Bournemouth, England) was associated with the Fountain Trust, Esher, Surrey, England; no further information was located.
Spirit, Working in Creation 293

Richardson, Paul Akers (b. Aug. 4, 1951, Stuart, VA), son of amateur church musicians, received his education at Mars Hill College (BMus in church music and voice, *summa cum laude*, 1973) and Southern Baptist Theological Seminary (MCM in voice and musicology, 1975, and DMA in church music, 1979) with additional study at Colgate Rochester Divinity School and Eastman School of Music; since 1977, has worked in various positions at Southern Baptist Theological Seminary, Louisville, KY, where he is presently Associate Professor and Chair of Doctoral Studies in Church Music; has served as minister of music in North Carolina, Indiana, and Kentucky; served two terms as Secretary-Treasurer and is now president-elect of The Hymn Society in the United States and Canada; was on the Editorial Committee for *The Worshiping Church* and one of the writers of the *Handbook to The Baptist Hymnal* (1992).
An Advent Prayer 141
As He Gathered at His Table, STUART 778

Rimbault, Edward Francis (b. June 13, 1816, London, England; d. Sept. 26, 1876, London) studied first with his father, Stephen Francis Rimbault, organist of St.

Giles-in-the-Fields, London, and a composer of note, and later with Samuel Sebastian Wesley and William Crotch; served as organist for a number of London churches, including St. Peter's, Vere Street, and St. John's Wood Presbyterian Church; was an outstanding musicologist and editor of the Motet Society; received honorary degrees from the universities of Harvard, Stockholm, and Göttingen; edited and published music of many kinds—madrigals, ballads, anthems and services, and compositions for piano and organ; produced editions of Tallis's *Cathedral Service and Order of Daily Service*, Este's *The Whole Book of Psalms* and Merbecke's (1550) *Book of Common Prayer Noted*. H

HAPPY DAY (attr.) 504

Rinkart, Martin (b. Apr. 23, 1586, Eilenburg, Saxony, Germany; d. Dec. 8, 1649, Eilenburg) attended the Latin School of Eilenburg, St. Thomas School, Leipzig, where he was a foundation scholar and chorister, and the University of Leipzig, where he studied theology and poetry; served Lutheran churches at Eisleben, Erdeborn, and Lyttichendorf; became archdeacon at Eilenburg and served through the horrors of the Thirty Years' War (1618-48); endured famine and pestilence while he gave himself and his possessions in serving others in that refugee center; officiated at as many as 40 funerals a day—possibly a total of 4500 during his lifetime; was a prolific poet, dramatist and musician, whose writings reflect his strong faith in difficult times. H

Now Thank We All Our God 374, 791

Rippon, John (b. Apr. 29, 1751, Tiverton, Devonshire, England; d. Dec. 17, 1836, London) was one of the most popular and influential dissenting (non-Anglican) ministers of his time; trained for the ministry at the Baptist College, Bristol; at age 22, became pastor of the Baptist church in Carter Lane, London, and served until his death; made a most important contribution to hymnody in his *Selection of Hymns from the Best Authors, Intended as an Appendix to Dr. Watts' Psalms and Hymns* (1787), which had wide use in England and America; in 1791 published a *Selection of Psalms and Hymn Tunes from the Best Authors*, and in subsequent editions added hymn tune names. H

All Hail the Power of Jesus' Name (adapt.) 93, 95
How Firm a Foundation (comp.) 612

Rist, Johann (b. Mar. 8, 1607, Ottensen, near Hamburg, Germany; d. Aug. 31, 1667, Wedel, near Hamburg) was the son of Kaspar Rist, a pastor, who dedicated Johann to the ministry; was educated at the University of Rinteln (1628) where he became interested in hymns, and at the University of Rostock where he studied classics and medicine, as a tutor for a merchant's sons; pastored at Edel [Wedel] (1635-67); produced about 680 hymns addressing all points of theology—intended for private use, they were not sung in worship during his lifetime; was made poet laureate by Emperor Ferdinand III (1644).

Break Forth, O Beauteous Heavenly Light (stanza 1) 158

Roberts, Daniel Crane (b. Nov. 5, 1841, Bridgehampton, Long Island, NY; d. Oct. 31, 1907, Concord, NH) was educated at Kenyon College, Gambier, OH, and served with the 84th Ohio Volunteers during the Civil War; was ordained a priest in the Protestant Episcopal Church (1866) and served parishes in Vermont and Massachusetts; in 1878 was appointed vicar of St. Paul's Church in Concord, NH, where he remained until his death; was president of the New Hampshire State Historical Society for a number of years. H
God of Our Fathers 419

Roberts, John (b. Dec. 22, 1822, Tanrhiwfelen, Aberystwyth, Wales; d. May 6, 1877, Vron, Caernarvonshire), known by his Welsh name, Ieuan Gwyllt, as a youth attended classes conducted by Richard Mills, who worked toward improving congregational singing in Wales; was a choir director at age 14 and a schoolteacher at 16; was ordained into the Calvinistic Methodist ministry and served churches in Aberdare and Llanberis in Capel Cock; in 1859, also founded the great music festival devoted to hymn tunes and texts, Gymanfa Ganu; edited *Llyfr Tonau Cynulleidfaol*, 1859, the official tunebook of the Calvinistic Methodists, and published *Swn y Iiwbili*, 1874, a translation of a Moody and Sankey hymnal. H
LLANFAIR (arr.) 40, 250, 258
ST. DENIO (harm.) 62, 373, 383

Robertson, C. R. W.; see **Davis, Katherine K.**

Robinson, George Wade (b. 1838, Cork, Ireland; d. Jan. 28, 1877, Southampton, England) studied at Trinity College, Dublin, and New College, St. John's Wood, London; became a Congregational minister and was co-pastor at York Street Chapel, Dublin, and later pastor at St. John's Wood, Dudley and Union Street in Brighton; published two books of verse: *Songs in God's World* and *Loveland*. H
I Am His, and He Is Mine 602

Robinson, Robert (b. Sept. 27, 1735, Swaffham, Norfolk, England; d. June 9, 1790, Birmingham) as a youth served as a barber's apprentice; after hearing George Whitefield preach on "The Wrath to Come," struggled spiritually for three years and finally found "joy and peace in believing"; in 1758 began preaching in a Calvinistic Methodist Chapel at Mildenhall, Suffolk, and later founded an independent congregation in Norwich; in 1761-90 pastored the Stone Yard Baptist Chapel in Cambridge, and was at the same time a farmer and merchant; was an eloquent spokesman for civil and religious liberty, American independence, and the abolition of slavery; wrote *A History of Baptism and Baptists* and other works. H
Come, Thou Fount of Every Blessing 45

Rodigast, Samuel (b. Oct. 19, 1649, Gröben, Thuringia (near Jena), Germany; d. Mar. 19, 1708, Berlin), son of a Lutheran pastor, received the MA degree (1671) at the University of Jena and became an instructor there (1676); was rector of the Greyfriars *Gymnasium*, Berlin (1680-1708), and was known

as a scholar and educator.
What God Ordains Is Always Right
82

Root, George Frederick (b. Aug.
30, 1820, Sheffield, MA; d. Aug. 6,
1895, Bailey's Island, ME) was a
popular American musician in the
19th century, remembered for Civil
War songs such as "Tramp, Tramp,
Tramp, the Boys are Marching";
became assistant organist at both
Winter and Park Street churches,
Boston (1839); assisted Lowell
Mason in teaching music in the
Boston public schools; moved to
New York in 1844 and taught in a
number of institutions, including
Union Theological Seminary and
the New York Institute for the
Blind, where Fanny Crosby was one
of his pupils; studied in Paris for a
year and upon returning, collaborated with Fanny Crosby in producing the cantata *The Flower-Queen*;
wrote for the Christy Minstrel
troupe under the pseudonym G.
Friedrich Würzel; in 1858 moved to
Chicago and was associated with
his brother in the music company
Root & Cady, which suffered great
losses in the Chicago Fire of 1871
and was dissolved; became affiliated with the John Church Company
in Cincinnati, but kept his residence in Chicago; was involved in
publishing some 75 important collections, and composed several
hundred songs.   H
QUAM DILECTA 796

Rosenmüller, Johann (b. *c*.
1619, Pelsnitz, Vogtland, Saxony;
d. Sept. 10 or 11, 1684,
Wolfenbüttel) was educated under
Tobias Michael at the University of
Leipzig, and then was a music
director at St. Thomas School in

Leipzig; spent some time in prison
because of improper behavior with
some of his students; pardon was
requested of Dresden (about 1655)
according to a story which is probably apocryphal (Julian); lived in
Hamburg, Germany, and then
Venice, Italy.
WUERTTEMBERG (attr.) 468

Rossetti, Christina Georgina
(b. Dec. 5, 1830, London, England;
d. Dec. 29, 1894, St. Giles,
London), daughter of Gabriele
Rossetti and Lavinia Plidori and sister of Dante Gabriel Rossetti
(painter and poet); precocious, privately published her first poetry in
1847; twice refused marriage; suffered from disfiguring Graves' disease; wrote fantasy, children's poetry, and hymns, sometimes using
the pseudonym Ellen Alleyne; had
she not died of cancer, might have
succeeded Tennyson as poet laureate. See Georgina Barriscombe's
Writers and Their Work: No. 189
(British Council and National Book
League, 1965), a brief biography
and select bibliography.
Love Came Down at Christmas
153
To Be Like Jesus 564

Routhier, Adolphe Basile (b.
May 8, 1839, St. Placide, Quebec,
Canada; d. June 27, 1920, St.
Irenee-les-Baines, Quebec) was edu-
cated at College of St. Thérèsa and
Laval University; entered the bar at
Kamouraska (Dec. 1851), eventual-
ly becoming a judge of the superior
court of Quebec (1873); ran as a
Catholic Conservative for the
House of Commons (1869), but
was not elected; traveled widely
and published his experiences as
well as columns in newspapers and

magazines; wrote the original French text to the Canadian national anthem, "O Canada!"
O Canada! 424

Routley, Erik (b. Oct. 31, 1917, Brighton, England; d. Oct. 8, 1982, Nashville, TN) was educated at Magdalen College, Oxford (BA, 1940), Mansfield College (1943 and BDiv, 1948) where he also was lecturer, and Oxford University (PhD, 1952); was ordained a Congregational minister (1943) and served churches at Wednesbury, Staffordshire, Dartford, Kent, Edinburgh, Scotland, and Newcastle-upon-Tyne; was president of the Congregational Church of England and Wales (1970-71); became visiting professor at Westminster Choir College, Princeton, NJ (1975), along with being director of the chapel (1978); wrote widely in hymnology and church music, including *The Church and Music* (1950), *The English Carol* (1958), *Music Sacred and Profane* (1960), *Hymns Today and Tomorrow* (1964), *Words, Music and the Church* (1968), *Church Music and The Christian Faith* (1978), *An English Speaking Hymnal Guide* (1979), *The Music Of Christian Hymns* (1981), and *The Divine Formula* (1985); edited or served on committees for these and other hymnals: *Congregational Praise* (1951) and co-editor of its *Companion* (1953), *Cantate Domino*, 3rd edition (1974), *Westminster Praise* (1976) and its *Companion* (1977), *Ecumenical Praise* (1977), *Festival Praise* (1979), and *Rejoice in the Lord* (1985). "In the kingdom of God duty and delight meet," was his life's theme and the title source of a memorial volume with a com-

plete bibliography, *Duty & Delight: Routley Remembered* (Hope Publishing Company, 1985).
All Who Love and Serve Your City 430
Church Musicians' Prayer 795
KANSFIELD 428
New Songs of Celebration Render 32
RENDEZ A DIEU (harm.) 32
SHARPTHORNE 571
ST. MAGNUS (descant) 268

Rowlands, William Penfro (b. 1860, Maenclochog, Pembrokeshire, Wales; d. Oct. 22, 1937, Swansea [Abertawe], Glamorganshire) was a schoolteacher and director of the highly renowned Morriston [Swansea] United Choral Society, and precentor of Tabernacle Congregational Church, Morriston (from 1892).
BLAENWERN 285, 325

Rowley, Francis Harold (b. July 25, 1854, Hilton, NY; d. Feb. 14, 1952, Boston, MA) received his education at Rochester University and Theological Seminary; was ordained to the Baptist ministry and served churches in Pennsylvania, Massachusetts, and Illinois; was greatly interested in both human and animal welfare, and served as president of the Massachusetts Society for the Prevention of Cruelty to Animals for 35 years; wrote several volumes, including *The Humane Idea* and *The Horses of Homer*; is memorialized in the Rowley School of Humanities at Ogelthorpe University, Atlanta, GA.   H
I Will Sing the Wondrous Story 500

Rowthorn, Jeffery (b. Apr. 9, 1934, Newport, Gwent, Wales)

attended Newport (Wales) High School (1944-52), Christ's College, Cambridge (BA, MA), Oriel College, Oxford (BLitt), and Union Theological Seminary, NY (Mdiv); was awarded an honorary DD from Berkeley Divinity School, Yale; was Associate Professor, Yale and Berkeley Divinity Schools and founding faculty member, Yale Institute of Sacred Music (1973-87); became Suffragan Bishop, Episcopal Diocese of Connecticut in 1987; served as co-editor (with Russell Schulz-Widmar), *A New Hymnal for Colleges and Schools* (Yale University Press, 1991); is married to a writer and lecturer, Anne, and they have three children.
Lord, You Give the Great Commission 715

Rubin, Steffi Geiser (b. May 10, 1950, Bronx, NY) attended Bronx High School of Science and Simpson College (BA with highest honors, 1973); has been a designer with New Vision Display, New York (1969-70), artist for American Board of Missions to the Jews (1972-73), creative director for Jews for Jesus (1973-80), and director of graphics (self-employed) with Now You See It (since 1980); has been leader of music at Emmanuel Messianic Congregation since 1984; authored many songs used by Jews for Jesus and the performing group, Liberated Wailing Wall.
The Trees of the Field (adapt) 272

Runyan, William Marion (b. Jan. 21, 1870, Marion, NY; d. July 29, 1957, Pittsburg, KS), the son of a Methodist minister, showed an interest in music when he was very young, and at age 12 often served as church organist; was ordained to

the Methodist ministry at 21 and held various pastorates in Kansas (1891-1903); was appointed evangelist for the Central Kansas Methodist Conference and served for some 20 years; wrote his first gospel song in 1915 and was greatly encouraged by D. B. Towner of Moody Bible Institute; in 1924 went to John Brown University, Sulphur Springs, AR, and served as pastor of the Federated Church, and editor of the *Christian Workers' Magazine*; moving to Chicago, was associated with the Moody Bible Institute, and served as editor for Hope Publishing Company, until his retirement in 1948; received the honorary Doctor of Letters, Wheaton (IL) College, 1948.   H
FAITHFULNESS 60

Sachs, Hans (b. Nov. 5, 1494, Nüremberg, Germany; d. Jan. 19, 1576, Nüremberg). Little is known about Hans Sachs, poet and cobbler in Nüremberg, Germany, a contemporary of Luther. He was a prolific writer of early German monophonic song in the Meistersinger tradition; over 6,000 of his works are extant.
WACHET AUF 131

Sacred Harp, The (1844); see **White, Benjamin Franklin**.
THE MORNING TRUMPET 278
BEACH SPRING 578
ALL IS WELL (this version) 595, 725

Sammis, John H. (b. July 6, 1846, Brooklyn, NY; d. June 12, 1919, Los Angeles, CA) moved to Logansport, IN, when he was 23, and became a businessman and an active Christian layman; later gave up business to serve as a YMCA secre-

tary and, as a result, felt called to the ministry and received theological training at Lane and McCormick Seminaries; in 1880 was ordained in the Presbyterian church, and served pastorates in Iowa, Indiana, Michigan, and Minnesota; moved to California in 1901 and was a faculty member of the Bible Institute of Los Angeles until his death.   H
Trust and Obey 523

Sandys, William (b. Oct. 29, 1792, London, England; d. Feb. 18, 1874, London) is remembered for his work in reviving interest in carols and carol singing; was educated at Westminster School and admitted to the bar in 1814, and was by avocation a musician and music researcher; had a very successful law practice, and from 1861 until his retirement was head of Sandys and Knott, Gray's Inn Square, London; among other works, published *Christmas Carols, Ancient and Modern* (1833), *Festive Songs, Principally of the 16th and 17th Centuries* (1848), and *Christmas-tide, Its History, Festivities, and Carols, with their music* (1852).   H
THE FIRST NOEL (attr.) 162

Sankey, Ira David (b. Aug. 28, 1840, Edinburgh, PA; d. Aug. 13, 1908, Brooklyn, NY) was America's most influential evangelistic musician, composer, and publisher in the last half of the 19th century; received his early education in the village of Edinburgh and attended high school in Newcastle, PA, when he moved there with his family in 1857; joined the Methodist Episcopal Church and served as Sunday school superintendent as well as choir director;

after serving in the Union Army during the Civil War, returned to Newcastle and worked with his father, a collector of internal revenue; was appointed secretary, and later president of the local YMCA; while attending the international YMCA convention in Indianapolis, IN (1870), became acquainted with Dwight L. Moody, and six months later joined him as soloist and songleader in his evangelistic work; conducted meetings with Moody throughout the United States and the British Isles for almost 30 years; published *Sacred Songs and Solos* in England, which is said to have sold more than 80,000,000 copies, and is still in print; collaborated with P. P. Bliss and others in editing *Gospel Hymns and Sacred Songs* (1875), *Gospel Hymns No. 2* (1876), *No. 3* (1878), *No. 4* (1883), *No. 5* (1887), *No. 6* (1892), and the collected *Gospel Hymns, Nos. 1-6* (1894). See *Sankey's Story of the Gospel Hymns* (Phila.: Sunday School Times, 1906).   H
TRUSTING JESUS 526

Sarum Primer (1514), an English translation of monastic prayers from earlier French sources (before 1490). The texts were gathered from hymns of the Sarum Rite dating to the 10th century or earlier— collected, by the church year, in a series of Sarum liturgical books in Latin.
God Be In My Head 837

Savonarola, Girolamo (b. Sept. 21, 1452, Ferrara, Italy; d. May 23, 1498, Piazzadella Signoria, Florence), son of a cultured merchant in the court of the Este family, was educated in the classics, including music and theology;

became a Dominican monk (1475), and moved to Florence, where he encountered the Medici family; wrote and preached widely, mostly in Florence and surrounding areas; attempted to reform the Catholic Church and the Florentine government and was martyred for heresy, although he remained loyal to the church, if not to the pope.
For Overcoming Adversity 665

Saward, Michael (b. May 14, 1932, Blackheath, Kent, England) describes himself as an "author, journalist, hymn-writer, broadcaster, lecturer—and amateur cricketer. . . . My style is deliberately punchy and I love to use strong, graphic illustration. I'm an earthy character"; received his education at Eltham College, University of Bristol (BA, 1955) and Tyndale Hall (Church of England Theological College); was ordained in Canterbury Cathedral in 1956 and served two curacies, 1956-64; served as warden at Holy Trinity Inter-Church Centre, Liverpool (1964-67), radio and television officer of the Church Information Office (1967-72), vicar of St. Matthew's, Fulham, London (1972-78), and, since 1978, vicar of Ealing, London; has been active in the area of church communications (especially radio and television), both in the Anglican Church and in inter-church conferences; was honored with the Winston Churchill Traveling Fellowship (1984); was "words editor" for *Hymns for Today's Church* (1982) and has written approximately 58 hymn texts, besides booklets, newspaper articles, and a book, *Don't Miss the Party* (1974).
Baptized in Water 758

King of the Universe 67
These Are the Facts 466
Who Honors Courage Here? 633

Schalk, Carl F. (b. Sept. 26, 1929, Des Plaines, IL) was educated at Concordia Teachers College, River Forest, IL (BS, 1952), Eastman School of Music, Rochester, NY (MMus, 1957), and Concordia Theological Seminary, St. Louis, MO (MA); early taught at Concordia Seminary, then returned in 1965 to Concordia Teachers College where he has stayed; served Zion Lutheran Church, Wausau, WI, as teacher and music director; directed music for the International Lutheran Hour radio program (1958-65); is a prolific hymn tune composer and a presenter at workshops on hymn writing.
FORTUNATUS NEW 228

Schlegel, Katharina Amalia Dorothea von (b. Oct. 22, 1697, Germany; d. date and circumstances unknown) was one of the group who contributed to the *Cöthnische Lieder*—29 hymns have been ascribed to her in the 1744 and 1752 collections, but only this one has been translated into English; according to Julian's *Dictionary*, was a lady attached to the ducal court at Cöthen; according to another source, may have been head of the Evangelical Lutheran nunnery at Cöthen.   H
Be Still, My Soul 530

Schlesische Volkslieder, 1842; see **Fairest Lord Jesus.**
CRUSADER'S HYMN 115

Schop, Johann (b. *c.* 1595, probably in Hamburg, Germany; d. *c.* 1665 Hamburg) was an active musi-

cian in the court at Wolfenbüttel (1615), and then a violinist in the court of Denmark; was director of town council music at Hamburg (1621) and, later, organist at St. James Church; composed musical settings for his friend Johann Rist's *Himmlische Lieder* (1641-43); compiled and composed *Geistliche Concerte* (1643), as well as some secular music.
BREAK FORTH, O BEAUTEOUS HEAVENLY LIGHT 158

Schrader, Jack (b. July 16, 1942, St. Louis, MO) is an arranger, composer, conductor, vocalist, organist, and pianist; attended Moody Bible Institute (church music, 1964) and University of Nebraska at Lincoln (BMusEd, 1966); was ordained in the Evangelical Free Church of America (1975) in which he has served several churches as minister of music, including Wheaton (IL) Evangelical Free Church for 15 years; directs the Singing Men of Oak Brook and the Hope Chorale; was a member of the editorial executive committee of *The Worshiping Church* and is currently Executive Editor of Hope Publishing Company.
BE STILL AND KNOW (arr.) 516
CANTIQUE DE NOEL (arr.) 160
CECELIA (arr.) 500
ACCLAMATIONS 781

Schubert, Franz (b. Jan. 31, 1797, Himmelpfortgrund, now Vienna, Austria; d. Nov. 19, 1829, Vienna) studied violin with his father, piano with his brother, and other aspects of music with his choirmaster; a boy singer with the Vienna Imperial Court chapel choir and school, also played violin, conducted, and, beginning in 1811,

composed much music, including many early *lieder* (songs); influenced and was influenced by major composers of his day in Vienna, yet recognition came primarily after his death; was a prolific composer of songs and song cycles, symphonies, occasional pieces, masses and other choral music, piano and organ works, and music for various instrumental and vocal combinations.
HOLY IS THE LORD 831

Schuler, George Stark (b. Apr. 18, 1882, New York, NY; d. Oct. 30, 1973, Sarasota, FL) received his training at the Chicago Musical College, Cosmopolitan School of Music, and the Moody Bible Institute, Chicago; was a member of the faculty of Moody Bible Institute for some 40 years; after retiring from Moody, served on the editorial staff of Rodeheaver Publishing Company for several years; wrote anthems and many gospel songs, and edited five songbooks and several piano and organ collections; authored some church music manuals, such as *Evangelistic Piano Playing, Gospel Song and Hymn Tune Composition,* and *Choral Directing.*   H
SCHULER 656

Schumann, Robert Alexander (b. June 8, 1810, Zwickau, Saxony, Germany; d. July 29, 1856, Endenich, near Bonn) studied law, but found music much more interesting and eventually overcame his mother's opposition to a musical career; studied piano with Friedrich Wieck and later married his daughter, Clara; became an accomplished pianist and composer and the editor of the Czerny exercises for

beginning students; injured his hand by over-strenuous practicing, which caused him to concentrate on composing, and to depend on his pianist-wife to popularize his music; developed mental instability and was committed to an asylum, where he died; founded *Die Neue Zeitschrift für Musik*, a critical journal, which is still being published; composed symphonies, chamber music, choral and organ pieces, but is perhaps best known for his solos for piano and for voice.   H
CANONBURY   574, 673, 761
SCHUMANN (attr.) 649

Schütz, Johann Jakob (b. Sept. 7, 1640, Frankfort-on-the-Main, Germany; d. May 22, 1690, Frankfort) studied law at Tübingen, returned to Frankfort and became a distinguished and respected lawyer; was a close friend of P. J. Spener, who founded the Pietist movement in the German Lutheran Church and influenced Bach; in later years, was influenced by J. S. Petersen and left the Lutheran communion in 1686, becoming a Separatist; published *Christliches Gedenckbüchlein* (1675).   H
Sing Praise to God Who Reigns Above 50

Schwartz, Stephen (b. Mar. 6, 1948, New York, NY), son of Stanley L. Schwartz (businessman) and Sheila Siegal Schwartz (teacher), was educated at Juilliard (1960-64) and Carnegie Tech (BFA, 1968); is married to Carole Ann Piasecki; has collaborated with Leonard Bernstein on several musicals and the theater piece *Mass*; was composer and librettist for *Pippin* and other broadway shows; received awards for *Godspell* (two

Grammy awards, Drama Desk, National Theater Arts Conference, and *Billboard*, 1971), and others.
GODSPELL 535

Schwedler, Johann Christoph (b. Dec. 21, 1672, Krobsdorf, Silesia, Germany; d. Jan. 12, 1730, Niederwiese) received his education at the University of Leipzig and became a popular preacher and writer of hymns; served as pastor at Niederwiese, near Greiffenberg, for almost 30 years, founding an orphanage there; wrote more than 500 hymns, mostly on the themes of God's grace and the believer's confidence, and published them in his *Die Lieder Mose und des Lammes, oder neu eingerichtetes Gesangbuch*, 1720.   H
Ask Ye What Great Thing I Know 224

Scott, Clara H. (b. Dec. 3, 1841, Elk Grove, IL; d. June 21, 1897, Dubuque, IA) attended the first musical institute held in Chicago by C. M. Cady in 1856; began teaching music at the Ladies' Seminary at Lyons, IA, in 1859; released many of her early songs in Horatio Palmer's collections; published *Royal Anthem Book* (1882), the first volume of anthems by a woman, and later, other collections; met an untimely death when she was thrown from a buggy by a runaway horse.   H
Open My Eyes, That I May See, SCOTT 557

Scottish Psalter (1615): ***The One Hundred Fifty Psalms of David***, published by Andro Hart (Edinburgh, 1615). The psalter was the source of all congregational participation in the churches of

Scotland until the mid-18th century. The earliest book (words) was *Gude and godlie Ballatis* (before 1546), but the 1615 edition became the major influence, offering a few melodies (interchangeable "common tunes") as well as many texts which have endured.
DUNDEE 73

Scottish Psalter (1650): ***The Psalms of David in Meeter. Newly translated and diligently compared with the Original Text and former Translations; More plain, smooth and agreeable to the Text than any heretofore*** (printed by Evan Tyler, Edinburgh, 1650). The Westminster Assembly of 1643 had called for a unified Psalter for England and Scotland. An edition was prepared in 1646 which incorporated texts of previous psalters, but the Scottish church was not satisfied with the Westminster versions and appointed John Adamson, Thomas Craufurd, John Row, and John Nevey to revise the Scottish Psalter—the version then adopted by the "General Assembly of the Kirk of Scotland" in Edinburgh, 1650.
The Lord's My Shepherd, I'll Not Want 330

Scriven, Joseph Medlicott (b. Sept. 10, 1819, Seapatrick, Co. Down, Ireland; d. Aug. 10, 1886, Bewdley, Rice Lake, Ontario, Canada) entered Trinity College in Dublin in 1835, but left to pursue an army career; was forced to give up his military ambitions because of poor health, and returned to Trinity College to complete his BA degree; moved to Canada where he taught school and served as a tutor;

was a member of the Plymouth Brethren, and devoted much time to humanitarian service without remuneration; was twice denied marriage because of the tragic and premature deaths of the expected brides; in later years suffered physically and financially, with periods of great depression; died by drowning and it is not known whether by accident or suicide; published *Hymns and Other Verses* (1869). H
What A Friend We Have in Jesus 622

Sears, Edmund Hamilton (b. Apr. 6, 1810, Sandisfield, MA; d. Jan. 16, 1876, Weston, MA) studied at Union College, Schenectady, NY, and Harvard Divinity School; was ordained a Unitarian minister but believed in and preached the divinity of Christ; held several pastorates in Massachusetts; co-edited the *Monthly Religious Magazine*, in which most of his hymns first appeared; wrote and published *Regeneration* (1854), *Pictures of the Olden Time* (1857), *Athanasia, or Foregleams of Immortality* (1858), *The Fourth Gospel, the Heart of Christ* (1872), and *Sermons and Songs of the Christian Life* (1875). H
It Came upon the Midnight Clear 170

Seddon, James Edward (b. Aug. 24, 1915, Ormskirk, Lancashire, England; d. Sept. 19, 1983, London) attended King George V grammar school, Southport, and earned associate degrees at London College of Music and Trinity College, London; served three curacies in England (1939-45); was a missionary to Morocco (1945-55), Home Secretary for the Church of England Missionary Society (1955-

67), and held two incumbencies (1967-80); wrote over 30 hymns, some in Arabic, while he was in Morocco.
Lord, Now Let Your Servant (para.) 343
Tell All the World of Jesus 742

Seerveld, Calvin (b. Aug. 18, 1930, Bayshore, NY) was the son of Lester Seerveld, a fishmonger, and Letitia van Tielen, a legal secretary and homemaker; attended Sayville High School, Long Island, NY, Calvin College, Grand Rapids, MI (BA), University of Michigan (MA), and Free University of Amsterdam, Netherlands (PhD); was Professor of English Literature and Philosophy, Belhaven College, MS (1958-59), Professor of Philosophy, Trinity Christian College, Palos Heights, IL (1959-72), and Senior Member in Philosophical Aesthetics, Institute for Christian Studies, Toronto (since 1972); has written psalm versifications and hymn texts as well as translations.
Savior of the Nations, Come (trans.) 138

Seiss, Joseph Augustus (b. Mar. 18, 1823, Graceham, MD; d. 1904, Philadelphia, PA), the son of a miner, was educated at Gettysburg College and Seminary; became a distinguished Lutheran leader and popular preacher, holding pastorates in Virginia, Maryland, and Pennsylvania; wrote a number of books, including *Lectures on the Gospels* and *Ecclesia Lutherana.* H
Fairest Lord Jesus (st. 4, trans.) 115

Sharp, Daniel (b. Mar. 8, 1947, Bloomington, IL) attended Wheaton (IL) College (BMusEd, 1969), Drake University, Des Moines, IA (MMusEd, 1970), and the University of Southern California (DMA, 1978); has served as minister of music at First Presbyterian Church, Pittsburgh, PA (1977-79), Grace Chapel, Lexington, MA (1979-90), Lake Hills Community Church, Laguna Hills, CA (1990-92), and St. Andrews Presbyterian Church, Newport Beach, CA (since 1992); was a member of the editorial committee of *The Worshiping Church.*
Congregational Commitment to Parents 765

Shaw, Martin Edward Fallas (b. Mar. 9, 1875, Kennington, Lambeth, Surrey, England; d. Oct. 24, 1958, Southwold, Suffolk) was the elder brother of Geoffrey Shaw, also a musician; studied at the Royal College of Music; started in theater music, then was organist at St. Mary's Church, Primrose Hill (1908-20), where Percy Dearmer was the priest, then at St. Martin's-in-the-Fields; collaborated with Dearmer in publishing several hymnals; served as Director of Music for the Diocese of Chelmsford (1935-45); composed choral, orchestral, and chamber music; edited and published *Additional Tunes in Use at St. Mary's, Primrose Hill* (1915), *Public School Hymn Book* (1919), *Songs of Praise* (1925) edited with Dearmer, and with both Dearmer and Ralph Vaughan Williams edited the *Oxford Book of Carols* (1928). See his partial autobiography *Up to Now* (1929). H
DANIEL (arr.) 397
NOEL NOUVELET (harm.) 159, 241
PURPOSE 750

Shepherd, Thomas (b. 1665, England; d. Jan. 29, 1739, Bocking, Essex) was ordained in the Church of England, but left in 1694 to become pastor of the independent Castle Hill Meeting House at Nottingham; moved to Bocking in 1700 where he first preached in a barn; after a chapel was finally built for his Bocking congregation, served there for almost 40 years. H Must Jesus Bear the Cross Alone? 658

Sheppard, Franklin Lawrence (b. Aug. 7, 1852, Philadelphia, PA; d. Feb. 15, 1930, Germantown, PA) graduated from the University of Pennsylvania in 1872 with highest honors and was a Phi Beta Kappa charter member; was put in charge of his father's foundry in Baltimore, which manufactured stoves and heaters; served the Zion Protestant Episcopal Church as organist and vestryman, and later joined the Second Presbyterian Church as music director; became President of the Presbyterian Board of Publication; served on the hymnal committee for the Presbyterian *Hymnal* (1911) and edited a Presbyterian Sunday School songbook, *Alleluia* (1915). H TERRA BEATA 335, 384

Sherwin, William Fiske (b. Mar. 14, 1826, Buckland, MA; d. Apr. 14, 1888, Boston) studied under Lowell Mason and became a faculty member at the New England Conservatory of Music in Boston; had great ability to organize and direct amateur choirs; was a Baptist, but was chosen by the Methodists to be their music director at the famous Lake Chautauqua Assembly in New York. H

BREAD OF LIFE 315
CHAUTAUQUA 319, 828

Showalter, Anthony Johnson (b. May 1, 1858, Cherry Grove, Rockingham Co., VA; d. Sept. 16, 1924, Chattanooga, TN) attended singing schools under B. C. Unseld, H. R. Palmer, and George F. Root, and at age 37, studied a year in Europe; published *Harmony and Composition* (1880) in his first year of teaching; worked in a branch office of Ruebush-Kieffer Music Company in Dalton, GA, for a time, and then founded his own company; published about 60 song books and edited the monthly periodical of his company, *The Music Teacher*; was widely known and respected as a conductor of singing schools throughout the southern states; was an elder of the First Presbyterian Church of Dalton, GA, and, for many years, their music director. H SHOWALTER 609

Shurtleff, Ernest Warburton (b. Apr. 4, 1862, Boston, MA; d. Aug. 24, 1917, Paris, France) received his education at Boston Latin School, Harvard University, and Andover Theological Seminary; served Congregational churches in California, Massachusetts, and Minnesota; in 1905 took up residence in Frankfurt, Germany, where he organized the American Church; in 1906 became director of Students' Atelier Reunions, working among American students in Paris; with his wife, participated in relief work during World War 1; wrote a number of books, including *Poems* (1883), *Easter Gleams* (1885), *Song of Hope* (1886), and *Shadow of the Angel* (1886). H Lead On, O King Eternal 747

Sibelius, Jean (b. Dec. 8, 1865, Tavastehus, Finland; d. Sept. 20, 1957, Järvenpää) is recognized to have been the most famous of Finnish composers; studied under Martin Wegelius, conductor of the Finnish Opera, and later in Berlin and Vienna; taught at the Helsingfors Music Institute and Philharmonic Orchestra School; devoted himself fully to composition after receiving a grant from the Finnish government; produced symphonies, choral music, orchestral and other instrumental works; published two principal sacred collections: *Five Christmas Songs* (1895) and *Musique religieuse* (1927).　H
FINLANDIA 507, 530

Siena, Bianco da; see **Bianco da Siena**.
Come Down, O Love Divine! 304

Sinclair, Jerry (b. Mar. 25, 1943, Calais, ME) began singing as a ministry while a teenager in northern Maine; moved to Oklahoma and then to California during the "Jesus Movement" of the 1960s; founded the performing group "The Chosen Ones" and worked with Arthur Blessit; recorded with Capitol Records and Manna Music ("Alleluia" in 1972); currently resides with his wife, Elizabeth, in Orange County, CA.
Alleluia, ALLELUIA 114

Skillings, Otis (b. July 27, 1935, Hamilton, OH), following high school (where he played trombone in award-winning bands), attended St. Paul (MN) Bible College; has served as minister of music at several churches, including Skyline Wesleyan Church, San Diego, CA, and First Evangelical Free Church,

Rockford, IL; has written many arrangements, compositions, and musicals for choir, orchestra, and soloists, including works for recording artists: The Hawaiians, The Spurrlows, Regeneration, The Couriers, Huntley Brown, and others; directs music for Chapel Baptist Church, Rockford, IL, and produces a community-wide Christmas concert; is active as a traveling musician and clinician; is married to Mervyl, also a musician, and they have two daughters and five grandchildren.
The Bond of Love, BOND OF LOVE 696

Skoog, Andrew L. (b. Dec. 17, 1856, Gunnarskog, Värmland, Sweden; d. Oct. 30, 1934, Minneapolis, MN), at the age of 10, followed his father as a tailor's apprentice; immigrated to America when he was 13 years old and settled with his family in St. Paul, MN; had formal education only to the sixth grade, but his search for knowledge brought success in many different fields, including teaching, photography, selling, writing, publishing, and printing; was a church musician (organist-choir director) in several churches in Chicago and Minneapolis; was editor-publisher of a popular Swedish language journal; wrote many hymns, hymn tunes, and anthems, and edited seven hymnals, including *Evangelii Basun I* (1881) and *Jubelklangen* (1886); had a part in the first three hymnals of the Mission Covenant Church, of which *Mission Hymns* (1921) was the last.　H
Day by Day and with Each Passing Moment (trans.) 367

Sleeper, William True (b. Feb. 9, 1819, Danbury, NH; d. Sept. 24, 1904, Wellesley, MA) studied at Phillips-Exeter Academy, the University of Vermont, and Andover Theological Seminary, and was ordained to the Congregational ministry; served in home mission work in Worcester, MA, and later in Maine, where he helped establish three churches; was pastor of Summer Street Congregational Church in Worcester, MA (his first mission assignment) for over 30 years; published a book of verse, *The Rejected King, and Hymns of Jesus* (1883). H
Jesus, I Come 448

Sleeth, Natalie Allyn Wakeley (b. Oct. 29, 1930, Evanston, IL; d. Mar. 21, 1992, Denver, CO) began piano study at age four; graduated from New Trier High School (1952) and Wellesley College (BA in Music Theory, 1952); was awarded an honorary doctorate by West Virginia Wesleyan College (1959) and Nebraska Wesleyan College (1990); lived in Nashville, TN, Dallas, TX, Evanston, IL, and Denver, CO; was an organist and composer of over 180 highly successful selections for church and school; published by AMSI, Sacred Music Press, Carl Fischer, Broadman Press, Hope Publishing Company, Hinshaw Music, and Sonos Music Resources; wrote a devotional book, *Adventures for the Soul* (Hope Publishing Company, 1987); with her late husband, Dr. Ronald E. Sleeth (d. 1985), had two children.
In the Bulb There Is a Flower, PROMISE 678

Smart, Henry Thomas (b. Oct. 26, 1813, London, England; d. July 6, 1879, Hampstead, London), born into a very musical family, received his early training from his father, and attended Highgate school; was largely self-taught, but served with distinction as organist of several leading London churches; became an authority on organ design and planned many outstanding installations; became totally blind when just past 50, but continued an active career; edited two hymnals, *Psalms and Hymns for Divine Worship* (1867) and the *Presbyterian Hymnal* (1875); was a prolific writer of music for choir and organ; also published *Choral Book* (1856) and *Collection of Sacred Music* (1863). H
LANCASHIRE 247, 747
REGENT SQUARE 174

Smith, Alfred Barney (b. Nov. 8, 1916, Wortendyke, NJ) studied at Moody Bible Institute and Juilliard School of Music, and received the AB degree in 1943 at Wheaton (IL) College; studied violin under Roderich Meakle and Leopold Auer; was youth soloist with the New York Philharmonic Orchestra (1933) and concertmaster of the Wheaton College Symphony Orchestra (1942-43); was the founder of Singspiration, serving as president from 1941 to 1962, editing and publishing many songbooks and *Inspiring Hymns* (1951); in 1972 founded Encore Publications, Montrose, PA, and published *Living Hymns;* has written approximately 500 songs; is still an active publisher through his company Better Music Publications in Greenville, SC, where he resides.
H
Surely Goodness and Mercy, SURELY GOODNESS AND MERCY 639

Smith, Deborah Davis (b. Mar. 3, 1958, Nashville, TN) is the wife of Michael W. Smith (below), whom she met in Nashville and with whom she collaborates in writing songs.
Great is the Lord, GREAT IS THE LORD 44

Smith, Edward Russell (b. July 18, 1927, London, Ontario, Canada) is better known by his professional name "Tedd Smith"; received music training at the Royal Conservatory of Music, London, Ontario, Canada, and Catholic University, Washington, DC; won the gold medal for piano performance in the Peel Music Festival and has had special training in orchestration, conducting, and composition; served as director of music at the Avenue Road Church (Alliance) in Toronto (1946-50), and since 1950 has been associated with the Billy Graham Evangelistic Association as pianist; was an arranger and recording artist for RCA Victor Records; has written approximately 40 hymn texts and tunes, and has published piano works, musicals, and a cantata; composes music for films, including the World Wide Pictures releases "The Hiding Place" and "Corrie." H
There's a Quiet Understanding, QUIET UNDERSTANDING 788

Smith, Henry (b. Feb. 3, 1952, Crossnore, NC) attended King College, Bristol, TN, and sang in the choir while completing a degree in psychology; taught himself to play the guitar, and is presently a songwriter in Richmond, VA, with some previous work in the medical field.

Give Thanks with a Grateful Heart, GIVE THANKS 496

Smith, Henry Percy (b. Dec. 1825, Malta; d. Jan. 28, 1898, Bournemouth, Hampshire, England) was educated at Balliol College, Oxford (BA, 1848 and MA, 1850), and became an Anglican clergyman (1849); served as curate at Eversley (1849-51) and at St. Michael's, Yorktown, Surrey (1851-68); became vicar of Great Barton, Suffolk, and later, chaplain of Christ Church, Cannes, France; was serving as canon of the Cathedral of Gibraltar at the close of his career (1892). H
MARYTON 651

Smith, John Stafford (b. 1750 [baptized Mar. 30], Gloucester, England; d. Sept. 21, 1836, London) studied with his father, Martin Smith, and with William Boyce; was chorister at the Chapel Royal, an organist, and composer of songs and anthems; arranged the tune which has become the National Anthem, but did not compose it; co-authored John Hawkins's *General History of the Science and Practice of Music* (1776-89).
STAR-SPANGLED BANNER (attr.) 423

Smith, Michael Whitaker (b. Oct. 7, 1957, Kenova, WV) moved to Nashville, TN (1978), working a "day" job and playing with local bands; became a staff writer for Paragon Music, then was associated with Meadowgreen Music (1981), and subsequently with Edward Grant Publishing Company; traveled with Amy Grant playing keyboards (1982); has written over 185

songs, which are recorded by himself as well as by Sandi Patti, Pat Boone, Larnell Harris, David Meece, and the Bill Gaither Trio; is married to Deborah Smith, and they have five children.
Great is the Lord, GREAT IS THE LORD 44
How Majestic Is Your Name, HOW MAJESTIC 61

Smith, Robert A. (b. Nov. 16, 1780, Reading, Berkshire, England; d. Jan. 3, 1829, Edinburgh, Scotland), the son of a weaver, was a string player and music teacher; became precentor, Abbey Church of Paisley (1807-1823), and psalmodist at St. George's Church, Edinburgh (1823); compiled the six-volume *The Scottish Minstrel* (1820-1824).
MARTYRDOM (adapt.) 208

Smith, Samuel Francis (b. Oct. 21, 1808, Boston, MA; d. Nov. 16, 1895, Boston, MA) is revered as the author of "America"; trained at Boston Latin School, Harvard University, and Andover Theological Seminary; while pastor of the Baptist church in Waterville, ME (1834-42), also taught modern languages at Waterville (now Colby) College; was pastor of the Baptist church, Newton, MA (1842-54); became interested in missions during his student days, and was secretary of the American Baptist Missionary Union for 15 years; visited mission fields of Asia and Europe and wrote *Rambles in Mission Fields* (1884); wrote approximately 100 hymns, mostly for special occasions; collaborated with Baron Stowe in producing *The Psalmist* (1843), a popular Baptist hymnal.   H
My Country, 'Tis of Thee 417

Smith, Walter Chalmers (b. Dec. 5, 1824, Aberdeen, Scotland; d. Sept. 19, 1908, Kinbuck, Perthshire) received his education at Aberdeen Grammar School and University, and at New College, Edinburgh; in 1850 was ordained in the Free Church of Scotland and served churches in London, Glasgow, and Edinburgh for a total of 44 years; pastored the Free High Church, Edinburgh (1876-94); was elected Moderator of the Free Church of Scotland in 1893, its jubilee year; published *Hymns of Christ and the Christian Life* (1876), *Poetical Works* (1902), and many other volumes.   H
Immortal, Invisible, God Only Wise 62

Snodham; see **Este, Thomas**.

Southern Harmony (1835); see **Walker, William** ["Singing Billy"].

Spaeth, Harriet Reynolds Krauth (b. Sept. 21, 1845, Baltimore, MD; d. May 5, 1925, Philadelphia, PA) attended Girls' High School, Philadelphia, and married Adolph Spaeth, president of the General Council of the Lutheran Church in America; was mother of music critic Sigmund Spaeth; served as organist at St. Stephen's Church in West Philadelphia; translated the *Church Book* (1868), *The Sunday School Hymnal* (1901), and two biographies; was active in charity work including aid to the Mary Drexel Home, Lankenau Hospital, and Lutheran Orphans' Home, all in Philadelphia.
Lo! How a Rose E'er Blooming (tr.) 163

Spafford, Horatio Gates (b. Oct. 20, 1828, North Troy, NY; d. Oct. 16, 1888, Jerusalem, Palestine) spent his early years in New York, and later moved to Chicago and set up a successful law practice; was a very active Presbyterian layman, and served as director and trustee for the Presbyterian Theological Seminary of the Northwest (now McCormick Theological Seminary); lost most of his fortune in the Chicago fire of 1871 and later his four daughters and his son (see "It Is Well With My Soul" 519); was for many years interested in the Holy Land and settled in Jerusalem in 1881; founded the American Colony in that city, whose story is told by another daughter, born later, Bertha Spafford Vester, in her book, *Our Jerusalem.*   H
It Is Well with My Soul 519

Sparrow-Simpson, William John (b. June 20, 1859, London, England; d. Feb. 13, 1952, Great Ilford, Essex) is best remembered as compiler of the text for John Stainer's famous oratorio *The Crucifixion* (1887); was educated at Trinity College, Cambridge, took Holy Orders and served various churches; became Chaplain at St. Mary's Hospital, Great Ilford, 1904; besides his collaboration with John Stainer, made literary contributions in the field of church history and theology.   H
All for Jesus! All for Jesus! 570
Cross of Jesus, Cross of Sorrow 214

Stafford, Ottilie (b. Feb. 12, 1921, Middletown, NY), the only child in a Seventh-day Adventist family, early became interested in music (which she has taught); was educated at Atlantic Union College (BA) and Boston University (MA and PhD); currently is professor of English at Atlantic Union College; as a member of the Seventh-day Adventist's Hymnal committee, notes, "Where better to combine an interest in poetry and an interest in music than in the great music of the church?"
Father, Grant Us Your Peace (tr.) 589

Stainer, John (b. June 6, 1840, Southwark, London, England; d. Mar. 31, 1901, Verona, Italy) was one of Britain's leading church musicians in the late-19th century; was a chorister at St. Paul's Cathedral, London, at age seven, and became a church organist at 14; was trained at Christ Church, Oxford, and St. Edmund Hall; was appointed organist at Magdalen College when he was 20 and at University College one year later; succeeded Sir John Goss as organist of St. Paul's Cathedral in 1872 and served in this capacity until failing eyesight forced him to retire in 1888; was knighted by Queen Victoria in 1888, and returned to Oxford University as professor of music until his death; wrote over 150 hymn tunes, plus anthems, cantatas and oratorios, including the well known work *The Crucifixion;* in a long list of publications, co-edited *Dictionary of Musical Terms* (1879), wrote the *Music of the Bible* (1879), and was musical editor for *Church Hymnary* (1898).   H
ALL FOR JESUS 570
CROSS OF JESUS 214
FOURFOLD [Amen] 820
GREENSLEEVES (harm.) 150
SEVENFOLD [Amen] 820
THE FIRST NOEL (arr.) 162
WYCLIFF 759

Stanford, Charles Villiers (b. Sept. 30, 1852, Dublin, Ireland; d. Mar. 29, 1924, St. Marylebone, London, England), musically talented as a child, at age 10 performed one of his compositions at Dublin Royal Theater; was a choral scholar at Queen's College, Cambridge (1870), and organist (1873) of Trinity College, Cambridge (BA, 1874 and MA, 1877); studied in Leipzig and Berlin with Carl Reinecke and Friedrich Kiel (1874-76); became professor of composition and orchestra at the Royal College of Music when it opened in 1883; held various other posts as music director and teacher of such notables as Walford Davies, Ralph Vaughan Williams, and Gustav Holst; was knighted in 1902 and is buried in Westminster Abbey.
ENGELBERG 127, 403

Stanislaw, Richard John (b. Nov. 29, 1939, Philadelphia, PA) is son of Alma Peterson, an immigrant from Latvia, and Benjamin Stanislaw, also of Latvian heritage; attended Haverford (PA) High School, Philadelphia College of Bible (BS, 1962), Temple University (BMusEd, 1966 and MMus, 1968), University of Illinois (DMA, 1976), Columbia (NY) University (post doctoral), and was a Fellow of the American Council of Education (1982-83); taught music in high schools in Philadelphia and Quakertown, PA (1964-69) and at Bloomsburg (PA) State College (1969-82); served as Vice President for Academic Affairs, Taylor University, Upland, IN (1982-92), and, since 1992, as President of King College, Bristol, TN; has presented numerous music workshops

and directed church choirs, most recently, First Presbyterian Church, Muncie, IN (1989-92); was music columnist for *Eternity* magazine (1971-1989); is a Staley Lecturer; authored *A Checklist of Four-shape Shape-note Tunebooks* (Institute for Studies in American Music, 1979) and is primary author of this *Companion*; was a member of the editorial committee of *The Worshiping Church*; is married (1964) to Rebecca Wetzel and father of three children.

Stassen-Benjamin, Linda (b. Sept. 19, 1951, IN) attended South Central High School, Ball State University, Muncie, IN, and El Camino College, Via Torrence, CA; composed and sang with recording groups "David" (1974-75) and "New Song" (1975-77); now writes for New Song Ministries.
Sing Alleluia to the Lord, SING ALLELUIA 771

Stead, Louisa M. R. (b. *c.* 1850, Dover, England; d. Jan. 18, 1917, Penkridge, near Umtali, Rhodesia) was converted at age 9, and later felt called to be a foreign missionary; came to America at age 21, and lived in Cincinnati, OH; at a camp meeting, volunteered for missionary service, but was not appointed because of poor health; married, but lost her husband when he drowned attempting to rescue a small child off Long Island, NY; with her daughter, Lily, moved to South Africa on her own and served as a missionary in the Cape Colony for 15 years; married Robert Wodehouse, a native of South Africa; in 1895, was forced by ill health to return to America, where Wodehouse served as a local

Methodist pastor; returned to Rhodesia when her health improved and was appointed to the Methodist Mission at Umtali; retired in 1911 but remained in Africa until her death.　H
'Tis So Sweet to Trust in Jesus 520

Stebbins, George Coles (b. Feb. 26, 1846, East Carlton, NY; d. Oct. 6, 1945, Catskill, NY) was raised on a farm in New York and studied music in Rochester and Buffalo; moved to Chicago in his early twenties and was a clerk at Lyon and Healy Music Company, and music director at the First Baptist Church; in 1874 became music director in the Clarendon Street Baptist Church, Boston, and later at Tremont Temple, Boston; in 1876 was persuaded by Dwight L. Moody to join him in evangelistic work; was associated with Moody and other leading evangelists for 25 years as song leader, choir organizer, composer, and co-compiler of many gospel song collections; collaborated with Ira Sankey and James McGranahan in preparing the 3rd, 4th, 5th, and 6th editions of *Gospel Hymns*; left the autobiography *Memoirs and Reminiscences* (1924).　H
JESUS, I COME 448
ADELAIDE 584
HOLINESS 540

Stennett, Samuel (b. 1727, Exeter, England; d. Aug. 24, 1795, London), the son of a Baptist minister, was assistant to his father at the Baptist Church in Little Wild Street, Lincoln's Inn Fields, and became pastor upon his father's death; was a prominent dissenting preacher of his time, who used his influence to support the principles of religious freedom; received the honorary DD degree, King's College, Aberdeen (1763); contributed some 38 hymns to John Rippon's *Selection of Hymns* (1787).　H
On Jordan's Stormy Banks I Stand 674

Steurlein, Johann [or **Steuerlein**] (b. July 5, 1546, Schmalkalden, Germany; d. May 5, 1613, Meiningen) studied law, was a town clerk in Wasungen, and then moved to Meiningen where he became mayor (*c.* 1640); a friend of Vulpius (GELOBT SEI GOTT 255), he composed choral works as well as texts.
WIE LIEBLICH IST DER MANN 375

Stites, Edgar Page (b. Mar. 22, 1836, Cape May, NJ; d. Jan. 7, 1921, Cape May) was born into a family whose ancestors came to America on the Mayflower; served during the Civil War, and was stationed in Philadelphia in charge of feeding transient troops; later was a riverboat pilot; was an active member of the First Methodist Church of Cape May for more than 60 years, and was a local preacher, who served for a time as a home missionary; frequently used the pseudonym "Edgar Page" on his hymns.　H
Trusting Jesus 526

Stock, Sarah Geraldine (b. Dec. 27, 1838, Islington, London, England; d. Aug. 27, 1898, Penmaenmawr, Wales), home missionary, was active in the British Sunday School movement; edited a hymnbook for the Church Missionary Society (1899); unmarried, worked with her brother

Eugene, an officer in the Society. Let the Song Go Round the Earth 726

Stockton, John Hart (b. Apr. 19, 1813, New Hope, PA; d. Mar. 25, 1877, Philadelphia), born into a Presbyterian home, was converted at a Methodist camp meeting and became a Methodist minister; held several pastorates in the New Jersey Conference and contributed to the development of church music in each; wrote many hymns and published two volumes: *Salvation Melodies* (1874) and *Precious Songs* (1875). H
Only Trust Him, MINERVA 443

Stone, Samuel John (b. Apr. 25, 1839, Whitmore, Staffordshire, England; d. Nov. 19, 1900, Finsbury, London) was educated at Charterhouse and at Pembroke College, Oxford; took Holy Orders (1862) and became curate of Windsor; succeeded his father as vicar of St. Paul's, Haggerston (1874); was appointed rector of All-Hallows-on-the-Wall, London (1890), and remained until his death; was a member of the committee which prepared the 1909 edition of *Hymns Ancient and Modern*; wrote and published *Lyra Fidelium* (1866), *The Knight of Intercession, and Other Poems* (1872), *Sonnets of the Christian Year* (1875), *Hymns* (1886), and *Order of the Consecutive Church Service for Children, with Original Hymns* (1883). H
The Church's One Foundation 689

Stookey, Lawrence Hull (Apr. 8, 1937, Belleville, IL) attended Swarthmore College (BA in English literature, 1959), Wesley

Theological Seminary (MDiv *magna cum laude*, 1962), and Princeton Theological Seminary (PhD on John Donne, 1971); pastored United Methodist churches in Maryland and Delaware, and has been Professor of Preaching and Worship, Wesley Theological Seminary, Washington, DC, since 1973; served on the revision committee for *The United Methodist Hymnal* (1989) and chaired its subcommittee on worship resources; authored four books on worship.
Epiphany Prayer 184

Storm, August Ludvig (b. Oct. 23, 1862, Motala, Sweden; d. July 1, 1914, Stockholm, Sweden) spent most of his life in Stockholm, where he attended elementary, trade, and agricultural schools and worked as an office clerk; was converted under the ministry of the Salvation Army and later joined the corps; served as finance secretary at the Army headquarters beginning in 1892, and was later promoted to lieutenant-colonel; in 1899 was permanently crippled with a serious back disorder, but continued to carry his responsibilities until his death; was a powerful preacher and a gifted hymnist. H
Thanks to God for My Redeemer 380

Strasburger Kirchenamt (1525); see **Greiter, Matthäus**.
OLD 113th 79

Struther, Jan (b. June 6, 1901, London, England; d. July 20, 1953, New York, NY), pseudonym of Joyce Torrens, was daughter of Henry Torrens and Eva Anstruther; was educated privately; married Anthony Maxtone Graham (1923);

348

wrote articles, stories and poems, and the novel *Mrs. Miniver* (1940); came to New York during the war and married A. K. Placzek (1948); died of cancer.
Lord of All Hopefulness 369

Sullivan, Arthur Seymour (b. May 13, 1842, Lambeth, London, England; d. Nov. 22, 1900, Westminster, London) is known for his music composed for Sir W. S. Gilbert's "Savoy Operas" (Gilbert and Sullivan operettas); was opposed to the use of secular tunes for church music; at age 12 became a chorister at the Chapel Royal, and at 15 had his first anthem published by Novello; studied at the Royal Academy of Music and also at Leipzig Conservatory (1858-61); held several organ positions before becoming professor of composition at the Royal Academy of Music (1866); in addition to his tuneful operetta music, wrote anthems, hymn tunes, and oratorios; edited *Church Hymns* (1874); was knighted by Queen Victoria (1883) and was made a member of the French Legion of Honor.   H
CALCUTTA (adapt.) 464
ST. GERTRUDE 748
NOEL (arr.) 643

Sweney, John R. (b. Dec. 31, 1837, West Chester, PA; d. Apr. 10, 1899, Chester, PA) showed musical gifts when he was very young, and at age 22 was teaching music in Dover, DE; directed the Third Delaware Regiment Band during the Civil War, and afterwards was professor of music at the Pennsylvania Military Academy for 25 years; for a number of years, served as director of music at the Bethany Presbyterian Church in

Philadelphia, and was a popular song leader for many summer assemblies; composed over a thousand hymn tunes and assisted in compiling some 60 collections of gospel songs, anthems, and Sunday school music, collaborating frequently with William J. Kirkpatrick.
H
STORY OF JESUS 199

Symeon, the New Theologian [The Younger] (b. 949, Paphlagonia, Galatia; d. Mar. 12, 1022), raised in the courts of Constantinople and influenced by Symeon the Pious, became a monk at Studion of Constantinople (977), moved to St. Mamas and was ordained a priest there (980); because of his defense of the older Symeon's theological disciplines, was exiled (1009) to St. Marina near Chrysopolis; wrote extensively, including sermons and *Hymns of the Divine Loves*, advocating a personal mystical union with Christ.
Prayer to Christ of Many Metaphors 117

Synesius of Cyrene (b. 365 or 375, Cyrene; d. between 414 and 430) was born into a distinguished family of Cyrene, a Greek city in N. Africa, whose lineage went back to Spartan kings; studied at Alexandria with Hypatia and became a Neoplatonist; converted to Christianity *c.* 400, and was elected Bishop of Ptolemais (409 or 410); was regarded as a great statesman and a man of eloquence; wrote 10 odes which have been translated, and of which *Hymnody Past and Present* (1937) says, "They are of great interest and beauty in their presentation of Christian devotion as seen through the eyes

of a Platonist philosopher."   H
Lord Jesus, Think on Me 462

Tabell, Roland (b. Dec. 3, 1934, Tacoma, WA) attended Queen Anne High School, Moody Bible Institute (1957), Wheaton (IL) College (BA, BMus, 1959), and University of Southern California (MMus); has served as minister of music and worship at Pasadena (CA) Covenant Church since 1961 along with some college and seminary teaching; has published several choral arrangements, including many tunes by Bryan Jeffery Leech, as well as the musicale *Resurrection*, also with Leech.
DUDLEY (arr.) 792
Trust in the Lord, TABELL 527

Taizé Community, a 20th-century monastic ecumenical (formerly French Reformed) fellowship in Taizé, Burgundy, France, is known as "La Colline" (the little hill). The community practices silent prayer, encouraged by mantra-like singing of short phrases (often historic and in Latin to accommodate the internationals), followed by long periods of absolute silence. Jacques Berthier is the resident composer of most of the music of the Community.
Gloria, Gloria 825
Jesus, Remember Me 822

Tallis, Thomas (b. *c.* 1505, Leicestershire, England; d. Nov. 23, 1585, Greenwich, Kent) is considered "the father of English cathedral music"; set texts in Latin and English for Catholic and Protestant royal courts; was organist at Waltham Abbey; a Gentleman of the Royal Chapel, served with William Byrd; was granted a music printing monopoly by Queen Elizabeth, the earliest such monopoly; provided tunes for Archbishop Matthew Parker's *The whole Psalter translated into English Metre* (*c.* 1560), including the famous CANON; is highly regarded for his church choral music and for his mastery of polyphony, evidenced in his motet for eight five-part choirs, *Spem in alium*.
TALLIS CANON 359, 360, 399
[GLORY BE] 810

Tappan, William Bingham (b. Oct. 24, 1794, Beverly MA; d. June 18, 1849, West Needham, MA) was apprenticed to a clockmaker in his early teens, and later moved to Philadelphia and worked in that profession; was very interested in the Sunday School movement, and secured a position with the American Sunday School Union, which he held until his death; was licensed as a Congregational minister (1840) and held evangelistic campaigns throughout the United States, always emphasizing the importance of the Sunday School; published 10 volumes, including *New England and Other Poems* (1819), *Poems* (1822), and *Gems of Sacred Poetry* (1860).   H
'Tis Midnight; and On Olive's Brow 220

Tate, Nahum (b. 1652, Dublin, Ireland; d. Aug. 12, 1715, London, England) is remembered for his association with the historic "Tate and Brady" Psalter; was the son of an Irish minister and author, and was educated at Trinity College, Dublin (BA, 1672); wrote principally for the London stage, adapting works of others, including Shakespeare; was named Poet

350

Laureate of England in 1692; produced his most significant contribution, *The New Version of the Psalms of David* (1696), in collaboration with Nicholas Brady, a psalter that was used for more than 200 years in the Church of England; was an intemperate and irresponsible man, who died in a "debtor's refuge."   H
As Longs the Deer for Cooling Streams (source) 331
While Shepherds Watched Their Flocks 172

Taylor, Cyril Vincent (b. Dec. 11, 1907, Wigan, Lancashire, England; d. June 20, 1991, Petersfield) was the son of a Church of England priest, a boy chorister at Magdalen College School (1918-23), then a student at Christ Church, Oxford (BA, 1929 and MA, 1935); was ordained in the Church of England and was precentor of Bristol Cathedral (1936-39), where he hosted the BBC while it was evacuated during World War 2; was BBC's producer in the Religious Broadcasting Department (1939-53), warden of the Royal School of Church Music (1953-58), vicar of Cerne Abbas, Dorsetshire (1958-1969), and precentor of Salisbury Cathedral (1969-75); retired to Petersfield but continued counseling and music editing, including work on supplements to *Hymns Ancient and Modern*; has several tunes in the *BBC Hymnbook* (Oxford, 1951).
ABBOT'S LEIGH 70, 715
MOWSLEY 180

Teresa [Mother], née **Agnes Gonxha Bojaxhiu** (b. Aug. 27, 1910, Skoppie, Macedonia, southern Yugoslavia [then under Turkish rule]) was called to become a nun at age 12 and at 18 went to India with the Loretto order, taking her first vows in 1928; taught at St. Mary's High School in Calcutta, and then became principal; left the convent's school to "help the poor, while living among them" (1946) and founded the Society of the Missionaries of Charity, an order that serves the sick and destitute; was awarded the Nobel Peace Prize "in recognition of her work in bringing help to suffering humanity" (1979); testifies publicly: "Because we cannot see Christ we cannot express our love to him; but our neighbors we can always see, and we can do to them what, if we saw him, we would like to do to Christ."
Serving the Poor 431

Tersteegen, Gerhard (b. Nov. 25, 1697, Mörs, Westphalia, Germany; d. Apr. 3, 1769, Mühlheim) was slated by his parents to become a Reformed Church minister, but his father's early death made university education impossible; was apprenticed to his brother-in-law, a merchant, and became a silkweaver; after five years of depression and spiritual dearth, made a new covenant with God and signed it with his own blood (1724); gave up his business, and afterward opened his home (called "The Pilgrim's Cottage") to all who needed spiritual counseling, encouraging, and renewal; worked outside the Reformed Church tradition, but is remembered as one of Germany's great hymnists and spiritual leaders; translated or paraphrased (in German) many classics from French and Latin sources, and

wrote 111 hymns, of which about 50 have been translated into English.　　　　　　　　　　　H
God Himself Is with Us 799

Teschner, Melchior (b. 1584, Fraustadt, Silesia; d. Dec. 1, 1635, Oberprietschen, Posen, Poland) was appointed cantor of the "Zum Kripplein Christi" Lutheran Church in Fraustadt (1609), and also taught in the parish school; in 1614 moved to nearby Oberprietschen where he served as pastor, and where he was succeeded by both his son and his grandson.　　　H
ST. THEODULPH 204

Theodulph of Orleans (b. *c.* 750; d. Sept. 18, 821, Angers, France) was born into a noble family (probably Italian), and became abbot of a monastery in Florence; in 781 was brought to France by Charlemagne and appointed abbot of Fleury and Bishop of Orleans; was Charlemagne's chief theologian and a proponent of education; in 818, after the emperor's death, was accused of conspiring with King Bernard of Italy against Louis I, was deposed of his bishopric and imprisoned at Angers; according to tradition, was later released by Louis, but he apparently died in prison, possibly from poison.　　H
All Glory, Laud and Honor 204

Thiman, Eric Harding (b. Sept. 12, 1900, Ashford, Kent, England; d. Feb. 13, 1975, London), son of a Congregational minister, attended Caterham School and Guildhall School of Music, F.R.C.O. (1921), and the University of London (DMus, 1927); became professor of Harmony, Royal Academy of Music (1931) and examiner for the Royal

College of Organists and London University; served as organist and choirmaster at Caterham Congregational Church (1917-20), Elm Road Baptist Church, Beckenham, Kent (1920-27), Park Chapel, London (1927-57), and City Temple, London (1957-75); composed music for piano, organ, choir (anthems and cantatas), and other instruments; was married, but had no children.
BINNEY'S 339

Thomas à Kempis (b. 1379 or 1380; d. 1471, Mount St. Agnes, Holland), born Thomas Hammerken, was sent to the Brothers' House of the Brethren of the Common Life, Deventer, Holland, a school for the poor, and there became known as Thomas à Kempis (Thomas from Kempen); was ordained a priest at Mt. Agnes, Zwolle, Holland (1413); authored biographies, tracts, and hymns, and wrote [or edited] the classic, *The Imitation of Christ* (*c.* 1427, printed 1471).
Grant Me, O Lord 544
O Love, How Deep, How Broad, How High (attr.) 193

Thomas, Edith Lovell (b. Sept. 11, 1878, Eastford, CT; d. Mar. 16, 1969, Claremont, CA), one of nine children of a singing Methodist minister and his musical wife, studied at Friends School, Providence, RI, Boston University (BRE, SRE, MEd), the School of Sacred Music of Union Theological Seminary, New York, and Wellesley College; was professor of music at Boston University (1918-31) and minister of music in nearby churches, including Christ Methodist Church, New York City; active in

Christian education, compiled several hymnals specifically for children, including *Singing Worship for Boys and Girls*, which sold over 250,000 copies.
ST. ANTHONY'S CHORALE (arr.) 37

Thomerson, Kathleen Armstrong (b. Feb. 18, 1934, Jackson, TN) graduated from the University of Texas (BMus, MMus), with additional organ study in Antwerp with Flor Peeters and in Paris with Jean Langlais; taught organ at Southern Illinois University and St. Louis Conservatory of Music; was music director at University United Methodist Church, St. Louis, MO, and an organ recitalist in America and Europe; is married to Jamie Thomerson and they have three children.
I Want to Walk as a Child of the Light, HOUSTON 539

Thompson, Will Lamartine (b. Nov. 7, 1847, Smith's Ferry, PA; d. Sept. 20, 1909, New York, NY), during his lifetime, was called "The Bard of Ohio"; received schooling at Mount Union College in Alliance, OH, and Boston Conservatory of Music, with further study in Leipzig, Germany; established the Will L. Thompson & Company music publishing firm with offices in East Liverpool, OH, and Chicago, IL; wrote many successful secular and sacred songs, and edited and published many collections. H
Softly and Tenderly Jesus Is Calling, THOMPSON 441
Jesus Is All the World to Me, ELIZABETH 491

Thomson, Mary Ann (b. Dec. 5, 1834, London, England; d. Mar. 11, 1923, Philadelphia, PA) spent her early years in England, then came to America and married John Thomson, first librarian of the Free Library in Philadelphia; was a member of the Church of the Annunciation, Philadelphia, where her husband served as the accounting warden; wrote many poems and hymns which appeared in *The Churchman*, New York, and *The Living Church*, Chicago. H
O Christians, Haste 731

Threlfall, Jeannette (b. Mar. 24, 1821, Blackburn, Lancashire, England; d. Nov. 30, 1880, Westminster, London) was left an orphan and spent most of her life in the homes of relatives; was disabled by an accident and became a permanent invalid, but maintained an attitude of exemplary love, cheerfulness, and serenity; read a great deal and wrote poems and hymns without effort, sending them anonymously to various periodicals; had her collected writings published in *Woodsorrel; or, Leaves from a Retired Home* (1856), and *Sunshine and Shadow* (1873). H
Hosanna, Loud Hosanna 203

Thring, Godfrey (b. Mar. 25, 1823, Alford, Somerset, England; d. Sept. 13, 1903, Guildford, Surrey) was trained at Shrewsbury School and Balliol College, Oxford, and was ordained a priest in the Church of England in 1846; served several curacies, and in 1858 succeeded his father as rector of Alford; was prebendary of East Harptree, Wells Cathedral (1876-93); edited and published *Hymns and Other Verses* (1866), *Hymns Congregational and*

Others (1866), and *A Church of England Hymn Book, Adapted to the Daily Services of the Church Throughout the Year* (1880), revised in 1882 with the title *The Church of England Hymn Book.*   H
Crown Him with Many Crowns (st. 2,3) 92
Jesus Came, the Heavens Adoring 194

Thrupp, Dorothy Ann (b. June 20, 1779, London, England; d. Dec. 14, 1847, London) is not well known among hymn biographers; wrote hymns for children, many of which appeared with the pseudonym "Iota," or with the initials "D.A.T.," or were left unsigned; released texts in such collections as W. Carus Wilson's *Friendly Visitor and Children's Friend* and Mrs. Herbert Mayo's *Selection of Hymns and Poetry for the Use of Infant Schools and Nurseries* (1838); edited *Hymns for the Young* (1830), in which all the works were unsigned.   H
Savior, Like a Shepherd Lead Us (attr.) 522

Timms, George B. (b. Oct. 4, 1910, Derby, England) was educated at Derby Grammar School, St. Edmund Hall, Oxford (M.A.), and the College of the Resurrection, Mirfield; was Deacon (1935), and then Priest (1936) at the Parish of St. Mary Magdalene, Coventry; served as curate of St. Bartholomew, Reading (1938-49), sacrist and succentor of Southwark Cathedral (1949-52), vicar of St. Mary the Virgin, Primrose Hill (1952-65), vicar of St. Andrew Holborn, London (1965-81), and archdeacon of Hackney (1971-81); wrote many hymns, including 14

in the *New English Hymnal* (1986), for which he chaired the editorial committee.
Father Eternal, Lord of the Ages 6

Tisserand, Jean (b. date unknown; d. 1494, Paris, France) was a Franciscan friar who founded an order for penitent women; is said to have written an office (worship service) commemorating the martyrdom of Franciscan monks in Morocco in 1220; is remembered for his Latin hymns, including "O Filii et Filiae," which was published after his death.   H
O Sons and Daughters, Let Us Sing 249

Tomer, William Gould (b. Oct. 5, 1833; d. Sept. 26, 1896, NJ) received his early musical training from attending singing schools and singing in the village choir in Finesville, NJ; began teaching school at age 17; served on the staff of General Oliver O. Howard (in whose honor Howard University is named) during the Civil War; after the war, worked as a government employee in Washington, and served as music director for Grace Methodist Episcopal Church; finally returned to New Jersey where he spent the last years of his life teaching school.   H
GOD BE WITH YOU 840

Toolan, Suzanne (b. Oct. 24, 1927, Lansing, MI), Society of Mary, studied at Immaculate Heart College, Hollywood, CA (BA) and San Francisco State University (MA); taught in high school (1953-80) and at Russell College (1960-70); directed choirs in churches and seminary (1960-86); was director of Mercy Center, a spiritual

retreat center (1981-88); wrote over 30 hymns and songs, many released by GIA Publications.
Two Fishermen, LEAVE ALL THINGS 654

Toplady, Augustus Montague (b. Nov. 4, 1740, Farnham, Surrey, England; d. Aug. 11, 1778, London) received his education at Westminster School, London and Trinity College, Dublin; was converted while a student in Ireland through a message brought by James Morris, a Methodist lay preacher; in 1762 was ordained in the Church of England and served various churches as curate before becoming vicar at Broadhembury, Devonshire, in 1766; moved to London, 1775, and preached at the French Calvinist Church in Leicester Fields; was an ardent Calvinist and an outspoken, bitter critic of John Wesley; published *Poems on Sacred Subjects* (1769), *Historic Proof of the Doctrinal Calvinism of the Church of England* (1774), and *Psalms and Hymns for Public and Private Worship* (1776). H
Rock of Ages, Cleft for Me 227

Torrens, Joyce; see **Struther, Jan**.

Tourjée, Lizzie Shove (b. Sept. 9, 1858, Newport, RI; d. Dec. 28, 1913, Auburndale, MA) was the daughter of Dr. Eben Tourjée, founder of the New England Conservatory of Music; received her education in Newton, MA, high school and Wellesley College (one year); married Franklin Estabrook (1883). H
WELLESLEY 486

Towner, Daniel Brink (b. Mar. 5, 1850, Rome, PA; d. Oct. 3, 1919, Longwood, MO), as a music educator at Moody Bible Institute, Chicago (1893-1919), had a profound influence on evangelical church music; received his early musical training from his father, Professor J. G. Towner, renowned teacher and singer, and later studied with John Howard, George F. Root, and George J. Webb; served several Methodist Episcopal churches in New York, Ohio, and Kentucky as music director; became associated in evangelistic work with D. L. Moody in 1885; in 1893 became director of the Music Department of Moody Bible Institute, which position he held until his death; received the honorary MusD degree from the University of Tennessee in 1900; died while leading music in an evangelistic meeting in Longwood, MO; is credited with composing over 2000 gospel songs and compiling 14 songbooks and hymnals, as well as writing textbooks on music theory and practice; is the subject of an unpublished thesis by Perry Carroll, New Orleans Baptist Theological Seminary. H
CALVARY 510
MOODY 472
TRUST AND OBEY 523

Tredinnick, Noel (b. Mar. 9, 1949, London), son of a school teacher, attended St. Olaves Grammar School, Guildhall School of Music (1967-70, organ and academic honors graduate), and London Institute of Education (1970-71); was music director at Langley Park School (1971-75); has been a professor and a member of the academic board at Guildhall

School since 1975, and organist and music director at All Souls Church, Langham Place, since 1972; is a conductor and arranger for BBC, among others, a member of the Jubilate Group, an editor for Oxford University Press, and an advisor with Royal School of Church Music; composes anthems, organ music, and hymn tunes.
A PURPLE ROBE (arr.) 217
BLOW THE WIND SOUTHERLY (arr.) 287
RACHEL (arr.) 102

Trier Manuscript (15th century). Trier, Germany's oldest city, occupied by France for some of its history, has a musical tradition which dates to St. Ambrose (*c.* A.D. 339-40); its extant organs (from *c.* 1364) are examples of early music instrument making; the Stadtbibliothek and Bistmarchiv museums contain manuscripts of ancient music known as *cantus trevirense*, which are identified by Trier Manuscript numbers.
JESU, DULCIS MEMORIA 322
PUER NOBIS 27, 136, 193

Troeger, Thomas Henry (b. Jan. 30, 1945, Suffern, NY) is the son of an inventor and mechanical engineer, Henry Troeger, and a grade school teacher, Lorena McDonald; was educated at Yale (BA in English, with honors, 1967) and Colgate Rochester Divinity School (BDiv, 1970); was ordained as a Presbyterian minister (1970); was associate minister of the Presbyterian Church, New Hartford, NY (1970-77), assistant professor of preaching and parish ministry, Rochester (NY) Center for Theological Studies (1977-91); has taught at the Iliff School of

Theology, Denver, CO, since 1991; has written more than 80 hymns, collected in *New Hymns for the Lectionary: To Glorify the Maker's Name* (1986) and *Make Our Prayer and Music One* (1992); married Merle Marie Butler, a lawyer.
Our Savior's Infant Cries Were Heard 438
The Hands That First Held Mary's Child 144
Wind Who Makes All Winds That Blow 294

Troutbeck, John (b. Nov. 12, 1832, Blencow, England; d. Oct. 11, 1899, London) was a graduate of Rugby School and Oxford University (MA, 1858); was precentor at Manchester Cathedral (1865), a canon of Westminster Cathedral (1869), and chaplain to Queen Victoria; translated the texts of works—including operatic libretti—by Bach, Beethoven, Brahms, and many others; wrote on theology and music.
Break Forth, O Beauteous (trans.) 158

Trueblood, David Elton (b. Dec. 12, 1900, Pleasantville, IA), an eighth generation Quaker, was educated at William Penn College (AB, 1922), Harvard University (STB, 1926), and Johns Hopkins University (PhD, 1934), and holds 14 honorary doctorates; has taught at Guilford College, Haverford College, Harvard University, Stanford University, Mount Holyoke College, and most recently at Earlham College, Richmond, IN; authored 36 books, and is a Swathmore Lecturer, Staley Lecturer, and Willson Lecturer; is active in Friends committees and leadership, and is Founder-

President of Yokefellows International; with wife, Virginia, has four sons, two daughters, and 15 grandchildren; now lives in Lansdale, PA.
Christ, Whose Purpose Is to Kindle 720

Tucker, Francis Bland (b. Jan. 6, 1895, Norfolk, VA: d. Jan. 1, 1984, Savannah, GA), son of an Episcopalian bishop, received his education at public schools in Lynchburg, VA, the University of Virginia (BA, 1914), and Virginia Theological Seminary (BDiv, 1920, DD, 1944); served in World War 1 in Evacuation Hospital No. 15 of the American Expeditionary Forces; was ordained an Episcopal priest (1920), and was rector of Grammer Parish, Brunswick County, Lawrenceville, VA (1920-25), St. John's, Georgetown, Washington, DC (1925-45), and Christ Church, Savannah, GA (1945-67), where he lived after his retirement, in the rectory that the parish gave him for life; was a member of the committee for *The Hymnal, 1940* in which six of his hymns and translations appeared; is a Fellow of The Hymn Society (1980).
All Praise to Christ 127
Awake, O Sleeper, Rise from Death 449
O Gracious Light, Lord Jesus Christ (trans.) 359
Our Father, by Whose Name 393

Tullar, Grant Colfax (b. Aug. 5, 1869, Bolton, CT; d. May 20, 1950, Ocean Grove, NJ), left motherless at an early age, was reared in hard circumstances by relatives; was converted at age 19 at a Methodist camp meeting; attended Hackettstown Academy for two

years, was ordained to the Methodist ministry and served briefly as a pastor; for 10 years was song leader for evangelist Major George A. Hilton; in 1893, with Isaac H. Meredith, founded the Tullar-Meredith Publishing Company, New York, publishers of church music; edited many hymnals and gospel songbooks, and wrote many original texts and tunes.   H
FACE TO FACE 684

Tye, Christopher (b. *c.* 1497; d. March, 1573, Doddington, Isle of Ely, England) was a boy singer at King's College, Cambridge, where he was also clerk (1537); was educated at Cambridge (BMus, 1537 and DMus, 1545) and honored by Oxford (DMus, 1548); was master of choristers, Ely Cathedral, intermittently between 1541-1561; as a result of the Reformation, received holy orders in the Anglican Church (1560) and served three parishes; was later organist to Queen Elizabeth's chapel; composed Catholic, Protestant, and secular vocal music.
WINCHESTER OLD (attr.) 172

Urwin, Ray W. (b. Feb. 1, 1950, Toledo, OH), composer, conductor, organist, harpsichordist, and accompanist, was educated at Rogers High School, Toledo, OH (1968), Oberlin College (BMus in organ, 1972), State University of New York at Stony Brook (MMus, orchestral conducting, 1976), and Yale University (MMusA, 1979 and DMA in organ, 1984), where he was awarded the School of Music Alumni Association Prize; has served as organist, director of music, or organist-choirmaster at

Trinity Episcopal Church, Toledo, OH (1967-70), First United Church of Christ, Oberlin, OH (1970-72), Memorial Lutheran Church, Toledo, OH (1972-74), Reformation Lutheran Church, Toledo, OH (1974), Temple Isaiah Reform Congregation, Stony Brook, NY (1975-77), Messiah Lutheran Church, Stauket, NY (1975-77), Immanuel Lutheran Church, Meriden, CT (1977-79), Cathedral Church of St. John, Wilmington, DE (1979-89), and St. Francis Episcopal Church, Palos Verdes Estates, CA (since 1989); contributed to *The Hymnal 1982* (Episcopal Church).
THOMAS MERTON 327

Vajda, Jaroslav John [Jan] (b. Apr. 28, 1919, Lorain, OH), son of a Lutheran pastor of Slovak descent, is a hymnologist with a specialty in Slovak poetry; graduated from Concordia Junior College (1938), Concordia Theological Seminary, St. Louis, MO (BA, BDiv, 1944); served Lutheran churches in Central City, PA (1942-43), Cranesville, PA (1945-49), Alexandria, IN (1949-53), and Brackenridge, PA (1953-63); edited *The Lutheran Beacon* (1959-63) and *This Day* (1963-71); served on the Commission on Worship of the Lutheran Church-Missouri Synod and the Inter-Lutheran Commission; has written and translated many hymns, an opera, and anthologies.
Greet Now the Swiftly Changing Year (tr.) 372
Up through Endless Ranks of Angels 264

VanDeVenter, Judson W. (b. Dec. 5, 1855 near Dundee, MI; d. July 17, 1939, Tampa, FL) attended the public schools at Dundee and Hillsdale College in Michigan; studied art, and for several years taught art and penmanship in public schools; was an active Methodist Episcopal layman, felt called to the ministry and was licensed as a local preacher; held evangelistic meetings in the United States, England, and Scotland; spent the last years of his life in Florida where he had an important influence on the young evangelist, Billy Graham (see **Crusade Hymn Stories**). H
I Surrender All 579

Van Dyke, Henry (b. Nov. 10, 1852, Germantown, PA; d. Apr. 10, 1933, Princeton, NJ) was an outstanding American preacher, author, and educator; was educated at Brooklyn Polytechnic Institute, Princeton University, and Princeton Theological Seminary; was ordained to the Presbyterian ministry and served in Rhode Island (1879-83) and at New York City's Brick Presbyterian Church (1883-99); beginning in 1900, was Murray Professor of English Literature at Princeton University for 23 years; in 1913 was appointed U.S. minister to the Netherlands and Luxembourg by President Woodrow Wilson; served as Moderator of the Presbyterian General Assembly and as chairman of the committee which prepared *The Book of Common Worship* (1905), and assisted in the 1931 revision; wrote many popular books, including *The Reality of Religion* (1884), *The Story of the Psalms* (1887), *The Story of the Other Wise Man* (1896), and *The Gospel for an Age of Doubt* (1896). H
Joyful, Joyful, We Adore Thee 20

Vaughan Williams, Ralph (b. Oct. 12, 1872, Down Ampney, Gloucestershire, England; d. Aug. 26, 1958, St. Marylebone, London) was a most significant English composer in the 20th century and strongly influenced contemporary hymnody; the son of Arthur Vaughan Williams, an Anglican priest, was born in the vicarage in Down Ampney; received early training in piano, violin, and theory; continued his formal education at Charterhouse School, the Royal College of Music, and Trinity College, Cambridge, with advanced music study in Berlin and Paris; served as organist and choirmaster of St. Barnabas Church, South Lambeth; was musical editor of *The English Hymnal* (1906); co-edited— with Martin Shaw and Percy Dearmer—*Songs of Praise* (1925, 1931); composed six symphonies, several major works for chorus and orchestra, operas, ballets, film music, chamber music and three organ preludes on Welsh hymn tunes; was a pioneer in researching English folk song, and used many of the tunes as settings for hymns.   H
DOWN AMPNEY 304
FOREST GREEN (arr.) 154, 340, 349
HYFRYDOL (arr.) 135, 263
KINGSFOLD (arr.) 192, 442, 559
KING'S WESTON 722
LASST UNS ERFREUEN (harm.) 259, 356
RANDOLPH 839
SINE NOMINE 751
SUSSEX CAROL (harm.) 168, 798

Venerable Bede; see **Bede**.

Vincent, Charles John (b. Sept. 19, 1852, Houghton-le-Spring, Durham, England; d. Feb. 23, 1934, Monte Carlo) at age 11 became a chorister at Durham Cathedral and at 16, organist at Monkwearmouth Parish Church; studied at Leipzig Conservatory for two years and received the BMus degree from Oxford; served several parishes as organist, including Christ Church, Hampstead, and was on the faculty of Trinity College, London, for many years; founded the Vincent Music Company, which later became Schirmer & Company; edited *The Organist and Choirmaster* and collaborated with John Stainer and D. J. Wood in producing the *Hymnal Companion to The Book of Common Prayer* (1890), *The Chant Book Companion*, and the *Anglican Organist*; composed many anthems, cantatas, and an oratorio, *Ruth*, as well as secular music, largely orchestral.   H
PAX TECUM (arr.) 598

Vleugel, Cornelius (20th century); no information was located on this American composer, whose name suggests Dutch ancestry.
VLEUGEL 57

von Fallersleben, H. A. Hoffmann; see **Hoffmann, Heinrich August**.
CRUSADER'S HYMN (comp.) 115

von Zinzendorf, Nicolas; see **Zinzendorf, Nicolas L. von**.

Vulpius, Melchior (b. *c.* 1560, Wasungen, near Meiningen, Thuringia, Germany; d. *c.* Aug. 7, 1615, Weimar) was Lutheran cantor at Weimar for approximately 14 years (1602-15); wrote many chorale melodies, published in *Cantiones Sacrae* (1602-04), which are still in use, but is best known for his contrapuntal settings of

established tunes in *Kirchengesänge und geistliche Lieder* (1604); also published *Canticum beatissimae* (1605), *Ein schön geistlich Gesangbuch* (1609), and a setting for the *Passion according to St. Matthew* (1612-14); dates for both his birth and death are uncertain, but was buried in Weimar on August 7, 1615.   H
GELOBT SEI GOTT 255

Wade, John Francis (b. 1711; d. Aug. 16, 1786, Douai, France) was a devout Roman Catholic Englishman who lived many years in Douai [Douay], France, a refuge for English citizens during the Jacobite rebellion of 1745; taught music and specialized in copying plainchant and other music for use in chapels of wealthy Roman Catholic families; collected his copied manuscripts in a volume, *Cantus Diversi pro Dominicis et Festis per annum* (1751), now preserved at Stonyhurst College in Lancashire, England.   H
ADESTE FIDELES 126, 173
O Come, All Ye Faithful (attr.) 173

Walch, James (b. June 21, 1837, Edgerton, Lancashire, England; d. Aug. 30, 1901, Llandudno, Caernarvonshire, Wales) studied music with his father and later with Henry Smart; became organist at Duke's Alley Congregational Church in Bolton at age 20, and served other churches (both Anglican and nonconformist) throughout his lifetime; conducted the Bolton Philharmonic Society (1870-1874); in 1877 moved to Barrow-in-Furness where he was a music dealer and honorary organist of the parish church; wrote hymn tunes and other church music.   H

TIDINGS 731

Walford, William W. (b. 1772, Bath, Somerset, England; d. June 22, 1850, Uxbridge) within the last few years has been determined to be the author of "Sweet Hour of Prayer"; was educated at Homerton Academy, to which he later returned as a tutor in the classics; was ordained to the Congregational ministry and served pastorates in Suffolk, Norfolk, and Middlesex; wrote *The Manner of Prayer* (1836) and an autobiography, edited by *John Stoughton* and published posthumously in 1851.   H
Sweet Hour of Prayer 623

Walker, William ["**Singing Billy**"**]** (b. 1809; d. 1875), with little formal education, was a traveling singing school teacher; compiled the four-shape notation *Southern Harmony and Musical Companion* (1835 and four later editions), which sold over 600,000 copies in antebellum rural United States; a facsimile with notes of the 1854 edition by Glenn C. Wilcox, was published by University Press of Kentucky, 1987; B. F. White was co-editor of *Southern Harmony*, but Walker, his brother-in-law, did not credit him; when seven-shape notation became popular, Walker published *Christian Harmony* (1866); attributed many tunes to himself which he had only gathered or harmonized.
CHARLESTON 430
DOVE OF PEACE (attr.) 768
WONDROUS LOVE (comp.) 212
ARISE (RESTORATION) 451

Wallace, William Vincent (b. June 1, 1812, Waterford, Ireland; d.

Oct. 12, 1865, Chateau de Bages, France), of Scottish descent, received his first musical training from his father; was challenged by hearing Paganini play, and became an accomplished violinist, giving his first concert in Dublin at the age of 15; in his recital career, traveled throughout the world and had an adventure-filled life; composed seven operas (which were popular in France), wrote tunes for four hymns of John Keble, a cantata, and a number of compositions for piano; because of failing eyesight, gave up writing and retired to the Pyrenees, where he remained until his death in 1865.　　　　H
SERENITY 607

Walsh, John (b. *c.* 1655-56, perhaps Ireland; d. Mar. 13, 1736, London, England), in London, published and sold English music and repertoire from the continent; also made and sold instruments, a flourishing business by 1690; was appointed instrument-maker-in-ordinary for William III (June 24, 1692), succeeding John Shaw, a contemporary of John and Henry Playford, whose style Walsh imitated; published Handel's music; printed and may have compiled *Lyra Davidica, or a Collection of Divine Songs and Hymns, partly new composed, partly translated from German and Latin Hymns, set to easy and pleasant tunes* (London, 1708). See journal articles of W. C. Smith in *The Library* for further information.
EASTER HYMN (comp.) 234
Jesus Christ Is Risen Today (comp.) 250

Walter, William Henry (b. July 1, 1825, Newark, NJ; d. 1893, New York, NY), as a boy, played the organ in Presbyterian and Episcopal churches in Newark; was organist at St. John's Chapel, St. Paul's Chapel, and Trinity Chapel, all in New York City; in 1865 was appointed organist of Columbia University, where he had received an honorary DMus degree; published a *Manual of Church Music* (1860), *The Common Prayer, with Ritual Song* (1868), and numerous anthems and services.　　　　H
FESTAL SONG 71, 670

Walton, James George (b. Feb. 19, 1821, Clitheroe, Lancashire, England; d. Sept. 1, 1905, Bradford, Yorkshire) was an English composer who edited *Plain Song Music for the Holy Communion Office* (1874), which contained his adaptation of the tune ST. CATHERINE from one of Henri F. Hemy's settings in Part II of *Crown of Jesus Music* (1864).　H
ST. CATHERINE (arr.) 556, 692

Walworth, Clarence Augustus (b. May 30, 1820, Plattsburg, NY; d. Sept. 19, 1900, Albany) graduated from Union College, Schenectady, and was admitted to the bar in 1841; originally a Presbyterian, studied for the Episcopal ministry at General Theological Seminary in New York (1842) but was influenced by the Oxford movement and became a Roman Catholic priest (1845) with the name Clarence Alphonsus; was one of the founders of the Paulist Order in the United States; for his last 34 years was rector of St. Mary's in Albany; published *The Oxford Movement in America* (1895), which explains his conversion to Roman Catholicism, and *Andiatorocté . . . and Other Poems* (1888); was blind for the last

10 years of his life.   H
Holy God, We Praise Your Name
(trans.) 3

Ward, Samuel Augustus (b. Dec. 28, 1847, Newark, NJ; d. Sept. 28, 1903, Newark) received musical training in New York City with Jan Pychowski and others; established a successful music store in Newark, NJ, and was involved in the musical life of the city; succeeded Henry S. Cutler as organist of Grace Episcopal Church in 1880; founded the Orpheus Club of Newark in 1889 and directed this group until 1900.   H
MATERNA 418

Ware, Henry, Jr. (b. Apr. 21, 1794, Hingham, MA; d. Sept. 25, 1843, Framingham, MA) graduated from Harvard in 1812 and became a member of the faculty of Exeter Academy in New Hampshire; was ordained to the Unitarian ministry in 1817 and became pastor of the Second Unitarian Church in Boston, where Ralph Waldo Emerson served as assistant pastor; taught at Cambridge Theological School (1830-42) as professor of pulpit eloquence and pastoral care; was editor of the *Christian Disciple*, which later became the *Christian Examiner*; left four volumes of writings which were published in 1846.
                                              H
Happy the Home When God Is There 389

Waring, Anna Laetitia (b. Apr. 19, 1823, Plas-y-Velin, Neath, Glamorganshire, Wales; d. May 10, 1910, Clifton, near Bristol, England) was brought up in a Quaker home, but at the age of 19 joined the Church of England; pub-

lished *Hymns and Meditations* (1850), which included 19 of her own hymns (the 10th edition contained 39); was a humanitarian who often visited the Bristol prisons, and was a strong supporter of the Discharged Prisoners' Aid Society.   H
In Heavenly Love Abiding 521

Warner, Anna Bartlett (b. Aug. 31, 1827, Long Island, NY; d. Jan. 22, 1915, near West Point, NY) wrote the famous children's hymn "Jesus Loves Me, This I Know"; made her home with her father and her sister Susan, a well known authoress, on Constitution Island in the Hudson River; with her sister, conducted Bible classes for the cadets at West Point and was consequently buried with military honors; wrote a number of novels for which she used her pseudonym "Amy Lathrop," and two collections of verse: *Hymns of the Church Militant* (1858) and *Wayfaring Hymns, Original and Translated* (1869).   H
Jesus Loves Me, This I Know 470

Warren, George William (b. Aug. 17, 1828, Albany, NY; d. Mar. 17, 1902, New York, NY), though largely self-taught, was an accomplished organist who served Episcopal churches in Albany, Brooklyn, and New York City; composed anthems and hymn tunes and edited *Warren's Hymns and Tunes as Sung at St. Thomas' Church* (1888); received an honorary DMus degree from Racine College (WI). H
NATIONAL HYMN 419

Warren, Norman Leonard (b. July 19, 1934, London, England) was educated at Dulwich College

and Corpus Christi, Cambridge (MA in music) and Ridley Hall Theological College; was ordained in the Church of England and served as vicar at St. Paul's, Leamington Spa (1963-77), rector of Morden (1977-89), and archdeacon of Rochester (since 1989); has written over 100 hymn tunes and some musical plays; has published numerous booklets for evangelism; was one of the musical editors of *Psalm Praise* (1973) and other hymnals, including *Hymns for Today's Church* (1982).
CREATOR GOD 513

Watson, Sidney (b. Sept. 3, 1903, Denton, Lancashire, England) was educated at the Royal College of Music, Keble College, Oxford (1925), and Oxford University (DMus); was assistant master at Stowe School and then precentor at Radley College; was organist at New College, Oxford (1933), and conductor of the Oxford Harmonic Society; taught music at Winchester College (1938-46) and Eaton (1946-55); became a fellow of the Royal College of Organists; served as organist at Christ Church Cathedral and conductor of the Oxford Bach Choir and Orchestra (1955-70); currently is retired at Aynho.
MORESTEAD 645

Watts, Isaac (b. July 17, 1674, Southampton, England; d. Nov. 25, 1748, Stoke Newington, London) has been generally acclaimed as "the father of English hymnody," the first to successfully challenge the long tradition of strict psalm singing; was educated at the Free School in Southampton and the nonconformist academy at Stoke Newington; was ordained and

appointed pastor of Mark Lane Independent Chapel, London (Congregational), in 1702; because of failing health, retired (1712) to live with the family of Sir Thomas Abney near Cheshunt, Hereford-shire, serving as tutor to the children and chaplain to the family; was a brilliant scholar and produced about 60 volumes on various subjects; wrote some 600 hymns and psalm paraphrases, most of which appear in three of his collections: *Hora Lyricae* (1706), *Hymns and Spiritual Songs* (1707), and *The Psalms of David Imitated in the Language of the New Testament* (1719).   H
Alas! and Did My Savior Bleed 208
At the Cross 512
Am I a Soldier of the Cross 668
Come, Holy Spirit, Heavenly Dove 298
Come, We That Love the Lord 22
We're Marching to Zion 596
Give to Our God Immortal Praise 16
I Sing the Mighty Power of God 52
I'll Praise My Maker While I've Breath 79
Jesus Shall Reign 745
Join All the Glorious Names 85
Joy to the World! the Lord Is Come 146
Nature with Open Volume Stands 222
O Bless the Lord, My Soul! 71
O God, Our Help in Ages Past 78
What Offering Shall We Give? 490
We're Marching to Zion 596
When I Can Read My Title Clear 681
When I Survey the Wondrous Cross 213

Webb, Benjamin (b. Nov. 28, 1819, London, England; d. Nov. 27, 1885, London) studied at Trinity

College, Cambridge (BA, 1842 and MA, 1845), where he knew John Mason Neale; was ordained and served in three parishes before becoming curate of Sheen, Staffordshire (1851), then vicar of St. Andrews, Wells Street, London, where Joseph Barnby was musician, and finally, prebend of Portpool in St. Paul's Cathedral, London (1881); was a hymn author and hymnal editor, and served as editor of the *Church Quarterly Review* (1881-85).
A Hymn of Glory Let Us Sing (tr.) 259
O Love, How Deep, How Broad (tr.) 193

Webb, Charles (b. Feb. 14, 1933, Dallas, TX) graduated from Southern Methodist University, Dallas (Bachelors and Masters, 1955), and from Indiana University (DMus, 1964); has taught at Indiana University's School of Music since 1958 and served as dean since 1972; performs extensively on piano and organ, including regular appearances with the Indianapolis Symphony; chaired the Service Music subcommittee for the *United Methodist Hymnal* (1989) and composed many of its descants and harmonizations.
CHEREPONI (arr.) 436

Webb, George James (b. June 24, 1803, Rushmore Lodge, Wiltshire, England; d. Oct. 7, 1887, Orange, NJ), the son of a well-to-do farmer, rejected his father's plans that he become a minister; studied organ at Salisbury Cathedral with Alexander Lucas and accepted the position of organist at a church in Falmouth; came to America in 1830 and settled in Boston, where he was organ-

ist of the Old South Church for 40 years; in 1833 was appointed professor at the Boston Academy of Music where he was associated with Lowell Mason; became president of the Boston Handel and Haydn Society (1840) and was well known as a choral and orchestral conductor; edited many publications, including *The Massachusetts Collection of Psalmody* (1840), *The American Glee Book* (with Lowell Mason as co-editor, 1841), *The Psaltery* (1845), *The National Psalmist* (1848), *Cantica Laudis* (1850), and *Cantica Ecclesiastica* (1859); served as editor for *The Music Library* (1835-36) and *The Musical Cabinet* (1837-40).   H
SCHUMANN (attr.) 649
WEBB 663

Webbe, Samuel (b. 1740, London, England; d. May 25, 1816, London) was first apprenticed to a cabinetmaker, and at the age of 20 turned to music; worked as a music copyist for a London publisher, which brought him to the attention of organist Carl Barbandt, who gave him lessons; was employed as organist of the Roman Catholic chapels at the Sardinian and Portuguese embassies in London, beginning in 1776; wrote a great deal of music, published in *A Collection of Sacred Music as Used in the Chapel of the King of Sardinia in London* (c. 1793), *A Collection of Masses for Small Choirs* (1792), *A Collection of Masses and Antiphons* (1792, compiled with his son, Samuel Webbe, the Younger), *Antiphons in Six Books of Anthems* (1818), and many collections of glees and catches, as well as instrumental music.   H
CONSOLATOR 613

Webbe, Samuel, the Younger [Jr.] (b. Oct. 15, 1768 or 1770, London, England; d. Nov. 25, 1843, Hammersmith, Middlesex) was the oldest son of Samuel Webbe (above) and an organist at the Unitarian Chapel, Liverpool (*c.* 1798-1817), the Spanish Embassy, London, and St. Patrick's Roman Catholic Chapel, Toxteth Park; composed songs, light music, masses, and piano and harp music.
RICHMOND (adapt.) 628

Webber, Christopher L. (b. Jan. 5, 1932, Cuba, NY) attended Princeton and General Theological Seminaries; was ordained in 1956 and taught briefly at General Seminary; held rectorships at various churches on Long Island before serving the international community at St. Albans, Tokyo; has served as rector of Christ Church, Bronxville, NY, since 1972; has been on several national church committees; has published numerous magazine articles and three books; is married to Margaret Elizabeth Rose Webber, and they have four children and one granddaughter.
Have Mercy in Your Goodness, Lord (vers.) 322

Weeden, Winfield Scott (b. Mar. 29, 1847, Middleport, OH; d. July 31, 1908, Bisby Lake, NY) is remembered as composer of the music for "I Surrender All," whose title is engraved on his tombstone; attended public school in Ohio and taught singing schools for a number of years before going into evangelistic work; was gifted with a fine voice and was an able song leader; late in life lived in New York City, the owner of a small hotel in lower Manhattan; compiled several collections, including *The Peacemaker* (1894), *Songs of the Peacemaker* (1895), and *Songs of Sovereign Grace* (1897). H
SURRENDER 579

Weir, Robert Stanley (b. Nov. 15, 1856, Hamilton, Ontario, Canada; d. Aug. 20, 1926, Lake Memphremagog, Quebec, Canada) was a jurist, who is otherwise known only for his English translation of the French anthem "O Canada!"
O Canada! (trans.) 424

Welsh tunes. For a study of these and other Welsh traditional melodies, see Alan Luff, *Welsh Hymns and Their Tunes* (Hope Publishing Company for Stainer & Bell, 1990).
ABERYSTWYTH 461
AR HYD Y NOS 366, 379, 610
ASH GROVE 53
BLAENWERN 285, 325
BRYN CALFARIA 283
CWN RHONDDA 271, 634, 669
EBENEZER 477
HYFRYDOL 89, 135, 263, 492
LLANFAIR 40, 250, 258
LLANGLOFFAN 422
RHOSYMEDRE 393
ST. DENIO 62, 383

Wesley, Charles (b. Dec. 18, 1707, Epworth, Lincolnshire, England; d. Mar. 29, 1788, London) is credited with 20 hymns in *The Worshiping Church*, more than any other author; was the 18th child and youngest son of Samuel and Susanna Wesley, and was educated at Westminster School and Christ Church College, Oxford; is referred to as one of the "first Methodists" since he and his brother John, along with George Whitefield, formed the "Holy Club" at Oxford, based on a disciplined approach to Bible study, worship, communion, and concern for the less fortunate; was ordained in the Church of England in 1735 and a year later accompanied his brother John to America as missionary to the colony in Georgia; returned to London in 1738 and met the Moravian leaders, William Law, Count Zinzendorf, and Peter Böhler, under whose influence he experienced his spiritual conversion; with John, traveled throughout the British Isles doing evangelistic work which led to the Great Awakening and notable spiritual, economic, and political changes; at his death, brother John wrote, "He had no disease; but, after a gradual decay of some months, 'the weary wheels of life stood still at last'"; was a spontaneous and prolific poet who wrote more than 6500 hymns, covering the entire span of Christian experience and theology; published 64 collections of hymns (listed in Julian's *Dictionary of Hymnology*, pp. 1259-60). H

A Charge to Keep I Have 659
And Can It Be That I Should Gain 473
Arise, My Soul, Arise 483
Christ the Lord Is Risen Today 234
Christ, Whose Glory Fills the Skies 562
Come, Let Us with Our Lord Arise 798
Come, Thou Long-Expected Jesus 135
Forth in Your Name, O Lord, I Go 397
Hail the Day That Sees Him Rise 258
Hark! the Herald Angels Sing 171
Jesus Christ Is Risen Today (st. 4) 250
Jesus Comes with All His Grace 468
Jesus Comes with Clouds Descending 283
Jesus, Lover of My Soul 461
Love Divine, All Loves Excelling 558
O For a Thousand Tongues to Sing 130
Praise the Lord Who Reigns Above 49
Rejoice, the Lord Is King 262
Soldiers of Christ, Arise 756
Ye Servants of God, Your Master 103

Wesley, John Benjamin (b. June 17, 1703, Epworth, Lincolnshire, England; d. Mar. 2, 1791, London) was a leader in the Great Awakening of the 18th century, which eventually led to the birth of Methodism; received his education at Charterhouse School and Christ Church, Oxford; was ordained in the Church of England and served briefly as curate under his father; returned to Oxford as a tutor (1729-35) and joined his younger brother Charles in the activities of the "Holy Club"; spent a brief and unpleasant time as a missionary to Georgia with the specific responsibility of parish priest in Savannah; became interested in hymnody through contacts with Moravians; in 1737 published his *Collection of Psalms and Hymns*, the first hymnal (other than a psalter) printed in America; returning to England, dated his conversion from a "heartwarming experience" at a meeting in Aldersgate in 1738; in some 30 years, traveled thousands of miles on horseback in evangelistic endeavor with his brother Charles; translated at least 30 hymns, most-

ly from German, and wrote about 27 original hymns; with Charles, co-produced and published many volumes, after carefully editing Charles's hymns to strengthen them; the contents of these books have been the backbone of English hymnody for almost 250 years.   H
I'll Praise My Maker While I've Breath (adapt.) 79
Jesus, Thy Blood and Righteousness (trans.) 481
Jesus, Thy Boundless Love to Me (trans.) 556
Give to the Winds Your Fears (trans.) 618

Wesley, Samuel Sebastian (b. Aug. 14, 1810, London, England; d. Apr. 19, 1876, Gloucester) was recognized as the outstanding English organist of his time and made notable contributions to church music; was a grandson of Charles Wesley and a chorister at Chapel Royal when he was 10 years old; at 16, began his career as organist, serving in five parish churches and four cathedrals—Hereford, Exeter, Winchester, and Gloucester; received both BMus and DMus degrees from Oxford University at the age of 29; published *The European Psalmist* (1872) which contained over 730 hymn tunes, of which 130 were his own; also composed liturgical-musical services, psalm settings, anthems, glees, and organ and vocal music.   H
AURELIA 689

Wesleyan Sacred Harp (1854); see **McDonald, William**.
O Happy Day That Fixed My Choice, HAPPY DAY (ref.) 504

Wesson, Ruth Janelle (Jan) Smith (b. Apr. 25, 1925, Greenville IL), daughter of a railroad car inspector and a housewife, graduated with honors from St. Louis High School (1942); is an active musician (soprano) and author of several hymn and song texts; is married to James Robert Wesson, and they have four children and 10 grandchildren.
They Asked, "Who's My Neighbor?" WHO'S MY NEIGHBOR 435

West, Martin (b. 1929); see **Wilson, John F.**

West, Melvin (b. Mar. 2, 1930, St. Paul, MN), son of Laurence P. West and Thelma Abel, showed early musical ability and had the support of his mother, who was a singer in the Lodi (CA) Central Seventh-day Adventist Church; was educated at Lodi Academy, Andrews University, Berrien Springs, MI (BA, 1952), University of Redlands (MMus, 1955), and Boston University (DMus, 1959); became a Fellow of the American Guild of Organists (1957) and was organist for the *Faith for Today* television program, as well as for Adventist, Congregational, Episcopal, and Unitarian churches; taught at Atlantic Union College, South Lancaster, MA (1953-59), Walla Walla (WA) College (1959-77), and other posts including Union College, Lincoln, NE; since 1982, has been director of music, Westminster Presbyterian Church, Lincoln, NE, and is active as an organ consultant.
DONA NOBIS PACEM (arr.) 589

Whately, Richard (b. Feb. 1, 1787, St. Marylebone, London, England; d. Oct. 8, 1863, Dublin, Ireland) was educated at Oriel

College, Oxford (BA, 1808, MA, 1812, BDiv and DDiv, 1825); was ordained (1814); became Bampton Lecturer (1822), and then principal of St. Alban's Hall, Oxford (1825); moved to Dublin where he was Anglican Archbishop (1831) and then chair of political economy at Trinity College, Dublin (1832); became a member of the Royal Irish Academy and the House of Lords (1833); wrote few hymns, but several books, including an apologetic for the historical Christ which was framed by questioning the historicity of the life of Napoleon.
God, Who Made the Earth and Heaven (stanza 3) 366

Whelpton, George (b. May 17, 1847, Redbourne, England; d. Nov. 25, 1930, Oxford, OH) came to the United States in 1851 at the age of four, and when he was 16, served with the Union Army in the Civil War; studied with Horatio R. Palmer at Lake Chautauqua School of Music, and became a choral director in Buffalo, NY (1903-25); associated with the Century Publishing Company, NY, and edited *Hymns of Worship and Service, The Church Hymnal,* and other compilations; after many years of service, accepted a similar position with the A. S. Barnes Company. H
DISMISSAL 842
[HEAR OUR PRAYER, O LORD] 817

Whinfield, Walter Grenville (b. Nov. 6, 1865, South Elkington, Lincolnshire, England; d. Apr. 26, 1919, Dodford, Worcestershire) received his music education at Magdalen College, Oxford; served as curate, West Hackney, London (1890), St. Mary's, Eastbourne (1890-97), Bromsgrove,

Worcestershire (1898-1908), and as vicar, Dodford (1908); published a collection of tunes (1902).
WORCESTER 11

White, Benjamin Franklin (b. Sept. 20, 1800, near Cross Keys, Union Co., SC; d. Dec. 5, 1879, Atlanta, GA) was one of 14 children of a Spartanburg farmer, Robert White; B. F. received only three years of formal education and some singing school instruction; moving to Hamilton, Harris County, GA (late 1830s), was editor of *The Organ*, a county newspaper, and a traveling singing school teacher; compiled *The Sacred Harp* (1844), the most influential of all the shape-note, end-bound, four-shape, pre-civil-war singing-school instruction books (see Joe S. James, *A Brief History of the Sacred Harp*, 1904; a facsimile of the 1859 edition was published by Broadman Press, 1968); was co-editor, without credit, with brother-in-law, William Walker, of *Southern Harmony* (1835), also very important in shape-note singing tradition. It is unlikely that B. F. White wrote all the tunes he attributed to himself; rather, he compiled and collected folk hymns already known at camp meetings and in the Second Great Revival; E. J. King (perhaps Joel King) appears on the title page of *The Sacred Harp* as a second compiler. See *The Sacred Harp: A Tradition and Its Music,* by Buell E. Cobb, Jr. (Athens, GA: University of Georgia Press, 1989).
THE MORNING TRUMPET (comp.) 278
BEACH SPRING 578

Whitfield, Frederick (b. Jan. 7, 1829, Threapwood, Shropshire,

England; d. Sept. 13, 1904, Croydon, London) received his education at Trinity College, Dublin, and was ordained in the Church of England; served churches in Otley, Kirby-Ravensworth, Greenwich, Bexley, and Hastings; wrote some 30 books of verse and prose, including *Sacred Poems and Prose* (1861 and 1864), which contained 26 hymns. H
O, How I Love Jesus 509

Whiting, William (b. Nov. 1, 1825, Kensington, London, England; d. May 3, 1878, Winchester, Hampshire) received schooling at Clapham School and Winchester College; was master of the Winchester College choristers for more than 35 years (1842-78); wrote *Rural Thoughts and Other Poems* (1851) and only this one hymn. H
Almighty Father, Strong to Save 358

Whittier, John Greenleaf (b. Dec. 17, 1807, Haverhill, MA; d. Sept. 7, 1892, Hampton Falls, NH) is acknowledged to be one of America's finest poets; was born of Quaker parents and worked on the family farm until he was 20; was largely self-taught, with a short period of study at Haverhill Academy; released his first poems in *Newburyport Free Press* (1825) and became editor of the *American Manufacturer* (1828); was named editor of the *New England Review* (1830), and in 1836 moved to Philadelphia, PA, where he became the editor of *The Pennsylvania Freeman*, an anti-slavery publication; published his first book, *Legends of New England* (1831), and followed it with numerous other works; once said, "I am really not a hymn writer, for the good reason that I know nothing of music"; nevertheless, several of his poems have found their way into common church use. H
Dear Lord and Father of Mankind 591
Immortal Love, Forever Full 607

Whittingham, William (b. 1524, Chester, England; d. June 10, 1579, Durham) entered Brasenose College at the age of 16, was elected a Fellow of All Souls (1545) and later studied in France at the University of Orleans; adopted John Calvin's views and, with John Knox, insisted on revising the Anglican Prayer Book; was appointed to draw up a Service Book which would show a compromise between the strict adherents to the Prayer Book and Calvinism; while in Geneva with Knox, turned several psalms into meter and included a total of 51 in the Service Book published in 1556; returned to England in 1560, and in 1563 became Dean of Durham; was buried at Durham Cathedral, where his tomb was destroyed by the Scots in 1640. H
The Lord's My Shepherd, I'll Not Want 330

Whittle, Daniel Webster (b. Nov. 22, 1840, Chicopee Falls, MA; d. Mar. 4, 1901, Northfield, MA) moved to Chicago in his mid-teens and worked as a cashier of the Wells Fargo Bank; served with Company B of the 72nd Illinois Infantry during the Civil War and, after being taken prisoner, was converted by reading the New Testament his mother had given him; was promoted to the rank of major at war's end and was there-

after known as "Major Whittle"; returned to Chicago and was treasurer of the Elgin Watch Company until 1873; became associated with D. L. Moody, who encouraged him to enter the field of evangelism; in many years of effective evangelistic work, was assisted by three capable singers: P. P. Bliss, James McGranahan, and George C. Stebbins; wrote most of his hymns late in life, and many bore the pseudonym "El Nathan."   H
I Know Whom I Have Believed 493
Moment by Moment 529

Wilkes, John Bernard (b. 1785; d. 1869) studied at the Royal Academy of Music and served as organist at several churches, including St. David's, Merthyr, and later at Llandaff Cathedral; was organist of the parish church of Monkland, near Leominster, where Henry W. Baker was vicar. (Baker was chairman of the committee which compiled the original edition of *Hymns Ancient and Modern*, 1861, and Wilkes made several contributions to that historic volume.)
                                                   H
MONKLAND (arr.) 59

Wilkinson, Kate Barclay (b. 1859, England; d. 1928) is not a well known individual in hymn history; according to sketchy reports, was a member of the Church of England, conducted a meeting for girls, and apparently was active in the Keswick Convention movement.   H
May the Mind of Christ My Savior 560

Willan, Healey (b. Oct. 12, 1880, Ballham, Surrey, England; d. Feb. 16, 1968, Toronto, Ontario, Canada) sang in the choir school of St. Saviour's, Eastbourne (on the English Channel); served as organist-choirmaster, Christ's Church, Wanstead, Essex, and St. John the Baptist Church, Kensington; came to Toronto Conservatory as head of music theory (1913) and organist-choirmaster of Toronto's St. Paul's Church; held various posts at Toronto University, finally becoming professor of the faculty of music (1937) and teaching until his resignation in 1950, after which he retained only his responsibility as university organist; also was precentor of the Church of St. Mary Magdalen during most of his career (1921-68); wrote on plainsong and composed, using chant idioms, along with writing extensive compositions for choir, organ, chamber groups, symphony orchestra, and other media.
WILLAN AGNUS DEI 833
WILLAN GLORIA 824
WILLAN KYRIE 821
WILLAN SANCTUS 829

Willard, Kelly Bagley (b. Aug. 18, 1956, Winter Haven, FL) was raised in Florida, giving herself to Christ in a local church at age 10; early played piano and composed, and was soon writing songs for The Archers, Seth, and Harlan Rogers; began solo performance after her marriage to Dan Willard (1977) with the album *Blame it On the One I Love* (1978); continued with a second album, *Willing Heart* (1981), and, following a time of spiritual renewal, *Psalms, Hymns, & Spiritual Songs*, and *Message from a King* along with contributions to the Maranatha Music Praise series and *Garden* (1991); with her husband and children, Bryan Asher and

Haylie Grace, lives in Nashville, TN.
Make Me a Servant, SERVANT 653

Williams. For Ralph Vaughan Williams, see **Vaughan Williams, Ralph**.

Williams, Aaron (b. 1731, London, England; d. 1776, London), a music teacher, publisher and music engraver, was clerk at the Scottish Church, London Wall; compiled and published *The Universal Psalmodist* (1763), *The Royal Harmony* (1766), *The New Universal Psalmodist* (1770), *Harmonia Coelestis* (a collection of noteworthy anthems, 6th ed., 1775), and *Psalmody in Miniature* (1778). An American edition of the *Universal Psalmodist* was published at Newburyport, MA, by Daniel Bailey in 1769, and entitled *The American Harmony*.   H
ST. THOMAS 22, 702

Williams, Clara Tear (b. Sept. 22, 1858, near Painesville Lake, OH; d. July 1, 1937, Caneadea, NY) is remembered by the gospel singer George Beverly Shea in a sketch in *Crusade Hymn Stories* (Hope Publishing Company, 1967); was born in the home of Thomas and Mary Evangeline (Searl) Tear, members of the Methodist Episcopal Church; after three years as a school teacher in Ohio (1879-82), joined "Sister Mary DePew" in evangelistic work, and continued in this work intermittently (and often alone) until 1890, traveling in Indiana, Michigan, Ohio, Pennsylvania, and New York, working first in Methodist Protestant churches, and later in Wesleyan Methodist groups; in 1895 married W. H. Williams, a lay preacher, and they lived successively in Canton, OH, Massillon, OH, Houghton, NY, and Philadelphia, PA, and finally retired in Houghton, NY; wrote several hymn texts and served as consulting editor for *Sacred Hymns and Tunes Designed for use in the Wesleyan Methodist Connection* (1900).   H
Satisfied 511

Williams, Peter (b. Jan. 7, 1722, Llansadurnen, Carmarthenshire, Wales; d. Aug. 8, 1796, Llandyfeilog) was educated at Carmarthen Grammar School and converted as a boy under the preaching of George Whitefield; was ordained at the age of 22 and became curate at Eglwys Cymmyn, where he began a school; in 1746, when he was opposed because of his vehement preaching, left the Church of England and joined the Welsh Calvinistic Methodists as an itinerant preacher; was expelled by the Methodists on charges of heresy, so built his own chapel in Carmarthen, and continued to minister; published a volume of Welsh hymns, *Rhai Hymnau ac Odlau Ysbrydol* (1759), *Hymns on Various Subjects* (1771), an annotated Welsh Bible, and a concordance.   H
Guide me, O Thou great Jehovah (trans.) 634

Williams, Robert (b. *c.* 1781, Mynydd Ithel, Anglesey, Wales; d. 1821, Mynydd Ithel), blind from birth, passed his life as a basketmaker on the island of Anglesey; was a capable musician in the exceptional Welsh tradition, having a good voice, a good ear, and a good memory; evidently wrote

hymn tunes, the custom of Welsh musicians.   H
LLANFAIR 40, 250, 258, 338

Williams, Thomas edited *Psalmodia Evangelica, a Complete Set of Psalm and Hymn Tunes for Public Worship* (1789). Nothing more is known about him.
TRURO 205, 243

Williams, Thomas John (b. 1869, Ynysmeudwy, Glamorganshire, Wales; d. Apr. 24, 1944, Llanelly, Carmarthenshire) was a student of David Evans of Cardiff; served as organist and choirmaster of Zion Church, Llanelly (1903-13), and at the Calfaria Church in the same community from 1913 until his death; composed many hymn tunes and some anthems.   H
EBENEZER 477

Williams, William (b. Feb. 11, 1717, Cefn Coed, Llanfairarybryn, Carmarthenshire, Wales; d. Jan. 11, 1791, Llandovery) was the son of a wealthy Welsh farmer who became known as both the "Sweet Singer of Wales" and "the Isaac Watts of Wales"; attended Llwynllwyd Academy to study medicine, but the preaching of Howell Harris in 1738 so challenged him that he entered the ministry; was ordained a deacon in the Church of England and served as a curate for three years, but was refused priest's orders because of his evangelical ideas; withdrew from the Established Church and became a popular itinerant preacher for the Calvinistic Methodist Church, traveling throughout Wales for 45 years; wrote more than 800 hymns in Welsh and some 100 in English, which appeared in such collections

as *Alleluia* (1745-47), *The Sea of Glass* (1752), and *Gloria in Excelsis, or, Hymns of Praise to God and the Lamb* (1771).   H
Guide Me, O Thou Great Jehovah (trans.) 634

Willis, Richard Storrs (b. Feb. 10, 1819, Boston, MA; d. May 7, 1900, Detroit, MI) received his education at Chauncey Hall, Boston Latin School, and Yale; studied composition in Germany for six years and became an intimate friend of Mendelssohn; from 1848 to 1852 served as music critic for the *New York Tribune, The Albion,* and *The Musical Times*, and from 1852 to 1864, *The Musical Times, The Musical World,* and *Once a Month*; edited and published *Church Chorals and Choir Studies* (1850), *Our Church Music* (1856), *Waif of Song* (1876), and *Pen and Lute* (1883).   H
CRUSADER'S HYMN (arr.) 115
CAROL 170

Wilson, David Gordon (b. Jan. 26, 1940, Greenwich, England) was educated at Colfe's Grammar School, Lewisham, University of Manchester (BS), Ridley Hall, and Clove College, University of Cambridge (MA, theology); was ordained in 1965 and has served parishes in London and Leicester; is an organist who served as editor and tune contributor to *Hymns for Today's Church* (London: Hodder and Stoughton, 1982) and other hymnals from the Jubilate Group.
A PURPLE ROBE 217
GLORIOUS COMING (arr.) 280
ONSLOW SQUARE 18
SPARKLE 323

Wilson, Emily Divine (b. May 24, 1865, Philadelphia, PA; d. June 23, 1942, Philadelphia) was the wife of John G. Wilson, a Methodist minister who served as district superintendent in the Philadelphia Conference and finally, as pastor of the Wharton Memorial Methodist Church, Philadelphia; with her husband, regularly participated in the Ocean Grove, NJ, summer assembly; generously contributed her musical and dramatic gifts to the service of God and the church.   H
HEAVEN 679

Wilson, Hugh (baptized Dec. 2, 1764, Fenwick, near Kilmarnock, Ayrshire, Scotland; d. Aug. 14, 1824, Duntocher, Dunbartonshire) was educated in the village school at Fenwick, and learned the shoe-making trade from his father; studied music and mathematics, and designed sundials in his spare time; after 1800 became a calculator and draftsman in the mills at Pollokshaws and then in Duntocher; was named "manager" of the Secession Church in Duntocher, and was one of the founders of the first Sunday School there; wrote and adapted many psalm tunes, but ordered the unpublished manuscripts to be burned after his death.   H
MARTYRDOM 208

Wilson, Ira Bishop (b. Sept., 6, 1880, Bedford, IA; d. Apr. 3, 1950, Los Angeles, CA), with the help of an older sister, learned to play the violin and organ, and began the study of harmony while still a youth; in 1902 entered Moody Bible Institute to prepare for musical evangelism but, in 1905, accept-ed a position as composer and editor with the Lorenz Publishing Company, Dayton, OH; was a contributing editor to Lorenz's periodicals, *The Choir Leader* and *The Choir Herald*, and editor-in-chief of *The Volunteer Choir*, frequently using the pseudonym "Fred B. Holton"; wrote a large number of seasonal choir cantatas, as well as numerous anthems and hymn arrangements; moved to Los Angeles in 1930, but continued his relationship with Lorenz.   H
Make Me a Blessing 656

Wilson, John Floyd (b. Mar. 24, 1929, Youngstown, OH) has been an editor for Hope Publishing Company since 1966; attended South High School, Youngstown, OH, Chicago Evangelistic Institute, American Conservatory of Music (BMus, 1954), and Northwestern University (MMus, 1959) with additional graduate work and composition study with Leo Sowerby and Anthony Donato; taught music at Mountain View Bible College (Didsbury, Alberta), Fort Wayne (IN) Bible College (now a campus of Taylor University), Moody Bible Institute, Chicago, IL, and was Director of the Music Department, Marion (IN) College (1964-66) (now Indiana Wesleyan University); served as minister of music at several churches including the First Methodist Church, La Grange, IL (1966-68) and the Village Church of Western Springs, IL (1971-81); in addition to his editorial duties, directed the Student Nurses' Choir at West Suburban Hospital, Oak Park, IL; conducts workshops and clinics; has written hymn texts and tunes, anthems, arrangements, and many full-

length musicals and cantatas; sometimes writes under the pen name Martin West; was a member of the editorial executive committee of *The Worshiping Church*; since 1989 has been serving as Pastor of Worship at Liberty Bible Church in Chesterton, IN, while continuing as Senior Editor at Hope.   H
[ALL THINGS COME OF THEE] 814
CAROL STREAM 463
CONNER 626
LEISURE TIME 398
LOVE TO CHRIST 706
O WALY WALY (arr.) 392, 499
[PSALM 19] (arr.) 329
[WRITE THESE WORDS] (adapt.) 812

Wilson, John Whitridge (b. Jan. 21, 1905, Bournville, Warwickshire, England; d. July 16, 1992, Guildford, Surrey) was raised in the Congregational tradition, joined the Church of England in his early 30s, and was organist at Guildford Methodist Church; attended Manchester Grammar School, Dulwich College, and Sidney Sussex College, Cambridge (honors in Physics, later, MusB); decided at age 23 to make music a career and studied at the Royal College of Music with Ralph Vaughan Williams and Gordon Jacob, among others, while living with his uncle, Sir Walford Davies, organist at St. George's Chapel, Windsor; became music master at Tonbridge School, then at Charterhouse (1947-65); taught at the Royal College of Music until 1980; was co-editor and researcher for *The Clarendon Hymn Book* (Oxford, 1936), *Hymns for Church & School* (1964), *Hymns and Songs* (Methodist supplement, 1969), and

collections for the Royal School of Church Music and the BBC; was a musical advisor and friend of Fred Pratt Green, Brian Wren, and other hymn writers. See *The Hymn* (Jan. 1993).
LAUDS 120
STUTTGART (desc.) 293

Winkworth, Catherine (b. Sept. 13, 1827, London, England; d. July 1, 1878, Monnetier, Savoy, France) is regarded as the foremost English translator of German hymns; lived most of her life near Manchester until she moved to Clifton (1862), to live with her father and sisters; was interested in educational and social problems and became secretary of the association for the promotion of higher education for women (1870); published two volumes, entitled *Lyra Germanica* (1853 and 1858), *The Chorale Book for England* (1863), and *Christian Singers of Germany* (1869).   H
All Glory Be to God on High (trans.) 10
Comfort, Comfort Now My People (trans.) 132
If You Will Trust in God to Guide You (trans.) 636
Jesus, Priceless Treasure (trans.) 119
Now Thank We All our God (trans.) 374
Praise to the Lord, the Almighty (trans.) 77
Wake, Awake, for Night Is Flying (trans.) 131

Winslow, John Copley (b. Aug. 18, 1882, Hanworth, Middlesex, England; d. Apr. 1, 1974, Godalming, Surrey) was educated at Eton and Balliol College, Oxford; took Holy Orders and lectured at St. Augustine's College,

Canterbury; after serving in India as a missionary, returned to England to become chaplain at Bryanston School (1942-48) and Lee Abbey, North Devon (1948-62). Lord of Creation 565

Wolcott, Samuel (b. July 2, 1813, South Windsor, CT; d. Feb. 24, 1886, Longmeadow, MA) was educated at Yale College (1833) and Andover Theological Seminary (1837); became a Congregational minister and then served as a missionary in Syria, but returned to the United States because of his health and pastored in Rhode Island, Illinois, and Ohio; wrote hymns during the last 17 years of his life. Christ for the World! We Sing 743

Wolfe, Lanny (b. Feb. 2, 1942, Columbus, OH) holds two bachelor's degrees and two master's degrees, from Ohio State University, San Jose (CA) State University, and Southern Illinois University (including a BS in business and MS in business administration); now serves at Jackson (MS) College of Ministries. Greater Is He That Is in Me, GREATER IS HE 525

Wood, James H. (b. Apr. 14, 1921, Rochester, MN) was educated at Macalester College (AB), Iowa University (MA), and Union Theological Seminary (SMD); was a member of the Robert Shaw Chorale (1951-52); has taught at Colorado A. & M. College, Bethany College, Duke University, and Southern Baptist Theological Seminary; was head of the music faculty at Morningside College, Sioux City, IA (1958-79), and at Frostburg State College, Frostburg,

MD (1979-86); has been active as a choral conductor and vocal soloist, and composed many choral compositions and arrangements; with his wife, Joyce, a piano teacher, retired to Owatonna, MN, in 1986. BEACH SPRING (arr.) 578

Woodward, George Ratcliffe (b. Dec. 27, 1848, Birkenhead, England; d. Mar. 3, 1934, Highgate, London) attended Gonville and Caius College, Cambridge (BA, 1872, MA, 1875); served at St. Barnabas, Pimlico (1874 and 1894-99), London Diocese (1899-1903), and St. Mark's, Marylebone, London (1903-06); translated Latin, Greek, and German hymns which were included in a number of collections, some of which he edited, including the *Cowley Carol Book* (1901 and later) and *Songs of Syon* (1904). PUER NOBIS (harm.) 136, 193

Woollett, Barbara Roach (b. Jan. 30, 1937, Southampton, England) is the daughter of Harry and Gertrude Lydia Jones Roach; was educated at the Sholing Secondary School, Southampton (1953); married David Woollett and has three children; calls herself a "housewife" and writes poetry and hymn texts; is a member of the Southampton Writers Circle and London's Fellowship of Christian Writers. God's Holy Ways Are Just and True (para.) 328 How Blest Are the People (para.) 706 How Long, O Lord (para.) 339

Wordsworth, Christopher (b. Oct. 30, 1807, Lambeth, London, England; d. Mar. 20, 1885,

Harewood, Yorkshire) was a nephew of the renowned English poet, William Wordsworth, and the son of Christopher Wordsworth, master of Trinity College, Cambridge; was educated at Winchester School and Trinity College, Cambridge, where he was acknowledged as a scholar and athlete; was ordained in the Church of England and served as headmaster of Harrow (1836-50), vicar of Stanford-in-the-Vale, Berkshire (1850-69), archdeacon of Westminster, and in 1869 was consecrated Bishop of Lincoln; a recognized Greek scholar, wrote a commentary on the entire Bible; was a prolific and spontaneous hymn writer who believed that "it is the first duty of a hymn to teach sound doctrine and thence to save souls"; published *The Holy Year, or Hymns for Sundays and Holy Days, and Other Occasions* (1862), with 117 original hymns and 82 others.   H
Alleluia, Alleluia! Hearts to Heaven 254
Songs of Thankfulness and Praise 190

Work, John Wesley, Jr. (b. Aug. 6, 1872, Nashville, TN; d. Sept. 7, 1925, Nashville), together with his brother, Frederick J. Work, was a leader in collecting, arranging, and promoting black spirituals; graduated from Fisk University (AB and MA) and returned to teach Latin and Greek at his *alma mater*; in 1923 became president of Roger Williams University, Nashville, TN, and served until his death; assisted in publishing several volumes, including *Folk Songs of the American Negro* (1907).   H
Go, Tell It on the Mountain 151
I'm New Born Again (arr.) 494

Wren, Brian A. (b. June 3, 1936, Romford, Essex, England) following a childhood with vivid memories of World War 2, attended a Congregational church and became active in the church choir; studied at New College, Oxford University (French, 1960) and Mansfield College (Theology); at Mansfield collaborated with tunesmith Peter Cutts, first on college songs, then on hymns; was minister at Hockley, Essex, then Consultant for Adult Education for the British Council of Churches; served on the Justice and Peace Commission of the Roman Catholic Church of England; was active in the United Reformed Church in England and the anti-poverty group Third World First; now lives in Rome, PA; calls his own writing "inclusive," "contemporary," and "trinitarian," and says, "In every hymn I write, I'm seeking to know God, and be known. Some hymns revisit familiar paths of doctrine, I hope in a refreshing way. Others are more exploratory." Wren has readily available collections of texts (Hope Publishing Company) which also include information about the hymns and suggestions for use: *Bring Many Names* (1989), *Faith Looking Forward* (1983), and P*raising a Mystery* (1986).
Christ Is Alive! 243
Christ upon the Mountain Peak 180
Great God, Your Love Has Called Us 779
I Come with Joy 768
Praise God for the Harvest 373
Thank You, God, for Water, Soil and Air 382
There's a Spirit in the Air 120
When Love Is Found 392

Wright, Priscilla (b. Oct. 2, 1928, Dallas, TX) attended Denver (CO) Metropolitan College (Administration, 1981-82), North Lake Community College, Dallas, TX (1983-84), and Christ for the Nations Institute of Biblical Studies (Theology, 1986-88); no other information has been located.
Fear Not, Rejoice and Be Glad 592

Wyeth, John (b. Mar. 31, 1770, Cambridge, MA; d. Jan. 23, 1858, Philadelphia, PA) learned the printer's trade as a youth and published tunebooks for many denominations and groups; lived and worked briefly in Santo Domingo, then in Philadelphia and Harrisburg, PA; with a partner, was editor of the Federalist newspaper *Oracle of Dauphin* for 35 years; was appointed postmaster of Harrisburg in 1793 by George Washington, but later was removed by John Adams because of the "incompatibility of the office of postmaster and editor of a newspaper"; was a non-musical Unitarian, but published *Repository of Sacred Music* (1810) and *Repository of Sacred Music. Part Second* (Harrisburg, PA, 1813; facsimile of 1820 second edition—Da Capo Press, 1964), which sold almost 200,000 copies and contained compositions of Reed, Holden, Swann, Holyoke, Billings and others; it captured folk tunes from the era and influenced all of the folk hymn, camp meeting, shape-note collections which followed it. Wyeth claims 58 of the tunes but probably only compiled them, with his musician-editor, Elkanah Kelsay Dare.
MORNING SONG (CONSOLATION) (comp.) 277
NETTLETON 45

Wyrtzen, Donald John (b. Aug. 16, 1942, Brooklyn, NY), son of evangelist Jack Wyrtzen, has been active in itinerant ministries since his youth—his early choruses were published in the *Word of Life* songbook series; graduated from Moody Bible Institute, Chicago (1963), The King's College, Briarcliff Manor, NY (BMus, 1965, alumnus of the year award, 1980), and Dallas Theological Seminary (ThM, 1969), with graduate work at North Texas State University while he was teaching at Dallas Bible College and Dallas Theological Seminary; has been a writer and editor for Singspiration Music (1970-89); received a Dove Award from the Gospel Music Association for "The Love Story" (1981); is now composing and orchestrating as a freelance artist in Nashville, TN, and teaching as an adjunct professor at Trinity Evangelical Divinity School, Deerfield, IL; is arranger, orchestrator, composer, and conductor of recordings and publications (over 2 million sold) for such performers as Steven Curtis Chapman, Michael Card, Steve Green, Larnelle Harris, and Carman; effectively works out his often-repeated goal of setting "God's truth to music in simple, attractive form"; with his wife Karen, has two children. See his *A Musician Looks At The Psalms* (Zondervan, 1988).
Worthy Is the Lamb, WORTHY IS THE LAMB 230

Young, Carlton Raymond (b. Apr. 25, 1926, Hamilton, OH), served in the Air Force (1944-46); graduated from Cincinnati College of Music (BS in MusEd, 1950), Boston University (BSacredTheo, 1953), and studied in Vienna and

Prague; was awarded an honorary doctorate by Ohio Northern University (1969); became a Methodist elder (1953), and has been minister of music at Church of the Savior, Cleveland Heights, OH (1953-56), Trinity Methodist Church, Youngstown, OH (1956-59), and Casa View Church, Dallas, TX (1971-74); was music editor, Abingdon Press (1959-64); taught church music at Perkins School of Theology and the School of the Arts, Southern Methodist University, Dallas, TX (1965-75), at Scarritt College, Nashville, TN (1975-78), and Candler School of Theology, Emory University, Atlanta, GA; is now director of programs in music and other arts, Scarritt-Bennett Center, Nashville, TN; was the editor of *The Methodist Hymnal* (1966) and co-author of its companion (1970) and editor of *The United Methodist Hymnal* (1989) and its *Companion* (1993); has been an editor at Hope Publishing Company since 1971 (Emeritus Editor since 1991).
CHARLESTOWN (arr.) 430
LET US BREAK BREAD (arr.) 776

Young, John Freeman (b. Oct. 30, 1820, Pittston, ME; d. Nov. 15, 1885, New York, NY) was trained at Wesleyan University, Middletown, CT, and Virginia Theological Seminary, Alexandria; was ordained in the Protestant Episcopal church and served dioceses in Texas, Mississippi, Louisiana, and New York, before being elected second bishop of Florida (1867); was keenly interested in architecture and responsible for many interesting church structures; was also involved in promoting education by establishing and re-opening

schools throughout the south; published *Hymns and Music for the Young* (1860-61) and edited *Great Hymns of the Church*, which was published posthumously in 1887 by John Henry Hopkins, Jr.   H
Silent Night! Holy Night! (trans.) 164

Zimmermann, Heinz Werner (b Aug. 11, 1930, Freiburg, Germany) studied composition with Julius Weismann (1946-48), with Wolfgang Fortner at Heidelberg School of Sacred Music (1950-54), and musicology with Thrasyboulos Georgiades at Heidelberg University; studied composition and theory at the State Music Academy, Freiburg (state diploma); taught at Heidelberg School of Sacred Music and Berlin School of Sacred Music (until 1975), then at the State Music Academy, Frankfurt-am-Main; has lectured frequently in the United States as a Fulbright Scholar (at Wittenberg University, Springfield, OH); was awarded the honorary DMus (Wittenberg, 1967); has published many choral and instrumental works, most in a refined jazz style.
LAUDATE PUERI 38

Zinzendorf, Nikolaus Ludwig von (b. May 26, 1700, Dresden, Germany; d. May 9, 1760, Herrnhut, Saxony), born to wealthy nobility, was educated at A. H. Francke's Adelspädagogium at Halle and at Wittenberg University, where he studied law; had a court post (1721-27), but resigned and was granted a preacher's license in 1734; established a center for Moravian refugees at his estate at Herrnhut, and later devoted him-

self completely to the Moravian community and became their bishop (1737); on grounds of unorthodoxy was banished from Saxony, and, during his absence, founded colonies of Moravian missionaries in Switzerland, England, Holland, North America, and the West Indies; was allowed to return to Herrnhut in 1748, and remained until his death; wrote over 2000 hymns, of which some 36 have been translated into English; had a profound influence on the lives and ministry (including the hymn writing) of John and Charles Wesley.　　　　　　　　H
Jesus, Thy Blood and Righteousness 481

Zundel, John (b. Dec. 10, 1815, Hochdorf, Germany; d. July, 1882, Cannstadt), educated in his native Germany, was first organist at St. Anne's Lutheran Church of St. Petersburg, Russia, and bandmaster of the Imperial House Guards; came to America in 1847 and spent 30 years here, 28 of them as organist at the Plymouth Church, Brooklyn, NY, where Henry Ward Beecher was pastor (the church was noted for quality in its preaching, organ playing and congregational singing); retired in 1880, and returned to his native Germany; published *The Choral Friend* (1855), *Psalmody* (1855), and *Christian Heart Songs* (1870); assisted Beecher in the preparation of the *Plymouth Collection* (1855), for which he wrote 28 hymn tunes.　　　　H
BEECHER 558, 701, 719

Tune Index

When the tune is used more than once,
the main entry is bold type.

A PURPLE ROBE
A Purple Robe, a Crown of Thorn
217
ABBOT'S LEIGH
**God Is Love, Let Heaven Adore
Him 70**
Lord, You Give the Great
Commission 715
Those Who Love and Those Who
Labor 394
ABERYSTWYTH
Jesus, Lover of My Soul 461
Wind Who Makes All Winds to Blow
294
ACCLAIM
Praise the Savior, Ye Who Know Him
125
ACCLAMATIONS
This Is the Threefold Truth 781
ACKLEY
He Lives 248
ADA
Redeemed, How I Love to Proclaim
It! 505
ADAMS
Where the Spirit of the Lord Is 604
ADELAIDE
Have Thine Own Way, Lord 584
ADESTE FIDELES
O Come, All Ye Faithful 173
O Come, Let Us Adore Him 126
ADORE THEE
Christ, We Do All Adore Thee 816
AFFECTION
My Jesus, I Love Thee 100
ALFORD
Ten Thousand Times Ten Thousand
746
ALL FOR JESUS
All For Jesus! All For Jesus! 570

ALL IS WELL
Come, Come, Ye Saints 595
Renew Your Church, Her Ministries
Restore 725
ALL SAINTS
God in Mercy Grant Us Blessing 344
ALL SAINTS, NEW
Macedonia 737
ALL THE WAY
All the Way My Savior Leads Me
641
ALL TO CHRIST
Jesus Paid It All 489
ALLELUIA
Alleluia 114
ALLELUIA NO. 1
Alleluia, Alleluia! Give Thanks 240
ALMSGIVING
By Christ Redeemed 789
Of All the Spirit's Gifts to Me 587
AMERICA
God Bless Our Native Land 421
My Country, 'Tis of Thee 417
AMSTERDAM
Praise the Lord Who Reigns Above
49
AMY
Good Shepherd, Take This Little
Child 760
ANDREWS
Heaven 25
ANGEL VOICES
Come to Us, Creative Spirit 407
ANGEL'S STORY
O Jesus, I Have Promised 648
ANNIVERSARY SONG
What Gift Can We Bring? 794
ANTIOCH
Joy to the World! the Lord Is Come
146

AR HYD Y NOS
For the Fruit of All Creation 379
God, Who Made the Earth and
Heaven 366
**Through the Love of God Our
Savior 610**
ARISE
Come, Ye Sinners, Poor and Needy
451
ARLINGTON
Am I a Soldier of the Cross? 668
ARMAGEDDON
Who Is on the Lord's Side? 666
ARNSBERG
God Himself Is with Us 799
ASCENDED TRIUMPH
Up through Endless Ranks of Angels
264
ASH GROVE
Let All Things Now Living 53
ASSAM
I Have Decided to Follow Jesus 576
ASSURANCE
Blessed Assurance, Jesus Is Mine 514
AU CLAIR DE LA LUNE
Jesus' Hands Were Kind Hands 412
AUCH JETZT MACHT GOTT
How Shall They Hear? 740
AURELIA
**The Church's One Foundation
689**
O Christ the Great Foundation 709
AUSTRIAN HYMN
**Glorious Things of Thee Are
Spoken 694**
Praise the Lord! O Heavens, Adore
Him 17
We Are Called to Be God's People
710
AWAY IN A MANGER
Away in a Manger 147
AZMON
O for a Thousand Tongues to Sing
130
BALM IN GILEAD
There Is a Balm in Gilead 611
BARIUM SPRINGS HOME
Our Savior's Infant Cries Were Heard

438
BATTLE HYMN
It Is God Who Holds the Nations
415
**Mine Eyes Have Seen the Glory
416**
BE STILL AND KNOW
Be Still and Know 516
BEACH SPRING
**Come, All Christians, Be
Committed 578**
God, Whose Giving Knows No
Ending 644
Lavish Love, Abundant Beauty 68
BEATITUDES
O How Blest Are the Poor in Spirit
603
BEATITUDO
Heal Us, Immanuel, Hear Our Prayer
411
**O for a Closer Walk with God
547**
BECK
Help Us Accept Each Other 437
BEECHER
God Is Here! 701
If My People's Hearts Are Humbled
719
**Love Divine, All Loves Excelling
558**
BELMONT
As Longs the Deer for Cooling
Streams 331
BEMERTON
Jesus, Stand Among Us 803
BENEDICTION
The Lord Bless You and Keep You
845
BENTON HARBOR
What a Wonderful Savior 488
BETHEL PARK
Glory to the Father 806
BIND US
Bind Us Together 690
BINNEY'S
How Long, O Lord? 339
BIRMINGHAM
Cast Thy Burden upon the Lord 815

BLAENWERN
   For Your Gift of God the Spirit 285
   **It Is Good to Sing Your Praises
   325**
BLESS HIS HOLY NAME
   Bless His Holy Name 36
BLOTT EN DAG
   Day by Day and with Each Passing
   Moment 367
BLOW THE WIND SOUTHERLY
   Spirit of Holiness 287
BOND OF LOVE
   The Bond of Love 696
BOURBON
   "Take Up Your Cross," the Savior
   Said 655
BOYLSTON
   A Charge to Keep I Have 659
BRADBURY
   Savior, Like a Shepherd Lead Us 522
BREAD OF LIFE
   Break Thou the Bread of Life 315
BRIDEGROOM
   Like the Murmur of the Dove's Song
   286
   **Not for Tongues of Heaven's
   Angels 597**
BROTHER JAMES' AIR
   The Lord My Shepherd Guards Me
   Well 615
BRYN CALFARIA
   Jesus Comes with Clouds
   Descending 283
BULLINGER
   I Am Trusting Thee, Lord Jesus 524
BUNESSAN
   Baptized in Water 758
   Christ Beside Me 543
   God of the Ages 363
   Morning Has Broken 362
BURLEIGH
   My Lord! What a Morning 279
CALCUTTA
   I Lay My Sins on Jesus 464
CALVARY
   At Calvary 510
CAMACHA
   Teach Me Thy Way, O Lord 586

CAMBERWELL
   At the Name of Jesus 266
CANONBURY
   How Blest Are They 673
   **Lord, Speak to Me, That I May
   Speak 574**
   We Bless the Name of Christ the
   Lord 761
CANTIQUE DE NOEL
   O Holy Night 160
CARLISLE
   We Give This Child to You 764
CARMICHAEL
   The Savior Is Waiting 446
CAROL
   It Came upon the Midnight Clear
   170
CAROL STREAM
   Heal Me, Hands of Jesus 463
CASWALL [BEMERTON]
   Jesus, Stand Among Us 803
CECELIA
   I Will Sing The Wondrous Story 500
CELEBRATION
   In the Presence of Your People 19
CELEBRATION '85
   When in Our Music God Is Glorified
   402
CHANNELS
   Channels Only 577
CHAPMAN
   One Day 196
CHARLESTOWN
   All Who Love and Serve Your City
   430
CHAUTAUQUA
   Lord, Our Lord, Your Glorious Name
   319
   O Lord Most High 828
CHEREPONI
   Jesu, Jesu, Fill Us with Your Love
   436
CHILDHOOD
   Greet Now the Swiftly Changing
   Year 372
CHILDREN PRAYING
   Lord, Listen to Your Children
   Praying 629

CHRIST AROSE
   Christ Arose! 235
CHRIST CHURCH
   Christ Is Made the Sure Foundation
   699
CHRISTE SANCTORUM
   Christ Is the World's Light 90
   Christ High-Ascended 734
CLAP YOUR HANDS
   Clap Your Hands 23
CLAY
   Fear Not, Rejoice and Be Glad 592
CLEANSING FOUNTAIN
   There Is a Fountain Filled with Blood
   467
CLONMEL
   We Praise You with Our Minds 401
CLOSER WALK
   Just a Closer Walk with Thee 561
COME LET US REASON
   Come, Let Us Reason 456
COMING AGAIN
   Jesus Is Coming Again 276
COMING SOON
   He Is Coming Soon 281
CONNOR
   Our Father 626
CONRAD
   Let All the World 24
   Through All the World 738
CONSOLATOR
   Come, Ye Disconsolate 613
CONVERSE
   What a Friend We Have in Jesus 622
CORONATION
   All Hail the Power of Jesus' Name 95
CRADLE SONG
   Away in a Manger 149
CREATOR GOD
   Safe in the Shadow of the Lord 513
CRIMOND
   O God, Whose Will Is Life and Good
   413
   The Lord Is Here! 777
   The Lord's My Shepherd, I'll
   Not Want 330
CROSS OF JESUS
   Cross of Jesus, Cross of Sorrow 214

CROSSROADS
   Let Us Draw Near! 631
CRUCIFER
   Lift High the Cross 229
CRUSADER'S HYMN
   Fairest Lord Jesus 115
CWM RHONDDA
   Christ Is Coming! Let Creation 271
   God of Grace and God of Glory 669
   Guide Me, O Thou Great
   Jehovah 634
DAMON
   Lord Jesus, Think on Me 462
   What Offering Shall We Give? 490
DANIEL
   Forth in Your Name, O Lord, I Go
   397
DARWALL
   Come, Let Us Praise the Lord 320
   How Sure the Scriptures Are! 312
   Rejoice, the Lord Is King 262
   We Come, O Christ, to You 86
DENNIS
   Blest Be the Tie That Binds 708
DIADEM
   All Hail the Power of Jesus' Name 93
DIADEMATA
   Crown Him with Many Crowns
   92
   Give to the Winds Your Fears 618
   Soldiers of Christ, Arise 756
DISMISSAL
   Lord, Let Us Now Depart in Peace
   842
DIVERNON
   Come, Share the Lord 782
DIVINUM MYSTERIUM
   Of the Father's Love Begotten
   145
   We Believe in God Almighty 693
DIX
   As with Gladness Men of Old
   181
   Christ, Whose Glory Fills the Skies
   562
   For the Beauty of the Earth 353
DOMINUS REGIT ME
   My Lord of Light Who Made the

Worlds 13
DONA NOBIS PACEM
**Father, Grant Us Your Peace
589**
Holy Lord 827
DOVE OF PEACE
I Come with Joy 768
DOWN AMPNEY
Come Down, O Love Divine! 304
DUDLEY
This Is a Time to Remember 792
DUKE STREET
Give to Our God Immortal Praise 16
I Know That My Redeemer Lives
239
Jesus Shall Reign 745
DUNCANNON
Lead Me to Calvary 211
DUNDEE
God Moves in a Mysterious Way 73
EARTH AND ALL STARS
Earth and All Stars 357
EASTER HYMN
Christ the Lord Is Risen Today 234
EASTER SONG
Easter Song 244
EBENEZER
O the Deep, Deep Love of Jesus 477
EIN' FESTE BURG
A Mighty Fortress Is Our God 43
EL NATHAN
I Know Whom I Have Believed 493
ELFAKER
Kind and Merciful God 455
ELIZABETH
Jesus Is All the World to Me 491
ELLACOMBE
Hosanna, Loud Hosanna 203
I Sing the Mighty Power of God 52
ELLERS
**Savior, Again to Your Dear
Name 835**
Search Me, O God 458
ELLSWORTH
Now I Belong to Jesus 503
EMMANUEL
Emmanuel, Emmanuel 140
ENGELBERG

All Praise to Christ 127
**When in Our Music God Is
Glorified 403**
ERMUNTRE DICH
Break Forth, O Beauteous 158
ES IST EIN' ROS' ENTSPRUNGEN
Lo! How a Rose E'er Blooming 163
EVENTIDE
Abide with Me, Fast Falls the
Eventide 365
EVERLASTING LOVE
I Am His, and He Is Mine 602
EVERY EYE
Every Eye Shall See 755
EWING
Jerusalem the Golden 754
FACE TO FACE
Face to Face 684
FAITHFULNESS
Great Is Thy Faithfulness 60
FAR OFF LANDS
Tell All the World of Jesus 742
FESTAL SONG
O Bless the Lord, My Soul! 71
Rise Up, O Saints of God! 670
FETTKE
Be Strong in the Lord 661
FIELD
God Be in My Head 837
FILITZ [BEMERTON]
Jesus, Stand Among Us 803
FILLMORE
I Will Sing of the Mercies 30
FINLANDIA
Be Still, My Soul 530
I Then Shall Live 507
FOR THE BREAD
For the Bread Which You Have
Broken 772
FOREST GREEN
**Amid the Thronging
Worshipers 340**
I Love You, Lord, My Strength, My
Rock 349
O Little Town of Bethlehem 154
FORTUNATUS NEW
Sing, My Tongue, the Glorious Battle
228

FOUNDATION
How Firm a Foundation 612
GARDEN
In the Garden 242
GATHERING
The Gathering 800
GELOBT SEI GOTT
Good Christians All, Rejoice 255
GENEVAN 42
Comfort, Comfort Now My People
132
GERMANY
All Things Are Yours 657
**Jesus, Thy Blood and
Righteousness 481**
Nature with Open Volume Stands
222
Where Cross the Crowded Ways of
Life 433
GIFT OF LOVE
The Gift of Love 593
GIVE ME JESUS
Give Me Jesus 551
GIVE THANKS
Give Thanks with a Grateful Heart
496
GLORIA
Angels We Have Heard on High 152
GLORIA III
Gloria, Gloria 825
GLORIFIED
Lord, Be Glorified 537
GLORIFY YOUR NAME
Glorify Your Name 10
GLORIOUS COMING
When the Lord in Glory Comes 280
GO TELL IT
Go, Tell it on the Mountain 151
GOD BE WITH YOU
God Be with You 840
GOD CARES
God Will Take Care of You 619
GOD IS SO GOOD
God Is So Good 75
GODSPELL
Day by Day 535
GORDON
My Jesus, I Love Thee 101

GREAT IS THE LORD
Great Is the Lord 44
GREATER IS HE
Greater Is He That Is in Me 525
GREATOREX
Glory Be to the Father 805
GREENSLEEVES
What Child Is This? 150
GREENWELL
I Am Not Skilled to Understand 480
GROSSER GOTT, WIR LOBEN DICH
Holy God, We Praise Your Name 3
HAIRSTON
Mary's Little Boy-Child 178
HALLELUJAH! WHAT A SAVIOR
Hallelujah! What a Savior 226
HAMBURG
When I Survey the Wondrous Cross
213
HANKEY
I Love to Tell the Story 498
HANOVER
Rejoice in God's Saints 749
Sing Praise to the Lord 346
The Kingdom of God Is Justice and
Joy 712
**Ye Servants of God, Your
Master 103**
HANSON PLACE
Shall We Gather at the River? 687
HAPPY DAY
O Happy Day That Fixed My Choice
504
HARROW WEALD
Father Eternal, Lord of the Ages 6
HE IS LORD
He Is Lord 97
HE LEADETH ME
He Leadeth Me, O Blessed Thought
635
HE TOUCHED ME
He Touched Me 410
HEARN
Jesus, Name Above All Names 106
HEAVEN
When We All Get to Heaven 679
HENDON
Ask Ye What Great Thing I

Know 224
Take My Life and Let It Be Consecrated 568
HERZLIEBSTER JESU
Ah, Holy Jesus 231
HICKS
Praise the Name of Jesus 128
HIS PRESENCE
Come into His Presence 122
HOLINESS
Take Time to Be Holy 540
HOLY IS THE LORD
Holy Is the Lord 831
HOLY MANNA
Brethren, We Have Met to Worship 802
God, Who Stretched the Spangled 54
Tell His Praise in Song and Story 347
HOUSTON
I Want to Walk as a Child of the Light 539
HOW MAJESTIC
How Majestic Is Your Name 61
HUDSON
At the Cross 512
HYFRYDOL
Alleluia, Sing to Jesus 263
Come, Thou Long-Expected Jesus 135
Fear Not, Rejoice and Be Glad 492
God, You Spin the Whirling Planets 51
Our Great Savior 89
I AM THINE
Draw Me Nearer 534
I HIMMELEN
In Heaven Above 682
I KNOW A FOUNT
I Know a Fount 485
I LOVE YOU, LORD
I Love You, Lord 124
I WANT TO BE A CHRISTIAN
Lord, I Want to Be a Christian 563
I WONDER AS I WANDER
I Wonder as I Wander 165
IL EST NÉ

He Is Born, the Divine Christ Child 177
IN BABILONE
Holy Spirit, Ever Dwelling 289
IN DULCI JUBILO
Good Christian Friends, Rejoice 157
INTO MY HEART
Into My Heart 444
IONA
Iona Gloria 826
IRBY
For Your Holy Book We Thank You 316
Once in Royal David's City 161
ISRAELI
Because He Died and Is Risen 588
ITALIAN HYMN
Come, Thou Almighty King 5
Christ for the World! We Sing 743
JACOB
Eternal Light, Shine in My Heart 545
JACOB'S LADDER [JACOB'S VISION]
As Jacob with Travel Was Weary 637
JESU DULCIS MEMORIA
Have Mercy in Your Goodness, Lord 322
JESU, MEINE FREUDE
Jesus, Priceless Treasure 119
JESUS, I COME
Jesus, I Come 448
JESUS IN THE MORNING
Jesus, Jesus, Jesus in the Morning 364
JESUS LOVES ME
Jesus Loves Me, This I Know 470
JESUS, REMEMBER ME
Jesus, Remember Me 822
JESUS SAVES
Jesus Saves! 728
JOYFUL NOISE
Make a Joyful Noise 31
JOYFUL SONG
Praise Him! Praise Him! 96
JUNGST
While by the Sheep We Watched 166
KANSFIELD

God of Love and Truth and Beauty 428

KING OF KINGS
King of Kings and Lord of Lords 110

KINGS OF ORIENT
We Three Kings of Orient Are 185

KING'S WESTON
When the Church of Jesus 722

KINGSFOLD
Make Room within My Heart, O God 559
O Come to Me, the Master Said 442
O Sing a Song of Bethlehem 192

KIRKEN DEN ER ET
Built on the Rock 705

KREMSER
The Works of the Lord Are Created 354
We Gather Together 376
We Praise You, O God, Our Redeemer 377

KUM BA YAH
Kum Ba Yah 630

LAFFERTY
Seek Ye First the Kingdom of God 447

LAKE AVENUE
Lord, We Worship and Adore You 832

LANCASHIRE
Lead On, O King Eternal 747
The Day of Resurrection 247

LAND OF REST
Jerusalem, My Happy Home 675
Lord, Who Throughout 200

LANDAS
My Faith Has Found a Resting Place 495

LANGLEY
Take My Life, Lead Me, Lord 566

LANGRAN
Here, O My Lord, I See You 783

LASST UNS ERFREUEN
A Hymn of Glory Let Us Sing 259
All Creatures of Our God and King 356
God's Holy Ways Are Just and True

328

LAUDA ANIMA
God the Father, Name We Treasure 766
Jesus Came, the Heavens Adoring 194
Praise, My Soul, the King of Heaven 26

LAUDATE DOMINUM
As Sons of the Day and Daughters of Light 704

LAUDATE PUERI
Praise the Lord! 38

LAUDES DOMINI
When Morning Gilds the Skies 99

LAUDS
There's a Spirit in the Air 120

LEAVE ALL THINGS
Two Fishermen 654

LEISURE TIME
Lord of All Leisure Time 398

LEMMEL
Turn Your Eyes upon Jesus 452

LENOX
Arise, My Soul, Arise 483

LEONI
God Is My Great Desire 336
The Battle Is the Lord's! 741
The God of Abraham Praise 66

LET US BREAK BREAD
Let Us Break Bread Together 776

LIVING
Living for Jesus a Life That Is True 569

LLANFAIR
Hail the Day That Sees Him Rise 258
Jesus Christ Is Risen Today 250
Let the Whole Creation Cry 40
Praise the Lord (ref.) 338

LLANGLOFFAN
O God of Every Nation 422

LO DESEMBRE CONGELAT
To a Virgin Meek and Mild 139

LOBE DEN HERREN
One Race, One Gospel, One Task 735
Praise to the Lord, the

Almighty 77
LOIS
Spirit, Now Live in Me 284
LONDONDERRY AIR
I Cannot Tell 109
Lord of the Church 717
LOVE ONE ANOTHER
This Is My Commandment 600
LOVE TO CHRIST
How Blest Are the People 706
I Love You, My Jesus 91
LOWLINESS
Who Is He in Yonder Stall? 195
LUX FIAT
Send Out Your Light and Your Truth
811
LYONS
O Worship the King 29
MACCABEUS
Thine Is the Glory 251
MADILL
Stir Your Church, O God, Our Father
718
MADRID
Come, Christians, Join to Sing 108
MAITLAND
Must Jesus Bear the Cross Alone?
658
MAJESTY
Majesty, Worship His Majesty 98
MALOTTE
The Lord's Prayer 632
MAORI
Search Me, O God 460
MARANATHA
Father, I Adore You 4
MARCHING TO ZION
We're Marching to Zion 596
MARGARET
Thou Didst Leave Thy Throne 198
MARION
Rejoice, Ye Pure in Heart 34
MARSH CHAPEL
Awake, O Sleeper, Rise from Death
449
MARTYRDOM
Alas! and Did My Savior Bleed? 208
MARYTON

O Master, Let Me Walk with Thee
651
MATERNA
America, the Beautiful 418
McAFEE
Near to the Heart of God 542
McKEE
In Christ There Is No East or West
695
MEECE
We Are the Reason 474
MEINEKE
Glory Be to the Father 807
MELITA
Eternal Father, Strong to Save 358
MENDELSSOHN
Hark! the Herald Angels Sing 171
MENDON
We Have a Gospel to Proclaim 714
MERBECKE
Lord, Have Mercy upon Us 823
MERCY
Holy Spirit, Light Divine 302
Holy Spirit, Truth Divine 303
MERLE'S TUNE
How Lovely, Lord, How Lovely 333
MESSAGE
We've a Story to Tell to the Nations
733
MIEIR
His Name Is Wonderful 87
MINERVA
Only Trust Him 443
MIT FREUDEN ZART
All Glory Be to God on High 8
Sing Praise to God Who Reigns
Above 50
MONKLAND
Let Us, with a Gladsome Mind 59
MOODY
Grace Greater than Our Sin 472
MORE LOVE TO THEE
More Love to Thee, O Christ 555
MORECAMBE
Spirit of God, Descend upon My
Heart 290
MORESTEAD
Lord of All Good 645

MORNING SONG
The King Shall Come 277
MORNING STAR
Brightest and Best of the Stars 182
God in His Love for Us 385
MOWSLEY
Christ upon the Mountain Peak 180
MUNICH
O Word of God Incarnate 310
MY SAVIOR'S LOVE
My Savior's Love 478
MY TRIBUTE
My Tribute 46
NAME OF THE LORD
In the Name of the Lord 113
NATIONAL HYMN
God of Our Fathers 419
NCHEU
His Battle Ended There 253
NEAR THE CROSS
Near the Cross 549
NEED
I Need Thee Every Hour 538
NETTLETON
Come, Thou Fount of Every Blessing 45
NEUMARK [WER NUR DEN LIEBEN GOTT]
If You Will Trust in God to Guide You 636
Wise Men, They Came to Look 186
NEW BORN AGAIN
I'm New Born Again 494
NEW BRITAIN
Amazing Grace! How Sweet the Sound 502
NICAEA
Holy, Holy, Holy! Lord God Almighty 2
NOEL
I Know Not Where the Road Will Lead 643
NOEL NOUVELET
Sing We Now of Christmas 159
Welcome, Happy Morning 241
NORTH PHOENIX
As We Gather Around the Table 770

NUN DANKET ALLE GOTT
Now Thank We All Our God 374
NUN KOMM, DER HEIDEN HEILAND
Savior of the Nations, Come 138
NYLAND
In Heavenly Love Abiding 521
O CANADA
O Canada! 424
O FILII ET FILIAE
O Sons and Daughters, Let Us Sing 249
O, HOW I LOVE JESUS
O, How I Love Jesus 509
O PERFECT LOVE
Lord Jesus Christ, Invited Guest 387
O Perfect Love 388
O QUANTA QUALIA
Here from All Nations 680
O STORE GUD
How Great Thou Art 21
O WALY WALY
An Upper Room Did Our Lord Prepare 767
Lord, I Was Blind 499
When Love Is Found 392
OASIS
As Water to the Thirsty 608
ODE TO JOY
Alleluia, Alleluia! Hearts to Heaven 254
Christ, Whose Purpose Is to Kindle 720
God Has Spoken by His Prophets 311
Joyful, Joyful, We Adore Thee 20
OLD HUNDREDTH
All People That on Earth Do Dwell 317
Praise God from Whom All Blessings 808
Praise God from Whom All Blessings 809
OLD 113th
I'll Praise My Maker While I've Breath 79
OLD 124th
We Will Extol You 348

OLD RUGGED CROSS
  The Old Rugged Cross 484
OLIVE'S BROW
  'Tis Midnight; and on Olive's Brow
  220
OLIVET
  My Faith Looks Up to Thee 552
OMNI DEI
  May the Grace of Christ Our Savior
  841
ONSLOW SQUARE
  Sing a New Song to the Lord 18
OPEN OUR EYES
  Open Our Eyes, Lord 536
ORWIGSBURG
  I Must Tell Jesus 621
PARADOXY
  Make Me a Captive, Lord 583
PARKSTONE
  Now Let Us Learn of Christ 567
PASS IT ON
  Pass It On 739
PASSION CHORALE
  O Sacred Head, Now Wounded 221
PATRICIA
  O How He Loves You and Me! 479
PAX TECUM
  Peace, Perfect Peace 598
PEARCE
  When He Shall Come 273
PEARLY GATES
  He the Pearly Gates Will Open 683
PENLAN
  We Come as Guests Invited 784
PEOPLE NEED THE LORD
  People Need the Lord 730
PERSONENT HODIE
  God Is Love—His the Care 400
  Long Ago, Prophets Knew 142
  **On This Day Earth Shall Ring
  175**
PICARDY
  Let All Mortal Flesh Keep Silence
  167
PISGAH
  When I Can Read My Title Clear
  681
PLAINFIELD

Nothing but the Blood of Jesus 471
PLEADING SAVIOR
  For the Life That You Have Given
  813
  **Jesus Calls Us o'er the Tumult
  580**
POSADA
  God's Love Made Visible 179
PRECIOUS LORD
  Precious Lord, Take My Hand 638
PROMISE
  In the Bulb There Is a Flower 678
PROMISED ONE
  The King of Glory Comes 134
PROMISED LAND
  On Jordan's Stormy Banks I Stand
  674
PROMISES
  Standing on the Promises 306
PUER NOBIS
  My Lord, You Wore No Royal Crown
  191
  O Love, How Deep, How Broad 193
  **O Splendor of God's Glory
  Bright 27**
  On Jordan's Bank the Baptist's Cry
  136
PURPOSE
  God Is Working His Purpose Out
  750
PYE
  My God, How Wonderful Thou Art
  65
QUAM DILECTA
  The Lord Is in His Holy Temple 796
QUEBEC
  Jesus, Thou Joy of Loving Hearts
  121
QUIET UNDERSTANDING
  There's a Quiet Understanding 788
QUIETUDE
  Lord, Now Let Your Servant 343
  **Speak, Lord, in the Stillness
  585**
RACHEL
  How Sweet the Name of Jesus
  Sounds 102
RANDOLPH

God Be with You 839
RATHBUN
    In the Cross of Christ I Glory 209
REDHEAD
    Go to Dark Gethsemane 225
REGENT SQUARE
    Angels from the Realms of Glory
    174
REGNATOR ORBIS [O QUANTA
QUALIA]
    Here from All Nations 680
REJOICE
    Rejoice in the Lord Always 606
RENDEZ A DIEU
    New Songs of Celebration Render 32
REPTON
    How Clear Is Our Vocation, Lord
    395
RESCUE
    Rescue the Perishing 736
REST
    Dear Lord and Father of Mankind
    591
RESURRECTION
    Because He Lives 238
REVIVE US AGAIN
    Revive Us Again 723
RHOSYMEDRE
    My Song Is Love Unknown 202
    **Our Father, by Whose Name
    393**
RICHMOND
    Lord, Teach Us How to Pray Aright
    628
ROCK HARBOR
    Let Heaven Rejoice 355
RUSSIAN HYMN
    Christ the Victorious 685
    God the Omnipotent! 427
    King of the Universe 67
RUSTINGTON
    God, We Praise You! 39
SAGINA
    And Can It Be That I Should Gain?
    473
ST. AGNES
    Come, Holy Spirit, Heavenly Dove
    298

Happy the Home When God Is
There 389
**Jesus, the Very Thought of Thee
112**
ST. ANDREW
    Not What These Hands Have Done
    476
ST. ANNE
    How Blest Are They Who, Fearing
    God 342
    **O God, Our Help in Ages Past
    78**
ST. ANTHONY'S CHORALE
    We, Your People, Praise You 37
ST. CATHERINE
    Faith of Our Fathers 692
    Jesus, Thy Boundless Love to Me
    556
ST. CHRISTOPHER
    Beneath the Cross of Jesus 216
ST. DENIO
    For Beauty of Meadows 383
    **Immortal, Invisible, God Only
    Wise 62**
ST. GEORGE'S, WINDSOR
    **Come, Ye Thankful People,
    Come 381**
    Songs of Thankfulness and Praise
    190
ST. GERTRUDE
    Onward, Christian Soldiers 748
ST. LEONARDS
    May the Mind of Christ My Savior
    560
ST. LOUIS
    O Little Town of Bethlehem 155
ST. MAGNUS
    The Head That Once Was Crowned
    268
ST. MARGARET
    O Love That Will Not Let Me Go
    531
ST. MATTHEWS
    Let Us Build a House of Worship
    793
ST. MICHAEL
    Stand Up and Bless the Lord 41
ST. MICHAEL'S

Your Hands, O Lord, in Days of Old 409
ST. PETER
In Christ There Is No East or West 697
ST. PETERSBURG
Great God, Your Love Has Called Us 779
ST. THEODULPH
All Glory, Laud and Honor 204
ST. THOMAS
Come, We That Love the Lord 22
I Love Thy Kingdom, Lord 702
SANDON
God of Our Life 370
Out of the Depths 465
SATISFIED
Satisfied 511
SCHULER
Make Me a Blessing 656
SCHUMANN
We Give Thee but Thine Own 649
SCOTT
Open My Eyes, That I May See 557
SECOND COMING
What If It Were Today? 275
SERENITY
Immortal Love, Forever Full 607
SERVANT
Make Me a Servant 653
SHALOM CHAVERIM
Shalom, My Friend, Shalom 599
SHARPTHORNE
What Does the Lord Require? 571
SHINE, JESUS, SHINE
Shine, Jesus, Shine 721
SHOWALTER
Leaning on the Everlasting Arms 609
SICILIAN MARINERS
Jesus, Come! for We Invite You 187
Lord, Dismiss Us with Your Blessing 834
SINE NOMINE
For All the Saints 751
SING ALLELUIA
Sing Alleluia to the Lord 771

SING, BELIEVERS
The Earth Belongs to the Lord 326
[SING TO THE LORD A NEW SONG] (ref.)
Sing to the Lord a New Song 324
SLANE
Be Thou My Vision 532
Christ Be My Leader 107
God of Creation, All-Powerful 48
Lord of All Hopefulness 369
Lord of Creation 565
SNYDOR [CHRIST CHURCH]
Christ Is Made the Sure Foundation 699
SOLID ROCK
The Solid Rock 517
SONG 13
Fire of God, Undying Flame 301
SONG 46
All Shall Be Well! 236
SOON AND VERY SOON
Soon and Very Soon 677
SOUTH PASADENA
"Let There Be Light!" 716
SPARKLE
Angels Bright, Heavens High 323
SPIRIT OF THE LIVING GOD
Spirit of the Living God 297
SPIRITUS VITAE
O Breath of Life 299
STAR-SPANGLED BANNER
The Star-Spangled Banner 423
STEPHANOS
Are You Weary, Heavy Laden? 453
STILLE NACHT
Silent Night! Holy Night! 164
STORY OF JESUS
Tell Me the Story of Jesus 199
STRENGTH AND STAY
We Trust in You, Our Shield 573
STUART
As He Gathered at His Table 778
STUTTGART
Spirit, Working in Creation 293
SURELY GOODNESS AND MERCY
Surely Goodness and Mercy 639
SURRENDER
I Surrender All 579

SUSSEX CAROL
Come, Let Us with Our Lord Arise 798
On Christmas Night all Christians Sing 168
SWEET HOUR
Sweet Hour of Prayer 623
SWEET, SWEET SPIRIT
Sweet, Sweet Spirit 291
SYMPHONY
We Are God's People 700
TABELL
Trust in the Lord 527
TACK, O GUD
Thanks to God for My Redeemer 380
TALLIS CANON
A Morning Prayer 360
An Evening Prayer 361
O God, Who Gives to Humankind 399
O Gracious Light, Lord Jesus Christ 359
TEMPUS ADEST FLORIDUM
Gentle Mary Laid Her Child 156
When the King Shall Come Again 337
TERRA BEATA
Great Is the Lord Our God 335
This Is My Father's World 384
THAT NAME
There's Something about That Name 104
THE BATTLE
The Battle Belongs to the Lord 672
THE FIRST NOEL
The First Noel, the Angel Did Say 162
THE LORD'S DAY
This Is the Day 801
THE MORNING TRUMPET
O, When Shall I See Jesus? 278
THE TREES OF THE FIELD
The Trees of the Field 272
THEODORIC [PERSONENT HODIE]
God Is Love—His the Care 400
Long Ago, Prophets Knew 142
On This Day Earth Shall Ring 175

THOMAS MERTON
Surely It Is God Who Saves Me 327
THOMPSON
Softly and Tenderly Jesus Is Calling 441
THROUGH IT ALL
Through It All 616
TIDINGS
O Christians, Haste 731
TO GOD BE THE GLORY
Sing Praise to the Father 9
To God Be the Glory 72
TOPLADY
Rock of Ages, Cleft for Me 227
TORONTO
So I Send You–by Grace Made Strong 732
TRENTHAM
Breathe on Me, Breath of God 295
TRURO
Christ Is Alive! 243
Ride On, Ride On in Majesty 205
TRUST AND OBEY
Trust and Obey 523
TRUST IN JESUS
'Tis So Sweet to Trust in Jesus 520
TRUSTING JESUS
Trusting Jesus 526
TRYGGARE KAN INGEN VARA
Children of the Heavenly Father 84
TYROL
A Man There Lived in Galilee 88
UNSER HERRSCHER
All Authority and Power 260
UPLIFTED EYES
I Lift My Eyes to the Quiet Hills 81
VENI CREATOR
Come, Holy Ghost, Our Souls Inspire 296
VENI EMMANUEL
O Come, O Come, Emmanuel 133
VICAR
Hope of the World 434
VICTORY
The Strife Is O'er, the Battle Done 233
VILLE DU HAVRE

It Is Well with My Soul 519
VLEUGEL
All Things Bright and Beautiful 57
VOX DILECTI
For Ages Women Hoped and Prayed 143
I Heard the Voice of Jesus Say 506
W ZLOBIE LEZY
Infant Holy, Infant Lowly 169
WACHET AUF
Wake, Awake, for Night Is Flying 131
WAKEFIELD
My Hope Is in the Lord 482
WALK WITH ME
I Want Jesus to Walk with Me 642
WAS GOTT TUT
What God Ordains Is Always Right 82
WAYFARING STRANGER
Bread of the World in Mercy Broken 774
WE WILL GLORIFY
We Will Glorify 118
WEBB
Stand Up, Stand Up for Jesus 663
WELLESLEY
There's a Wideness in God's Mercy 486
WEM IN LEIDENSTAGEN [BEMERTON]
Jesus, Stand Among Us 803
WEN-TI
May the Lord, Mighty God 843
WER NUR DEN LIEBEN GOTT
If You Will Trust in God to Guide You 636
Wise Men, They Came to Look 186
WERE YOU THERE?
Were You There? 218
WESTMINSTER ABBEY
Hark! the Voice of Love and Mercy 475
WHITTLE
Moment by Moment 529
WHO'S MY NEIGHBOR
They Asked, "Who's My Neighbor?" 435

WHOLE WORLD
He's Got the Whole World 518
WIE LIEBLICH IST DER MAIEN
Sing to the Lord of Harvest 375
WILLAN AGNUS DEI
O Lamb of God 833
WILLAN GLORIA
Glory Be to God on High 824
WILLAN KYRIE
Lord, Have Mercy upon Us 821
WILLAN SANCTUS
Holy, Lord God of Hosts 829
WINCHESTER OLD
While Shepherds Watched Their Flocks 172
WONDERFUL GRACE
Wonderful Grace of Jesus 497
WONDROUS LOVE
What Wondrous Love Is This 212
WOODLANDS
Tell Out, My Soul 350
WOODWORTH
Just As I Am, without One Plea 445
WORCESTER
Glory Be to God the Father 11
WORDS OF LIFE
Wonderful Words of Life 309
WORSHIP AND ADORE
We Worship and Adore You 33
WORTHY
Thou Art Worthy 116
WORTHY IS THE LAMB
Worthy Is the Lamb 230
WUERTTEMBERG
Jesus Comes with All His Grace 468
WYCLIFF
Lord, We Bring to You Our Children 759
WYE VALLEY
Let Your Heart Be Broken 429
Like a River Glorious 594
WYLDE GREEN
Thanks to God Whose Word Was Spoken 313
ZEUCH MICH, ZEUCH MICH
God in Mercy Grant Us Blessing 344
ZUVERSICHT
Jesus Lives and So Shall I 246

Bibliography

General Reference Works

ASCAP Biographical Dictionary. 4th ed. Compiled for the American Society of Composers, Authors and Publishers by Jaques Cattell Press, R. R. Bowker, New York & London, 1980.

Baker's Biographical Dictionary of Musicians. 8th ed. Rev. Nicolas Slonimsky. New York: Schirmer [Macmillan], 1992.

Blume, Friedrich, et al. *Protestant Church Music.* New York: Norton, 1974.

Chase, Gilbert. *America's Music.* Rev. 3rd ed. Urbana: U of Illinois P, 1987.

Dictionary of American Biography. 22 vols. New York: Scribner's, 1928-58.

Dictionary of National Biography. 68 vols. London, 1885-1901.

Dictionary of National Biography. Supplements 1 and 2. London, 1901 and 1902.

Fischer, Albert Friedrich Wilhelm. *Kirchenlieder-Lexicon.* Gotha: Friedrich Andreas Perthas, 1878.

Gaster, Adrian, ed. International *Who's Who in Music and Musicians' Directory.* 9th ed. Cambridge, England: I.W.W.M., International Biographical Centre, 1980.

Hitchcock, H. Wiley, ed. *The New Grove Dictionary of American Music.* New York: Grove's Dictionaries of Music, 1986.

Julian, John, ed. *A Dictionary of Hymnology.* New York: Scribner's, 1892. New York: Dover, 1957.

Koch, Edward Emil. *Geschichte des Kirchenlieds und Kirchengesängs.* Stuttgart: Chr. Belser'schen, 1866.

Long, Kenneth R. *The Music of the English Church.* New York: St. Martin's, 1975.

New Catholic Encyclopedia. 15 vols. New York: McGraw, 1957.

New Grove's Dictionary of Music and Musicians. 6th ed. 20 vols. Washington, DC: Grove's Dictionaries of Music, 1980.

The New Oxford History of Music. (11 volumes) London: Oxford UP, 1957-.

Randel, Don Michael, ed. *The New Harvard Dictionary of Music.* Cambridge: Belknap Press of Harvard UP, 1986.

Wolff, Dr. Eugen. *Des Deutsche Kirchenlied des 16 and 17 Jahrh.* Stuttgart, n.d.

Hymnal Handbooks

Adams, Jere V., ed. *Handbook to The Baptist Hymnal.* Nashville: Convention Press, 1992.

Avery, Gordon. *Companion to the Song Book of the Salvation Army.* 4th ed. London: Salvationist Publishing and Supplies, 1970.

Bock, Fred, and Bryan Jeffery Leech. *The Hymnal Companion* (a companion to *Hymns for the Family of God*). Nashville: Paragon, 1979.

Bucke, Emory Stevens, Fred D. Gealy, Austin C. Lovelace, and Carlton R. Young. *Companion to the Hymnal: A Handbook to the 1964 Methodist Hymnal.* Nashville: Abingdon, 1970.

Covert, William C., and Calvin W. Laufer. *Handbook to the Hymnal.* Philadelphia: Presbyterian Board of Christian Education, 1935.

Dearmer, Percy, and Archibald Jacob. *Songs of Praise Discussed.* London: Oxford UP, 1933.

Erickson, J. Irving. Sing It Again! *A Handbook on The Covenant Hymnal.* Chicago: Covenant Press, 1985.

Farlander, Arthur, Leonard Ellinwood, et al. *The Hymnal 1940 Companion.* New York: Church Pension Fund, 1949.

Frost, Maurice, ed. *Historical Companion to Hymns Ancient and Modern.* London: William Clowes, 1962.

Haeussler, Armin. *The Story of Our Hymns. The Handbook to the Hymnal of the Evangelical and Reformed Church.* St. Louis: Eden, 1952.

Higginson, J. Vincent. *Handbook for American Catholic Hymnals.* New York: Hymn Society of America, 1976.

Hooper, Wayne, and Edward E. White. *Companion to the Seventh-day Adventist Hymnal.* Washington: Review and Herald, 1988.

Hostetler, Lester. *Handbook to the Mennonite Hymnary.* Newton, KS: General Conference of the Mennonite Church of North America, 1949.

Hughes, Charles W. *American Hymns Old and New; Notes on the Hymns and*

Biographies of the Authors and Composers. NY: Columbia UP, 1980.

Hustad, Donald P. *Dictionary-Handbook to Hymns for the Living Church.* Carol Stream, IL: Hope, 1978.

Kelynack, William S. *Companion to the School Hymn-Book of the Methodist Church.* London: Epworth, 1950.

Lightwood, James T. Ed. and rev. Francis B. Westbrook. *The Music of the Methodist Hymn-Book.* London: Epworth, 1955.

Macmillan, Alexander. *Hymns of the Church, A Companion to The Hymnary of The United Church of Canada.* Toronto: United Church Publishing, 1935.

Martin, Hugh, ed., et al. *The Baptist Hymn Book Companion.* Rev. ed. R. W. Thomson. London: Psalms and Hymns Trust, 1967.

McCutchan, Robert G. *Our Hymnody: A Manual of the Methodist Hymnal.* 2nd ed. New York: Abingdon, 1942.

McKim, LindaJo H. *The Presbyterian Hymnal Companion.* Louisville: Westminster/John Knox, 1993.

Milgate, Wesley. *Songs of the People of God; A Companion to the Australian Hymn Book / With One Voice.* London: Collins Liturgical Publications, 1982 (with corrections 1985).

Moffatt, James, and Millar Patrick. *Handbook of the Church Hymnary with Supplement.* Rev. ed. London: Oxford UP, 1927.

Parry, K. L., and Erik Routley. *Companion to Congregational Praise.* London: Independent Press, 1953.

Polack, William G. *The Handbook to the Lutheran Hymnal.* 3rd ed. rev. St. Louis: Concordia, 1958.

Reynolds, William Jensen. *Hymns of Our Faith, A Handbook for the Baptist Hymnal.* Nashville: Broadman, 1964.

—-. *Companion to Baptist Hymnal.* Nashville: Broadman, 1976.

Ronander, Albert C., and Ethel K. Porter. *Guide to the Pilgrim Hymnal.* Philadelphia: United Church, 1966.

Sanchez, Diana. *The Hymns of the United Methodist Hymnal.* Nashville: Abingdon, 1989.

Schoenhals, Lawrence R., ed. *Companion to Hymns of Faith and Life.* Winona Lake,

IN: Light and Life, 1980.

Seaman, William A. *Companion to the Service Book and Hymnal*. Commission on the Liturgy and Hymnal, 1976.

Statler, Ruth B., and Nevin W. Fisher. *Handbook on Brethren Hymns*. Elgin, IL: Brethren Press, 1959.

Stulken, Marilyn Kay. *Hymnal Companion to the Lutheran Book of Worship*. Philadelphia: Fortress, 1981.

Taylor, Gordon. *Companion to the Song Book of The Salvation Army*. London: International Headquarters of The Salvation Army, 1989.

Wake, Arthur N. *Companion to Hymnbook for Christian Worship*. St. Louis, MO: Bethany, 1970.

Watson, Richard, Kenneth Trickett, et al. *Companion to Hymns & Psalms*. Peterborough, Great Britain: Methodist Publishing, 1988.

Young, Carlton R. *Companion to The United Methodist Hymnal*. Nashville: Abingdon, 1993.

General Hymnology

Bailey, Albert Edward. *The Gospel in Hymns*. New York: Scribner's, 1950.

Barrows, Cliff, ed. *Crusade Hymn Stories*. Chicago: Hope, 1967.

Benson, Louis F. *The English Hymn*. New York: George H. Doran, 1915. Richmond: John Knox, 1962.

Brown, Theron, and Hezekiah Butterworth. *The Story of the Hymns and Tunes*. New York: George H. Doran, 1906.

Clark, Keith C. *A Selective Bibliography for the Study of Hymns; The Papers of the Hymn Society of America XXXIII*. [Fort Worth, TX], 1980.

Clark, W. Thorburn. *Stories of Fadeless Hymns*. Nashville: Broadman, 1949.

Colquhoun, Frank. *Hymns that Live*. Downers Grove, IL: InterVarsity, 1980.

Colson, Elizabeth. *Hymn Stories*. Boston: Pilgrim, 1925.

Davies, James P. *Sing with Understanding*. Chicago: Covenant, 1966.

Dearmer, Percy, Ralph Vaughan Williams, and Martin Shaw. *The Oxford Book of Carols*. London: Oxford UP, 1928 and later editions.

Douglas, Charles W. *Church Music in History and Practice*. New York: Scribner's, 1937. Rev. Leonard Ellinwood, 1962.

Ellinwood, Leonard. *The History of American Church Music*. New York: Morehouse-Gorham, 1953.

Emurian, Ernest K. *Living Stories of Famous Hymns*. Boston: Wilde, 1955.

Erickson, J. Irving. *Twice-Born Hymns*. Chicago: Covenant, 1976.

Eskew, Harry, and Hugh T. McElrath. *Sing with Understanding*. Nashville: Broadman, 1980.

Foote, Henry Wilder. *Three Centuries of American Hymnody*. Cambridge: Harvard UP, 1940.

Hall, Frederick. *Know Your Hymns?* Boston: Wilde, 1944.

Hutchings, Arthur. *Church Music in the Nineteenth Century*. London: Oxford UP, 1967.

Knapp, Christopher. *Who Wrote Our Hymns?* Denver: Wilson Foundations, 1925.

Laufer, Calvin W. *Hymn Lore*. Philadelphia: Westminster, 1932.

Liemohn, Edwin. *The Chorale*. Philadelphia: Muhlenberg, 1953.

Lovelace, Austin C. *The Anatomy of Hymnody*. New York: Abingdon, 1965.

Mable, Norman. *Popular Hymns and Their Writers*. London: Independent Press, 1946-1951.

Miller, L. David. *Hymns: The Story of Christian Song*. Philadelphia: Lutheran Church Press, 1969.

Northcott, Cecil. *Hymns We Love*. Philadelphia: Westminster, 1954.

Patrick, Millar. *Four Centuries of Scottish Psalmody*. London: Oxford UP, 1949.

—-. *The Story of the Church's Song*. Scottish Churches Joint Committee on Youth, Edinburgh, 1927. Rev. for American use by James Rawlings Sydnor. Richmond: John Knox, 1962.

Pratt, Waldo S. *The Music of the French Psalter of 1562*. New York: Columbia UP, 1939.

Reynolds, William Jensen. *Songs of Glory*. Grand Rapids: Zondervan, 1990.

Reynolds, William Jensen, and Milburn Price. *A Survey of Christian Hymnody.* Carol Stream, IL: Hope, 1987, 3rd Edition.

Roff, Lawrence C. *Let Us Sing: Worshiping God with Our Music.* Norcross, GA: Great Commission Publications, 1991.

Routley, Erik. *A Panorama of Christian Hymnody.* Chicago: GIA Publications, 1979.

—-. *An English-Speaking Hymnal Guide.* Collegeville, MN: Liturgical Press, 1979.

—-. *Christian Hymns Observed.* Princeton, NJ: Prestige, 1982.

—-. *Church Music and Theology.* Philadelphia: Fortress, 1960.

—-. *Hymns Today and Tomorrow.* New York: Abingdon, 1964.

—-. *The English Carol.* Westport, CT: Greenwood, 1973.

—-. *Twentieth Century Church Music.* New York: Oxford UP, 1964.

Rudin, Cecilia Margaret. *Stories of Hymns We Love.* Chicago: John Rudin, 1945.

Ryden, Ernest Edwin. *The Story of Christian Hymnody.* Rock Island, IL: Augustana, 1959.

Schilling, S. Paul. *The Faith We Sing.* Philadelphia: Westminster, 1983.

Sheppard, W. J. Limmer. *Great Hymns and Their Stories.* Rev. ed. London: Lutterworth, 1950.

Smith, C. Howard. *Scandinavian Hymnody from the Reformation to the Present.* Metuchen, NJ: Scarecrow, 1987.

Smith, H. Augustine. *Lyric Religion: The Romance of Immortal Hymns.* New York: Appleton, 1931.

Stanislaw, Richard J. *A Checklist of Four-Shape Shape-Note Tunebooks.* I.S.A.M. No. 10. NY: Institute for Studies in American Music, Brooklyn College of the City University, 1978.

Stevenson, Robert. *Protestant Church Music in America.* New York: Norton, 1966.

Sydnor, James Rawlings. *A Short Bibliography for the Study of Hymns; The Papers of the Hymn Society of America, XXV.* [Fort Worth, TX], 1964.

—-. *Hymns: A Congregational Study.* Carol Stream, IL: Agape, 1983.

—. *Hymns and Their Uses.* Carol Stream, IL: Hope, 1982.

Thompson, Ronald W. *Who's Who of Hymn Writers.* London: Epworth, 1967.

Ethnic and Special Use Music

Buchanan, Annabel Morris. *Folk Hymns of America.* New York: Fischer, 1938.

Ehret, Walter, and George K. Evans. *The International Book of Christmas Carols.* Englewood Cliffs: Prentice, 1963.

Jackson, George Pullen. *Another Sheaf of White Spirituals*. Gainesville: U of Florida P, 1952.

—. *Down-East Spirituals and Others*. Locust Valley, NY: Augustin, 1943.

—. *Spiritual Folk-Songs of Early America*. Locust Valley, NY: Augustin, 1937. New York: Dover, 1964.

—. *White and Negro Spirituals, Their Life-Span and Kinship*. Locust Valley, NY: Augustin, 1943.

—. *White Spirituals in the Southern Uplands*. Chapel Hill, NC: U of North Carolina P, 1933. Hatboro, PA: Folklore, 1964.

Lovell, John, Jr. *The Forge and the Flame.* New York: Macmillan, 1972.

Luff, Alan. *Welsh Hymns and Their Tunes.* Carol Stream, IL: Hope for Stainer & Bell, 1990.

Work, John W. *American Negro Songs and Spirituals.* New York: Bonanza, 1940.

Gospel Hymns

Emurian, Ernest K. *Forty True Stories of Famous Gospel Songs* Natick, MS: Wilde, 1959.
Gabriel, Charles H. *The Singers and Their Songs.* Winona Lake, IN: Rodeheaver, 1915.
Hall, J. H. *Biography of Gospel Song and Hymn Writers.* New York: Revell, 1914.

Hustad, Donald P., ed. *Fanny Crosby Speaks Again.* Carol Stream, IL: Hope, 1977.

Kerr, Phil. *Music in Evangelism.* Glendale, CA: Gospel Music Publishers, 1939.

Lillenas, Haldor. *Modern Gospel Song Stories.* Kansas City, MO: Lillenas, 1952.

Rodeheaver. Homer A. *Hymnal Handbook for Standard Hymns and Gospel Songs.* Winona Lake, IN: Rodeheaver, 1931.

Sankey, Ira D. *My Life and the Story of the Gospel Hymns.* New York: Harper, 1906.

Sanville, George W. *Forty Gospel Hymn Stories.* Winona Lake, IN: Rodeheaver, 1943.

Showalter, A. J. *The Best Gospel Songs and Their Composers.* A. J. Showalter, 1904.

Smith. Oswald J. *Oswald J. Smith's Hymn Stories.* Winona Lake, IN: Rodeheaver, 1963.

Stebbins, George C. *Reminiscences and Gospel Hymn Stories.* George H. Doran, 1924.

Terry, Lindsay L. *Stories Behind Popular Songs and Hymns.* Grand Rapids: Baker, 1990.

Hymn Tunes

Frost, Maurice, ed. *English and Scottish Psalm and Hymn Tunes, c.* 1543-1677. London: Oxford UP, 1953.

Lightwood, James T. *Hymn Tunes and Their Story.* London: Epworth, 1935.

Mason, Henry L. *Hymn Tunes of Lowell Mason.* Cambridge: Harvard UP, 1944.

McCutchan, Robert Guy. *Hymn Tune Names, Their Sources and Significance.* New York: Abingdon, 1957.

Parker, Alice. *Creative Hymn Singing.* 2d ed. Chapel Hill, NC: Hinshaw, 1976.

—. *Melodious Accord: Good Singing in Church.* Chicago: Liturgy Training Publications, 1991.

Routley, Erik. *The Music of Christian Hymnody.* London: Independent Press, 1957.

Zahn, Johannes. *Die Melodien der deutschen evangelischen Kirchenlieder,* 1893. Hildesheim: G. Olms, 1963.

One-Author Collections

Clarkson, Margaret. *A Singing Heart.* Carol Stream, IL: Hope, 1987.

Colvin, Tom. *Fill Us with Your Love.* Carol Stream, IL: Hope, 1983.

Daw, Carl P., Jr. *A Year of Grace.* Carol Stream, IL: Hope, 1990.

—. *To Sing God's Praise.* Carol Stream, IL: Hope, 1992

Dudley-Smith, Timothy. *Lift Every Heart.* Carol Stream, IL: Hope, 1984.

—. *Songs of Deliverance*. Carol Stream, IL: Hope, 1988.

Green, Fred Pratt, and Bernard Braley. *The Hymns and Ballads of Fred Pratt Green*. Carol Stream, IL: Hope, 1982.

Green, Fred Pratt. *Later Hymns and Ballads and Fifty Poems*. Hope, 1989.

Huber, Jane Parker. *A Singing Faith*. Philadelphia: Westminster, 1987.

Kaan, Fred. *The Hymn Texts of Fred Kaan*. Carol Stream, IL: Hope, 1985.

—. *Planting Trees and Sowing Seeds*. Carol Stream, IL: Hope, 1989

Murray, Shirley Erena. *In Every Corner Sing*. Carol Stream, IL: Hope, 1992.

Routley, Erik. *Our Lives Be Praise*. Carol Stream, IL: Hope, 1990.

Vajda, Jaroslav J. *Now the Joyful Celebration*. St. Louis, MO: Morning Star Music, 1987.

Wren, Brian. *Bring Many Names*. Carol Stream, IL: Hope, 1989.

—. *Faith Looking Forward*. Carol Stream, IL: Hope, 1983.

—. Praising a Mystery. Carol Stream, IL: Hope, 1986.